THE FUTURE OF
THE INTERNATIONAL LEGAL ORDER
VOLUME IV

*The Structure of the
International Environment*

# THE FUTURE OF THE
# INTERNATIONAL LEGAL ORDER

### EDITED BY CYRIL E. BLACK
### AND RICHARD A. FALK

Volume I. *Trends and Patterns.* 1969.
Volume II. *Wealth and Resources.* 1970.
Volume III. *Conflict Management.* 1971.
Volume IV. *The Structure of the International Environment.* 1972.
Volume V. *Toward an International Consensus.* Forthcoming.

Written under the auspices of the
Center of International Studies,
Princeton University

A list of other Center publications
appears at the back of the book.

# THE FUTURE
# OF THE INTERNATIONAL
# LEGAL ORDER

## VOLUME IV

## *The Structure of the*
## *International Environment*

EDITED BY CYRIL E. BLACK
AND RICHARD A. FALK

PRINCETON UNIVERSITY PRESS
PRINCETON, NEW JERSEY, 1972

Copyright © 1972 by Princeton University Press

All Rights Reserved

L.C. Card: 68-20866

ISBN: 0-691-09221-4

This book has been composed in Linotype Baskerville

Printed in the United States of America
by Princeton University Press

# Foreword

THIS SERIES has been organized and edited under the auspices of the Center of International Studies, Princeton University, with the assistance of a grant from the Ford Foundation. The views presented in these volumes are those of the authors of the individual chapters, and do not necessarily represent those of the contributors as a group, of the Center of International Studies, or of the Ford Foundation.

This volume completes the substantive aspects of this enterprise, and the arguments and interpretations set forth in the first four volumes will be presented to an international group of specialists in 1972 for their evaluation and criticism. The results of this evaluation will be the subject of Volume V, tentatively entitled *Toward an International Consensus*.

The editors wish to thank Mrs. Nancy Baldwin Smith for the careful attention she gave to the preparation of this manuscript for publication; and to acknowledge once again the assistance of Marjorie Putney of the Princeton University Press and Jane G. McDowall, June Traube and Mary Merrick of the staff of the Center of International Studies at Princeton University.

CYRIL E. BLACK
RICHARD A. FALK

# Introduction

THE ISSUES of conflict management are in a sense as old as human societies and present new problems today primarily because of the destructiveness of modern weapons, but the issues with which this volume is concerned are relatively recent consequences of the scientific and technological revolution and are in significant respects unprecedented. Until the modern era states have been primarily concerned with national security, and even the most autocratic of traditional empires never exercised much direct authority at the local level where four-fifths or more of the population normally conducted its affairs. Until almost within memory of persons now alive, human affairs were conducted primarily at the local level, and such interstate activities as trade, war, and ecclesiastical administration normally left most people unaffected.

Today this is no longer the case. The increasing specialization characteristic of the process of modernization has resulted in an ever-expanding exchange of goods and services that has made some aspects of human activity virtually worldwide and has extended many others beyond the confines of individual countries. It was a difficult task to establish a customs union (1819–44) in the course of the unification of Germany, and the Interstate Commerce Commission (1887) in the United States met for many years with considerable opposition from local interests; but today the European Economic Community has gone a long way toward reducing economic barriers between its members and the international regulation of trade is accepted by most states as essential for the protection of common interests. In earlier times, and in less-developed societies today, it was rare for individuals to stray far from their native habitat; but in more developed societies it is common for people by the millions to move from one country to another in search of a better way of life. In the realm of international production it has been estimated that the proportion of the overseas production owned or controlled by advanced societies is likely to rise from one-quarter to one-half of the world output of commodities produced between 1970 and 2000.

These and many other aspects of human activity have long since broken the bounds of the local community, but the politically sovereign states that form the basic framework for human activity have not changed to meet new needs. Instead, in response to demands of ethnic groups for self-determination and independence, the political situation of the world has stabilized into an increasing number of independent sovereignties. It is in fact one of the central dilemmas of the modern era that as the scope of many aspects of human activity—

the exchange of goods and services, the organization of professions, the advancement of knowledge—has assumed worldwide proportions, the political sovereignties that represent the principal instrumentalities for the mobilization and allocation of resources have tended to become narrower and more exclusive. Even aspects of human activity that have been in some degree international for many centuries, such as trade, currencies, and religious organizations, have tended to be adversely affected by the growth of the modern state. At the same time the scientific and technological revolution has led to the development of common problems of a global character—food, population, ocean resources, water and air pollution, in addition to the difficult problems of conflict management—that cannot be adequately solved except by international efforts.

It is easy to portray this situation as a consequence of short-sightedness—the increasing concentration of states on selfish concerns, or the fear of local interest groups that they will lose privileges based on the exploitation of fellow human beings if they permit the local and national instruments of coercion that they control to elude their grasp. Such factors certainly play a role, but the underlying sources of the dilemma represented by the increasing emphasis on the exclusive rights of states in a time of expanding human activity are more complex. What is not adequately recognized is that the apparently "international" character of earlier relationships, when many peoples were united by a few world religions, by trade and commerce circulating on newly-opened ocean trade routes, and by travel unrestricted by passports and frontier regulations, was limited to a very small proportion of humankind. The effective economic and social environment as well as the political framework for most individuals was the local community, and only in recent times has the advancement of knowledge and technology permitted the development of human capabilities to the point where many individuals can now begin to share the benefits and responsibilities of a worldwide community.

The political organization of human societies has of course been influenced by this process, but political organization is much less flexible than knowledge, commerce, or religion, since it is the instrumentality that regulates relations of individuals and groups within societies and also regulates their relations with other societies. Changes in political organizations cannot be made without loss of privileges by some individuals and groups at the expense of others. There is nothing that human beings prize more highly, even at the cost of sacrificing their sons in civil and international war, than the maintenance and advancement of their personal security and status within the framework of familiar and reliable political institutions.

The problems of humankind with which this volume is concerned thus involve the means by which states as participants in the international system can cope with problems that are international in scope. Political systems are among the most rigid of human institutions, concerned as they are with the security of societies in a competitive world. Only as a result of revolutionary turmoil have they been transformed thus far to perform integrative functions at a national level, and it took the unprecedented tragedy of two world wars to bring six West European states to the point of evolving a type of confederation, although of extremely limited character. It is not difficult, nor is it necessarily unrealistic, to imagine that in the long run global political institutions endowed with adequate sovereignty will be devised to cope with problems that are worldwide in their scope, but this is not the issue with which this volume is concerned. There are many problems that call for institutional management of a global character, but we do not believe that it lies within the capacity of the present system of states to alter to this extent the attitudes, values, and sources of support necessary for such a transformation within the near future that is the time boundary we have imposed upon our enterprise of inquiry and speculation.

We have instead set for ourselves the more modest, and in our view more realistic, task of exploring the adjustments in the present international system that are minimally necessary and practicable. With this purpose in mind, we have approached this subject from two perspectives: a discussion of the international legal aspects of the most important problems of the development of the human environment, and an analysis of the institutions, agencies, and movements that must be further adapted to the rapidly changing needs of humankind.

Institutions, like laws, acquire authority less from the amount of coercion available to give them effect than from their acceptance as a necessary means for achieving common objectives. National institutions have gained such acceptance in the modern era, but most people still perceive international institutions as remote and marginal. Harold D. Lasswell's introductory chapter discusses the process by which a change of identity may occur, and the nature of the obstacles that must be overcome. In considerable degree the transfer of identity from locality and province to national state which most nations have experienced offers precedents for the problems and illuminates the possibilities for further developments. Modern communications nevertheless afford national states a much stronger hold on human loyalties than that possessed by more local entities a century or more ago, and one cannot assume that internationalism will have the same emotional power that nationalism exhibited at an earlier stage of societal growth.

In the relation of human beings to the global environment, it is the former that represent the dynamic factor both in growing numbers and in increasing demands per capita. Mary Ellen Caldwell examines the extent to which population pressures may lead to international disputes. Solutions to the population problem along such lines as migration, food relief, and birth control all call for international instrumentalities more developed than those now available. The need for more sophisticated instruments of international management are also stressed in the chapter of Dennis Livingston on science and technology, and of Howard J. and Rita F. Taubenfeld on man's efforts to modify the earth's weather. Livingston discusses the impact of the scientific and technological revolution on weapons, communications, human rights, and environmental problems that transcend national boundaries, and stresses the role of treaties, conventions, and other forms of international cooperation in meeting their challenge. The Taubenfelds focus more particularly on the human capacity to modify the environment either intentionally, as in the case of weather management, or through neglect leading to the various forms of air and water pollution. Both types of modification threaten the interests of states in ways that can only be dealt with by innovative forms of international regulation.

It was through the development of ocean-borne commerce that the modern world began to evolve in the sixteenth century, and today the oceans have again become an international frontier although of different dimensions. While continuing their important role as the principal highway for the transportation of bulky cargoes, the oceans have now become an international frontier offering possible sources of food, minerals, and energy as well as locations for the placement of nuclear weapons and a repository for waste disposal. In exploring this subject, L. F. E. Goldie reviews customary international law of the oceans, which was concerned primarily with fishing, commerce, and the rights of riparian states, and explores the range of problems that must be solved if these traditional codes are to be adapted to deal with the awesome new problems and prospects created by modern technology. A variety of international institutions, including the United Nations, have concerned themselves with these problems, and the frustrations thus far experienced in their efforts to adapt national interests to world community welfare provide a good example of the deep-seated rigidities that the international management of the environment will have to overcome in the decades ahead.

Human beings are people as well as populations, and their welfare, rights, and responsibilities become a matter for international concern when economic development and social change affecting many peoples occur at the initiative of a relatively few affluent countries. Expectations regarding the treatment of human beings tend to spread more rapidly than the economic growth needed to sustain them, and there is already a respected tradition by which international standards are established by such bodies as the International Labor Organization, the World Health Organization, and the United Nations Children's Fund. In discussing this sphere of international activity, Leon Gordenker places particular emphasis on the problems faced by the less-developed countries in trying to implement standards set by the most highly developed, and stresses the desirability that the latter should take greater responsibility in regard to such problems as disease and food that call for resources of a magnitude that only they possess.

Human rights in the more traditional political sense have also become a matter of formal international concern as a result of the minorities treaties following the First World War and the United Nations Commission on Human Rights and its Subcommissions. John Carey discusses these developments, and the parallel European and Inter-American efforts, with particular concern for the authority accorded the United Nations Subcommission for the Prevention of Discrimination and Protection of Minorities in 1967 to inspect the many written complaints by individuals that were being received. The right to inspect such complaints is accompanied by a limited right to publicize them, and this prerogative suggests the need for investigative procedures, and finally, for a capacity to take remedial action. These and related developments may be criticized as no more effective than the right of citizens to petition their sovereign in much earlier times, but it is from beginnings such as these that systems of adjudication evolve. The changing status of individuals as subject to international law is reviewed by Hans W. Baade in terms of the international sanctions that evolved after 1919 in regard to crimes against peace and humanity, and such contemporary developments as the efforts by the Geneva Convention of 1949 to modernize the humanitarian side of the law of war. In this, as in most other comparable fields, a very significant gap remains between the degree of international consensus thus far achieved and the kind of implemented consensus on which domestic legal systems are normally based.

The chapters in Part I are concerned with significant problems of transnational scope and refer to international institutions primarily in terms of their applicability to specific situations. The authors of the chapters in Part II are concerned with the institutions themselves, and explore their varied capabilities for development into more significant actors and more effective problem-solving instrumentalities. Of these institutions none is more important than international law itself, and in exploring this subject Gidon Gottlieb makes the distinction between the traditional conception of international law in terms of a vertical model, based on a pyramid of legal authority presided over by governmental institutions of society-wide competence, and a horizontal model based on more decentralized and dispersed arrangements of authority. The vertical model sees international law as a less effective version of domestic law because it is less centralized, whereas the horizontal model views international law as a distinctive system that relies upon reciprocal and voluntary modes of compliance and cannot be usefully compared with domestic legal orders. Horizontal systems do not depend on enforcement agencies such as police and courts characteristic of vertical systems, but rely upon intergovernmental agreements as to applicable normative standards. Professor Gottlieb reviews legal precedents that illustrate these two approaches to law, and discusses the prospects for the development of a system of international law that would depend not on a transition from national states to a world state, but on a transformation of the modes of interaction of existing political entities.

The domestic, regional, and global actors in the international system that are explored in the chapters by Richard Lillich, Joseph Nye, and Donald McNemar may be said to illustrate the vertical side of the international system, to use the terminology introduced by Gottlieb. The role of domestic courts in the international legal order is illustrated by the decisions of the United States courts, and their not inconsiderable capacity for playing an active role in the development of international law is demonstrated. Regional and global institutions have historical precedents, but the extent of their present development is essentially a recent phenomenon, and in most respects still possess only a pale reflection of the authority and effectiveness of the national state.

A more horizontal approach to international law is reflected in the chapters of James Sewell on functional agencies and Gerald A. Sumida on transnational movements. Sewell notes that functional agencies are in most respects no less dependent than international bodies on the initiative of nation-states; but he also points out that they have a life of their own because of their functional focus on problems that require international solutions, and that their participation in such solutions leads to a greater commitment on the part of member states than is the experience of less problem-oriented international bodies. The wide range of international movements and economic structures described by Sumida have in some cases a tradition of activity going back to much earlier times, and in contrast to functional agencies their membership is normally composed of individuals and of associations rather than of governments. However, the growth of this kind of transnationalism is one of the most dramatic trends now visible in international society, making it especially important to take these actors into account in a description of the future of the international legal order.

In their concluding chapter, Harold and Margaret Sprout present a view of human affairs that stresses the close relation between the peoples of the world to their environment, and the marked change in this relation that is resulting from the rapid growth of population and the increasing depredation of the environment that is a consequence of industrialization and urbanization. Until quite recently human beings have taken their environment as much for granted as the air they breathed, but the Sprouts have been exploring the ecological perspective since the 1930's with a view to understanding the problems inherent in the international management of the environment which now loom as large as the management of conflict. Their broad view of these problems provides a framework for relating the pressing issues presented in Part I of this volume to the instrumentalities discussed in Part II.

This fourth volume of *The Future of the International Legal Order* concludes the review of the principal problems and institutions in terms of which the evolving world order can be assessed. This review has been designed to provide a basis for determining the extent to which there is an international consensus on the next steps that should be taken in the effort to meet the challenges of the scientific and technological revolution, and to meet them with processes and institutions adequate to the task of assuring order, welfare, and justice under rapidly changing conditions. Inherent in the approach of these volumes is the view that the establishment of such a consensus, and concurrently the further intensive study of issues on which there is significant disagreement, is as important to world order as the transformation of formal political institutions. In world society, no less than in individual states, changes in consciousness pertaining to norms and to the agenda of issues may be more important than institutional changes, and could be capable of fostering the transformation of behavior and policies needed to meet the crises of our times.

*The Editors*
C. E. BLACK
R. A. FALK

# Contents

# Part I

# Man and His Environment

## CHAPTER 1

# Future Systems of Identity in the World Community

### HAROLD D. LASSWELL

#### INTRODUCTION

THE MOST conspicuous institutions of government and law in the world arena are the nation states and the transnational network of intergovernmental organizations. They affect and in turn are affected by the transnational political parties and pressure organizations that operate between official agencies and private groupings. The public order institutions of today's world are not strong enough to provide even minimum security from the threat or fact of war.[1]

Our immediate problem is the examination of "identity." The public order of nation states depends on many factors, among which the patterns by which individuals identify with such states play an important part. An obvious question is whether a comparable asset can be mobilized for the strengthening of world public order, or whether world political institutions must precede world loyalty. In any case the future will continue to be affected by the predispositions of all whose nationalistic loyalties are expressed in ways that perpetuate the institutions of world division and war.

As usual, history confirms the fact that many different roads may lead to the same Rome. In feudal times "nationality"—the sense of belonging to a people of distinctive language or general culture—was compatible with political disunity. Political "nationalism" has sometimes arisen after a period of subjection to a rule perceived as oppressive (as in contemporary Africa). Nationalism has also emerged as a movement aimed at uniting a divided people into a single body politic (as in nineteenth century Germany and Italy). The principal characteristic of nationalism as a system of political identity is the sense of belonging to an actual or potential body politic that rightfully is or should be as free as any other. Expressed negatively, this implies freedom from external control. Affirmatively, nationalism embodies a demand for equal access to whatever decision arenas make authoritative and controlling commitments. The "negative" aspect is phrased in terms of "sovereignty"; the "positive" in demands for "recognition" and "admission" to processes for clarifying common in-

[1] On minimum security see, for instance, M. S. McDougal and F. P. Feliciano, *Law and Minimum World Public Order* (New Haven 1961).

terests. The "positive" ideologists celebrate a "Federation of Free Nations" and a "Parliament of Man." [2]

## POLITICAL IDENTITY

The question is whether a sense of political identity comparable to nationalism is developing or can develop in support of a world-inclusive system of public order. Will a transnational identity arise the object of which is the whole nation of man? Will such an identity mobilize enough intensity of support on a sufficiently large scale to become a significant factor in future world politics?

A political identity is a shared perspective on the self as a participant in politics; it is held with sufficient intensity by enough people to achieve at least a minimum threshold of effect on political outcomes.

It is everyday knowledge that we are each linked by multiple loyalties to many territorial and pluralized groups, and that under various circumstances we give priority to different identities. At times we are aware of conflicting loyalties, especially when the claims of larger and smaller identities seem to be mutually incompatible.[3] Ordinarily we cope with latent incompatibilities by diverting attention to other matters. The cement of society is the strategy of avoidance, supplemented by creative ambiguity in the solution of many incipient contradictions.

As a means of investigating the significance of any factor in the political process, we utilize a conceptual map of the whole process. Briefly:

Participants ⟶
Perspectives ⟶
Arenas ⟶
Base Values ⟶
Strategies ⟶
Outcomes ⟶
Effects ⟶

1. Participants, or the individuals and groups who interact politically. The world arena includes organized groups: nation states, intergovernmental structures, transnational political parties, transnational pressure groups, other transnational private associations. Can transnational, world-inclusive identity systems affect the composition of the world arena?

[2] On the literature of "nation" and "nationalism," Karl W. Deutsch, *Nationalism and Social Communication: An Inquiry into the Foundations of Nationality* (New York and Cambridge, Mass. 1953)

[3] Harold Guetzkov, *Multiple Loyalties* (Princeton 1955)

2. Perspectives, or the subjective events (symbols) that refer to politics. Included are symbols of identity (such as designations of territorial and pluralistic groups), demands (preferences and volitions regarding outcomes [values]), expectations (matter of fact references to past, present, and future events). The perspectives are also patterned as political myths: doctrines, or philosophies; formula, or legal codes; miranda, or popular versions of group character and fate. Can a growing sense of inclusive identity generate expectations and demands of great intensity and scope? Can such an enlarged self-image achieve stability by elaborating a comprehensive political myth?

3. Arenas, or the organized or unorganized setting in which political interactions occur (global, subglobal). Can a system of transnational and world identity contribute to the organization of a globally inclusive arena?

4. Base Values, or the assets available to participants for strategic use. Can the vitalized self-image of world community marshal and direct the use of economic and other resources in ways that strengthen public order?

5. Strategies, or the manipulations that precede outcomes, such as diplomatic, ideological, economic and military campaigns. Can the emerging system of identity stimulate the plans and operations required to consolidate and to sustain a strong and inclusive set of political institutions?

6. Outcomes, or the flow of successes or failures in votes or fights. Will the governments, parties, and pressure associations that identify themselves with a world image succeed in making themselves effective at the moments of final commitment to at least minimum public order decisions?

7. Effects, or the significance of outcomes for value accumulation and distribution, and for the innovation, diffusion, and restriction of institutions. As time passes will the self-image of man acting politically influence the various sectors of the world community in ways that cumulatively strengthen a public order of peace and dignity?

## INDICATORS

Political identities are components of act-systems. They are preceded by drives or impulses at the unconscious or preconscious level; and they are accompanied and followed by words, gestures and other modes of expression. In short, an identity is an attitude composed of perspectives and operations (behaviors). Identities have both direction and intensity.

Our estimates of future world politics will be more operational if we keep in mind the state of the art that is variously called the study of political attitudes, opinions, or sentiments.[4] The difficulties of investigating perspectives of identity—or, in fact, any perspectives—are only partly overcome. By introspection we are able to experience and describe one stream of subjective events (perspectives) directly (our own). Our everyday working postulate is that other people experience perspectives that are parallel to, though not necessarily congruent with, our own. Hypotheses about perspectives enable us to discover the often complex indicators that permit us to predict, explain, or even empathize with the thoughts and feelings of others.

Direct introspection of the primary ego (the "I," "me") must be supplanted by indirect inferences when we investigate other people. The fundamental indicators are words (or word equivalents such as gestures), deeds (overt acts that involve more than expression), resource manipulations (which involve weapons, machines, and similar features of the environment). (For a brief summary of the procedures available for studying indicators consult Note A at the end of this chapter.)

## DYNAMICS

We are concerned with the dynamics of identity. We have suggested that the most important fact about an identity is that it is part of an action system. In schematic terms an act is a completed sequence of events that passes from the phase of preconscious impulse to subjectivity and expression. Acts are part of "interacts" when they are precipitated by the human or physical environment, or are perceived as successful or not depending on the response. Exposure to an environment stimulates a predisposition to act in ways that are perceived as maximizing (optimalizing) results. The symbols of self ("I," "me," "thou," "we") mark the boundaries of an identity. They depend on expected and realized net consequences. The members of an aggregation of people possess a common identity to the extent that they share identifying symbols with sufficient intensity to influence behavior significantly.

In some circumstances the advantages of publicly affirming a group identity are obvious. Those who vote on the winning side of a plebiscite in a disputed territory may expect to be value-indulged in many ways. They can look forward to better political careers than the losers, and to benefits in terms of jobs and contracts, prestige, admission to educational facilities, and the like.

It will not do to rely solely on a specific behavioral commitment in

4 W. Phillips Davison, *International Political Communication* (New York 1965); Herbert C. Kelman, ed., *International Behavior: A Social-Psychological Analysis* (New York 1965); and relevant articles in the *International Encyclopedia of the Social Sciences*.

predicting the future. Subjectivities count. In private plebiscite voters may reassert their "basic identity" (telling family and friends that they are still at heart as they were before, and that some day an opportunity will arise to demonstrate it in action). In some cases there may be no private behavioral expressions, even when the individual keeps alive his basic identity by internal fantasy (in the same way that devoted espionage agents may continue underground and out of contact with their principal for years). Some persons, at least, are able to preserve an identity system by internal rewards (value indulgences), enjoying a quiet sense of moral superiority from their steadfastness, savoring a sense of secret knowledge, or imagining eventual gratifications in the "real world."

It is not difficult to see how the dissemination of an established identity system depends on "expected and realized net value consequences." Early socialization usually takes care of the matter. Results are obtained by a flow of environment exposures that reward identity-affirming behavior and deprive identity-denying or indifferent behavior. During early years the developing personalities of the young incorporate appropriate symbols of identity, expectation, and demand as part of their stable perspectives. These self-images mobilize and guide an impulse to appropriate completion. They guide attention, opinion, belief, loyalty, action, and organization.

Of special relevance to our task are the circumstances in which self-images are redefined and intensities are redistributed among identities. When does an identity system become more inclusive? Less? A general hypothesis is that the boundaries of a system of political identity (a political self) tend to be enlarged to include those who are perceived as similar to the self in politically salient ways. Boundaries are restricted to exclude those who are perceived (in the same terms) as incompatible.

The paradigm for an enlarging identity system in a group is the perception of a common threat of value deprivation and of possible joint action to prevent loss or even to obtain value gains. A shared field of attention thus generates a map of expectation. If the situation continues the participants stabilize the boundaries of their enlarged self-image. They remain durably oriented toward defending and extending the value position of the self in the sectors perceived as a common interest.

A stably enlarged identity becomes part of a group culture that includes a decision process that (1) protects basic institutions, and (2) interacts supportively with the civic order. The civic order is composed of the institutions whose policy processes rely on less severe crisis sanctions than are at the disposal of the institutions of public order.

One classic sequence of enlargement moves from a loose league or confederation of bodies politic to the formation of a more perfect federal or unitary union in a larger body politic. For example: the confederation of the thirteen British colonies in North America; later, the formation of a "more perfect" federal union. Complex readjustments of identity precipitated, accompanied, and consolidated those developments. For instance, the self-system of the colonists was restricted to exclude Great Britain, and the self-system of the British was restricted to exclude the colonies. Among the colonials particular identities were enlarged to include the new body politic.

The paradigm covers the restriction as well as the enlargement of identity systems. The analysis includes situations in which those who share a common self-image perceive one another as sources of deprivation rather than indulgence. This is what happened when the colonies became estranged from Britain.

After these preliminary considerations we turn to future sequences of world politics and systems of identity. We postulate as a desirable goal the achievement of substantial progress toward a world order of peace, welfare, and social justice. Our developmental construct assumes that this goal is possible, and outlines a sequence of conditions and strategies by which the goal can be approximated. No estimates of probability are made beyond the "possible."

## A PROJECTION: GLOBAL INTERACTIONS WILL INCREASE IN FREQUENCY

This means that more people around the globe will take one another into consideration in their decisions and choices. To take other people into consideration does not necessarily imply such overt interchanges as travel, trade, or communication. That the official or unofficial elite of a given country takes another country "into consideration" may be demonstrated by internal indicators: references to external affairs in speeches and other statements by top executives; references in legislative sessions, cabinet discussions, military and civilian administrative agencies, reports of intelligence, planning, and appraisal services. Indicators that external events are taken "into consideration" by the rank and file of the community include: political party platforms, resolutions of pressure associations, news and comment in mass media, references in school textbooks, sermons, and other forums specialized to various institutions.

While it is true that the content of communication media are not direct measures of perspective, no one would seriously challenge the assertion that more or less frequent references to the external environment probably indicates more or less consideration of foreign affairs.

### World Attention

Chart 1 projects the probable shape of the world attention curve in coming years and summarizes the rising trend that has been affected by the growth of mass media, literacy, and various forms of interchange in the last hundred years. The projection is to be understood in several ways. For example, it indicates the changing percentage of foreign news and comment in elite and popular media of all countries.

The chart is generalized for all countries, but it is unlikely that the degree of "external consideration" will be uniformly distributed through the world community. For instance, we know that attention to the external environment is greater per capita in small countries with active direct transnational contact than in the big powers (Table 1).

Is the inference that the big states ought to be broken up into smaller entities as a means of increasing the perceived involvement of the world's population with one another? This may be the implication; but it is highly improbable that China, the Soviet Union and the U.S.A. will divide into independent states in the immediate future.

The picture we have drawn needs to be qualified in order to emphasize the degree of contrast between the elite and the rank and file. The elite media of the globe pay more regular attention to the ex-

Chart 1

World Attention
(Developmental Construct)

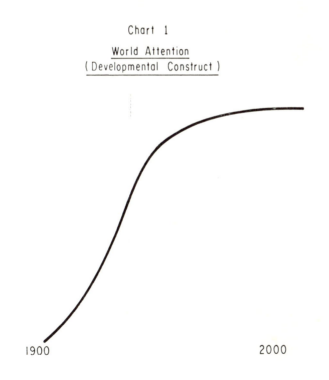

1900                                        2000

TABLE 1

ITEMS OF FOREIGN MAIL SENT PER CAPITA

(IN 1960 OR NEAREST REPORTED YEAR)

| | |
|---|---:|
| *Top 10% of countries* | |
| British Guinea | 53.80 |
| Malta and Gozo | 37.01 |
| Switzerland | 31.81 |
| Luxembourg | 31.53 |
| Ireland | 31.35 |
| Hong Kong | 21.49 |
| Singapore | 18.45 |
| *Bottom 10% of countries* | |
| India | .17 |
| Angola | .15 |
| Thailand | .13 |
| Burma | .10 |
| Indonesia | .06 |
| Laos | .03 |
| Uruguay | .01 |

(From Bruce M. Russett, Hayward R. Alker, Jr., Karl W. Deutsch, Harold D. Lasswell, *World Handbook of Political and Social Indicators* [New Haven 1964], Table 33)

ternal environment than the popular media. Granting that the "consideration" of the foreign environment will increase, it is probable that a gap will continue to separate elites from broader levels of the population (Table 2). We shall presently evaluate the significance of this gap.

Table 2 can be construed as confirming hypotheses based on the maximization postulate that elite members of the world community focus on other elite members because they recognize that they have more at stake than rank and file members perceive that they—the rank and file—have at stake. Military, diplomatic, business, and other elites

TABLE 2

WORLD ELITE PRESS

| *United Nations information items per issue* | |
|---|---:|
| 50 elite newspapers | 3.1 items |
| 1,209 daily newspapers | 1.3 items |

(UNITAR Panel on Communications Information, 1969)

are often immediately involved in cross-boundary activities affecting their power, wealth, and other value positions. Hence they expect to pay differential attention to those parts of the environment that may affect the maintenance or improvement of their position.

ATTENTION AND IDENTITY

We have not dealt explicitly with the significance of an increased frequency of transnational attention for identity systems. In order to do this we must take into account what we know about the interplay of several zones of interaction: zones of attention, opinion, action, organization and identity (see Chart 2).

Chart 2

World Zones

(Frequent Not Inevitable Distribution)

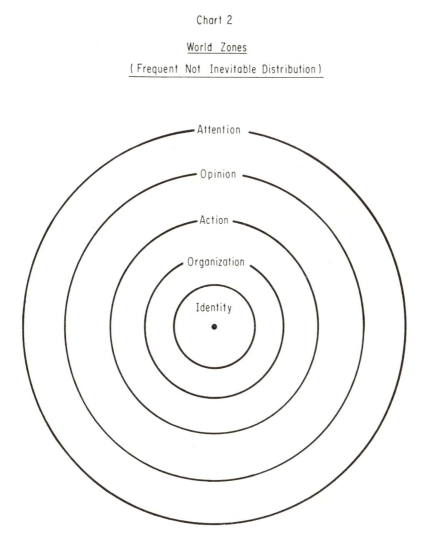

Thinking of the chart in world terms the globe and its environment are included in the attention zone in two senses: first, the earth's inhabitants constitute an audience; second, the earth and its environment are objects of reference. People formulate opinions (demand) about what policies ought to be adopted and executed on a scale that is smaller than the attention zone; that is, people see and hear about things they do not think of trying to change. An opinion is more than a designation, since it includes at least some minimum degree of stress toward action. It took a long time for part of the outer spatial environment to become a target of opinion. The zone of action is smaller than the other two, as a rule, since communication media, for example, can mobilize attention and opinion well beyond the area of effective action (as in reference to outer space). An organization zone typically lags behind action zones (as in the case of transnational organizations that do not include all the nation states with some level of trade and other direct or indirect contact). Identity zones appear to lag behind organization. Does this suggest that identity systems must play a small and belated part in achieving a larger unity of action? Or are some factors amenable to change?

Suppose we reexamine the broad picture outlined in the chart. It need not be taken as depicting an invariant sequence. Granted that a few pioneers thought that the earth was round and that it could be circumnavigated, it is clear that no striking changes of attention or opinion occurred until action was taken—as in the European Age of Exploration.

The activity areas of military and civilian explorers, adventurers, missionaries, traders, and scholars precipitated active rivalries and conflicts among imperial organizations until the occupiable globe was finally covered in the scramble for Africa at the end of the nineteenth century. Organization areas tended to include all activity areas, often following a buildup of attention and opinion. One result of the sequence was greatly to enlarge the scope of many identity systems until they transcended localities, regions, and even continents. Once consolidated, a national or imperial identity tended to support the political structure, and to provide incentives for expansion.

An important proposition that emerges from these reflections is that identities may outrun organizational areas. Consider the following: the ideology of Christendom in the fifteenth or sixteenth centuries was not restricted to the territorial limits of Europe as they were left at the end of the Crusades. Those who were associated with the mission of the Roman church perceived themselves as trustees of all men everywhere. Hence they were identified with universal man, with an obligation to fit all mankind into the organizational structure of the church. All men who allowed themselves to be converted to Christianity were eligible for inclusion in the church and its approved secular institutions. The inference is that the identification of members of the elite of Spain, Portugal, and other countries with all men conceived as potential Christians provided incentives that affected the timing, direction, and magnitude of their expansionist operations. The significance of these symbolic factors is not negated by the observation that other factors combined to influence demands, expectations, and identities and to redefine effective ideologies.

Clearly the sharing of a common set of identifying symbols makes it possible for larger numbers of people to act together more quickly than if common cues are missing. Differences of local culture, class, interest, and personality were partially overcome by invoking established predispositions to accept a degree of common leadership. We note in this connection the frequent lament that the opportunity to establish a closer identifying link with Asia was lost when the Vatican decided to forbid its missionaries to incorporate native customs into their services.[5]

## FUTURE IDENTITIES AND DECISIONS

Although the degree of effective identity attained in the past was too weak to bring about a comprehensive system of world order, it is pertinent to ask whether the accelerating pace of global interaction paves the way toward intense identification with a universal vision and program that will be capable of moving the peoples of the globe toward a more satisfactory state of affairs. There is little doubt that the scientific and critical view of the physical, biological, and cultural realms will be ever more widely shared by the school teachers, scientists, journalists and, in general, by the influential people of every nation, city, and town in all parts of the world. This common universal map underlines the threats and opportunities inherent in a scientifically based technology that accelerates the interactions between man and his environment. The dangers of nuclear and biological weaponry will be a continually disturbing theme. The menace of polluted space, air, water, soil, and foodstuffs will be brought home to ever-widening circles in developed and developing countries. The possibility of "The Andromeda virus" or its equivalent will pass from

---

[5] In 1940 the Secretary of *Propaganda Fide,* Monsieur Celso Constantini, commented: "The Emperor was on the verge of conversion. If he had been converted, all China would almost certainly have followed the example of the Son of Heaven. The sad conflict of the Rites was probably the main cause of alienating the Emperor from the Christian religion." As a recent writer put it, "The modern churchman, accustomed to make every possible concession to native opinion, finds it strange that the Church was willing to lose China and India for points of custom." Maria Luisa Ambrosini with Mary Willis, *The Secret Archives of the Vatican* (Boston 1969), 262.

an occasional fantasy to a perpetual alert.[6] These cumulative threats will be accompanied by marvelous contributions to every human value. Many diseases and defects will succumb to laboratory science. New materials will enable many physical characteristics of man to change faster than most animals molt. Genetic engineering will come progressively closer to the deliberate planning of modified forms of life. Educational procedures will speed up the acquisition of linguistic, logical, and mathematical skill, and pave the way in early years for the acquisition of sophisticated tools of thought about ego and society.

Such a world map continually emphasizes the identity of "man," not of specific forms of parochial man (the nation of man not subnations of man). The iteration of emphasis on "our" position in outer space, "our" polluted land and sea and air, "our" threat of annihilation by uncontrolled conflict or disease or procreation, "our" opportunities to master knowledge on behalf of a world commonwealth of peace and dignity—all these cognitive references to man-in-context enlarge the boundary of the self with which the individual ego identifies. "Self" references guide the formation of demands for policies that diminish immediate and potential deprivation, and augment immediate and potential indulgence. The enlarging identity system defines the limits of tolerable action. Some actions—including inactions— become unthinkable. Such predispositions are among the preconditions of a more perfect public order. A broadening and intensifying identity system is at once an initiator and a censor of the range of permissible decisions in the world community.

The foregoing scenario projects a sequence that culminates in worldwide institutions that are both authoritative and controlling. It implies that on fundamental questions of war and peace the elite (and the rank and file) of the Superpowers and the weaker powers are willing to be outvoted. It means that the institutional process is effectively supported even where specific decisions are repugnant to significant elements in the world community. Obviously this requires a huge emotional investment in disciplining the self in the light of the common map of world realities.

We emphasize that the projection requires no drastic reconstruction of the formal structures of decision. Not the formal structures but the facts of control must change. As mass violence is perceived as less and less tolerable, the instruments for policing trouble spots are tacitly permitted to become more prompt and efficient. The presence of the inspectors, conciliators and arbitrators representing the United Nations will be commonplace. Revenue bases will be made available to

---

[6] The reference is to the title of a novel outlining the consequences of acquiring a destructive virus from extraterrestrial sources.

the organs of transnational order, whether in the form of licenses for exploiting the riches of the oceans, the ocean bed, the earth core, or outer space. Transnational civil servants will multiply as the permeability of boundaries increases. (For a systematic guide to Decision Phases see Note B at the end of the chapter.)

Intelligence services are more inclusive, rapid, and realistic in reporting recent developments and formulating plans of action. Promotional activities are less segregated and more interspersed among nations and regions. Prescriptions are more quickly made as the legislative role of the U.N. Assembly is perceived and accepted. Prescriptions are invoked with increasing frequency and effect in transnational, national, and subnational arenas. Agencies of application expand. Obsolete prescriptions are more quickly terminated and the appraisal of the functioning of public order institutions is more realistic and expeditious.

## Diffusion and Restriction

In assessing this "construct" it is appropriate to ask why it has not been effective up to the present. Why are we still in the throes of a suicidal arms race?

The broad answer, of course, is that the institution of war is supported by the institutions of a politically divided world in which the expectation of violence is a basic fact of life. Hence decision-making presidents, prime ministers, kings, or chiefs of staff are in a vulnerable position. If the ceremonial and effective elites of the great powers openly initiate a change in international public order that seems to subordinate them to other powers, they are vilified by political opponents in their Communist, Socialist, Republican, Democratic, Labour or Conservative parties. The question is whether the accelerating impact of the common world map will so modify systems of identity that members of sub-elites and mid-elites will refrain from blocking initiatives that contribute to the consolidation of a more potent and instantaneously operative system of public order. As systems of identity with *all* men eclipse identities with *some* men, the prospects of universal public order are improved.

A question is whether the mobilization of transnational incentives to support public order can occur simultaneously. The implication is that parallel developments occur throughout the globe to the extent that elite and mid-elite perspectives are so altered that important breaches of public order are perceived as intolerable among both officeholders and opposition. The strategy of simultaneity would appear to be the line of action that is most promising if the global forces on the side of peace and dignity are to assist in realizing the potentials here outlined.

## THE STRATEGY OF SIMULTANEITY

It has been lack of simultaneity that acts as a veto on the initiatives that might be taken to strengthen global agencies of inspection and policing. When the U.S.A. is in an accommodating phase, the Chinese and Soviet Russian elites are not necessarily so. And the U.S.A. may drag its feet on another day. The task is to multiply the number and intensity of involvements on the part of young and old, persistently active or intermittently active, who are warmly disposed to effective change in political systems.

We bear in mind the psychological mechanisms that in the past have operated so efficiently in inhibiting the growth of an active identity inclusive of humanity. I refer, for example, to the self-reference effect. What happens when people are first exposed to a larger environment either by travel or communicated images? Their focus of attention is altered and to some extent this alters the cognitive map. But exposure does not necessarily or even typically produce an expansion of the boundaries of the self to take in the new environment. It is worth noting that an early manifestation of the self-reference effect is to increase the amount of preoccupation with the original self. Consider the standard tourist: he sees the chopsticks of China, the sarongs of Southern Asia, or the mosques of the Near East in terms of his familiar self-image—whether the reference frame is Iowa, Provence, or the Hokkaido. Hence it is typical to find a quantitative (if not a relative) increase in self-references. In fact, the self-reference effect is part of the learning process, since it comprehends the new by noting likeness with or difference from the familiar. This is the sense in which waves of increased parochialism are to be predicted when a population is first exposed to a wider environment. This mechanism helps to explain why our increasingly interactive and interdependent world can be described up to the present as exhibiting less localism without, however, achieving an intense and universal identity with man.

It will be possible to follow the changing structure of world identities in future years by giving particular attention to increasing reactivity on matters touching world order. The changes can be shown by properly analyzed "occurrences," such as controversies over policies that appear to restrict the scope of national systems for the benefit of transnational order. Proposals that at an earlier date would not be taken seriously will become major features of party platforms and of statements by public leaders. Suppose, for instance, that the proposal to establish a system of transnational tribunals authorized to issue writs of habeas corpus becomes a major question everywhere. (Executives would be required to show cause for detaining an individual beyond a brief period.) Or imagine that the proposal to turn

10 percent of all national budgets over to the U.N. is "practical politics." Or that a worldwide scandal develops when some generals, industrialists and scientists try to develop a secret arsenal of biological weapons for the use of a single country. The salient point is that as a transnational identity is more generally and intensely held the deprivation of what is now perceived as the common interest is more bitterly resented. Public or private individuals or organizations that seem to block progress are objects of opprobrium for the performance of acts which were previously accepted without a ripple of protest.

As a means of rendering contingencies more vivid, consider the role of significant occurrences in a past case, such as the demand of the thirteen North American colonies for independence of Britain and recognition as Americans. It is easy to write a history of the movement that describes it as a series of dramatic conflicts between the colonies and the mother country. For instance, "The Stamp Act Crisis" of 1764–66 included the passage of various acts by Parliament, the convening of the Stamp Act Congress by the colonists, and the repeal of the offending acts by Parliament. No one doubts that the "confrontation" increased the sense of identification of the colonists with one another, the perception of their common interest, and the assessment of the new self as sufficiently powerful to affect decisions. This analysis, however, does not go far enough. A key question is whether the predispositions of the colonists had changed so that by 1764 they perceived their common interests with some clarity and acted with dispatch in attempting to affect results.

When the colonial press is analyzed (as has been done in an important study by Richard Merritt) [7] it becomes clear that predispositions had indeed changed, and that the reactivity of the 1764–66 period is partly to be understood in terms of the shift. From 1735 to 1775 colonial newspapers increased their attention to symbols of America while maintaining a rather steady interest in Britain. The American share grew from 13.2 percent in the decade 1735–44 to 34.3 percent in 1765–75 (an increase of 160 percent). In the last two pre-Revolutionary years 54.2 percent of the total symbol count was American.

Of particular relevance to our expectations about the future is the finding that the changing balance of self-references followed a cyclical pattern that was modified toward the end of the period when the downward trend after an attention peak was arrested.

The transformation of identity symbols (and presumably of perspectives) was neither a sudden illumination nor a simple straight line sequence. Rather the flow of events can be described, in Merritt's

[7] Richard L. Merritt, *Symbols of American Community, 1735–1775* (New Haven 1966).

words, as a "learning process" that "seemed to progress rapidly at some stages, to hold relatively steady in others, and in some cases even to decline." [8] Our developmental construct holds that the changing identity system of the effective elements in the world community will be indicated as their shared map of expectation portrays the common predicament and opportunity of man. The map aids in recognizing as enemies of progress all individuals, social groups, and procedures that block the realization of an inclusive world order capable of providing at least minimum security. Transnational loyalties will contribute to their own further growth by increasing the reactivity of more and more participants in the world arena against whatever stands in the way. As cycles of commitment rise and fall, the degree of drop-off will be less and less.

## INEQUALITIES

A complicating factor in forming and maintaining a wider unity is the inequitable distribution of control over the shaping and sharing of values. One is never quite sure whether the monumental edifices of a great urban center will serve as instruments for a strategy of awe that will impress the "back country," or whether, on the contrary, they will turn into a strategy of provocation for the zealots, tribesmen, and rustics who rail at the iniquities of Babylon.

One forecast is fairly sure: the life styles of the elite everywhere in the world will continue to converge. Every top manager, engineer, scientist, and public figure will demand prompt access for himself and his family to the best medical care; he will use his influence to arrange adequate facilities in his locality, and will travel in emergencies to the best centers. No matter how variegated the life styles may be in many respects, the elite classes will insist on sharing the "in" arts, sports, fashions, and manners of their opposite numbers in the most prestigious centers. Even today it is possible to travel around the globe from capital to capital—national or provincial—as a guest of the local elite, or a paying guest at the local Hilton (or sub-Hilton), without drastic change in eating, sleeping, or toilet habits. You may swap a Volkswagen or a limousine for a camel or an elephant or an odd creature called a horse. But the chances are you won't. And your receiving set can keep you clued in to "God's country" or "Marx's country," though this electronic tether to home base is blended with familiar static from rock or Bach.

Lined up around every center is a girdle of sub-centers; and around every sub-center is a girdle of satellites. Lined up around every elite is a sub-elite. For life-styles all necks are craned on the man above (or

8 Merritt (fn. 7), 59.

on the man above him). Besides any implications for power or money, the formal or informal hierarchies give or withhold respect (including the criteria for respect). And respect may depend on skills in "consumption" not "production"; on knowledge by quotation, not discovery; on propriety, not righteousness; on ingratiation, not affection.

The structure of equality-inequality in any community configuration approximates a design that is graduated and many-channeled, or segmented and fused. In industrialized communities where spatial and vertical mobility are relatively high, the span between the upper and the lower tenth may be great as to income, but the political process may be kept comparatively smooth as the political "brokers," "mediators," or "arbitrators" compromise or integrate articulate interests. Many escalators are available in every sector of society: politics, economics, enlightenment (science and information), health, education, popularity, respect, ethics, and religion. In communities with limited access to the global pattern of science-based technology segmentation implies sharp differences in the permissible life-styles of urban and rural areas, of tribesmen and modernized men, or among castes and classes. Such a society has few escalators and the dominant elite is usually quick to call on the army or police forces of the center to mobilize the coercion necessary to enforce public order. (This is the structure of countries with large landholders, small merchants and artisans, and tribal or peasant agriculture.) [9]

The recurring threat to the political stability of graduated and multi-channeled communities is that the communities with little command over capital resources may bring drastic pressure to bear on their political system to obtain outside assistance. Hence the political elite is cross-pressured to keep the support of both the outside sources and the internal population. Its members are vulnerable to parochial and demogogic movements led by dissident and ambitious members of the central elite, or by figures from the lesser strata. The top elite is the component of the world community most likely to be aware of world interdependence and hence of the precariousness of many policies. It is also in a position to join the political game in a larger arena, and to aim at obtaining respect and other assets from transnational activities. At the same time, as indicated above, it is a possible target of internal attack for failing to erase inequality.

Obviously mid-elite elements occupy a pivotal position in determining the future. The prospects of a more secure system of world public

[9] Among the vast number of pertinent studies see Edward Dew, *Politics in the Altiplano; The Dynamics of Change in Rural Peru* (Austin, Texas 1969). An attempt to generalize a segmented model to the world arena is Michael Barkun, *Law Without Sanctions; Order in Primitive Societies and the World Community* (New Haven 1968).

order depend on the cognitive map of the mid-elite, and on the intensity with which they commit themselves to parochial or to transnational ends.

As exposure to world culture rises, the prospect will probably improve of simultaneous initiatives throughout the globe on behalf of peace and dignity.

## INTEREST COALITIONS

We must not underestimate the potential effect of interest coalitions that block the measures required to strengthen global institutions. A principal tactic will continue to be the mobilization of parochial systems of identity to nullify the strength of more universal orientations. Such coalitions will occur in all powers, whether they are strong or weak, graduated or segmented, multi-channeled or fused. A brief reminder of those who may expect to benefit by these tactics: leaders of political factions or parties who hope to stigmatize officials as agents of a foreign power; officers of naval, land, air, or space forces who fear appropriation cuts; contractors for weapons who fear a shrinking market; leaders of managerial, scientific, skilled or unskilled work forces who fear layoffs; community leaders who are apprehensive about lost income and taxes; manufacturers of semi-processed products, fearful of foreign competition, who link high tariffs with strategic considerations; agricultural and other extractive operators who fear foreign competition and also use strategic arguments; foreign investors in mining and other enterprises that may be vulnerable to expropriation if military considerations lose importance; mass media which increase circulation and advertising revenue by xenophobia; religious organizations secretly fearful of local revolution and expropriation if military influence is reduced; landholders and other elite groups with similar fears; middle income groups apprehensive of internal violence and disorder if "pacifist and internationalist" tendencies gain strength; "revolutionary" parties fearful that if autonomy is in any way compromised revolutionary measures already adopted will be endangered by counterrevolutionary forces; race-conscious groups distrustful of arrangements that seem to give other races a potential veto on important matters; nationalistic groups apprehensive that foundations of love and loyalty are crumbling away.[10]

## THE REGIONAL AND THE UNIVERSAL

The groups that mobilize power to block universal public order may favor lesser consolidations at a regional level or along ideological

[10] Pertinent studies are abundant. A research report that emphasizes the expansion, not the narrowing, of perspective is, for instance, in Ithiel de Sola Pool, "Effects of Cross-National Contact on National and International Images," Chap. 4 in Kelman (fn. 4).

lines. There is no consensus about the degree to which high levels of regional integration foster or endanger the prospects of an inclusive system of public order capable of providing at least minimum security for all. Competent analysts of power-balancing processes have always recognized the tendency for all participants in a military arena to arrange themselves in two hostile groups, spatially segregated rather than interpenetrative. The classical pattern approximated under conditions of acute and active conflict is a compact "encircled" and a less compact "encircling" coalition. In modern world history the ultimate model is rarely approximated, and if it is at least partially achieved, the inner stresses of the various bodies politic often generate conflicts that disrupt such an alignment. (For instance, Russia was unable to fight World War I to an end on the Entente side, and Germany "collapsed" under pressure in 1918 and 1945.)

The important point in evaluating a successful regional movement appears to be the perspectives of those who bring it to fruition. If the elite expects to segregate the region from extraregional contact, such an ideology will resist tendencies to keep alive a continuing critical appraisal of its successes or failures. If, on the contrary, whatever degree of integration is achieved is always open to reappraisal, and if it is viewed as possible to modify existing arrangements on a territorial or pluralistic basis as a means of accommodating complex patterns of transnational interest, the results will be quite different. In the latter case, the preconditions are present for the evolution of global patterns of a pluralistic, interpenetrative character.

The significance of elite perspectives is brought out in Daniel Lerner's study of the members of the French elite from 1955 through 1965 (survey years were 1955, 1956, 1959, 1961 and 1965). A definite transformation occurred. The change was to move toward a pragmatically based pluralism, or "expathy" which was associated with the political modes of tolerance, negotiation, compromise, and consensus (as contrasted with dogmatism, intransigence, conflict, and coercion).[11] Such perspectives limit self-segregating tendencies toward autarky. They are compatible with flexible participation in larger communities (Europe, Euratlantica, or the whole world community).

In connection with the analysis of the place of regional integration in world politics it is pertinent to consider the past and prospective role of religions or secular movements with universalistic and radical ideologies. If such a movement were to succeed totally, it would expand

[11] Daniel Lerner and Morton Gorden, *Euratlantica; Changing Perspectives of European Elites* (Cambridge, Mass. 1969), 306. See Bruce M. Russett, *International Regions and the International System; A Study in Political Ecology* (Chicago 1967); further, Bert Landheer, *On the Sociology of International Law and International Society* (The Hague 1966).

its regionally segregated base until it encompassed the globe. In the past no world revolutionary radical movement has achieved universality. It has stopped short, and its regional base which at first was relatively segregated has become more interpenetrative with other global areas. Is it likely that in the future a coercive world revolutionary ideology will bring peace and order to the earth? Or will such initiatives once more end as regional blocs whose early structure, at least, is relatively segregated, not interpenetrative?

In considering the problem we are obliged to evaluate "developmental constructs" that emphasize the principal political movements of the past 200 years and of the future.[12] Consider the "moral and legalistic" symbolisms of the French Revolution, the "economic" vocabulary of the Socialist-Communist Revolutions, the "racist" language of the Nazis. The segregated pattern of dispersal of "races" on the globe is a standing invitation to mobilize collective action along the superficially plausible lines of bodily likeness and difference: "white" Europe, America, and Australia; "Black" Africa; "Brown" Asia. "Afro-Asia," for instance is a symbol that shrewdly fuses geographical, racial, religious, and "anti-white imperialist" connotations.

Past world revolutionary movements have failed of universality and become regional movements owing to the strength of restrictive factors from without and within. The French Revolutionary wave that spread from Paris, the Russian Revolutionary wave from Moscow, the Nazi Revolutionary wave from Berlin, had this in common with the religious revolutions of an earlier age (such as the Protestant Reformation): they were restricted from without by the elites of territorial areas that were changed by the partial incorporation of features borrowed from the new threat. Restriction from within occurred as vested interests were partially stabilized short of a united world.

A more far-reaching mechanism was restriction by functional differentiation, a process in which the distinctive core of a challenging ideology was counteracted and superseded in the name of an equally distinctive myth. Such were the sequences mentioned above: "rights of man" gave way to "proletarian socialism," and they were both confronted by the nominal biology of "Aryanism." Are we at the end of the racist-biological appeal? Or is the explosion of biological knowledge drawing a map of expectation that will eventually be utilized by political leaders to glorify a master-race of superbrains? Will the new ruling caste be brought into being by genetic engineers who will blend the "superstrains" of every race? Will the immediate future see steps

---

[12] For the concept see H. D. Lasswell, *World Politics and Personal Insecurity* (New York 1935; reprint, Cambridge, Mass. and New York 1965). For the constructs see, for instance, H. D. Lasswell and D. Lerner, eds., *World Revolutionary Elites; Studies in Coercive Ideological Movements* (Cambridge, Mass. 1966).

toward revival and completion of the dream of realizing the dignity of man on a global scale under the leadership of a vanguard of innovative intellectuals?

## MASS ACTION

Whatever happens it will undoubtedly be affected by the attitudes of the young and by the expectations of the old about the orientation of the young. Today's world is both disturbed and impressed by alienated youth. The theme of alienation has accompanied the expansion of industrial society. The image of the factory worker and the agricultural laborer as disengaged proletarians was a Marxist creation with scientific plausibility and agitational strength. Post-Marxian thinkers have extended the search for, and the discovery of, alienated groups to include many components of contemporary society: The "old" and the "new" middle classes (or "middle income skill groups"), "women," "intellectuals," "artists," "students," "youth." [13]

The "youth" appear to have the potential for collective action on the massive scale necessary to break down many surviving perspectives and operating arrangements the net effect of which is to keep the institution of war alive. We know that "crowd psychology" is an ever-present threat that haunts the security forces of established orders. A "crowd" is generated by simultaneous exposure to a common focus, and the "communications revolution" has created a world network that reaches the tens of millions rather than the thousands. An emerging common culture of rhythm, spontaneity, and love is inflaming the imaginations of youth in upper, middle, and lower layers of society in many countries. Among the gifted and educated young the obvious universality of scientific knowledge is fostering another wave of concern for parochial social arrangements—arrangements which subordinate knowledge to the pursuit of power by political parties and nation states, to the search after profits by private or public corporations, to the pursuit of glory by rival scientists or teachers or institutes, to the service of influential clients by physicians and professionals. The question is often posed: if knowledge is for man why not serve man directly through institutions directly connected with institutions of world public or civic order?

In this context a relevant point is whether the preconditions are imminent for another outpouring of mass emotionality in crusades. Specific forms, of course, would be generated by the cultures of our time. Perhaps we may see the mobilization of youth by the millions who surge to the wartorn spots of the globe, saturate military bases and front lines with youth brigades, and demand peace, dignity, and an end to fighting.

[13] See Pt. I of Kelman (fn. 4).

Any such movement will spread consternation among the elites who fear the dissolution of the social systems from which they benefit. They will be fearful that the loss of the young will weaken them more than the hypothetical enemy, and pave the way, not for a world of peace and dignity, but for a victorious oligarchy run by "the other side."

## THE SPECTER OF OLIGARCHY AND CASTE

If we assume that the elite classes of the component parts of the world arena remain under great pressure from "below," owing to continuing inequality, the possibility must not be overlooked that the principal elites will identify with one another against "mass" discontent. Such perceptions of common interest may enable them to consolidate a global system of public order that transcends those specific ideologies originally employed to obtain or to maintain power. It is not necessary for the "common threat from below" to be expressed through the channel of a single transnational organization in order to contribute to the development of a unifying perspective among elites. It is sufficient for simultaneous parallel pressures to erode the foundations of all established orders.

When we consider the factors affecting the evolution of a sense of common identity among political elites in the future, we must emphasize the role that a "common other" will probably play in the process. The fact of being treated as a distinct identity is a factor that contributes to the redefinition of any self-system. The English writers whose articles and letters appeared in colonial newspapers preceded writers on this side of the Atlantic in identifying both the land and its people as "American." The available indicators suggest that Englishmen began to identify the colonial population as "Americans" persistently after 1763, a decade before the Americans themselves did so.[14] If parallel "initiatives from below" stigmatize top governmental executives, legislators, military and industrial figures as belonging to one "transnational establishment" regardless of their diversities of color or political myth, the members of all elites are likely to perceive themselves in the same way.

Of obvious importance is the future of political strategies. Will the expansion of science-based technology help to transform the traditional balance between the use, by established elites, of symbolic and of nonsymbolic instruments?

The enormous importance of communication—of the symbolic instrument in diplomacy and propaganda—has been acknowledged in the manuals of statecraft in every society of record. Symbols are almost always cheaper than guns, and in any case they are routinely employed in the family and in other primary environments as means of trans-

14 Merritt (fn. 7), Chap. 7.

mitting accepted attitudes toward authority. Once incorporated in the self-system of the young these symbolic patterns are defended by internal monitors. The conscience inflicts automatic symptoms of anxiety on the incipient rejector of authority. Mass media, too, when kept under elite control, exclude from popular attention whatever is presumed to be an upsetting (a liberating) experience.

However, symbolic means are not entirely satisfactory. They are subject to grave limitations as a tool of self-perpetuation. Managers of mass media are prone to misread the predispositions of their audiences and to select material that inadvertently undermines the credibility of the system. The symbols used in the early socialization process may suffer from similar myopia on the part of parents, teachers, and educational administrators. There is also the relatively unpredictable creativity of human beings, whose innovative brilliance is not always tamed either by early rigidities of perception or by later twinges of conscience.

A further complication is that the process of communication itself inaugurates new, even though often transitory situations. Such alignments occur every time people fall into new listening or conversational groups. The perspectives cultivated in these situations are not necessarily in accord with accepted beliefs, faiths, or loyalties.

From time immemorial elites have supplemented symbols by the use of nonsymbolic instruments such as blows, body mutilation, or violent death; or by denials of food, shelter, and medical care. Chemicals are a favorite weapon, especially poisons (outlined, for example, in Kautilya's *Arthasastra* or in the "how to do it" manuals of the alchemists).

For some time now it has been feasible to complicate ordinary medical (or employment) examinations by the use of tests designed to reveal conscious or even unconscious indicators of faulty loyalty, that is of incomplete identity with the established order. Given the growing refinement of knowledge, the crude instruments of lie detection now available are obsolescent. And whatever the rate of advance in the next twenty years toward genetic control, this weapon will eventually appeal to the practical imagination of political elites who will see in genetic engineering a means of rendering most of the population incapable of rebellion. The temptation to rely on such a "final solution" will increase.

If temptations of the kind are to be prevented or nullified, much more than simple denunciation is necessary. The challenge is to evolve countervailing strategies of humanization. The dehumanizing tendencies of science-based technology are expressed in the "apathetic fallacy," the opposite of the pathetic fallacy of romanticism. The apathetic fallacy treats man as a thing (a machine), and sacrifices empathy, or the concern for entering as far as possible into the experience of others.

To a degree we must rely on the communication media provided by the technoscientific revolution to conduct a "counterrevolution of humanity," if not, in fact, of "life." Given the accelerating rate of exposure to and interaction with life styles, we have been dilatory in employing the media to provide opportunities for insight and understanding between persons whose upbringing has separated them by culture, class, interest, and personality.

The counterrevolution of the humane must go much further than this. For instance it is necessary to make our devastated urban and nonurban environments livable.

## IN CONCLUSION

Transnational systems of identity will be widely shared by the educated and power elites and mid-elites of all countries. As global interactions rise in frequency more and more participants in the world community will take one another into account. Their self-image will share a cognitive map in which all human beings are shown to be vulnerable to the destructive consequences of science-based technology unless an inclusive decision process is made adequately authoritative and controlling. The map will also emphasize the vast value indulgences that result from a properly mastered technology.

The cognitive map will affect the world political process by circumscribing the range of tolerable policy alternatives. It will do so by representing the consequences of escalated conflict in matter of fact and vivid terms. Some risks are "unthinkable." There is also an affirmative effect. The expectation map stimulates the release of creative initiatives to take advantage of the positive payoffs of common action to master science-based technologies.

The progressive involvement of elite and mid-elite elements in a common system of identity and a homogeneous life-style has positive consequences for world public order. These elite components can mobilize the rank and file of the world community in ways that help to overcome the effects of parochial socialization. The global process of interaction will contribute to the formation of active and inclusive zones of attention, opinion, action, belief, faith, loyalty, and organization. Without fanfare it will be possible to change authoritative and controlling perspectives in such a way as to integrate a world public order of peace, security, and dignity.

We have not underestimated the strength of the spatially restrictive factors that will continue to work in favor of continuing the present structure—a divided world that sustains the institution of war. Nor, on the other hand, have we neglected to weigh the factors that strengthen world order, though at the cost of human dignity.

It is generally agreed that the task is to strengthen predispositions that mobilize identities with, and support for, policies which aid in transforming the world community into a comprehensively graduated, interpenetrative, and many-channeled system of public and civic order.

## NOTE A
### Indicators of Identity

A major difficulty in estimating identity systems is that immediate behavior (which includes communications), when taken literally, is not always a reliable basis for predicting subsequent behavior. There may be deliberate deception, as when the voters in a plebiscite declare themselves in favor of one identity while clinging to a different commitment. Public expressions do not necessarily coincide with private or inner perspectives. Yet systematic estimates of the latter may be more reliable predictors of future behavior in international crises than estimates inferred solely from public expressions.

A further complication is that when people are trying to be candid, they are often in error about themselves. They often underestimate the deep religious, racial, and regional biases acquired in formative years, or deny the intensity of repressed hostilities that frustrate a conscious ideal of patient self-control in a crisis.

A pervasive error on the part of political analysts is to treat an immediate situation as an accurate exemplar of future situations. What is meant is not that the members of a group deliberately deceive, or that they mistake their own predispositions. The point is that the situation is probably not sufficiently congruent with future situations to provide a dependable prevision of perspectives and behaviors. During a given period the specific environments of a group are insufficiently diverse to bring about a complete disclosure of group predispositions. During intercrisis periods, in particular, the analyst may not have an opportunity to observe how people are predisposed to cope with a sudden threat to life or to the establishment with which they are identified. This means that knowledge is always somewhat incomplete as a basis of inferring response to future contingencies.

Several strategies are open to a political analyst who recognizes the problem. He may examine current (or past) situations in order to locate sub-situations where individuals can be found whose predispositions are unusual, or where the environment is exceptionally severe or mild. Although a given period may be one of general peace and prosperity, parts of a country may be affected by the memory of recent hardship or by a localized recession. Intense study of these contexts may provide clues to the strength of tendencies toward factionalism, secession, or utopianism. Perhaps the inference is that such acts will occur on a large scale under contingencies to which a probability may be tentatively assigned.

Another strategy of investigation is to arrange experimental or prototyping situations. The aim is to discover latent predispositions among group members. The experiments may be designed to present policy problems in which competing or conflicting identities are mobilized (religious versus party loyalty, race versus economic group, etc.).

A strategy that commends itself to an increasing extent is to provide for improved world coverage during the immediate and more remote future. The plan is to make it easier for political analysts to keep in closer touch with a realistic map of changes in systems of identity and to observe them in context. The program also enables the analysts to benefit from participation in continuing seminars that allow them to project the future, and to benefit from the feedback of data as events unfold. Seminar members can also benefit by attempting to improve their bases of inference. They engage in critical discussion as to why previous projections were correct or incorrect.

More important than forecasting the future is changing it. This calls for commitment to such overriding goals as peace and dignity. It also requires creative orientation toward knowledge of the past and estimates of the future. Creativity is expressed in the invention of policy objectives and strategies that optimalize results. This includes exposure to the discipline of estimating the probability that one's own interventions will have the results sought (and of evaluating feedback as the future appears). Many "leader" types are impatient of such discipline. But they may be partly protected by advisers who undergo such exposure.

Some institutions already provide limited coverage of changing systems of identity. In the accessible parts of the globe sample surveys rely on data obtained by short interviews administered by trained and trusted investigators. Short interview results are often supplemented by case studies of communities, conducted by diversified techniques of gathering and processing data. Pioneered by social anthropologists, these procedures include participating in the life of the society, and noting words (gestures and postures), deeds, and resource management in ordinary or special circumstances.

Where political barriers stand in the way of survey and depth research, an indirect indicator of perspective is the content of the public media available to audiences. It is plausible to assume that the symbols of identity used by the media that regularly reach a given audience correspond to the systems of identity current among audience members. Some news commentators assume an obvious "we" and "they."

Strictly speaking, the contents of any medium of communication are the most satisfactory indicators of the outlook of those who control it. The official press, radio, and television are examined in search of indicators of official plans and assumptions. Such material shows how the controlling group perceives the identity system of its audience. For years, there may be no news of certain minority groups. Suddenly the "Blacks," or the "Untouchables," or "Youth" make headlines. Presumably these groups are perceived by official or private controllers of media as sufficiently important to receive more attention. Evidently the national identity is in process of redefinition. Hence the strategies of selection employed by media controllers indicate the perceived composition of the politically relevant "self" and "other."

Clearly, the words uttered by, or addressed to, a group provide indicators of the direction and intensity of political attitudes. Two other categories of indicator are exceedingly significant: the performance of deeds (overt acts beyond words), and the manipulation of resources. Participants in a political process signalize the intensity of their involvement by making human and physical resources available for a cause. The fluctuating intensity of support for a "Jewish national home" in Palestine can be estimated approximately by dollar contributions, size of membership rolls of Zionist organizations, frequency of attendance, class representativeness of the members (upper, middle, lower), assistance by other associations (political parties and "orders," pressure groups and gangs, official agencies). Where open agitation is not permitted the indicators would be the volume of undercover assistance (political, economic, etc.). In terms of the political process map we have been summarizing the "base values" and "strategic operations" of a political participant who is expressly concerned with identity questions.

The discussion has gone far enough to suggest that for our purposes the most desirable indicators are trustworthy communications which are supplemented but not supplanted by other indices. Our principal concern is with the number and location of individuals who achieve at least a minimum level of identity with and impact on world public order. The preferred indicators are trustworthy communications that exhibit explicit identity with man, a disposition to regard war as intolerable, and a tendency to support innovations likely to do away with it.

We emphasize the desirability of a trustworthy communication because it is necessary to avoid the mistaken inferences that depend only on public behavior. We have already commented that in some plebiscites voting has been done under coercive conditions that led to grossly mistaken conceptions of identity systems, and to erroneous forecasts of future political behavior. Similarly, the ruling elites and the intellectuals of an area may mistake the seeming calm of a given period, exhibited by a given social category, as implying a strong system of identity that fosters the continuation of an established order. Is it necessary to adduce examples? Some reminders: the underestimation in the U.S.A. of the involvement of many segments of the black population and of youth with the political order; the mistaken assumptions of the European colonial powers concerning the political attitudes of colonial peoples; the mistaken images of peasant loyalty entertained by the elites of France, Russia, and most of the countries where the structure of society was "feudal"; the miscalculations of British tenacity made by the effective leaders of Germany in two world wars.

## NOTE B

### Decision Phases

The development of public order institutions can be analyzed in detail by examining outcomes that are part of the total flow of decision.

Intelligence ⟶
Promotion ⟶
Prescription ⟶
Invocation ⟶
Application ⟶
Termination ⟶
Appraisal ⟶

The arrows could point in both directions and could be drawn vertically to indicate interactions within the structures and functions of the decision process as a whole.

As a system of public order becomes more inclusive, facilitating changes occur at all phases. The intelligence outcomes are the transmission or withholding of information relevant to policy action. Among the structures specialized to this phase are the overt and covert agencies (census, espionage), and planning commissions. Official agencies may be supplemented by unofficial agencies (private press).

The promotion phase is the active mobilization of support for major policies. In modern states the political party and the pressure group network specialize in this function.

The prescribing phase is the crystallization of general policies. This is the chief role of legislatures and of the treaty process.

The invoking phase is the provisional application of prescriptions to concrete situations. The initial steps in a police or administrative action are typical.

The terminating phase is the ending of a prescription and the disposition of claims generated when the prescription was in force. Special structures are set up to cope with war or state succession problems.

The appraisal phase is the assessment of success or failure in achieving public policy and the provisional assignment of responsibility.

The seven phases of decision utilize the governmental channels to perform five tasks. The constitutive task allocates power among the participants in the decision process itself. It covers the authoritative and controlling arrangements relating to the use of power as a base value for power purposes. Thus it includes the territorial division of power and the separation of powers among the organs that make the decisions enumerated above (intelligence, etc.).

The supervisory task of government is to provide a means of settling private controversies that are referred to it for settlement (e.g. disputes over contracts, alleged wrongs). The regulatory task is to maintain the fundamental structures in every sector of society that are entitled to protection (e.g. the family institution). The enterprisory task is to administer activities that are carried on through community-wide organizations (other than the institutions specialized to the power process itself). The sanctioning task is to obtain conformity to public policy by managing deprivations and indulgences.

The role of public authority and control in various societies can be described in terms of a map of the social process: participants striving to optimalize preferred outcomes (values) through institutions affecting resources. My colleagues and I find it convenient to employ eight value-institution categories to analyze any social process. In brief: the power value is the shaping and sharing of important, enforceable decisions; power institutions are law, government and politics. The enlightenment value is the shaping and sharing of knowledge of the social and natural context; enlightenment institutions include mass media and agencies of research. The wealth value is the shaping and sharing of claims to resources; the wealth institutions are, for example, the specialized extractive, manufacturing, financing, and commercial operations. The well-being value is the shaping and sharing of safety, health, and comfort; well-being institutions include operations that specialize in conserving or destroying life. The skill value is the shaping and sharing of competences in occupational, professional, and artistic expression. The affection value is the shaping and sharing of love and friendship with particular persons, and of loyalty to symbols of group identity; affection institutions include families, friendship groups, and fraternal associations. The respect value is the shaping and sharing of recognition; respect institutions include social classes and castes. The rectitude value is the shaping and sharing of the norms and applications of responsible conduct; rectitude institutions include ethical and ecclesiastical associations.

# CHAPTER 2

# Population

## MARY ELLEN CALDWELL

### INTRODUCTION

IN 1962, Sir Charles Galton Darwin, grandson of the great naturalist, speculated about the future of mankind in *The Next Million Years*.[1] He admitted the essential irrelevance of that grandiose projection and the world remains indifferent to its pessimistic conclusions. He succeeded, however, in focusing attention upon the fact that human beings find it difficult to identify with their own unborn. The effects of this psychic inability in the human race are many. Among them is an unwillingness to accept a present responsibility for assuring a habitable environment for their children, to say nothing of their unconcern for their children's children. Indeed, Sir Charles denied the existence of a strong procreative desire in most of the human family. Reproduction of the human species, like that of other animal life, appears to be grounded in, and guaranteed by, the sexual instinct, not the parental. Sir Charles predicts that unless the essential "wild beast" in man is changed, the central question for humanity will continue to be what it has always been, the problem of "the starving margin." Science confirms that this is an ecological truth for other forms of life, and Sir Charles doubts that mankind is capable of willing his own existence as an exception to that rule.

These studies on the future of the international legal order proceed on two basic assumptions. The first is that a large number of us who are alive today will live to share the consequences of current decisions about that future. By limiting our inquiry to the near future of ten to twenty years, we may avoid the speculative generalizations that so often accompany projections to a more distant time. Many of us have a large stake in the immediate future and our concern for it does not demand species-specific altruism or an unnatural concern for descendants whom we shall never see. In 1990, persons born in 1930 at the beginning of the Great Depression will be sixty years old. The children of post-World War II affluence will be at the peaks of their productive careers. Those yet to be born in 1972 when this series of studies is completed will be eighteen. Thus, the audience for whom we are making projections and offering recommendations comprises a global population of which many of us will be a part and whose life experience spans well over half a century.

[1] London 1952.

A second assumption is the widespread belief that studies such as these may influence decisions to be made by those now living, in ways that will serve the value preferences of most human beings. Basic among those values is the desire to live.

Recently, that urge to live has taken on a new quality—the desire to live well. The fundamental issues raised in this volume are focused on whether we can or should intervene in the natural order of things in order to perpetuate and universalize a quality of life that has been attained by relatively few people in this century.

Even if Sir Charles' belief that the starving margin of humanity has been and always will be our major problem is a correct one, the past fifty years have introduced an element that may affect human response to that dismal fact of life. It is the new awareness by people everywhere that human misery can be alleviated. Science and technology have made it possible to broadcast around the globe the message that life can be lived more comfortably and more abundantly than ever before. As tangible proof of that new truth, science and technology have also made it possible to reduce dramatically the death rate all over the world. For the first time in history, the suffering, starving margin of the human family can perceive an alternative. Instead of slipping into eternity in tragic lassitude, the poor and ill-fed can be expected to behave quite differently from their predecessors. Demands and disorder, rather than prayers and despair, are likely to shape the process of sharing the world's food in the foreseeable future. In a global society attuned to egalitarian concepts of human rights and dignity, the starving margin is apt to claim equal access to the granaries of the rich. Given the dimensions of the population problem, its causes and expected trends, and the perspectives attending individual claims to a right to life, what are the prospects that the international legal order can act to tame the wild beast that Sir Charles says still resides in us?

Richard A. Falk has asserted that the population issue is closely intertwined with all principal dimensions of the future of international order.[2]

The prospect of mass distress and international catastrophe arising from projected population increases is a virtual certainty. As such, questions of population policy should be shifted from the legally reserved domain of "domestic jurisdiction" to the domain of "international concern." Population projections, and even present levels of population, are bound to imperil, if not negate, the attainment of almost every human right set forth in the Declaration of Human

[2] Richard A. Falk, "World Population and International Law," 63 *American Journal of International Law*, 517–18 (July 1969).

Rights and in the Covenant of Economic and Social Rights. The same reasoning that underlies the internationalization of questions of genocide and racial oppression applies to population policy. The entire logic supporting a global legal policy on matters of fundamental human rights and on issues of peace and security establishes the case for the international status of population problems: (1) a failure to adopt rational and humane population policies on the national level causes serious adverse consequences on the international level; (2) a failure to adopt rational and humane population policies on the national level violates minimum world community standards applicable to group welfare within national boundaries.

Because international lawyers have exhibited little professional concern with population problems, the effort is made here to elaborate the logical case for their international status. It begins with a description of prevailing trends in population size, distribution, and composition in the world's major regions, and describes ways in which internal population pressures may become matters of international concern. The wide variations in population growth rates among various regions of the world prompts inquiry into the "fertility motives" of peoples in those regions. Similar inquiries are made into the justifications given by political elites in support of pro-natalist or anti-natalist national policies. Against this backdrop, several suggested solutions are examined and evaluated, and specific recommendations are made for immediate international action to ensure a decade of lead-time for designing solutions to the larger problem of finding a balance between man and his finite resource environment, the Earth.

### I. The Human Family: Now and Twenty Years from Now

Demographers and population analysts have amassed an enormous literature portraying the past, present, and future of people and their distribution throughout the world. Numbers, age, sex, and race; education and skill; creed, ideology, and folklore; health and economic status; all these and more are relatively known or knowable facts about millions in human communities. It would be an impossible task to summarize their findings here. It is essential, nevertheless, that we grasp some notion of who now inhabits the earth and the extent to which the present composition of world population is expected to be the same or substantially different in the next twenty years.

One mid-1968 population estimate for the world's major regions shows the following distribution of the global total of 3.5 billion people presumed to be alive at that date (see Table 1). By the year 2000, the populations in Africa, Asia, and Latin America, already comprising 2.5 billion of the world's total, will have doubled. Those

TABLE 1

THE RICH AND THE POOR: NUMBERS NOW AND THEN

| Area | Population Estimates (mid-1968 millions) | Per Capita National Income (U.S. $) | No. of Years to Double Population |
|---|---|---|---|
| WORLD | 3,479 | 493 | 35 |
| Africa | 333 | 123 | 31 |
| Asia | 1,943 | 128 | 32 |
| Latin America | 268 | 344 | 24 |
| North America | 222 | 2,793 | 63 |
| Europe | 455 | 1,069 | 100 |
| Oceania | 18.5 | 1,636 | 39 |
| U.S.S.R. | 239 | 928 | 63 |

SOURCE: Table 9-5. William Petersen, *Population* (2d edn., New York 1969), 328–32. From data compiled by the Population Reference Bureau, Washington, D.C.

regions happen also to be poorer than the remaining areas of the world. Assuming continued growth at current rates of natural increase, the poorer peoples could attain their promised inheritance of the earth by the year 2000.

Not only are their numbers increasing with fantastic speed, but the poorer countries are also expected to contribute an ever-growing share of the total population growth of the world as a whole. John J. Durand has estimated that the richer nations are becoming proportionately less significant in the overall growth of the human family. Table 2 shows

TABLE 2

THE RICH WILL BE FEWER: SHARE OF TOTAL POPULATION GROWTH

| Period | Europe, U.S.S.R., North America, Oceania, Japan (percent) | Africa, Latin America, Asia (except U.S.S.R. and Japan) (percent) |
|---|---|---|
| 1900–1950 | 31 | 69 |
| 1950–1965 | 22 | 78 |
| 1965–2000 | 11–14 | 86–89 |

SOURCE: John J. Durand, "A Long-Range View of World Population Growth," 369 *The Annals of The American Academy of Political and Social Science* (1967), 7.

the progressive diminution in the rate at which the richer countries are contributing to world population growth.

What are the implications of these patterns of increase? Unfortunately, the economics of coping with rapidly multiplying population in developing areas and the insidious beliefs of many political elites that "people are power" present a twin-barreled threat to the world at large.

## A. People and World Power

In language calculated to perpetuate a power politics theory of international relations, Philip Hauser has contrasted French political preeminence in 1800 with its diminished state in 1910 in the following terms: [3]

> In Europe in 1800, for example, France with a population of some twenty-seven million conducted her foreign relations vis-à-vis a less developed Russia of some thirty-seven million persons, a Germany of less than twenty-five millions, an Italy of eighteen millions, a United Kingdom of some sixteen millions. The United States at that time had little more than five million inhabitants. By 1910, however, a France of less than forty million faced a Germany of sixty-five million; Russia had a population of 140 million; the United Kingdom forty-five million; Italy thirty-five million. The United States in 1910 had grown to ninety-two million.

The same suggestion is made in Colin Clark's array of world powers, covering a much longer span of time; see Table 3.

Today the leadership in several of the most densely populated underdeveloped countries has adopted vigorous policies of fertility control, but decision makers in other areas have declined to do likewise. Recalling the words of Juan Bautista Alberdi, a 19th century political thinker, "to govern is to populate," officials in Argentina, for example, are actively seeking to encourage a domestic population explosion, notwithstanding the fact that the country's 1.3 percent annual economic growth rate is one of the lowest in Latin America.[4] Moreover, in terms that sound spurious to Western ears, it is argued in some of the poorer countries that birth control is being promoted to effect a form of genocide, or to keep poor countries economically dependent upon the wealthy nations of the world.

Demographer Kingsley Davis has enumerated four reasons why population size is regarded by some as a major determinant of national

[3] Introduction, by Philip M. Hauser, ed., *Population and World Politics* (Glencoe, Ill. 1958), 17.
[4] *Columbus* (Ohio) *Dispatch,* UPI, March 6, 1969, 25A.

TABLE 3

POPULATION AND WORLD POWER STATUS
(Millions)

| 1670 | (Minimum 1 million) | 1770 | (Minimum 6 million) |
|---|---|---|---|
| Turkey | 25 | Russia | 33 |
| France | 20 | Turkey | 30 |
| Russia | 16 | France | 24 |
| Spain-Portugal | 7 | Austria | 20 |
| England | 6 | U.K. | 14 |
| Poland | 5 | Spain | 9 |
| Netherlands | 1 | Prussia | 6 |
| 1870 | (Minimum 27 million) | 1970 | (Minimum 100 million) |
| Russia | 78 | China | 670 |
| Germany | 41 | India | 550 |
| Austria-Hungary | 40 | U.S.S.R. | 245 |
| U.S.A. | 39 | U.S.A. | 205 |
| France | 36 | Indonesia | 120 |
| U.K. | 31 | Pakistan | 110 |
| Italy | 27 | Japan | 100 |

SOURCE: Colin Clark, "World Power and Population," *National Review* (May 20, 1969), 481.

and, thus, international power.[5] The first two are tied to economic theory: (1) the magnitude of the total population is the principal factor in the size of the labor force, which, in turn, is the principal determinant of gross national productivity, and (2) given the adequacy of resources, the larger the population integrated into one economic system, the greater the potential advantages of scale to be gained from mass production and mass distribution. If all of the other variables in the economic growth equation are adequate, then there can be no quarrel with these generalized assertions. However, among states that rely upon such rationalizations in support of pro-natalist policies there exist wide variations in present levels of technology, organizational infrastructure and skill, investment capital, and distribution systems. Declining per capita income during periods of admitted gross national economic growth in such states provides the clearest indicator that numbers and exploitable resource bases alone are insufficient to ensure domestic economic strength.

The third and fourth justifications catalogued by Davis are: (3) a large population is necessary to furnish age groups for a sizable conventional army and to sustain losses in fighting strength, and (4) con-

[5] Kingsley Davis, "Population and Power in the Free World," in Hauser, ed. (fn. 3), 199.

solidation of victory in war often requires sizable occupation forces. However distasteful the prospects, one cannot lightly dismiss this kind of thinking. This century, indeed this decade, has witnessed enormous loss of life in war, by both great and small nations, and national security is a foremost concern among those currently taking part in disarmament and peace negotiations at various capitals in the world. But here again, all other things are seldom equal. Small nations may have other internal and external assets that offset mere differences in domestic manpower. Similarly, more populous nations may be correspondingly weak internally, to a degree that reduces the threat value of mere population size.

In a world where leaders of large and small nations alike must somehow meet their constituencies' demand for a better life, it is far more relevant to aspire to the levels of stability and production already attained by numerous middle-sized and smaller states than to gamble on the sheer force of numbers in the primitive world power game.

Julius Stone, exploring the prevailing concepts of international justice, has made quite clear the necessity for projecting further the domestic principles of distributive justice into the international legal order—to assure some minimal material endowment and rights of personality among individuals throughout the world.[6] His call for intensified efforts to expand the numerous technical and assistance programs undertaken by the United Nations and other multilateral operations clearly demands serious consideration and action in the next two decades. Implementation of such efforts would be greatly enhanced if there were any indication that responsible world leaders had abandoned the dangerous and unsound economic and military rationales to justify unrestrained population increase.

## B. Impacts of Differential Growth on Wealth Distribution

Recent trends and the predictions embodied in Table 1 support the old maxim that, barring radical intervention, the rich will get richer while the poor get poorer. With few exceptions, the underdeveloped areas with high rates of population increase will be proportionately worse off in human goods and values in 1990 than they are today. Professor Falk suggests several detrimental consequences of population growth in such areas: [7]

(1) the effort to feed increasing populations will reduce the capacity of national governments to take other steps to improve the quality

6 Julius Stone, "Approaches to the Notion of International Justice," in Cyril E. Black and Richard A. Falk, eds. *The Future of the International Legal Order* (Princeton 1969), I, 372–460.

7 Falk (fn. 2), 516–17.

of life for their population through better housing, health, education, welfare services, and leisure facilities; (2) the rapid increase in urban populations in conditions that already are often unbearably overcrowded is likely to induce rising rates of crime, riot, disease, and acute emotional distress; (3) increases in population tend to be accompanied by exponential increases in pollution of air and water supplies; (4) many poor countries experiencing an increasing growth in population are also, as a consequence, more vulnerable to various forms of political extremism involving recourse to large-scale violence at home and abroad.

That these trends are being borne out in fact is quite evident in studies of the adverse effects of crowding as more and more people aggregate in cities and metropolitan areas.

## C. Effects of Urbanization and Global Crowding

During the past century and a half, urbanization has been viewed as an index of technological and economic development, and there is every prospect that migration to the cities all over the world will continue apace in the next twenty years. Demographers warn, however, that mere aggregation is not a hopeful sign. The current flow of rural poor into the cities of underdeveloped countries is not the same phenomenon as was nineteenth and twentieth century urbanization in Europe and North America. The latter movement was both antecedent to technological advancement and a result of it; the former is often a mere relocation of dispossessed rural peoples into urban encampments. Whether the movement from the hinterlands to the big cities is direct, or by way of intermediate migration to small urban centers, the receiving metropolitan communities are rapidly losing their ability to absorb the immigrant masses. In some areas, the cities themselves are becoming ruralized. In others, the volatile potentials of unemployed masses of hungry poor pose dramatic crisis possibilities in domestic politics. Such crowding threatens the safety, stability, and civility of the receiving cities.

As people shift from one socioculture to another, behavior that was useful in the former setting is often maladaptive to the new. The psychiatrist, Dr. Eugene Brody, has described the individual migrant's situation as follows: [8]

The migrant leaves behind the supports and stresses of the donor system from which he departs, including the push factors which contributed to his decision to move. He loses the support of social and

[8] Eugene B. Brody, "Migration and Adaptation: The Nature of the Problem," in *American Behavioral Scientist*, XIII (No. 1, September/October 1969), 7.

geographic familiarity, of longterm relationships and values which were built into him while growing up. At the same time he is freed of some of the threats of disease and hunger, of the obligations to perform in expected ways and of certain stressful relationships. He is welcomed by the receptor networks or must deal with resistances in the host system to which, lured in part by pull factors, he comes. He is excited by new stimuli and opportunities and fearful of the new threats and the unknown. Between the systems, en route, he must cope with a series of transitional factors which color his perceptions, attitudes and capacity to deal with the host environment. And his adaptation throughout is shaped by internal motives for moving which may have little to do with environmental push or pull factors.

The aggregate psychological and physical consequences of an increasingly crowded society, populated by such migrants, are becoming clearer. The editors of a well-known medical journal have labeled the undeniable effects "people pollution." [9] Citing studies by physicians, research scientists, and others, including the authors of a recent United Nations report, they predict that "continued urbanization, even in wealthy countries, is likely to increase incidence of a long list of physical and social ills: tuberculosis, parasitosis, skin diseases, diarrhea diseases, malnutrition, bowel infections, respiratory infections, venereal diseases, mental breakdowns, psychosomatic illnesses, suicide attempts, crime, drug dependence, and antisocial behavior." Urbanization in some of the more affluent countries has taken on this character and, together with problems of racism, is posing comparable domestic problems, notably in the United States.

### D. Racism: Amelioration or Exacerbation?

Racial tension and conflict are not new, but in the twentieth century they have taken on some new characteristics which are relevant to our consideration of population increase. The culminating event of European dominance over much of the nonwhite world was the political emancipation of most colonial territories. Quite naturally, anti-white sentiment was a potent political weapon among indigenous leaders during decolonization. In the ensuing period of internal instability and economic distress, racism continues to be a powerful argument against white economic imperialism. In a near future populated predominantly by poorer nonwhites whose numbers increase at rates calculated to make them even poorer, only a fool would predict a reduction in international racial tension and fear. The problem of racism is further complicated by the fact that nonwhite minorities in

---

[9] "People Pollution," *Medical World News* (December 19, 1969), 28.

the United States and elsewhere in the affluent West have begun to exert their political strength to attain total civic, social, and economic equality with the white man. The unfortunate coincidences of color, poverty, and population increase, coupled with efficient communication of both truth and half-truth about racial perspectives, are likely to intensify existing conflicts. The affluent white minority of the world in Europe, North America, U.S.S.R., and Oceania, can be expected to be the domestic and international targets of politicized racism in future claims by nonwhites for their share of the world's wealth. It is impossible to predict at this juncture whether backlash or enlightened distributive justice will be the prevailing white mode by 1990.

## E. Youth and Age

Just as modern communications have helped to universalize perspectives about the good life and about the unhappy condition of nonwhite peoples, the mass media have also helped to intensify the eternal struggle between fathers and sons. Recent decades have produced an intense mutual identification of the youth of all countries. Student dissent and the contagion of political activism among the young may be approaching epidemic proportions.

Table 4 illustrates the extent to which persons under the age of twenty-five are expected to comprise the numerical majority of the world's population in the next thirty years. Note that the balance in favor of the young is greater in the poorer, essentially nonwhite areas.

TABLE 4

THE NEAR FUTURE BELONGS TO THE YOUNG

| Area | 1965 | | 1980 | | 2000 | |
|---|---|---|---|---|---|---|
| | Percent under 25 | Percent 65 and over | Percent under 25 | Percent 65 and over | Percent under 25 | Percent 65 and over |
| WORLD | 53.9 | 5.2 | 54.2 | 5.8 | 50.8 | 6.4 |
| Africa | 62.5 | 2.7 | 62.7 | 2.8 | 61.8 | 3.2 |
| Asia | 56.7 | 3.9 | 55.8 | 4.5 | 49.1 | 6.0 |
| Latin America | 60.6 | 3.4 | 61.1 | 3.9 | 57.8 | 4.3 |
| North America | 46.8 | 9.1 | 47.1 | 9.4 | 46.9 | 8.9 |
| Europe | 40.0 | 10.6 | 38.2 | 13.1 | 37.4 | 13.1 |
| Oceania | 47.7 | 7.7 | 47.6 | 8.3 | 48.7 | 8.5 |
| U.S.S.R. | 44.7 | 6.9 | 43.5 | 9.5 | 42.9 | 11.2 |

SOURCE: Table A2.1, Age Composition of the World, Major Areas, Medium Variant of U.N. Projections: U.N. Department of Economic and Social Affairs, *World Population Prospects*, Population Studies, No. 41 (1966).

## TABLE 5

DEPENDENCY RATIOS, MAJOR WORLD AREAS,
1960 AND 1975

| Area | $\dfrac{\text{Population Aged } 0\text{-}14,\, 65+}{\text{Population Aged } 15\text{-}64} \times 100$ | | $\dfrac{\text{Economically Inactive}}{\text{Economically Active}} \times 100$ | |
|---|---|---|---|---|
| | *1960* | *1975* (proj.) | *1960* | *1975* (proj.) |
| WORLD | 70 | 75 | 150 | 156 |
| Africa | 79 | 85 | 130 | 135 |
| Asia | 76 | 79 | 161 | 166 |
| Latin America | 80 | 86 | 181 | 190 |
| North America | 67 | 63 | 146 | 140 |
| Europe | 54 | 59 | 126 | 133 |
| Oceania | 66 | 66 | 167 | 162 |
| U.S.S.R. | 58 | 64 | 122 | 129 |

SOURCE: Françoise Leridon, "Prévisions de population active: Trois publications internationales," *Population,* 17 (1962), 97–120, as cited in William Petersen, *Population* (2d edn., 1969), 73.

While many of those under twenty-five will be economically dependent infants (see Table 5) and politically impotent, it is not unlikely that student groups and young adults may exhibit more cohesive force than they do today. Whether their influence will become organized in the international arena is difficult to assay.

## F. Ideologies

Even less easy to predict is the international political complexion of the globe in 1990. In 1955, it was assumed that the West and the Communist bloc each controlled about one-third of the world's population. The other third was not committed and East-West strategies were designed to effect political alignments with states in that "third world." Today it is generally recognized that this is no longer the case. Major changes are taking place within the political camps of both East and West, and the uncommitted nations are increasingly resistant to cooperation among themselves and to external affiliation. What seems most likely during the next twenty years is progressive disorganization of traditional power blocs and the possible emergence of new ones that polarize the rich and the poor, the white and the nonwhite, the industrialized capital exporters and the underdeveloped consumers.

## G. *Ecological Effects*

However important the focus upon predicted polarities among the earth's peoples for the contingencies of the next two decades, the most significant effects of the present pace of human reproduction are ecological. The ultimate struggle will be free of generational, racial, economic, and ideological distractions; it will be man's battle to remain alive in a poisoned and depleted environment. Whoever they are and wherever they live, the six billion people of the year 2000 will aspire to a standard of comfort and vitality that can be sustained only at the expense of outrageous exploitation of soil, energy, air, and water. Industrialization is the Janus-faced god of modern progress: the benefactor of the few who have, in turn, generated massive depletion of resources and wholesale pollution of earth, air, and water. By 1980, the United States alone will probably consume more than 83 percent of the raw material resources consumed in the world that year. This consumption pattern exhausts soils, fills the air and waters with unwholesome effluents, generates thermal and chemical imbalance that imperil the global ecosystem, and threatens life for all men.

Nevertheless, this industrial capacity to produce creature comforts is the unquestioned model of those still in want. Therein lies its ultimate danger. Short-range measures designed to accelerate economic and industrial growth to effectuate his brothers' aspirations may turn out to be the most lethal threat to his species ever designed by man. Atomic annihilation is possible, but not inevitable; environmental pollution, in the long run, is lethal and probably inalterable.

## II. POTENTIALS FOR INTERNATIONAL CONFLICT

Just as community leaders seldom project trends and potentials far enough ahead to forecast probable and possible futures, individuals rarely perceive the relationships between abstractions, such as "population density" and "personal discomfort." Instead, what demographers would describe as responses to population pressures are perceived by individuals as personal, familial, and local community phenomena. A typical response by individuals or groups to "overpopulation" in a family or community is emigration. If the receiving communities are unable to provide satisfactory relief, other behavioral modes may be employed by those who have "jumped from the frying pan into the fire." These mechanisms include further migration, and both active and passive adaptation to the circumstances of the new community. Because the very presence of migrants in the new location causes dislocations for the original inhabitants, the latter also undertake forms of self-protection and readjustment. Whether organized or not, such efforts by both indigenous and migrant populations to cope with the environmental changes brought about by a rapid increase in numbers produce massive social and economic disorganization. In countries where parochial identifications are relatively intense, the problems resulting from population pressure are generally perceived as political dysfunction and are experienced as regional or national disorder. Unemployment, poor housing, inadequate health and educational facilities, and the general pall of hopelessness provide the tinder for political explosion.

Once the fiery potentials are recognized by incumbent leaders, the problems caused by population pressures may be projected into the realm of international politics in a number of ways. The government may invoke external assistance to preserve domestic peace and tranquility. The dispossessed themselves may migrate, legally or illegally, into less populous territories beyond national boundary lines as cheap labor or as squatters on lands theretofore unoccupied and, to their way of thinking, therefore unclaimed. In the absence of voluntary international migration, if adjacent territories are thinly populated, a revival of ancient border quarrels or the occurrence of "provocations" by a vulnerable target may give rise to international conflict. The stakes are high if the dispute involves the potential acquisition of new territory and exploitable resources for the overpopulous state.

Another strategy may be employed if the economic conditions in one segment of a country are more favorable than those in other parts. The more favored inhabitants may take anticipatory self-protection by way of secession, and thus raise the usual array of international questions concerning domestic jurisdiction and the rights of peoples to self-determination.

This list of available techniques for projecting domestic population-resource issues into the international arena could be expanded, but there is little need to do so here. The abundance of real or imagined grievances within the human family, combined with wit and desperation, will provide endless rationalizations for these and similar responses to the demands of an indignant starving margin and of those who find the starving at their doors.

### III. Why Some Peoples Wax While Others Wane

Except for the preceding discussion of private migration motives, attention has been focused upon aggregate patterns of human reproduction and group characteristics and demands. It is necessary, at this juncture, to shift inquiry to the individual.

With few exceptions in recorded history, the decision to reproduce has been a matter of private volition, encouraged or discouraged by community opinion, but rarely coerced by official intervention. Among groups possessing the requisite information and the techniques for effectively controlling fertility, the psychocultural predispositions that guide choice are of the utmost importance. Some demographers have attempted to classify the motives that account for high and low birth rates. For example, Donald J. Bogue's thesis is that birth rates reflect individual efforts to satisfy certain human needs. Thus, both high and low birth rates are subject to change when perceived needs change. His "international" lists of fertility motives provide an interesting array of the diverse explanations given by individuals and social groups to justify family size.

TABLE 6

INTERNATIONAL LIST OF FERTILITY MOTIVES

| *High-Fertility* | *Low-Fertility* |
|---|---|
| HEALTH | |
| Children often die; large families required to produce living adults | Preserve the health of the mother; assure healthy children; lessen worry and overwork on the part of the parents |
| ECONOMIC CONDITION | |
| Children are an economic advantage (child labor); children provide social security in old age | Everyday general expenses are less; avoid worsening present poor economic condition; gain a higher standard of living, more comfort, afford better house; permit saving for the future, including retirement; desire to avoid subdividing property among many children; family able to have money for recreation |
| FAMILY WELFARE | |
| Children can help with work around the house; big families are happy families; children from big families have better personalities; children are needed to continue the family name; children help to strengthen the clan | Improve children's lot in life (education, career); happier family life (less tension); opportunity to do a better job of rearing children; avoid overcrowding of house; more peace and quiet in the home; easier to find a more desirable house or apartment |
| MARRIAGE ADJUSTMENT | |
| Large families promote good marriage adjustment between parents | Provides husbands and wives more leisure together; improves sexual adjustment (by reducing fear of unwanted pregnancy) |

TABLE 6 (*Continued*)

INTERNATIONAL LIST OF FERTILITY MOTIVES

| *High-Fertility* | *Low-Fertility* |
|---|---|
| **PERSONALITY NEEDS** | |
| Ego support (demonstration of male virility); companionship (parents need children to love) | Facilitates realization of ambitions (by permitting parents to pursue occupational or vocational objectives); facilitates self-development (especially of talented wives); facilitates participation in social activities; reduces worry about the future (avoids danger of childbearing when one is too old and the danger of leaving orphan children) |
| **COMMUNITY AND NATIONAL WELFARE** | |
| Large families are good for the community or nation (make the nation strong) | Helps avoid overpopulation (overcrowding); helps community meet demands for education and other community services; helps nation in economic development; helps keep down delinquency (social problems of youth); helps reduce welfare burden on the community |
| **MORAL AND CULTURAL** | |
| Large families are God's will; large families promote morality (help to prevent divorce, infidelity); tradition (the community expects large families); high status of large families in the community | |
| **CONTRACEPTION** | |
| Disliked for aesthetic or health reasons, or on grounds of inconvenience | |

SOURCE: Donald J. Bogue, *Principles of Demography* (New York 1969), 840–41.

These anecdotal justifications are far from exhaustive. The high-fertility motives do not include, for example, the frustrated question of an Indian woman unable to adhere to rhythm: "Can the butter refuse to melt when it is close to the fire?" Nor does it cover political exhortations to white South Africans to have more babies to redress the disparity of increase between whites and blacks in that nation.[10] Bogue might have included pseudo-Darwinistic claims by other elites to have a natural right (and duty) to reproduce in greater numbers

[10] See *New York Times*, May 18, 1969, p. 2.

than their inferior fellow beings. Similarly, the catalogue of low-fertility motives appears to be less an international list than a repertoire of Western middle-class arguments for family planning. If the trend toward higher rates of delinquency among the children of affluence continues in the West, the model of suburban comfort may become less attractive in the future than it has been in the recent past. In like manner, widespread attribution of delinquency and family disorganization to the absence of the mother from the home may diminish the appeal of mothers' personality development motives as outlined by Bogue.

Bogue is probably correct in his hypothesis that adherence to high-fertility motives is everywhere steadily declining. If, as he thinks, "most populations of the world subscribe to a great many of the low-fertility motives and . . . this adherence is rapidly on the increase," [11] there may be a sufficient basis in world perspectives for a significant downward trend in population growth during the next two decades.

A more systematic analysis seems to be called for, however, to make a case for such optimism. It would begin with the premise that human decisions seldom turn on a single value. The context of human preferences provides a rich array of choices among goods or between lesser evils. Ultimately, the policies adopted by, and in the name of, the larger community can be shaped to reinforce or undercut the consequences of those individual choices. Using a framework somewhat different in scope and content from that employed by Bogue, we may be able to describe that broader context in a way more meaningful for both national and international understanding.

In any one person's lifetime, he is likely to make very few decisions that are motivated by an explicit desire to preserve or enhance the existence of mankind as a species. The opportunity and the power, in this atomic age, to make such decisions are the province of a very small political and military elite. To be sure, such decisions are neither made in the privacy of the bedchamber nor comparable with those made there. Thus, to reproduce or not to reproduce is a question directed not toward love of the whole of humanity, but of smaller segments of the species in both time and space. History occasionally records ethnocentric or nationalistic pro-natalist movements, but in larger and more widely dispersed social groups the procreative motive is more likely to be personal than communal. For the vast majority of people now living, as well as for those who have ever lived, reproduction is a function of that intimate social group that comprises the family. Whether nuclear, as in the contemporary West, or extended, tribal, or clan, familial society is the effective domain regulating affec-

---

[11] Donald J. Bogue, *Principles of Demography* (New York 1969), 842.

tion relationships, sexual expression, and their reproductive effects. It is in the name of preserving the values of this social unit that both pro-natalist and anti-natalist policies are rationalized. The greatest resistance to contraception and family planning is found in the family unit; and, paradoxically, the most effective implementors of population limitation are members of families who seek to maximize the happiness and satisfactions obtainable from a family life free of stress. As with most human values, demands for affection are occasionally inconsistent and contradictory. More often, however, they are complementary and subject to alternative choice, each of which produces some satisfaction of felt needs.

In traditional folk and agrarian societies, the large family, which was an economic asset, was quite naturally a symbol of success. Community deference was paid to the fertile and the fecund. In the societies that developed during industrialization, status perspectives shifted from procreative to anti-natalist. The normal ideal for the highly mobile, acquisitive, nuclear family dependent on wages is two, three, or four children. Larger families are excused as the rich man's prerogative, because he can afford them, or condemned as the poor man's badge of indolence and vulgar passion. In these societies, the "haves" alternate between chastising the socially inferior "have nots" for moral depravity and enlightening them about the virtues of hard work and self-restraint.

Enlightenment is a potent instrument in the war against ignorance and it may be the ultimate weapon in effecting population control. Among most peoples, however, there exists no comprehension of the community impacts of high fertility rates. In societies solidly grounded on the family as an economic and cultural unit, the larger social effects of unlimited reproduction are never conceptualized. Even in affluent communities, such as the United States, private decisions to have a "wanted baby," not unsophisticated mistakes, account for occasional upward trends in national birth rates. The cumulative effect of millions of such decisions is appreciated by the individual citizen only after the fact—when the time comes for paying new taxes and higher tuitions for education, for securing competent medical care, recreational opportunities, and rewarding careers for the offspring of that earlier procreative tide. Whatever may be said for raising the level of enlightenment in reproductive man, knowledge alone is not likely to produce stable, widespread modification of his essential bent. What is needed is a more direct appeal to his sense of self-preservation.

Where rates of infant mortality are high, there tends to be general morbidity among old and young alike. For people unaware of the very basic relationships between sanitation and health, sickness and death are mere phases in the natural order and progression of life. For them, there exists no motivation for changing that order. Even after "death control," by way of massive public health campaigns, has become a reality, old attitudes and practices persist, and parents tend to reproduce at the same rates, for reasons that are no longer valid. Patterns of childbearing which once demanded ten live births to ensure two living adults persist long after the risk of infant death has been effectively curbed. Among social groups that have attained a higher level of physical vitality, a greater premium is placed upon the physical and mental health of the parents as well as that of their offspring. Population curbs, such as contraception and, more recently, abortion on socioeconomic grounds, are voluntarily adopted by great numbers of individuals who might otherwise dissipate their health and vitality by having their biologically-possible quota of children. If appeals to individual well-being are persuasive, it is essential that those affected be endowed with certain skills in order to attain desired health objectives.

The techniques employed by man to reduce his family size are many. Some demand a rather high level of scientific technology; others require either a control of the sexual instinct or a disregard for the claim to life of the newborn and the aged. Those that demand outward migration are socially complex, but always require that the extracommunity environment be available to receive the continuous flow of surplus young adults. In most cultures there is a general unwillingness to abandon or destroy the aged, either because of reverence for the old or of a moral rejection of euthanasia. Similarly, in most contemporary societies, infanticide is not viewed as an acceptable mode of coping with the social problems created by the birth of an unwanted child. Continence, *coitus interruptus,* and the rhythm method demand a fairly high level of skill and an intense motivation to restrain otherwise natural sexual instincts. Artificial contraceptives—mechanical and chemical—also require individual intelligence, skill, and, in most cases, a sophisticated technology for production and distribution of essential devices and material. Abortion, long practiced by the human family, and sterilization demand extraordinary medical skill to avoid high rates of infection and death. In short, whatever the means employed— volitional and/or technological—certain minimal skills are prerequisite to the successful practice of family limitation.

A cynic has remarked that the automobile is Western man's bribe for not having "another child." This observation may be correct, but it omits the even larger role of the motor car in Western rates of population growth; its contribution to air and water pollution and to slaughter on the highways has accelerated Western death rates as well. Nevertheless, the general premise seems to hold. The enticements of middle-class comfort do appear to account for many private decisions relating to family size. Upwardly mobile wage earners in economies which do not depend upon a large measure of child labor are more likely to perceive the tangible benefits of smaller families. The positive correlation between advanced economic development and low fertility, so pronounced in Western societies, has given rise to both optimism and pessimism among the population experts. The optimists view economic development as the *sine qua non* for decreasing rates of population growth. The pessimists agree, in principle, that development is the key factor, but fear that contemporary man has neither the will nor the capacity to create the necessary economic framework for avoiding imminent catastrophe.

Opponents and proponents of population control are wont to invoke ethical or rectitude norms in support of their respective positions. Here again the range of complementary value preferences in the domain of responsible decision is quite apparent. Historically, religious and ethical prescriptions have played a large role in regulating sexual behavior and questions relating to the taking of human life. These norms have had direct impacts upon patterns of procreation and rates of population increase. Religious mandates have been varied: each and every marriage act must remain open to the transmission of life; sons are required for ceremonial honorifics to the dead; celibacy is the highest moral ideal. Whatever the context and despite the intended effects of these rules for sexual practice, humans everywhere have seldom responded in a single or uniform way. Roman Catholic communities in Ireland have effectively reduced their numbers by migration and deferred marriage, notwithstanding the Biblical injunction to increase and multiply. Jamaican women of all religious persuasions have been found to adopt contraceptive practices introduced by family planners. The religious poor in certain Andean communities are known to induce abortions and to engage in clandestine infanticide when the pressure of a tenth or twelfth mouth to feed becomes unbearable. On the other hand, ethical norms embodying the principle of the sanctity of life have been instrumental in movements to effect death control, and they are potent forces in contemporary efforts to improve the quality of life for humanity as a whole. The norms that command individuals to preserve their bodies as temples of the spirit through temperate living, that require spouses to care for each other in sickness and in health, and that demand that parents feed and nourish the young, all form the basic framework for broader conceptions of individual responsibility, for the self and for others, in social contexts likely to include limitations upon otherwise unrestrained reproduction.

It is against the point-counterpoint of these value preferences and demands that organized societies formulate natal policies. Whether explicit or implicit, those policies are calculated to increase, decrease, or stabilize population growth. By complex systems of rationing wealth, power, respect, and other values, community decision makers influence individual choices related to reproduction.

In the international arena, growing global concern about the long-range effects of disparate rates of population growth has only recently prompted efforts to influence the influencers. There are close parallels between individual-community (or national) relationships, and those that obtain between nations and the world community as a whole. Just as national policies both reflect and shape individual choices in pro-natalist or anti-natalist ways, international policy may also be employed to support policy choices within the several nation states. For this reason, it is altogether appropriate to investigate the various ways in which the international legal regime can and should undertake to do so in the next ten to twenty years.

## IV. Where Is "The Population Problem?"

Most of the foregoing discussion presupposes that there exists, in some parts of the world at least, a serious problem of overpopulation. The rather violent terms "baby boom" and "population explosion," so fashionable in the West, reflect attitudes of fear that basic values may be threatened by the burgeoning growth of the human species. The "starving margin" conjures up a vision of hapless multitudes scrambling for wholly inadequate food supplies, or a Calcutta where [12]

> . . . misery radiates outward . . . dusty streets straggle away in every direction lined with tiny shacks built of metal scraps, pieces of old baskets, strips of wood, and gunnysacks. In the dark interiors of the shacks, small fires glow through the smoke, and dark faces gaze out at children playing in the urinous-smelling, fly-infested streets. In a few years the children who survive . . . will grow taller and thinner and stand in the streets like ragged skeletons, barefoot, hollow-eyed, blinking their apathetic stares out of grey, dusty faces.

Many theorists who project demographic possibilities beyond the next ten to twenty years are predisposed to base their calculations on such assumptions. They venture long-range predictions of the total number of human beings that could be sustained by the finite food resources of the earth and its waters.

Other demographers base their estimates on some fundamental assumptions about human values. They posit that a given per capita income is the probable value preference for both "have" and "have-not" peoples, and proceed from there to define overpopulation in

[12] Philip Appleman, *The Silent Explosion* (Boston 1965).

terms of a community's ability to attain rates of economic growth that exceed rates of population increase.

Less sophisticated views are widely entertained, however, among many otherwise responsible elites. Some, for example, perceive no domestic population problem if, within national boundaries, there are substantial areas of unexploited land. To them, population density is the principal indicator of national welfare and is the most obvious guide for population policy. Some believe that national income and productivity are more appropriate indices, but they often fail to see the essential danger involved when per capita incomes do not keep pace with accelerating gross national productivity.

Given this diversity of perception and evaluation, it is not surprising that the world's various opinion leaders disagree on the basic question of whether there is a population "problem." Even among those who share the view that the world or some of its parts is susceptible to overpopulation, there are differences of opinion as to when, where, and under what conditions that state of affairs is likely to occur. Thus, policy recommendations directed toward solutions of actual and potential population problems vary from expert to expert, and population policies differ from state to state.

It was noted earlier that a few of the poorer, densely populated countries have adopted anti-natalist policies, including in some cases vigorous programs of family planning and birth control. Among them are India, Indonesia, Korea, and Taiwan. Others, equally disadvantaged, have expressly supported pro-natalism. Elsewhere, in countries such as the United States, for example, where rates of natural increase are relatively low, comprehensive population policies have not been expressly articulated, but the whole system of value distribution within those countries is calculated to maintain a stable balance between population and exploitable resources. In still others, such as Australia, with vast undeveloped natural resources, notwithstanding high rates of natural population increase, official policy strongly supports selective immigration and other pro-natalist measures designed to secure a more favorable population-resource ratio. These are but a few examples of the broad spectrum of official response in contemporary nation states to internal rates of population increase or decline.

Edward A. Ackerman of the Carnegie Institution has estimated that two-thirds of the world's peoples live in technologically deficient areas and that the other one-third enjoys a more advanced technology.[13] In each of these major areas (technology-deficient and technology source) are regions of high and low population-resource ratio. His analysis is best described graphically in Fig. A.

[13] Edward A. Ackerman, "Population, Natural Resources, and Technology," 369 *The Annals of The American Academy of Political and Social Science* (1967), 84–97.

FIGURE A

|   | Technology Deficient + | (China, | | Technology Source + | (Western |
|---|---|---|---|---|---|
| I | High Population-Resource Ratio | India, Indonesia, Korea, Egypt, Pakistan, Iran) | III | High Population-Resource Ratio | Europe, Japan) |
| II | Technology Deficient + Low Population-Resource Ratio | (Africa, Latin America) | IV | Technology Source + Low Population-Resource Ratio | (U.S.A., U.S.S.R., Canada, Australia) |

SOURCE: Edward A. Ackerman, "Population, Natural Resources, and Technology," 369 *The Annals of The American Academy of Political and Social Science* (1967), 84–97.

If one accepts Ackerman's premise that the quality of life is better in the richer nations, the examples given to illustrate his four categories make it clear that pro-natalist policies are most appropriate for countries that have advanced technology and a relatively low population-resource ratio (IV). Population policies that reinforce stable or slightly decreasing rates of natural increase are more rational for nations in category III. Pro-natalist policies are acceptable for countries in category II if, and only if, those countries are able to develop more advanced technologies. To the extent that unrestrained population increase exceeds rates of economic and technological development, such countries will be unable to provide comfortable living standards for their peoples even though they may possess vast quantities of unexploited natural resources. Nations in category I have the most complex and difficult set of problems, for they must find ways to reduce the population-resource ratio (fewer people *or* more resources) and at the same time to advance their technological capacities. Otherwise, they are destined to be mankind's starving margin, troubled and troublesome in the world community at large.

## V. SHORT-RANGE OPTIMISM

For those who retain some faith in our ability to overcome immediate threats of starvation among large parts of the world's poor, the recent seed-fertilizer revolution has brought new hope. Even the population pessimists admit that the development of Sonora 64 wheat, IR-8 rice, and other miracle grains, plus the happy occurrence of good weather in the past couple of years, have given the problem-solvers some extra time. But to take comfort in the likelihood that new pro-

## TABLE 7

ESTIMATES OF FUTURE WORLD POPULATION BY REGIONS,
ASSUMING CONDITIONS OF LINEAR DECLINE OF
GROWTH RATE TO ZERO BY 2000
(Millions)

| Area | 1965 | 1970 | 1980 | 1990 | 2000 |
|------|------|------|------|------|------|
| WORLD | 3,276 | 3,562 | 4,061 | 4,463 | 4,527 |
| Africa | 309 | 345 | 409 | 455 | 473 |
| Asia | 1,814 | 1,979 | 2,262 | 2,456 | 2,524 |
| Latin America | 244 | 274 | 332 | 374 | 388 |
| North America | 215 | 231 | 259 | 277 | 284 |
| Europe | 445 | 465 | 497 | 518 | 525 |
| Oceania | 17.5 | 19.3 | 22.6 | 24.9 | 25.6 |
| U.S.S.R. | 232 | 249 | 279 | 298 | 305 |

SOURCE: Table 20-1, Donald J. Bogue, *Principles of Demography* (1969), 835.

ductivity in food supplies is the solution to the ultimate threat of
overpopulation is a myopic attempt to avoid the issue. It is realistic
to rejoice over the development of new food production techniques if,
and only if, a zero growth rate is attainable within the near future—
ten to thirty years. One demographer, Donald J. Bogue, believes that
the latter goal is a feasible one. In a paper originally presented at a
1966 Conference on World Food Resources,[14] Bogue asserted that "It
is now technically possible and operationally plausible that the world
population growth will slacken at a pace such that it will equal about
five billion persons in the year 2000, and when this point is reached
growth rates in all of the major world regions will have declined to
zero or so very nearly so that there will be little anxiety about a
population crisis." The effects of such a decline were calculated by
him to result in the relative numbers of people in the world's major
regions shown in Table 7.

Bogue's evidence in support of this view is based upon what he believes to be significant trends in population control. Among them are:
(1) grass roots approval of voluntary fertility control in the critical
areas of Asia, Latin America, and Africa; (2) aroused political leadership in countries around the world; (3) accelerated research activity
and improved technology in contraception methods and distribution;
and (4) the slackening of scientific progress in the techniques of "death
control." Encouraged by the rates at which fertility reduction programs are being implemented all over the underdeveloped world,
Bogue asserts that the exponential curve of population growth and its

[14] See revised version in Bogue (fn. 5), 828–67.

reciprocal, the exponential curve of contraception adoption, "cannot both be valid simultaneously in the future." It is from this posture of optimism that Bogue calls for intensified efforts to reinforce population deceleration trends.

## VI. Strategies for the Near Future: Feasibility and Long-Range Impacts

Whether or not the exact numbers can be foretold, it is clear beyond doubt that the family of man is growing at rates unprecedented in history. Recent trends in food production indicate that if the environment remains relatively stable, it will be technologically possible to sustain virtually all of the people now alive and those to be born by 1990, even if rates of natural increase are not reduced at all. If, however, one or more of the world's major grain-producing areas should experience crop failure for two consecutive years, there is a fairly high risk that large masses of people might die of starvation within that time. Such a contingency has so great a potential for international conflict that wise policy makers everywhere in the world should at once review and modify current programs for production, storage, and distribution of emergency food supplies for famine relief wherever it may occur.

Population experts agree that our present and probable future capacity to extract and distribute food for human beings is finite, and is not likely to keep pace with man's current reproduction rates. As Robert S. McNamara stated in the spring of 1969, agricultural technology has permitted us to "buy two decades of time, admittedly the barest minimum of time" during which we might reduce world population to manageable proportions. Policies for the next ten to twenty years will be shortsighted indeed if they do not take this fact into account. Acceleration in economic development and deceleration of population increase must be pursued with equal vigor if we are to exorcise Sir Charles' "starving margin" from man's future history.

There are thus three mandates for the immediate future: emergency food relief programs, effective reduction in the rates of population increase, and economic development of the hitherto poorer regions of the world. The first of these has been the object of extensive investigation by the Food and Agricultural Organization and the OECD. The recommendations embodied in the latter's 1968 report, *The Food Problem of Developing Countries*,[15] provide a ready-made agenda for consideration by decision makers of the contemporary international community. In considering feasible policies for dealing with population control and economic development, two questions must be asked

[15] OECD, *The Food Problem of Developing Countries* (Paris 1968).

and answered. The first is whether the present state of Western peoples in the Northern Hemisphere is a natural, a typical, or a possible state for all humanity for all time. The second question is whether responsible leaders among both "have" and "have not" nations may be expected to go beyond vague optimism about the future and to accept some disagreeable conclusions about ways to cope with the presently unstable state of population growth and economic development.

## A. Emergency Food Relief

In July 1969, Addeke H. Boerma, the director general of the Food and Agricultural Organization, reported to the United Nations Economic and Social Council that world food production in 1968 increased by over 2 percent and kept at least abreast of population growth. Food production declined in Latin America because of drought, but there was a substantial increase in the Far East. The FAO report noted that the food requirements of developing countries are expected to increase at an average yearly rate of 3.9 percent until 1985 and warned that "a long, arduous, and extremely expensive struggle" would be necessary to achieve an equivalent increase in food production.[16]

That report was far more pessimistic than the earlier FAO study for 1965.[17] The latter account indicated that from 1954–55 to 1964–65 world food production increased by about 30 percent, while world population increased by 22 percent. During that decade, a little more than one-fourth of the total addition to food production was available to increase per capita food consumption. Despite the advances in agricultural science and technology which have brought about dramatic increases in food productivity since 1966, the world food situation is a precarious one, and destined to become even more acute as population increases and surplus food supplies shrink.

In his 1968 report to the Council of the OECD, Secretary General Thorkil Kristenson also was concerned with the current food production problem. He noted that the following phenomena coincided during the first seven years of the United Nations Development Decade (1960–70): [18]

1. Food production in the developing countries, taken together, grew more slowly than demand.

2. The area of good new land that could easily be brought under cultivation in developing countries was sharply reduced.

---

[16] *International Herald Tribune,* July 18, 1969, p. 3.

[17] FAO, *The State of Food and Agriculture 1965* (Rome 1966), Tables I-1, I-2, and I-3.

[18] OECD (fn. 15), 10.

3. The population of developing countries grew at an increasing rate.

4. The surplus stocks of grain in North America were exhausted mainly through exports to less developed areas.

5. Development aid from the richer countries did on the whole not increase.

6. The debt burden of many developing countries rose rapidly.

This resume of trends is not a bright one. Kristenson noted with alarm that the partial failure of the monsoon in India in two consecutive years demonstrated the precarious state of our current capacity to meet world food demands. What is desperately needed is a new scheme for emergency food relief.

Food aid started on a large scale in 1954 with the passage of United States Public Law 480. Other countries, including Australia and Canada, and certain multilateral agencies, such as the UN-FAO, have contributed substantial amounts of food aid to needy nations, but the bulk of food assistance, until recently, was provided by the United States. In 1965, food aid represented 33 percent of the United States' gross aid disbursements. Since that time, surplus stocks of food for emergency relief have been virtually exhausted, but in the several donor countries there is a surplus capacity for the production of relief supplies.

An important distinction should be made at this point between emergency or famine relief and contributions, by way of food supplies, to the long-range economic development of food-importing countries. Emergency relief is designed to prevent or allay imminent starvation; general food aid is a part of an overall program intended to sustain and develop the poorer nations' productive capacities. Food serves, in both cases, to reduce mortality and to raise levels of human vitality to their full potential.

The concept of starvation is sometimes expanded to cover both absolute and relative nutritional deficiencies.[19] It includes, for example, deaths directly attributable to the lack of any food, as well as to deaths from diseases caused by gross nutritional deficiencies in available food supplies. Human mortality from these causes may be the result of the total failure of food supply, of a population's lack of means to obtain that which is available, or of inadequate patterns of selection, preparation, distribution, or consumption of nutritious edibles. Some experts on nutrition also label malnutrition and states of frequent hunger as forms of starvation.

As food surpluses decline throughout the world, starvation either

[19] Norman W. Desrosier, *Attack on Starvation* (Westport, Conn. 1961).

as a relative or as a total nutritional deficiency in its most dreadful manifestations is a real possibility for large numbers of the world's poor. One aspect of the problem, then, demands that ways be found to provide a world food reserve against the evil day of acute food shortage when food-producing nations experience disastrous crop failure. The other is more closely related to the continuing needs of food-importing countries for adequate supplies of grains and other foodstuffs under market conditions that they can afford.

The responsibility for meeting both types of world food needs rests, ultimately, upon producer countries which have the requisite capacity to produce a surplus supply. Efforts should be made to secure a greater degree of cooperation among all such nations in the production and distribution of surpluses to cope with chronic and emergency food shortages of other countries. During the next ten to twenty years, ways should also be found to depoliticize the question of providing aid to famine-struck populations. Cold war issues are of little concern to the victims of starvation in India or China, where famine is wont to occur; they were of still less interest to Biafran millions caught in the cross-fire of a military strategy that used hunger as a primary weapon. In addition to creating a global conscience that would abhor such examples of man's inhumanity to man, efforts should be made to invoke human intelligence as well. It can be predicted, for example, on the basis of a single calculation, that gross food needs in developing countries will rise dramatically in the next ten to twenty years. Assuming that current mortality rates will remain stable, today's children in those nations who now consume small quantities of food will, by 1990, require adult portions. Table 5, above, which projects a long-range decrease in the percentage of persons under twenty-five, supports a prediction that a larger proportion of the earth's population will then be adults, and therefore will need more food. It is also quite clear that wherever economic development does occur in the poorer regions of the world, additional per capita income is likely to create a high-income elasticity of demand for more and better food.[20] Add to these facts the well-known consequences of rapid population growth—inevitable reduction of agricultural land per capita, and retardation of capital formation for investment—and it becomes clear that inaction today is a denial of both conscience and elementary intelligence.

While knowledge and good will do not necessarily make problem solving simple, they do provide a favorable environment for creative solutions. The decade of the 1960's saw the rise and demise of several food aid programs. Expert analysis of their strong points and their

[20] OECD (fn. 15), 15.

failures should provide us with valuable lessons about how food needs and demand might be more adequately met in the future.[21]

## B. Population Deceleration

In 1966 the United Nations published population projections to the end of this century. One projection shows that if present fertility and mortality rates remain constant for the next thirty years, world population will reach 7.5 billion by the year 2000. The other three projections—high, low, and medium variants—were based on assumptions that birth rates may decline. The high projection predicts a global population of 7 billion, the medium variant 6.1 billion, and the low, 5.4 billion. The high projection indicates that the less developed areas of Africa, Asia, and Latin America will have an aggregate population of about 5.4 billion in the year 2000, whereas the remaining more developed areas will total about 1.6 billion. These figures represent a 170 percent population increase in the less developed areas as against a 60 percent increase among the more affluent.

Given these estimates, let us now reconsider Donald J. Bogue's suggestion that the rates of population increase around the globe *can* be reduced to zero by the year 2000.[22] If the world population growth rate were to decline uniformly to zero in the next thirty years, Bogue's calculations of that linear decline would result in approximately the same proportionate distribution of people in the seven major regions (see Table 7, above). The rank order of regions would not be disturbed, and the richer nations would still comprise about 30 percent of the world's total numbers. The populations of Asia, Europe, Africa, Latin America, and the U.S.S.R., respectively, would continue to be greater numerically than that of North America. Asians and Europeans would outnumber the Russians; Africa would maintain its numerical superiority over Latin America. Oceania would then have fewer than 26 million inhabitants—one-tenth of the population expected in the United States and one one-hundredth that of Asia.

In the light of what we already know about the supposed power advantages that attach to mere numbers, what is the likelihood that all of the countries in all of these regions will be willing to perpetuate their current positions in population rank order? Asia can maintain its regional preeminence no matter what population policy is adopted. Zero growth rates begun tomorrow would not in thirty years subordinate Asian populations to second place in people-power.

The reported beliefs of many Latin Americans about the power

[21] See, for example, the recommendations of the OECD (fn. 15).
[22] See text at fn. 11.

function of sheer numbers is far from encouraging. Intra-American national rivalries, the hardy survival of culture patterns that place high priority upon virility and fecundity, and the moral suasion presumably effected by the *Humanae Vitae* encyclical of 1968 are not calculated to produce in Latin America an instant shift in policy or practice consistent with Bogue's formula.

The situation in Africa is unclear. North of the Sahara, the United Arab Republic and Tunisia have been supporting family planning programs for economic and health reasons. South of the Sahara, five countries have adopted governmental policies favoring family planning. Most of the newer states have yet to express fully their perspectives about the power implications of large populations. So many complex cultural and economic factors are at work in Africa's diverse regions that it is difficult to find any empirical basis for prediction about the population policies that may obtain there.

Since the peoples in these three regions already constitute an overwhelming majority of contemporary mankind, and in view of the complicated logistics required to disseminate information and to modify procreative perspectives and practices, it hardly seems likely that a zero growth rate can be realized in a short thirty years. Nevertheless, because human beings *ought* to prefer population stability once their numbers have reached some articulated maximum, serious attention should be given now to the matter of attaining such a goal. The National Academy of Sciences in its 1963 annual report, *The Growth of World Population,* concluded that, other than the search for lasting peace, no problem is more urgent. The alternatives to this goal are so costly in terms of human misery and death that there should be no quarrel among world leaders that population deceleration to a growth rate of zero is one ultimate aim of the international legal order.

It was noted above that accelerating rates of natural increase in population usually render it more difficult to accumulate wealth for investment and development. Where that is the case, deceleration of those rates should produce the opposite and more favorable effect. Thus, in the poorer countries that are reproducing at the highest rates, the politically powerful demand for economic development may be achieved more quickly by reducing population growth than by some other long-range means. A number of developing countries have already embarked on such a course for that purpose. Their example is the strongest empirical evidence that can be mustered in support of Bogue's belief that zero growth rates are possible in our time. It should be evident that it requires fewer resources to prevent a birth than to produce one person's lifetime share as a consumer of national output. Moreover, if reductions in the birth rate are gradual, the effects of the resulting age redistribution can bring about favorable conditions for economic growth in the countries which need it so desperately. For a period, at least, declining fertility reduces the ratio of children, who consume but do not produce, to adults of working age, who are available to produce when supplied with enough capital. This very reduction in the numbers of nonproducing consumers tends to result in greater savings and investment of output. In his economic-demographic model designed to illustrate these relationships in less-developed countries,[23] Stephen Enke admits that there are ways of raising individuals' incomes other than that of reducing human fertility, but he makes a persuasive case for birth control as the one factor having the highest association among progeny, savings, and innovation.

Although the mushroom growth of the city, produced by massive migration patterns all over the world, poses enormous problems for economic development, the situation thus created is not necessarily hopeless. For a number of reasons, metropolitan population deceleration programs may become effective principally because so many people are living so closely together. Cities have more medical manpower and facilities per capita than rural areas; they have more effective transportation and communications systems; and their very congestion serves to reinforce the suggestion that life might be better for individuals and families alike if only there were fewer people. Even where systematic family planning has not been undertaken, birth rates in the cities are consistently lower than those of neighboring rural hinterlands. Given these factors, it seems evident that intensive programs to provide birth control information and family planning services in the cities would be more economical than in the rural areas where there are fewer medical personnel, less efficient transportation and mass communication systems, and where children serve as productive members of the agricultural work force. In time, the very success of urban programs for population deceleration is likely to be self-reinforcing and to provide an additional impetus for expansion into the rural sector as well.

Demographer Kingsley Davis has seriously questioned whether family planning alone will be an effective means for controlling fertility.[24] Realistic government policy of lowering the birth rate, he says, might include some additional coercive and persuasive strategies. His "catalogue of horrors" would permit official action to: [25] "squeeze consumers through taxation and inflation; make housing very scarce by limiting

[23] Stephen Enke, "Birth Control for Economic Development," *Science*, CLXIV (May 16, 1969), 748.
[24] Kingsley Davis, "Population Policy: Will Current Programs Succeed?" *Science*, CLVIII (November 10, 1967), 730.
[25] Same, 739.

construction; force wives and mothers to work outside the home to offset the inadequacy of male wages, yet provide few child-care facilities;
encourage migration to the city by paying low wages in the country
and providing few rural jobs; increase congestion in cities by starving
the transit system; increase personal insecurity by encouraging conditions that produce unemployment and by haphazard political arrests."
Assuming that no government would institute such hardships for the
single purpose of controlling population growth, he suggests that
officials begin to develop attractive substitutes for family interests, so
as to avoid having to turn to hardship as a corrective. The specific
measures required for developing such substitutes are not easy to determine in the absence of research on the question. Perhaps it is in
order to suggest that the agenda for assuring a stable international
legal order in the next ten to twenty years include accelerated research
efforts along these lines.

It was emphasized above that race, an old and troublesome issue in
human affairs, continues to be politicized in ways that are harmful
for the international order. Even here, however, there is reason to
believe that the demand for a healthy, productive, and satisfying life
may be universal, transcending racial and cultural boundaries. This
hope receives some support from data on the adoption of family planning programs or practices among peoples all over the globe. Bernard
Berelson's 1967 tabulation of official efforts to reduce rates of population growth is instructive (Table 8). At that time twenty countries,
representing about two-thirds of the developing world, had adopted
official policies and instituted large-scale family planning programs
financed by public funds.[26] Although sub-Saharan Africa is not well
represented in this array, a great number of the so-called nonwhite
peoples in the world have already begun to move in the direction of
population deceleration.

Leaving aside as presently unanswerable the question of racial or
ethnic obstacles to an effective program for global population reduction, let us reexamine the implications of the current age distribution
in the major regions of the world. As of 1965, only 40 percent of those
in Europe were under 25 years of age, while in Africa and Latin
America over 60 percent of the total population were in that age group
(see Table 4, above). Several contradictory trends among the youth in
various parts of the world make it difficult to predict the degree of
stability that is attainable in the current family planning effort. Among
them are the development in the Western countries of a new sexual
morality, accompanied by widespread practices of contraception and a

---

[26] Bernard Berelson, "National Family Planning Programs: Where We Stand,"
from *Fertility and Family Planning: A World View.* University of Michigan Sesqui-
centennial Celebration Conference, November 1967.

TABLE 8

THE STATUS OF FAMILY PLANNING IN
DEVELOPING COUNTRIES, 1967

| Population (millions) | Official Policy and/or Program | Something Official | Nothing Official |
|---|---|---|---|
| OVER 500 | China (1962?) India (1952, 1965) | | |
| 100–500 | Pakistan (1960, 1965) | Indonesia | |
| 50–100 | | | Nigeria Brazil |
| 25–50 | Turkey (1965) U.A.R. (1965) S. Korea (1961) | Mexico Philippines Thailand | Burma |
| 15–20 | Iran (1967) Colombia (1967) | | Congo Ethiopia N. Vietnam S. Vietnam |
| 10–15 | Morocco (1966) Taiwan (1964) Ceylon (1967) | Peru Algeria Nepal | Sudan Tanzania N. Korea |
| UNDER 10 | Malaysia (1966) Kenya (1966) Chile (1966) Tunisia (1966) Hong Kong (1964) Honduras (1965) Singapore (1966) Jamaica (1966) Costa Rica (1967) Mauritius (1965) Barbados (1966) | Venezuela Cuba Guatemala Dominican Republic | Africa— 31 countries Asia— 12 countries Latin America— 9 countries |

demand for unrestricted abortion, but with no well-defined program suggesting restriction on reproduction. On the contrary, the movement is highly individualistic, appealing more to personal rights than to communal responsibilities. While there appears to be an increase in illegitimate births, for example, among teenagers for whom the newer contraceptive techniques are not generally available, it is still too early to appraise the twin effects of more liberal sex practices and wide-spread use of contraceptives among the young adults of the 1960's.

Another factor, in the developing countries especially, is the present and probable future retrogression in programs for mass public education. In those economies that experience declining per capita income, per capita expenditures for public schools are also likely to decline. Since voluntary birth control requires both knowledge and acquired preferences for limiting procreative behavior, the process of creating and maintaining effective patterns of birth-limiting behavior is a function of the basic educational systems. If the children in such areas cannot go to school they are likely to be effectively cut off from the sources of technical knowledge as well as from the broader value-shaping experiences that are necessary for the success of family planning programs.

Another disquieting fact has been recently reported from Taiwan, where massive efforts toward fertility control during the past five years have been remarkably successful among adults. These reports suggest that different attitudes now prevail among Taiwan's younger people. They have begun to marry at an earlier age, and their reproductive activity now threatens to nullify the gains made by their elders in gross population reduction.

A fourth and rather ironic factor reflects the basic biology of man. As human beings become stronger, healthier, and more productive, they also become more reproductive. Studies of natality in India, for example, show that people accustomed to daily hunger are relatively disinterested in sexual activity. Once their vitality has been restored at harvest time, they experience a heightened interest in reproductive behavior, with the result that birth rates show a radical increase in the ninth month following the harvest, and the magnitude of the increase is a function of the success or failure of the harvest. The same phenomenon is probably associated with the "baby booms" that occur among the comfortable middle classes of the West. On the basis of this and similar evidence, demographers predict that successful maternal and child health care programs in the developing countries will produce a new population control problem: a new generation endowed with the physical vitality and sexual interest to create a new wave of population growth.

Despite the enormous furor created by *Humanae Vitae* in both religious and political circles, its effect as a brake on population control programming has probably been overrated. The principal area of concern is Latin America, but during the one year following promulgation of the encyclical the population experts and planners have not reported any major change or setback in the rate of adoption of family planning programs. Indeed, the radical split among respectable theologians on the theological issue of the *magisterium* as related to the contents of the encyclical has given faithful Catholic parishioners some avenues of alternative thinking in this delicate realm of individual conscience and decision.

It thus seems from this examination of expected political, economic, and sociocultural trends that there do exist some bases for optimism about the future success of noncoercive methods of population control. Two additional developments of a technical nature are also relevant to the probable future of rates of natural increase. One is the developing war against DDT. Numerous scientists around the world are succeeding in their efforts to have governments limit or ban its use on the grounds that the chemical has proven to be an ecological disaster. If they are successful in preventing its future use and unsuccessful in finding an acceptable substitute to eradicate the malaria-bearing mosquito, then the "death control" curve is likely to go upward in certain areas where the birth rates are high and unrestricted. To those accustomed to using all available means of keeping people alive, this prospect is indeed harsh and calls for an altruism (or fear) of a somewhat different order than that evoked by the ordinary eradication campaign. The second scientific fact is related to the pace at which contraceptive techniques more effective than the IUD or the pill are being developed. David Sanford, writing for *The New Republic*,[27] has charged that pharmaceutical companies are not conducting research that might lead to safer, more effective contraceptive devices for use in developing countries because "they have profitable drugs and are not eager to spend millions of dollars on perfecting other methods which, once produced, would be cheaper and less lucrative than present methods."

In both of these cases, national and international decision makers are called upon to take some decisive action designed to bring about scientific developments consistent with well-conceived population goals.

## CONCLUSION

Those responsible for the future of the international legal order can never do nothing. Perpetuating the status quo is action. Given the current trends in population increase and its attendant hazards to the life and welfare of mankind as a whole, some way must be found to subject the population problem to rational decision.

We have seen that during the next ten to twenty years the international legal order will have thrust upon it three principal population issues: (1) the invention of new mechanisms for dealing with the problem of starvation in a world barely able to keep food production abreast of a rapidly growing community of food consumers; (2) the intensification of existing anti-natalist practices and the initiation of other sociocultural programs designed to provide individual incentives for reducing rates of population increase to zero; and (3) the development of human, natural, and technological resources to their fullest potential throughout the globe in order to realize the universal aspiration for an abundant life.

[27] David Sanford, "More Studies, More People," *The New Republic* (May 24, 1969), 14.

Fortunately, a number of international groups are already giving serious attention to both the first and the last issues. Ever since the failure of Sir John Boyd-Orr's grand proposal for a World Food Board,[28] efforts have been made by international organizations, both governmental and private, to work out suitable world food reserve schemes. The widely publicized Biafran tragedy has spurred the interests of some international jurists in devising ways to avoid the recurrent use of mass starvation as a weapon of war. Similarly, the vast resources of many wealthy nations and extensive programs initiated by international organizations are being brought to bear on the total resource development of the presently underdeveloped world. All of these efforts require additional funding and a constant infusion of sound theory and innovative thinking, if they are to attain reasonable objectives in the next ten to twenty years.

Rapid deceleration in the rate of population increase has not yet become an articulated goal for the principal participants in the international legal order. As Thorkil Kristenson stated in his 1968 OECD report, the question of an absolute maximum that our planet could sustain is hardly meaningful. "The problem is *how* we want future generations to live and there can be no doubt that every billion people added will make the solution of the food problem and a number of other problems more difficult." [29] While most theorists agree that at some point in time a zero rate of increase will become necessary to ensure global peace, security, and human welfare, the questions of when and how to attain that goal is just now emerging as an important agenda item among world leaders.

Even though anticipated food yields during the next twenty years may not demand immediate action to reduce rates of population growth, world leaders would be remiss in their obligations to the species if their policies within that period did not take into account the predicted ecological disasters likely to come thereafter.

Kingsley Davis [30] and Garrett Hardin [31] have presented a grave challenge to decision makers everywhere on this issue. They view the present commitment by a few states to voluntary family planning—dependent upon millions of individual wills—as a foolish reliance upon an unstable, unpredictable decision process. They feel that such

[28] The proposal was designed: to stabilize prices by buffer stock schemes; to hold a world food reserve against famine; to finance surplus disposal programs to needy people; to cooperate with a credit-issuing agency; and to coordinate bodies dealing with individual commodities. The proposal was never implemented. See FAO, *So Bold An Aim* (Rome 1955), 80, 83.

[29] OECD (fn. 15), 101.

[30] Davis (fn. 24), 730.

[31] Garrett Hardin, "The Tragedy of the Commons," *Science*, CLXII (December 13, 1968), 1243.

reliance condemns the world to a tragic and impossible ideal. "Unfortunately," says Hardin, "this is just the course of action that is being pursued by the United Nations. In late 1967, some 30 nations agreed to the following: 'The Universal Declaration of Human Rights describes the family as the natural and fundamental unit of society. It follows that any choice and decision with regard to the size of the family must irrevocably rest with the family itself and cannot be made by anyone else.' " [32] Hardin reluctantly suggests that "if we love the truth," we must openly deny the validity of this premise embodied in the Declaration, even though it is promoted by the United Nations, and we should also "join with Kingsley Davis in attempting to get Planned Parenthood-World Population to see the error of its ways." [33]

Lest we be too harsh on current international efforts, it is well to recall that only in December 1962 the United Nations General Assembly concluded the first debate in its history devoted entirely to the subject of population. At that time, by a vote of 69 affirmative, 27 abstentions, and no negatives, the member states adopted a major resolution calling for intensified programs of international cooperation in population matters. By 1968, a small population trust fund had been created in the population division of the United Nations secretariat. With the aid of government contributions of over $1.5 million, the secretariat has already recruited and trained a number of demographic advisers who are working in Asia, Africa, and Latin America to help governments organize national programs. Other specialized agencies, such as the World Health Organization, the Food and Agriculture Organization, and the United Nations Children's Fund are also discussing cooperation through the United Nations Development Program. In January 1970, the United States alone pledged $7.5 million to the United Nations Fund for Population Activities. The pledge met half of the United Nations' goal of $15 million for 1970.[34] This program and other population growth issues are likely to be on the agenda for the future of the international legal order for the next ten to twenty years. It is our responsibility to ensure that the questions thus raised are answered with dispatch and reason.

[32] U Thant, *International Planned Parenthood News*, No. 168 (February 1968), 3.
[33] Hardin (fn. 31), 1246.
[34] *New York Times*, January 24, 1970, p. 2.

# CHAPTER 3

# Science, Technology, and International Law: Present Trends and Future Developments

## DENNIS LIVINGSTON

### INTRODUCTION: A FRAMEWORK FOR ANALYSIS

THE PURPOSE OF this chapter is to analyze the public policy issues and significant trends raised by developments in science and technology for international law over the next few decades.[1] The analysis is carried out by focusing on those activities in which international law plays a role that are the most open to influence from science and technology. Six such fields or management areas have been chosen: (1) international law; (2) conflict; (3) economic development; (4) human rights; (5) environmental alteration; (6) science and technology.

These are the areas in which international law, through its rules and procedures, seeks to impose a framework of management the legal structure of which is devised under the impetus of science and technology. "Management" is not meant to connote some form of supranational governmental control, but more simply the establishment, through the international legal process, of patterns of expectations among international actors regarding the legitimacy of the spectrum of behavior made possible for actors by developments in modern science and technology. The patterns involved may run the gamut from full acceptance of the appropriateness of a given activity, to demands for new definitions of permissible conduct in the case of novel forms of behavior.

The first management area for international law is international law itself; this area looks to the internal affairs of international law—its structural operation. The five other areas involve the relevant legisla-

---

[1] While many publications have dealt with specific areas in which the relationships of science, technology, and international law could be traced (arms control, the oceans, outer space, nuclear energy), there have been few attempts to study this topic macroscopically. The exceptions include Charles Rousseau, "Scientific Progress and the Evolution of International Law," *Impact of Science on Society,* v (Summer 1954), 71–92; Oscar Schachter, "Scientific Advances and International Law-making," 55 *California Law Review,* 423–30 (May 1967); C. Wilfred Jenks, "The New Science and the Law of Nations," 17 *International and Comparative Legal Quarterly,* 327–45 (April 1968), and *Law, Freedom and Welfare* (London 1963), 33–49; Howard J. Taubenfeld, "Science, Technology, International Law and International Accommodation," in S. F. Seymour, ed., *Washington Colloquium on Science and Society: First Series* (Baltimore 1967), 114–30.

tive output of the legal system—its external influence on those components of the world social process comprised by the five fields. This output within each area can entail several forms: (1) rules: the rights, claims, and obligations of international actors; (2) organization: forums of interaction for actors and decision-makers; (3) jurisdiction: spheres of applicability of national and international law systems.

Science, technology, and international law do not confront each other in a vacuum, but operate within and impinge upon the general international political system. The major values which characterize relationships among system actors can be important components influencing the nature and direction of the confrontation, that is, the kinds of issues that are perceived as salient for international law at any given time, and the ways they are developed or resolved. Two global value-clusters may be identified as relevant here; each contains potentially conflicting elements: (1) the desire for national security: the desire for security from annihilation by weapons of mass destruction; (2) the desire for higher standards of material wealth: the desire for maximum realization of human potential: the desire for an environment inhabitable by man.

The process by which these values, techniques, and rules of the game interact is complex. The fields of science and technology, and the components of international law and international relations, simultaneously impact on each other throughout a planetary physical/social space, creating a gestalt from which emerges new or revised guidelines effecting the modes of behavior that lead into it. International law, thus, is not a passive recipient of whatever forces impinge on it, but an active part of the process of structuring global life in a manner consonant with the interests of the international community.

Table 1 summarizes the issues and trends to be taken up in the sections to follow.

## TABLE 1

### SCIENCE, TECHNOLOGY, AND INTERNATIONAL LAW: AN INVENTORY OF TRENDS

| Management Area | Trends Influenced by Science and Technology | Converging Effects of Trends |
|---|---|---|
| International Law | Improving access to data<br>Facilitating holding of codification conferences<br>Developing non-treaty sources of international law<br>Enhancing conclusion of treaties based on inspection and verification<br>Coopting technical experts into the legal process<br>Influencing man's perception of reality | Rationalization of the international legal process |

TABLE 1 (*Continued*)

SCIENCE, TECHNOLOGY, AND INTERNATIONAL LAW: AN INVENTORY OF TRENDS

| Management Area | Trends Influenced by Science and Technology | Converging Effects of Trends |
|---|---|---|
| Conflict | Extending methods of waging war<br>Extending methods of exerting coercion<br>  Propaganda<br>  Blockade and boycott<br>  Technological disruption<br>  Selective release of information and equipment<br>  Exclusion from international organizations and programs<br>  Electronic surveillance<br>Extending arenas and causes of conflict<br>Predicting national bellicosity | Manipulation of states by techniques of indirect intervention |
| Economic Development | Widening the brain drain and technology gap<br>Promoting access to resources and their exploitation<br>  International rivers<br>  Nuclear energy<br>  Continental shelf and offshore fisheries<br>  Outer space<br>  Deep sea-bed<br>  Atmosphere<br>Setting prices for agricultural commodities<br>Monitoring resources by satellite | Exploitation and allocation of sharable resources on an equitable basis |
| Human Rights | Experimenting on human beings for medical purposes<br>Carrying out organ transplants<br>Developing genetic engineering<br>Gathering data on human groups for social and behavioral sciences | Provision of guidelines for encroachments on human bio-social integrity |
| Environmental Alteration | Spreading environmental pollution<br>  Threshold levels<br>  Identification of polluters<br>  Legal consequences of pollution<br>  Institutional structures<br>Disrupting the environment with large-scale technological projects<br>Disrupting the environment with large-scale scientific experiments<br>Threatening conservation of fish and wildlife<br>Expanding human population | Regulation of national environmental activities and promotion of a healthy environment: international ecological law |
| Science and Technology | Lessening barriers to the advancement of scientific research<br>Protecting the output of scientific research and technological invention<br>Promoting diffusion of scientific and technological information, equipment, and personnel | Expansion of scientific research and diffusion of its results: the international law of science |

## THE MANAGEMENT OF INTERNATIONAL LAW

The area of interest here is the operational structure of international law itself; particular patterns of legal doctrines are the concern of the following five sections. Several trends may be analyzed regarding the influence of science and technology on this structure.

The first is improving access to data on the part of legal scholars and decision-makers. There is clearly a flood of information potentially useful to concerned individuals—texts of international agreements, decisions of national and international tribunals, national policy statements, documents of international organizations, and the like; the great problem is making it available in coherent form. Other technical fields, such as medicine and chemistry, have faced similar problems and are accumulating experience in making the information explosion manageable by the use of computers to index, abstract, and process relevant data. However, the utility of computers for international law will not be fully ascertained until a number of serious issues are resolved, including the choice of index or abstract code to be utilized and of material to be coded, training of programmers skilled in legal affairs, establishment of secure access lines to the computers, and designing programs capable of rendering the output in the national languages of users.[2] If these difficulties are overcome, one can conceive of the setting up of legal computer utilities in major institutions around the world, open to use by individuals simultaneously on a shared-time basis, analogous to the World Data Centers organized during the International Geophysical Year.[3] Besides making data retrieval for international law more efficient, a major benefit to the legal process could result insofar as greater participation of scholars from the less-developed areas in international legal affairs is enhanced by the improved availability of information open to them.

A second trend involves the relationship of modern communications and transportation technology to the feasibility of holding the large, multilateral codification conferences which have become so characteristic of contemporary international law, and from which have

[2] Julius Stone, *Social Dimensions of Law and Justice* (Stanford 1966), 687–96; Wesley L. Gould, "Inventory and Retrieval of Literature as Aids to Interdisciplinary Approaches to International Law," 59 *American Society of International Law Proceedings*, 98ff. (1965); David Harris, "Computers and International Law," 15 *International and Comparative Legal Quarterly*, 551–53 (April 1966); Richard W. Edwards, Jr., "Electronic Data-Processing and International Law Documentation," 61 *American Journal of International Law*, 87–92 (January 1967).

[3] The Geneva World Peace Through Law Center has ambitious plans for the establishment of a world legal center to house conferences of interested groups, a computer containing the statutory law of all countries, indexes to high court decisions of all countries, and copies of all treaties. World Peace Through Law Center, *Proposed Plan for the Computerization of Law Internationally* (Geneva 1968).

emerged important pieces of international legislation. However convenient it has become for states that can afford to do so to send delegations to the wide variety of such meetings held annually, and to maintain contact with them while abroad, it is possible that future face-to-face gatherings for the purpose of structuring international law will become unnecessary, except for ceremonial occasions, because of developments in communications. Wall-size, global, 3-d, color TV, telex and facsimile devices for rapid transmission of documents, and regional computer libraries could result in a situation in which, "Long before the year 2000, man will be able to communicate instantaneously —in sound, sight, in written message and in exchanged computer information—with anyone anywhere. . . . In a crisis, delegates to the United Nations will be able to 'meet' at once, discuss issues and vote on them, without flying to New York." [4]

Third, science and technology affect the utility of nontreaty sources of international law. The development of customary norms begins with national officials transmitting to one another their varying claims regarding the allocation of global resources and their characterizations of each others' activities. If states are willing to communicate in the first place, the facility with which messages may be exchanged could lessen the time needed for the establishment of accepted ways of behavior derived from national experiences. In addition, the growth in the use made by international organizations of the declaratory resolution as a quasi-legal guide to national activities may be traced to the novelty of such activities made possible by technology. The declaratory resolution is a necessary device for providing a sense of the international community regarding how states are to behave in a new arena pending the establishment of binding rules.[5] This was the case, for example, in outer space: the Treaty on Outer Space (1967) was preceded by a U.N. declaration of principles on the subject. The same evolution will probably occur with respect to national exploitation of the resources of the seabed.

Science and technology may enhance the negotiation and continuing viability of the kind of treaty which relies for its enforcement on technical verification that its provisions are being fulfilled. While the completion of such treaties will require, in part, the presence of a feeling of mutual interest among the parties involved, the existence of technology applicable to the detection of treaty violations may itself serve as the catalyst to convince the parties that adhering to the treaties will not unreasonably strain their national security. In these

---

[4] David Sarnoff, "TV Revolution Ahead!" *Readers' Digest*, XLV (March 1966), 66–67; see also Arthur C. Clarke, *Profiles of the Future: An Inquiry into the Limits of the Possible* (New York 1962), 193–96.

[5] Schachter (fn. 1), 425–27.

cases, there would thus exist a virtual requirement for the fulfillment of certain technological prerequisites before the given international discussions could be undertaken. Arms control treaties fall within this category; some means of national or international technical verification will also be needed for whatever treaties emerge from the current interest in regulating man's impact on the global environment.

The cooptation of the technical expert into the international legal process is a trend that has been in existence for some time, paralleling a similar development at the national level and for essentially the same reasons: as the issues that enter the public forum become increasingly linked to the consequences of work in science and technology, policy makers, from judges to conference delegates, need the services of individuals able to translate the technical components of an issue into more understandable terms.[6] A multiplicity of roles has already become available to the expert in international lawmaking— he may serve as an adviser to international tribunals, as the actual judge in a contentious proceeding, as a participant in national delegations to international legal conferences, or as an adviser to officials in national and international organizations dealing with science and technology. In the future, it is probable that the international call on qualified persons will increase, especially as a routine part of the operation of functional international organizations whose mandate includes "legislative oversight" with regard to treaties of interest to their members. Even more interesting is the possibility that scientists will choose to influence the legal process more directly, acting through their own professional and international organizations to ensure that their interests are not harmed by national activities. Examples of this process are already apparent in the efforts of scientists to prevent undue encroachment on their research by treaties regulating state behavior in exploiting the continental shelf and using the radio band-width.[7]

Perhaps the most general and subtle influence of science and technology are their cultural effects on the way man perceives reality and his place in it. The great discoveries of Galileo, Darwin, and Freud have had such influences on man's world view, impacting in due course on his social institutions. International law is not immune from this

[6] Gillian M. White, *The Use of Experts by International Tribunals* (Syracuse 1965).

[7] In the shelf case, the International Council of Scientific Unions sent a series of resolutions via UNESCO to the Geneva conference negotiating the treaty, expressing their apprehension that too broad a grant of discretion to states to define for themselves permissible conditions for continental shelf research could be detrimental for such research. Myres S. McDougal and William T. Burke, *The Public Order of the Oceans: A Contemporary International Law of the Sea* (New Haven 1962), 701–02, 713–16, 721–24. On the radio-frequency dispute, see R. L. Smith-Rose, "Allocation of Frequencies for Radio Astronomy and Space Science," *Nature*, CCIII (July 4, 1964), 7–11.

process; one scholar has conveniently summarized how the legal community has reflected, in its own fashion, the theories and methods of science:

> Determinism, measurement, continuity and impersonality were the basic principles of nineteenth century science. They belong to the same intellectual world as the Austinian theory of law and the positivist theories of international law. The revolutionary developments in mathematics, the physical sciences, the biological sciences and the social sciences have profoundly changed the fundamental assumptions of contemporary thought. Discontinuity, uncertainty and chance are now recognized to be inherent in the laws of nature . . . [reflecting this,] speculative writings on jurisprudence . . . have emphasized the element of uncertainty in general legal principle, custom and judicial decision. There is now an increasing acceptance of the same general intellectual attitude by writers on international law.[8]

It may be that the next great step in man's perception of his place in life will come from findings of the space program and astronomy. The visual confirmation we have been given of the unity of the earth's biosphere, the growing possibility that this planet may be the only abode of life in the solar system, and the discovery of mysterious phenomena in deep space which portend the existence of vast and powerful forces hitherto unknown, may merge to deeply impress on mankind the fragility and humbleness of its existence, and the consequent imperative for managing its affairs with diligent prudence.

The converging effects of these trends is toward the rationalization of international law, the more efficient and organized use of the materials, skills, and forums comprising the legal process. This is not to imply that disputes will be more easily settled, statesmen more enlightened, or legislative conferences more farsighted, for science and technology only provide the tools that man may use, not the purposes of their use. But as participants in the process benefit from speedier access to the information they need, greater contact with each other, and increased ability to tap other individuals with specialized skills, the qualitative functioning of international law should also improve.

## THE MANAGEMENT OF CONFLICT

The devices and techniques by which states attempt to coerce each other in the achievement of national goals have been traditional sub-

---

[8] Jenks, "New Science" (fn. 1), 327–28; Floyd Matson, *The Broken Image: Man, Science, and Society* (Garden City, N.Y., 1966).

jects of international legal regulation. In the twentieth century, such attempts to guide and restrain the use of force have been heavily influenced by developments in science and technology, as well as by ideological disputes. Four patterns describing this influence can be traced.

First, science and technology have led to an extension of the methods of waging war, which in turn have conditioned the effectiveness of the international rules of war and the maintenance of a position of stabilized deterrence among the great powers. As to the rules of war, international law has long attempted to ensure that, if war must be waged, it be done as humanely as possible, with the minimum destruction, in the light of military objectives, to human lives and property. This principle has been subjected to great strain: the destructive power of the new weapons makes due respect for civilian safety in military arenas difficult, and the development of industrialization and mass armies has opened to attack every sector of a nation at war on the ground that anything can contribute to the military effort. Yet herein lies the irony. It is open to question whether there will ever again be a great power war: the perfection of nuclear weapons capable of destroying viable national existence has damped any inclinations of their possessors to wage war on each other. Nothing short of defense against a prior attack by such weapons would seem to justify their use in wars for limited ends.

This condition of deterrence has engendered a certain amount of stability in great-power relations, or at least increased their reluctance to use provocative force in their mutual affairs, but at the same time the scope and intensity of internal (civil) wars and wars among the less-developed states seem to be increasing, and great-power states sometimes give covert aid to one side or the other. Therefore, in spite of the prohibition of unilateral, aggressive, armed attack by the U.N. Charter, international law will remain intensely concerned in the future with imposing restraints on national discretion regarding the methods of warfare. Besides elaborating suitable guidelines applicable to internal wars, particular issues on the agenda may arise from the experience of the Vietnam and Nigerian conflicts, including bombing of civilians, blockades which result in mass civilian deaths, the use of tear gas and herbicides, and the international registration of governmental arms sales to the less-developed areas.

Advances in weapons technology threaten not only the traditional rules of restraint regarding weapons use, but also the maintenance of stabilized deterrence among the great powers. Since the balance of terror is premised in part on the expectation by each side that the

TABLE 2

INTERNATIONAL ARMS CONTROL LEGISLATION AND WEAPONS OF MASS DESTRUCTION

| Weapon | Existing Legislation | Proposed Policies | Detection Technology |
|---|---|---|---|
| Nuclear Bomb | Nuclear Test Ban Treaty (1963)* Treaty on the Non-Proliferation of Nuclear Weapons (1968) Treaty for the Prohibition of Nuclear Weapons in Latin America (1967) Antarctic Treaty (1959) US-USSR Agreements on Averting Nuclear War and on Communications Link (1971) de facto national control of key information | No first use of nuclear weapons; comprehensive test ban; additional atom free zones | Optical and radiation-detecting satellites; Large Aperture Seismic Array; fallout monitoring stations |
| Diversion of Fissionable Materials | Treaties in above category Statute of the International Atomic Energy Agency (1956) Convention on the Establishment of a Security Control in the Field of Nuclear Energy (1957) European Atomic Energy Community Treaty for the Cooperative Development of Uranium Enrichment Plants (1970) | Reduction in production of fissionable materials and their diversion to peaceful uses | IAEA reporting and inspecting system; satellite inspection of nuclear plants |

| | | | |
|---|---|---|---|
| Nuclear Weapon Delivery Vehicles | | | Satellite inspection |
| Orbiting Weapons of Mass Destruction | Treaty on Outer Space (1967) | | Manned and unmanned satellite inspection |
| Antiballistic Missiles (ABM) and Multiple Independently Targeted Reentry Vehicles (MIRV) | | Destroy obsolete models; reduce numbers of current models | Satellite inspection for ABM's |
| | | Moratorium on production during U.S.–Soviet Strategic Arms Limitation Talks; ultimate ban on production | |
| Implanting weapons of Mass Destruction on the Seabed | Treaty on the Prohibition of the Emplacement of Nuclear Weapons and Other Weapons of Mass Destruction on the Sea-Bed and the Ocean Floor and in the Subsoil Thereof (1971) | | Underwater acoustical arrays; submarine observation |
| Chemical and Bacteriological Weapons | Protocol for the prohibition of the use in war of asphyxiating, poisonous, or other gases, and of bacteriological methods of warfare (1925). Convention on the Prohibition of Biological Warfare and of the Production of Biological Weapons (1971) Unilateral national policy | | |

* Dates given in parenthesis following treaty titles are those in which the treaties were opened to signature.

other will not achieve a sudden, qualitative breakthrough in weaponry —in particular, a nuclear first-strike capability—the possibility of this happening poses the dangers of a continuing, escalating arms race and a potential breakdown in world security. International law has responded by promoting arms control as the methodology for slowing down national progress in the technology of mass destruction.

As Table 2 indicates, the international community attempts to place several types of obstacles in the way of national development of particularly destabilizing weapons systems. Production or acquisition of a weapon may be banned outright. This is the goal of the present nuclear powers in blocking the diffusion of atomic weapons to non-nuclear states and in prohibiting the orbiting of such devices. That the inhibition of weapon development need not be accomplished by international agreement is illustrated by the policy announcement of the Nixon administration, in November 1969, unilaterally renouncing the use of bacteriological warfare and the possession of such weapons, and reserving the use of chemical weapons for defensive purposes only. But the political and technical difficulties involved in carefully defining categories of prohibited weapons are also illustrated here by the inclusion of toxins (dead, but poisonous, bacteria products) in the U.S. ban, but the exclusion of CS (an incapacitating, non-lethal tear gas) and herbicides, in spite of a U.N. resolution interpreting the latter substances as outlawed chemical weapons within the terms of the Geneva Protocol. Another technique of inhibition lies in the prevention of the diversion to this purpose of material that would be useful in the manufacture of a banned weapon; particular concern focuses on the fissionable materials produced as a by-product in nuclear reactors or exchanged in trade among states. Bilateral and international systems of inspection have been instituted to monitor this cycle of production and disposal. When appropriate, suspension of production— or of the initiating of production—of a weapons system may be suggested by states; such proposals for a moratorium have been made regarding U.S. and Soviet employment of antiballistic missiles and multiple warhead missiles (MIRV's).

In all of this, the availability of technology that can aid the detection of violations of arms-control agreements has proven extremely beneficial, since the principal devices used, reconnaissance satellites and seismic arrays, can be operated by individual states to check up on the activities of other states without intrusion on the territories of the latter. Indeed, in the absence of further progress in negotiating agreements regulating weapons technology and with the development of more exotic types of weapons (such as laser beams mounted on satellites or remote-controlled robot weapons), states may rely increasingly on national means of verification to establish the status of their opponents in the arms race.[9]

Science and technology have not only expanded the destructive power of weapons, but, as a second general influence, have extended methods of coercion of a relatively nonmilitary, nonforceful nature. As a result the international doctrine prohibiting interference by one state in the internal affairs of another, already breaking down in a technologically interdependent world, has been put under further strain, especially when means are available to states to affect each others' internal affairs without direct intervention across a border.

One such technique is the radio transmission of propaganda from one state to the citizens of other states, a widespread practice on the part of countries of all degrees of economic development. The national response to unwanted broadcasts from abroad has been to prevent citizens from receiving them by local law and by jamming. International law, in turn, has attempted to establish minimum standards for the content of broadcasts, represented in the Convention Concerning the Use of Broadcasting in the Cause of Peace (1936), which forbids signatories from broadcasting statements disruptive of internal order in foreign territories, constituting an incitement to war, or harmful to good international understanding because of incorrect information transmitted. However, the relevance of such general guidelines to a world in which propaganda broadcasting is a common, convenient way for states to inform the people of neighboring countries of their positions on issues is dubious; indeed, it has been suggested that the engagement of states in propaganda activities short of incitement to riot be deemed an allowable and desirable form of coercion, compared to much more destabilizing forms such as armed subversion.[10] It is also true, however, that in future governments will have to face the prospect of direct radio and television broadcasts, via satellites, of programs transmitted from one country into the receivers of citizens of other countries. The free marketplace of ideas is one tolerated more in rhetoric than reality by many governments, so some combination of international supervision of direct broadcast transmission and a standard international right of reply to damaging broadcasts will have to be worked out.

The economic blockade or boycott should be an important tool of coercion in an age of interdependence. When the domestic prosperity

[9] On future weapons, see Nigel Calder, ed., *Unless Peace Comes: A Scientific Forecast of New Weapons* (New York 1968), and U.S. Congress, House Committee on Foreign Affairs, *Strategy and Science: Toward a National Security Policy for the 1970's* (Washington 1969).

[10] Richard A. Falk, "On Regulating International Propaganda: A Plea for Moderate Aims," 31 *Law and Contemporary Problems*, 622–34 (Summer 1966).

of most nations is dependent to an important degree on international trade for access to natural resources or goods not available internally, such dependence should make countries vulnerable to pressure if the flow of needed materials is reduced or eliminated. However, the blockade has proven an imbiguous and clumsy weapon in international affairs, for a state which finds itself the object of such a maneuver can attempt to find substitutes or alternative markets for the materials in question—a task made easier in the absence of careful political planning and tight coordination among the states applying pressure. This has been the lesson of attempts at the blockade of Israel by the Arab League Boycott Committee, of Rhodesia by the U.N., and of Biafra by Nigeria.[11] In spite of the ultimate victory of the federal forces in the latter case, the mass civilian hardship resulting in Biafra from Nigeria's blockade only prolonged the Biafrans' will to resist, and stimulated their search for technically ingenious solutions to make up for the reduced supply of key commodities, such as oil.

A possibly more effective technique of coercion is what might be called technological disruption. The most dramatic instance of this is the hijacking of airplanes or their attempted destruction on the ground by individuals seeking asylum in certain countries, or acting in retaliation against the government of the airline. The ability to disrupt the flow of international air traffic is a particularly potent weapon available to quasi-governmental or private groups, as seen in the efforts of Palestinian Arabs to make the flight of passengers and cargo to Israel an unsafe proposition on any airline. In controlling such maneuvers, international law is handicapped by the multiplicity of jurisdictions potentially involved, and by the traditional discretion granted to states in deciding what to do with individuals requesting political asylum. The Convention on Offences Committed on Board Aircraft (1963) does provide for the return of hijacked airlines to the country of registration, and for the free transit for passengers and crew, but it is silent on the question of requiring the country of asylum to try or to extradite the hijacker. The International Civil Aviation Organization hopes to close this loophole by recommending amendments to the convention and by its Convention for the Suppression of Unlawful Seizure of Aircraft (1970). Meanwhile, it has not escaped the attention of the airlines and the pilots' international associations that they have private pressures of their own available, such as threatening global

[11] Instructive case studies may be found in Herbert Feis, "The United States and the Italo-Ethiopian War," in Joel Larus, ed., *From Collective Security to Preventive Diplomacy: Readings in International Organization and the Maintenance of Peace* (New York 1965); Ronald Segal, ed., *Sanctions Against South Africa* (Baltimore 1964); Ralph Zacklin, "Challenge of Rhodesia: Toward an International Public Policy," *International Conciliation*, No. 575 (November 1969), 36–63.

strikes if corrective action by governments is not taken. In the future, even more serious possibilities of disruption will be possible as the transportation, communications, and information network of the world grows tighter. One can conceive of sabotage of key links in a communications satellite system, of a central nuclear power plant, or in the lines of a computer utility, resulting in great havoc to the community. As the ante for such technological blackmail goes up, states may have to consider the creation of some sort of "international technological police force," a sophisticated body of trained and equipped individuals empowered to investigate and apprehend those who attempt the serious crime of technological disruption.

Analogous to a blockade, states have utilized the selective release of scientific information or technological equipment as a technique of nonforceful coercion. If the subject matter involved is one of particular importance to the target state, such denied access may be sharply felt, not only by governments but by elite groups dependent on the information or material; these groups may in turn bring pressure to bear on their own officials. But the effectiveness of this technique is open to the same problems as economic blockade in general—target states may find other sources of material they need and evolve their own paths toward achieving technological goals. For example, U.S. predominance as a supplier of plutonium and enriched uranium for atomic power plants has given it a potential influence not unnoticed in the receiving states of Japan and Western Europe. That three of the latter consequently plan to develop their own sources of supply is indicated by their formulation of a treaty (1970) for the cooperative development of uranium enrichment plants by the gas ultracentrifuge method.

Closely related to this is what Friedmann has called the "sanction of nonparticipation," [12] the exclusion of states from participating in international scientific and technical organizations and programs. The potential power of this technique rests on the apprehension generated when one is excluded from taking part in an endeavor which is manifestly beneficial. Of course, the efficacy of this method depends on how badly the target state needs the services of the group from which it is excluded, while the group which excludes a state from participating in its work may end up harming itself more than anything else. Threats to expel South African from the U.N.'s technical specialized agencies may be of this type. On the other hand, the very real reliance for their viability by middle- and small-power states on international technical aid and scientific cooperation makes the nonparticipation sanction a possibly more credible threat for them.

12 Wolfgang Friedmann, *The Changing Structure of International Law* (New York 1964), 88–95.

The use of electronic surveillance methods may or may not be viewed as a threat by the target state. Apparently the two superpowers accept as a contribution to the stabilization of their relations the routine monitoring of each other's affairs by spy satellites, planes, and ships, since such data-gathering gives the opponent a more accurate estimate of one's own capabilities, and presumably makes him more wary of initiating an all-out war. The Soviet Union and its allies have indicated the limits of such tolerance by their hostile action against intelligence ships and planes which intrude into their territorial airspace or waters. The controversy raised over such cases as the U-2 spy plane and the *Pueblo* intelligence ship, and the continuing improvement in surveillance operations by satellites may lead to the phasing out of the former instruments in favor of the latter.

The potentially most far-reaching technique of coercion becoming available is the manipulation by a state of the environment located within its territory or outside its jurisdiction in such a way as to effect repercussions within the territory of other states.[13] One possible example of this was the decision several years ago by Syria and Lebanon to divert the Banias and Hasbani Rivers, two headwater tributaries of the Jordan, so as to affect Israel's ability to pump water from Lake Tiberias to the Negev Desert; in return, Israel's destruction of the East Ghor Canal in Jordan can be viewed as an environmental component of the general strategy of putting pressure on surrounding Arab governments to control the activities of guerrilla groups based in their territories. But the most dramatic and serious example of the ecological weapon has been the use of anti-plant chemicals by the U.S. in South Vietnam. This seriousness lies in the fact that the U.S. is carrying out in that country what amounts to a massive ecological experiment, without any real knowledge of the possible long-term effects of its activity on local inhabitants, wildlife, or land. There have been reports, however, regarding the laterization (hardening) of Vietnamese soil, destruction of Cambodian rubber trees, and birth defects caused in experimental animals subjected to two of the defoliants used (2,4,5-T and 2,4-D).[14] It is such potentially disastrous implications of large-scale alteration of the environment that has led Prof. Arthur Galson of Yale to propose that just as "the willful destruction of an entire people and its culture" has been condemned by mankind as the

[13] The gruesome possibilities are strikingly explained by Gordon J. F. MacDonald, "How to Wreck the Environment," in Calder (fn. 9), 181–205.

[14] Sheldon Novick, "The Vietnam Herbicide Experiment," *Environment*, x (January–February 1968), 20–21; "Mission to Vietnam," *Scientific Research*, iv (June 9, 1969), 22–30; Midwest Research Institute, *Assessment of Ecological Effects of Extensive or Repeated Use of Herbicides* (Kansas City, Mo., 1967); *New York Times*, December 7, 1969; December 31, 1969; January 14, 1970; March 15, 1970.

crime of genocide, so "the willful, permanent destruction of an environment in which a people can live in a manner of their own choosing be similarly considered as a crime against humanity, to be designated by the term *ecocide*." [15] Long before any such ecocide convention is concluded, it is possible that states, confronted by additional environmental weapons that may become available in the future (such as weather modification), will tacitly agree to a "no first use of ecological intervention" principle, analogous to the no first use concept for nuclear weapons—which, of course, are also ecological weapons.

A third influence of science and technology on conflict management is the extension of the arenas and causes of conflict. Progress in transportation and communications has enabled the industrialized countries to transport large numbers of troops, their equipment, and supporting forces, to foreign locations in a relatively short time, and to maintain constant contact with troops in the field. Characteristic are the developments, in the U.S., of the Lockheed C-5 Galaxy troop transport plane and the Defense Department's own communications satellite system. While these capabilities enhance the interventionary capacity of the great powers, they may also be put to use some day by the U.N. to extend its policing and peacekeeping activities swiftly around the globe. Besides gaining states faster access to traditional territorial arenas, technology has opened up new areas—the continental shelf, Antarctica, the deep ocean, and outer space—in which states have the opportunity to continue the competition for resources that has so often marked disputes on land. While the most efficient route for the community as a whole would be the common management of sharable resources available in these areas, states resort to the games of sovereignty when the stakes are high. One example of a potential conflict area opened up by technology is the scramble for the exploitation of the resources of the continental shelf; while the states surrounding the North Sea have peacefully resolved the issue of allocating access rights to the shelf they share in common, such a process is more problematical among those states (Japan, Taiwan, and China) bordering the oil field beneath the East China Sea off the Ryukyu Islands.

Finally, it is possible that work under way in the behavioral sciences will eventually lead to the ability of skilled individuals to predict with some accuracy the probability of national bellicosity. This might be achieved by the computer storage, manipulation, and comparative analysis of data regarding a large variety of factors relevant to national life. If it turns out that the degree of aggressive behavior of a state can be positively correlated with key indicators, such as domestic un-

[15] Speech delivered to the Washington, D.C., Conference on War and National Responsibility, February 1970.

rest and economic status,[16] the international community may possess a tool which makes possible the anticipatory prevention of conflict. In particular, the finding of a high probability that a certain state was a potential threat to world peace could prove helpful to those advocating an interventionary role for the appropriate international organization in that state, on the grounds that inaction would lead to a situation destabilizing for the international system if allowed to continue unchecked.

Concluding this section, the most striking trend that emerges is the growing ability of states possessing the requisite skills to operationalize their national policies vis-à-vis other states without directly intervening within the latter. Such action-at-a-distance intervention may include a variety of coercive and noncoercive activities, from manipulating atomic explosions so that the radioactivity drifts over enemy territory, to direct broadcasting of propaganda from satellites, to competition for resources in internationalized arenas. Given the desire of most states to avoid overt destabilizing gestures, a premium is placed on coercive measures that are relatively covert, informal, and nonmilitary in nature, in contrast to the traditional means of employing force. The value of such transnational techniques from the national perspective is that they can be undertaken outside the borders of the target state, while leading to effects within it—on its territory and its social processes.[17] But great problems ensue from the level of the international system, which must evaluate the propriety of the newer methods of coercion. Guidelines for judging retaliatory intervention include the degree to which the acting state interferes with the rights of third parties, the proportionality of the action to the alleged delict, and attempts made by the acting state to gain the prior authorization of an international organization for actions defined as sanctions. While the international community is already attempting to apply these guides to judge the suitability of such moves as airplane highjacking, substantial legal innovativeness will be necessary to deal with the permissibility of the variety of national behavior made possible by the methods of indirect intervention.

## THE MANAGEMENT OF ECONOMIC DEVELOPMENT

Given the continuing desire on the part of the materially less-advanced peoples of the world to promote their economic growth in the direction of the standards prevailing in the industrialized coun-

---

[16] R. J. Rummel, "A Foreign Conflict Behavior Code Sheet," *World Politics*, XVIII (January 1966), 283–96.

[17] John H. Herz, *International Politics in the Atomic Age* (New York 1959); Andrew M. Scott, *The Functioning of the International Political System* (New York 1967), and *The Revolution in Statecraft: Informal Penetration* (New York 1965).

tries—which modern communications have shown them—economic modernization will remain a powerful goal for the rest of the century. Clearly, science and technology have a major role to play in this process,[18] a proposition to which international law has responded in a general way by postulating, as a goal for states, that described in the International Covenant on Economic, Social, and Cultural Rights (1966) as the "right of everyone . . . to enjoy the benefits of scientific progress and its applications." More particular areas of concern can be grouped around five policy patterns.

The first issue involves the related subjects of the brain drain and the technology gap, which agitate relations among the industrialized countries as well as between the latter and the less-developed areas.[19] The brain drain refers to the migration of individuals from their home countries to the industrialized world in order to receive technical training or to practice their professions there permanently. Such movement results from, and may accentuate, the economic disparities existing between countries, especially differences in pay scales and professional opportunities. It will not be easy for international law to ease the situation because matters of immigration have traditionally been reserved for states to handle as they wished, and because interference with the decisions of individuals to seek employment where they judge market conditions most fitting might itself violate human rights. International legislation might be forthcoming on those aspects of the issue most amenable to agreement, such as limiting the stay of foreign graduate students in the countries where they receive their training. The technology gap refers to the fact that technological skills with regard to such key industries as computer and electronic component manufacturing appear to be lodged in a relatively small number of companies with headquarters in the U.S. and Western Europe. International law can make positive contributions to the problem by promoting cooperation in the exchange of managerial talent among countries needing particular organizational skills, and through agreements among states that firms holding patents in other countries work them within a specified period or let the state involved open up bids for licenses from indigenous businesses.

Second is the vital problem of giving the less-developed areas access to natural resources and a share of the wealth that results from their exploitation. Both jurisdictional and allocational questions are in-

[18] Sherman E. Katz, "The Application of Science and Technology to Development," *International Organization*, XXII (Winter 1968), 392–416; Claire Nader and A. B. Zahlan, eds., *Science and Technology in Developing Countries* (New York 1969).

[19] U.S. Congress, House Committee on Government Operations, *Scientific Brain Drain from the Developing Countries* (Washington 1968); "Technological Gaps: Their Nature, Causes and Effects," *The OECD Observer*, XXXIII (April 1968), 18–29.

volved: whose set of laws applies to the control of resources spatially located, and how does the appropriate legal system determine the criteria for allocating access to and exploitation of the resources? Advances in science and technology have given rise to these questions by opening up new methods of exploiting resources and new territories in which they may be found.

On the land, a traditional concern of international law has been the uses made of international rivers. Whereas the primary utilization in the past of such rivers was for navigation, advances in technology and increasing power needs of industrial countries have made it feasible and necessary to subject river systems to a multiplicity of uses—irrigation, flood control, recreation, and power generation—not all of which may be compatible with the interests of all states within the system. The principle that has emerged from experience in this field is that inclusive, equitable use of a river system should be made in the light of the interests of all parties; if a state wishes to utilize an international river, it is obligated to consult with other riparians regarding possible effects of the project on their own reasonable enjoyment of the river, and to negotiate with them methods of preventing serious damage to their use of the system.[20] In practice, protracted disputes which have developed among riparians have erupted around the amount and quality of water to be delivered among them upon completion of a project. But the general acceptance of a norm prohibiting unilateral cooptation of a sharable resource has important applicability for other areas as well, as does the institutional arrangement adopted for many river systems—international river commissions to provide just administration of inclusive rules and cooperative development projects.

Acquiring skills relevant to the application of nuclear energy for peaceful purposes is regarded by many developing countries as vitally important for the achievement of a modern industrial infrastructure. Particular interest has focused on using nuclear explosives to excavate land for the construction of canals and harbors and for gaining access to underground oil and gas. But the nuclear technology involved in such excavation is equivalent to that used in the construction of nuclear weapons, while these weapons, in turn, make use of one of the by-products of nuclear power reactors, plutonium. There are, thus, two competing values: the desire of less-developed areas to make full use of the atom to aid their economic and technological progress, and

20 U.S. Department of State, *Memorandum on Legal Aspects of the Use of Systems of International Waters* (Washington 1958); A. H. Garretson, R. D. Hayton, and C. J. Olmstead, eds., *The Law of International Drainage Basins* (New York 1967); International Law Association, *Final Report of the Committee on the Uses of the Waters of International Rivers* [Helsinki Conference] (London 1966).

the desire of the nuclear-weapon states to maintain the status quo in the number of countries able to manufacture such weapons. Involved negotiations aimed at balancing these values have led to two major treaties. One, the Treaty for the Prohibition of Nuclear Weapons in Latin America (1967), is a regional attempt to establish an atom-free zone while still permitting parties to use nuclear energy for peaceful purposes, including explosions, under IAEA safeguards. The global Treaty on the Non-Proliferation of Nuclear Weapons (1968) also provides for safeguards against the nonpeaceful diversion of fissionable materials or explosives, but they are not to inhibit the fullest cooperation in the peaceful uses of atomic energy. This cooperation is to include provision by the nuclear-weapons states of nuclear explosive services, at cost, for projects in the non-nuclear-weapons states. The latter have already organized themselves, at a conference in 1968, to push for the release of the fullest possible information by nuclear states of the relevant technology, the donation of special funds and fissionable material by nuclear states for distribution by the IAEA, and the establishment of a nuclear explosion service to approve and supervise the carrying out of peaceful atomic explosions.[21]

As to "new" territories opened for exploitation by science and technology, the jurisdictional question was solved for the continental shelf by granting states "sovereign rights" for the purposes of exploration and exploitation, according to the Convention on the Continental Shelf (1958). The degree to which less-developed states can take advantage of this provision depends, of course, on their technological capabilities or willingness to lease extraction rights to foreign companies. Unlike the situation just described for nuclear energy, there is no positive obligation for the technically-endowed countries to promote the requisite skills among their poorer neighbors. A similar case exists for high seas fisheries; while access has been granted by long custom and law to all comers, the vital factor now is possession of modern techniques of locating, catching, and preserving fish, skills not lacking solely among the less-developed countries. International fishery commissions have attempted to recommend conservation standards scientifically sound for the species within their purview, but have scarcely dealt with determining criteria for the actual allocation of catch in any one area or season among participating fleets of diverse fishing capabilities, not to mention between the latter and needy nonparticipating nations.

21 E. A. Martell, "Plowing a Nuclear Furrow," *Environment*, XI (April 1969), 3–13, 26–28; David B. Brooks and John V. Krutilla, *Peaceful Uses of Nuclear Explosives: Some Economic Aspects* (Baltimore 1969); Mason Willrich, *Non-Proliferation Treaty: Framework for Nuclear Arms Control* (Charlottesville, Va. 1969); Lawrence Scheinman, "Nuclear Safeguards, the Peaceful Atom, and the IAEA," *International Conciliation*, No. 572 (March 1969).

In contrast to most fisheries, the exploration and use of outer space have been mandated by the Treaty on Outer Space (1967) to be carried out "for the benefit and in the interests of all countries, irrespective of their degree of economic or scientific development," but, like the high seas, space and extraterrestrial bodies are open to access on the basis of nondiscrimination. Although present economic considerations weigh against the possibility of the routine mining and transporting to earth of materials obtained in space, the development over the next decade of reusable booster rockets will bring the cost of space trans-port sharply down, and it is probable that the moon and translunar space will become the locale of industries able to take advantage of the prevailing physical conditions.[22] If any economically valuable re-sources are located in space and are amenable to use there or on the earth, international law will have to supplement the space treaty with a more detailed legal code regarding their ownership, allocation, and the dispensation of any profits realized.

While the exploitation of the resources of the deep seabed and sub-soil has attracted great attention, it is unrealistic to expect a rich wind-fall of resources over the near future because of the economic cost of extracting, processing, and distributing whatever is obtained from the ocean floor, and because of the inhibiting effects on companies of legal uncertainties regarding ownership of resources in this domain. Still, deep-sea technology is proceeding rapidly toward enabling man to live and work for extended periods on the ocean floor and toward increas-ing his mobility within the ocean via a variety of deep-sea submergence vehicles. Already oil companies extend their rigs deep into the conti-nental shelf and extractive industries look forward to handling organic deposits, manganese nodules, and placer minerals from the ocean as well.[23] In U.N. discussions over what to do with recoverable resources, a general principle receiving wide approval has been that the resources should be exploited in the interests of the international community, including the possible reservation of some of the value received from them for direct contribution to economic development. Two legal/ political issues confront the international community in realizing the full potential of the oceans: defining the boundaries of the seabed (or the limits of the continental shelf) and defining the nature of the regime to operate for the seabed. Given the overlapping interests of

[22] Lincoln P. Bloomfield, ed., *Outer Space: Prospects for Man and Society* (New York 1968); U.S. Space Task Group, *The Post-Apollo Space Program: Directions for the Future* (Washington 1969).

[23] Edmund A. Gullion, ed., *Uses of the Seas* (Englewood Cliffs, N.J. 1968); U.N. Secretary-General, *Resources of the Sea* (New York 1968) (E/4449); U.S. National Commission on Marine Science, Engineering, and Resources, *Our Nation and the Sea* (Washington 1969); U.S. Department of the Interior, National Petroleum Coun-cil, *Petroleum Resources Under the Ocean Floor* (Washington 1969).

the great power states in maintaining maximum accessibility to the seabed for their industries, in assuring the security of offshore coastal areas, and in appealing to the good will of the less-developed areas, it is possible that the ocean floor will be internationalized in the same sense as outer space—not subject to national appropriation and open to all who can enter—with the addition that a small, but significant, percentage of profits realized by national operations will be turned over to international development agencies.[24]

One additional arena is likely to be opened up for more sustained exploitation—the atmosphere. Efforts at such weather-control and modification activities as obtaining rain from clouds and diverting hurricanes are still at a primitive stage, but any success in achieving operational control would have great impact on all the sectors of economic development. Pressures for some kind of international supervision or regulation of these activities may be even greater than in national exploitation of deep-sea and outer-space resources, because of the immediate impact any diversion of rainfall by one state would have on the economic life of another. It is therefore likely that the international community will in due course engage in debates over such issues as the jurisdiction of clouds passing through national airspace, liability for damages caused from weather modification, and the forms that might be taken by international groups established (analogous to river commissions) for the just allocation of the resources of air basins.[25]

Besides dealing with the distribution of human and natural resources, a third concern of international law is the relation of prices for primary agricultural commodities to developments in science and

[24] A U.S. draft resolution before the U.N. Committee on the Sea-Bed in 1968 held that any statement of principles on this issue should provide for "dedication as feasible and practicable of a portion of the value of the resources recovered from the deep ocean floor to international community purposes." U.S. Congress, House Committee on Foreign Affairs, *The Oceans: A Challenging New Frontier* (Washington 1968), 109; Arvid Prado, "Who will control the seabed?" *Foreign Affairs*, XLVII (October 1968), 123–37; Elisabeth Mann Borgese, *The Ocean Regime: A Suggested Statute for the Peaceful Uses of the High Seas and the Sea-Bed Beyond the Limits of National Jurisdiction* (Santa Barbara, Cal. 1968); Louis Henkin, *Law for the Sea's Mineral Resources* (New York 1968); Committee to Study the Organization of Peace, *The United Nations and the Bed of the Sea* (New York 1969). At its twenty-fourth session, the U.N. General Assembly, with the U.S. and Great Britain in the negative, declared that, pending the establishment of a seabed regime, states and persons should refrain from exploiting its resources or making claim to that area (A/RES/2524 D [XXIV]). *International Legal Materials*, IV (March 1970), 422–23. Note also the UN Declaration of Principles Governing the Sea-Bed GA Res. 2749, XXV (1970).

[25] Howard J. Taubenfeld, *Weather Modification and the Law* (New York 1968); Robert G. Fleagle, ed., *Weather Modification: Science and Public Policy* (Seattle 1969); Bruce W. Atkinson, *The Weather Business: Observation, Analysis, Forecasting, and Modification* (Garden City, N.Y. 1969); J. W. Samuels, *Draft Protocol on Weather Modification* (Geneva 1971).

technology. Many of the less-developed countries are heavily dependent on the foreign exchange they receive from sale of their produce to purchase capital goods needed for economic development. If prices for these commodities swing too low, development budgets and the balance of payments status of all countries can be greatly affected. To insure the maintenance of prices adequate to the continuance of economic development, international commodity commissions have been organized which attempt to relate agricultural output to world supply and demand, including the setting of minimum and maximum prices and of national quotas. Paradoxically, progress in scientific agriculture, while necessary to feed hungry populations, may prove detrimental to attempts at maintaining minimum prices for key commodities, insofar as this progress results in an increase in crop yields beyond prevailing world demand. This has been the case with wheat: the International Grains Arrangement (1967) collapsed in the summer of 1969 under a glut of the world wheat market partly because of good weather, but also because of improved production resulting from better irrigation methods, fertilizers, and wheat strains. Future threats to the stability of commodity price arrangements may come from the development of synthetic substitutes (for example, for coffee), extension of growing areas and seasons by using new crop strains, improvements in irrigation via atomic energy desalination of sea water, and the growth of aquaculture.[26] The greater food production that should result will in turn influence the potentially conflicting goals of feeding the hungry, maintaining price stability, improving the balance of trade, reducing the cost of storage of surplus commodities, and eliminating one-crop dependency.

Fourth, current work in the technology of satellite remote sensing using multispectral photography promises enormous dividends for the global management of resources. What is involved is the taking of pictures of the earth from space by earth resources satellites or manned spacecraft (such as Apollo 9), using instruments which record the status of a given area by simultaneously detecting radiation emissions across the wave-length spectrum. Such means can indicate the health of crops, topography of coastlines, urban density and land use, movements of wildlife, presence of minerals, and conditions in the seas, all information of vital importance for any international legislation seeking to establish a true worldwide system of economic utilization and conservation of resources.[27] The international community must very soon

---

[26] Clifford N. Hardin, ed., *Overcoming World Hunger* (Englewood Cliffs, N.J. 1969); Sherret S. Chase, "Anti-famine Strategy: Genetic Engineering for Food," *Bulletin of the Atomic Scientists* xxv (October 1969), 2–6; Lester R. Brown, *Seeds of Change: The Green Revolution and Development in the 1970's* (New York 1970).

[27] National Academy of Sciences–National Research Council, Division of Engi-

place on its agenda the question of the most suitable forum for the establishment of a global resource data-retrieval network, proprietary rights in the information gathered, and means by which such information will be distributed to subscribers to the system. The U.S. might well operate such a system pursuant to the supervision of an international group such as the Food and Agricultural Organization, following the communications satellite model.

Finally, it is clear that fundamental to a wise husbanding of natural resources is an effective world population-control program. Rising populations, combined with the demands for better standards of living heard from newly-articulate nations, mean an inevitable, continuing drain on the world's supply of raw materials, a supply which is not inexhaustible. Of particular concern is the fact that should the developing areas of the world achieve the standard of industrialization now prevailing in the Western world, the demand on resources would be staggering, even if there should be no further rise in the per-capita call on resources on the part of the Western nations—an unlikely prospect. Under these circumstances, it is at least problematical if such materials as iron, copper, and lead will remain in adequate supply by the year 2000; even new means of extracting resources from the seas, waste material, and deeper veins themselves require the expenditure of energy.[28] It is always possible that forms of obtaining energy which are now exotic, such as the processes of magneto-hydrodynamics, solar cells, and, above all, atomic fusion, will become widely available, continuing the historical cycle whereby techniques for gaining presumably exhausted minerals have been supplanted by more modern methods that open up new sources. But it would be foolhardy to take this trend for granted; thus, any contribution international law makes to slowing down population growth will directly influence the rate of resource use and the possibilities for global economic development.

Concluding this section, it is apparent that a major force for innovation in international law will be the desire for social justice felt by the inhabitants of the third world. This force has been evident throughout the subjects that have been discussed, comprising a global demand on the industrialized countries to use the wealth derived from science and technology for the benefit of all mankind. Two principles follow from this: the just allocation of sharable resources, and the provision

---

neering, *Useful Applications of Earth-Oriented Satellites: Systems for Remote Sensing Information and Distribution* (Washington 1969); U.S. Congress, House Committee on Science and Astronautics, *Earth Resources Satellite System* (Washington 1969).

[28] Charles F. Park, Jr., *Affluence in Jeopardy* (New York 1969); National Academy of Sciences–National Research Council, Committee on Resources and Man, *Resources and Man* (New York 1969).

of the technical aid requisite to enable countries lacking the necessary skills to join in the exploitation of these resources. The precise obligations that result from these principles vary according to the nature of the resource and the technological prerequisites involved. In some cases, such as the use of international rivers or fishing on the high seas, a state may be required only to follow inclusive community rules mandating exploitation of the resource in a way that does not harm the equivalent interests of all users. In other cases, such as the peaceful uses of atomic energy, states with the relevant skills may undertake a commitment to share them with states that do not. And it may be that if access to the potential resources of outer space, the seabed, and the atmosphere, or to the results of resource satellite sensing, are necessarily restricted because of the large capital investments required, then those states or international organizations carrying out such work may be requested to put aside a portion of the economic profits or information recovered, for diffusion in the form of development assistance.

## THE MANAGEMENT OF HUMAN RIGHTS

Developments and possibilities in science and technology pose profound implications for the protection of human rights, in particular, of the right of privacy. It is not simply the general right to be left alone in the confines of one's home or business that is threatened, but nothing less than man's biosocial integrity. In response, both national and international legal systems are compelled to elaborate new definitions of the human right of privacy and provide safeguards for it.[29] Emerging patterns can be grouped around biological and social science trends.

The subjection of human beings to medical experimentation is the only topic to be analyzed here that has already received some international legal attention. The Hippocratic Oath's ethical injunction to do no harm to patients, and its development over the past century by national medical societies and public health services, were the bases of provisions in the Nuremberg Code (1947), which applied to Nazi physicians, and in the Declaration of Helsinki (1964) of the World Medical Association that the medical subject must give his voluntary, informed consent before he submits to experimentation. This rule received codification in treaty form for the first time in the provision of the International Covenant on Civil and Political Rights (1966) that "no one shall be subjected without his free consent to medical or scientific experimentation." However obvious this principle may seem, its application to specific cases is fraught with difficulty because of the wide latitude of interpretation possible to the physician, and

---

[29] Moses Moskowitz, *The Politics and Dynamics of Human Rights* (New York 1968); Louis B. Sohn, *Science, Technology and Human Rights* (New York 1970).

to the peer groups which regulate his activity, of the extent to which patients—especially elderly persons and prison inmates—have been fully and reasonably informed of the possible effects of experiments on themselves. Even the conscientious doctor must weigh such complex variables as the ability of the subject to comprehend what he is told, the subject's right to reject an experiment on emotional grounds, the doctor's own vested interest in carrying out the experiment, and potential benefits which may result from the experiment to the patient and/or society.[30] Thus, more detailed codes and administrative regulations will be needed for the principle of freedom of consent to have operational meaning.

These considerations would also apply to experimental procedures involved in the transplantation of organs. But additional serious issues have been raised by the achievement of heart transplants, made possible by advances in the techniques of tissue typing and immunosuppressive drugs (to combat the body's natural defense against the intrusion of foreign matter), spare-part surgery, heart respirators, and heart-lung machines. These issues include the definition and determination of death, criteria for performing heart transplants, rights of the donor and his relatives regarding removal of his organs, liability potentially incurred by medical teams, and criteria for terminating the mechanical maintenance of a donor's life. Several national and international groups, including the Council for International Organizations of Medical Sciences, have been working on defining and gaining consensus for the necessary criteria. A possible international code is evolving along the following lines: the medical team that determines the availability and death of the donor should be separate from the team performing the transplant; the latter team should be well trained and experienced in the operation; a uniform tissue act should establish the right of an individual to declare in advance his desire to give up his organs upon death; and death should be defined as some combination of total cessation of brain functions, awareness, breathing, and reflexes.[31] Useful as these efforts are, they will surely be subjected to further strain in the future, as the medical sciences perfect such developments as viable

[30] William J. Curran, "Legal codes in scientific research involving human subjects," *Lex et Scientia*, CXI (April–June 1966), 65–73; M. H. Pappworth, *Human Guinea Pigs: Experimentation on Man* (Boston 1967); Bernard Barber, "Experimenting with Humans," *The Public Interest*, VII (Winter 1967), 91–102; Walter Goodman, "Doctors Must Experiment on Humans: But What Are the Patients' Rights?" *New York Times Magazine*, July 7, 1967, pp. 12ff.

[31] Peter Hawthorne, *The Transplanted Heart: The Incredible Story of the Epic Heart Transplant Operations by Professor Christian Bernard and His Team* (Chicago 1968); Edwin Diamond, "Are We Ready to Leave Our Bodies to the Next Generation?" *New York Times Magazine*, April 21, 1968, pp. 26ff.; Brian Richard Boylan, *The New Heart* (New York 1969); "Board on Medicine Proposes Criteria for Heart Transplants," [NAS] *News Report*, XVIII (March 1968), 1–3.

mechanical organs, brain transplants, man-machine link-ups (cyborgs), freezing of organs or whole bodies for later revival, and the laboratory creation of life.

Present and potential advances in genetic engineering add to the complexities of the questions raised in the other components of the biomedical sciences. While further research is necessary before the full implications of genetic developments and the codes of behavior they may require are understood, it is none too soon to consider the issue. Already, enough knowledge has accumulated about the relationships of individuals' genetic makeup to their physical well-being for hospitals to establish genetic counselors available to couples planning marriage or children, while a foundation of statutory and case law is emerging at the national level for such relevant topics as abortion, contraception, and artificial insemination. There is ample reason to expect in the near future the perfection or development of such techniques as clonal reproduction of humans, choice by parents of their children's sex, surgery *in utero,* implantation of embryos and stored genetic material in artificial wombs or human recipients, and, perhaps after the turn of the century, shaping of physical and personality traits (including intelligence) by precise manipulation of the genes.[32] International law must become involved in the genetic policy-making process which will decide the uses to which such work may be put, if for no other reason than that international problems are inherent in these possibilities—determination of sex of offspring could effect national economic development, while cloning (exact duplication of the body) and alteration of the human body could have military uses. More basically, the appropriate forum for dialogue on the directions in which man wishes to guide his evolution is the international community as a whole. Discussions on necessary guidelines will probably range, and rage, around the obvious "who" and "what" questions: what will be the criteria, according to whose decisions, by which certain physical and personality traits are deemed eugenically desirable, and others not, for transmission to later generations?

Threats to human privacy and individuality from the social and behavioral sciences involve attempts to gather and collate data about, or perform experiments on, groups of people as a whole. Areas of concern include the establishment of computer data centers, electronic surveillance (tapping and bugging), and behavioral science experimentation. To date, interest in these matters at the international level

[32] John D. Roslansky, ed., *Genetics and the Future of Man* (New York 1966); Gordon Rattray Taylor, *The Biological Time Bomb* (New York 1968); Albert Rosenfeld, *The Second Genesis: The Coming Control of Life* (New York 1969); Robert L. Sinsheimer, "The Prospect for Designed Genetic Change," *American Scientist,* LVII (Spring 1969), 134–42; Robert Prehoda, *Extended Youth: The Promise of Gerontology* (New York 1969).

has only arisen when one state has impinged on the interests of another, as in cases of the surveillance of foreign embassies or of social science studies being carried out by one country within another (the Project Camelot affair). Serious international bargaining on these topics may occur in future in order to alleviate the tension that can arise in such cases, and particularly as attention focuses on possible misuses of personal data stored in the data banks of international organizations and multilateral corporations. The kinds of norms that emerge could include provisions for the fully informed consent of host countries (as well as test subjects) involved in behavioral experiments, and rules for the release of computer data only to previously authorized persons, in coded form, on a need-to-know basis.[33]

In conclusion, it is apparent that the response of international law to biosocial threats to human integrity varies according to the nature of the threat. In some instances, all that may be possible at the international level are general moral or ethical codes of a recommendatory nature, with the elaboration of detailed rules left to the national level. This has been the case with medical experimentation and heart transplants, where national medical societies and governmental agencies have attempted to oversee the scientific judgments of researchers in these fields. In other instances, it may be possible for international legislation to codify appropriate norms directly; this could happen with regard to cross-national behavioral field research and the operation of international data banks. Finally, there are subjects on which more information is needed, such as genetic engineering, so that discussions on feasible regulatory systems can proceed on an informed basis. The international community has initiated, in fact, the first steps in obtaining greater information on the dangers science and technology pose to privacy. In January 1968, the Council of Europe's Consultative Assembly requested the Committee of Ministers to have the Committee of Experts on Human Rights "study and report on the question whether, having regard to Article 8 of the [European] Convention of Human Rights, the national legislation in the member States adequately protects the right to privacy against violations which may be committed by the use of modern scientific and technical methods." [34] A similar request was made to the U.N. by several states participating in the twentieth anniversary celebration of the U.N. Declaration of Human Rights (1948) in December 1968.

[33] National Academy of Sciences, *Privacy and Behavioral Research* (Washington 1967); National Academy of Sciences–Social Science Research Council, *Behavioral and Social Sciences: Outlook and Needs* (Washington 1969); Alan Westin, *Privacy and Freedom* (New York 1967) and "The Snooping Machine," *Playboy*, xv (May 1968), 130–32, 152–57; U.S. Congress, House Government Operations Committee, *Privacy and the National Data Bank Concept* (Washington 1968).

[34] "Big Brother's Return," *Forward in Europe* (February–March 1968), 18.

THE MANAGEMENT OF ENVIRONMENTAL ALTERATION

In view of international law's traditional image as a social process relatively slow to respond to contemporary public issues, it may be surprising that, in fact, the increasing global concern with man's effects on the environment has resulted in action at the international, as well as the national, level. Yet it would be ironic if this were not the case. The coexistence among life forms, and the relationships between the latter and their natural surroundings, extend throughout the planetary biosphere; any efforts to restrict attempts to counter deleterious alterations of this web to the political units within which the human species chooses to reside would be ultimately inadequate.

That they have a mission to perform in the environmental field has not escaped the attention of international organizations, including those—like NATO, OECD, the Council of Europe, and the U.N. Economic Commission for Europe—not traditionally identified with this topic. This developing concern will culminate in general conferences on the environment to be held by the ECE in Czechoslovakia in 1971, and by the U.N. as a whole in Sweden in 1972. Meanwhile, during the 1960's the docket of international law has also been seized by the case of man versus the environment, with the relevant output taking the form of treaties, a handful of international court decisions, and the declarations of international groups. While this response has not always been far-sighted—great bursts of activity seem to follow awareness of the latest disaster—and the obligations imposed on states not easily enforced, sufficient work has been done to warrant the classification of a new sub-field of international law: international ecological law. It is composed of norms and doctrines involving the causes and cures of environmental disruption, and is applied to phenomena whose loci may be wholly within a state, transnational, beyond the jurisdiction of any state, or any combination of these. Analysis of the issues involved will be taken up from the perspective of five functional areas: environmental pollution resulting from the disposal and emission of the fuel and by-products of industrial civilization; environmental disruption caused by large-scale technological projects; similar alteration caused by large-scale scientific experiments; threats to the conservation of wildlife; and the growth of population.[35]

35 On environmental issues in general, see Max Michelson, *The Environmental Revolution* (New York 1970); Jean Dorst, *Before Nature Dies* (Boston 1970); Keith Reid, *Nature's Network* (Garden City, N.Y. 1970); Garrett de Bell, ed., *The Environmental Handbook: Prepared for the First National Environmental Teach-In* (New York 1970); President's Council on Recreation and Natural Beauty, *From Sea to Shining Sea* (Washington 1968); U.S. Congress, House Committee on Science and Astronautics, *Environmental Quality* and *Managing the Environment* (Washington 1968); Barry Commoner, *Science and Survival* (New York 1967); Don Fabun, ed., "Ecology: The Man-made Planet," *Kaiser News*, No. 1 (1970).

TABLE 3

INTERNATIONAL LAW, ENVIRONMENTAL POLLUTION, AND THE CONSERVATION OF WILDLIFE

| Type of Pollution | International Legal Response | Nature of Response |
|---|---|---|
| General Environment | Council of Europe's Declaration on the Management of the Natural Environment of Europe (1970)<br>Proposals for a U.N. Declaration on the Human Environment<br>International Health Regulations (1969)<br>Nordic UN Associations' International Declaration of Environmental Rights (1969) | Policy statements intended to guide national and international bodies in their activities affecting the environment |
| Oil Pollution of the High Seas | Convention on the High Seas (1958)<br>Convention for the Prevention of Pollution of the Sea by Oil (1954, amended 1962 and 1969)<br>Convention on the Conduct of Fishing Operations in the North Atlantic (1967)<br>International Convention on Civil Liability for Oil Pollution Damage (1969)<br>International Convention Relating to Intervention on the High Seas in Cases of Oil Pollution Casualties (1969)<br>Agreement for Co-Operation in Dealing with Pollution of the North Sea by Oil (1969)<br>Torrey Canyon case (Britain and France vs. Barracuda Tanker Corp.) (settled out of court, 1969)<br>International Convention on the Establishment of an International Fund for the Compensation of Oil Pollution Damage (1971) | Legal regimes bar dumping of specified types of oil in high seas zones by ships, establish ship liability rules, detail responsibilities of coastal states in cases of accidental oil spills, promote cooperation in oil spill monitoring |
| Pollution of International Rivers (sewage, detergents, and thermal pollution) | Treaties regulating international river systems; e.g., U.S.–Canadian Boundary Water Treaty (1909), India-Pakistan Indus Waters Treaty (1960)<br>Conventions on the International Commissions for the Protection of the Moselle (1956), the Rhine (1963), and the Sarre (1963) Against Pollution | Legal regimes establish principles for the abatement of existing and prevention of future pollution in river systems, organize international bodies to propose and monitor water quality standards, provide for negotiation of disputes |

TABLE 3 (*Continued*)

INTERNATIONAL LAW, ENVIRONMENTAL POLLUTION, AND THE CONSERVATION OF WILDLIFE

| Type of Pollution | International Legal Response | Nature of Response |
|---|---|---|
| | European Agreement on the Restriction of the Use of Certain Detergents in Washing and Cleaning Products (1968) Convention on the International Water Preservation Commission (1959) World Health Organization's International Standards for Drinking Water (1958) *Lake Lanoux Arbitration* case between France and Spain (1957) U.N. Economic Commission for Europe's Declaration of Policy on Water Pollution Control Council of Europe's Europe Water Charter (1968) and draft Convention on the Protection of Fresh Water Against Pollution (1969) | |
| Disposal of Chemical and Biological Weapons in the Ocean | U.S. policy statements and administrative regulations | Attempt to impose strict safety standards; prior notification to other nations |
| Radioactive Pollution of All Environments | Nuclear Test Ban Treaty (1963) Antarctic Treaty (1959) Treaty for the Prohibition of Nuclear Weapons in Latin America (1967) Convention on the High Seas (1958) Convention on Third Party Liability in the Field of Nuclear Energy (1960) Convention on Minimum International Standards Regarding Civil Liability for Nuclear Damage (1963) Convention on the Liability of Operators of Nuclear Ships (1962) U.S. bilateral agreements with countries regarding visits of the *Savannah* and nuclear submarines Settlement of Japanese Claims [by U.S.] for Personal Injuries and Property Damages Resulting | Elimination of new radioactive materials discharged into the air, space, and under water, and in Latin America and the Antarctic, due to the testing of nuclear weapons; establishment of quality standards for discharge of spent radioactive material into rivers and seas; determination of safety standards for operating land- and sea-based nuclear reactors and of liability settlement in case of nuclear reactor accident |

| Type of Pollution | International Legal Response | Nature of Response |
|---|---|---|
| | from Nuclear Tests in the Marshall Islands in 1954 (1955) | |
| | IAEA Ad Hoc Panel report on Radioactive Waste Disposal into the Sea (1961) and Panel of Experts' Report on Disposal of Radioactive Wastes into Fresh Water (1969) | |
| | U.S. payment of damages to Palomares, Spain, farmers | |
| | IMCO draft Convention on Maritime Carriage of Nuclear Substances (1971) | |
| Pesticide Pollution | Unilateral national laws and administrative regulations regulating use of pesticides (U.S., Canada, Western Europe) | Phase out use of persistent pesticides, especially DDT, by specified dates |
| Air Pollution (industrial processes, automobiles, and high altitude airplane exhaust. *Trail Smelter* case between U.S. and Canada (1941) | Council of Europe's Declaration of Principles on Air Pollution Control (1968) | Proposals to establish legal and financial responsibilities of states for modifications of the atmosphere, and air quality standards for regional basins |
| Extraterrestrial Contamination | Treaty on Outer Space (1967) | Treaty members are to avoid adverse changes in Earth's environment due to contamination by returning spacecraft or personnel |
| Noise Pollution (automobiles, airplanes) | U.N. draft convention on road traffic (1965) National legislation on overflight by supersonic airplanes | Prohibit use of car horns in built-up areas; ban land overflight by supersonic transports |
| Conservation of Wildlife | Convention on Fishing and Conservation of the Living Resources of the High Seas (1958) Numerous regional fish conservation treaties; e.g., European Fisheries Convention (1964), International Convention for the Conservation of Atlantic Tuna (1966) Bilateral treaties on migratory birds; e.g., U.S.–British (for Can- | Treaties establish rules for fish catch based on "maximum sustainable yield" and for negotiating fish disputes among states; prohibit poaching and trade in endangered species; regulate hunting seasons for particular birds and animals; promote cooperation and |

| Type of Pollution | International Legal Response | Nature of Response |
|---|---|---|
| | ada) Migratory Birds Convention (1916) <br> Convention of Nature Protection and Wildlife Preservation in the Western Hemisphere (1940) <br> African Convention for the Conservation of Nature and Natural Resources (1968) <br> IUCN's draft Convention on the Export, Import, and Transit of Certain Species of Wild Animals and Plants (1970) <br> East African Animal Interpol (1969) <br> Antarctic Treaty (1959) <br> Agreed Measures for the Conservation of Antarctic Fauna and Flora (1964) <br> International Plant Protection Convention (1951) <br> International Convention for the Protection of Birds (1950) <br> Convention on Wetlands of International Importance, Especially as Waterfowl Habitat (1971) <br> IUCN's draft Convention on Conservation of the World Heritage (1971) <br> IUCN's draft Convention on Conservation of Certain Islands for Science (1971) | founding of national parks and game reserves within a region |
| Population Control | Declaration on Population by World Leaders (1966) <br> U.N. Declaration on Discrimination Against Women (1967) <br> Teheran Conference on Human Rights' Resolution on Human Rights Aspects of Family Planning (1968) | Statements support the family-planning approach, with the spread of relevant education, as a basic human right |

Future international pollution agreements suggested by Sweden at the March 1970 preparatory meeting for the 1972 environment conference:
1. Prohibition of the discharge of oil by ships into the oceans
2. Prohibition or reduction of the use of persistent pesticides
3. Identification and control of additives harmful to the environment
4. Radical reduction in the sulphur content of heating oils
5. Rules for the transportation of toxic substances
6. Rules for the storage and final disposal of radioactive substances

TABLE 4

INTERNATIONAL ORGANIZATIONS WITH GENERAL ENVIRONMENTAL OVERSIGHT

| International Organization | Principal Subsidiary Organ(s) Concerned with the Environment |
|---|---|
| United Nations | Preparatory Committee for the U.N. Conference on the Human Environment<br>Office of Science and Technology<br>U.N. Economic and Social Council<br>Specialized Agencies: UNESCO, IAEA, IMCO, WMO, WHO, ILO, FAO, ICAO |
| U.N. Economic Commission for Europe | Senior Advisors to the ECE Governments on Environmental Problems<br>Committee on Water Problems |
| Organization for Economic Cooperation and Development | Environment Committee |
| International Council of Scientific Unions | Special Committee on Problems of the Environment<br>Special Committee on the International Biological Program |
| International Social Science Council | Standing Committee on Environmental Disruption |
| North Atlantic Treaty Organization | Committee on the Challenges of Modern Society |
| Council of Europe | Committee for the Conservation of Nature and Natural Resources |
| International Union for Conservation of Nature and Natural Resources | Ecology, Legislation, and Survival Service Commissions<br>International Youth Federation for Environmental Studies and Conservation<br>International Council of Environmental Law |
| International Joint Commission | International Lake Erie and Lake Ontario–St. Lawrence River Water Pollution Boards |
| International Union of Biological Sciences | International Association for Ecology |
| Inter-Parliamentary Union | Special Committee for the Conservation of Nature |
| International Union of Pure and Applied Chemistry | Division of Applied Chemistry |
| International Geographical Union | Commission on Man and Environment |
| World Federation of Engineering Organizations | Committee on Environmental Engineering |

TABLE 4 (Continued)

INTERNATIONAL ORGANIZATIONS WITH GENERAL ENVIRONMENTAL OVERSIGHT

| International Organization | Principal Subsidiary Organ(s) Concerned with the Environment |
| --- | --- |
| International Union of Local Authorities | |
| Commission of the European Communities | |
| Council for Mutual Economic Assistance | |
| International Institute for Environmental Affairs | |
| Friends of the Earth | |

Environmental pollution in its myriad forms has proven a difficult problem for international law to handle, partly because the mix of potential polluters involved—local and national governments, businesses, and private individuals—makes it a complex task to assign overall responsibility, establish liabilities, and enforce damages awarded. But the difficulty also lies in the diverse nature of the threat; the effects of pollution may be as direct as the eutrophication of a river resulting from nutrients dumped into it by households and factories, or as indirect and subtle as the persistent pesticides ingested into the food chains of animals. Pollution is a continuing, cumulative process of degradation, and not all of its interrelationships are presently understood or easily traced. In the light of these considerations, it is not surprising that a certain amount of improvising and after-the-fact reaction have taken place at both the national and international levels, as policy makers struggle to adapt familiar institutional forms to the requirements of a newly-recognized public issue.[36]

Work in international law on the pollution problem has coalesced around the clarification of three issues. The first is both political and technological, involving the definition of threshold levels beyond which damage to the environment calling for corrective action may be said to have occurred, and the tracking down of such pollution to its source.

[36] Some of the material in this part is derived from my article, "Pollution Control: An International Perspective," *Environment*, x (September 1968), 172–82; see also Abel Wolman, "Pollution As An International Issue," *Foreign Affairs*, XLVII (October 1968), 164–75; U.N. Secretary-General, *Problems of the Human Environment* (New York 1969) (E/4667); U.N. Food and Agricultural Organization and UNESCO, *Conservation and Rational Use of the Environment* (New York 1969) (E/4458); U.N. Economic Commission for Europe, *Report of the Meeting of the Preparatory Group for the Meeting of Governmental Experts on Problems Relating to Environment* (New York 1969) (E/ECE/726); UNESCO, *Intergovernmental Conference of Experts on the Scientific Basis for Rational Use and Conservation of the Biosphere: Final Report* (Paris 1969) (SC/MD/9).

Obviously, it is necessary to know that some level of pollution calling for remedial response exists, and where it originated, before legal and diplomatic activities can begin against those at fault. That these tasks are not easy, even from a technical standpoint, was illustrated in the Rhine fish kill of 1969, when authorities from the riparian states encountered difficulty establishing its cause (industrial, agricultural, or ship sewage) and its place or places of origin. The addition of politics to the search for threshold standards is inevitable, given the economic and prestige factors involved in international cases of pollution: this may have been a factor, for instance, in the disagreement between scientists from the U.S. Atomic Energy Commission and their Japanese colleagues over the possibility that the nuclear submarine *Swordfish* was the source of radioactivity detected in Sasebo harbor in May 1968, and over the question of whether or not the level detected endangered life. Perhaps the most progress toward defining international standards has been made in the area of oil pollution of the high seas, where the relevant treaties delimit the amount of oil or oily wastes that may be deposited by ships of various tonnages in specified zones.[37] The treaties dealing with civil nuclear reactors become applicable simply upon the occurrence of a nuclear "incident" causing nuclear damage, while the IAEA and International Commission on Radiological Protection continue their work on determining tolerable radiation levels for disposing of radioactive wastes. Existing and proposed treaties on fresh water pollution usually embody the concept of deleterious pollution, entailing "substantial damage" done by one state to another by the nature of the river water passed between them. Work is being done on international air and noise pollution by the Council of Europe and U.N. specialized agencies (WHO, ILO, and ICAO).

However elegant quality standards become, they will mean little in practice if polluters cannot be identified. Here technology may aid in the cure of its own excesses as detection equipment becomes more sophisticated. For example, the detection of oil slicks left by ships at sea may be greatly enhanced by the microwave radiometer, a device sensitive to the particular microwave emissions of oil and water and easily adapted to installation in light planes. Most interesting in this regard is the possibility that the International Biological Program will approve the establishment of a global monitoring network, many of whose components already exist, for the detection of alterations in the

[37] Richard Petrow, *In the Wake of Torrey Canyon* (New York 1968); Edward Cowan, *Oil and Water: The Torrey Canyon Disaster* (Philadelphia 1968); U.S. Congress, House Committee on Merchant Marine and Fisheries, *Report on International Control of Oil Pollution* (Washington 1967); Ved P. Nanda, "The 'Torrey Canyon' Disaster: Some Legal Aspects," 44 *Denver Law Journal*, 400–25 (Summer 1967); "Oil Pollution of the Sea," 10 *Harvard International Law Journal*, 316–59 (Spring 1969).

environment; the network, consisting of twenty stations by 1972, would use mechanical, animal, and plant sources as monitors, and could be an extremely effective way of applying pragmatically the concern being expressed by governments about the quality of the environment.

The legal consequences following the determination of the fact of pollution are another issue for the international community. Major principles involved are the degree of state responsibility in various situations, and the nature and scope of liability to be assessed. Under existing treaties and court cases, it is the state that has been held responsible for the quality of the water and air that it sends to its neighbors; this quality should not have so deteriorated by uses made of the water or air in the first state as to cause serious injury to other states.[38] Where oil pollution in the high seas or radioactive material from nuclear reactors is involved, the owner or operator of the vessel or facility (assuming his state has signed the requisite treaty) is responsible. In these cases, detailed systems of liability have been worked out, specifying such matters as the nature of liability involved (absolute or based on fault), limits to the amount of liability that can be assessed, appropriate forums for litigation of disputes, and insurance requirements to be met; it is usually up to each signatory state to operationalize these clauses by passage of local law. Currently on the agenda of international law is the problem of extending this system to the assessment of liability for damages done by space vehicles or pursuant to exploitation of the resources of the seabed.

The final pollution issue involves the kinds of institutional structures that should be established for the more efficient undertaking of pollution control activities. In some cases, no formal international mechanism, except that needed for monitoring, may be necessary; thus, without holding any conferences on the matter, several of the industrialized nations are acting in parallel, but unilaterally, to restrict or abolish the use of the more persistent agricultural pesticides within a few years. The negotiation of the appropriate treaties may also be sufficient, as in the case of those arms control agreements that ban outright the testing of nuclear weapons (thereby eliminating one source of new radioactivity) in all but underground environments. But for air and water pollution a step beyond this could be required—

---

[38] In the *Trail Smelter Dispute,* a U.S.–Canadian tribunal declared that "under the principles of international law . . . no State has the right to use or permit the use of its territory in such a manner as to cause injury by fumes in or to the territory of another or the properties therein, when the case is of serious consequences and the injury is established by clear and convincing evidence." "First Decision," 33 *American Journal of International Law,* 182–212 (January 1939), and "Final Decision," 35 *American Journal of International Law,* 716 (October 1941). On water pollution, see the *Lake Lanoux Arbitration* in 53 *American Journal of International Law,* 156–71 (January 1959); A. P. Lester, "River Pollution in International Law," 57 *American Journal of International Law,* 828 ff. (October 1963).

the creation of new international bodies designed to deal with regional pollution problems beyond the capacity of individual states to handle satisfactorily and too consistent to be dealt with on an *ad hoc,* case by case, basis. It is significant that the OECD plans to work out environmental control standards for the voluntary adoption of European member countries, pursuant to its investigations of economic growth. This modest start may well be supplemented in the next decade by the growth of regional international organizations concerned with international drainage and airshed basins, and empowered to deal with such matters as the assessment of responsibility for cleaning up existing pollution, the establishment of liability for cases of future pollution, the fair apportionment of abatement costs, the arbitration of pollution disputes, and the drafting, administration, and enforcement of regional quality standards.[39]

Large-scale technological projects comprise the second functional problem area for environmental management. It is possible to contemplate projects of such magnitude that their undertaking would lead, for better or worse, to widespread environmental alteration. Already, it seems, the construction of the Aswan High Dam has promoted the spread of snail-borne schistosomiasis, and has led to such silting that the U.A.R. may end up with less agricultural acreage than it had before the project.[40] In the future we may have to face radioactively-contaminated ground water and even earthquakes caused by the detonation of large underground atomic explosions, or the massive ecological disruption that could accompany the construction of huge reservoir and pipeline systems designed to move fresh water from Siberia and the North American Arctic to more populated territories to the south.

At the national level, the pressures of informed and coordinated public opinion may impress governments with the necessity of not implementing such plans unilaterally without taking into serious account their ecological implications, even before binding international obligations to this effect are negotiated or acknowledged. Thus, the U.S. Department of the Interior has drawn up regulations to ensure that each step in the program to lay an oil pipeline from the Arctic North Slope south to Valdez, Alaska, is taken in the context of careful investigation and continual inspection of its environmental consequences, lest permanent damage be caused to the tundra, with serious disruption of animal migratory patterns.

[39] U.N. Economic Commission for Europe, *Tentative Suggestions for the Establishment of International River Pollution Control Bodies in Europe* (New York 1959) (Annex III of E/ECE/340) and *Conference on Water Pollution Problems in Europe* (New York 1961).

[40] Garrett Hardin, "To Trouble a Star: The Cost of Intervention in Nature," *Bulletin of the Atomic Scientists,* XXVI (January 1970), 17–20.

The development of a global ecological consciousness could lead to similar expectations among states—large-scale technological projects would be permissible if the government involved indicated active awareness of its environmental responsibilities. Such expectations would be particularly legitimate if the projects were planned for internationalized areas (outer space and, eventually, the seabed), or if they were carried out with the economic and technical assistance of international organizations. One treaty already provides this "checking in" with other concerned parties before a state proceeds with a project; the Treaty for the Prohibition of Nuclear Weapons in Latin America (1967) stipulates that a party contemplating the explosion of a nuclear device for peaceful purposes furnish the Agency established by the treaty and the IAEA with information on the plans, possible radioactive fallout, and measures to be taken to avoid danger to the territories of other parties. Furthermore, officials of the agencies may observe the explosions.

Similar perceptions of what is defined as responsible, and therefore permissible, state behavior have arisen around the subject of large-scale scientific experiments. Much of the experience with this form of environmental intrusion has resulted from a series of projects, designed at least in part to give militarily useful information, carried out by the U.S. over the last decade. These include Project Starfish, the explosion in 1962 of a hydrogen bomb 250 miles above the Pacific, with consequent damage to several satellites and interruption of the Van Allen belts; and Project West Ford, the orbiting in 1963 of a thin band of copper dipoles for experimentation with a prototype interference-free communications system. The controversy raised in the scientific community by such potentially disastrous tampering with the environment as Starfish implied led to a significant restructuring of procedures the next time around. Westford was reviewed before and after launch by both national and international bodies (ICSU and the International Astronomical Union); as a result, much of the information dealing with the project was declassified, and the launch date was postponed once.[41]

In the context of this experience, President Kennedy made a speech to the National Academy of Sciences a month before his death explaining that the government had established procedures to assure expert review before such experiments were undertaken; every effort would be made to publish relevant data needed for open discussion by the

41 Eugene B. Skolnikoff, *Science, Technology and American Foreign Policy* (Cambridge, Mass. 1967), 84–92; American Association for the Advancement of Science, "The Integrity of Science," in Gerald Holton, ed., *Science and Culture: A Study of Cohesive and Disjunctive Forces* (Boston 1967), 291–99, 318–22; Andrew G. Haley, *Space Law and Government* (New York 1963), 11–12, 268–71.

scientific community. While this commitment is potentially self-serving and open to interpretation in any given case in the light of national security, it is an important recognition of the necessity of responsible behavior by a great power—a power capable of setting precedents in spheres of activity that it dominates by reason of technological superiority. The principles of full prior consultation and data sharing within the international community will probably be stressed even more in the future.

Concern for the conservation of wildlife is not new in international law, but the ecological perspective has pervaded the conservation movement in recent years as much as it has other segments of environmental management. Working to ensure the continuance of other species is now perceived as not merely a moral imperative, but a matter of survival insurance for man himself, who is only one among other animals bound together in the interdependence of life.[42] The role of international law is to preserve and protect wildlife from purposeful destruction carried out for food and fashion, and from indirect destruction resulting as a by-product of technological civilization. The species of most interest to international law are those that inhabit international areas (the high seas and Antarctica), whose migratory patterns carry them across national boundaries, or who are on the verge of extinction.

Different patterns for regulation and enforcement have been used in relation to the different contexts in which man encounters wildlife. For fish, migratory birds, and rare animals, international regulations have sought either to ban outright hunting of the species or to allow hunting under specified conditions, relating to the time of year, type of weapons, and locations. Historically, primary attention has been paid to the conservation of living marine resources. The goal here has been not so much to preserve nearly extinct species, as to ensure that the food fish on which nations heavily rely are not pushed to that point by overexploitation. While standards cannot be as precise as those for pollution control, the guiding principle has been the achievement of the "maximum sustainable yield," a rate of catch high enough to make efficient use of the stock available, without taking so much that future reproduction cannot make up for present loss. But the application of this standard is as subject to nontechnical factors as it is in pollution. The general goal of conservation must compete with the desires of given coastal states to maintain monopolistic control of offshore fishing, in order to protect inefficient local fishermen from

---

[42] U.S. Department of the Interior, Bureau of Sport Fisheries and Wildlife, *The Right to Exist* (Washington 1969); U.S. Congress, Senate Committee on Commerce, *Endangered Species* (Washington 1968); James Fisher, Noel Simon and Jack Vincent, *Wildlife in Danger* (New York 1969).

technologically more advanced foreign fleets and to reserve offshore fish for expanding national populations. A balancing process has ensued in which coastal states may enforce genuine conservation laws in offshore contiguous zones, while the interests of the community as a whole are maintained by assuring access to high-seas resources by all who can obtain them. To ensure that good conservation practices are followed on the high seas, over a dozen fishery conservation commissions, of varying degrees of effectiveness, have been established to compile scientific data, calculate total annual fish yields, and settle disputes among parties.[43]

For endangered species of birds and animals, it has not proven sufficient to regulate hunting seasons or establish sanctuaries. More active efforts have been necessary to renew species nearly exterminated by illegal hunting. At both national and international levels these efforts have taken the form of programs carefully designed to "nurse" a vanishing species back to health in the controlled environments of wildlife survival centers, and international lists of endangered species have been drawn up, prohibiting the catching of certain wildlife for trade.

It is difficult enough to regulate man's direct predation on other species; but wildlife is also threatened by industrial civilization itself, a matter not so amenable to treaty regulation. Insofar as pollution—particularly that from persistent pesticides—is brought under control, wildlife in general will benefit. Sensitivity of governments to the ecological consequences of their large-scale scientific or technological projects would have similar results. Some such projects have already aroused the concern of informed groups, with varying effects: Britain in 1967 proposed to build an air base, radio, and tracking station on Aldabra Atoll in the Indian Ocean; the Soviet Union has been constructing a pulp-mill factory near Lake Baikal in Siberia; and the U.S. has carried out several underground nuclear explosions on Amchitka Island in the Aleutians. All three locations are the habitats of unusual or endangered species. Britain eventually shelved the project, as much for budgetary as ecological reasons; the Soviet government has attempted to include purification plants in its complex; and the U.S. has taken special care to remove sea otters from the test site. Although controversy on these issues has not been stilled, it is significant that the governments involved found it necessary to respond publicly to both domestic and international concern about the pollution and the threats to wildlife involved in such projects. Once again, the evolution

[43] James A. Crutchfield, ed., *The Fisheries: Problems in Resource Management* (Seattle 1965); Douglas M. Johnston, *The International Law of Fisheries: A Framework for Policy-Oriented Inquiries* (New Haven 1965); Norman J. Padelford, *Public Policy and the Uses of the Sea* (Cambridge, Mass. 1969); L. F. E. Goldie, "The Oceans' Resources and International Law—Possible Developments in Regional Fisheries Management," 8 *Columbia Journal of Transnational Law*, 1–53 (Spring 1969).

of a norm of national responsibility for the environment may be detected.

Efforts to slow down the growth rate of the human population must be a fundamental component of international ecological law, for it is this growth, coupled with by-products of the science and technology necessary to support it, that triggers the overall threat to the environment and to the achievement of human rights. The resolutions and declarations of international organizations within the last few years have acknowledged the existence of the population problem and have stressed family planning as a human right. But this is a very modest first step. For some time to come, international law will be involved in the work of establishing international consensus and guidelines on such issues as the desirability of positing national and global population goals (possibly a zero growth rate); the necessity for governmental intervention to close the gap between voluntary family planning and the achievement of lower population growth rates; and the promotion of a philosophy that stresses the qualitative aspects of life over progress defined in terms of ever-higher levels of GNP.[44]

In conclusion, the thrust of international ecological law is to promote the acceptance of two basic principles. One is the extension to environment-related activities of the traditional norm that a state is not entirely at liberty to do as it wishes within its territorial sphere. The other points to the establishment of a new human right, freedom from the harmful effects of environmental alteration: this right has already received codification as a general principle in the International Covenant on Economic, Social, and Cultural Rights (1966), which obligates signatories to improve all aspects of environmental hygiene as a contribution to the realization of everyone's right to enjoy the highest attainable standard of physical and mental health.

As to the application of these principles, it is possible to describe a cluster of shared expectations emerging in the international community with regard to state responsibilities in the environmental realm: a state should consult with all concerned parties, on the basis of openly-available information, about any contemplated environmental alteration which is considered by them to be potentially harmful; a state should engage in the negotiation of inclusive rules regulating the equitable apportionment of sharable resources; and a state should

[44] Moskowitz (fn. 29), 113–22; Richard A. Falk, "World Population and International Law," 63 *American Journal of International Law*, 514–20 (July 1969); Georg Borgstrom, *Too Many: A Study of Earth's Biological Limitations* (New York 1969); Richard N. Gardner, "Toward a World Population Program," *International Organization*, XXII (Winter 1968), 332–61; Garrett Hardin, "The Tragedy of the Commons," *Science*, CLXII (December 13, 1968), 1243–48; Bernard Berelson, "Beyond Family Planning," *Science*, CLXII (February 7, 1969), 533–43.

accept such liability as accrues to it in case of harm resulting from
deleterious use of its territory.[45]

In all of this, international law makes use of traditional components
of the legal process to define and handle the issues involved—the negotiation of treaties, the establishment of international organizations
for coordination and administration, and the interplay of diplomatic
relationships. But it must be questioned whether traditional forms are
sufficient to deal with a crisis of this nature. Fish will not conveniently
remain within the boundaries man chooses to draw for their control;
pesticides will be carried by air and water to wherever the dictates of
geography deposit them; and the cumulative effects on local flora and
fauna of altering the landscape for human purposes may be undetected for years. It is possible that nothing less than a new world order
will be needed to deal seriously with the man/environment nexus, an
order which perceives the planet and its resources as a whole, to be
managed in the interest of all living things.[46] In achieving this, international law will have to engage in an unprecedented effort at international social invention, purposefully innovating new structural relations among international and transnational actors. The goal would
be to operationalize in the legal-political realm the moral principle
that the conservationist Aldo Leopold called the ecological conscience:
"A thing is right when it tends to preserve the integrity, stability, and
beauty of the biotic community. It is wrong when it tends otherwise." [47]

## THE MANAGEMENT OF SCIENCE AND TECHNOLOGY

While previous sections have explored the response of international law to the consequences of developing science and technology,

[45] Skolnikoff (fn. 41), 88–92, 306–12; American Association for the Advancement
of Science (fn. 41), 291–92, 310–18; Jenks, *Law* (fn. 1), 39–47; David Davies Memorial
Institute, "Draft Rules Concerning Changes in the Environment of the Earth," in
C. Wilfred Jenks, *Space Law* (New York 1965), 430–39; C. Wilfred Jenks, "Liability
for Ultra-Hazardous Activities in International Law," in Hague Academy of International Law, 117 *Recueil des Cours*, 105–200 (The Hague 1967). The UNESCO
*Biosphere Conference*, 31, suggested that the U.N. General Assembly might "Consider the advisability of a Universal Declaration of the Protection and Betterment
of the Human Environment" (Recommendation 17). See also the David Davies
Memorial Institute, *Principles Governing Certain Changes in the Environment of
Man* and *International Means of Conservation of Natural Resources* (London 1968
and 1969), and World Peace Through World Law Center (Carl August Fleischer),
*Draft Convention on Environmental Cooperation among Nations* (Geneva 1971).

[46] Suggestions for new, comprehensive international environmental organizations
have been made by Richard A. Falk (Address: "Inability of Traditional Forms of
Legal and Political Order to Adapt to Pollution Problems") and Richard R. Baxter
at the Conference on International and Interstate Regulation of Water Pollution,
Columbia University School of Law, March 1970; George F. Kennan, "To Prevent
a World Wasteland: A Proposal," *Foreign Affairs*, XLVIII (April 1970), 401–13.

[47] Quoted in Thomas Merton, "The Wild Places," *The Center Magazine*, 1 (July
1968), 44.

the present one is concerned with the roles international law has taken on under the necessity of providing an international framework for guiding the progress of science and technology themselves. While international law is often perceived as buffeted about by new discoveries and inventions, it is also the case that international law in its turn influences science and technology. Indeed, the relevant legal output has grown to such an extent in recent years that it is possible to list as a major trend the evolution of an international law of science. This law is an expression of the belief that the fulfillment of such community goals as economic development, intellectual progress, and social justice depends heavily on achievements in science and technology, and their widespread diffusion. The international law of science is carried out by norms that seek to alleviate national barriers to international cooperation in science and technology and to make more efficacious such cooperation as does take place. These trends will be analyzed within the categories of the advancement, protection, and diffusion of science and technology.[48]

Science is advanced by international law when international legal regimes aid in the removal or regulation of barriers to the undertaking of research carried out within or among states. The trend that has become evident here, reflecting the high value placed by the international community on basic scientific research, is the development of a norm according to which interference with such research is to be eliminated to the maximum extent possible. Interference with research may be reasonable or unreasonable, depending on how important the free pursuit of knowledge is judged to be in the light of other goals being sought in a given context, with which this pursuit could itself potentially interfere.

Even at the purely national level the concept of freedom of research has already received community recognition and acknowledgement in general terms in the International Covenant on Economic, Social, and Cultural Rights (1966), which holds that signatory states "undertake to respect the freedom indispensable for scientific research and creative

[48] The material in this section is adapted from my article, "An International Law of Science: Orders on Man's Expanding Frontiers," *Bulletin of the Atomic Scientists*, xxv (December 1968), 6–10. Some attempts to date to investigate international legal questions raised by scientific research have been made in relation to the high seas: Thomas A. Clingan, Jr., "Scientific Inquiry in the Oceans: Legal Regulation and Responsibility," *Lex et Scienta*, vi (April–June 1969), 77–91; William T. Burke, *International Legal Problems of Scientific Research in the Oceans* (Washington 1967). On general cooperation in science and technology, see Daniel Behrman, *Web of Progress: UNESCO At Work in Science and Technology* (Paris 1964); U.S. Congress, House Committee on Science and Astronautics, *The Participation of Federal Agencies in International Scientific Programs* (Washington 1967); W. B. Walsh, *Science and International Public Affairs: Six Recent Experiments in International Scientific Cooperation* (Syracuse, N.Y., 1967).

ability." While even so broad a statement is further qualified in its application by the Covenant, and enforcement is limited to the submission of reports by states on their achievements in attaining Covenant rights to the U.N. Secretary General, the goal expressed sets the stage for the international legal process to undertake more specific definitions of the nature of permissible interference.

This is being done contextually, according to the kinds of barriers inhibiting the free flow of research activities. The research under consideration is that which impinges on the international system, because of its location, transnational effects, or reliance on individuals or materials from more than one country. International experience to date in this field is summarized in Table 5.

## TABLE 5
### INTERNATIONAL RESPONSE TO INTERFERENCE WITH SCIENTIFIC RESEARCH

| Barrier to Research | International Response | Nature of Response |
|---|---|---|
| Lack of necessary equipment or skilled personnel available to state or international community | Treaties and activities of international organizations promoting cooperation in research; e.g., U.S.–Australian Agreement on the Ultra-Violet Survey of Southern Skies (1961), Convention for the Establishment of the European Space Research Organization (1962) | States pool expenses and material in their joint research endeavors |
| Different national systems of measurement and terminology | Activities of the International Council of Scientific Unions and its constituent organizations, the International Bureau of Weights and Measures and the International Organization for Standardization; UNESCO/ICSU World Science Information System (1972) | International agreements on standardization of scientific constants and nomenclature |
| Uncertainty about access to internationalized areas | Fishery conservation treaties providing for relevant research, Treaty on Outer Space (1967), Antarctic Treaty (1959) | Freedom of scientific investigation permitted, subject to community regulations |
| National protective legislation inhibiting free flow of scientific equipment and publications | Beirut and Florence Agreements (1949 and 1950) facilitating the importation of educational, scientific, and cultural materials; Paris Convention Concerning the International Exchange of Publications (1958) | Elimination of tariff and equivalent barriers among signatories in relation to trade in scientific material |

TABLE 5 (*Continued*)

INTERNATIONAL RESPONSE TO INTERFERENCE WITH SCIENTIFIC RESEARCH

| Barrier to Research | International Response | Nature of Response |
|---|---|---|
| Conservation of wildlife, potentially interfering with collection of scientifically valuable specimens | Fish conservation treaties; Agreed Measures for the Conservation of Antarctic Fauna and Flora (1964) | Provision of exemptions for collection of specimens among protected species, under specified conditions |
| National legislation or policy limiting access of foreign scientific expeditions to territorial domain | Convention on the Continental Shelf (1964) | Requests to undertake scientific investigations on its continental shelf are "normally" to be granted by the coastal state |
| International regulation of dangerous products useful in research | Single Convention on Narcotic Drugs (1961); Convention on Psychotropic Substances (1971) | Signatories may import or manufacture, under national license systems, narcotics necessary for medical or scientific use |
| Operation of commercial enterprises, especially broadcasting, potentially interfering with research | 1959 Geneva Radio Regulations Revision (1963); administrative regulations of International Telecommunications Union | Allocate specified frequencies of radio bandwidth in radio astronomy and space science services |
| Accident occurring to large-scale scientific experiment carried out in international arena | Agreement on the Rescue of Astronauts, the Return of Astronauts, and the Return of Objects Launched into Outer Space (1968); UNESCO draft Convention on the Legal Status of Ocean Data Acquisition Systems (1972) | State in whose territory astronauts or spacecraft accidentally land is to undertake search, rescue, and return operations; safety rules for ocean data systems |
| National activities that threaten serious alteration of the environment | U.S. policy statements; Outer Space Treaty (1967) | States agree to undertake international consultations before instigating activities that might cause potentially harmful interference with space activities of other states |
| Liability incurred from damages resulting from experiments | Convention on Liability for Damage Caused by Objects Launched into Outer Space (1971) | States are absolutely liable to pay compensation for injury to life or property caused by space objects |

Two types of response are evident from the international behavior described in the table. Where the barrier to research comes from a lack of coordination among the states involved, to the extent that they are not getting the maximum utility from their mutual scientific enterprises, the reaction is an attempt to eliminate the relevant barriers. This lack of coordination is an unreasonable interference with research, as no competing international goals would be served by allowing it to continue. Thus, various combinations of European countries have chosen to pool their resources so that all may benefit from joint research done in such subjects as space sciences, molecular biology, and atomic physics: an international conference in 1969 proposed the "Systems Internationale," a modification of the metric system, as the set of measurement units most suitable for acceptance throughout the world; and the Antarctic and space treaties have facilitated access by research teams to these areas by declaring them open to all who can enter. In such ways, national blocks to the fullest cooperation in science are progressively eliminated.

Where the barrier to research arises from attempts to maintain other goals, then interference with full freedom of research may be reasonable and even necessary. The thrust of this experience is an effort to reconcile the value of allowing maximum freedom to carry out research with other desirable, and possibly competing, goals. When there has been a potential clash in the concomitant realization of these goals, a careful balancing process has taken place in which the desirability of permitting unfettered scientific experimentation has been matched against the necessity of preventing this work from interfering with the competing activity to such a degree as to render the effectuation of the latter futile. The search is for that framework within which research may be reasonably interfered with, when necessary to ensure the enhancement of other values which the international community has defined as also important.

The procedure often followed, as outlined in Table 4, has been to allow for the undertaking of research under conditions that constitute an exception to the usual rules applied to the subject. It may be necessary for the researchers to obtain a license, specifying the conditions of their work, or to obtain some kind of permission to proceed from other relevant parties. Thus, regimes for the protection of certain types of wildlife or for the control of trade in narcotics provide for the obtaining of necessary research material under national licensing procedures; portions of the radio frequency band-width are set aside for the exclusive use of equipment supporting the astronomical sciences; before a state can perform certain kinds of space experiments it may need the *de facto* agreement of other states before proceeding; and permission from national officials is required, though normally granted, for scientific expeditions wishing to carry out research on continental shelves. According to this experience, interference is unreasonable when there is no provision under the given regime for scientists to obtain the information, equipment, or specimens they may need. It is reasonable when scientists are allowed to pursue their needs, subject to requirements designed to protect the fulfillment of other goals— maintenance of territorial integrity, protection of local industries, conservation of wildlife, control of drug abuse, and so on.

Whatever the achievements to date in operationalizing this formula, the balancing process involved will most probably become increasingly complex and difficult in future as the international community continually shifts the emphasis and priorities given to possible goals. In particular, as described in the previous section, the execution of large-scale experiments designed to modify the environment may be severely circumscribed, nationally and internationally, as general concern for the quality of life rises.

The protection of scientific and technical knowledge is attained by the network of treaties formulated to promote international cooperation in patents and copyrights. Here the goal is to enable scientists and inventors to spread the output of their work globally by providing them with suitable protection and reward when this work is used in foreign countries; the international system, in turn, benefits insofar as expensive and time-consuming duplication of effort is avoided when all countries have maximum access to the science and technology being undertaken in any one of them. The major barrier to full free trade in science and technology is the multiplicity of national regulations established by states for the taking out of patents and copyrights by nationals, and by foreigners wishing to register their claims. Correspondingly, the long-term international trend, extending back to the nineteenth century, has been to facilitate the registration of claims across borders to the maximum extent possible.[49]

Two major treaties exist in the copyright field, designed to protect the author's rights in his literary, scientific, and artistic output—the Convention Concerning the International Union for the Protection of Literary and Artistic Works (1967 revision) and the Universal Copyright Convention (1952). Both treaties operate by guaranteeing that authors in one country belonging to the system receive, in other member countries, the same rights they give their own nationals; the first

[49] Max Sorensen, "Institutionalized International Co-operation in Economic, Social and Cultural Fields," in Max Sorensen, ed., *Manual of Public International Law* (New York 1968), 653–56; Arpad Bogsch, *The Law of Copyright under the Universal Convention* (New York 1968). On the matter of "scientists' rights"—the protection of basic scientific discoveries, apart from patent or copyright questions—see UNESCO Secretariat, "The Right to Scientific Property," *Impact of Science on Society*, v (Spring 1954), 47–68.

treaty also contains detailed provisions concerning minimum protection foreign authors may claim. In an attempt to coordinate the work of the organizations that oversee the maintenance of the conventions, and to explore the possibilities of even closer cooperation, a Convention Establishing the World Intellectual Property Organization (1967) has been negotiated; WIPO will provide a central administration replacing the United International Bureaux for the Protection of Intellectual Property (BIRPI).

The Revision of the Paris Convention for the Protection of Industrial Property (1967) provides for a system similar to that of the copyright conventions, under which member states allow nationals of other members the same rights for patents and trademarks that they allow their own nationals. This procedure, however, has not proved capable of dealing with the problems arising from the great numbers of patent applications presently being filed among the countries of a technologically interdependent world. The duplication of effort involved in the filing, search, and examination of patents, for their novelty relevant to the state of the art, results in large and unnecessary expense for patent offices of the industrialized nations, for multinational business corporations interested in protecting their inventions in the countries in which they operate, and for the less-developed states lacking the equipment and experience properly to judge applications. As a result, BIRPI is sponsoring an International Patent Co-Operation Treaty (1970), which would establish a single international patent application and search; if the result is favorable, a patentability certificate would be issued, on the basis of which member states in which the inventor filed would issue their patents.

Even this step would not yet imply a true universal patent, good anywhere, but the future should see continuing effort in this direction, greatly aided by the possible computerization on national and regional levels of patent examinations. An important prototype for the global patent may be established by the European Common Market, which is planning for a European patent system available to all the countries of that continent.

The advancement of knowledge is promoted when barriers to the carrying out of research are progressively reduced; knowledge and its fruits are protected, enabling their most efficient international utilization, by guaranteeing suitable rewards to creative individuals. Scientific knowledge is further diffused by treaties and norms dealing with the international exchange of scientific information and personnel.

A good example of international legislation which mandates a general obligation on signatories to engage in such diffusion is the Protocol of Amendment to the Charter of the Organization of American States (1967), which holds that "The Member States shall extend among themselves the benefits of science and technology by encouraging the exchange and utilization of scientific and technical knowledge in accordance with existing treaties and national laws." The philosophical premise behind such a clause is not only that it is good *per se* to internationalize the findings of science and technology, especially when this involves transfer from the richer to less-developed areas, but that cooperation in scientific matters will somehow promote more political friendliness among the states involved. Whatever the validity of this belief, countries like the United States have formulated many treaties relating to the exchange of personnel and data in such areas as space tracking, meteorology, water desalination, pollution control, and atomic energy, for both the prestige these agreements may bring and the usefulness of cooperation among the individuals involved. The constitutions of many of the international scientific organizations, including the technically-oriented U.N. specialized agencies, also often provide for the widest possible dissemination of information relating to the subjects under their jurisdictions.

But it is in international arenas that the strongest obligation has arisen on the part of states conducting research there to share whatever knowledge is gained. This is true of the Antarctic and outer space, in particular. States signatory to the Antarctic Treaty (1959) are to exchange scientific personnel between expeditions and states and to make scientific observations from Antarctica "freely available"; while the Treaty on Outer Space (1967) obligates members, to the greatest extent possible, to inform the international scientific community of the nature, conduct, locations, and results of their space programs.

An interesting possibility in the future is that states will use the inducement of permitting access to particular scientific or technical information to gain the adherence of other states to desired policies. This is the other side of the coin of the possibility described in the section on conflict management, whereby states could deny access to information as a sanction or deterrent. Permitting access could be a selective way of diffusing especially sought-after data from science and technology. In a general way, the U.S. engaged in this process by offering the non-nuclear countries the benefits of cooperation that could ensue from their participation in the Treaty on the Nonproliferation of Nuclear Weapons (1968), which imposes on the nuclear states which sign it a positive commitment to provide data, under appropriate safeguards, to non-nuclear signatories on the peaceful uses of atomic energy.

In conclusion, to speak of international law influencing the development of science and technology is a modest claim, considering the activities described in this section. They are eminently useful, but do not yet add up to anything like full-blown international assessment and control of the directions in which science and technology may go—

a matter to be taken up below. On the other hand, to contribute to the progress of science and technology by breaking down barriers to research, protecting the output of skilled individuals, and promoting the global diffusion of this output entails a subtle factor: the values represented by these aspects of the international law of science are basically congruent with some of the essential components of the value system of science itself, in particular, the belief that the scientific enterprise should be open to all who are qualified to practice it and that knowledge resulting from this work should be diffused widely and rapidly to all who can use it. In this way, international law may enhance its own future by proving sympathetic, though not subservient, to these major secular values of our time.

## CONCLUSION

It is clear from the material in this chapter that developments in science and technology raise fundamental questions about the doctrines and institutional structures of the international legal system. This occurs because the system attempts to operate according to the basic premise, from a previous era, that the nation-state is and ought to be legally supreme and functionally viable within its territorial domain—a premise increasingly obsolete, at least at the functional level. The issues discussed here have been those with impact or effects transcending national borders, whatever their loci of origin, making it difficult for even the most powerful countries to conduct their affairs without some sense of the value-goals of the international community as a whole. The response of international law to this challenge has been to detail the nature of the appropriate global guidelines for community behavior made possible by science and technology, to influence the course taken by science and technology themselves, and to attempt the anticipation of norms that could be needed to regulate future forms of international activities.

Characteristic in the first response is the elaboration of principles designed to provide international actors with common baselines, as they engage in processes not wholly amenable to the control or regulation of any one of them. All five of the operational management areas discussed here have evidenced trends that converge toward attempts to define such baselines, including rules to guide the indirect intervention of states in each others' territories, to provide for the efficient sharing of community resources on a just basis, to protect human beings from unreasonable encroachments on their physical and social personalities, to safeguard the environment from unreasonable degradation from the by-products of industrialization, and to promote the undertaking and diffusion of scientific and technological research. Each cluster of rules, in turn, implies a value that the international community has decided deserves enhancement: the maintenance of the relative stability of the international political system; the equitable allocation of resources opened up by science and technology for the economic benefit of all nations; the fullest realization of humanity's biosocial potential in a manner consonant with the individual's integrity; the provision of an environment esthetically pleasing and without long-term threats to the viability of human life; and the widest use possible for the benefit of mankind of the fruits of science and technology. It is possible that, in due course, some of these values—particularly that related to the environment—will achieve the status of *jus cogens*, preemptory norms of international law from which substantive laws are not to derogate.[50]

In the meantime, international law over the next few decades will be involved in a state of creative tension brought on by two competing processes. On the one hand, the evolution of community baselines appropriate to world order will continue, along with the evolution of international bodies equipped to manage the earth's human and natural resources on a more rational basis than can be provided by individual states (present international river, fishery, and commodity commissions provide first-generation models of this process); this evolution entails a centralization of the norms and organizations of international law. On the other hand, a more centrifugal process is also observable. The impact of technology on international law itself has been to open up the number and variety of actors who may become involved in the legal process; less-developed states, concerned individuals, private organizations, quasi-governmental entities, and transnational movements all may influence the development of norms. At the same time, influence is also dispersed to those states possessing modern technological infrastructures, as they are able actually to undertake activities made possible by technology that establish precedents for whatever norms eventually emerge. In responding to the challenges of science and technology, international law is thus caught in the paradox of centralizing its norms and organs, while decentralizing its process.

Merely responding to external forces, however, is not the only role possible for international law. It can also attempt to guide developments in science and technology in the direction of fulfilling values such as those previously mentioned. The development of an international capacity for technological assessment is made necessary because of the potentially deleterious consequences that may result from work in science and technology. While the study of technology assessment is quite recent on the national level—and not until 1970 was a bill

[50] Egon Schwelb, "Some Aspects of International *Jus Cogens* as Formulated by the International Law Commission," 61 *American Journal of International Law*, 946–75 (October 1967).

introduced in the U.S. Congress to establish a formal Office of Technology Assessment within that body—it is not premature to consider international involvement with technology's consequences.[51] In fact, such assessment already takes place internationally, albeit on an *ad hoc,* dispersed, and often after-the-fact basis. Many of the issues discussed in previous sections involved the variety of ways in which international law is attempting to evaluate and control developments of international importance resulting from science and technology, in such areas as medical experimentation on humans, exploitation of the resources of space and the oceans, survival of wildlife, and protection of scientific discoveries. All such processes involve choices: certain effects of science and technology are to be encouraged by the community, while others should be controlled or suppressed; certain lines of scientific investigation are to be supported, and others discouraged. A representative sample of the kinds of international forums in which assessment now takes place is given in Table 6.

In the future, states may deem it desirable to draw together the various functions dispersed throughout the system relevant to assessment into a more centralized agency. Such an agency would have the general task of investigating, evaluating, and suggesting suitable controls for the international ramifications of technology. More specifically, the agency could encompass the following range of activities:

(1) Collection, evaluation, and publication of data describing current and potential developments in science and technology and their effects on international institutions and the environment;

(2) Recommendation, on the basis of such studies, that international organizations channel their support toward certain lines of endeavor over others;

(4) Detection of harmful environmental alterations by a global monitoring system;

(5) Liaison and coordination with national assessment boards;

(6) Mediation and fact-finding services at the request of states

51 National Academy of Engineering, Committee on Public Engineering Policy, *A Study of Technology Assessment* (Washington 1969); Library of Congress, Legislative Reference Service, *Technical Information for Congress* (Washington 1969); National Academy of Sciences, Committee on Science and Public Policy, *Technology: Processes of Assessment and Choice* (Washington 1969); U.S. Congress, House Committee on Science and Astronautics, *Technology Assessment Seminar* and *Technology Assessment* (Washington 1967 and 1970); Raphael G. Kasper, ed., *Technology Assessment—The Proceedings of a Seminar Series* (Washington 1969); Raymond S. Bauer, with Richard S. Rosenbloom and Laurie Sharp—and the assistance of others, *Second-Order Consequences: A Methodological Essay on the Impact of Technology* (Cambridge, Mass. 1969); Charles Schwartz, *et al.,* "Science and Social Controls," *Bulletin of the Atomic Scientists,* xxv (May 1969), 21–36; Harvey Wheeler, "Bringing Science under Law," *The Center Magazine,* ii (January 1969), 56–60; John Lear, "Predicting the Consequences of Technology," *Saturday Review,* liii (March 28, 1970), 44–46.

## TABLE 6

### Examples of International Technological Assessment

| Forum | Functions |
| --- | --- |
| U.S.–World Health Organization | Drug monitoring network |
| International Whaling Commission | Sets quotas for catch on species basis (largely ineffective) |
| Rhine Pollution Commission | Sets recommendatory standards for states to enforce; monitors pollution levels |
| U.N. Committees on Outer Space and the Sea-Bed | Attempt to anticipate legal issues in areas of concern |
| Regulatory International Organizations (IMCO, ICAO, ITU, etc.) | Elaborate administrative rules and carry out "legislative oversight" regarding treaties within their purview |
| International Scientific Organizations (UNESCO, CERN, ESRO, etc.) and Cooperative Programs (International Biological Program, etc.) | Funding of research in areas deemed important or amenable to cooperative endeavors |
| Bilateral Scientific Cooperation (U.S. space and pollution control programs) | Same considerations as international cooperation, plus strengthen relations with allies |
| IAEA (safeguard system against diversion of fissionable materials) | Actual inspection and enforcement of rules regarding a technology which states have previously assessed as important and amenable to some international control |
| ICSU Committee on Space Research's Consultative Group on Potentially Harmful Effects of Space Experiments | Committee of respected experts judging allegedly harmful effects of technology and scientific experiments; no enforcement powers |
| Swedish Seismic Array System | Neutral nation monitoring underground atomic testing |
| National Action Taken under Art. 9 of Outer Space Treaty | One country requests information or consultations with another regarding potentially harmful space activities of latter |

which disagree about the potentially harmful effects of each others'
large-scale projects or scientific experiments;

(7) Recommendations that states suspend such activities or undertake them only pursuant to suggested guidelines.

This agency could be established most appropriately by the U.N.
General Assembly, UNESCO, and the International Council of Scientific Unions, to which its reports would be transmitted. It could focus
at first on potential environmental effects of projects funded by international organizations; the latter, indeed, might be required to send
reports on these effects to the agency before projects are initiated (departments of the U.S. Government are now required to make similar
studies). Functions (6) and (7) would amount to an institutionalization
of obligations already encumbent upon states signatory to the outer
space treaty and many river-basin treaties. The agency need not be
large; functions (1)–(4) could be contracted to other institutions, in a
way analogous to the operation of the proposed U.S. Office of Technology Assessment. Thus, environmental monitoring could be accomplished by tying together already existing systems under the World
Health Organization, International Biological Program, and World
Meteorological Organization; international river and fishery commissions could undertake studies of technologies affecting their fields, and
so on.[52]

Finally, it follows from the assessment process that international
law must be conscious of the future. It is obviously too late to patch
together treaties affecting technology after the latest disaster has occurred, whether it be an oil spill, fish kill, or airplane hijacking. A bit
more creativity is needed within the legal system for the anticipation
of frameworks, at least, for the kinds of principles that will be needed
as a result of the fruition of presently forseeable technology. In effect,
this is done by international organizations that pass declaratory resolutions regarding areas on which there is not enough information or
agreement to negotiate binding obligations, and by the recommendations that come from such groups as the U.N. International Law Commission and the General Assembly's Committees on the Peaceful Uses
of Outer Space and the Sea-Bed. But a more purposive effort is required for the broad-scale projection of alternative political and social,
as well as technological, futures and for the determination of the effects
of each possible future on international law.[53] In turn, international

---

[52] Dennis Livingston, "International Technology Assessment and the United Nations System," 64 *American Society of International Law Proceedings*, 163–71 (September 1970).

[53] On futurology methodology, see R. U. Ayres, *Technological Forecasting and
Long-Range Planning* (New York 1969); James R. Bright, ed., *Technological Forecasting for Industry and Government: Methods and Applications* (Englewood Cliffs,

legal scholars and policy-makers can engage in the process of formulating a global law, embodying the highest consensus of the international community, that influences the evolution of that alternative future envisioned as most beneficial for the inhabitants of Spaceship Earth.

---

N.J. 1968); Erich Jantsch, *Technological Forecasting in Perspective* (Paris 1967). For attempts at projecting international political futures, see Herman Kahn and Anthony J. Wiener, *The Year 2000: A Framework for Speculation on the Next Thirty-Three Years* (New York 1967); Theodore J. Rubin, E. M. Krass and A. H. Schainblatt, *Projected International Patterns*, 2 vols. (Santa Barbara, Cal. 1967); Charles A. McClelland, *Research Potentials and Rules in Predicting International Futures* (Holloman AFB, New Mexico, 1968); Daniel Bell, ed., *Toward the Year 2000: Work in Progress* (Boston 1969), 310–23; Saul Friedlander, "Forecasting in International Relations," in Bertrand de Jouvenel, ed., *Futuribles*, 2 vols. (1963 and 1965), II, 27–52; Johan Galtung, "On the Future of the International System," *Journal of Peace Research* (No. 4, 1967), 305–33; Richard A. Falk, *The Status of Law in International Society* (Princeton 1970), 554–69.

# CHAPTER 4

# Modification of the Human Environment

### HOWARD J. AND RITA F. TAUBENFELD

WITHIN THE framework of "The Structure of the International Environment" and "The Future of the International Legal Order," we take the question of modification of the human environment to relate to those changes in the natural environment, intended and inadvertent, made or makable by men, which have caused or may cause friction between groups large enough to create international tensions when problems arise between them. The need for and possibility of creating such modifications may also patently form the basis for international cooperation.

Without the necessity or possibility of making sharp delimitations, there are, broadly, three types of modification of the environment with which we will be concerned, though in differing degrees. These include (1) conscious attempts to modify the environment, temporarily or permanently. As examples, we will cite the efforts in many countries to modify the weather and the high altitude nuclear tests of several years ago which were in part studies of distortion of the electromagnetic spectrum. (2) There are also activities which inadvertently cause unintended changes in the human environment which are generally agreed to be, once they are observed, detrimental and are of a type which nations have made attempts to deal with. Prime examples include the fallout from nuclear testing and pollution of the seas and seacoasts by oil. (3) The third category involves activities which clearly cause changes in the environment inadvertently or as a byproduct and have not yet been dealt with extensively by the international community. Indeed, they often appear to be of a nature which, in the present and foreseeable international system, is probably not amenable to international correction, even assuming that some national basis for "correction" could be evolved and generally accepted. In a sense some inadvertent environment modification is ubiquitous. Thus each time open land, or forest, or farm is converted to a building, there is an effect on the local climate. A city has weather different from that of the undeveloped area which it replaces. Industrialization changes the climate of an area, of a country, and thus inexorably affects, to whatever small degree, the world weather system. Some changes of this type may have little or no effect on another nation, some may cause substantial though unintended changes in climate and pollution levels elsewhere.

The Secretary-General of the United Nations has warned, in his

report on "Problems of the Human Environment" (E/4667) of a looming crisis of the human environment caused by the explosive growth
of human populations, the unforeseen impact of new and powerful
technology, unplanned urbanization with its problems of slums, disease, crime, and inadequate educational facilities, the loss of space and
agricultural land, and the pending extinction of many forms of plant
and animal life. Indeed the specific purpose of a UN Conference on
the Human Environment set for 1972 is the "concentration on the
need for action by public authorities at the local, national, regional,
and international levels, to deal with the problems of planning, management, and control of the human environment for economic and
social development." Patently, this paper can deal with only a portion
of this broad spectrum. We will focus most directly on some aspects
of major measurable induced changes in the physical environment,
both intentional and inadvertent, leaving analysis of such general,
broad-gauge social problem issues, which incidentally imply major
changes in the human environment, both physical and psychic, as
population increase, urbanization and slum creation, and the like, to
other papers in this volume.

## I. Intentional Modification [1]

We will first discuss some human activities which are specifically
designed and undertaken to cause changes in the physical environment
of man including weather modification, the use and diversion of rivers,
high altitude nuclear tests, and Project West Ford. Each of these has
raised or may raise questions of sharing, control, and conflict in the
international community.

### Weather Modification Activities [2]

As weather modification activities, we here include "any artificially
produced changes in the composition, or dynamics of the atmosphere.

[1] Unlike the tripartite division of activities used in this paper, the Secretary-General's Report suggests a tripartite division based essentially on the approach that
some problems are inherently "local" and hence appropriate for local (national)
action; that some are more properly national in scope and thus may readily have
international implications; and that some are inherently regional or worldwide and
require international efforts and regulation. It turns out that activities do not divide
neatly on such a basis and the Report does not carry through very far with this
division. Inherently local, normally unregulated, or locally regulated phenomena
like the weather may also have important international repercussions yet their
modification may not promise to be very well suited to effective international regulation in the current international system. In any case the activities analyzed by use
will by definition fit primarily into the second and third of these categories; they
will imply some international effect.

[2] The authors of this paper have prepared a study for the US Department of
State entitled "The International Implications of Weather Modification Activities,"
published by the Office of External Research, June, 1968. An article based on that
study appears in xxiii, *International Organization* (1969), 808ff.

Such changes may or may not be predictable, their production may be deliberate or inadvertent, they may be manifested on any scale from the microclimate of plants to the macro-dynamics of the worldwide atmospheric circulation." [3] At this time, scientific opinion has shifted to the view that man can, in certain circumstances and at certain places, modify at least local weather conditions in limited ways. Man can now dissipate certain "cold" fogs in limited areas for short periods. Many believe that he can increase rainfall or snowfall by perhaps 10–15 percent in a local area in narrowly limited circumstances and that he can probably convert hail into less dangerous forms of precipitation, also in narrowly limited circumstances. [4] He is conducting experiments to learn more about such phenomena as hurricanes and lightning. He still needs to learn much more and to develop faster computers before he can begin to think of safely undertaking intentional modification on anything more than a local and highly selective basis. Nevertheless, it is clear that even the limited effects thus far produced do not stop at some predetermined boundary; both nationally and internationally, attempts to modify weather can be expected to cause dislocations and friction. While it is not clear that large-scale changes in weather or climate can be artificially induced, it is the possibility of weather changes of these types which implies the most difficult international problems. It is also not clear that, if undertaken, such major changes will have to be of the type which imply that some states must lose desirable or valuable weather if others are to gain it. A review of the projects suggested indicates that this is likely. [5] Indeed even local changes in the weather *status quo* achieved so far have regularly produced complaints as well as congratulations. With the development of increased knowledge about weather, and given the fact that weather modification is a potential weapon, it seems certain that there

[3] The definition is that used by the U.S. National Academy of Sciences. See "Weather and Climate Modification—Problems and Prospects," 1, Summary and Recommendations, Publication No. 1350, National Academy of Sciences-National Research Council (Washington 1966), 1.

[4] The principal basis for current local weather modification to date has normally involved the use of cloud "seeding" with silver iodide crystals. For a general survey, see Report of the Special Commission on Weather Modification, *Weather and Climate Modification* (SNF-1965). The Soviet Union claims success in the hail field.

[5] The international implications of weather modification activities are suggested by the fact that many countries are already active in studying these phenomena. In addition to the United States, countries with field programs include the Soviet Union, with a program reportedly two or three times that of the United States, Argentina, Australia, Canada, France, Italy, Japan, Kenya, Korea, and Tunisia. Studies are also under way in Germany, Great Britain, India, Israel, and Switzerland. See National Science Foundation, *Weather Modification*, Seventh Annual Report, 1965 (hereinafter cited as NSF); Eighth Annual Report, 1966; Ninth Annual Report, 1967. See also "Weather Modification and Control," A Report for the Use of the Committee on Commerce, U.S. Senate, April 27, 1966, Report No. 1139, 89th Congress, 2nd Session, esp. 45–46.

will, in time, be increased wide-scale experimentation in weather modification and that man, who has already modified weather inadvertently on an important scale, and by conscious effort on a smaller scale, will also, in time, have at least some substantial capacity to "control" weather, that is, to modify it consciously on a regional national, continental, or even intercontinental scale. We elsewhere explored some of the implications of the approaching development of weather modification technology for the current international system and came to the conclusion that international institutional innovation is implied by man's emerging capacity to modify the weather.[6]

The need for new international arrangements to deal with weather modification has already been recognized by the World Meteorological Organization, which has stated:

> . . . the complexity of the atmospheric processes is such that a change in the weather induced artificially in one part of the world will necessarily have repercussions elsewhere. This principle can be affirmed on the basis of present knowledge of the mechanism of the general circulation of the atmosphere. However, that knowledge is still far from sufficient to enable us to forecast with confidence the degree, nature or duration of the secondary effects to which a change in weather or climate in part of the earth may give rise elsewhere, nor even in fact to predict whether these effects will be beneficial or detrimental. Before undertaking an experiment on large-scale weather modification, the possible and desirable consequences must be carefully evaluated, and satisfactory international arrangements must be reached.[7]

We can foresee at least two stages of possible international frictions on weather modification, first the experimental stages, and second, the operational stages. As to the first, the problem is that, since weather knows no boundaries, even modest experiments in the weather field and even local weather modification activities may have an impact in other countries, however unintended; yet there is no reason to feel persuaded that any firm international controls over the safety of

---

[6] See studies cited in fn. 2.

[7] See WMO, *Second Report on the Advancement of Atmospheric Science and Their Application in the Light of Developments in Outer Space*, Geneva, WMO Secretariat (1963).

On risks in weather modification to the world ecosystem, see Sargent, "A Dangerous Game: Taming the Weather," *Scientist & Citizen*, IX (No. 5, May 1967), 81–88. To the extent that the existence of national boundaries has already caused limitations on programs of weather modification, see the testimony of Dr. Irving Krick, Hearing on S. 22 and S. 2016 Before the Committee on Commerce, 89 Cong., 1st and 2nd Sess., pt. 102, 405 (re the Columbia River Basin) [hereinafter cited as Hearings]. On the eventual need for an "International Weather Control Commission" see *Hearings*, 38 (Dr. Pierre St. Amand), 423.

weather experimentation will be reliably imposed on the nations. They have not been established over potentially hazardous national research programs in other security-suffused fields of knowledge, such as, for example, outer space. It should also be noted however that, precisely because weather knows no boundaries and is inherently an international phenomenon, there have been some indications that at least in the preliminary, basic, knowledge-seeking stages, international cooperation may be more necessary in the study of weather modification than it has in the exploration of outer space. Nevertheless, the development of cooperative operations to date has been slow. Few, if any, seem to have been undertaken, even on a nonregulated, voluntary cooperation basis.[8]

Conflicts which may arise out of actual weather modification operations involve the possibility that weather modification and control activities may prove to be in the nature of constant sum games, or, rather, they may normally entail inverse payoffs so that there will normally be losers as well as gainers. To the extent that there must be "losers" (even if this means only that states must deal with any unwanted change of some sort), as well as gainers, international conflict over changes is inevitable. In predicting the future, Dr. Edward Teller some years ago nominated "weather" as the probable cause of the "last war" on earth.[9]

Weather modification is also clearly a potentially strategic activity. On the interest of the armed forces in developing a capability of modifying the environment to their own advantage or to the disadvantage of an enemy, Dr. St. Amand, a Navy scientist, stated: "We regard the weather as a weapon. Anything one can use to get his way is a weapon and the weather is as good a one as any."[10] Not only are weather

[8] In early July, 1967, for example, there were press reports of a U.S.–Cuba arrangement permitting overflights of Cuba by U.S. planes studying hurricanes and techniques for "modifying" them. The U.S.–Cuba arrangement did not involve joint attempts to modify these storms. The U.S. has sought and received permission from Canada to seed clouds on the Canadian portion of the Great Lakes in circumstances where all effects anticipated would occur in U.S. territory.

[9] And Dr. Teller told the Senate Military Preparedness Subcommittee in November, 1957:

Ultimately, we can see again and again that small changes in the weather can lead to very big effects. . . .

Please imagine a world in which the Russians can control weather on a big scale, where they can change the rainfall over Russia, and that—and here I am talking about a very definite situation—that might very well influence the rainfall in our country in an adverse manner. . . .

What kind of a world will it be where they have this new kind of control, and we do not? [Cited by Clinton P. Anderson in "Resources for the Future," *Science and Resources: Prospects and Implications of Technological Advance*, Henry Jarrett, ed. (Baltimore 1959), 60–61.]

[10] *Hearings* (fn. 7), 33. On military short-run interests in weather phenomena

information and general surveillance possible from many weather information-collecting devices, and local weather-modification capacity likely to be useful in military maneuvers, but there also remains the possibility, perhaps remote, that major weather-switching may become a very important new alternative total weapon.

Granting the lack of specific international agreements dealing with weather modification, there are nevertheless already in existence certain international norms which may be of service in this and other areas of technological development to be discussed hereafter. In addition the cases of conflicts arising from weather modification activities already litigated in the United States are also useful in pointing the problems we can expect in time at the international level. These include, among others, problems of proof of causation of alleged harm, of governmental immunities, of concepts of "ownership" of an ephemeral resource (e.g., the water content of clouds), of compensation to "losers," of definition of and proof of a "loss," of a decision as to the permissible types of loss. Given the nature of the nonintegrated, horizontal international system of order, it is likely that, internationally, these issues, particularly the questions of whose rights are to be defended, those of the states whose citizens wish to modify or those of the states whose citizens will be damaged thereby, are likely to be even more complicated.

In cases of international conflict of interest, the alternative approaches to conflict resolution cover the usual range: from reliance on legal dispute settlement by an international court, a technique relatively little used by the states, to reliance on regulation and negotiation within established formal organs for international technical or political cooperation, to reliance on international diplomacy and power outside international organizations. Mixtures of the latter two techniques are of course normal.

Although conflict resolution through courts remains generally unpopular with the states, there is existing general international law which seems relevant to weather modification activities and to others to be discussed hereafter. Indeed, the fact that a few related international cases exist suggests that, if the threatened international harm is relatively minor and an isolated case, legal-type conflict resolution might be relied on. Moreover, even if legal processes are in fact eschewed in favor of negotiations, these latter may be expected to refer back to the general guidelines implicit in the relevant international legal analogies which can be cited by the disputants.

General international law now appears to give a state the right to

---

which influence military operations, see remarks by Dr. C. W. Sherwin, same, 156, 161. Weather modification efforts could possibly produce or eliminate concealment in military operations, for example.

maintain its national territory free of external interference and to protect the lives, property, and interests of its nationals when threatened from any quarter.[11] This can possibly be extended to include its interests in its own weather. States also claim the airspace above their national territory and waters, and seem certain to assert rights of "ownership" or control of the clouds and other weather phenomena in national airspace.[12] International law also imposes duties on a state "not to allow knowingly its territory to be used for acts contrary to the rights of other States." [13]

Combining these concepts, there does seem to be an inherent *status quo* bias as far as disturbing weather modifications would be concerned. It appears that a state is internationally responsible if its acts or those of its citizens, while not intended to be harmful, do in fact cause damage (unwanted change) in another state. The best known international case in point, the *Trail Smelter Arbitration* between Canada and the United States, supports this conclusion. Canada was held responsible for the injury and damage resulting in the United States from fumes and deleterious matter emitted from a smelter located in British Columbia and deposited over an area of the State of Washington, and was obliged to pay damages on the theory that a nation incurs liability under international law when it permits or fails to act reasonably to prevent conduct within its territory which causes injury in the territory of another state.[14] Future operations were to conform to a specific set of restrictions designed to prevent injury as much as possible.

All this seems to indicate that a nation could assert some legal rights to its initial weather conditions and that a legal approach to the protection of these may be useful where the stakes are small and the issues are narrow. But there are obvious difficulties in such a *status quo* biased, legalistic approach. Social adaptation to socially desirable change normally implies some redistribution of power and welfare. It is not normally accommodated primarily through exclusively legal processes in any society. In a country, the legislature and/or the executive can and normally do set laws specifying norms and guidelines for public policy, on new issues arising out of new technological opportunities and on other major conflicts of interests which the courts can be expected to respect.

There is clearly much less effective "government" to define and or-

---

[11] Cf. U.N. Charter, Arts. 2(7), 51.

[12] On accepted sovereignty in airspace, see Chicago Convention on International Civil Aviation, Dec. 7, 1944, USTIAS No. 1591, Art. 1.

[13] Corfu Channel Case (1949) *I.C.J.* Rep. 4, 22.

[14] See 35 *American Journal of International Law*, 684ff. (1941). See also the *Corfu Channel Case* and L. F. L. Oppenheim, *International Law*, 8th ed., H. Lauterpacht, ed. (London 1955), 290–91, 365.

ganize the pursuit of the "public good" in the face of important new technological opportunities in the international system, and no legislature to establish legal guidelines for international courts in handling conflicts arising therefrom, on the basis of majority rule decision-making. (Although the UN provides a forum for the discussion of international norms, and claims are sometimes made for the legally binding force of some unanimously accepted General Assembly decisions, it remains true that new law in this system is made only ponderously and by the agreement of the sovereigns.) The courts in the international system cannot be expected to function effectively from the community viewpoint on issues involving major social contests or conflicts of norms or major social changes in response to new technological opportunities, without guidance from appropriate community-wide organs of definitive political decision-making. The weakness of these in major international political conflict issues in part rationalizes the fact that a far narrower group of cases is in fact submitted by the states for legal decision to an international jurisdiction than would be likely within a model well-developed, well-integrated state.

In the absence of organs of "fair," definitive norm-making and efficient law-making emphasizing the requisites of the community, each state is at present likely to tend to assert the right to attempt to induce changes in the weather—for example, in its own favor, for the good of *its* public. If at some point the pursuit of the important interests of one state implies some compromise of the "rights" of other states—for example, of those which are in the role of defenders of the initial weather *status quo*—then the challenging nations are unlikely to allow international courts, applying conservative *status quo* biased legal reasoning largely unguided by general public policy considerations in the light of the new technological opportunities, to thwart their free pursuit of their own important public purposes. Yet a system in which many actors simultaneously seek to pursue their own interpretation of their own maximum social benefits from new opportunities open to all is likely to involve important direct clashes of interest. In a society in which there is no ultimate central decision-making, order-providing hierarchy, such political, distributional conflicts are likely to produce conflagrations. In sum, if important redistributionary opportunities to change the weather in favor of some states became possible, the presently limited central institutions of political choice of the international system are unlikely to be able to contain the implied conflicts of interest securely. Indeed the special difficulties of the international community in adapting peacefully and in the public interest to new technological opportunities permeates all the discussions in this paper.

## Modification of International Waters

Questions of use of international waters, including diversion and pollution, are distinct, with pollution perhaps falling more appropriately under our second category, inadvertent modification of the environment, but the two categories and their control are so intimately related that some overlap is unavoidable. In fact, there are relatively few broadly acceptable general legal norms concerning the shared use and the pollution of international rivers and drainage basins. While the principles of equitably-shared use and of restraint in pollution have long been considered desirable, it is not possible to say, at present, that there are generally accepted rules of international law requiring that all international rivers be kept free for the use of all, or barring their pollution or special restrictive use by riparian states.[15] However many multination river authorities have been established on the basis of mutual convenience of the parties. Some of these have operated, for example, to build port facilities and to keep channels dredged.[16]

Again, while the law is as noted, not fully settled, the principle of no use which will harm the interests of another state has been accepted by some international and national tribunals.[17] Treaties and other agreements have dealt with this problem.[18] Even where the pollution is unintentional, as where irrigation use in the nation of first use leaves a murderous salt residue in the water delivered to the second state using the water, there seems to be an inclination today to make reparation to the second user, though not necessarily to discontinue the use.[19]

[15] See, International Law Association, Report of Prof. Olmstead, "Waters of International Rivers," *Report of the 51st Conference* (Tokyo) (1964), 119ff. The study of river problems is of special interest since efforts at rain-making may have a direct effect on the rivers.

[16] There are special treaty arrangements dealing with use and control of specific rivers—the Rhine, the Danube, the Columbia, etc.

There are also special treaty arrangements concerning pollution: The Euratom Treaty, for example, deals with potential radioactive pollution of all waters affected by Euratom experiments and activities. See also, in general, Friedrich J. Berber, *Rivers in International Law* (London and New York 1959).

[17] See the Lake Lanoux Arbitration (France and Spain), (1957), *International Law Reports*, 101, esp. 123; 62 *Rev. Gén de Droit Intl. Pub.*, 79 (1958), trans. 53 *American Journal of International Law*, 156 (1959).

[18] See E. J. Manner, "Water Pollution in International Law," in Aspects of Water Pollution Control, WHO (Public Health Papers) (Nov. 13, 1963), 53, 68; A. P. Lester, "River Pollution in International Law," 57 *American Journal of International Law*, 828 (1963).

[19] See the U.S.–Mexico arrangements concerning the Colorado River, 59 *Stat.* 1219, T.S. No. 994; Timm, "Water Treaty Between United States and Mexico," *Department of State Bulletin*, x (1944), 282. In recent years, the United States has had to make adjustments due to pollution of Mexican land by water from the Colorado which, on delivery to Mexico, was laden with salt pollutants picked up in the course of irrigation use in the United States. The United States has made efforts to improve the quality of the water delivered. See below pp. 133–34.

Summing up the matter, a State Department Memorandum of April 21, 1958,[20] suggested that "an international tribunal would deduce the applicable principles of international law to be along the following lines:

2(a) Riparians are entitled to share in the use and benefits of a system of international waters on a just and reasonable basis.

3(a) A riparian which proposes to make, or allow, a change in the existing regime of a system of international waters which could interfere with the realization by a coriparian of its right to share on a just and reasonable basis in the use and benefits of the system, is under a duty to give the coriparian an opportunity to object.

(b) If the coriparian, in good faith, objects and demonstrates its willingness to reach a prompt and just solution by the pacific means envisaged in article 33(1) of the Charter of the United Nations, a riparian is under a duty to refrain from making, or allowing, such change, pending agreement or other solution.

*Comment.* It seems clear that there is no rule of international law that a riparian must have the consent of coriparians as a condition precedent to the use and development within its territory of a system of international waters. In other words, a coriparian does not have what in effect would amount to a veto over changes in the system.

However, in current international practice no riparian goes ahead with exploitation of its part as a system when a coriparian may possibly be adversely affected, without consulting the latter and coming to an understanding with it. It is to be noted that the latter's consent need not be expressly given; having been given an opportunity to object, its silence may be taken as consent.

Thus it is suggested that co-riparians have a right to an opportunity to object to changes in the river system detrimental to themselves and, in fact, in current international practice, few riparians go ahead with exploitation of their parts of a system—when co-riparians may possibly be adversely affected—without consulting the latter and coming to an understanding with them.

Similar patterns, relying ultimately on voluntary mutual accommodation sometimes arranged within organs of international cooperation, may emerge for other deliberate modification activities among states sharing the same watersheds, weathersheds, etc., if effects are likely to be felt across borders. Some may organize formal multinational au-

[20] Department of State Memo., April 21, 1958, by W. L. Griffin, "Legal Aspects of the Use of Systems of International Waters," S. Doc. No. 118, 85th Congress., 2d Sess. (1958).

thorities for control and management of other regional resources on the basis of agreed policies or principles and agreed rules of decision-making and perhaps claims-processing. Yet this concept of nonobligatory accommodation and often little or no shared operations may not prove adequate to avert grave conflicts of interest whenever the resources in question are not readily shareable. It has not always worked well in the case of rivers. Thus both Israel and the Arab States involved stated in the pre-June 1967 period that the other's attempt to interfere with its use, present and prospective, of the waters of the River Jordan would amount to "aggression" and would lead to armed resistance.[21]

Thus the sharing of international resources like water is not now principally obtained on the basis of recognized, generally-agreed, legal norms or rules even when grave international conflicts exist. Peaceful use and peaceful sharing are sometimes facilitated by the existence of formally organized cooperation among co-riparians. We can contrast this with the process for division of disputed waters within a nation like the United States. If such dispute issues are not settled cooperatively, administratively, or by legislative action they are if necessary normally resolved definitively by the courts. Such authoritative institutions of final decision-making on pure conflict issues backed ultimately by overwhelming central enforcement powers do not exist in the international community.

Thus the approach to resolving international conflicts over water has stressed mutual cooperation and accommodation, the creation of specialized international administrative machinery where possible, and, in cases of grave conflict, political negotiations or political contests among the sovereigns. All evidence suggests the probability of a similar development emphasizing voluntary regional cooperation among neighbors *in re* such other intentional modifications as weather modification. Whether this proves adequate to preserve international stability depends in part on the shareability and importance of the modification's results.[22]

[21] See Kathryn B. Doherty, "Jordan Waters Conflict," *International Conciliation,* No. 553 (May 1965), esp. 1, 35.

[22] There is an important caveat: even where there are incentives to cooperation, special problems for technical cooperation exist *in re* weather control. Joint projects in weather modification conducted over the sovereign territory of any nation might disclose strategic information, for example, as to the vulnerability of the nation. Weather neighbors would have to be good, trustworthy, political neighbors if such weather-modification operations were to be shared with security. Even between good neighbors one might foresee the necessity of a regional scurity system for control of strategic information obtained from joint weather operations. This is unlikely to be welcomed by security-sensitive national states. A compromise stressing the national operation of an internationally regulated, coordinated program is more likely.

*Other Intentional Changes in the General Environment*

One other class of cases of intentional modification of the physical environment which has already engaged the world's attention involves changes in the earth's environment which do not cause identifiable specific losses. The two principal cases thus far involve primarily American experiments; one was Project West Ford, an attempt to place copper "needles" in orbit around the earth in 1961 and 1963; the other was the series of high altitude nuclear explosions, conducted before the Test Ban Treaty of 1963 barred testing in the atmosphere and in outer space.

In general, nations and their scientists have demanded an undiminished, undistorted, freely observable outer space. These claims have been made both generally and with respect to specific national operations in space. Project West Ford, for example, the effort to place a band of copper needles in orbit for communications purposes, was attacked by scientists in several countries, and by government spokesmen in a few, as a potential interference with radio astronomy and with other observation techniques as well. It was denounced as a "dangerous" unilateral interference with the cosmos. When it was pointed out that such allegations were excessive, and, on the facts, untrue, it was opposed as at least the forerunner of a scientifically undesirable "cluttering" up of space.[23]

Similarly, high-altitude nuclear explosions were opposed by some scientists as creating distortions in the Van Allen Belt, making the study of the earth's natural environment more difficult, causing interference with scientific and other satellites in orbit, and constituting a menace, present and future, to man in space.[24] The Soviet bloc called

[23] On Project West Ford, see John Johnson, "Pollutions and Contamination in Space," in Maxwell Cohen, ed., *Law and Politics in Space* (Montreal 1964), 37ff. The first attempt to discharge the needles failed.

For an attack on West Ford, see A. C. B. Lovell and M. Ryle, "Interference to Radio Astronomy from Belts of Orbiting Dipoles (Needles)," *Journal of the Royal Astronomical Society*, III (1962), 100–08, and D. G. Blackwell and R. Wilson, "Interference to Optical Astronomy from Belts of Orbiting Dipoles (Needles)," same, 109–14. See also the Soviet writer Georgi Zhukov, "Problems of Space Law at the Present Stage." Report presented to Fifth Colloquium on the Law of Outer Space, International Institute of Space Law, September 25–28, 1962 (Varna, Bulgaria 1962) mimeo, 37 pp.

The Space Science Board of the National Academy of Sciences has concluded that the West Ford dipoles had not in fact interfered with radio or visual astronomy, but it was stated in the report that this "should not be taken either as an endorsement of the experiment or as tacit agreement to the launching of another similar belt without further discussion." See *NASNRC Press Release*, March 26, 1964, and Space Science Board, US Space Science Program: Report to COSPAR 153–4 (1964).

[24] On the high altitude tests, see Johnson (fn. 23); Sir Harrie Stewart Massey, *Space Physics*, 208 (Cambridge 1964); Howard Taubenfeld, "Nuclear Testing and International Law," 16 *Southwestern Law Journal*, 365, 397 (1962).

such experiments "acts of aggression" and contrary to international law, to the UN Charter, and to UN Resolutions.[25] Yet the high altitude tests were, themselves, in part, designed as an interesting scientific experiment.[26] While some of these criticisms have been obviously polit-

[25] Soviet bloc comments include the following:
Statement by the Soviet Government on the United States high altitude nuclear explosions: "In connection with the resumption of nuclear weapon tests by the United States, the Soviet Government has already declared that by undertaking such operations the United States Government is perpetrating an aggressive act. . . . Any aggressive acts that endanger peace by whatever side they may be perpetrated are now resolutely condemned by the peace-loving states."
A/AC. 105/C.2/SR 5, Legal Sub-committee on Outer Space, 21 August 1962 (Mr. Misha—Albania), 5: "The United States Government's experiments flagrantly violated the principles of the United Nations Charter and of the General Assembly's resolutions . . . they were a crime against science and humanity, and acts of aggression."
"American Diversion in Space," *International Affairs*, No. 12 (Moscow 1961), 117–18: "Hence there is no difference in principle between the behaviour of a state which in peacetime would lay mines or set up minefields on the high seas, and states which clutter up space with copper needles hampering research and representing a hazard both to the movement of sputniks and the life of cosmonauts. In both cases there is an indisputable international lawless act, a hostile action of a state with regard to other states."
[26] On interference generally, see David Davis Memorial Institute of International Studies, *Draft Rules Concerning Changes in the Environment of the Earth*, passim (and sources cited).
Sir Bernard Lovell, a noted critic of many U.S. efforts, has written (*Saturday Evening Post*, Feb. 22, 1964, pp. 10, 14):

It is now time for concern about the ethical standards which man must apply to embryonic dangers which are not obvious. We cannot afford to wait until the dangers become practically apparent, since some experiments may create an irretrievable condition. . . .
[As an example, he described the ozone layer.] . . . it happens that ozone is rather easy to destroy. And if it is intentionally or accidentally removed, then the ultraviolet radiation would penetrate to earth. If this happened for a sufficiently long period, then human beings might suffer severe sunburn and possible sterilization. Further, the temperature distribution in the atmosphere could be radically altered and, in the state of our present knowledge, no one could predict what climatic changes might occur.
It is not difficult to estimate that a few tons of suitable contaminant, deposited in the atmosphere 25 miles above the earth, would destroy the ozone over several miles for a few hours . . . a rocket launched from earth to land a man on the moon might burn up 2,000 tons of fuel in its passage through the earth's atmosphere . . . [and] the launching of one such rocket a week might well lead to a permanent transformation of the conditions in the high atmosphere, according to recent study by the Advanced Research Project Agency.
. . . when one turns from the contamination as an accidental by-product to an intentional act, an ugly array of possibilities is revealed. To begin with, specially selected substances could be deposited in great quantities at precise altitudes. . . . The American [ARPA] report states that 25 tons of fluorine would be sufficient to depopulate the ionosphere of electrons and so blot out all long-distance radiotelephony. The deposition of large quantities of gases like carbon monoxide at an altitude of 25 miles might radically alter the temperature distribution and climatic conditions by absorbing some of the sun's infrared radiation. . . .
The human race therefore faces a critical situation in the next few decades, because there is at the moment little evidence of the moral and legal controls

ically self-serving, for example, the Soviet attacks on US high-altitude tests when the Soviet Union has in fact done the same thing,[27] they have been widespread enough to indicate a general interest around the world in protecting nature's *status quo* even where no specific damage to nations, persons, or property could be shown or was foreseeable. Note too that the United States has not repeated the "needles" experiment.[28]

Moreover, after much maneuvering in the United Nations, all major powers agreed in the 1963 UN resolution on Outer Space [29] that

> In the exploration and use of outer space, States shall be guided by the principle of co-operation and mutual assistance and shall conduct all their activities in outer space in the due regard for the corre-

---

which must be enforced if man's continued life on earth is not to be jeopardized by the accidental or intentional results of space research. There are large areas of uncertainty, so that it is not yet possible to assess whether various other space activities may affect man more directly than in the inhibition of his study of the cosmos.

[27] A/AC. 105/C. 1/1, Committee on the Peaceful Uses of Outer Space, 5 June 1962, Statement by the Soviet Government on the United States high-altitude nuclear explosions: "The high-altitude nuclear weapon tests being carried out by the United States of America can have extremely harmful consequences—the disturbance of the upper conducting layers of the earth's atmosphere over vast areas, the appearance of radio-wave absorption areas and the appearance of a new radiation zone in space immediately surrounding the earth." *New York Times*, Jan. 24, 1963, p. 5, col. 4, which reported that the Telstar satellite had come up with a new find: a flood of radiation poured into space immediately after the Soviet Union's high-altitude nuclear tests in late October.

[28] In a somewhat similar situation, there were, in 1966 at least, proposals in the United States to orbit a reflecting satellite, a "space mirror" to illuminate the dark areas of the world at night. The Department of Defense was reportedly also "curious." Astronomers objected. See Bryce Nelson, "Reflecting Satellite: NASA Study Causes Concern Among Astronomers," *Science*, CLV, No. 3760 (January 20, 1967), 304, 306. In May, 1967, a Report by the NRC Space Science Board on the concept of orbiting large reflecting mirrors concluded that there was no overwhelming evidence that scientific damage would result from the deployment of a single reflector system. It recommended, however, that such a satellite should not be considered in the future unless the ability to destroy it by ground signals were an inherent part of the design, and unless detailed studies of its effects on ecology, biology, and astronomy were previously conducted and made public. The report could see no scientific merit for such a satellite system commensurate with its cost to the public and its nuisance to science. A report was prepared by the Board's Committee on Potential Contamination and Interference from Satellites, as a result of NASA's 1966 announcement that it had asked five aerospace companies to study the feasibility of orbiting large reflecting mirrors that could illuminate land masses at night. Dr. Donald F. Hornig, Special Assistant to the President for Science and Technology, confirmed in a letter to NAS President Dr. Frederick Seitz that the Government no longer had plans for such a project. See NAS-NRC-NAE *News Report*, 5/67, 2 (May 25, 1967).

On proposals to do cloud experiments using colored vapors, see *Washington Star*, March 31, 1967.

[29] Res. 1962 (XVIII), Dec. 24, 1963, par. 6.

sponding interests of other states. If a State has reason to believe that an outer space activity or experiment planned by it or its nationals *would cause potentially harmful interference with activities of other States in the peaceful exploration and use of outer space,* it shall undertake appropriate international consultation before proceeding with any such activity or experiment. A State which has reason to believe that an outer space activity or experiment planned by another State would cause potentially harmful interference with activities in the peaceful exploration and use of outer space may request consultation concerning the activity or experiment. [Emphasis added.]

Even more recently, the Outer Space Treaty [30] of January, 1967, provides, in Article 9, that

States parties to the treaty shall pursue studies of outer space, including the moon and other celestial bodies, and conduct exploration of them so as to avoid their harmful contamination and also adverse changes in the environment of the earth resulting from the introduction of extraterrestrial matter and, where necessary, shall adopt appropriate measures for this purpose. If a state party to the treaty has reason to believe that an activity or experiment planned by it or its nationals in outer space, including the moon and other celestial bodies, *would cause potentially harmful interference with activities of other states parties in the peaceful exploration and uses of outer space,* including the moon and other celestial bodies, it shall undertake appropriate international consultations before proceeding with any such activity or experiment. A state party to the treaty which has reason to believe that an activity or experiment planned by another state party in outer space, including the moon and other celestial bodies, would cause potentially harmful interference with activities in the peaceful exploration and use of outer space, including the moon and other celestial bodies, may request consultation concerning the activity or experiment. [Emphasis added.]

Perhaps this does not precisely attempt to defend nature's *status quo.* It does attempt to assure all states' rights to explore and use the resources in question presumably in unspoiled condition. All experiments presumably induce some changes in the *status quo* of nature. How much is too much is bound to be a contentious issue when scientists themselves disagree and tend to take positions favorable to their own interests in the experiments in question.

The treaty is self-policed and involves no enforcement technique. It appears to demonstrate the likelihood of international efforts to

[30] See *Department of State Bulletin,* LV (1966), 953–55.

prevent at least certain perceived general dangers. We cannot be sanguine about self-policed controls over valuable phenomena and resources. Nations which believe that a particular activity is truly vital or even very valuable to their national interests may well be willing to risk the censure which such an unpopular act might involve, as the Soviet Union did in renewing its nuclear testing program in the fall of 1961, and the United States in proceeding with West Ford (although the United States did not continue such testing).

Even so, in the course of these UN discussions, the US representative stated that it was his government's belief that, *according to established principles of international law,* states should take all reasonable steps to avoid activities which limited the free use of space by others [31] and, as early as 1962, the Committee on Space Research (COSPAR) established a Consultative Group on Potentially Harmful Effects of Space Experiments consisting of scientists from the Soviet Union, India, Sweden, the Netherlands, the United States, and the United Kingdom, to study all questions relating to possible harmful effects of proposed space exploration and to make recommendations to COSPAR. The United States reports its efforts to COSPAR and consults with other states concerning these matters. Again, we can conclude that evidence suggests that prior consultations, at least, are recognized by the states as necessary to maintain international amity in the face of consciously induced prospective changes in the physical environment. It can be expected that this would suffice only where important damage to a particular nation is not expected or can be compensated for adequately on agreed standards.

## Concluding Note: Intentional Modifications

If we take the general international regime for the use of international rivers as an analogy for prospective regimes for the control of international cross-border modifications, such as weather operations, we must note that, except where special international regimes have been negotiated, the general regime relies primarily on voluntary consultation and cooperation, and mutual agreement among co-riparians. No state has an automatic legal veto over the actions of other states even when these affect its traditional use of the river's waters. Except where especially negotiated, there are few or no shared operations. Moreover, regional cooperation is quite likely to be more difficult to negotiate for weather control, for example, or at least more demanding of mutual trust, because of the possibilities for surveillance as a by-product of weather-modification activities, and the likelihood that, unlike the simpler river control problems, operations may lead to substantial

[31] A/AC. 1/SR, 1289, G.A.O.R., 1st Committee, 3 December 1962 (Mr. Gore–U.S.A.), 3.

losses as well as gains to individuals and might upset the ecological balance in the region of operation.

Analogous experience suggests that the international control of national programs of scientific experimentation in weather and other modifications, even those which may bring damages to some states or to all states, promises to be difficult to achieve on the basis of mutual agreement of sovereigns. The realities are that scientific evaluations and prognostications as to implied costs, dangers, and benefits often differ. Scientists do not relish sacrificing their freedom to experiment when *they* regard it as sufficiently safe. States have proved unwilling to yield a veto, much less control over their own partly strategic, scientific research programs to other states or to international bodies. They have pursued experiments despite objections. Such international bodies or agreements as have been evolved have either been advisory, as with COSPAR, or have provided for largely self-interpreted, self-enforced international cooperation to control even major risks arising from nationally-devised and nationally-run experimentation—as is the case in general with experimentation in outer space. On this record we can doubt that international control of, for example, weather experimentation, which is designed to assure that such activities will be technically and/or politically safe for mankind, will be easy to negotiate among the present jealous, highly sensitive, sovereigns of the international community, so conscious of their national security.[32]

## II. INADVERTENT MODIFICATION

Although the division is necessarily somewhat arbitrary and based in part on what must be changing political considerations, it seems

---

[32] We do not here detail the other side of the coin, the history of international cooperation in scientific activities and in technical cooperation. See the studies cited in fn. 1.

The world has a limited experience with allocations of scarce resources by technical cooperation, such as through the International Telecommunications Union (ITU). The ITU allocates bands of frequencies for *types of use* rather than to specific users. The nations assign specific frequencies to users by normal national reactioning procedures. These assignments are registered with the ITU on a "first come–first served" basis. Many frequencies can be widely shared or, rather, used in several geographical regions. Nonetheless violations of frequency assignment, both inadvertent and intentional, apparently are common. Ordinarily most complaints are resolved within the ITU framework. In addition neighboring countries enter into bilateral or multilateral agreements to provide additional controls over radio and television. In general one writer has analogized the role of the ITU to that of a policeman who can only "stand on the street corner and cry 'foul,'" when states violate their legal obligations. Given the mutual interest of the parties in orderly sharing, in the case of these still essentially shareable radio frequencies, in which some frequencies remain unassigned, this approach has apparently not led to dangerous international conflict or grave technical discords. But such favorable circumstances and shareability cannot be anticipated for all cases of international modification of the physical environment.

useful to deal first with some major human activities which are generally recognized as inadvertently having harmful effects on the physical environment of man, and which have proved to be at least partially amenable to international control or accommodation. We later briefly discuss inadvertent modification of the style and quality of living such as those which accompany population increase.

## Nuclear Testing

A near-classic case of inadvertent modification of the physical environment, of course, is that of nuclear testing. The testing of new weapons was deemed essential to their development, but has caused modest, but potentially cumulative and lethal or distorting, changes in the world environment.[33]

After conducting a formidable series of nuclear tests in the atmosphere, the United States and the USSR, yielding to both internal and external pressures, in the "thaw" of 1963, managed to agree to a Nuclear Test Ban Treaty in that year. The Treaty prohibited tests in the atmosphere, the seas, and outer space, and barred testing within a country's territory if the effects might be carried beyond its borders.[34] The Treaty, while not affecting the use of nuclear weapons in war which could also be expected to affect the human physical environment, has been accepted by most of the states of the world, and has apparently dramatically reduced the threat of a radioactive fallout problem from nuclear testing at least.

Nevertheless, the Treaty has a patent *status quo* bias; if atmospheric testing is deemed essential to the creation of a nuclear weapons capacity, and if a state seeks such a capacity, in the present international system, it can be expected that it *will* test. Thus Communist China and Gaullist France rejected the ban and have continued to test nuclear devices in the atmosphere, ignoring adverse world comment. While this testing has been on a small scale, the attitude of these states is indicative of the predominant universal concern for state survival and power, regardless of anticipated, possible, generalized adverse effects on the total world environment.

Moreover, even the remaining permissible tests—those underground— have begun to give concern, at least in the United States. Testing underground has been suggested as the cause for instability and earth-

[33] As with most disturbing results of technological advances, the effects of actions taken are often not perceived in advance. Thus, while the general hazards of radioactive fallout were understood, it was not known until after the event, for example, that lichens have an extraordinary capacity for concentrating strontium 90. Since reindeer feed on lichens, and certain northern peoples use reindeer as a source of food, a special health hazard was presented in some areas of the world.

[34] Note that the 1959 Antarctic Treaty had already barred, for Parties, *all* nuclear explosions in Antarctica.

quake phenomena in the western states. These tests and others proposed for Amchitka Island in October 1969 brought forth predictions of possibly serious earthquakes and tsunamis elsewhere, e.g., in Hawaii and Japan.[35] Underground tests may also give rise to release of radioactivity into the atmosphere by accidental "venting," may contaminate underground water, and may damage property due to ground-shock caused by the explosion itself. Thus far, however, there seems little world outcry concerning underground tests and, given the nature of the international system in which each state is ultimately responsible for its own self-defense, it seems unlikely that the major nuclear powers will yield to a total ban on testing short of an overall, convincingly secure, acceptable and accepted, arms control program.[36]

## Inadvertent Modification: Pollution of Air, Land, and Water

As population and technology advance, man puts great pressure on land, water, and air to accept the results of his progress.[37] The resultant "pollution" modifies the environment in many ways, directly and indirectly.

Pollution of the environment comes primarily from the interaction of land use with the demands placed upon water and air. The alterations are both chemical and physical in nature. Farming, water resources development, the building of cities, and construction of transportation systems not only alter the land surface but affect air temperature, density, and movement. The dependence of industry and metropolitan growth upon combustion results in the pollution of water and air by increasing the amount of specific chemical compounds already present as well as adding new ones. Pesticides used in agriculture, the home, and industry constitute an original pollution burden since they do not naturally occur in air, water, and land. Clearly, environmental pollution is a social problem and while man individually may help to reduce the contamination of his environment, needed and effective control can only be achieved by concerted social and political action. Senator Muskie emphasized this point when he said, "In a society as complex as ours, where practically everything we do to maintain life and produce

[35] See the review article by Luther J. Carter, "Earthquakes and Nuclear Tests: Playing the Odds on Amchitka," *Science*, CLXV, No. 3895 (Aug. 22, 1969), 773–76.
[36] Note also that such important states as Japan, India, Communist China, Israel, and West Germany are not parties to the Nuclear Nonproliferation Treaty.
[37] There is now a vast literature. See the Secretary-General's Report (E/4667). Useful, brief reports are U.S. Department of Agriculture, *Environmental Improvement (Air, Water, and Soil)*, 1966 and NAS/NRC, *Waste Management and Control*, Pub. No. 1400 (Washington 1966); National Science Foundation, *Human Dimensions of the Atmosphere*, NSF 68-18 (Washington 1968).

goods and services results in contamination of the environment, public decisions and actions are needed to improve the environment." [38]

Some effects of pollution are relatively local and dramatic. Smog in Los Angeles [39] and killing fogs in London, Donorra, Pa., and elsewhere are well publicized and lamented. Yet, other, potentially very important effects of pollution are relatively unknown outside of scientific circles. Thus, worldwide industrialization has rapidly increased the carbon dioxide ($CO_2$) in the atmosphere, an increase of perhaps 10 percent in the last hundred years. This, most believe, has caused a temperature rise of a few degrees centigrade in the stratosphere and a few tenths of a degree in the troposphere. Extrapolations indicate a more rapid rise by the end of the century although recent measurements seem to indicate that this heating up of the earth, this "greenhouse effect" may, for unknown reasons, now have stopped. If it should continue, if the atmosphere should heat up and the glaciers and ice melt, vast changes in man's environment would follow. To be most fanciful, for example, a total melting of the Antarctic's ice would raise the level of the oceans by about 100 feet around the world. No continent would look the same. While this is an unlikely eventuality, it is noteworthy that a combination of tiny individual activities could culminate in a vast and certainly unintended overall change.

Within some countries, conscious efforts are being made to deal with various forms of pollution (and "modification") and to preserve the quality of the environment—though at economic levels which most experts consider too modest. The United States has not only a national, state, and regional park system, but has adopted local, state, and national legislation (the "Clean Air" Acts of 1963 and 1965, etc.). European cities preserve parks, and "green belts" are planned for new cities in the United Kingdom, which adopted its Clean Air Act in 1956 and a Radioactive Substances Act in 1960. France adopted water pollution control legislation in 1963. Some international arrangements exist as well, as noted earlier, and we will next briefly examine a few of these.[40]

[38] John T. Middleton, Comments, in *Environmental Improvement* (fn. 37), 53.
The 1965 Report of the Environmental Pollution Panel of the President's Science Advisory Committee (U.S.) noted similarly that: "The production of pollutants and an increasing need for pollution management are an inevitable concomitant of a technological society with a high standard of living. Pollution problems will increase in importance as our technology and standard of living continue to grow."
[39] Estimates are that, in the Los Angeles area, some 15,000+ tons of pollutants are released into the atmosphere daily, over 90 percent of it from automobiles. Yet the area has developed in a way highly dependent on automotive transport.
[40] See generally Abel Wolman, "Pollution as an International Issue," *Foreign Affairs*, XLVII (Oct. 1968), 164–75.

1. *Radioactive Wastes.* The disposal of radioactive waste material presents both national and international aspects and will grow as the use of nuclear power grows. Some of these materials, such as krypton 85 and tritium, retain their potency for long periods. Burial on the land raises the threat of a menace to local populations; burial at sea raises the issue of contamination of sea resources and, as nature's cycle is completed, of the land as well. The visits of nuclear-powered surface ships and submarines to foreign ports have also led to allegations of nuclear pollution.[41]

The nations are aware of the problems involved and some action has been taken, but nuclear issues remain delicate matters for international negotiators.[42] The 1958 Geneva Convention on the High Seas has an article dealing with radioactive pollution, and asking each state to take into account relevant international standards in preventing pollution of the seas through the dumping of waste. As yet, no other general treaties deal with the specifics of this issue.[43] Such a treaty is being prepared by the International Atomic Energy Agency (IAEA), whose *Ad Hoc* Panel reported on this issue in 1961, recommending against the use of the seas for highly radioactive wastes but suggesting that certain wastes could be deposited in approved locations.[44]

There is also the Brussels Convention on the Liability of Operations of Nuclear Ships of 1962, which makes operators absolutely liable for damage to life or property anywhere in the world for damage caused by the ship or its waste products. Liability is limited to $100 million and there are several escape clauses, but the Treaty is again an evidence of international concern. Since warships are included, the United States has not become a party but does negotiate bilateral arrangements for visits to foreign ports by its warships and by the nuclear ship Savannah. In time, however, it seems likely that there will be substantially greater international cooperation in this matter; the interest expressed in the UN in the floor of the high seas and in the preservation of marine resources offers some assurance that the gener-

[41] See the controversy caused by the visit of the nuclear submarine USS Swordfish to Sasebo, Japan in May, 1968. A brief rise in the radioactivity of harbor waters was detected in this period. An inspection team from the U.S. Atomic Energy Agency found that the ship was not responsible. Some Japanese scientists objected that in their own studies they had been denied access to all the information available from the ship. See *New York Times*, May 15, 1968, May 26, 1968, June 3, 1968; *Christian Science Monitor*, May 28, 1968.

[42] See Wolman (fn. 40), 172.

[43] Dennis Livingston, "Pollution Control: An International Perspective," *Scientist and Citizen* (Sept. 1968), 172–81. Livingston argues that, even now, a state which used unreasonable and unsafe methods of disposal and thus endangered the reasonable use of the seas by others would be violating the right of free use of the seas and that actual harm caused could give rise to an international claim (p. 174).

[44] Report of the *Ad Hoc* Panel, "Radioactive Waste Disposal into the Sea." IAEA Safety Series No. 5, 1961.

ally acknowledged threat from nuclear pollutants will be seriously considered by the states. The problem remains to create alternative socially preferable disposal sites and techniques.

2. *Petroleum and the Seas.* In recent years, a few maritime disasters—the sinking of the Torrey Canyon off England, the breakup of the Ocean Eagle at San Juan, Puerto Rico, the seepage from a well in the Santa Barbara channel—have focused attention on a problem which was already becoming difficult in various forms as oil replaced coal as a fuel at sea and as oil tankers increased in numbers and size. In each case, complicated legal issues developed. In each case, there was a destruction of sea life and a loss of the use of beaches. Moreover, we remain ignorant of easy ways to clean up the long-lasting remnants of the oil leaks.

In the case of the Torrey Canyon,[45] for example, which was carrying 117,000 tons of Kuwait oil, masses of detergent, some 3 million gallons, were sprayed on the petroleum and the wreckage was attacked by the Royal Navy and the RAF with 160,000 pounds of high explosives, 10,000 gallons of kerosene, 3000 gallons of napalm and rockets. No major oil fires were set but the ship was destroyed. For many weeks the beaches were heavily polluted by the oil and some 10,000 sea birds were estimated to have died from various connected causes. On the other hand, marine life was relatively unaffected by the oil but was slaughtered near the shoreline by the detergents used in efforts to clear the oil. Both technology and law will need to advance to deal with similar catastrophes more adequately.

An International Convention for the Prevention of Pollution of the Sea by Oil has been in existence since 1954 and was amended in 1962.[46] The amended Convention, which is now in force, bars the discharge from tankers of over 150 tons gross tonnage of oil or oily mixture into a prohibited zone of all waters within fifty miles of land in general and of greater distances for some specified areas (e.g., 100 miles off the northeastern US). After May 1970, the limitations will apply to almost all ships over 500 gross tons. *All* discharge of oil *anywhere* is barred to ships over 20,000 gross tons if they were contracted to be built after May 1967 except if the master finds "special circumstances." Even then, discharge in the prohibited zones is barred. Governments are to promote the provision of facilities to receive oil wastes at its ports. Tankers and other ships must keep records showing discharge

[45] On the Torrey Canyon see Angela Croome, "Oil from the Torrey Canyon," *Sea Frontiers*, xiv, No. 3 (May–June 1968), 138–49.

[46] International Convention for the Pollution of the Sea by Oil, May 12, 1954, July 26, 1958, 12 UST 2989 (T.I.A.S. 4900). Amendments, April 11, 1962–May 18, 1967. See generally Livingston (fn. 43), 172–74; Wolman (fn. 40), 172–74.

operations. Violations are set by the state of the ship's registry and severe penalties are to be imposed. Each member may report violations by another country's vessels to that country. In addition, the 1958 Geneva Convention on the High Seas calls for Parties to adopt laws preventing oil pollution of the seas through uses made of the waters, and of the seabed.[47] Many states have adopted legislation limiting oil discharges in prohibited zones near the coasts, in harbors, and the like, as did the United States in the amended Oil Pollution Act of 1961.

Clearly, there will be problems in obtaining cooperation, even after governments become parties to these arrangements and even after technology for dealing with the problems becomes better understood.[48] States with large fleets may not adhere; state rule may vary in severity and enforceability. Such legislation is by nature difficult to enforce. Similar legislation against litter is dependent on compliance by numerous, generally unsupervised actors. There are also necessary "loopholes" (discharge to secure the safety of the ship, etc.). The nations have recognized the problems and are generally amenable to seeking to prevent changes in the seas and sealife due to oil,[49] but, especially in view of the known political power of oil interests, it can be expected that successful regulation of these far flung activities will be slow to develop.

3. *Some Further Words on River Pollution.* We noted in the first section the state of international acceptance of rules dealing with the diversion and use of international rivers. We need here to add a bit more on the inadvertent pollution of these waterways. Even when this problem is recognized by riparian states, issues of conflicting self-interest have often made an improvement of the environment difficult. Thus international projects to prevent pollution in the Danube basin, the Rhine, and the Meuse have all run into political difficulties. For example, an International Commission for Protection of the River Rhine against Pollution was formed in 1950 by Switzerland, France, Luxembourg, West Germany, and the Netherlands and, in 1965, these countries signed a treaty undertaking to study the pollution problem

[47] Convention on the High Seas, April 29, 1958, 13 UST 2312 (T.I.A.S. 5200).

[48] See the opposition by the U.S. oil industry to closer federal regulation of offshore oil leasing and to requirements that the "potential effect of the leasing program on the total environment, aquatic resources, esthetics, recreation and other resources" be considered and that these other elements receive protection. See *New York Times,* Aug. 3, 1969, Sec. 1, p. 37, col. 3.

[49] In May 1967, several governments met in London at the headquarters of the Intergovernmental Maritime Consultative Organization (IMCO) to discuss avoidance of "the hazards presented by the carriage of oil or other noxious or hazardous cargoes" and a long list of preventative measures was developed. All will take time to implement. See Wolman (fn. 40), 173–74. The Assembly of IMCO met on these questions in November 1968 as well.

and recommend the actions needed to protect the Rhine against pollution. Yet Wolman notes that "What they, and others, have failed to do was to come to grips with the hard-core questions as to who was to institute corrective measures and who was to pay for them." [50] These are issues which can be expected to cause basic difficulty in dealing with any of the complex problems involved in changes of man's environment. As the International Law Association pointed out in 1964, it had more trouble in dealing with the water pollution problem than with any other in international law and, because of the conflicts of interest involved, no rule of law "would . . . be completely pleasing to any interested state."

An interesting situation touched on earlier involves the United States, Mexico, and the waters of the Colorado River, which has also been an internal problem over the years within the United States. For over half a century the two countries discussed a division of the waters at the diplomatic level. In 1944 a treaty was finally evolved which provided that Mexico was to receive some 1.5 million acre feet annually.[51] In the US Senate, before the treaty was consented to, the issue of the quality of the water to be received by Mexico was discussed and it was suggested that Mexico take the water "regardless of quality." Since it was obvious that Mexico would not accept a treaty with such express language in it, the section dealing with quality was left vague.

In fact much of the water delivered to Mexico passed through irrigation projects along the Colorado, and over the years its salinity rose. Mexico raised many protests, especially after extremely alkaline lands in Arizona went into use. Conditions in Mexico became so aggravated that, in 1965, the US agreed, at its own expense, to build a by-pass drain to carry heavy saline waters around the Mexican diversion works. This, however, is at best a temporary solution.[52]

Such problems are not and will not be unique. In addition to the examples already noted, there is, for example, a Convention regarding Lake Constance signed by Germany, Austria, and Switzerland and several other agreements covering European rivers. Throughout Latin America there are already some two dozen international agreements, yet these cover only some 15 percent of the 68 international river basins there. All of these agreements are limited in functions and uses covered, and in very few has there even been an effort to create the organizations needed to implement controls.[53] Thus, despite the con-

[50] Wolman (fn. 40), 169.
[51] United States–Mexican Water Treaty, 1944, 59 *Statutes* 1219 (TS 994).
[52] For an account of the problem, see Wolman (fn. 40), 170–71; Livingston (fn. 43), 178.
[53] See generally Wolman (fn. 40), 170–71. He suggests (p. 171) that the agreements between India and Pakistan on the uses of the Indus River and on the

clusion reached by the UN's Economic Commission for Europe in 1961 that "in accordance with established principles of customary international law no state should pass on its waters to its neighboring states in such a polluted condition that this water would seriously damage the interest of its neighboring states,"[54] it cannot be said that the problems involved have been much more than recognized. Fair solutions and effective institutions for control to ensure maximal joint use and benefit are still largely in the future.

4. *Air Pollution.* Air pollution has only recently become of international concern. Reports by authors indicate concern by Sweden that industrial activities in the UK and Central Europe are affecting the air over Sweden, and by Switzerland that air pollution from France is affecting the scenic views from Geneva. France, Germany, and Luxembourg have interconnected problems arising from air pollution generated by industrialized regions on their borders.[55] In 1966, the US and Canada asked their International Joint Commission to study air pollution along their border.

It is not as yet possible to point to any major international efforts. The World Health Organization and the Economic Commission for Europe have been studying air pollution for several years. A draft declaration prepared by a group of experts for the Council of Europe's Committee of Ministers contains a declaration of principles on air pollution covering industrial, thermal, vehicular, and other sources of pollution, and may serve as a guide to Council governments. In the Carpathian region, the governments are reportedly jointly studying the problems of regional pollution. Recall too, as noted in Part I, that the Trail Smelter Arbitration was concerned broadly with this form of pollution and set out guidelines forbidding preventable harm across borders. This is, again, a set of problems on which joint action seems both necessary and perhaps possible, if undertaken firmly before major vested interests in polluting develop. The source of pollution is usually

---

diversion of the flood waters of the Ganges River into the Hooghly River, which will reduce the incursions of salt water from the sea to the major intakes of fresh water for Calcutta, are more hopeful signs of the possibility of international accommodations. These agreements also deal expressly with efforts to avoid other kinds of pollution. See 55 *American Journal of International Law*, 797 (1961). Another exception may be the U.S.–Canadian Boundary Water Treaty of 1909 which seeks to avoid pollution. (See 36 *Statutes* 2448.)

54 See ECE, *Conference on Water Pollution Problems in Europe* (March 17, 1961), 7. See generally *International Law Association*, Final Report of the Committee on the Uses of the Waters of International Rivers, 1966 (Helsinki, Report of the Conference).

55 On the prospective problems caused by auto pollution in Europe, see Wolman (fn. 40), 169. See also Livingston (fn. 43), 177–78.

identifiable and internationally-pressed claims seem likely to be decided in favor of the defenders of the environment. Nevertheless the ultimate right of a state to industrialize is also likely to be strongly asserted in practice. Perhaps the most that can be hoped for in general is that the best modern standards of care will be imposed on potential polluters by the cooperative actions of the states. This does not seem very comforting, since it has already failed to thwart environmental pollution by the small proportion of already industrialized states. It remains debatable whether the developing regions will look with favor on an international attempt to credibly impose higher standards of care on all parties. Such a credible program would normally be necessary if none were to be especially disadvantaged owing to extra costs of unilaterally maintaining superior standards against pollution.

5. *Pesticides*. Last, a brief word on a problem of inadvertent pollution now springing to both national and international attention. The effective development of DDT in the 1940's was considered an immense boon to mankind, and has resulted in the near-elimination of such diseases as malaria in many parts of the world. Now it appears also to have serious and perhaps permanent effects on other aspects of the world's ecology, effects which pass beyond the borders of the states in which it is used. Some American states and some countries, such as Sweden, have already banned its use. Many newer compounds exist. If no complete substitute can be found, however, decision-makers around the world may be faced with a precise problem in balancing— malaria versus the other now-demonstrated effects of DDT on the environment. We hope that such a Hobson's choice can be avoided. Certainly generally acceptable evaluations of such widely-used contaminants are necessary. Yet it must be remembered that relatively few governments today do much in the way of internal control over the use of drugs, pesticides, or the like. Since international machinery for making politically difficult choices which would be binding on states is rudimentary, their use is not likely to be effectively internationally controlled in the near future, at least not unless excellent substitutes for the deleterious compounds prove readily available, or a very strong international consensus on the value judgments implied is constructed, as is at present perhaps the case with some narcotics.[56] Once international norms concerning the use of pesticides were negotiated, however, international technical cooperation monitoring and facilitating their implementation might well be undertaken on the basis of mutual national interests.

[56] See I. Waddell, "International Narcotics Control," 64 *American Journal of International Law*, 310–23 (April 1970).

*Inadvertent Modification: The Style and Quality*
*of the Human Environment*

The kinds of inadvertent modification of the environment to be mentioned last are those inherent in man's movement toward a large population in an industrialized world. In a literal sense, each new child, each new house built, each street paved, changes the world environment.[57] Perhaps in a total world state, allocations of population and physical resources could be made on a world scale with world norms, goals, and expectations, as defined by world-choice institutions, in view. Yet changes in fundamental cultural patterns normally take place slowly. Even within a modern national state, it is difficult to impose change in relevant social standards on such basic, private choices as the appropriate size of families, and it is difficult to prevent or reverse such movements as migration from the farm to the city— certainly, at least, without massive totalitarian controls.

In a world of essentially self-defending nations, it seems likely that even if risks to the quality of the human environment definable on relevant world-group standards are foreseen, it is not likely to be possible to do more than exhort a state to do its best to follow an approved pattern of behavior or standards. A state can be urged to help prevent or minimize undesirable population growth or pollution from industry; it is hard to believe that it could be asked not to grow in size and power and not to industrialize. People plus industry mean power. The problems are obvious when we note that some nations are densely populated; some are relatively open. Can we think of a practical way of redistributing such populations—from China, say, to Australia within the present world system? Without something of the sort some nations will continue to seek continued (selective) population growth while others are to be urged to attempt population control. Surely the effective arguments in such cases will be those that appeal to the self-interests of the relevant states and to their desires to achieve per capita economic growth, and not to the interests of world community.

As nations industrialize, cities *will* supplant countryside and perhaps jungle and tundra; roads *will* be built through former wildernesses; factories *will* rise to sully or supplant the original native ecology. International action could be conceived of, in theory at least, to exhort for the preservation of the best of the present environment or even to call for a return to a more "pristine" *status quo ante,* but effective international enforcement action would have to be imposed on the nu-

---

[57] Note the patterns of change in atmosphere and weather caused by the existence of cities, of jet contrails, etc., related in Thomas J. Fleming, "Smog Is Changing our Weather," *This Week Magazine* (August 11, 1968), 3–5.

merous unwilling challengers to the *status quo,* and is indeed unlikely. The underdeveloped areas are not humanity's "National Parks." Most of the world has chosen to seek change, not ecological stability. Development and industrialization have been chosen as less burdensome than the continuation of present poverty, disease, and relatively short life-expectancy in the developing states. The best hope would be that this widely-sought change could be induced to fulfillment with optimal safety and welfare for all on rational world-standards. Again it is difficult to feel sanguine about defining or pursuing such a goal in the present decentralized world system. This does not necessarily mean that less than optimal (from the world point of view) compromises which nonetheless allow human survival are unlikely. We have muddled through in the past. How well we do so this time may depend heavily on the future technology of cheaply and simply controlling population and industrial pollution (with its deleterious climatological and health by-products), primarily on a local or national basis and in response to local or national incentives.

## CONCLUSIONS

As usual, we are faced with a spectrum of possibilities. The net international political effect of man's capacity to modify his environment must depend importantly on the scope and reversibility of his technological achievements and their by-products. For conscious weather modifications, the extent to which they must affect other states deleteriously, irreversibly, seems very important. If a dispute over the international partition of the potential gains from deliberate weather or environment modification is implied by the circumstances, and therefore must be minimized and contained, some generally accepted, reliably enforced, decision-norms and rules and effective international political procedures for division of the gains—and probably for compensation for the losses—must be established, or we can expect severe, possibly disastrous conflict. In short, both more clear-cut norms and new institutions for their enforcement would become necessary.

We have elsewhere argued [58] that an approach to conscious modification of the environment which permits states to make their own efforts (or even to be aided) to become better off—*so long as other states are not damaged except in their loss of relative strength or privileges* [59]—would appear to be the minimum conservative (initial

[58] See studies cited in fn. 2.

[59] Of course it must be noted that in the present system states indeed have to care about their relative power positions. Suppose, for example, that Mexico became much wealthier and therefore much more powerful as a result of agreed, intentional, modification activities while the U.S. stayed about as well off as it was. Would that not upset the balance of power of the two nations? Or, perhaps a

*status quo* biased) rule of thumb to seek to establish with reference to the international interest in controlling such modifications. Where such an approach cannot be adequate, because some states must lose importantly even when international compensation is used to broaden its field of applicability, all other possible attempts are called for to convert harmful conflict-ridden modification situations into cooperative ones. A credible national security guarantee to the losers, from the international community or from their allies, is the minimum that would seem to be required if peace is not to be threatened. Such an approach could apply to unintended as well as to explicit attempts to modify man's environment.

As for inadvertent modification of the environment, what makes it less dangerous politically than designed modification is that it *is* inadvertent. The type of problems included can be expected to grow with industrialization—as they have for New York and New Jersey which cannot go to war over them. (N.B. So far, they have not solved them either.) Since they can be expected to grow they can no doubt lead to serious international misunderstandings, but again, in a world in which the desire and right to industrialize a native resource base are generally asserted, the costs of industrialization, like acts of God, are less likely to lead inevitably to conflagration. Of course, effective control of deleterious inadvertent modification of the environment would be greatly aided by the development of simple, inexpensive, antipollution technology, preferably locally applicable. Some cases may even appear to be reasonably good candidates for effective regional cooperative ventures, however, securely defended either by the nations

---

better example, suppose Siberia prospered and no one else was damaged. Such relative redistributions in practice normally cannot long be thwarted, especially if the states which will benefit in the long run can go it alone, or go it at least without the cooperation of those who will lose in the relative (power) redistribution. States may even be willing to fight to prevent such an occurrence. But it is awkward in the latter part of the Twentieth Century and would appear inconsistent with the U.N. Charter to insist internationally on a state's *relative* privileges, and no state advances legal claims of a type which would mean that no one could grow in welfare and power relative to the current balance. The U.S. has not insisted officially, for example, that the poor weak states must stay poor, underdeveloped, nonintegrated power fragments. Rather, if anything, it has pressed for and assisted recovery from war damage, and for development in integration in Europe and elsewhere, whatever the imputable effects on the relative power position of the United States. The key seems to be to find some way to assure the relative losers that they nonetheless remain essentially secure, at least in their ability to defend their own survival on their own standards, given their remaining power assets and their reliable allies. In addition, of course, insofar as states could rely on the organized international community to preserve their security, they would have less reason or need to rely on their own survival resources and therefore on the maintenance of their own relative power. The development of reliable organs of international security should make major changes in welfare and power potentially safe and more acceptable to all affected parties.

on their own, or as organized into alliance systems, or into an effective international security system.

Some attempt can be made to minimize the creation of new problem regions. In general, for inadvertent modification, its prevention, or its effective local control where feasible, is clearly politically easier than cure or than interregional or international control. Therefore, insofar as the location of new industrialization is consciously planned and controlled, it would seem wise for national planners to investigate *inter alia* the suitability from a "pollution" viewpoint of proposed new urban centers. "Modification" and pollution expertise could become a standard type of technical assistance to nations with inadequate domestic resources of the type needed to effectuate such surveys. In addition, attention should be called on the international level, as it is now in the UN and specialized agencies, to local, national, and international cooperative approaches to minimize the development of further pockets of harmful modifications. Internationally-sponsored study of the techniques of environmental preservation, and internationally-organized exchanges of information as to relevant technology and the appropriate standards for and the promising political avenues of social control of the environment, have already been initiated and should be continued and expanded.[60] These efforts could lead to the negotia-

---

[60] The Report of the U.N. Secretary-General (E/4667) usefully summarizes a modest, generalized approach as follows (pp. 22-23):

(a) The universality of environmental problems results in an important amount of work being carried out both in developed and developing countries as an attempt to meet these problems;

(b) This work however is mainly conducted by traditional instrumentalities on a fragmentary basis without integrated approach at the national level and without sufficient overall view at the international level;

(c) While preventive action would usually be preferable on many grounds, developments affecting the environment are usually not planned or conducted in such a way as to prevent or minimize harmful consequences, thus leading to the need for difficult costly and imperfect corrective measures;

(d) There is a considerable amount of scientific and technological knowledge which is available and not being applied or properly applied; most problems of the human environment appear amenable to solution by wise and proper management, including not only protection from degradation but rational utilization and improvement for future generations; such management requires appropriate administrative measures, and practices, enlightened economic and social planning and support of national and international legislation;

(e) However, there is need for further research on certain scientific and technological problems particularly on global, physical and biological phenomena, on sociocultural factors, on non-polluting techniques and on rational and conservative use of resources.

(f) There would be great advantages in developing further international action in the field of the human environment such as the promotion of research and monitoring programmes (which are under way or being planned), educational and technical assistance programmes (which could be significantly developed), and arrangements for technical meetings and specialized studies. A major area for international action will be in world-wide or regional legislation, standardization and conventions.

tion of international conventions establishing relevant minimum general norms or standards which local, national, regional, and international governmental units could be called upon to strive to fulfill.

In sum, then, in addition to internationally-fostered study and general standard-setting for the control of inadvertent modification, technical assistance in national industrial-location planning should be offered, where necessary, both to developing states and to those which are already experiencing harmful changes. Also, as noted, the need for, potentials of, and appropriate capacities of organized international technical cooperation in international resource conservation, in "poison" and pollution control, and in operational regional airshed and watershed authorities should also be seriously studied for problem areas as soon as possible.

For those major environmental discomforts likely to be caused simply by population increase, and by the pressure of more men and states for the "better"—more politically and economically secure if more hectic (industrialized)—life, it may be appropriate again to urge socially responsible behavior, the necessity of explaining the costs to the group and to the states themselves, of initiating cooperative programs, offering technical assistance, pointing up the problems.[61] As other papers in this volume indicate, however, the solutions to this class of issues may be far more dependent on advances in psychology, sociology, and technology and the facilitating arts of politics and government than, for example, on conscious efforts to limit the world's population growth or to ration industrialization by international approaches in the present and foreseeable world system.

In general, for modest ecological challenges, international exhortation and standard-setting plus international technical cooperation, based essentially on mutual interest in environmental conservation which would reinforce basically national control programs, and organized, operational regional control of multistate resources where necessary, may well suffice to enable the present international community to "muddle through" adequately. If a genuine ecological crisis should develop which threatened human survival and imposed on states and their citizens the necessity of rationing the right to industrialize and to procreate, major modifications of the world political system would probably be required—its conversion into something like a responsible world government to assure that the optimal distribution, on world standards, of the scarce rights to life, power, material welfare, and security was to be achieved fairly, peaceably, and with maximum feasible human dignity for all.

[61] Same.

CHAPTER 5

# The Management of Ocean Resources:
# Regimes for Structuring
# the Maritime Environment

## L. F. E. GOLDIE

### I: INTRODUCTION

THE SEA constitutes some 71 percent of the earth's surface. It and its riches have always challenged or charmed men into seeking to gain a livelihood from it—frequently at great risk. From long before classical times sympathetic magic, religion, and law have regulated Man's uses of the sea. Today, however, as never before, science, engineering, and available capital are permitting new exploitations of the maritime environment and new means of gaining wealth, respect, knowledge, adventure, and power. These new uses, no less than others which are now emerging or can be anticipated in the near future, can only be fitted into the slowly developed customary rules—evolved at different points of time during the past two millennia as Procrustes' victims were fitted into their host's infamous bed—by fictions which distort facts, or by meaningless interpretations of the earlier experience.

The international law of the sea lacks the many essential institutions and rules and even, to a large extent, the necessary language to manage effectively the maritime resources now available to man, or shortly to become so; it will prove inadequate as an impartial framework of claim and decision for the equitable distribution of jurisdictions, titles, and values with respect to those resources and to the wealth which science and technology are developing. Accordingly, this chapter will review some of the harmful effects of retaining traditional international law unchanged, in regulating man's new relationship with the sea, and will investigate critically some possible blueprints for managerial regimes within the framework of emerging international law.

### II: EMERGING PROBLEMS

#### A. Biological Resources

Edible fish constitute perhaps the oldest, and certainly the most valuable, of the biological resources of the sea. But, from the most ancient times to the present, mankind has had only one approach, the most primitive, to the harvesting of this resource—that of the hunter and collector. This is as true of the Australian aborigine wading in a mangrove creek at low tide as it is of a modern trawler fleet scouring the ocean, supported by a spotter plane and equipped with radar. Today we stand on the brink of great changes. Mankind may eventually need, in order to survive, to change from the hunter of fish to the herdsman and shepherd of some species and the farmer and cultivator of others—thereby changing fundamentally his ecological, social, economic, and legal relations to the sea.[1] It may well become necessary for him to cultivate and process algae and plankton, if only to feed the fish and animals which he will himself eat. The effect on international law of such a revolution calls, as a preliminary step, for the complete rejection of Grotius' time-honored premise that the fish resources of the sea are inexhaustible, so that all may fish freely without detriment to others. Second, the emerging or discernible future uses of the seas demand the transformation of the relevant rules of international law into regimes which make maximum use of ocean exploration and exploitation, establish functional standards for the equitable allocation of the benefits derived from those activities, and formulate new concepts of jurisdiction, access, proprietorship, and answerability.

## B. Mineral Resources

### 1. FOSSIL FUELS UNDER THE SEABED

For a considerable time oil has been won from shallow seabed areas. But recent improvements in technology have made oil drilling economically feasible beyond the 200 meter bathymetric contour line [2] (the outer limit of the continental shelf as defined in terms of depth).[3]

---

[1] Experiments are already being conducted in fish farming by analogies with battery methods. See "On Flatfish Farm," *Economist*, CCIIIV, No. 6596 (1970), 51.

[2] For an outline of this trend off the coasts of the United States, see Goldie, "The Exploitability Test—Interpretation and Potentialities," *Natural Resources Journal*, VIII (1968), 434–36, esp. fns. 1 and 2, the accompanying text, and Appendix 1 [hereinafter cited as Goldie, "Exploitability Test"].

[3] See Convention on the Continental Shelf, April 29, 1958 [1964], 1 U.S.T. 471, T.I.A.S. No. 5578, 499 U.N.T.S. 311 [hereinafter cited as Continental Shelf Convention]. This Convention came into force on June 10, 1964, see 499 U.N.T.S. 312, note 1. The other conventions which the 1958 United Nations Conference on the Law of the Sea at Geneva produced were: Convention on the Territorial Sea and the Contiguous Zone, April 29, 1958 [1964], 2 U.S.T. 1606, T.I.A.S. No. 5639, 516 U.N.T.S. 205 [hereinafter cited as the "Convention on the Territorial Sea and the Contiguous Zone"]. This Convention came into force on Sept. 10, 1964, see 516 U.N.T.S. 206, note 1; Convention on the High Seas, April 29, 1958 [1962], 2 U.S.T. 2312, T.I.A.S. No. 5200, 450 U.N.T.S. 82 [hereinafter cited as the "Convention on the High Seas"]. This Convention came into force on Sept. 30, 1962, see 450 U.N.T.S. 83, note 1; Convention on Fishing and Conservation of the Living Resources of the High Seas, April 29, 1958 [1966] 1 U.S.T. 138, T.I.A.S. No. 5969, U.N.T.S. 285 [hereinafter cited as the "Convention on Fishing"]. This Convention came into force on March 20, 1966, see 559 U.N.T.S. 286, note 1.

This technological trend [4] will become intensified as demand increases.[5] Thus *Our Nation and the Sea* tells us that: "Twenty-two countries now produce or are about to produce oil and gas from offshore sources. Investments of the domestic offshore oil industry, now running more than $1 billion annually, are expected to grow an average of nearly 18 percent per year over the coming decade. Current free world offshore oil production is about 5 million barrels per day or about 16 percent of the free world's total output." [6]

As claims to develop more offshore oil and gas resources go out into deeper and deeper regions, they will inevitably give rise to even more acute problems of jurisdiction over the deep-sea areas where the fuels are mined and title over the commodities won, and over transportation, pollution, and liability. More fundamentally, however, these developments may raise acute issues of scarcity, access, and division of the products. In addition to fossil fuels, the subsoil of the seabed is now providing sulphur, sand, gravel, and aragonite—vast quantities of this last having recently been discovered in the Bahamas.[7] These also threaten the possibility of major pollution.

[4] Already experimental drillings have been conducted through over 11,000 feet of water into the sediment beneath. See the report of the "Glomar Challenger's" drilling through 11,720 feet of water and a further 472 feet of sediment in the Gulf of Mexico to discover oil in submarine salt domes in *New York Times*, Sept. 24, 1968. This report also indicates that the depth of 17,567 feet was also drilled. See also *New York Times*, Sept. 1 and Nov. 26, 1968, p. 28, cols. 2–7; May 13, 1969, p. 29, cols. 1–5. The *New York Times* reported discoveries by the U.S. Navy research ship "Kane" of clues to "oil rich salt domes" in the deep ocean off the west coast of Africa. A miscellany of facts recently revealed in the *New York Times*, Saturday, Aug. 30, 1969, p. 25, cols. 6–7 and p. 27, cols. 4–6, in connection with oil exploration plays on the continental shelf and slopes of the United States and Canadian Atlantic coasts, should be noted. These include: (1) permits have been issued for the exploration of 260 million acres or nearly 410,000 square miles of seabed; (2) the Shell Oil Company will use a semisubmersible rig, the Sedco H, which will drill as deep as 25,000 feet while sitting on the seabed under 100 feet of water, or afloat through 800 feet of water; (3) most of the areas now being explored are within 200 miles of the largest cities of the United States. Other areas are close to major Canadian cities; and (4) like the North Sea, and in contrast with the Gulf and Southern California coasts, most of this area is extremely turbulent.

[5] For projections of increases in both demand for and production of offshore oil "twenty years from now" see Commission on Marine Science, Engineering, and Resources, *Our Nation and the Sea* (1969), 122–30 [hereinafter cited as *Our Nation and the Sea*]. The Commission has also published three volumes of *Panel Reports*, I, *Science and Environment* (1969); II, *Industry and Technology: Keys to Ocean Development* (1969); III, *Marine Resources and Legal-Political Arrangements for Their Development* (1969) [hereinafter cited as "*Panel Reports*" and prefixed by the appropriate volume number. Page citations to the Panel Reports are prefixed by the Roman numeral indicating the appropriate Panel, *e.g.*, page citations to the International Panel are prefixed by VIII].

The Commission was appointed by President Johnson on Jan. 9, 1967, pursuant to the Marine Resources & Engineering Act of 1966, 80 Stat. 203 (1966), 33 U.S.C.A. §1101 (Supp. 1967).

[6] *Our Nation and the Sea* (fn. 5), 122.

[7] See fn. 293.

## 2. SURFICIAL DEPOSITS

Writing some five years ago, Dr. John Mero could tell us that: "[S]ub-stantial engineering data and calculations show that it would be profitable to mine [from the sea] materials such as phosphate, nickel, copper, cobalt and even manganese at today's (1964) costs and prices. And I firmly believe that within the next generation, the sea will be a major source of, not only those metals, but of molybdenum, vana-dium, lead, zinc, titanium, aluminum, zirconium and several other metals as well." [8] And he added: "But most important, the sea-floor nodules should prove to be a less expensive source of manganese, nickel, cobalt, copper and possibly other metals than are our present land sources." [9]

While these minerals may be increasingly won from the sea, they undergo a cycle of constant renewal [10] which, for the foreseeable future, will continue to add a quantity of nodules to the store already on the seabed greater than that taken for human use.

The question remains, however, whether a contemporary equivalent of Grotius' demand of open access to fisheries is applicable here. Some submarine areas will offer far better possibilities of return on outlay than others, although they may be very expensive to discover and to start using. Those who foot the bill may well claim protection for their investment. Accordingly, the gathering of nodules may also gen-erate claims that access should be restricted, and consequently create problems of jurisdiction and title. If those nodules are to be bene-ficiated, i.e. processed, on the spot, possibly problems of pollution will also be encountered.

### 3. MINERALS IN SUSPENSION

Apart from the metal-rich waters of such special, and currently little understood, phenomena as submarine hot brines—for example those of the deeps of the Red Sea and the Atlantic II deep,[11] the sea carries many chemicals and metals in suspension. Substantial industries already extract sodium chloride (in the form of common salt), potas-sium chloride, magnesium chloride, sodium sulphate, magnesium

[8] John L. Mero, *The Mineral Resources of the Sea* (Amsterdam 1965), 275.

[9] Mero (fn. 8), 280. See also Mero, "Review of Mineral Values on and Under the Ocean Floor," Marine Technology Society, *Exploiting the Ocean*, 61 (Transactions of the 2d Annual MTS Conference and Exhibit, June 27–29, 1966, Washington 1966) [hereinafter cited as Mero, "Mineral Values"]; I, *Panel Reports* (fn. 5), 1-32; III, *Panel Reports*, VII-106-71; and Cord-Christian Troebst, *Conquest of the Sea*, trans B. Price and E. Price (New York 1962), 180–93.

[10] See Mero, "Mineral Values" (fn. 9), 76.

[11] See III, *Panel Reports* (fn. 5), VII-107 and the authorities cited therein at fns. 23–27.

metal, and bromine.[12] Processing the extraction of these resources,[13] like the beneficiation of nodules from the sea floor, could give rise to waste and pollution problems. It should be remembered, too, that seawater could become an increasingly important source of fresh water, serving urban areas and irrigating arid lands.[14] It is possible to imagine political and legal problems arising in such areas not unlike those presented by the distribution of the waters of international river basins. As at other points in this study, managerial conciliation [15] blueprints might well serve the interests of the region. Again the Grotian assumptions of an inexhaustible resource, allowing open access to all comers, must be replaced by the recognition that here, too, the resource is exhaustible, and that brines and other by-products may pollute the environment. Hence regimes of restricted access and equitable systems of allocation are needed.

## C. Generating Power from the Sea

In volume 2 of its *Panel Reports* the Commission on Marine Science, Engineering, and Resources distinguished between two categories of "[m]ajor power generating concepts to exploit the ocean's potentials," [16] namely: (1) The use of the sea as an environment; and (2) harnessing the energy in the sea.

### 1. USE OF THE SEA AS AN ENVIRONMENT

The seabed may well provide an environment for establishing nuclear power stations. At 150–200 foot depths they would be below the level of all except minor disturbances caused by storms. Because this ideal depth is not encountered on the Atlantic and Gulf coasts of the United States sufficiently close to shore (approximately within 20 miles of the coast), certain added costs such as building relay stations or embedding the structure in the seabed might be necessary in such places. Indeed an embedded reactor design, appropriate even for the less than optimal

---

[12] See Mero (fn. 8), 25–52. Note especially Table II for a list of the degree of concentration and of total quantities of 60 of the elements in sea water.

[13] See, however, for an indication of the cost which would, at the present state of the art and of demand, make this development prohibitive in most parts of the sea where special concentrations do not occur, III, *Panel Reports* (fn. 5), VII-101.

[14] For an outline of this process, see G. Young, "Dry Lands and Desalted Water," *Science* CLXVII (No. 3917, 1970), 339. See also, especially for the concomitant problems of disposal of waste and pollution, III, *Panel Reports* (fn. 5), VII-223-32.

[15] For an introduction of the concept of managerial conciliation or cooperation regimes see Goldie, "The Oceans' Resources and International Law—Possible Developments in Regional Fisheries Management," 8 *Columbia Journal of Transnational Law* (1969), 1, 17–18, 45–51 [hereinafter cited as Goldie, "Fisheries Management"]. See also §VC below.

[16] II, *Panel Reports* (fn. 5), VI-213. See also III, *Panel Reports*, VII-233-34.

areas, has been studied.[17] The main savings which submarine nuclear power plants could make would be land cost, low costs in constructing the radiation shield, avoidance of possibly expensive claims which might arise out of gradually "leaking" radioactivity giving rise to illnesses such as leukemia, and elimination of the myriad claims possible in the event of a nuclear disaster on the scale which might arise on dry land. Should power stations located on or under the seabed be increasingly used as a means of easing the problems of population growth and crowding on land, important legal problems of protecting the marine ecology would arise. For it should be remembered that such plants could create risks not only of radioactive pollution, but also of heat pollution, leading to local eutrophication and other deleterious losses to the quality of the area's animal and plant life. Building and running these power stations might, furthermore, adversely affect the use of the sea as a source of beauty and pleasure. Again, the question of the sort of liability to be imposed on operators for the harm their underwater stations might do could not be deferred. Finally, the issue of the degree of pollution to be accepted as "tolerable" in the sea would have to be faced. Here again, the traditional "free-for-all" would be most inappropriate.

2. HARNESSING TIDAL ENERGY [18]

Possibly because of the friendly and relaxed atmosphere of the dispute (reflected in the French judge delivering a very learned opinion unfavorable to his own country's claims), the recondite investigations of Anglo-Norman feudal land tenures, and the learned disquisitions on the history of the Norman Duchy in which the International Court of Justice indulged itself in the *Minquiers and Ecrehos Case*,[19] that litigation has seemed to lack both drama and modernity to commentators. But the underlying conflict which led to this display of antiquarian erudition actually pointed to the future more than do most of the cases adjudged by the International Court of Justice. France did not dispute English Normandy's rule over the islets and reefs of the Bay of Granville out of a pious desire to vindicate dead heroes' titles. She wished to exclude Jerseymen engaged in collecting crabs, oysters, and lobsters for the London market from those locations where the Commission du Plan had called for the building of power stations,

---

[17] Same, VI-215.

[18] There are other potential sources of power in the ocean—wave motion, currents, thermal gradients, and geothermal sites. An attempt to harness wave energy to operate a generator has been made on the Algerian coast. See II, *Panel Reports* (fn. 5), VI-217. But these are all in the far more distant future than are the plans to generate electricity from the tides.

[19] I.C.J. [1953], 47.

designed to generate [20] approximately a quarter of France's electricity from the tides of the English Channel.[21]

The French decision to harness the tides for the generation of electrical power is not unique, although it would appear to be in advance of other countries. Nearly one hundred sites for commercially feasible tidal power plants exist in the world, and Great Britain,[22] the United States, Canada, India, Australia, New Zealand, the Soviet Union, Argentina, Brazil, Spain, Germany, and Mexico are all engaged in studying the possibilities of this source of power.[23] In fact, Great Britain has had the possibility of harnessing the Bristol Channel's tides under review since 1918.[24] In addition to France, only Canada, the United States, and the Soviet Union, however, have begun to implement their plans.[25]

This new use of the sea, although it seems at first so beneficial and apparently without deleterious side-effects, could also impose difficult legal problems. The *Minquiers and Ecrehos Case* highlights its potential conflict with fisheries. In addition, the barrages, channels, and holding basins could clearly change the whole complex dynamic of an estuary—perhaps greatly and irreversibly accelerating its decay into a swamp. Where an estuary is international,[26] perhaps a supranational agency or a multinational public enterprise with built-in safeguards protecting other uses might well provide the only effective institutional blueprint.

On the other hand, a supranational agency directed to the shared use of an estuary for the purpose of generating electric power might so strongly reinforce the interests supporting specific use, that, reciprocally, it would further weaken the effectiveness of those claiming recognition for its fishery, recreational, residential, and aesthetic uses. Such a supranational agency should, accordingly, be widely enough conceived to include at least some representation of the interests it might threaten, or should include some deference to them in its mandate. A system of compensation for the substantial diminution or exclusion of existing uses should also be formulated.

[20] See Judge Carneiro's closing comments, same, 66.

[21] *I.e.,* the La Rance Tidal Project near St. Malo, see II, *Panel Reports* (fn. 5), VI-216.

[22] R. Charlier, "Harnessing the Energies of the Oceans," *Marine Technology Society Journal,* III (1969), 59.

[23] Same.

[24] Same, 63. Had either the 1933 or the 1945 River Severn projects been brought to fruition, "they would have paid off within ten years." Same.

[25] Same, 59; see also 65–67, and II, *Panel Reports* (fn. 5), VI-217–19.

[26] An international power project has been proposed for Passamaquoddy Bay, on the Bay of Fundy between the State of Maine and the Canadian Province of New Brunswick. See II, *Panel Reports* (fn. 5), VI-217–19.

## D. Health, Therapy, and Recreation

In addition to deriving drugs from the sea,[27] mankind may also use its surface and volume for health, therapy, and recreation. Dr. Cousteau has described how cuts and sores, which proved obstinate and hard to cure in the heat and other adverse conditions ashore, healed in 48 hours or less under the Red Sea in Conshelf II.[28] Perhaps hospitals for injury and accident victims and major surgery cases might be advantageously established underwater? In addition, psychotherapy may develop concepts, arising from the universal symbolism of the sea, calling for restful sanatoria, especially for hypertension and anxiety cases, to be developed in the oceans or on the seabed.[29]

With the spread of leisure, of education, and of the popularity of scuba diving, underwater activities, no less than surface recreations such as sailing, surfing, speedboat racing, and cruising, may become increasingly popular. Underwater activities may even come to be more appealing than surface ones, since they offer an intellectual dimension lacking in surface water-sports. Scuba diving by amateur naturalists could make contributions to the many nascent underwater sciences. Would it be beyond the realms of practicality to forecast mass production of inexpensive underwater recreation and/or research vehicles and vessels? What would be the liability of extra-hazardous submarine enterprises, such as nuclear power stations, to persons engaging in these activities? What precautions should be demanded? Whatever the answers to these questions may be, it is already clear that the traditional open access for all uses and users provides an inappropriate and inadequate regime for the future.

## E. Scientific Research

At the outset a definition should be stipulated. Unless otherwise expressly stated or demanded by the context, the term "scientific research" and its grammatical variations and synonyms will be used to indicate disinterested academic, scholarly, and naturalistic investigations by qualified persons and institutions. It should not be confused with either "exploration" for commercial purposes, or defense experimental activities which might incidentally include scientific research. On the other hand, publication of the results of such research should

---

[27] See II, *Panel Reports* (fn. 5), VI-190–97.

[28] Jacques-Yves Cousteau, "Working for Weeks on the Sea Floor," *National Geographic*, XXIX (1966), 498.

[29] See, for an interesting confirmation of this theoretical possibility, Wilford, "Learning from a Sojourn under the Sea," *New York Times*, July 12, 1970, §4 (The Week in Review), p. 10, cols. 1–2.

not be mandatory; it should be at the discretion of the research worker or institution involved.[30]

In addition to the factors mentioned in the immediately preceding subsection, academic marine sciences are developing very rapidly, and may well become involved in one of the major confrontations of exclusive and inclusive claims to use of the oceans' volume and floor. At a time when more and more countries have scientific research ships —whether owned by university, private, or government laboratories [31]— many coastal states are seeking more than ever before to restrict scientific research activities off their shores.[32] Increasingly, ocean and outer space research activities may become intimately connected in a number of ways. The ocean seems to be the location for the recovery of space vehicles on their return to earth. In addition, buoys could come to provide valuable links in combined ocean and outer space research, and in communications activities.

Finally, the freer marine scientific research is allowed to become, the more likely pollution, radiation, eutrophication, ecological imbalance and other man-made abuses of the sea may be discovered and rectified by appeals to public opinion. Claims made in this connection may well vie with many of the most time-honored uses of the sea—such as its treatment as the ultimate depository of all kinds of garbage (including poison gas containers and waste nuclear materials) and as the arena of contemporary preemptive military competition.

## F. Weather Forecasting and Control

Weather prediction began on dry land. For a considerable time, however, prediction has increasingly come to depend upon reports from ships at sea. More recently, weather satellites have provided additional

[30] This requirement in art. 5, para. 8 of the Continental Shelf Convention is not necessarily beneficial to research. Indeed, it should be properly viewed as creating, in favor of coastal states, restrictions on the freedom of the sea which had not existed previously. Because applications to conduct even purely scientific projects off their shores may arouse some states' suspicions, those applications will probably be met by time-consuming delays in receiving the consent which cannot "normally" be withheld—delays, moreover, which may well be as effective as withholding consent by rendering the research plan useless. In this way apprehensive states could prevent the scientific publication of discoveries concerning their coastal regions.

[31] See, e.g., list of scientific research ships registered by the maritime nations of the world in 1, Panel Reports (fn. 5), 1-14. For a survey of the growth of marine science research activities see same, 1-2-3, 1-13-19.

[32] Papers delivered by William L. Sullivan, Jr., Department of State, Daniel S. Cheever, Director, Department of International Affairs, University of Pittsburgh, at "Science and International Organization" session (Thursday, June 26, 1969) of the Law of the Sea Institute's Fourth Annual Summer Conference, "National Policy Recommendations," at Kingston, R.I., June 23-26, 1969. (These papers are to be published in the Conference's Proceedings.)

dimensions of prediction. A foreseeable system of long-range forecasting may come into operation which will be conducted by means of a complex and computerized combination of weather and communication satellites, buoys, and the more traditional modes of collecting weather data, so that a comprehensive intergovernmental knowledge of the "ocean-earth-atmosphere" physical system can be continuously and accurately kept up to date [33] by means of a highly sophisticated version of the already-projected "World Weather Watch." [34] Ultimately, perhaps, technological advances and developed procedures of intergovernmental cooperation may lead from weather prediction to weather control on a comprehensive basis.

## G. Transportation

As the great corporations, which in this century are exploiting the planet's petroleum resources, move their activities out into the deep ocean, they will need to transport their crude oil and their gas to centers of population. The logistical problems will be solved, in the main at least for this century, by means of giant tankers.[35] Although, eventually, pipelines may well come to provide means of transporting the great bulk of gaseous, liquid, and fine-grain materials between continents, or from seabed operations in the deep ocean, many decades will elapse before the greater proportion of bulk cargoes will cease to be carried in ships of increasingly gigantic dimensions.[36] On the other hand, this observation does not deny the probability that, in the near future, pipelines will be used increasingly to bring gaseous, liquid, and pulverized products of deep-ocean mining ashore. But this mode of transportation faces not only great technological problems, but also problems of the political stability of the coastal states on whose lands

[33] See I, *Panel Reports* (fn. 5), II-11–14, II-58–62.

[34] See also Sub-§ H 4 of this Section, below.

[35] See Troebst (fn. 9), 97–98, where the author projects the following possible developments in ocean transportation:

> Eventually man will use regular convoys of submarine barges, towing behind them a chain of enormous, sausage-like containers. The United States Rubber Company and several European firms have already designed rubber containers for surface transportation of various liquid cargoes. Bigger versions, 20 feet in diameter and 360 feet long, would be ideal for high-seas traffic. Every "rubber sausage" of this size could hold 182,000 gallons of freight and several of them could be towed by a single submarine tanker. Admiral Momsen is convinced that by 1980 such submarine barge trains will be almost a mile long, transporting some seventy-five different liquids ranging from oil, petrol, alcohol and acids to fine-grained materials like cement or grain. One great advantage would be that no reloading would be necessary if the purchaser was located inland. Tugs could continue to convey the goods by river to the point nearest the final destination.

[36] For a projection of the growth of tankers and bulk carriers over the period 1970–2000, see Table 4, I, *Panel Reports* (fn. 5), III-67. See also the textual matter accompanying this Table.

the pipelines debouch. Both giant tankers and pipelines present international lawyers with hard problems of pollution and of liability.[37] In addition, the threat of continuing day-to-day oil pollutions should not be overshadowed by more headline-grabbing ones. They are even more injurious to the environment than are the relatively infrequent massive oil spills. The Commission on Marine Science, Engineering and Resources tells us:

> Pollution of the marine environment through massive oil spills has received increasing public notice because of several recent dramatic situations involving damaged tankers. These occurrences highlighted the ease with which natural resources and the economic life dependent upon them could be wiped out by one unfortunate incident, and focused attention on the possibility of other such incidences. Yet the most pervasive pollution comes not from headlined oil spills but from the many activities that take place every day underwater. There are about 16,000 oil wells off the continental United States, and the number is increasing by more than one thousand a year. There is rightful concern that oil well blow-outs, leaks in pipelines, and storm damage can cause pollution that could ruin large parts of commercial fisheries, sportsfishing, and recreational areas.[38]

## H. Defense and Military Security Problems

### 1. SUBMARINE PENS AND FORTS

In the near future, when men have learned to establish semipermanent dwellings under the sea,[39] naval authorities will see the need to establish permanent fixed submarine maintenance facilities, research and communications stations, storage depots, and repair works (in the beginning, perhaps, miniature San Diegos, Gibraltars, Maltas, and Guantanamos). These could be built on the seabed or in the subsoil; or they could float suspended at various depths below the surface of the sea. However constructed and placed, these installations would need pro-

---

[37] For a brief indication of these see § VII A below.

[38] I, *Panel Reports* (fn. 5), III-52–53.

[39] In discussing the use of the sea floor for human residence the Commission on Marine Science, Engineering and Resources could write, in II, *Panel Reports* (fn. 5), VI-16: "By the year 2000 colonies in the sea floor will be commonplace because industries will operate profitably at sea and people will be there to support them. . . . By the year 2000 the U.S. industry with the highest sales volume, employment and earnings may well be one intimately associated with the oceans."
These probabilities not only give rise to thoughts on the strategic uses of the seabed and subsoil as ancillary to dry land objectives and power confrontations, but also on the independent strategic needs of the seabed colonies and industries themselves. That is, the human seabed world may not, in the long run, so much redress the balance of the dry-land world, as call for its own balances and power stabilizations.

tection, not only from discovery and from espionage, but also from the direct exercise of either secret or overt force. Only a worldwide disarmament of the seabed can prevent these possibilities from becoming fact in the not too distant future.

## 2. FIXED OR "HARDENED" SUBMARINE THERMAL TORPEDO SITES

While fixed or "hardened" submarine rocket installations would simply be the equivalent of a moored Polaris submarine on the seabed—a loss of some 90 percent of its utility—there may be a considerable future for fixed installations for thermal torpedoes which could be automatically launched. Many of the issues which have already been discussed in connection with submarine naval bases, workshops, supply depots, and establishments could be relevant to these installations. Here, too, a state may rely on either secrecy or, alternatively, on possible regional treaty regimes. The possibility of such establishments coming into existence might be precluded by the 18-Nation Committee on Disarmament meeting in Geneva reaching agreement on the demilitarization of the seabed, and if this agreement were implemented, on the one hand, by the United States and the Soviet Union, and on the other, by a resolution of the General Assembly of the United Nations. This, indeed, would appear to be the benefit which the United States–Soviet Union draft treaty banning nuclear weapons from the seabed offered.[40]

## 3. POLARIS SUBMARINES, DEEP DIVING SYSTEMS, MOBILE RESEARCH LABORATORIES, AND TELECHIRIC SYSTEMS

The units indicated in this heading include the many types of submarines, deep submersibles, bottom crawlers, remote-controlled ("telechiric" = "distant hand") vehicles and surface vessels which have recently been, or are now being, developed. Three-dimensional mobility will be their distinguishing characteristic.[41]

## 4. SUBMARINE HUNTING SYSTEMS

Secrecy and surprise, as well as the nuclear warhead of its weapons, provide the Polaris submarine with its awesome authority. This submarine warship's invulnerability depends on the difficulty, in the present state of the art, of finding it and keeping track of it—a function also of the present-day inability of radar to operate effectively under water, and of the short range of sonar and the slow traveling speed of its signals. On the other hand, there are many types of equipment

[40] For text see *New York Times*, Oct. 8, 1969, p. 6, cols. 1–5; for commentary, p. 1, col. 1 and p. 6, cols. 5–6.
[41] See next subsection (§I) below.

which could be combined, with a little imagination, to limit the Polaris submarine's authority by ending its potential of surprise. One such combination has already been publicly proposed for peaceful uses —General Dynamic's "World Weather Watch" system. This is, briefly, to add to the present-day meteorological system of land stations, supplemented by measurements in the upper atmosphere and the reports of the weather satellites, a worldwide network of giant data-collecting ocean buoys. The data, it is suggested, could be instantaneously relayed to central positions by communications satellites. Could not such a system be adapted to submarine watching? If the buoys were in close enough proximity they could utilize various means of submarine detection and relay their findings to central receiving systems for analysis.

## I. Three-Dimensionally Operating and Bottom-Crawling Vehicles

Industry and scientific research may shortly be developing bottom-crawling vehicles and vessels capable of navigating through the volume of the sea at great depths. Some of these systems could be manned. Others could be remotely controlled. Clearly, apart from Article 14, Paragraph 6, of the Convention on the Territorial Sea and the Contiguous Zone, and the Convention on the High Seas (especially the provisions relating to a ship's nationality, the slave trade, piracy, hot pursuit, and pollution), little has been developed in international law and practice to regulate the interactions of these novel systems with other uses and claims. It is extremely doubtful whether such vessels would fall within the Continental Shelf Convention—unless they were engaged in the exploration or exploitation of the resources of a coastal state's shelf and remained there. But would such vessels, navigating outside territorial waters and engaged in scientific research above the shelf (and hence beyond the scope of Article 5, Paragraph 8, of the Continental Shelf Convention), or submersible military units, long be permitted immunity from coastal states' continental shelf jurisdiction?

## J. A Provisional Observation

Men have very frequently, possibly too frequently, domesticated the social challenge of new knowledge, new technologies, and the consequent new social relationships by means of legal fictions—by falsely postulating as premises untrue (but reassuringly familiar) ascriptions of legal characteristics to the new and challenging facts. By this path they reach conclusions which give comfort, but fail to accommodate to all the impending possibilities for social change inherent in the new knowledge and the new technologies.[42] Strange as it may seem in

---

[42] An example of the resort to legal fictions in order to obtain the comfort of familiarity from novel and unfamiliar circumstances is to be found in discussions

the context of the vaunted rationalism of the present time, this has been particularly true in recent writings on the application of international law to activities in the deep oceans and in outer space. What is needed today is not the overstretching of analogies—to present the appearance (but not the fact) that time-tested concepts of continued vitality are still in use—but the formulation of new blueprints and rules, and new ideas to underpin them. In the pages which follow, after a review of the current law, some novel ideas and blueprints are offered for examination and testing.

### III: The Traditional International Law of the Sea

#### A. General International Law

Traditionally, international law distinguished between two categories of seas; those under the sovereignty of the coastal state by reason of a number of labels—territorial waters, internal waters, historic waters,

---

of the Allied bombardments of Hiroshima and Nagasaki with the atomic "Thin Man" and "Fat Man" bombs. They were originally justified, and have been traditionally defended since, on the ground that these atomic bombs merely provided a more efficient and economic bombing raid effect—the bombing raids themselves being justified as "retaliation."

Here again the use of the familiar, as an analogy, is misleading. To equate atomic and hydrogen bombs to fire plus high explosives is simply false. Radioactive fallout and radiation sickness, as well as the bombs' known genetic effects, make analogies even with traditional poisonous gases misleading, if comforting. These analogies are used to clothe the horrors of the future with the ill-fitting dress of the familiar present.

Nuclear weapons are neither war explosives nor war gases. Their legal classification is *sui generis* (as, indeed, are the legal problems of the continental shelf, mining claims in the deep oceans, the uses of outer space, weather modification, and the multitude of new human activities and powers which modern science has made possible). This argument, of course, does not rule out the use of analogies in problem-solving. There is a great difference between, on the one hand, drawing on the successful experience of the past and adapting that experience to present circumstances and, on the other, announcing that novel situations are to be classified as if they did not differ from successfully-solved past problems and, hence, are to receive the same solutions—regardless of essential differences between the earlier and the later problems.

A possibly less hair-raising example of the use of familiar, but irrelevant, categories to domesticate the intellectual challenge of new developments may be found in what I have called, elsewhere, the *"Duchess of Sutherland fallacy"* after the once-obscure Scottish decision, Duchess of Sutherland v. Watson, v, Scots L. R., 158 XL, Sc. Jur., 119 (Ct. of Sess. 1868), in which the pretense of an untrue state of facts, namely that sessile sea animals are *partes soli* of the seabed and therefore appertain to the proprietor of the *solum*. In my study "Fisheries Management," I cite examples to underscore the extent to which this fiction has permitted international fisheries relations to get out of hand (fn. 5), 13–23. See also Goldie, "Sedentary Fisheries and Article 2(4) of the Convention on the Continental Shelf—A Plea for a Separate Regime," 63 *American Journal of International Law* 86 (1969) [hereinafter cited as Goldie, "Sedentary Fisheries"].

and those beyond the sovereignty of any state—the "free high seas" being viewed as *res extra commercium* whether as *res nullius* or as *res omnium communis*. In recent years some novel doctrines have been developed for the affirmance of coastal states' claims to extend their exclusive authority farther and farther out from their coasts, into the maritime areas which were formerly characterized as "free high seas." Although these doctrines pay lip service to the freedom of the seas, like the older formulations of territorial and internal waters they fall within the general category of exclusive rather than shared claims to exploit a resource or to exercise a jurisdiction. They are thus little more than sophisticated variations on the older theme of exclusivity and include: contiguous zones, zones of specialized jurisdiction, the continental shelf doctrine, and conservation zones. Such claims resemble the older concepts in that the competences they justify arise from the unilateral enclosing action of coastal states, and remain exclusively vested in those states. This enclosure movement, this trend of ever-increasing jurisdictions, should be a matter of concern for international lawyers. One may usefully stigmatize it with the satirical name this writer has already proposed, namely "Roe's Law." [43]

At this point a caveat should be entered. To point to the trend of these newer forms of exclusive competence as further legal weapons in the armories of coastal states, in their pursuit of power on and under the high seas at the expense of inclusive uses (a truism), is not to assert that these jurisdictions, and especially the contiguous zone, do not differ from territorial waters (a false statement). Yet assertions to this effect are frequently made. While they are understandable as part of the rhetoric of governments and publicists at pains to justify extravagant territorial claims, they are not acceptable as objective statements of legal analysis. It is surprising, to say the least, to find them in documents where the arguments or presentations have nothing to gain therefrom. For example, the Commission on Marine Science, Engineering, and Resources critically comments on the definition of "the Con-

---

[43] Formulated in a comment from the floor during the Panel on "Regimes of the Deep Sea Bed" (Monday, June 23, 1969) at the Law of the Sea Institute's Fourth Annual Summer Conference "National Policy Recommendations," at Kingston, R.I., on June 23–26, 1969. It is named in honor of the fictitious casual ejector in what is surely one of the most famous of all legal fictions, the Action of Ejectment as a protection of freehold titles. By Roe's many trespasses one jurisdiction (that of the Court of King's Bench) was expanded at the expense of others (those of the Courts of Common Pleas and Exchequer) greatly to swell its judges' revenues. Roe's law may be formulated as follows: (1) Jurisdiction tends to expand to occupy the subject-matter allocated for its exercise; (2) Subject-matter in (1) above tends to expand until confronted by an equal and opposite subject-matter of a countervailing jurisdiction.

tiguous Zone" in Article 24 of the Geneva Convention on the Territorial Sea and the Contiguous Zone [44] as follows:

> Although the Convention seems to restrict the purposes for which national control may be exercised in the contiguous zone, the coastal nation's authority is not, in fact, so limited. This is true, because one way or another, coastal nations claim permanent, exclusive access to the living resources of the sea up to 12 miles and more from the baselines from which the breadth of the territorial sea is measured. Thus, the United States has passed laws and regulations prohibiting foreign vessels from fishing in its 12-mile "exclusive fisheries zone" without its permission.[45]

These asseverations disagree with three leading authoritative studies in the field, namely those by Gidel,[46] McDougal and Burke,[47] and

---

[44] See fn. 2. Article 24 is as follows:

1. In a zone of the high seas contiguous to its territorial sea, the coastal State may exercise the control necessary to:
   (a) Prevent infringement of its customs, fiscal, immigration or sanitary regulations within its territory or territorial sea;
   (b) Punish infringement of the above regulations committed within its territory or territorial sea.
2. The contiguous zone may not extend beyond twelve miles from the baseline from which the breadth of the territorial sea is measured.
3. Where the coasts of two States are opposite or adjacent to each other, neither of the two States is entitled, failing agreement between them to the contrary, to extend its contiguous zone beyond the median line every point of which is equidistant from the nearest points on the baselines from which the breadth of the territorial seas of the two States is measured.

[45] *Our Nation and the Sea* (fn. 5), 50; III, *Panel Reports* (fn. 5), VIII-12-13.

[46] Gilbert C. Gidel, *Le Droit International Public de la Mer*, III (Paris 1934), 11–22. Compare especially p. 14 where Gidel writes:

> La "zone de haute mer contiguë aux eaux territoriales" ou, plus brièvement, la "zone contiguë," est, répétons-le, l'espace où l'Etat riverain exerce, au delà de la limite des eaux territoriales, certaines compétences rigoureusement spécialisées et auxquelles il ne saurait prétendre sur le reste des espaces appartenant à la haute mer. Etant donné qu'elle commence seulement au delà de la limite des eaux territoriales, la zone contiguë forme une partie de la haute mer; mais cette partie de haute mer est dotée, à raison de sa situation géographique proche des côtes, d'un statut juridique particulier qui n'est pas celui des autres espaces de haute mer. D'autre part la zone contiguë se distingue essentiellement de la mer territoriale. Dans la mer territoriale, l'Etat riverain peut prétendre, sous les limitations résultant du droit international, à l'exercice du faisceau des compétences dont l'ensemble constitue la souveraineté. Dans la zone contiguë, l'Etat riveraine ne peut prétendre qu'à l'exercice de compétences fragmentaires, limitativement déterminées.

Note, however, that Gidel includes "protection des richesses de la mer" among the "compétences fragmentaires, limitativement déterminées." Unlike the opening sentence of the paragraph just quoted in the text from *Our Nation and the Sea*, however, Gidel does not see this inclusion as negating the specific quality of the coastal state's authority or as undermining the zone's quality as "de la haute mer."

[47] M. McDougal and W. Burke, *The Public Order of the Oceans* (New Haven 1962), 518–19. Note especially:

> The argument is often made that the recognition of a variety of contiguous

Shalowitz.[48] By asserting that the addition of coastal states' exclusive fisheries authority to their other specific powers in the contiguous zone changes that concept from one of a collection of specific and restricted purposes, *Our Nation and the Sea* tends to throw its weight behind the avoidable and pernicious thesis that the contiguous zone, like the territorial sea, provides coastal states with "un faisceau des compétences." [49]

Unlike *Our Nation and the Sea*, Gidel saw no inconsistency between the specificity of the contiguous zone doctrine and the inclusion of coastal states' exclusive fisheries within its terms. For him these were merely further examples of the separate and restrictively defined specific competences within the scope of the coastal states' contiguous zone. On the other hand, not only does the Geneva Convention on the Territorial Sea and the Contiguous Zone not include exclusive fisheries within the zone but, further, legislation [50] and a multilateral treaty [51] promulgated since that time have been drafted to vest *ipso jure* in the coastal state the exclusive fisheries zones which they created, or the creation of which they authorized. Exclusive fisheries zones may, despite Gidel's characterization of them, be viewed as an independent category of international law, rather than as added specific instances

---

zones for different purposes is no improvement over an extension of the territorial sea to include all such zones since the same authority is being recognized, so it is asserted, under different labels. Limited authority for specific purposes is not, however, the same as comprehensive authority for all purposes. States do frequently have particular objectives which they seek by extending limited authority seaward, such as in the control over fisheries, smuggling of guns, customs surveillance, and prevention of other undesirable activities, and both their concern for limited objectives only and their reciprocal claims for limited authority are very often completely genuine. Recognition by the general community of particular contiguous zones for particular purposes is not, therefore, tantamount to an invitation to the states to create comprehensive zones for all purposes.

(Footnotes omitted, but note fn. 202.) See also the distinction between "sovereignty" and "jurisdiction" made at 82, fn. 182.

48 See 1 A. Aaron L. Shalowitz, *Shore and Sea Boundaries* (Washington 1962), 238, where the author writes:

The term "contiguous zone" in international law may be defined as an area of the high seas, outside and adjacent to the territorial sea of a country, over which it exercises control for special purposes, such as the protection of its revenues and health laws. The origin of this doctrine goes far back into history, but the first attempt to codify it as a principal of international law was in 1930 at the Hague Codification Conference. No agreement was reached on the matter, but nations continued to claim various rights of control for different purposes in areas beyond the traditional 3-mile limit.

49 See fn. 45.

50 See Fisheries Limits Act (U.K.), 1964, c. 72. Contrast, Act to Establish a Contiguous Fishery Zone Beyond the Territorial Sea of the United States, 80 Stat. 908 (1966), 16 U.S.C.A. §§1091–94 (Supp. 1967). It is submitted that resort to contiguous zone terminology in the United States statute is at best otiose and at worst misleading.

51 European Fisheries Convention, *done,* March 9, 1964, Cmnd. 2355.

of the protective competences within the contiguous zone doctrine. This writer suggests that the recognition of coastal states' exclusive competence over offshore fisheries as an independent legal category should be the preferred position. Proposing the recognition of coastal states' exclusive rights over fisheries beyond their territorial seas as a separate category of legal competence is not fatal to supporting Gidel's central concept of contiguous zones as being essentially part of the high seas, and not assimilable under any conditions to territorial waters. The competences which still remain within the category of contiguous zones are still separate and specific rights to exercise authority on the high seas.

## B. Pollution and Responsibility for Harms

Since the seventeenth century the high seas have come to be held to be a common zone of open access to resources. The tragedy of a common zone and of its open-access resources is that any act of wastage, pollution, or overproduction which may, on balance, be disadvantageous to the actor when property is private, or access is controlled, will balance a private gain against a shared detriment (shared by all the other users). Hence, in the case of the high seas for example, not only is pollution permitted, but it becomes more advantageous than it could be in a private or closed-access environment, since the polluter is, at best, required to suffer an infinitesimally small share of the disutility arising from his polluting act, and can enjoy, alone, all the economies which he can derive from it. A response which conventional wisdom offers is that the sea is an "infinite sink" [52] in which pollutants will disappear, but if, by chance, a polluting act does cause harm, the polluter will answer to the victims of his fault. Such conventional wisdom, however, fails to take account of reality in at least two ways. First, the *Stratton Commission Report* tells us: "To many the oceans are the ultimate repository of all pollutants. The oceans' ability to assimilate waste material is immense; for every person on earth there is the equivalent ocean volume of one square mile, 500 feet thick. But the oceans are not infinite, and they must not be considered the ultimate solution for waste disposal problems." [53]

Second, international lawyers have traditionally adhered to the dogma that state sovereignty and autonomy are inconsistent with a thesis that, in international law, states may be held to act at their peril. Hence the great majority of writers in the field have rejected arguments claiming that strict liability, let alone absolute liability canvassed in this article, may be imposed on states, even when these arguments have only contemplated certain special situations and certain

[52] I *Panel Reports* (fn. 5), III-60.     [53] *Our Nation and the Sea* (fn. 5), 74.

narrow sectors of legal relations. Thus we find the following statement in Oppenheim: "An act of State injurious to another State is nevertheless not an international delinquency if committed neither wilfully and maliciously nor with culpable negligence." [54]

Despite this prevailing conservatism, the *Trail Smelter*,[55] *Corfu Channel*,[56] and *Lac Lanoux* [57] cases clearly point to the emergence of strict liability as a principle of public international law.[58] In none of these cases did the issue of fault prevail. Although *Trail Smelter* might have seemed to turn on the Anglo-American doctrine of nuisance, this was because of the inclusion, in the *compromis,* of a reference to the decisions of the United States Supreme Court in the exercise of its original role in settling controversies between the states of the United States. If *Trail Smelter* is to be viewed as an application of public international law, rather than of common law, the irreducible minimum of the relevant general principles of law which it deposits after the refining out of the idiosyncrasies of the common law is the strict liability which Canada owed to the United States. This interpretation is further strengthened when it is recalled that no issue of fault was tried in the case. Again, in *Corfu Channel,* Albania's liability lay in the presence of mines in her territorial waters, not in any malevolence or neglect which would have had to be proved by the applicant state.

In the *Lac Lanoux* arbitration the Tribunal clearly considered strict liability to govern in the event of its finding for Spain. It said: "It could have been argued that the works would bring about a definitive pollution of the waters of the Carol or that the returned waters would have a chemical composition or a temperature or some other characteristic which could injure Spanish interests. Spain could then have claimed her rights had been impaired. . . ." [59]

[54] L. F. L. Oppenheim, *International Law,* 8th edn., H. Lauterpacht, ed. (London 1955), I, 343. See also Sohn and Baxter, "Convention on the International Responsibility of States for Injuries to Aliens" (Draft No. 12 with *Explanatory Notes*) 43–44, 50–52, 171–76, 188–90 (mimeo., April 15, 1961). Compare Michael Hardy, "International Protection against Nuclear Risks," 10 *International and Comparative Law Quarterly,* 739, 752–53 (1961) [hereinafter cited as Hardy, "Nuclear Risks"].
For another method of imposing strict liability mitigated by varying maximum amounts of damages payable, see Art. 11, Convention on Damage Caused by Foreign Aircraft to Third Parties on the Surface, Rome, October 7, 1952, 310 U.N.T.S. 181, 188 (No. 4493, registered by the International Civil Aviation Organization on September 9, 1958) [hereinafter cited as Rome Convention on Damage to Third Parties on the Surface].

[55] 3 UNRIAA 1905, 1938 (1938 and 1941).
[56] 1949 I.C.J. 4.
[57] 12 UNRIAA 281 (1957); 53 *American Journal of International Law,* 156 (1959).
[58] Goldie, "Liability for Damage and the Progressive Development of International Law," 14 *International and Comparative Law Quarterly,* 1189, 1226–31 (1965) [hereinafter cited as Goldie, "Liability for Damage"].
[59] 12 UNRIAA 281, 303 (1957); 53 *American Journal of International Law* 156, 160–61 (1959).

In addition to these three cases, the United States Government's *ex gratia* payments to the Japanese Government for injuries sustained by fishermen from the latter country as a result of the 1954 hydrogen bomb tests in the Pacific has an auxiliary, but only an auxiliary, function. During March and April 1954 the United States conducted a series of nuclear tests at the Pacific Proving Grounds in the Marshall Islands. As a result of miscalculations some Japanese fishermen, and some of the inhabitants of the Marshall Islands (*e.g.* those on Rongelap Island),[60] were injured by hydrogen bomb tests carried out on March 1. (It should, perhaps, be noted that although Professor McDougal and Mr. Schlei write of a "series of miscalculations" as occasioning the injuries,[61] negligence on the part of the United States has not been established. Furthermore, whether a case could be made out in terms of *res ipsa loquitur* [62] is doubtful.) After the incident diplomatic action culminated in an exchange of notes between Japan and the United States. The resulting agreement entered into force on January 1, 1959.[63] The United States paid two million dollars to the Japanese Government on the understanding that the sum would be distributed in an

[60] See, for a background on this *ex gratia* payment on compassionate grounds, Settlement of Japanese Claims for Personal Injuries and Property Damages Resulting from Nuclear Tests in the Marshall Islands in 1954, Tokyo, January 4, 1955 [1955-1] U.S.T. & O.I.A. 1, T.I.A.S. No. 3160. See also *Department of State Bulletin*, xxx (1954), 598–99; xxxi (1954), 492, 766; xxxii (1955), 90–91.
A similar *ex gratia* payment on compassionate grounds was appropriated for certain residents of Rongelap Island in the Pacific Island Trust Territory in respect of fallout injuries following the explosion of an atomic bomb at Bikini Atoll on March 1, 1954. See Committee on Interior and Insular Affairs, *Providing for the Settlement of Claims of Certain Residents of the Trust Territory of the Pacific Islands*, H.R. Rep. No. 110, 88th Congress, 1st Session (1963); Committee on Interior and Insular Affairs, *Providing for the Settlement of Claims of Certain Residents of the Trust Territory of the Pacific Islands*, H. R. Rep. No. 1193, 88th Congress, 2d Session (1964); and Public Law No. 88-485 (August 22, 1964), 78 Stat. 598 (1964).
[61] See McDougal & Schlei, "The Hydrogen Bomb Tests in Perspective: Lawful Measures for Security," M. McDougal & Associates, *Studies in World Public Order* 763, 764 (1960). See also 64 *Yale Law Journal*, 648, 649 (1955).
[62] The difficulty of characterizing this case in terms of *res ipsa loquitur* is illustrated by Williams v. United States, 218 F. 2d 473 (5th Circuit, 1955) in which a jet aircraft (an Air Force B-47) exploded in mid-air causing deaths, personal injuries, and property damage. The Court of Appeals for the Fifth Circuit held that at the time of the trial the engineering and scientific knowledge necessary for the manufacture, maintenance, and flying of jet aircraft was so novel and specialized that a court could not confidently extrapolate circumstantial evidence to find the defendant negligent. See, however, Ybarra v. Spangard, 25 Cal. 2d 486, 154 P. 2d 687 (1944). But see, for criticism of this latter case, Seavey, "*Res Ipsa Loquitur: Tabula in Naufragio*," 63 *Harvard Law Review*, 643 (1950). For an explanation of special circumstances in Ybarra v. Spangard, see Prosser, "*Res Ipsa Loquitur* in California," *Selected Topics on the Law of Torts*, 302, 362–63 (1953). See also Goldie, "Liability for Damage" (fn. 58), 1197–99, 1232–33.
[63] See fn. 60. See also *Department of State Bulletin*, xxxii (1955), 90–91. For background facts, same, xxxi (1954), 492, 766; xxx (1954), 598–99.

equitable manner at the discretion of the Japanese Government.[64] This payment reflects the United States concern and sense of moral obligation, despite the lack of proven fault on its part. Its concern reflects a basic sentiment of justice, and may stand as an important signpost for future legal evaluations of the liability to be ascribed to developing scientific activities—particularly when placed in perspective with the *Trail Smelter, Corfu Channel,* and *Lac Lanoux* cases.

This writer has suggested the following policy argument in support of incorporating these more stringent obligations of good neighborliness in international law:

> A municipal system has sufficient authority to prohibit ultrahazardous activities which are not socially beneficial. International law, on the other hand, is still largely a system of permissive and facultative norms. The practicality, therefore, of seeking to outlaw many activities which are not conducive to the general utility may be questioned. It would be more in keeping with the present state of international law's development to argue for the regulation of these activities, and for the imposition of stringent responsibilities and high maximum monetary levels of liability upon them. Hence, if they may not be prohibited, their potentiality for harm can be reduced by the imposition of either strict liability or absolute liability.[65]

This emerging international law principle, and its development into the principle of "channeling," [66] is thus in the process of becoming incorporated into the international treaty law governing liability for nuclear harms.[67]

## C. The 1958 Geneva Conventions on the Law of the Sea [68]

Although guided by the ideal of "progressive development," as well as faithful to the task of codification, the Geneva Conventions on the

[64] Same, XXXII (1955), 90–91.
[65] Goldie, "Liability for Damage" (fn. 58), 1221.
[66] See §VII below.
[67] The four agreements on liability for nuclear harms are: Convention on Third Party Liability in the Field of Nuclear Energy, Paris, July 29, 1960 (OEEC Doc. No. C (60) 93), 8 *European Yearbook* 202 (1960); Convention on the Liability of Operators of Nuclear Ships, Brussels, May 25, 1962, 57 *American Journal of International Law* (1963); British Institute of International and Comparative Law, Special Publication No. 6 (1965), *Developments in the Law of the Sea, 1958–1964,* 196. It should be noted that this convention is not yet in force, since it has not been adhered to as called for in its art. 24, para. 1. 1; Convention Supplementary to the (OEEC) Paris Convention, 1960, Brussels, January 31, 1963, 2 *International Legal Materials* 685 (1963); International Convention on Civil Liability for Nuclear Damage, Vienna, May 21, 1963 (IAEA Doc. No. CN.12/46), 2 *International Legal Materials* 727 (1963). There is a fifth, embryonic agreement in a draft sponsored by the Inter-American Nuclear Energy Commission.
[68] For the citations of these conventions, see fn. 2.

Law of the Sea, and their attendant Resolutions and Protocols, did little more than cast the traditional pattern of the international law of the sea into an authoritative form, consecrate several emerging doctrines (for example, that of the continental shelf) as existing law, and introduce some reforms.[69] The one exception to this disappointing record is the Geneva Conference's reformulation of Articles 50–60 of the International Law Commission's 1956 *Articles Concerning the Law of the Sea* [70] into the *Convention on Fishing*. In this Convention the possibility of creating special fishery regimes which fall into neither traditional category—that of seas subject to state sovereignty or that of free high seas—was formulated. Although now in force,[71] this Convention has proved to be the Cinderella of the four which the 1958 Conference produced.[72] One may hope, however, that while the Convention on the Continental Shelf, which so far has generated the most interest, as both scholarly writings and political invocations attest, may come to be left behind by technological, economic, and political events,[73] the Convention on Fishing will come into its own. Further-

[69] In contrast with at least three of these conventions, the resolutions adopted by the United Nations Conference on the Law of the Sea held at Geneva Feb. 24–April 27, 1958, represented a number of pioneering but necessary ideas.

[70] International Law Commission, "Articles Concerning the Law of the Sea," xi U.N. GAOR, Supp. No. 9 at 4, 9–10, [1956], 2 *Year Book of the International Law Commission*, 256, 262–63, U.N. Doc. A/3159 (1956). These draft articles were, in their turn, based on a draft preamble and six draft articles submitted by Dr. Garcia Amador at the 296th Meeting of the International Law Commission. See International Law Commission, "Summary Records of the Seventh Session," [1955], 1 *Year Book of the International Law Commission*, 1, 76–77. See also International Law Commission, "Provisional Articles Concerning the Regimes of the High Seas," x, U.N. GAOR, Supp. No. 9 at 3, 10–13, [1955], 2 *Year Book of the International Law Commission*, 21, 28–31, U.N. Doc. A/2934 (1955). Judge Jessup has been credited with this line of thought in the progressive development of the international law of fisheries. See Bishop, "The 1958 Geneva Convention on Fishing and Conservation of the Living Resources of the High Seas," 62 *Columbia Law Review,* 1206–07 (1962); see also 1212.

Draft article 60 deals with "[f]isheries conducted by means of equipment embedded in the floor of the sea" and, interestingly, reflects principles first included in the International Law Commission's 1951 draft article on sedentary fisheries. See International Law Commission, "Report Covering the Work of its Third Session, 16 May–27 July, 1951," [1951] 2 *Year Book of the International Law Commission*, 123, 143, U.N. Doc. A/1858 (1951). This latter became art. 13 of the Convention on Fishing. For a review of the needed distinction to be drawn between sedentary fisheries properly so-called and those conducted by means of permanent or semi-permanent installations embedded in the floor of the sea, see Goldie, "Sedentary Fisheries" (fn. 42), 88–89.

Failing a separate regime, sedentary fisheries, like the fisheries governed by art. 13, should be taken out of the regime of the Continental Shelf Convention and brought within that of the Convention on Fishing. See also §iii C 5 below.

[71] See fn. 12.

[72] For a discussion of this point, see Goldie, "Fisheries Management" (fn. 15), 3.

[73] On the obsolescence of three of the important rules of the Continental Shelf Convention, see Goldie, "The Contents of Davy Jones's Locker—A Proposed Regime

more, some of the managerial regimes it makes possible could provide models for regimes governing resources other than fisheries—for example, submarine oil and gas, and hard minerals on or under the sea floor, and the prevention and control of pollution.[74] In this way many of the problems which the Continental Shelf Convention did not resolve might well be answered.

Aside from such advances as the Geneva Conventions in general may represent, states have been able to modify their own maritime legal relations. The means to which they have resorted have, under favorable circumstances, made it possible to establish, for example, regional fishery authorities with competence to conduct research and even to exercise independent regulatory powers. On the other hand, a critical review of some of the existing maritime regimes' shortcomings may provide cautionary tales to point up the weaknesses which later draftsmen would do well to avoid. For, in the main, they still reflect much that is counter-productive in the traditional and conceptualistic approach to international law. Furthermore, the influence of that approach extends from those areas where regimes have failed to replace the traditional order to those where treaty regimes now provide the governing rules. Traditional concepts only too often provide arguments for asserting claims and pressing advantages in the course of negotiating a treaty as well as in its subsequent interpretation. Thus a rhetoric has only too often been built into treaty regimes which inhibits them from furnishing more original approaches, from recognizing a wider range of equities, and from providing more inclusive precedents for international cooperation in the development and exploitation of a high seas fishery.

## D. The Continental Shelf Convention

Unlike the Convention on Fishing, the Continental Shelf Convention does not create procedures for departing from the traditional dichotomy between coastal states' exclusive and community inclusive claims. In reinforcing that dichotomy it represents an aspect of the contemporary march of state jurisdiction into the ocean. In addition, the encroachment of states into the ocean under the banner of the continental shelf doctrine during the 1940's and 1950's had become gener-

---

for the Seabed and Subsoil," 22 *Rutgers Law Review*, 1, 3–4 (1967) [hereinafter cited as Goldie, "Davy Jones's Locker"]; Goldie, "Exploitability Test" (fn. 2), 434; "Sedentary Fisheries" (fn. 42), 86–91.

[74] See, *e.g.*, for a tentative approach, Agreement for Co-operation in Dealing with Pollution of the North Sea by Oil, *done* June 9, 1969, entered into force August 9, 1969, [1969] Gr. Brit. T.S. No. 78 (Cmnd 4205); and International Convention Relating to Intervention on the High Seas in Cases of Oil Pollution Casualties, *done* November 29, 1969, not yet entered into force, IMCO Doc. LEG VII/3, Annex I.

ally accepted as developing international customary law by the time of its restatement in the convention. Although the Convention is now in force, issues regarding the degree to which it codifies custom are still important, especially as growing dissatisfaction with it may lead to alteration. Apart from the issue of customary law, the main problems it creates relate to the outer limits of states' continental shelf jurisdiction, the nature of the rights the doctrine confers, and the anomalous position of sedentary fisheries and of freedom of scientific research.

1. CUSTOMARY LAW

Almost since states first began to invoke the continental shelf doctrine to justify their extensions of jurisdiction into seabed areas beyond territorial waters, writers have expressed a fuzzy uncertainty as to the degree this state practice has created customary rules. As early as 1952 J. P. A. François could report:

> Les réponses de quelques Etats font preuve d'une certaine hésitation au sujet de la question *lex lata* ou *lex ferenda*. A mon avis, il faudrait faire une distinction: le principe de la "souveraineté" de l'Etat côtier sur le plateau continental, tout en maintenant la liberté de la mer surjacent pourrait être considéré déjàmaintenant comme *lex lata*, comme principe générale de droit, mais toutes les questions de détail se trouvent encore dans la phase de *lex ferenda*.[75]

Professor François' term, "principe générale de droit," in the context of this quotation is distinguishable from Article 38. 1.c of the International Court of Justice's Statute which provides a source of international law other than custom.[76] In addition, Professor François' term relates to a principle already existing as law, in contrast to those adverted in aleana c., which provide materials for judicial legislation [77] rather than direct attention to emerging state practice in the international arena. Indeed if Article 38.1 c also called for the classification of, for example, coastal states' continental shelf proclamations of jurisdiction it would merely be duplicating the function of aleana b. and creating confusion.

[75] International Law Association, *Report of the Forty-fifth Conference* (Lucerne 1952), 145. See also, International Law Commission, "Fourth Report on the Regime of the High Seas, the Continental Shelf and Related Subjects," 106, 108 U.N. Doc. No. A/CN.4/60 (François rapporteur) (mimeo. Feb. 19, 1953, [1953], 2 *Year Book of the International Law Commission* (1953), 1.

[76] For the possibility of combining customary international law with general principles of law as meant in art. 38.1.c of the I.C.J. Statute see Goldie, "Some Comments on Gidel's Views," 3 *University of Western Australia Law Review*, 108, 119–20 (1954); the same, "A Problem of Double Classification in International Law," 38 *British Year Book of International Law*, 218, 240–48 (1962).

[77] See J. Stone, *Legal Controls of International Conflict* (1954), 144–45.

After the Continental Shelf Convention came into force, the problem of knowing which rules had become customary became one of knowing which of the convention's provisions should be viewed as codifying preexisting custom, and hence generally binding, or, alternatively, which, lacking the authority of customary law, are binding by force of the agreement only. Recently the International Court of Justice, by eleven votes to six, held that while certain provisions of the convention did embody preexisting customary rules, others did not.[78] The majority relied on Article 12, Paragraph 1, of the convention to confirm their position; and to indicate which of its provisions could be regarded as embodying customary international law that paragraph provides: "At the time of signature, ratification or accession, any State may make reservations to articles of this Convention other than to articles 1 to 3 inclusive."

While this interpretation may well set at rest problems of indicating which clauses are, and which are not, the embodiment of customary international law, it creates or at least lends itself to a number of other difficulties.[79] In particular one may question the argument that because a treaty provision is not open to reservations it therefore codifies a rule of customary international law. As Judge Sorensen said:

[T]he faculty of making reservations to a treaty provision has no necessary connection with the question whether or not the provision can be considered as expressing a generally recognized rule of law. To substantiate this opinion it may be sufficient to point out that a number of reservations have been made to provisions of the Convention on the High Seas, although this Convention, according to its preamble, is "generally declaratory of established principles of international law." . . . The acceptance, whether tacit or express, of a reservation made by a contracting party does not have the effect of depriving the Convention as a whole, or the relevant article in particular, of its declaratory character. It only has the effect of establishing a special contractual relationship between the parties concerned within the general framework of the customary law embodied in the Convention. Provided the customary rule does not belong to the category of *jus cogens*, a special contractual relationship of this nature is not invalid as such. Consequently, there is no incompatibility between the faculty of making reservation to certain articles of the Convention on the Continental Shelf and the recog-

---

[78] North Sea Continental Shelf Cases, I.C.J. [1969], 3.

[79] For an indication of some of these see Goldie, "Sedentary Fisheries and the North Sea Continental Shelf Cases—A Paradox Revealed," 63 *American Journal of International Law*, 536 (1969) [hereinafter cited as Goldie, "Continental Shelf Cases"]. In addition to the problems in the text of that study, see also same, 538, fn. 6. The issue indicated in that footnote will be discussed briefly in sub-§3 here.

nition of that Convention or the particular articles as an expression of generally accepted rules of international law.[80]

If this argument is taken *e converso,* it becomes abundantly clear that the mere fact of falling within Article 12's prohibition against reservations should not be treated as a basis for bringing the provisions of the first three articles within the scope of customary international law.

This writer would suggest, as an alternative to the Court's view, that the difficult and delicate problem of determining which rules of the convention reflect customary international law should be best approached from Professor François' point of view, and those rules which reflect both general principles of law[81] and general practice should be viewed as having become customary law.

## 2. THE OUTER LIMITS OF THE CONTINENTAL SHELF

Article 1 of the Continental Shelf Convention provides the following definition:

> For the purpose of these articles, the term "continental shelf" is used as referring (*a*) to the seabed and subsoil of the submarine areas adjacent to the coast but outside the area of the territorial sea, to a depth of 200 metres or, beyond that limit, to where the depth of the superjacent waters admits of the exploitation of the natural resources of the said areas; (*b*) to the seabed and subsoil of similar submarine areas adjacent to the coasts of islands.

Clearly this Article provides two criteria for determining the adjacent[82] submarine zones over which a coastal state may exercise its continental

[80] I.C.J. [1969], 3, 248. For expressions of similar points of view, see: Vice-President Koretsky, same, 163–64; Judge Lachs, same, 223–25; Judge Morelli, same, 197–98, "[i]t goes without saying that a reservation has nothing to do with the customary rule as such," same, 198.

[81] See fn. 75 and the accompanying text. But note the articles cited in fn. 76.

[82] The concept of "adjacency" here includes both "contiguity"—i.e., where there may be intervening depths greater than 200 meters between the shelf regions claimed and the coastal state's dry-land area but a general shelf configuration—and "continuity" where there are no such deeper intervening regions. See A/CN.4/60, and note especially the submission of Special Rapporteur J. P. A. François at 104: "The Rapporteur feels that the expression 'contiguous to the coast' does not preclude submerged areas separated from the coast by a narrow channel of more than 200 metres depth from being considered in certain circumstances as 'contiguous to the coast.'"

The proposal in this paper is that, rather than extend the notion of the contiguous continental shelf to include submarine areas separated from the main mass of the legal continental shelf area "by a narrow channel," but geographically remaining a part of that mass, the term "adjacent continental shelf" be employed to describe such separated areas.

Finally "adjacency" should be distinguished from the concept of Continental Borderlands. In the latter there is an inherent notion of geographical unity. Although a geographical unity also exists, as a fact, in any given situation of

shelf claims—its "sovereign rights" [83] over exploration and exploitation activities—namely that of the depth of two hundred meters and that of exploitability. It is important to know whether this legal concept of the continental shelf was intended to have any reference to the geographical entity of the same name.

(a) *The Ocean Rim—And the Two Hundred Meter Isobath.* Several different definitions of the continental shelf in terms of the configuration of the ocean bottom, rather than man's capabilities to exploit it, have been suggested by various writers. For example the geographer Bourcart, in his leading treatise *Géographie du Fond des Mers, Etude du Relief des Oceans,*[84] has defined the world's continental shelves as the submarine land masses which lie beneath the shallow sea areas between the shores and the *rupture du pente,* or "break of slope," *i.e.,* the first substantial falloff, whatever the depth. Bourcart has also described this zone as the "ocean rim." [85]

Bourcart's concept is predicated on a vision of the continental abyss. Lying offshore, but underneath the oceans and between the shores and the depths, a shallow shoulder extends, in many places, for some distance seaward. This terminates in a steeper slope and plunges into the ocean depths. At the point where the slopes become steeper and pitch downward, Bourcart saw the terminating point of the continental shelf. Here definition reflects geographical reality. Other geographers, noting that, despite local variations,[86] in general the average depth of the break in slope tends roughly to approximate that of the 200 meter, or the 100 fathom, bathymetric contour line,[87] have proposed one or the

---

adjacency, it is not a necessary concept to its application. Adjacency, as described by François in the passage just quoted, rests upon propinquity rather than unity.

[83] Continental Shelf Convention, art. 2, para. 1.

[84] (1949).

[85] In submitting the view that the continental slopes can be more flexibly conceived of as the "ocean rim" Bourcart writes, at 126: "La rupture de pente séparant le Plateau du Rebord semble constante sur tout le pourtour des mers. Quelle que soit la reduction du Plateau, elle peut suffre à le définir."

[86] In terms of geographical reality the continental slopes may begin at any depth. In parts of the world the break in slope occurs at only 50 fathoms, in others not until the depth of 200, or even 500, fathoms is reached.

[87] For a treatment of these two isobaths, i.e., the 200 meter and the 100 fathom contour line as being approximately equivalent, see the International Law Commission's 1956 "Commentary to the Articles Concerning the Law of the Sea," U.N. Doc. A/3159 at 41, 2 *Year Book of the International Law Commission* [1956], 265, 296.

There may, however, be a considerable variation of lateral distance on the bed of a gently sloping continental shelf area. Since a meter is approximately 39.37 inches, it may be seen that the 100 fathoms isobath is less in depth than that of 200 meters. The former is merely 7200 inches while the latter is 7874 inches. The difference of 56 feet, 2 inches (or just over 2 feet more than 9 fathoms) means that the 100 fathom bathymetric contour line will always be within that of 200 meters on the seabed. Depending on the degree of the submarine slope down into the deeper zones, and

other of these two isobaths as the determinant of the shelf's outer limits. They seek to establish one (or even both as alternatives) of these lines as criteria having no reference to any physically-existing break in slope, but as possessing the considerable advantage of offering a standardized if abstract working definition. The 200 meter isobath has received, furthermore, the support of the International Committee on the Nomenclature of Ocean Bottom Features of the International Association of Physical Geography at Monaco (a member of the International Council of Scientific Unions).[88]

Following the majority of geographers, the International Law Commission proposed in 1956,[89] and the 1958 Geneva Conference on the Law of the Sea accepted, the 200 meter bathymetric contour line in preference to the physical break in slope as one of the two criteria [90] for determining the existence of the continental shelf for legal purposes. To a lawyer especially the 200 meter bathymetric contour line, the test in terms of a fixed depth, has considerable advantages over that of the break in slope supported by the geographical realists; it avoids the definitional and legal difficulties attendant upon this latter test's application in concrete situations which admit of contradictory

---

its general configuration, any equivalence laterally on the surface of the continental shelf or slope region between them can only form a very rough approximation indeed. Since that possible approximation of the isobaths is exceedingly rough, they should not be used interchangeably. In this chapter, following the drafts of the International Law Commission, and especially that of 1956, and the 1958 Geneva Convention on the Continental Shelf, reference will be made to the 200 meter bathymetric contour line or isobath in preference to the 100 fathom line.

[88] The International Hydrographic Bureau, Monaco, has now accepted the following definitions, *International Hydrographic Review*, XXXI (May 1954), 97: "*Continental Shelf*," "*Shelf Edge*" and "*Borderland*." The zone around the continent, extending from the low water line to the depth at which there is a marked increase of slope to greater depth. Where this increase occurs the term "Shelf Edge" is appropriate. Conventionally its edge is taken at 100 fathoms (or 200 meters) but instances are known where the increase of slope occurs at more than 200 or less than 65 fathoms. When the zone below the low water line is highly irregular, and includes depths well in excess of those typical of Continental Shelves, the term "*Continental Borderland*" is appropriate.

"*Continental Slope*." The declivity from the outer edge of the continental shelf or continental borderland into great depths.

"*Borderland Slope*." The declivity which marks the landward margin of the continental borderland.

"*Continental Terrace*." The zone around the continents, extending from the low water line to the base of the continental slope.

See also M. Mouton, "The Continental Shelf," 85 Hague Academy of International Law, *Recueil des Cours* (1954-1), 343, 348, fn. a.

[89] Article I of the Commission's 1951 Draft Articles adopted the test of exploitability for determining the extent of the "legal" continental shelf. For the addition of the 200 meter line criteria in later drafts, and in the Convention, and the complex drafting history of these two tests, see Goldie, "Davy Jones's Locker" (fn. 73), 7–8, fn. 12, and 58–65. See also fn. 92 below.

[90] The other test being the "exploitability test."

and competing, but equally supportable, theses of the line where the actual break in slope occurs, for this may involve wide areas, horizontally, when an "old" and gradually sloping ocean rim is involved.

(b) *The Shelf's Delimitation in Terms of "Exploitability."* Article 1 provides a second basis for advancing coastal states' claims over submarine regions beyond territorial waters and beyond the 200 meter isobath, namely "where the depth of the superjacent waters admits of the exploitation of the natural resources of the said areas." [91] This second criterion is frequently known as the "exploitability test." Can the two criteria or tests which that Article contains, namely the test of the 200 meter bathymetric contour line and that of exploitability, be taken in conjunction? The history of the exploitability test in the deliberations of both the International Law Commission and the 1958 United Nations Conference on the Law of the Sea at Geneva show that it was intended to have a function supplementary to that of the 200 meter isobath test. Originally it was intended to permit a coastal state to exercise sovereign rights over continental shelf activities carried out on the continental slopes and in the continental borderlands in continuation of activities begun, or connected with those carried out, in the zone between its territorial sea and the 200 meter bathymetric contour line.[92] The test was thus a practical measure, and one intended to give a practical solution to day-to-day problems which would arise if the 200 meter bathymetric contour line were accepted as a complete and final cut-off line.[93] Be that as it may, the exploitability test no

[91] *I.e.,* "Submarine areas adjacent to the coast but outside the area of the territorial sea."

[92] On the checkered history of this test in the International Law Commission's drafts see citations in fn. 89. On the exploitability test's evaluation by the International Law Commission in 1956 as a subordinate and supplementary concept see the Commission's Commentary on art. 67 (the Commission's version of what later became art. 1 of the Continental Shelf Convention) A/3159 at 41–42, 2 *Year Book of the International Law Commission* [1956], 296–97. For views on the status of the exploitability test at the 1958 United Nations Conference on the Law of the Sea at Geneva, see II *United Nations Conference on the Law of the Sea, Geneva, Official Record (Plenary Meetings)* (1958), 12–13, U.N. Doc. A/CONF. 13/38, Sales No.: 58.V.4, Vol. II (1958) [hereinafter cited as A/CONF.13/38], and VI, *United Nations Conference on the Law of the Sea, Geneva, Official Records (Fourth Committee)* (1958), U.N. Doc. A/CONF. 13/42, Sales No.: 58.V.4, Vol. VI at 2 (Gros), 4 (Cutteridge), 9 (Alvarez Aybar), 19 (Whiteman), 24 (Buu-Kinh), 26–27 (Gomez Robledo), 31–32 (Patey), 34 (Carbajal), 40 (Whiteman), 42 (Nikolic, Wershof, Jhirad); but for a contrary view see same, 5 (Rubio), 6 (Krispis), 10 (Caicedo Castilla), 16 (Barros), 17 (Rosenne), 25 (Garcia Amador), 29–30 (Carty), 33 (Ruiz Morena), 37 (Quarshie).

On possible contraposed evaluations of the clause inserting the test see, W. Burke, *Ocean Sciences, Technology and the Future Inter-National Law of the Sea,* Mershon National Security Program, Pamphlet Series No. 2 (1966), 54–55, and Goldie, "Davy Jones's Locker" (fn. 73), 11–14.

[93] For a discussion of the factors which have led to the expansion of the meaning of the exploitability test, despite the considerations which led to its adoption, see Goldie, "Davy Jones's Locker" (fn. 73), 2–4, 8–11, and esp. fn. 15.

longer has merely the supplementary function and subordinate status envisaged for it in 1958.

Admittedly, both of the tests for determining the submarine regions to be designated the "continental shelf" of the coastal state for the purpose of the Convention do not necessarily conform to offshore geographical reality—neither test is adequately congruent with the facts regarded as definitive of the physical shelf or pedestal—the geographers' notion of the part the continental shelf plays in the depiction of the world's oceanographic features. On the other hand, the definition of the continental shelf ascribable to a coastal state by reference to the 200 meter bathymetric contour line may, perhaps especially in the seclusion of the study and the abstracting atmosphere of the conference chamber and the courtroom, give an impression of having at least a tenuous connection with Bourcart's "ocean rim." Although in any given case the coincidence of the break in slope with the 200 meter bathymetric contour line will be accidental, and the geographical and the legal shelves could be widely divergent, yet many publicists and the International Law Commission have observed a general if perhaps abstract and theoretical congruence. On the other hand, no designation of a submarine region as a continental shelf defined in terms of the exploitability test need have any verisimilitude with the physical geography of the oceans' contours. That test is clearly quite independent of the geographical and oceanological concept of the pedestal upon which the land masses rest. Indeed, it is as free of any empirical connection with the ocean rim as are the much-criticized claims of exclusive competence over vast areas of the oceans which Chile, Ecuador and Peru, and other Central and South American states assert (the "CEP" claims [94]), and as indeterminate—although on different grounds.

[94] Insofar as the "bioma" and "eco-system" theories, which are usually deployed in support of the "CEP" claims (i.e., claims by Chile, Ecuador and Peru), may be viewed as involving continental shelf concepts at all, they have some relevance to the present discussion. See e.g., v, *United Nations Conference on the Law of the Sea, Geneva, Official Records (Third Committee)* (1958), 6–7 (Peru) U.N. Doc. A/CONF. 13/41, Sales No.: 58.V.4, Vol. v (1958); Chile, Ecuador and Peru Declaration on the Maritime Zone, Santiago, Chile Aug. 18, 1952. For a reproduction of this and the Parties' accompanying declarations and agreements (together constituting the "Santiago Declaration"), as well as subsequent and supplementary declarations and agreements, see B. MacChesney, *Situation Documents and Commentary on Recent Developments in the International Law of the Sea* (Naval War College Blue Book Series No. 51, 1956), 265–89, see also Stefan Bayitch, *Interamerican Law of Fisheries, an Introduction with Documents* (New York 1957), 42–47; Barry Auguste, *The Continental Shelf—the Practice and Policy of the Latin American States with Special Reference to Chile, Ecuador and Peru* (Geneva 1960), 187–92, and *U.S. Department of State, Santiago Negotiations on Fishery Conservation Problems* (1955). For a polemical defense of the CEP claims and policies, see e.g., Cisneros, "The 200 Mile Limit in the South Pacific: A New Position in International Law with a Human and Juridical Content," *American Bar Association Section of International and Comparative Law, 1964 Proceedings,* 56 (1965). Particular note should be taken of

The exploitability test's indeterminacy depends, no less than does that of the CEP claims, on factors which were not in the contemplation of the Law of the Sea Conference in 1958, when the participants agreed to its adoption. They saw it as ancillary to the 200 meter test.

Certain present-day developments, although mainly (but not entirely) in their experimental stages, have inspired some publicists to give a new significance to the exploitability test. This could become a means of validating ever-increasing encroachments upon the inclusive uses of the high sea. They argue, for example, that recent improvements

---

the criticism administered to the CEP claims in Kunz, "Continental Shelf and International Law: Confusion and Abuse," 50 *American Journal of International Law*, 828, 835–50 (1956).

Interestingly, as at the time of this writing, August 31, 1969, Chile, Ecuador, and Peru have only been able to add Costa Rica and El Salvador to the band of states asserting "CEP claims." While it is true that a number of states have added to their continental shelf claims, claims to the "epicontinental sea" (i.e., the volume of the waters superjacent upon a continental shelf) off their coasts, and to the superambient air above that "sea," this type of claim is distinguishable from the CEP type. So far the five "CEP countries" have not been successful in persuading other Latin American states to assert specifically CEP claims to adjacent seas. Nor has the Organization of American States adopted this position as that of the collectivity of Western Hemisphere nations. Indeed it has not, as a body, recognized state claims to epicontinental seas as valid. Thus, for example, at the Inter-American Specialized Conference on "Conservation of Natural Resources: The Continental Shelf and Marine Waters," Ciudad Trujillo, Dominican Republic, March 15–28, 1956, see the *Final Act* of the Conference, *Organization of American States Conferences & Organizations Series*, Number 50, Doc. No. 34. 1-E-5514 (1956), the CEP states were unable to gain the Conference's agreement to the "bioma" and "eco-system" theories, or to declare that either the waters above a continental shelf region, or waters extending from the shores of a coastal state for some such distances as that of at least 200 sea miles appertain to the coastal state either on the basis of the continental shelf doctrine or on that of some other theory. The Conference observed (in Resolution I of the Conference, the "Resolution of Ciudad Trujillo," *Final Act*, 13–14) that:

2. Agreement does not exist among the states here represented with respect to the juridical régime of the waters which cover the said submarine areas. . . .
6. Agreement does not exist among the states represented at this Conference either with respect to the nature and scope of the special interest of the coastal state, or as to how the economic and social factors which such state or other interested states may invoke should be taken into account in evaluating the purpose of conservation programs. . . .
Therefore, this Conference does not express an opinion concerning the positions of the various participating states on the matters on which agreement has not been reached. . . .

For the views of inter-American legal experts see: Inter-American Council of Jurists, "Resolution XIII, Principles of Mexico on the Juridical Regime of the Sea, C: Conservation of the Living Resources of the High Seas," *Final Act of the Third Meeting*, XXXVII, Doc. No. CIJ-29 (English) (1956), for comments of governments see same, 50–59; Inter-American Juridical Committee, *Opinion on the Breadth of the Territorial Sea*, OAS Official Doc. OEA/Ser. I/VI.2 (English CIJ-80) (1966), 24–42.

For a general analysis and review, together with some constructive proposals of the CEP legal dilemmas and problems, see Goldie, "Fisheries Management" (fn. 15), 31–38, 41–51.

in depth- and direction-drilling for oil and gas, the "Glomar Challenger's" discoveries, Captain Jacques-Yves Cousteau's I, II, and III, the United States Navy's Sea-Lab III, the development of the new submersibles by the aerospace industry, Edwin Link's Man-in-Sea Project, and the growing conviction that there is a beckoning wealth of mineral nodules on the surface of the seabed (as well as subsoil minerals including petroleums existing at great depths on and under the ocean floor), have all given, in recent times, a new importance to the exploitability test—an importance which could eclipse that of the 200 meter bathymetric contour line.

Emerging expectations that science and technology are about to usher mankind into "[a] new environment of golden promise"[95] are quickening interest in either defining the outer extent of what the exploitability test allows in terms of settled criteria, or redefining the shelf in terms of depth or, perhaps, maximum distance from the coast. Many of the proposed exegetics on the exploitability test have been quite thoroughly investigated already and will not be the subject of further review here.[96] In addition, the planning needs among transnational technostructures have led to a public contention as to the "meaning" of the exploitability test as it is presented in Article 1 of the Continental Shelf Convention.[97] This has become as recondite and formal as the theological debates of the third and fourth centuries A.D., when schism over words helped to mask rivalries among the successors to the Roman Empire competing for booty.

The outcome of a discussion of the various interpretations[98] of the exploitability test is that there are no adequate assurances that it will not be used to justify extravagant shade-claims of sovereignty over the seabed and subsoil. While it is true that such claims may never extend, as Professor Georges Scelle[99] feared they might, out to a median line or *Thalweg* in the deep oceans, yet it is equally true that coastal states seem to be accelerating the march of their offshore claims out into the oceans. It is also clear that this march is today being spurred by the exploitability test's obscurity of meaning.

[95] For a timely and valuable airing of this subject, see L. Henkin, "International Law and 'the Interests'; The Law of the Seabed," 63 *American Journal of International Law,* 504 (1969).

[96] See, e.g., Goldie, "Davy Jones's Locker" (fn. 73), 8–21.

[97] For a further development in this debate see below, subsection (c) of this section. For an indication of some of the major interests in play, generally, in the complex contention over exclusive and inclusive maritime claims see IV below. See also Goldie, "Davy Jones's Locker" (fn. 73), 8–21.

[98] For a critical and comparative appraisal of the main interpretations of the exploitability test which have been offered see Goldie, "Davy Jones's Locker" (fn. 73), 8–21.

[99] G. Scelle, "Plateau Continental et Droit International," 59 *Revue Générale de Droit International Public,* 5 (1955).

*(c) The Intermediate Zone.* The contention which now exists between those who advocate a "broad" continental shelf and those advancing a "narrow" one [100] has given rise to the proposal of a third position, namely that of the "intermediate zone."

Some writers who favor the narrow continental shelf have suggested what would appear to be a compromise between their position and that of the broad-shelf advocates. Following these writers, the Commission on Marine Science, Engineering, and Resources, and its International Panel [101] have proposed the definition and demarcation of an "Intermediate Zone." In brief, this is to be defined as a zone engrossing the areas beyond the two hundred meter isobath which the broad-shelf advocates claim should be included in the coastal state's zone of exclusive rights under the continental shelf regime. It should perhaps include the "Continental Borderlands" or "Continental Terraces" [102] of the seabed. In order to assure it a relatively fixed and certain definition, the International Panel has suggested the following lines of demarcation (the practicality of which I do question): "[I]t is recommended that the outer limits of the intermediate zone be defined in terms of the 2,500 meter isobath or 100 nautical miles from the baselines for measuring the breadth of the territorial sea, whichever alternative gives the coastal State the greater submarine area for the purposes for which the intermediate zone is created." [103]

In this area only the coastal state or its licensees, "which may or may not be its nationals," [104] are to be "authorized to explore or exploit the mineral resources of the intermediate zone." [105] On the other hand, that zone is not to be permitted to fall within the scope of coastal states' continental shelves. It must always remain within the international regime for deep-ocean mining.[106]

But the Commission's selection of the 2500 meter isobath as providing the outer limit of the intermediate zone is questionable. The concept of the intermediate zone has been offered by the supporters of

[100] The "broad" continental shelf may be defined as the extension of the coastal states' exclusive continental shelf jurisdiction out to the "continental rise" or "toe" of the slopes where the continental pedestal joins the abyssal plains. The "narrow" continental shelf may be defined as the region of coastal states' exclusive continental shelf jurisdiction out to, and terminating at, the 200 meter bathymetric contour line. For a discussion and evaluation of the "broad" and "narrow" continental shelf theories respectively, see L. Henkin, *Law for the Sea's Mineral Resources* (ISHA Monograph No. 1, 1968), 37–41, 45–46.

[101] *Panel Reports* (fn. 5), VIII-34–35, *Our Nation and the Sea* (fn. 5), 151. See also Henkin (fn. 100), 46–48.

[102] See fn. 88.

[103] III, *Panel Reports* (fn. 5), VII-34–35.

[104] Same, VII-35.

[105] Same.

[106] For an outline of the Commission's recommended regime for deep-ocean mining see same, VIII-35–44, and *Our Nation and the Sea* (fn. 5), 146–51.

the narrow shelf as a middle and mediating position between the view they profess and that of the wide-shelf advocates. That isobath, one may presume, is put forward as indicating the outer limits of the broad continental shelf, as representing the "true" geological or topographical "boundary" on the sea floor between the crust of the deep ocean basins and the continental land masses. This geological "boundary" is said to exist as an empirical fact. One may be confident, therefore, that it does not exist in all places at exactly the 2500 meter isobath.[107]

Despite the intermediate zone's attractiveness as a compromise between the wide shelf and the narrow shelf parties, I suggest that it has some fatal flaws. First, in practice there might well develop contests between coastal states and the international regime as to the modalities of control. Whereas mining activities in the zone would be regulated by the international authority, coastal states may well demand a further say in what goes on in the zones fronting upon their continental shelves. This could be asserted by imposing conditions in the licenses they grant. If the coastal states' demands for a dominating position become intense, the conditions they stipulate for granting their licenses might well become of greater practical importance than the international regime's regulations. This latter authority might, indeed, subside into a residual revenue-collecting regulatory agency. The chances of this possibility becoming an eventuality are enhanced when one recalls how contemporary events in maritime law and policy reflect the greater pressure and authority of exclusive state claims over international claims.[108]

Since it is conceived of as a compromise, the intermediate zone may in effect be merely a temporizing and temporary legal institution, ready and poised to be merged into whichever of the two adjoining regimes may come to exercise the stronger attraction. On this count it may be seen as no more than a compromise of the moment.

In place of an intermediate zone, *tout court,* there is the proposal[109] that a seabed zone with similar geographical boundaries and dimensions to those of that proposed zone be marked out. But in place of one institutional concept, which may not be feasible in many parts of

[107] Compare Committee on Deep Sea Mineral Resources of the American Branch of the International Law Association, Interim Report, x (1968) [hereinafter cited as American Branch Report] with Department of the Interior, National Petroleum Council, *Petroleum Resources under the Ocean Floor* (Washington 1969), 67. Note should be taken that the American Branch of the International Law Association's "Interim Report" was published on July 8, 1968, but that no further or final report has been published as of the date of this writing, namely December 28, 1969. These two documents are the main vehicles of the "wide shelf" advocates.

[108] For a discussion of this process see Goldie, "Davy Jones's Locker" (fn. 73), 13.

[109] See Goldie, "Where is the Continental Shelf's Outer Boundary?" to be published in 1 *Journal of Maritime Law and Commerce.*

the world, a number of variants could be developed to suit more closely the political geography and community histories of various regions and communities.

While the geographical areas of the intermediate zones of, for example, the greater part of such countries as Australia, Canada, the Soviet Union, or the United States might well be absorbed into those countries' exclusive continental shelves, in other areas, for example off the Caribbean submarine slopes of Central America or the Gulf Coast of the United States, on the northern continental borderlands and slopes of the North Sea bed, or on the slopes eastward of the Strait of Hormuz, political and economic factors militate against individual countries gaining exclusive rights over "broad shelves." In such regions submarine areas beyond the "narrow" continental shelf should be regulated by means of a managerial regime of conciliation and/or cooperation [110] established by all the states of the region.

Finally, in other areas, where the facts of political and physical geography could, *ceteris paribus,* lend the offshore zones beyond the 200 meter bathymetric contour line to the regional managerial regime blueprint, but where local internal political instability, territorial rivalries, irredentism, or long-lived hatreds (for example, perhaps, off West Africa, or the Horn of Africa) preclude the formation of such a regime, the zone should be administered under the international regime to be established to regulate the resources of the deep-ocean bed. Such a take-over should not be accomplished, however, until a local regime of managerial cooperation had been tried. Furthermore, it should be conducted as a trust for the countries (as a group) which have been unable to combine effectively to administer the submarine areas in terms of a regime of administrative or managerial conciliation.

Thus, in place of the Commission's single blueprint of its intermediate zone, there should be a variety of them, each adapted to the physical, economic, and political realities of its offshore region and its mainland. These blueprints need not be exact replicas of the three kinds I have just outlined. But all of them should have in common the capability of balancing the region's inclusive and exclusive claims so as to achieve both maximum political stability and economic return with the minimum of friction.

A criticism of this proposal questions whether it is marketable in the present state of the world. Would it be acceptable to developing countries? At first blush it would seem to favor the "have" countries, as many large "have" states would get still more submarine resources under their exclusive control, while many "have-not" states (for ex-

---

[110] For an introduction to managerial conciliation or cooperation regimes see Goldie, "Fisheries Management" (fn. 15), 17–18, 45–51.

ample those in Central America and the Caribbean) would not get as much. A persuasive reply would point out, in the first place, that small states wouldn't get much under the Stratton Commission's proposals either, and landlocked states would get nothing. Furthermore the Stratton Commission's intermediate zone is more likely to assure to small coastal states the possibility of acquiring rights to future boundary disputes than it is to assure them additional resources in economic quantities. Second, it could be pointed out that, under the present proposals, not only "have" states would enjoy valuable increments to their offshore resources, but also a number of large and medium-sized "have-not" countries, for example Nigeria, Brazil, India, Argentina, the Federation of Malaysia, and Indonesia would also stand to gain.

Third, one may further support the present proposals by indicating that the formation and dissolution of federal polities in many parts of the world show that it is not impossible for a "Balkanized" region to federate, and thereby become, possibly, a more stable factor in international politics. If one takes such polities as Canada and the United States as examples, it is possible to point out that federations can enjoy the benefits of extensive offshore areas because they manage to hold together, despite internal centrifugal forces and dissensions. Hence, it may be possible to view the advantages these suggestions offer to larger polities as providing added inducements, under propitious conditions offshore, for the formation of new federations. One example may suffice: concern about a possible failure of these proposals to make adequate provisions for the Central American States would not be so pressing if they were to federate, or if the Republic of Grand Colombia could be reestablished. In brief, this blueprint may assist in inhibiting "Balkanization" and even reverse the trend. This same argument can be applied, *mutatis mutandis,* to many other Balkanized regions.

Finally, these proposals were intended to bestow the advantages of federation upon the regulation of exploring and exploiting the seabed and subsoil resources of offshore zones beyond the two hundred meter isobath when the coastal states are in no mood to federate. A supranational managerial regime may offer the means of removing some of the more deleterious results of that unhappy political condition from the administration of offshore resources beyond the two hundred meter isobath. Furthermore the landlocked states of the region could also participate.

3. THE RIGHTS CONFERRED

(a) *Opinions of the Learned.* A number of writers and speakers are constantly referring to countries' offshore continental shelf rights as being their "mineral estate"; in different ways they employ expressions which assume that doctrine and convention, alike, confer territorial rights or rights which are more easily assimilable under that category than any other. This error has been compounded by the formulation of the Outer Continental Shelf Lands Act of 1953.[111] The general contours of the territorial fallacy have already been exposed in the discussion of the contiguous zone. Accordingly, the more general points there will not be repeated. They will merely be specifically applied in the discussion which follows. The scope, and the limits, of the rights which the convention, as well as the continental shelf doctrine, conferred were plotted in Article 2, paragraph 1. It is as follows: "The coastal State exercises over the continental shelf sovereign rights for the purpose of exploring it and exploiting its natural resources."

This formula, apart from substituting the words "jurisdiction and control" (not "sovereignty," it should be noted), follows the International Law Commission's 1951 draft Article 2. Gidel has commented as follows on that draft article:

> It was impossible to frame a more plain spoken—indeed outspoken—rejection by the International Law Commission of the whole notion of a general power of control and jurisdiction exercisable by a coastal State over the extra territorial continental shelf; it "conceded" that control and jurisdiction only for limited and specified purposes. To emphasize this point, para. 7 of the Commentary on Art. 2 once more sets out the limitations on the powers which the Commission was prepared to concede to the coastal State in relation to the continental shelf.[112]

It is submitted that, like coastal states' rights in their contiguous zones, the sovereign rights they enjoy in continental shelf areas are also separate and restrictively defined specific competences.[113] As I have written elsewhere:

> Thus the limitation of the ambit of the power remains. Power is specialized and is limited to particular purposes. In addition, Article 3 of the 1951 and 1953 drafts remains the same. It makes a formal reservation of the superjacent waters from the exercise of the privilege. But Article 3, if taken alone, can effect only a formal compromise in the conflict of interests involved in contradictions between the freedom of the high seas on the one hand, and the continental shelf doctrine on the other.[114]

111 67 Stat. 462, 43 U.S.C. §§1331-43 (1964). See also Goldie, "The Exploitability Test" (fn. 2), 434–36 and Appendix I.

112 Gidel, "Continental Shelf" (fn. 46), 100.

113 See e.g., McDougal and Burke (fn. 47), 82, fn. 182.

114 Goldie, "Some Comments on Gidel's Views" (fn. 76), 108, 113.

And:

> The International Law Commission considers that the term to describe the rights of coastal States should be "sovereign rights" rather than "jurisdiction and control" or "rights of sovereignty." . . . The term chosen as intended to import, on the one hand, the completeness of the powers of the coastal State necessary for and connected with the exploration and the exploitation of the natural resources of the continental shelf, and, on the other, the limitation of the object of the right to the natural resources of the seabed and subsoil, excluding such miscellaneous matters as wrecked ships, sunken bullion, free navigation on the high seas and fishing or swimming and bottom (demersal) fish.[115]

Finally, it is regretted that a widespread tendency is emerging which seeks to construe *dicta* by the majority of the International Court of Justice in the *North Sea Continental Shelf Cases* in the hope that judgment can be made to shed some respectability upon the territorial fallacy.[116]

The foregoing interpretation, greatly limiting the scope of the coastal state's range of claimable authority, would support the view that such activities as three-dimension explorations and research activities in the volume of the waters above the shelf, including those having military relevances, could be justified as pertaining to the freedom of the sea. Similarly, it would hold that all activities on the seabed, not actually derogating from, or interfering with, the coastal state's exclusive rights over exploring for and exploiting the shelf's mineral and sedentary fishery [117] resources, are beyond the reach of the coastal state's jurisdiction.

(b) *Communis Error Facit Jus?* The most highly qualified of the scholars and publicists who pioneered the early formulations of the continental shelf doctrine, whose early writings foreshadowed much of the form it received at the hands of the International Law Commission, and whose professional standing lent it much of the weight needed for acceptance, saw it as having a limited and specialized jurisdictional scope. On the other hand, early practice, some of which antedated the initial scholarly work, was not so clear-cut. In 1942 the United Kingdom's Order in Council,[118] which was promulgated pur-

---

[115] Goldie, "Davy Jones's Locker" (fn. 73), 17 (footnotes omitted). See also III, *Panel Reports* (fn. 5), VIII-16.

[116] See *I.C.J.* [1969], 3, 37.

[117] As to the indeterminacy of this concept, however, see sub-§5 of this Section, and the studies cited there.

[118] Trinidad and Tobago Submarine Areas of the Gulf of Paria (Annexation) Order in Council [1942], 1 Stat. R&O 919, 1 *Laws and Regulations of the Regime of the High Seas (United Nations Legislative Series)*, 44 U.N. Doc. ST/LEG/Ser. B/1, Sales No.: 1951.V.2 (1951).

suant to the Gulf of Paria Treaty,[119] purported to annex the affected submarine areas to the then Colony of Trinidad and Tobago. As the Order had been made under the authority of the Colonial Boundaries Act, 1895,[120] it asserted that the Colony's "boundaries" had been "extended." There is a paradox in the fact that, although she has long been a foremost champion of the freedom of the seas, Great Britain has, in the context of continental-shelf proclamations taking effect in non-European waters, consistently followed the Colonial Boundaries Act formula. This has been applied on behalf of both territories which fall within the ambit of that statute,[121] and noncolonial states for whose international relations she assumed responsibility.[122] On the other hand, her own North Sea claims are merely in terms of "sovereign rights." [123] In addition to these two categories of rights asserted by one country at different times and regarding different regions, states have laid claim to a wide variety of rights.[124] Indeed, counting in the former British Colonies, the states which have asserted full sovereignty

[119] Treaty Relating to the Submarine Areas of the Gulf of Paria Between Great Britain and Venezuela, signed Feb. 26, 1942, 205 L.N.T.S., 121, [1942], Great Britain T.S. No. 10 (Cmd. No. 6400).

[120] 58 and 59 Vict. c. 34.

[121] For example:

(a) Bahamas: *Bahamas (Alterations to Boundaries) Order in Council* (Made under the *Colonial Boundaries Act*), 1895, 58 and 59 Vict. c. 34) Statutory Instruments, 1948, No. 2574. See also *Petroleum Act*, Bahamas Acts No. 1 of 1945;

(b) British Honduras: *British Honduras (Alteration of Boundaries) Order in Council* (Made under the *Colonial Boundaries Act* 1895, 58 and 59 Vict. c. 34) Statutory Instruments No. 56 of 1949;

(c) Falkland Islands: *Falkland Islands (Continental Shelf) Order in Council* (Made under the *Colonial Boundaries Act*, 1895, 58 and 59 Vict. c. 34), Statutory Instruments, 1948, No. 2100;

(d) Jamaica: *Jamaica (Alteration of Boundaries) Order in Council* (Made under the *Colonial Boundaries Act*, 1895, 58 and 59 Vict. c. 34) Statutory Instruments 48, No. 3574;

(e) North Borneo: *North Borneo (Alteration of Boundaries) Order in Council,* June 24, 1954 (Made under the *Colonial Boundaries Act*, 1895, 58 and 59 Vict. c. 34) Statutory Instruments 1954, No. 838.

(f) Trinidad and Tobago: *Trinidad and Tobago Submarine Areas of the Gulf of Paria (Annexation) Order* (1942), 1, Statutory Rules and Orders 919, and see *Submarine (Oil Mining) Regulations* (Government Notice No. 87 of 1945).

[122] See, e.g., the following Proclamations made by Great Britain on behalf of Arab States under her protection. Each Proclamation was entitled "Proclamation with respect to the sea-bed and subsoil of the high seas of the Persian Gulf," these were, Abu Dhabi, June 10, 1949; Ajman, June 20, 1949; Bahrein, June 5, 1949; Dubai, June 14, 1949; Kuwait, June 12, 1949; Qatar, June 8, 1949; Ras el Khaimad, June 17, 1949; Sharjah, June 16, 1949; Umm al Taiwan, June 20, 1949 (for a discussion of the rights of the Sheikdoms and of their concessionaires, see *Abu Dhabi Oil Arbitration Award* by Lord Asquith of Bishopstone (1952), 1 *Int. L. Q.*, 247).

[123] See long title to the Continental Shelf Act 1964, 1964 c. 29. See also same, §1(1).

[124] For an illustrative classification of these claims up to the time of writing that study, see Goldie, "Australia's Continental Shelf: Legislation and Proclamations," 3 *International and Comparative Law Quarterly*, 535, 552–54 (1954) [hereinafter cited as Goldie, "Australia's Continental Shelf"].

over their adjacent continental shelves (and including those which extend their claims to the superincumbent sea and air space, the "epicontinental sea") exceed in number those which, like the United States, merely assert a claim to "jurisdiction and control," or, like Great Britain with respect to the North Sea zones appertaining to her, follow the formula of Article 2, paragraph 1 of the Continental Shelf Convention.

Propelled by the increasing uses of the shelf, many of which may fall outside the scope of the coastal states' authority on a strict reading of the convention, and induced by the growing acceptance by the international community and by publicists of an increasing assimilation of continental shelf rights to territorial rather than extraterritorial concepts, a "common error" may eventually come to give an accumulating authority to the notion that, at least landward of the two hundred meter bathymetric contour line coastal states are justified in exerting plenary power over the seabed and subsoil. Because of its contingent nature, the exploitability test is unable to vest sovereignty over areas not at present exploited.[125] Beyond the two hundred meter line coastal states' competences should, therefore, remain specialized and limited.[126]

It is still too early to assert dogmatically that either theory, namely that which complies with the original concept enunciated by the doctrine's early framers, or that which recognized coastal states' enjoyment of plenary sovereignty over the extent of the shelf measured in terms of depth (and excluding the waters above it), has emerged as definitive. On the other hand, the preponderance of contemporary practice would tend to point to the latter as the more likely victor. This, in turn, may call for the reinterpretation of the competences the doctrine confers on coastal states in the light of *communis error facit jus*.

### 4. THE PROBLEM OF ADJACENT AND OPPOSITE STATES

When it held, in the *North Sea Continental Shelf Cases*,[127] that the equidistance rule, as formulated in Article 6 of the Continental Shelf Convention, was not a rule of customary international law, the International Court of Justice sent the parties back to the negotiating table. In holding as they did, the majority removed one premise of the Dutch and Danish bargaining counters. Those countries had simply negotiated on the footing that the equidistance rule provided a fall-back position from which they could not be budged unless they were offered sufficiently attractive alternatives. In removing the equidistance crutch

[125] See above, sub-§C 2(b).
[126] See, Goldie, "Davy Jones's Locker" (fn. 73), 17. See also III *Panel Reports* (fn. 5), VIII-16.
[127] See fn. 58.

from Denmark and the Netherlands, and in providing guidelines,[128] the Court, laudably, was seeking to force the parties to negotiate genuinely. This may well develop into an important doctrine in international law.

## 5. SCIENTIFIC RESEARCH

Scientific research has been distinguished from both economic exploration and military testing.[129] Be that as it may, its present protection by the relevant provisions of the Continental Shelf Convention is inadequate. The relevant paragraphs of Article 5 state that:

1. The exploration of the continental shelf and the exploitation of its natural resources must not result in any unjustifiable interference with navigation, fishing or the conservation of the living resources of the sea, nor result in any interference with fundamental oceanographic or other scientific research carried out with the intention of open publication.

[128] The Court's guidelines were as follows:
(A) the use of the equidistance method of delimitation not being obligatory as between the Parties; and
(B) there being no other single method of delimitation the use of which is in all circumstances obligatory;
(C) the principles and rules of international law applicable to the delimitation as between the Parties of the areas of the continental shelf in the North Sea which appertain to each of them beyond the partial boundary determined by the agreements of 1 December 1964 and 9 June 1965, respectively, are as follows:
   (1) delimitation is to be effected by agreement in accordance with equitable principles, and taking account of all the relevant circumstances, in such a way as to leave as much as possible to each Party all those parts of the continental shelf that constitutes a natural prolongation of its land territory into and under the sea, without encroachment on the natural prolongation of the land territory of the other;
   (2) if, in the application of the preceding sub-paragraph, the delimitation leaves to the Parties areas that overlap, these are to be divided between them in agreed proportions or, failing agreement, equally, unless they decide on a régime of joint jurisdiction, user, or exploitation for the zones of overlap or any part of them;
(D) In the course of the negotiations, the factors to be taken into account are to include:
   (1) the general configuration of the coasts of the Parties, as well as the presence of any special or unusual features;
   (2) so far as known or readily ascertainable, the physical and geological structure, and natural resources, of the continental shelf areas involved;
   (3) the element of a reasonable degree of proportionality, which a delimitation carried out in accordance with equitable principles ought to bring about between the extent of the continental shelf areas appertaining to the coastal State and the length of its coast measured in the general direction of the coastline, account being taken for this purpose of the effects, actual or prospective, of any other continental shelf delimitations between adjacent States in the same region.
[1969] I.C.J. 4, 53–54.
[129] See fns. 30–32 and the accompanying text.

And:

> 8. The consent of the coastal state shall be obtained in respect of any research concerning the continental shelf and undertaken there. Nevertheless, the coastal state shall not normally withhold its consent if the request is submitted by a qualified institution with a view to purely scientific research into the physical or biological characteristics of the continental shelf, subject to the proviso that the coastal state shall have the right, if it so desires, to participate or to be represented in the research, and that in any event the results shall be published.

The significance of the inclusion of the qualifier "unjustified" in paragraph 1's formulation in terms of navigation and fishing, and the omission of that significant qualifying adjective from that paragraph's clause relating to scientific research should be reviewed in the light of paragraph 8. The 1958 United Nations Conference on the Law of the Sea at Geneva missed the opportunity of declaring a "freedom of research, experiment and exploration" [130] as a freedom of the high seas, while drafting either the Convention on the High Seas [131] (Article 2 of which enunciated a selection of such freedoms) or the Convention on the Continental Shelf. This omission is to be regretted, especially since the United Kingdom had, in 1955–56,[132] advocated such a freedom as a fifth freedom of the high seas, to be inserted in Article 2 of the International Law Commission's 1955 Draft Articles on the Regime of the High Seas (later Article 27 of the Commission's 1956 Articles concerning the Law of the Sea [133] and, with significant changes, Article 2 of the Convention on the High Seas). The International Law Commission, although composed of men of learning and of savants, did not see fit to insert into any of its drafts for a Continental Shelf Convention a protection of the preexisting freedom of scientific research at the time it was formulating the terms of the expansion of states' authority over the seabed and subsoil of the continental shelf—thereby rendering the freedom of scientific research in that region more precarious than before. The protections now in Article 5 of the Convention on the Continental Shelf, limited as they are, were added at the

---

[130] Quoted from United Kingdom's Reply (transmitted by a Note Verbale dated March 15, 1956, from the United Kingdom Delegation to the U.N.), 2 *Year Book of the International Law Commission* [1956], 80, U.N. Doc. A/CN.4/99/Add. 1 (1956) suggesting the addition of a fifth item to the freedom of the seas article (art. 2) of the Commission's 1955 Provisional Articles on the Regime of the High Seas, International Law Commission, "Report Covering the Work of its Seventh Session," 10, U.N. GAOR, Supp. No. 9 at 2, 3, 2 *Year Book of the International Law Commission* [1955], 19, 21, U.N. Doc. A/2934 (1955).

[131] *Done.* April 29, 1958, [1962] 2, U.S.T. 2312, T.I.A.S. No. 5200, 450 U.N.T.S. 82 [1962].

[132] See fn. 111 and the accompanying text. See also 1 *Year Book of the International Law Commission* [1956], 29–32.

[133] 2 *Year Book of the International Law Commission* [1956], 253, 259.

1958 United Nations Conference on the Law of the Sea at Geneva as a result of discussions in the Fourth Committee of that conference,[134] a stylistic change in the Drafting Committee,[135] and the agreement of the 9th Plenary Meeting of the Conference.[136] Apart from noting that the Fourth Committee's deliberations point to a search for a balance between the interests of scientific research and the claims of coastal states to exercise discretionary authority and control over their contiguous and adjacent continental shelves, the *travaux préparatoires* are of little assistance in determining the intended scope of the freedom to engage in scientific research.

The difference in formulation, in paragraph 1 of Article 5 between the protection to be accorded to "fundamental oceanographic or other scientific research" and that to be accorded to "navigation, fishing and the conservation of the living resources of the sea," call for elucidation. For, while the latter (the economic) group of activities are to be protected only from "unjustifiable" interference, scientific work which is intended to culminate in "open publication" appears to be protected from all interference—the qualifying adjective "unjustified" having been dropped from interference with this latter class of activities. Does this mean that Article 5, paragraph 1, is mandatory and ambulatory, in that all forms of continental shelf exploration and exploitation activity which might, conceivably, interfere with the types of scientific research [137] falling within the clause are prohibited? Or does it merely seek to protect scientific work actually to be undertaken, or in the process of being conducted, *in situ?* An affirmative answer to the first question would lead to the stultification of many business-oriented exploration and exploitation activities, because they might possibly impair future scientific research. An affirmative response to the second question might lead to the complete foreclosure of the interests of possible future research. Clearly neither of these answers was contemplated by the draftsmen.

Common sense tells us that although paragraph 1 is silent as to whether certain exploration and exploitation activities may set limits to the freedom of scientific research, that freedom is not altogether without those restraints which would enable exploration and exploitation activities to be reasonably carried on. To construe the paragraph as excluding all interference, even those interferences which might

---

134 A/CONF. 13/42 (fn. 92), 81–91, 119–20.

135 A/CONF. 13/38 (fn. 92), 15. And see First Report of the Drafting Committee Articles and Final Clauses Adopted by the Fourth Committee (U.N. Doc. A/CONF. 13/L.13) (mimeo, April 21, 1958), A/CONF. 13/38 at 92–93.

136 A/CONF. 13/38 (fn. 92), 15.

137 The question of the classes of scientific research activities which are within these protections is also open ended. Compare e.g., the observations of Sorensen, A/CONF. 13/42 (fn. 92), 82, with Schaeffer, same, 89. See also 82 (Mouton), 83 (Ranukusomo), 84 (Sangkhadul) and 87 (Rouhani).

arise from necessity, or from the claims of higher social values specifically operating in an individual context, would make the freedom of scientific research into a tyrant governing all other uses of the resources of the world's continental shelves. But if exploration and exploitation activities may, in special circumstances, also justifiably interfere with scientific research, one should ask why, then, was the modifying adjective "unjustifiable" excluded from the description of the prohibited interferences with scientific research, but included in that of the prohibited interferences with navigation, fishing, and the conservation of the living resources of the sea? This writer would suggest that the answer lies in the fact that if the term "unjustifiable" were used in the two distinct contexts of scientific research and economic activity without any further modifications, then there would be a danger that governments and international agencies might feel impelled to give both uses the same meaning and operation. On the other hand, the justifications of an interference with navigation and fishing are very different from those which would uphold an interference with scientific research. Thus, the submission here is that the omission of the term "unjustifiable" from the clause relating to the freedom of scientific research thereby indicates that the continental shelf exploration and exploitation activities which should be permitted to interfere with this freedom must be justified by entirely different criteria from those permitting interference with navigation, fishing, and the conservation of the living resources of the sea.

Paragraph 8 formulates certain duties which reciprocally bind coastal states and those individuals and institutions that engage in the scientific research activities indicated by the article; but clearly its main thrust is the protection of the "sovereign rights"—the discretionary powers—of coastal states. Hence it would appear that the only limitations on those states' authority to grant or withhold consent at will is the provision that their consent is not to be "normally" withheld. The limits for applying this important modifying adverb "normally" are not indicated. While it remains in the paragraph it provides a temptation for coastal states which may be uncertain as to the policies they should apply or bureaucratically suspicious of research plans to treat many genuine applications for the conduct of original research as outside the norm. Individual bona fide scientific projects could, when the claims are considered, be diverted, modified, and even frustrated by states complying with the letter of paragraph 8. This writer's suggestion is, therefore, that there should be, in addition to the obligations of "not normally withholding . . . consent" on the part of the coastal state, the provision of a positive duty of supporting, or at least of respecting, as a freedom of the seas, bona fide scientific researches carried out on that state's contiguous and adjacent shelves, and, in addition, of restraining its nationals from interfering with those researches. The paragraph should, accordingly, include positive obligations of protection and assistance, and of the recognition of a general freedom of research, experiment, and exploration on the continental shelf. On the other hand, these obligations, and this freedom, should be formulated so as not to stultify the coastal state's essential requirements of survival. Nor should the freedom of scientific research be permitted to expose the coastal state helplessly to espionage. Finally, a state should, when issuing exploration or exploitation licenses with respect to its continental shelf, bear in mind their effect on existing, impending, or even planned research (when known to that state's officials) and make both noninterference with the research activity, and nondestruction (from the researchers' point of view) of its subject matter, a condition of granting the license. In sum, these proposed amendments to the Continental Shelf Convention are all intended to implement the consideration that exploration and exploitation policies should be developed which take into account the enormous value of scientific research in the development of the shelf region. They should, furthermore, be subordinate to the needs of research.

Eventually an international agency, perhaps under the general direction of COSPAR, should be established with authority to sponsor scientific research beyond territorial waters. A sanction protecting research sponsored by that body could be the denial of research cooperation and, in instances calling for a severe response, the denial of scientific information through the sponsoring agency, to states refusing their consent or harassing the researchers.

## 6. SEDENTARY FISHERIES [138]

Almost from the time of the formulation of the sedentary fisheries provisions of the Continental Shelf Convention,[139] its indeterminacy has

[138] A definition should be stipulated at the outset of this discussion. The term sedentary fisheries will be used to indicate the species caught, not the equipment used. There are fisheries, sometimes denominated sedentary, which are "exercised with permanent or semipermanent installations, weirs, or pound nets, or 'sero's' as they are called in Malay. The sero's are bambu [sic] stakes standing in the seabed in comparatively shallow waters." See Mouton (fn. 88), 441. See also Gidel (fn. 46), I, 488; McDougal and Burke (fn. 47), 653–54; A. Papandreou, *La Situation Juridique des Pêcheries Sédentaire en Haute-Mer* (Athens 1958), 146; art. 13 of the Convention on Fishing.

The definition just stipulated would appear to be more in keeping with traditional usage. See, e.g., C. 6921, [1893–94], CX, *Parliamentary Papers* (1893), 759, 822. It was a thesis, moreover, which Sir Cecil Hurst echoed in "Whose is the Bed of the Sea?" 4 *British Year Book of International Law*, 34, 40 (1923–24). See also E. de Vattel, *Law of Nations*, White ed. (London 1787) bk. I, ch.?. XXIII, §287; Oppenheim (fn. 54), I, 628–29; Goldie, "The Occupation of Sedentary Fisheries Off the Australian Coasts," 1 *Sydney Law Review* (1953), 84; Goldie, "Australia's Continental Shelf" (fn. 124), 543–48, 559–60. But cf. McDougal and Burke (fn. 47), 661–62.

This writer has discussed in greater detail the issues raised briefly in this Section, see Goldie, "Sedentary Fisheries" (fn. 42), 86; "The Continental Shelf Cases" (fn. 79); and "Fisheries Management" (fn. 15), 13–22.

[139] *I.e.*, art. 2, para. 4.

permitted the extension of the province of sedentary fisheries from the sessile creatures of the benthos which were once their main, if not their only, living resource, to bottom-crawling and even possibly swimming crustaceans. This indeterminacy gives a graphic illustration of the danger, indicated above,[140] inherent in ascribing familiar legal characteristics to novel situations—a practice which tends to make law the occasion of conflicts rather than the means of their solution. It can be seen, for example, as contributing to the "Lobster War," which arose between Brazil and France over the arrest on January 2, 1962, of the French ship "Cassiopee," [141] and to the contention between the United States and Japan over king crabs.[142] This legal indeterminacy and fictional reasoning should be contrasted with the clearer categories of oceanographers.[143]

[140] See §1 J above, and §VIII below.

[141] See 67 *Revue Générale de Droit International Public*, 133 (1963); 69 (1965), 120; and Azzam, "The Dispute between France and Brazil over Lobster Fishing in the Atlantic," 13 *International and Comparative Law Quarterly*, 1453 (1964). It is significant that both states felt justified in invoking art. 2, para. 4 in support of their respective positions, although neither state is a party to the Continental Shelf Convention. They both assumed, wrongly it is submitted, that the paragraph's addition of sedentary fisheries embodied customary international law. For a contrary view, see Goldie, "Continental Shelf Cases" (fn. 79), 536.

[142] Agreement Between the Government of the United States of America and the Government of the Union of Soviet Socialist Republic Relating to Fishing for King Crab, signed Feb. 5, 1965 [1965] 1 U.S.T. 24, T.I.A.S. No. 5752, 541 U.N.T.S. 97, extended and amended Jan. 31, 1969, T.I.A.S. No. 6635. Although the Agreement originally only encompassed the king crab, the latest amendment brings another species of crab, tanner crab, under its terms—thus further extending the concept of the "natural resources" of the continental shelf. Agreement Between the United States of America and Japan relating to the King Crab Fishery in the Eastern Bering Sea, signed Nov. 25, 1964 [1964], 11, U.S.T., 2076, T.I.A.S. No. 5688, 533 U.N.T.S. 31, extended and amended on Nov. 29, 1966 [1966], 11, U.S.T. 2191, T.I.A.S. No. 6155, extended and amended Dec. 23, 1968, T.I.A.S. No. 6001. Like the Agreement with the Soviet Union, the most recent amendment to this Agreement extends its coverage to tanner crabs. For another recent United States extension of the sedentary fisheries concept from king crab to tanner crab, see Dept. of Interior Reg. §§295.1, 295.2, xxx Feb. Reg. 16114 (1968).

[143] The standard oceanology work, Harald Sverdrup, Martin Johnson and Richard Fleming, *The Oceans—Their Physics, Chemistry, and General Biology*, 2nd edn. (New York 1946), 280–81, tells us:

> [T]he population of the sea may be divided into three large groups—namely, the benthos, nekton, and plankton, the first belonging to the benthic region and the other two to the pelagic region.
>
> In the *benthos* . . . are included the sessile, creeping and burrowing organisms found on the bottom of the sea. Representatives of the group extend from the high-tide level down into the abyssal depths. The benthos comprises (1) sessile animals, such as sponges, barnacles, mussels, oysters, crinoids, corals, hydroids, bryozoa, some of the worms, all of the seaweeds and eel grasses, and many of the diatoms, (2) creeping forms such as crabs, lobsters, certain copepods, amphipods, and many other crustacea, many protozoa, snails, and some bivalves and fishes, and (3) burrowing forms, including most of the clams and worms, some crustacea, and echinoderms.

The submission is that the legal category of sedentary fisheries should be limited to only the biological category of sessile forms of the benthic division—the burrowing

Thus has the addition of biological resources to the category of the "natural resources" of the shelf led to confusion, and to encroachments on the freedom of fishing on the high seas. Unless this movement is checked, there are very strong probabilities that it will continue, and even, perhaps, accelerate—as more and more claims are asserted that additional species should be brought within the category of "resources of the continental shelf." As a preliminary step in helping to hold back the further development of this "enclosure movement," the proposal is that the resources of the continental shelf which are to be subjected to a coastal state's sovereign rights should be limited to mineral resources. In place of overloading the concept of the continental shelf and that of "its" resources (thereby rendering the notion of the resources of the continental shelf more indeterminate than its limitation to minerals would require), sedentary fisheries existing on continental shelf areas (as measured by the 200 meter isobath) should be brought within a separate regime from that provided by the Continental Shelf Convention.[144] Sedentary fisheries on seamounts beyond the continental shelves of coastal states should not be within the proposed regime,

---

and creeping forms being excluded. This strict view of sedentary fish would, unlike art. 2, para. 4, exclude from the category organisms such as the trochus, green snail, and the "sacred chank of India and Ceylon," to quote a phrase from Bailey, "Australia and the Law of the Sea," 1 *Adelaide Law Review*, 1, 11 (1960), as well as shrimps, lobsters, and langoustes. They would then be eligible to qualify for enlightened regional regimes for the conservation and profitable exploitation under the Convention on Fishing.

144 See, Goldie, "Sedentary Fisheries" (fn. 42), passim. This study contains, at 97, a proposed Draft Article on Sedentary Fisheries which is as follows:

(1) The regulation of sedentary fisheries may be undertaken by a state in areas of the high seas contiguous to its territorial waters, where such fisheries have long been maintained and conducted by nationals of that state, provided that non-nationals may enjoy, subject to the principle of abstention, such historical privileges as they may have acquired by long usage. Such regulation will, however, not affect the general status of the areas as high seas.

(2) The resources of sedentary fisheries within the scope of this Article are living organisms which, during the adult life are permanently or biologically connected with and are incapable of movement on the seabed or in the subsoil of the high seas.

(3) The coastal state's exclusive authority over a sedentary fishery within the scope of this Article shall be exercised to ensure the good management of the fishery. In particular, that state's regulation of the fishery should prohibit biologically wasteful practices and promote economically efficient procedures for the production and marketing of the resource.

(4) A state may not assert claims under this Article to exercise jurisdiction over sedentary fisheries conducted beyond the two hundred metre bathymetric contour line lying seaward off its shores and beyond territorial waters, being the contour line defining, in terms of depth, the continental shelf area subject to its sovereign rights as provided in the Convention on the Continental Shelf done at Geneva on 20 April 1958.

(5) This Article shall not apply where states have established a treaty regime to regulate the conservation of and access to any specific sedentary fishery, unless the treaty establishing that regime so provides.

but should be the subject of special regional arrangements. The Convention on Fishing offers adequate procedures for their creation.[145] These regional regimes should be independent of both the continental shelf regime and the proposed sedentary fisheries regime. In addition, provision should be made for the possibility of states of a region agreeing to a special regional cooperation regime for sedentary fisheries situated on their continental shelves. A major advantage which all of these proposals have in common is the possibility of eliminating the present dependence of influential thought on the *Duchess of Sutherland* fallacy.

Should the Sedentary Fisheries Article this writer has proposed, or some similar set of principles, fail to be accepted, then, as second best, sedentary fisheries beyond territorial waters would be more appropriately regulated under the Convention on Fishing than under the Convention on the Continental Shelf. The former Convention would provide appropriate procedures for establishing a regional regime of cooperation in terms of its Article 4, or perhaps of its Articles 7 and 9. Reliance on these procedures would bring about, in the long run, greater net advantages to the regional fishery by treating the resource as a single unit than would barren disputes as to the characterization of benthic creatures in terms of the resources of the continental shelf, or, alternatively, of the high seas, in order to establish coastal states' separate, divisive, and exclusive claims.

## IV: EMERGING SOCIO-POLITICAL PROBLEMS

*A. The Impact of International Technostructures* [146]

### 1. INTRODUCTION

Professor John K. Galbraith has pointed to the imperatives of technology and planning in the development of the modern corporation—of the technostructure. Apart from some brilliant comparative and illustrative examples he has, in the main, restricted his field of vision to the giant corporations which operate mainly in the domestic United

---

[145] See, §V A below. See also Goldie, "Fisheries Management" (fn. 15), 10–18.
[146] This term has been adapted from J. Galbraith, *The New Industrial State* (Boston 1967), 82. On the other hand, whereas Professor Galbraith coined the term to describe enterprises usually described as capitalistic, but also to include public or socialist ones (see same, 339), this writer would like to give it a further currency and add other instrumentalities to those primarily engaged in providing the goods and services to be obtained from the "market place." I would like to extend its denotations to include other social structures, especially those extensively engaged in planning the employment of technological and human resources which provide services, in the light of received (or developing) theories or doctrines to maximize the respect, status, and well-being of its planned constituent members. This would include the Armed Services among other administrative departments of government—also the Corps of Engineers could provide an outstanding example.

States. Although the international operations of the United States Steel Corporation may be left out of consideration without giving a distorted analysis of its internal relations and its business operations, the history of the Standard Oil Corporation, and those of its mightiest offshoots, Standard Oil of New Jersey, Socony Mobil's Standard of California, and Esso, have marched majestically across the world in search of markets no less than of sources of supply. In engaging in international competition for markets and sources of supply, these oil companies have been able to rely upon the diplomacy of the United States to underpin their overseas long-term planning no less than the more domestically-oriented corporations of this country's technostructure have been able to rely upon government contracts to stabilize their prices and to underpin much of their domestic long-term planning. The means of governmental support has varied in accordance with the goals and the theaters of action, but the fact of essential support re- mains—the grammar may change, but the logic remains the same.

It would, however, be an error to suppose that all internationally-oriented enterprises make similar or even reconcilable demands on the Government. There may be great divergencies between different types of enterprises operating in the same area. Thus the policies which the oil companies [147] wish the United States to espouse regarding the exploitation of the minerals of the seabed may well be in opposition to those of enterprises which look forward to mining hard minerals from the deep-ocean floor.

In addition, the United States Navy has, as a most important plan- ning entity, its own interests, doctrines, and theses. These may, or may not, depending on circumstances, harmonize with theories and doc- trines held by the navies of other countries. They might, further, run counter to the interests, doctrines, and planned expectations of Ameri- can, foreign, and international business enterprises. The doctrines championed by the United States Navy may be summarily indicated as representative of the "Blue Water School." The legal doctrinal aspects of this approach include an emphasis on the freedom of the

[147] The policies ascribable to this country's international oil companies are those published by the National Petroleum Council. Accordingly, in the discussion which follows its publication, *Petroleum Resources Under the Ocean Floor* (fn. 107), will be treated as the source material for the oil industry's thesis regarding the winning of oil from the subsoil of the seabed. The *Interim Report* of the American Branch of the International Law Association's Committee on Deep Sea Mineral Resources may be viewed as an early expression of the same interest group's views. Although that *Interim Report* was published on July 19, 1968 it has not, as of this time of writing (December 30, 1969) been followed up by a "Final" Report. On the other hand the three versions of *Petroleum Resources Under the Ocean Floor* both follow it in a time sequence and reflect an increasing responsiveness to some of the criticisms made of the *Interim Report* by members of what Professor Galbraith has called "the educational and scientific estate."

seas, and the limitation of maritime zones under the exclusive competence of coastal states to the smallest areas which can be made diplomatically acceptable. This viewpoint has been traditionally influential
in the shaping of United States foreign policy and has important
strategic and commercial justifications. Nevertheless, it has not gone
unquestioned in the past, and today, in the international petroleum
industry, it is confronted by a most formidable opponent.

2. THE PETROLEUM INDUSTRY AND THE STRATTON COMMISSION

In July 1968 the American Branch of the International Law Association's Committee on Deep Sea Mineral Resources [148] offered, in its
*Interim Report,* the conclusion that:

> Since exploration and exploitation of undersea minerals is likely
> to occur earlier in the shallower waters of the oceans adjacent to the
> continents than in the abyssal depths, it follows that if jurisdictional
> uncertainties arise to impede such operations during the next several
> decades, such problems will be primarily related to the scope of the
> mineral jurisdiction which is already vested exclusively in the coastal
> states by the "exploitability" and "adjacency" criteria of jurisdiction
> which now appear in the Continental Shelf Convention. This un-
> certainty, if necessity for its resolution occurs, might be removed by
> consultation, among the major coastal nations which are capable
> of conducting deep sea mineral development, looking toward the
> issuance by those states of parallel ex parte declarations. These
> declarations might appropriately restrict claims of exclusive sea-bed
> mineral jurisdiction, pursuant to the exploitability and adjacency
> factors of the Continental Shelf Convention, to (i) the submerged
> portions of the continental land mass, limiting this provisionally to
> a depth of, say, 2,500 meters, or (ii) to a stated distance (say 100
> miles) from the baseline, whichever limitation encompasses the larger
> area. Such declarations might appropriately recognize special cases.
> Two such classifications suggest themselves: (i) In the case of states
> whose coasts plunge precipitously to the ocean floor (e.g., on the
> west coast of South America), the suggested 100-mile limit on sea-
> bed mineral jurisdiction would automatically operate on the deep
> ocean floor. (ii) In the case of narrower enclosed seas, the principle
> of adjacency might appropriately carry coastal mineral jurisdiction
> to the median lines, even though these are beyond the continental
> blocks. [149]

[148] American Branch Report (fn. 107). Note, however, Professor L. Henkin's "Dissenting Statement," same, XXI.
[149] (Preprint copy) (mimeo. March 1969), 77–104 [hereinafter cited as "National
Petroleum Council Report"].

The National Petroleum Council's recent publication *Resources Under the Ocean Floor* has more recently offered a conclusion which bears some striking resemblances to that of the American Branch Committee of the International Law Association—leaving aside the earlier publication's denomination of either a bathymetric contour line, or a line of distance (whichever should encompass the larger area), as a "provisional" delimitation of the shelf's outer limits. The National Petroleum Council argued that:

> Moreover, since the plunge of the slope has often been locally overlapped extensively by the sediments of the continental rise, a boundary just oceanward of the base of the slope, to include the shelf, the slope, and the landward portion of the continental rise, where developed, most closely approaches the true ocean-bottom boundary between continental and oceanic areas and is the most natural and appropriate outward limit of a country's sovereign rights over bottom resources. A boundary thus drawn gives recognition to the natural oceanward extension of the domain of each coastal nation and the inclusion under its jurisdiction of that suboceanic territory over whose natural resources the coastal nation is most practically suited to exercise control.
>
> In summary, given a recognition of the above scientific facts, it is apparent that the outer edge of the continent is a far more logical choice than the outer edge of the geological continental shelf as the limit of coastal-nation exclusive jurisdiction over the natural resources of the seabed and subsoil. The participating nations at Ciudad Trujillo in 1956 and at Geneva in 1968 wisely declined to limit the coastal nation's exclusive jurisdiction to the geological continental shelf or to the 200-meter isobath.[150]

The "broad" continental shelf [151] which the National Petroleum Council advocates was rejected by the Commission on Marine Sciences, Engineering, and Resources. It wrote: "There is little question but that the NPC view of adjacency extends too-far beyond the 200 meters, the depth of most geological shelves of the world. Considering the totality of its interests in the oceans, the United States would never have accepted the Convention on the Continental Shelf as NPC now reads it." [152]

I very strongly suggest that the main criticisms I leveled at the American Branch Committee Report during the Deep-Sea Mining

[150] Same, 103–04.
[151] See fn. 100.
[152] III, *Panel Reports* (fn. 5), VIII-20. See also *Our Nation and the Sea* (fn. 5), 144–45.

Session [153] of the International Law Association's Fifty-third Biennial Conference at Buenos Aires on August 25–31, 1968, apply, *mutatis mutandis,* to the relevant pages of the National Petroleum Council's Report.

While the deep ocean sciences and engineering technologies advance, and markets fluctuate in response to production and need, the exploitability test must always have a contingent operation. Even the probability of a brilliant future for human exploitation of the resources of the ocean bed and its subsoil cannot remove the contingent and uncertain qualities of time and utilization. In contrast with that discussion, the Petroleum Council Report entirely ignores the contingent quality of the exploitability test. In contrast with the clear words of Article 1 of the Continental Shelf Convention, the National Petroleum Council interprets the exploitability test as a sanguine beneficiary might ignore intermediate interests (not unlike, perhaps the "hero" of *Kind Hearts and Coronets?*) and interpret a contingent gift in his favor as one which had immediately vested in him.

Second, the whole underlying assumption of the National Petroleum Council Report's presentation of the exploitability test—as capable of denominating a boundary within which a total submarine "mineral estate" of all available resources appertains to the coastal states—fails (as it must) to examine the meaning of the key term "exploitability" as it appears in the context, and against the background, of its use in Article 1. This is clearly a legal solecism also. It is mistaken to assimilate coastal states' exclusive continental shelf rights to territorial notions. Those rights should be seen, as they were originally conceived, and as they were originally drafted, namely as being specific and limited extraterritorial competences over exploration and exploitation activities on and under the shelf.[154]

Someone reading the *National Council Petroleum Report* or the *American Branch Committee Report* may well begin to wonder why such an elaborate construction was attempted in the first place—and reiterated in the second. There would appear to be a simple answer. Both *Reports* express the position of those who are pressing for wide

[153] Goldie, International Law Association 53rd Biennial Conference, Buenos Aires, "Comments from the Floor at the Deep-Sea Mining Session" (mimeo. Aug. 26, 1968), 9–10 [hereinafter cited as Goldie, "Deep-Sea Mining Comments (ILA)"].

[154] International Law Commission, "Articles Concerning the Law of the Sea: Part II, Section III, The Continental Shelf," [1956] 2 *Year Book of the International Law Commission,* 256, 297; A/CONF. 13/42, 50–72. See especially 51–52 (Münch), 52 (de la Pradelle), 52–53 (Garcia Amador), 54–55 (Souter), 65 (Mouton), 66 (Molodtsov), 68 (Gutteridge). Gidel evaluated the coastal states' rights over the continental shelf as follows: "The consequence of the restricted and specialized nature of the rights of the coastal State is that their exercise should leave the use of the high seas as intact as possible." Gidel, "The Continental Shelf," trans. Goldie, 3 *University of Western Australia Law Review,* 87, 96 (1954) [hereinafter cited as "Gidel, 'Continental Shelf' "].

continental shelves.[155] Surely it would have been better to have frankly advanced the policy arguments favoring a wide shelf,[156] than to have engaged in an exegesis which has tended to becloud the debate by directing attention from what is needed to what may, or may not, have been intended over a decade ago at the 1958 United Nations Conference on the Law of the Sea at Geneva—or even earlier by the International Law Commission.

However, the present tendencies of states to engage in cartographical chauvinism in asserting offshore claims might well preclude the possibility of this accurate but restrained interpretation. Accordingly, the proposal is that coastal states' shelf jurisdiction be given a single boundary, namely that of 200 meters, or, at the most, the 550 meters [157] bathymetric contour line, and that the exploitability test be eliminated altogether.[158] On the other hand, the alternatives to the "Intermediate Zone," proposed in an earlier section of this paper,[159] should be added to the possible alternatives of the exploitability test.

3. ENTERPRISES MINING HARD MINERALS FROM THE OCEAN FLOOR

Spokesmen of other industries interested in the possibilities of the seabed of the high seas have been critical of the National Petroleum Council's identification of the major oil companies' interest with those of the nation. For example, Mr. Malcolm R. Wilkey, General Counsel, Kennecott Copper Corporation, has written: "A particular industry advocate who equates any change in the U.S. position, which conceivably might affect his particular industry, with a sacrifice of the national patrimony . . . is not particularly helpful in reaching a well considered overall evaluation of the true United States national interest." [160]

---

[155] See fn. 100.

[156] Henkin (fn. 100), 25–36.

[157] This is the line of demarcation which Senator Pell is now proposing. See S. Res. 33, 91st Cong. 1st Sess., art. 6. This latter line is identical with that proposed by the United Kingdom and the Netherlands delegations in the Fourth Committee of the 1958 United Nations Conference on the Law of the Sea at Geneva. See Netherlands and the United Kingdom of Great Britain and Northern Ireland, Proposal, U.N. Doc. A/CONF. 13/C.4/L.32, VI, *United Nations Conference on the Law of the Sea, Geneva 1958, Official Records (Fourth Committee)* at 6 (Mouton), 36 (Gutteridge), 41 (Gutteridge), 44 (Mouton), 45 (Mouton), 46 (Mouton), 47 (Mouton), 48 (Gutteridge)—a comment on the uncertainty of the International Law Commission's draft Article 67, 135 (for the text of the United Kingdom–Netherlands proposal), A/CONF. 13/42.

[158] See Goldie, "Davy Jones's Locker" (fn. 73), 21–22; also "Exploitability Test" (fn. 2), 451–52. Note, however, the problems faced in this regard, and the proposals for their solution, same, 452–55.

[159] See §III C 2(c) above.

[160] M. Wilkey, "The Role of Private Industry in the Deep Ocean," IV, Symposium on Private Investments Abroad, Southwestern Legal Foundation, Dallas, Texas, June 18–20, 1969 [hereinafter cited as Wilkey].

The same writer refers to the National Petroleum Council's position as "Waving the Flag 20,000 Leagues Under the Sea." [161]

Having dealt with the National Petroleum Council's wide-shelf thesis, Wilkey then criticized the Stratton Commission's "Freezing the Boundary at 200 Meters" [162] on the grounds that, being specific, it would "impair our bargaining ability (and agility)." [163] It makes no provision for a reciprocal act of self-limitation by other states.[164]

Unlike Kennecott, which still mainly looks to dry land resources for its expectations of the future, Deep Sea Ventures looks entirely to the ocean's mineral resources. In this vein, its President Mr. John Flipse, anticipates the increasingly advantageous winning of nickel, copper, cobalt, and manganese from the high seas.[165] But, like Kennecott, Deep Sea favors the narrow continental shelf approach.[166] Lately Mr. Flipse has expressed himself much more unequivocally in favor of the Stratton Report than has Mr. Wilkey.[167] Both spokesmen, furthermore have taken up positions on the regime of the deep ocean which are very similar to that already outlined in this chapter and presented in "Davy Jones Locker." [168]

## 4. THE "BLUE WATER" NAVIES

The support which the United States Navy (and possibly, in the future, that of the Soviet Union) gives to the freedom of the seas stems from its need to maximize its freedom of movement by limiting the extent of the exclusive jurisdiction of coastal states. This point of view, which dominant naval powers have all, from time to time, entertained, stems

[161] Same, 17.

[162] Same, 20.

[163] Same.

[164] Same, 21. Wilkey calls for "strict reciprocity by other nations" and the abandonment of the 200 meter isoboth as a continental shelf boundary "if other nations did not reciprocate completely." Same.

[165] See e.g. paper presented by Flipse at Law of the Sea Institute, University of Rhode Island, *National Policy Recommendations* (Fourth Annual Summer Conference (mimeo. June 23, 1969) [hereinafter cited as Flipse, U.R.I. Paper]. See also Flipse, Statement Before the Subcommittee on Oceanography of the House Merchant Marine and Fisheries Committee Concerning the Report of the Commission on Marine Science, Engineering, and Resources, passim (mimeo) [hereinafter cited as Flipse, Statement Before the House Subcommittee on Oceanography]; the same, Statement Before the Senate Commerce Committee's Special Study on United Nations Suboceanic Lands Policy Hearings of September 23 and 24, 1969 Concerning Policy Considerations Germane to the Peaceful, Beneficial, and Economic Exploitation of the Resources of the Deep Ocean Floor, passim (mimeo) [hereinafter cited as Flipse, Special Study].

[166] See Flipse, U.R.I. Paper (fn. 165), 3–4; same, Statement Before the House Subcommittee on Oceanography (fn. 165), 15–16; and same, Special Study (fn. 165), 15, 16.

[167] Same.

[168] See §III C 2(b) above, and Goldie, "Davy Jones's Locker" (fn. 73), 18–21; "Exploitability Test" (fn. 2), 450–52, and "Deep-Sea Mining Comments (ILA)" (fn. 153), 9–10.

from their enlightened self-interest. The greater the extent of the free high seas, the greater their room for maneuver in times of peace and for the application of force in times of maritime violence. Today a new dimension is added. Technology is increasing the ways of using the seabed, including the development of many types of vessels which can navigate and engage in a multitude of specialized activities.[169] While these new tools add to the flexibility and power of high-seas navies, they also provide coastal states with both the excuse for and the capability of asserting jurisdictions which encroach even further into the high seas. The Continental Shelf Convention, for example, limits states' sovereign rights over activities on their continental shelves to the exploration for and the exploitation of the natural resources there, but the quantity and types of activities are all likely to increase greatly. Hence not many states, one may safely say, would look with equanimity upon naval powers invoking the freedom of the seas to justify fortifying their shelves, or using them for supporting three-dimensional and telechiric weapons. It is also possible to imagine a hostility, on the part of coastal states, toward the use of the volume of waters above their continental shelves by three-dimensionally operating foreign naval vessels. Thus a challenge is presented which may well induce coastal states to respond by further adding, in terms of both distance and competences, to their claims of exclusive authority offshore.

The recent draft agreed to by the United States and the Soviet Union [170] purporting to limit the location of fixed launching installations of nuclear weapons or other weapons of man's destruction in the seabed and subsoil, to a contiguous zone of no more than twelve sea miles in width and extending from the baselines from which territorial waters are measured, could have had a salutary effect in this context. One can only regret, therefore, the action of the General Assembly in rejecting this draft.[171] This action may not only reduce the chances of disarmament in an important potential area of contention, but also create insecurities and excuses leading to another round of unilateral encroachments into the high seas.

## B. Developing Countries' Claims

While the Soviet Union has been reluctant to recognize any special regime to govern deep-ocean minerals above and beyond the privileges which the doctrine of the freedom of the high seas allows, and the

[169] For an indication of at least some of these developing capabilities, see §1 H above.

[170] *New York Times,* Oct. 8, 1969, p. 6, cols. 1–5.

[171] *New York Times,* Dec. 12, 1969, p. 6, cols. 1–2. But see now *New York Times,* April 21, 1970, p. 4, cols. 3–5.

United States supports only a limited regime—a registry [172]—many of the developing countries have, at least initially, supported a strong international agency with power to grant concessions and obtain substantial revenues in return. These revenues are viewed as being distributed for development purposes among the countries with the strongest cases for its allocation to them. Thus many of them, at least up to December 1969, have tended to see their national interests as being best represented in the position taken by Ambassador Pardo of Malta on August 18, 1967,[173] and developed by him subsequently in numerous speeches and drafts. On the other hand, the four resolutions [174] passed by the General Assembly on December 15, 1969 (and

[172] See, for a statement of the United States position, Press Release by the United States Mission to the United Nations, Aug. 29, 1969, Press Release USUN-90(69) [hereinafter cited as USUN-90(69)]. The core of the United States thesis is to be found at 2 where the following statement occurs:

> In our view, a registry should operate under internationally agreed criteria for registration, exploration. Agreed criteria and procedures should include the following elements: 1) Acceptable procedures to verify compliance with established operational standards. 2) Effective procedures for settlement of disputes. 3) Provisions for liability for damages arising from exploitation of seabed resources. 4) Provision to avoid any unjustifiable interference with the exercise of the freedoms of the high seas, or with the conservation of the living resources of the seas, or any interference with fundamental scientific research carried out with the intention of open publication. 5) Acceptable criteria for commercial exploration and for exploitation, governing such matters as the types of resources to be exploited under a claim, the size of the claim, the duration and termination of the claim, the accommodation of multiple uses of the seabed and the water column, and the relation between exploration and exploitation rights. 6) Acceptable criteria governing operations designed to further objectives of conservation and to reduce to an acceptable minimum pollution and danger to human life. And 7) criteria establishing eligibility of the claimant and criteria governing minimum performance requirements. Governments, we believe, should be responsible for adherence by their nationals to these internationally established criteria and provisions.

The position adumbrated in the above quotation is very similar to that outlined in this writer's "Davy Jones's Locker" (fn. 73). See § VI B2 below.

In addition to counseling a limited regime, the United States has also counseled against haste. Thus in USUN-90(69) at 3 the following evaluation is expressed:

> [O]ur Delegation has cautioned that the development of seabed resources beyond the limits of national jurisdiction will be slow. All of the necessary technology is not yet available, although the essential elements appear to be on the verge of development. Nor are we forced by the threat of scarcity to bear the high costs that exploitation of seabed resources would presently entail. But some courageous explorers may be willing to enter this new frontier if we show them that they can operate within a favorable economic and legal climate.

[173] *Note verbale* date Aug. 17, 1967, from the Permanent Mission of Malta to the United Nations Addressed to the Secretary-General, xxii, U.N. GAOR, Annexes, Agenda Item 92, at 1–2, U.N. Doc. A/6695 [hereinafter cited as A/6695].

[174] A Request for Views of Member States on an Early Convocation of a Conference on the Law of the Sea, G.A. Res. 2574A (xxiv); Continuation of the Work of the Committee of the Peaceful Uses of the Sea-Bed, G.A. Res. 2574B (xxiv); Request to the Secretary-General to Prepare a Study in Depth of an International Machinery

especially the fourth), may signal a *volte-face* in those countries' positions.

Although still supporting the eventual emergence of strong international machinery,[175] developing countries now appear to be prepared to insure the satisfaction of their own needs by also giving support to the broad, continental-shelf approach. Two points should be stressed in noting this change of position. First, clearly many developing countries are concerned that if the developed countries continue to oppose a strong international agency then the narrow-shelf thesis would work greatly toward the economic vulnerability of the poorer countries, since a maximum area of high seas would be open to exploitation without any obligations being incurred to the developing world. Such countries reason that if they cannot jointly gain a distributable income from the exploitation of the high seas then they should individually maximize their opportunities for sharing in the wealth of the oceans, by extending their claims of exclusive competence as far seaward as possible. Second, it should be pointed out that a number of developing countries have always endorsed the broad-shelf thesis. Known mineral wealth under their continental slopes has beckoned their claims of competence there no less surely than the same resources have beckoned technologically-advanced exploiters.

These interests led to the General Assembly's Moratorium Resolution. What its legal status is need not detain us. There are those who will argue that, lacking the support of the technologically-advanced countries, and especially that of the United States and the Soviet Union, this Resolution is ineffective to abridge the privileges which the traditional doctrine of the freedom of the high seas accords to the exploiters of the oceans' resources. Be that as it may, clearly the developing countries have stated a principle of significance to them. Although not directly enforceable, that principle may provide those countries with an addition to their rhetoric and a basis for pressing further claims. Second, the developing countries' refusal to define the limits of national jurisdiction should be noted. This leaves open the options of states to proclaim further exclusive competences over increasingly extensive sea areas.[176]

Unless states can reach agreement on both the nature of the regime

---

Having Jurisdiction over the Area Beyond National Jurisdiction, G.A. Res. 2574C (XXIV); Declaration that States and Individuals are Bound to Refrain from Exploiting Resources Beyond the Limits of Jurisdiction Pending the Establishment of an International Regime, G.A. Res. 2574D (XXIV). The fourth Resolution will be hereinafter cited as the "Moratorium Resolution."

[175] See, e.g. Resolution 2574C (XXIV).

[176] Shortly after the Moratorium Resolution was agreed to the Uruguayan Government joined the CEP countries and Argentina in claiming territorial waters for a width of 200 sea miles. *New York Times*, Dec. 27, 1969, p. 31, col. 6 (City Edition).

which will replace the present open-access system—spelled the freedom of the high seas—and the extent of the national jurisdiction of coastal states, the developing and the technologically-advanced states would appear to be on a collision course. Even if the National Petroleum Council could persuade the Government of the United States to adopt a broad continental shelf the scope of other interests in the United States, including the Defense Department, would be greatly curtailed if other states were to follow such a lead. A similar restriction would be imposed if foreign countries were to respond to extended claims by the United States, as the original CEP countries responded to the Truman Proclamation, by asserting an extensive maritime jurisdiction.

Alternatives to the CEP model include, where geography is favorable, the extended baselines of the "archipelago" doctrines of Indonesia and the Philippines, or of such systems of enclosures as those favored by Norway, Iceland, and, perhaps, Canada in the near future.

## V: FINGERPOSTS IN SOME NEW DIRECTIONS

Law may be regarded in many ways, as an authoritative repository of a community's long-term as well as short-term value system, as providing procedures for beneficial human interaction, for reducing tensions or distributing satisfactions, as a language controlling society, or as a set of complex techniques for ordering human relations to reduce an initially inhospitable nonhuman environment to a knowable and exploitable form. In this sense it provides the skeleton for the management of resources and the frame of reference for their allocations. Discussion of law, while emphasizing any one of these qualities, is necessarily shot through with all of them. In this discussion, emphasis will be upon the last, while law as description of values and societies, and as language, will not be shunned.

### A. The 1958 Convention on Fishing

The Convention on Fishing offers the beginning, at least, of a new direction. It creates the possibility of bypassing the traditional dichotomy of the sea's status. Unlike the other conventions which were signed at Geneva in 1958 and which mainly restate or confer substantive rights and prescribe substantive rules, this Convention, with the exception of recognizing the special interests of coastal states in adjacent fisheries, offers facilities of which states may avail themselves to establish fisheries conservation and development regimes. Article 3 provides that, where the nationals of one state fish a stock on the high seas, that state may adopt conservation measures to govern its own nationals there. Article 4 contemplates the situation where the nationals of two or more states fish on the high seas for a single stock. Any such state may request the other (or others) to engage in negotiations to establish a conservation regime. Paragraph 2 of this Article permits any of the parties to invoke the procedures of Article 9 in the event of a failure to reach an agreement within twelve months. Article 5 lays down the conditions and the procedures for extending the regimes contemplated in Articles 3 and 4 to states outside those regimes. These include the fundamental principle of nondiscrimination.

Article 6 recognizes the special interest of coastal states in the maintenance of the productivity of a fishery on the high seas adjacent to their territorial seas,[177] their right to take part in research and regulation of the fishery even if their nationals do not engage in the fishery,[178] and their authority to request other states engaging in the fishery to enter into negotiations with them to establish a conservation regime.[179] This Article also forbids noncoastal states whose own nationals are engaged in a fishery on the high seas, but adjacent to the territorial waters of a coastal state, from enforcing any conservation measures opposed to those adopted by the coastal state.[180] Such noncoastal states may, however, enter into negotiations with the coastal states in order to formulate "measures necessary for the conservation of the living resources of the high seas in that area."[181] The machinery of Article 9 is available if, in any of the above situations, the states concerned are unable to agree, within twelve months, to conservation measures regulating the fishery.[182] Where states fail to reach agreement within six months, a coastal state may, with a view to the maintenance of the living resources of the sea, unilaterally adopt measures of conservation binding on the nationals of other states.[183] This power may only be exercised if the "following requirements are fulfilled":

(a) That there is a need for urgent application of conservation measures in the light of the existing knowledge of the fishery;

(b) That the measures adopted are based on appropriate scientific findings;

(c) That such measures do not discriminate in form or in fact against foreign fishermen.[184]

These measures are only temporary, pending the agreement of the other states concerned.[185] If no agreement can be reached, any of the parties may invoke the procedure in Article 9. But, subject to the requirements of Article 10, paragraph 2 (which will be indicated below), the measures adopted by the coastal state will remain in force until a

---

177 Para. 1. See, for a discussion of this new concept, Francisco V. Garcia-Amador, *The Exploitation and Conservation of the Resources of the Sea,* 2nd edn. (Leyden 1963), 196–98, 201-03.

178 Para. 2.

179 Para. 3.

180 Para. 4.

181 Same.

182 Art. 8, para. 2.

183 Art. 7, para. 1.

184 Art. 7, para. 2.

185 Art. 7, para. 3.

special commission called into being under Article 9 gives its decision.[186] When two or more of the states unilaterally regulate a common fishery, problems of establishing the boundaries of the conservation zones of each may well become acute. Article 7, paragraph 5, provides that "[t]he principles of geographical demarcation as defined in Article 12 of the Convention on the Territorial Sea and Contiguous Zone" [187] shall govern.

The Convention on Fishing recognizes the possibility that a noncoastal state may have a special interest in the conservation of the resources of a fishery, even when its nationals do not engage in fishing that resource.[188] That noncoastal state may request that state (or states) whose nationals do engage in the fishery to take necessary measures for conservation. Should the negotiations continue for twelve months without agreement, the state initiating them may have recourse to the procedure contemplated in Article 9.[189]

Articles providing for the judicial settlement of disputes arising out of the interpretation or application of the four 1958 Geneva Conventions on the Law of the Sea are contained in a separate *Optional Protocol of Signature Concerning the Compulsory Settlement of Disputes*.[190] Article 9 of the Convention on Fishing provides for a procedure for the settlement of disputes alternative to that of the *Optional Protocol* and to those laid down in Article 33 of the United Nations Charter.[191] Neither the machinery nor the modalities of settlement which Article 9 contemplates are necessarily judicial. It provides for an *ad hoc* commission of five members named by agreement among

[186] Art. 7, para. 4.

[187] See fn. 3. Art. 12 reads as follows:

1. Where the coasts of two States are opposite or adjacent to each other, neither of the two States is entitled, failing agreement between them to the contrary, to extend its territorial sea beyond the median line every point of which is equidistant from the nearest points on the baselines from which the breadth of the territorial seas of each of the two States is measured. The provisions of this paragraph shall not apply, however, where it is necessary by reason of historic title or other special circumstances to delimit the territorial seas of the two States in a way which is at variance with this provision.

2. The line of delimitation between the territorial seas of two States lying opposite to each other or adjacent to each other shall be marked on large-scale charts officially recognized by the coastal states.

[188] Art. 8, para. 1.

[189] Art. 8, para. 2.

[190] *Done* April 29, 1958, 450 U.N.T.S., 169. This Optional Protocol came into force on Sept. 30, 1962. See same, 170, fn. 1. Parenthetically, it should be noted that the United States is not a party to this Protocol.

[191] Para. 1, Art. 33 of the United Nations Charter reads, in part: "The parties to any dispute, the continuance of which is likely to endanger the maintenance of international peace and security, shall, first of all, seek a solution by negotiation, enquiry, mediation, conciliation, arbitration, judicial settlement, resort to regional agencies or arrangements, or other peaceful means of their own choice."

the disputing states. If those states fail to agree on a commission within three months, any one of their number may request the Secretary-General of the United Nations to name the commission within a further three months' period. The Secretary-General is called upon to make his appointments under this paragraph in consultation with the disputing states, the President of the International Court of Justice, and the Director-General of the Food and Agriculture Organization, from among "well qualified persons being nationals of States not involved in the dispute and specializing in legal, administrative or scientific questions relating to fisheries." [192] The parties are given a right to name to the commission their own nationals, who may partake fully in the proceedings on an equal footing with the members, but without the right to vote or to participate in writing the commission's decisions.[193] Although the commission may be viewed as having an arbitral or conciliating function, this provision is less of a concession to the claims of national sovereignty than is the provision of "national judges" in Article 31(3) of the Statute of the International Court of Justice. The remaining paragraphs of Article 9 set out certain procedural and jurisdictional provisions. In particular, it should be noted that the special commissions are required to remain within the scope laid down in "these articles and . . . any special agreements between the disputing parties regarding the settlement of the dispute." [194] Decisions by the commission established under this Article "shall be by majority vote." [195]

Article 10, paragraph 1, provides that when commissions are called to settle disputes under Article 7, they shall apply the criteria set out in paragraph 2 of that Article.[196] When disputes arise under Articles 4–6 and 8, the following criteria are called for:

(a) Common to the determination of disputes arising under Articles 4, 5 and 6 are the requirements:
   (i) That scientific findings demonstrate the necessity of conservation measures;
   (ii) That the specific measures are based on scientific findings and are practicable; and

[192] Convention on Fishing, art. 9, para. 2.
[193] Art. 9, para. 3.
[194] Para. 6.
[195] Para. 7.

[196] For those criteria, see above the text accompanying fn. 102. Art. 10, para. 2 provides: "The special commission may decide that pending its award the measures in dispute shall not be applied, provided that, in the case of disputes under Article 7, the measures shall only be suspended when it is apparent to the commission on the basis of *prima facie* evidence that the need for the urgent application of such measures does not exist."

(iii) That the measures do not discriminate, in form or in fact, against fishermen of other States.

(*b*) Applicable to the determination of disputes arising under Article 8 is the requirement that scientific findings demonstrate the necessity for conservation measures, or that the conservation programme is adequate, as the case may be.[197]

Article 11 provides necessary enforcement measures. "[T]he provisions of paragraph 2 of Article 94 of the Charter of the United Nations shall be applicable to [the] decisions" of the special commissions. Any recommendations which accompany a commission's decisions "shall receive the highest possible consideration." [198]

## B. Arbitration and Conciliation: Some New Developments

The alternatives to judicial settlement which the Convention on Fishing provides invite further consideration. Often when disputing states stand on what they view to be their legal rights to a resource not only do international tensions mount, but also golden opportunities for developing that resource are lost. A purely legal dispute tends, further, to focus attention upon the analysis of the claims put forward, and their validity, rather than upon that of the resource's development potentialities. In contrast with the barrenness of purely legal disputes, the flexible procedures which the Convention on Fishing offers disputants include the possibility of developing a fishery and of re-allocating its products in the light of new equities arising from its increased productivity or value.

The settlement which the "good offices" (and more than simply good offices [199]) of the International Bank for Reconstruction and Development achieved in the dispute between India and Pakistan over the waters of the Indus River provides a valuable object lesson from another touchy area of international relations—that of international rivers. By raising extensive credits, and by working with engineers and administrators whose focus of interest centered far more upon the development of the resource than upon disputes about its distribution

---

[197] Art. 10, para. 1.

[198] Art. 11.

[199] Professor Baxter points out that:

> While the International Bank of Reconstruction and Development referred to its role as one of "good offices," its function actually went beyond "good offices" or "mediation" in the technical senses of those terms. As the real differences were brought to light, the Bank was forced to play a more active part in working out a solution. The Bank pursued its own enquiries into the facts, and it was the Bank which at various stages suggested principles upon which the agreements might be based—a process which might be described as "continuing conciliation."

Richard R. Baxter, "The Indus River," in A. H. Garretson, R. D. Hayton and C. J. Olmstead, eds., *The Law of International Drainage Basins* (New York 1967), 443, 477.

at the current level, the factual basis of the dispute was changed—with salutary results. As Professor Baxter has written: "Instead of there being a limited and insufficient quantity of water to quarrel over the supply of water would be increased to a level that would permit the needs of both parties to be satisfied. The slate was wiped clean of the existing rights and obligations of the parties whatever they might be considered to have been." [200]

He concluded his analysis of the dispute over the waters of the Indus River and of the International Bank of Reconstruction and Development's "continuing conciliation" with the observation: "The possibility of adjusting the dispute is enhanced if the mediator or conciliator is authorized not merely to divide the existing water supplies but to work out a scheme for the wider and more effective use of the water resources within the basin. The argument that both parties can secure more water from the basin through cooperative effort offers, if not a guarantee of success, at least some inducement for the parties to work together." [201]

In the Indus Valley case the authority of the Bank's continuing conciliation was augmented by the credits it raised for the purpose of developing the resource.[202] As a practical matter, it cannot be assumed that funds of the magnitude of those raised by the Bank for the Indus Valley project would be available to develop a common international fishery. Furthermore, such financial power as that brought to bear by the Bank in the interest of amicable settlement would not, in most cases at least, be at the disposal of the commissions established under Article 9 of the Convention on Fishing. On the other hand, the devel-

---

[200] Same, 476.

[201] Same, 478.

[202] The amounts committed by the contributing states to the Indus Basin Development Fund by Dec. 31, 1968 (in U.S. dollar equivalents as determined by the International Bank for Reconstruction and Development for accounting purposes at that date) were as follows, according to a letter dated Jan. 28, 1969, from Piero Sella, Esq., Assistant General Counsel, IBRD, to this writer and held in this writer's files:

| | |
|---|---:|
| Australia | $ 26,061,000 |
| Canada | 36,246,361 |
| Germany | 51,600,000 |
| IBRD Loan and IDA Credit | 138,540,000 |
| India | 168,803,200 |
| Pakistan | |
|   in £ Sterling | 1,188,000 |
|   in Rupees | 371,824,292 |
| United Kingdom | 91,288,270 |
| U.S.A. | |
|   dollar grant | 295,590,000 |
|   dollar loan | 121,220,000 |
|   rupees | 235,000,000 |
| Total | $1,537,361,123 |

opment of a fishery and the enhancement of its value to the participating states need not involve the great capital outlays that the development of a river basin would generally entail. In the case of a fishery, development may well be relatively inexpensive in terms of infrastructure and investment outlays; it may be dependent on research, restraint of fishermen, and cooperative planning with existing or marginally improved equipment. And even if the lack of financial power may deprive the commission of a veiled coercive authority, the common sense inducements of a developed resource which a continuing conciliation would muster, could well provide the conciliators with an authority which the parties could voluntarily concede as a matter of enlightened self-interest on all sides.

## C. Conciliation and Management: Blueprints for Fisheries Regimes

Regimes which have been brought into being to regulate international fisheries have been successful to the extent that they have managed to dispense with "the Geneva language of international idealism" and "accommodate to the *realpolitik* of the averagely selfish." [203] Accordingly, various forms of fisheries regimes will be reviewed as models, and as adaptable, *mutatis mutandis* and to the extent practicable, to other resource-winning uses of the sea. They will be canvassed in terms of the following blueprints: (a) National Quotas; (b) Agent State; (c) Administrative Conciliation; and (d) Multinational Public Enterprises. This offering will be in the light of the following criteria: (a) Goals; (b) Participants; and (c) Measures.

### 1. CRITERIA

(a) *Goals.* Generally, management regimes may be viewed as guided by one or more of the following goals: (i) to improve the stock of a fishery, thereby implementing the goal of conservation as well as goals relating to the rewards the fishery has to offer its participants; (ii) to facilitate coastal states' domestic policies, be they guided by a call to create employment opportunities [204] or to use the fishery to contribute to their domestic economies; (iii) to protect and enhance the rewards of the fishermen; and (iv) to generate a value in the right to fish itself, part or all of which would be recoverable, by means of license fees, royalties, or taxes to be applied on behalf of the fishery regime as a whole to defray such costs as research, administration and control, etc. The strategy best suited for realizing these goals may, in most cases, be that of controlling access—a procedure which, in its turn, inevitably

---

[203] To adapt a phrase from George Orwell, a pragmatic idealist.

[204] Christy has graphically characterized this possible goal as "a form of unemployment insurance." F. Christy, "Fisheries Goals and the Rights of Property" (mimeo. Sept. 1968), 13, 19.

calls for the joint action of all states engaging in the fishery to delegate, for the benefit of all, a part of each separate authority, and to surrender the preexisting right to act preemptively. The advantage for each participant is that, as the whole fishery increases in value, so will the shares available to the participants grow—over and above what each of them might have originally taken from the resource by acting unilaterally to preempt what it could. Ultimately, the Santiago Declaration [205] and the Convention on Fishing have as their goals the welfare of the fishermen and the communities they support. The difference lies in the means. The Santiago Declaration places its trust in preemptive conduct,[206] the Convention on Fishing looks to the scientific cultivation of the fishery. While preemptive conduct may not reduce the fishery to levels below that of the maximum sustainable yield, it will never ensure that the fishery is conducted with a maximum saving of cost and a maximum economic return. That is, the emphasis of the Santiago Regime on the individual sovereignties of the CEP states as the bearers of exclusive fishing rights, and as individually authorized to enforce each of its own restrictions and regulations against the fishermen of third states in the maritime zone proclaimed by that state, indicates the regime's orientation. It is not so much directed toward joint control of the Humboldt Current fishery for cultivation and economic development purposes as toward collaborative efforts in the vindication of separate claims—the goal being not so much the rational management of the fishery as simply the acquisition of the greatest possible share of the Current's existing wealth. Such an orientation, it is suggested, must almost inevitably lead to the inefficient use of fishermen and gear, since each state will tend to make the greatest effort to appropriate the largest share of the catch. In contrast with such a state of affairs, the submission here is that the regime should also look to the maximization of the rewards of the fishermen and toward "saving the cost of fishing" [207] by establishing a supranational authority. This would achieve a functional integration of the resources used with policies of enhancement, thus maximizing the utility of the resource as a whole.

(b) *Participants.* It is suggested that the parties to the Santiago Declaration should be entitled to invoke the principle of abstention against all states not asserting a claim to fish in the Humboldt Current waters, at the point of time when those declarant states begin to

[205] See fn. 94.

[206] For an analysis of this point see Goldie, "Fisheries Management" (fn. 15), 31–33.

[207] See, Francis Christy and Anthony Scott, *The Common Wealth in Ocean Fisheries: Some Problems of Growth and Economic Allocation* (Baltimore 1965), 223 [hereinafter cited as Christy and Scott]. See also Goldie, "Fisheries Management" (fn. 15), 19–23.

negotiate, but not against other states with bona fide established claims to participate in the fishery—even if physically prevented by *force majeure*. Diplomatic protests against the arrest of fishermen and vessels for fishing on the high seas beyond territorial waters as recognized in international law, but within the limits claimed, for example, by the CEP states, or similar protests against unilateral CEP legislation establishing the maritime zones of at least 200 sea miles as provided for in the Santiago Declaration, or approaches to renegotiate the Santiago Declaration on other bases than those of the CEP states' unrecognized claims to maritime zones, or proposals to have differences regarding CEP, similarly exclusive, and unrecognized claims respecting maritime zones made the subject of arbitral or judicial settlement, should each and all be viewed as evidencing a bona fide claim to participate in the fishery. All states which have taken any one or more of the above steps should, therefore, be entitled to participate in the negotiations to establish a truly viable international regime to regulate and conserve the fishery of the Humboldt Current. The cut-off date, the "critical date" [208] after which no further state should be permitted to participate, should be a date indicated in the proposing countries' invitation to negotiate the regime's establishment and within a reasonable time thereafter. The "reasonable time thereafter" should allow a sufficient period of time for any uninvited state to lodge a claim to participate in the negotiations—the acceptance or rejection of such a claim also being a matter for compulsory arbitral or judicial settlement. This proposal would not work an injustice to the states actively participating in, or interested in, the fishery. On the other hand, it would be responsive to the comment made in Christy and Scott that: "The extent of historical involvement, however large and inefficient, is obviously important in arriving at agreements on the distribution of resources. New countries, with small fleets and short histories, however, will quite naturally complain of the unfairness of this approach." [209]

The procedure outlined above is intended to give "new countries with small fleets and short histories" their day to be heard. The only category of possible claimants are those who feel that they may have future contingent interests arising from newly developing economic, demographic, or cultural patterns which this proposal may seem to exclude forever. One answer to such an objection is that this touches upon one of the major infirmities of international law, namely its defective and piecemeal machinery for adjusting its rules and institu-

[208] For a discussion of the generalization of the critical date concept from territorial disputes to all international disputes involving temporal issues, see Goldie, "The Critical Date," 12 *International and Comparative Law Quarterly*, 1251 (1963).
[209] Christy and Scott (fn. 207), 212.

tions to social change, and that such a deficiency is not limited to the problems of fisheries. Emerging or future or contingent claims should not be viewed as blocked by fisheries settlements here and now. Nor should they be permitted to block settlements in this, any more than in any other, area of international law. One should remember, furthermore, that these claims are not as likely to be blocked or hampered by existing treaties, as such, as by *inertia* and the power and influence which might, in any given issue, be available to uphold the *status quo*. This observation is not to deny, on the other hand, the urgency of the problem of international law and social change as a general problem and not simply as a problem of fisheries. It should be a major concern of us all in every area of international law.

(c) *Measures*. First, the regime under discussion should emphasize the importance of both biological and economic research, so that the regulation of total catches would be not only limited in terms of the survival of fish populations, but also guided by criteria ensuring the optimum uses of capital and fishermen so as to ensure the maximum economic rent for the fishery.

Second, all forms of discrimination between the fishermen of different nationalities should be eliminated—except insofar as the principle of abstention [210] creates equities in favor of nations which have engaged in the extensive cultivation and improvement of a fishery, by the application of scientific principles and the imposition of restraints upon their own fishermen.

## 2. ALTERNATIVE REGIMES

When two or more states establish a common fisheries regime, there are a number of models. Four of these have already been indicated as subjects for the present discussion.

(a) *National Quotas*. Some agreements provide for the apportionment of a total permissible catch among the participating nations. Canada and the United States, for example, have agreed to apportion the annual catch of salmon within a treaty area.[211] Similarly, the parties to the International Convention for the Regulation of Whaling,[212] who were engaged in pelagic whaling, agreed in 1962 [213] to the alloca-

---

210 For a discussion of the "Principle of Abstention," see, Goldie, "Fisheries Management" (fn. 15), 28–31; and "Sedentary Fisheries" (fn. 42), 95–96.

211 See International Convention for the High Seas Fisheries of the North Pacific Ocean, [1953] I, U.S.T. 330, 391, T.I.A.S. No. 2786, 205 U.N.T.S. 65, 96–97.

212 Signed Dec. 2, 1946, 62 Stat. 1716, T.I.A.S. No. 1849, 161 U.N.T.S. 72.

213 See Arrangements Between Japan, the Netherlands, Norway, the Union of Soviet Socialist Republics, and the United Kingdom of Great Britain and Northern Ireland for the Regulation of Antarctic Pelagic Whaling, signed June 5, 1962, 486 U.N.T.S. 263. Supplementary Arrangements for the Regulation of Antarctic Pelagic Whaling were also signed by the above countries. See 486 U.N.T.S. 271.

tion of quotas [214] among themselves. An example attesting to the proprietorial (or quasi-proprietorial) nature of these rights is provided by
the United Kingdom's sale of its quota to Japan in 1964.[215] Professor
Crutchfield has strongly supported this as a solution to the present
chaotic results of uncontrolled access and unlimited takes.[216] Theoretically, it makes each national fishing industry independent of the others,
and each can arrange to take its quota in the manner best suited to
its social, economic, and technological situation without fear of being
preempted by other countries' fishermen. Christy and Scott, however,
demonstrate clearly the difficulties of this solution.[217] They point out
that it does not eliminate the incentives of members to race each other
in bringing in their quotas, resulting in over-large capacity and short
seasons. Second, they point out that the probability of having to split
national quotas into sub-areas would induce fishermen to race in those
sub-areas, resulting in incentives for fleets larger and swifter than
would otherwise be warranted. Finally, they argue that a national
quota, having monopoly characteristics, might serve to retard technical
progress and inhibit the entry of more efficient producers.[218] To these
points this writer would like to add the following consideration: resistance at the 1958 Geneva Conference on the Law of the Sea to the
principle of abstention stemmed very largely from a suspicion that
this was an attempt to stamp the *status quo* in international fisheries
to the exclusion of possible future contingent claims, which, in the
present fluid situation of world fisheries, might come to be strongly
pressed. A national quota system, insofar as it also may be characterized as a system allocating proprietorial, or quasi-proprietorial, rights,
is even more vulnerable to the criticism already outlined than is the
principle of abstention, in that its advantages are not made contingent upon good husbandry.[219] Nor would a system of national quotas
necessarily contain qualities which could ensure the protection of
developing fisheries similar to those inherent in the principle of abstention. Accordingly, unlike that principle, it could be available for the
support of the *status quo* without the attachment of the fiduciary

[214] Art. 3 of the 1962 Arrangements authorized the following quotas: Japan—33%;
the Netherlands—6%; Norway—32%; U.S.S.R.—20%; United Kingdom—9%. For a
comprehensive history, see Douglas Johnston, *International Law of Fisheries: A
Framework for Policy-Oriented Inquiries* (New Haven 1965), 396–411.

[215] See, e.g., Exchange of Notes Between the United Kingdom and Japan, signed
Jan. 6, 1964, T.S. No. 18 (1964), Cmnd. 2337.

[216] Crutchfield, "Management of the North Pacific Fisheries: Economic Objectives
and Issues," 43 *Washington Law Review*, 283, 303–05 (1967).

[217] Christy and Scott (fn. 207), 209–10.

[218] See also McDougal and Burke (fn. 47), 508–10.

[219] For a discussion of the principle of abstention, see Goldie, "Fisheries Management" (fn. 42), 28–31.

conditions which tend to make the latter principle both acceptable to developing countries and advantageous to the general welfare of the fishery to which it is applied.

(b) *Agent State*. The Fur Seal Convention between Russia, Japan, the United States, Great Britain, and (later) Canada [220] provides the leading example of the "agent state" approach. Christy and Scott describe it as follows: "[I]t is unique among all conservation treaties in that it appoints two 'agents'—the United States and Russia—to carry out the management and harvesting of the herds on their islands. Pelagic sealing is prohibited, and provision is made for sharing the proceeds amongst the signatories. In effect, the agreement creates sole ownership in each of the two areas." [221]

On the basis of this model, one or more of the participating states may come to be accepted as the "fishing agents" of a community of states in a regime. The other members' claims to participate would then become converted into claims for compensation. Fishing regimes could consist of all the states of a region and even of the world. A scheme of this kind would be sufficiently inclusive to envisage that states with merely contingent future interests in the fishery might also be entitled to negotiate for membership. These states may thereupon be enabled to trade off their claims for a share in the fishery for other gains which might be collateral to the fishery, or independent of it— merely coinciding with other interests of the leading states engaged in the fishery regime. In this context, the principle of abstention could be further developed so as to relate to the appointment of, and the equitable rewards to be recognized as vesting in, the regime's "agent states," also the compensation due to the abstaining states, the necessary qualifications for such compensation, and the trade-offs which could be utilized in the satisfaction of claims to be an "agent state," or merely to participate in the fishery.

(c) *Administrative Conciliation*. The managerial emphasis of "administrative conciliation," in contradistinction to continuing conciliation, has already been indicated.[222] The procedure of administrative conciliation, as a means of allocating rights to exploit a fishery in which the fishermen of a number of both coastal and overseas states participate, would involve a number of very important differences

[220] The first of these treaties, the Convention Between the United States and Other Powers Providing for the Preservation and Protection of Fur Seals, was signed July 7, 1911, 37 Stat. 1542. The most recent was signed in 1957 and amended in 1963. See Interim Convention on Conservation of North Pacific Fur Seals, [1957] 2 U.S.T. 2283, T.I.A.S. No. 3948, 314 U.N.T.S. 105, and the Protocol Amending the Interim Convention . . . [1964] 1 U.S.T. 316, T.I.A.S. No. 5558, 494 U.N.T.S. 303.

[221] Christy and Scott (fn. 207), 196.

[222] See Goldie, "Fisheries Management" (fn. 15), 17–18.

from the continuing conciliation of a dispute over the waters of an international river basin. For example, a system of dams, barrages, irrigation canals, and water collection networks can only be established once the basic allocations have been settled. Thus, this conciliation may be seen as "continuous" only for as long as there are outstanding differences in the means of developing the river system and in the distribution of the waters it can be made to yield. The greater the area of settlement becomes, the smaller the area for conciliation. With a fishery the process may be far otherwise. There need not be any agreed distribution which becomes final and forms the basis of costly construction works and changes in the use of land—changes which can only be reversed at great human and economic cost. Indeed, fluctuations in the market, changes in the feeding, migration, or spawning habits of the stock, and developments in conservation knowledge and in fishing gear and techniques, might, in fact, call for a continuing reappraisal of the basic criteria of the resource's distribution among the countries involved. Administrative, or managerial, conciliation does not indicate a process of widening the area of agreement by building on previously settled aspects of a dispute; rather it means the continuous management of the development and distribution and redistribution of the resource in terms of continuously changing controlling factors. To carry out its task effectively, a conciliation commission would have to operate without any goal of achieving final solutions.

A special agreement creating a fisheries regime independently of the Convention on Fishing, or under Articles 4 and 5, or one invoking Article 9, could instruct the commission it sets up to administer the fishery without planning to wind up its work. Alternatively, such a commission might well be called upon to establish a permanent administrative group to carry on the task of administrative conciliation. In either case, the institution of an impartial administrative agency would be a most effective instrument for enhancing the efficiency and value of the fishery as well as for achieving a just distribution of its product. The fishery as a whole would, furthermore, be better served if the administrative agency could be invested with supranational powers. If this necessary transfer of power could be achieved, the agency would be in a position to administer the fishery as a single unit and without regard to the special claims of the sovereign states through which, otherwise, it would have to operate. (Only too often such special claims have had a severely distorting effect.) In effect, a supranational authority could be treated as an efficient substitute for the agent state, in addition, it would be able to achieve greater equities between a number of states than could the "agent state" model.

(d) *Multinational Public Enterprises.*[223] Properly designed, a multinational public enterprise could effectively combine the advantages of the agent state solution with that of administrative conciliation. Such an enterprise could either engage directly in the multinational fishery or, alternatively, give licenses to fish to fishermen who complied with the standards it would set for gear, employment policies, and economic efficiency. In either case, the enterprise would have to be accorded a monopoly of the fishery. It would enjoy the advantages of the agent-state approach, as it would be the delegate of all the states participating in the regime. It would, in addition, avert the disadvantage of that approach since no state, or group of states, need be placed in a favored position. It would also provide the regime with the advantages of the administrative conciliation procedure, since its blueprint should include a politically-oriented commission with authority to give overall direction to the corporation in the light of the values, demands, expectations, and contributions of the participating states. The corporation would have the further advantage, and one which multinational public enterprises have in common, of building transnational habits of cooperation and of problem-solving coterminous with the area of the regime rather than with that of any state within it.[224]

Before examining some of the more salient relevant features of a blueprint for the proposed multinational public enterprises, the basic point should first be made that entities of this kind are utilized in many and diverse areas of international economic activity, and each of them springs from pragmatic and functionalist roots. They are brought into being when states seek to attain common ends "by making use of the present social and scientific opportunities to link together particular activities and interests, one at a time, according to need and acceptability, giving each a joint authority and policy limited to that activity alone." [225] Second, although they are called upon to fulfill very divergent tasks, these entities "possess certain common characteristics which distinguish them from other international organizations. They perform economic tasks of a public nature, for which they require the long-term investment of capital and a permanent organization. They generally perform operational functions, and are vested with a power of direct action." [226] As Professor Wolfgang Friedmann

223 For the choice of this term, from among a number of others see C. Fligler, *Multinational Public Enterprises* (IBRD Study 1967), 7–8 [hereinafter cited as Fligler]. For a more detailed application of this blueprint to international fisheries, see Goldie, "Fisheries Management" (fn. 15), 47–51.

224 See, e.g., Fligler (fn. 223) 10; Inis Claude, *Swords into Plowshares* (New York 1964), 348.

225 D. Mitrany, "The Prospect of Integration: Federal or Functional," *Common Market Studies*, IV (1965), 119, 135. See also D. Mitrany, *A Working Peace System* (Chicago 1966), 41.

226 Fligler (fn. 223), 7.

has pointed out, quoting President Roosevelt's characterization of the Tennessee Valley Authority, they are "clothed with the power of government, but possessed of the flexibility and initiative of private enterprise." [227]

An enterprise such as that to be considered for the management of a multinational regional fishery should include provisions resolving questions as to the constituent instrument, juridical personality (and nationality, if any), structure and control, powers, privileges and immunities, and the settlement of disputes.[228] This writer has already outlined the structure of an international public enterprise conceived of to manage a regional fishery,[229] and has applied the lessons learned from studies of such enterprises in other fields.[230]

## VI: SOME PROPOSED REGIMES FOR DEEP-SEA MINING

### A. Some Theories in Review

#### 1. A BRIEF CONSPECTUS [231]

The dilemmas created by the growing need and the developing engineering capability on the one hand, and the ineptitude and primitiveness of the applicable legal doctrines on the other, have induced a number of writers to propose alternatives to the present regime. The offered blueprints vary greatly, but they are all guided by the need to secure titles and transactions arising out of ocean-bed enterprises, to

[227] W. Friedmann, "International Public Corporations," 6 *Modern Law Review*, 185–86 (1943).

[228] Certain other important topics, such as "capital structure and method of financing," "governing law," and recruitment of personnel have been omitted as not bearing sufficiently on the central theme of this study. For a discussion of the former topic, see, e.g., Friedmann (fn. 227), 192–95; and for the latter two topics, see Fligler (fn. 223), 82–92, 107–09.

[229] See, Goldie, "Fisheries Management" (fn. 15), 47–51.

[230] International public enterprises are deservedly becoming an important topic of study for international lawyers. In addition to the works already cited, the following represent a useful selection: J. Sewell, *Functionalism and World Politics* (Princeton 1966); A. Hanson, *Public Enterprise and Economic Development* (London 1965); R. Baxter, *The Law of International Waterways* (Cambridge, Mass. 1964), 91–148, 306–41 (but note the writer's conclusion at 340–41 and his "Articles on the Navigation of International Canals" at 343–45); W. Friedmann, *The Changing Structure of International Law* (New York 1964), 216–20; H. Finer, *The T.V.A. Lessons for International Application* (Montreal 1944), passim; Johnson, "International Co-operation in Satellite Communications Systems," 61 *Proceedings of the American Society of International Law*, 24 (1967); Note, "Corporations Formed Pursuant to a Treaty," 76 *Harvard Law Review*, 1431 (1963); Sereni, "International Economic Institutions and the Municipal Law of States," 96 *Recueil des Cours* (1959-I), 133; Clive Parry, "The International Public Corporation," in *The Public Corporation: A Comparative Symposium*, W. Friedmann, ed. (Toronto 1954), 495; and see Friedmann, "A Comparative Analysis," in same, 541, 593–94.

[231] See, for a fuller review of the theories briefly foreshadowed here, Goldie, "Davy Jones's Locker (fn. 73), 25–38.

achieve an equitable allocation of the benefits which the oceans offer, and to safeguard inconsistent uses so that they do not lead to conflicts which cannot be resolved by international diplomatic procedures or adjudication. The suggested alternative regimes are: (a) to divide the bed of the oceans among coastal nations, an alternative which has a very strong resemblance to the position of those who advocate the interpretation of the exploitability test in Article 1 of the Continental Shelf Convention which permits states to advance into the ocean basins until they meet along median lines. Whether in the form of an exegesis of Article 1 of the Continental Shelf Convention or of a new Convention, this is the proposal most hospitable to chauvinism and greed [232]—it is one, moreover, which ratifies the enclosure movement which the late Professor George Scelle foresaw as the inevitable and baneful consequence of the continental shelf doctrine; [233] (b) To apply the doctrine of *occupatio terrae nullius* as assumed and made to serve, for example, in the Guano Island Act of 1856 [234] to the ocean's seabed and subsoil—this has also been called "the 'flag nation' approach"; [235] (c) To establish an international agency with power to grant leases and extract revenues therefrom. There are four main versions of this recommendation, namely, (i) Senator Pell's more recent resolution proposing a Declaration of Legal Principles Governing the Activities of States in the Exploration and Exploitation of Ocean Space,[236] and his proposed Treaty on Principles of Governing the Activities of States in the Exploration and Exploitation of Ocean Space; [237] (ii) Ambassador Pardo of Malta's proposals in the General Assembly of the United Nations [238] and in the *Ad Hoc* Committee to Study the Peaceful Uses of the Sea-Bed and Ocean Floor Beyond the Limits of National Juris-

[232] S. Bernfeld, "Developing the Resources of the Sea—Security of Investment," 2 *The International Lawyer*, 67 (1968).

[233] Scelle, "Plateau Continental" (fn. 99).

[234] 11 Stat. 119 (1856), 48 U.S.C. §§1411–17 (1964). The main proponent of this theory, Mr. Northcutt Ely, does not make reference to the Guano Islands Act. Be that as it may, there is clearly a very close parallel between that long-established statute and this current proposal. Indeed, the great majority of the proposals in this category bear closer resemblances to the use of the doctrine of occupation in the Guano Islands Act than they do to more traditional uses of this doctrine.

[235] N. Ely, "American Policy Options in the Development of Undersea Mineral Resources," 2 *The International Lawyer*, 215 (1968). Dr. Christy has characterized this thesis as "the 'flag nation' approach"; see his "A Social Scientist Writes on Economic Criteria for Rules Governing Exploitation of Deep Sea Minerals," 2 *The International Lawyer*, 224 (1968).

[236] S. Res. 33, 91st Cong., 1st Sess. See also S. Res. 263, 90th Cong., 2nd Sess.; S. Res. 186, 90th Cong., 1st Sess.; and *Hearings on S. J. Res. 111, S. Res. 172, and S. Res. 186 Before the Senate Committee on Foreign Relations, 90th Cong., 1st Sess.,* (1967).

[237] 114 Congressional Record (daily edn. March 5, 1968), 2199-2202. This was later incorporated into Senator Pell's S. Res. 263, above.

[238] See A/6695 (fn. 173), 1–2.

diction,[239] and the Committee on the Peaceful Uses of the Sea-Bed and Ocean Floor Beyond the Limits of National Jurisdiction; [240] (iii) the Commission to Study the Organization of Peace's Seventeenth [241] and Nineteenth Reports; [242] and (iv) Professor Scelle's proposal in 1955.[243]

## 2. A CRITICAL APPRAISAL OF THE INTERNATIONAL AGENCY BLUEPRINTS

Two criticisms of these last three groups of proposals are immediately relevant. Unlike Senator Pell's proposals, the Commission to Study the Organization of Peace's Reports and Professor Scelle's article fail to accommodate freedom of scientific research. Second, in seeking to banish politics, the three sets of blueprints for an international leasing agency make their initial acceptance the more unlikely—since they deny any role to the states whose consent is a condition precedent to establishing the regime they advocate. In addition, the rejection of politics may well be equivalent to the rejection of the balance wheel of the agency's efficient operation in international affairs.

(a) *The Need to Ensure Freedom of Scientific Research.* Senator Pell affirms the "freedom of scientific investigation in ocean space." Other blueprints for an international licensing or leasing authority have failed, even, to propose the extension out to the bed and subsoil of the "Great Seas" (Mr. Bernfeld's phrase) [244] of the limited privileges assured to science in the Continental Shelf Convention. Yet here is a crucial issue. The exercise of the freedom of disinterested scientific research might very easily conflict in a number of ways with the pur-

---

[239] See e.g., "Reply by Malta to Secretary-General," March 6, 1968, Note by Secretary-General at 29–32, U.N. Doc. A/AC. 135/1 (mimeo. March 11, 1968).

[240] See "Representative of Malta, Statement in the Legal Sub-Committee of the Committee on the Peaceful uses of the Sea-Bed and Ocean Floor Beyond the Limits of National Jurisdiction" (Press Release, mimeo, March 30, 1969). See also, "Malta, Draft Resolution," U.N. Doc. A/AC 138/11 (mimeo., March 18, 1969). Ambassador Pardo also gave a full statement of his position in his address at the 62nd Annual Meeting of the American Society of International Law, see American Society of International Law, *Proceedings of the Sixty-Second Annual Meeting (April 25–27, 1968)* (1968), 216.

[241] The leading Statement of this doctrine is Commission to Study the Organization of Peace, *New Dimensions for the United Nations: The Problems of the Next Decade* (17th Report, 1966), 41–46 [hereinafter cited as *Seventeenth Report*]. See also Statement of Clark Eichelberger, Commission to Study the Organization of Peace, *Hearings on S. J. Res. 111, S. Res. 172, S. Res. 186 Before the Senate Committee on Foreign Relations,* 90th Cong. 1st Sess. (1967), at 39–43.

[242] Commission to Study the Organization of Peace, *The United Nations and the Bed of the Sea* (Nineteenth Report, 1969) [hereinafter cited as *Nineteenth Report*].

[243] See Scelle, "Plateau Continental" (fn. 99), 57–61.

[244] He indicated a sense of his meaning for this phrase, see Bernfeld (fn. 232), 68, in the following passage: "By the 'Great Seas of Mankind' I include the Atlantic, Pacific, Indian and Arctic Oceans after excluding from each of them those bodies of water *sui generis* such as closed or partially closed seas, bays, estuaries, straits, channels, and the like." See also 70, 73, 75.

chased rights of the states' or international organization's licensees or lessees, in a way which could greatly restrict the scope of their operations (by threat of being subject to an easement, as it were, of scientific research), and hence reduce their value. Without being subject to the possibility of having to defer to the needs of scientific research, the licensees or lessees would enjoy greater leeway in the exercise of their economic rights, which were originally conferred in terms of economic efficiency. Thus economic efficiency may be seen as in conflict with freedom of scientific research, and proposals emphasizing it would appear to contain a strong implication either of support for its abolition or, at least, of sympathy for fobbing off claims made on the strength of the value it underpins.[245]

(b) *The Banishment of Politics.* Despite their failure to include a future for the freedom of scientific research, in general it is true to say that all three of the proposals for an international licensing and/or leasing agency are very attractive and worthwhile. On the other hand, they suffer from a second defect. This lies in their attempt to banish politics from the processes of their agencies' decision-making. Professor Scelle states this to be an avowed goal—at least as far as it could be feasible.[246] The *Seventeenth* and *Nineteenth Reports'* model is that of an independent agency which is required to exercise its authority "in accordance with the principles of economic efficiency." [247] Hence purely political motivations would necessarily be minimal in the agency's operation. The assumption underlying the proposals to be put forward later, by contrast, is that the suggested institution should not only be able to operate within the system of contemporary international politics, but should drawn its strength from it—for these are the very politics upon which the development of a stable regime governing the resources of the seabed and subsoil of the oceans will necessarily depend, in the first instance for acceptance, and continuously thereafter for effective survival. Second, in contrast with the other proposals for an international organization with authority to allocate seabed resources, this paper's proposals are far more limited, ambitious as they may appear in comparison with some other proposals and when viewed against the backdrop of the contemporary system. In place of

245 For a fuller discussion of this point see Goldie, "Davy Jones's Locker" (fn. 73), 37, 52–53.

246 One should add that Professor Scelle also viewed the complete banishment of politics from his proposed agency as an impractical ideal. On the other hand, he was clearly determined to reduce their significance by recourse to administrative processes—which he felt were inherently freer of the taint of politics—to as great an extent as possible. See Scelle, "Plateau Continental" (fn. 99), 59–61.

247 See *Seventeenth Report* (fn. 241), 44. See also *Nineteenth Report* (fn. 242), 16–17. In the latter publication the *Seventeenth Report*'s emphasis on economic efficiency was retained, but its emphasis would appear to be modified slightly.

an international administrative agency, the proposal here is for the establishment of a comprehensive treaty regime which would take into account the national security problems of coastal states, secure a significant role in the process of decision for interested states, assure internationally-supported exclusive titles to take mineral resources from the seabed and subsoil of the oceans below the 200 hundred meter depth without derogating from the rights of interested states to retain control of those resources, and give effective expression to claims advanced in terms of a proposed freedom of scientific research to be exercisable both on the continental shelf and beyond.

## B. Registration Regimes

### 1. THE COMMISSION ON MARINE SCIENCE, ENGINEERING, AND RESOURCES

Among the recommendations the Commission on Marine Science, Engineering, and Resources published in early 1969 was its proposed "international legal-political framework" [248] to govern the exploration of deep-ocean mineral resources. It recommended, first, that each coastal state's continental shelf be redefined as ending at either the two hundred meter isobath or fifty nautical miles from the baseline from which the territorial sea is measured, whichever gave the coastal state the greater area. Second, it proposed the establishment of an "intermediate zone" [249] for areas beyond that shelf. Third, it put forward a blueprint for an international registry authority. Under the registry plan "only a nation or an organization of nations, should be eligible to register a claim." [250] The claim, in its turn, would be worked by public or private business enterprises—the states enacting appropriate legislation and extending their civil and criminal laws to the relevant exploration and exploitation activities.[251] Fourth, the "framework" also contained provisions for an International Fund,[252] into which would be paid a

---

[248] See III, *Panel Reports* (fn. 5), VIII-35–43; *Our Nation and the Sea* (fn. 5), 141–51.

[249] This was described in III, *Panel Reports* (fn. 5), VIII-34–35, as an area where only the "coastal State or its licensees, which may or may not be its nationals" may explore for or exploit the zone's "mineral resources." In all other respects, however, the intermediate zone was to fall under the regime governing the deep sea. The Zone's geographical limits were then defined as follows: "[I]t is recommended that the outer limits of the intermediate zone be defined in terms of the 2,500 meter isobath or 100 nautical miles from the base-lines for measuring the breadth of the territorial sea, whichever alternative gives the coastal State the greater submarine area for the purposes for which the intermediate zone is created." See also *Our Nation and the Sea* (fn. 5), 151.

[250] *Our Nation and the Sea* (fn. 5), 148. See also III, *Panel Reports* (fn. 5), VIII-36. Cf. Goldie, "Davy Jones's Locker" (fn. 73), 44–45.

[251] For the "Powers and Duties of Registering Nations" see *Our Nation and the Sea* (fn. 5), 150. See also III, *Panel Reports* (fn. 5), VIII-39.

[252] *Our Nation and the Sea* (fn. 5), 149–50, III *Panel Reports* (fn. 5), VIII-38–39.

portion of the value of production to finance marine scientific activity, resources exploration and development, "particularly food-from-the-sea-programs" [253] and international aid for developing countries.

The Stratton Commission's "international legal-political framework" calls for state action, and only state action, at the international level.[254] States register their "claims" [255] or "Zones of Special Jurisdiction." [256] Enterprises, be they public or private,[257] operate within the municipal-law scope of what the nation state obtains internationally. This two-step approach, and the reliance on municipal law to regulate the technostructures actually engaged in exploration and exploitation activities, require a clear statement of the legal quality [258] of the title,[259] that is, the bundle of rights conferring jurisdiction and control short of "sovereign rights" [260] which an administering state may exercise within

[253] Same.

[254] *Our Nation and the Sea* (fn. 5), 148. See also, III, *Panel Reports* (fn. 5), VIII-39. Cf. Goldie, "Davy Jones's Locker (fn. 73), 45–46.

[255] This is the term used in *Our Nation and the Sea* (fn. 5), 148–51 and III, *Panel Reports* (fn. 5), VIII, 36–40. It would, when asserted by a state as contemplated in the above Reports, appear to be more or less homologous with the term "Zones of Special Jurisdiction" cited in fn. 261.

[256] For an explanation of Zones of Special Jurisdiction see Goldie, "Davy Jones's Locker" (fn. 73), 40–41, 43–45.

[257] The term "enterprise," denoting an economic or business entity operating under the municipal law of a registering state, may be publicly or privately owned, or it could be an independent public corporation. It could also be a local entity ultimately owned and controlled by foreign individuals or corporations, or be itself a foreign corporation or a foreign or multinational public enterprise. The nature and qualities of the enterprises the participating states permit to engage in exploration and exploitation activities in their Zones of Special Jurisdiction are matters for the municipal laws and policies of each of them.

[258] The term "quality" of an administering state's interest or "title" in this context means the manner of holding title, and indicates the sources of its validity. It is to be contrasted with the quantity of such a state's interest, *i.e.,* the scope and duration of the rights allowed. The quantity of a state's interest has usually been well covered in the published works on the subject.

[259] "Title" in the present context is a shorthand term to indicate the bundle of rights of jurisdiction and control (see next footnote and the accompanying text) which an administering state may exercise over specific resources in its zone of special jurisdiction (see fn. 261).

[260] The concept of sovereign rights was formulated by the International Law Commission and adopted in art. 2, para. 1, of the Continental Shelf Convention. This term is clearly distinguishable from "sovereignty," since it is specialized and restricted to the carrying out of the purposes of exploring and exploiting the resources of the seabed and its subsoil. On the other hand, it does include the recognition that the coastal state's rights, limited and specific as they may be, are permanent, exclusive and proprietary. See the International Law Commission's commentary on art. 68 of its Articles Concerning the Law of the Sea, International Law Commission, "Report Covering the Work of its Eighth Session," 1956, 2 *Year Book of the International Law Commission* 253, 298, U.N. Doc. A/3159. Accordingly, the term "jurisdiction and control" has been selected, despite its early association, in art. 2 of the International Law Commission's 1951 Draft Articles on the Continental Shelf and Related Subjects, and in President Truman's Proclamation With

the area of its claim, or zone of special jurisdiction [261] for the period assigned, and with respect to the resources made the subject of its rights. The "framework" should, furthermore, unequivocally prescribe its formula for the general, regime-wide, basis for the transnational recognition, protection, and vindication of these rights.

(a) *The Quality of States' Titles.* The Stratton Commission has proposed the establishment of an International Registry Authority [262] with which states would register their claims to explore, and subsequently exploit, specific resources in a defined area for a certain time. The Commission also considered that contentions as to claims should be governed by the "first-come, first-registered" principle. The argument has been made [263] that, despite its use of the word registry, and its invocation of certain land registry shibboleths, the Commission either did not intend to establish a true registry system (*i.e.,* one that has the effect of deriving title from the register) or, if it did so intend, it did not effectively carry out its purpose. The core of this argument is that the creation of title under a registry system is necessarily both a dispository and judicial act, and that neither of these legal criteria were sufficiently complied with. In addition it was pointed out that, if the Commission did intend to establish a dispository body, then the distinction it sought to draw between its own proposals and, for example, those of the Commission to Study the Organization of Peace, were, so far as the essentials of dispositions was concerned, a distinction without a difference.

This formal analysis leaves the question of the Commission's intention open. Perhaps it did intend to formulate a registration regime but, in omitting certain essentials, it failed to achieve its purpose, or it may have intended all along to propose a regime more analogous to domestic recording than to registration systems.

The problems attendant on a recording system are very different from those which have just been reviewed. Since recording merely evi-

---

Respect to Natural Resources of the Subsoil and Sea Bed of the Continental Shelf, Sept. 28, 1945, 10 Fed. Reg. 12303 (1945), with ideas of permanence, exclusivity, and proprietorship. It is arguable that since this term was supplanted by "sovereign rights" in order to indicate those qualities more clearly, it is available to indicate a legal concept which does not include permanent rights of full proprietorship, or *dominium,* let alone sovereignty, or *imperium,* over seabed areas.

[261] "Zones of Special Jurisdiction" have been defined as areas in which "states may exercise exclusive authority over the exploration for and exploitation of the specific mineral resources for which the authority was originally sought." Goldie, "Davy Jones's Locker" (fn. 73), 40. For a discussion of the limited and contingent nature of this concept, same, 43-48.

[262] *Our Nation and the Sea* (fn. 5), 147-49.

[263] See Goldie, "Two Neglected Problems in Drafting Regimes for Deep-Ocean Resources" (to be published) [hereinafter cited as Goldie, "Neglected Problems"].

dences title, the validity of that title depends on rules which the system presumes. In the case of the ocean floor beyond national jurisdiction, these would be occupation and prescription. Indeed, the "first-come, first-registered" policy of the Stratton Commission's proposals seem to reflect the worst aspects of occupation. One may say "worst aspects" advisedly, since they are not mitigated by the requirement of notice which article 34 of the General Act of the Berlin Congo Conference of 1885 required.[264] Of course a recording system is itself a means of giving notice. Unlike the giving of notice which should be called for, recordation, including the "registration" the Commission recommends, merely notifies the world of a completed fact—a *fait accompli* which, in its turn, derives its strength from winning the race to the record book. Winning this race may also amount to giving notice; but that notice is a triumphant proclamation, not an invitation to test the equities.

(b) *Transnational Recognition.* A problem which treaty draftsmen have frequently not sufficiently faced in the past is the contingent and relative nature of titles in transnational commerce, once they have passed beyond the jurisdiction which created them. International law does not impose duties equivalent to those called for in the full faith and credit clauses of federal constitutions, and so nation states are, largely, free to consult their own policies when faced with the issue of whether or not to recognize a foreign disposition of property rights. Such policies may, and normally do, include "that of fostering the element of stability and unity essential to an international order in which many aspects of life are not confined within the limits of any single jurisdiction"[265]—a policy of enlightened economic self-interest. On the other hand, a particular state's local values might well demand deference to a local policy which denies effectiveness to the call of such an internationally-oriented policy. Furthermore, the domestic law rules in which a generous policy of recognition may be embodied, are, from the international point of view, not the particular applications of an international rule of law, but merely the reflection of a propensity of domestic courts and of states—a propensity which might be limited by other claims upon the actor. The exclusive authority of states in this connection was felicitously summed up by von Savigny in the following brief pair of propositions:

(1) Every State is entitled to demand that its own laws only shall be recognized within its bounds;

264 Feb. 26, 1885, 10 Martens Nouveau Recueil 2d 384, 396. Art. 35 of the General Act contains a classic definition of occupation, same, 396–97.
265 Von Mehren and Trautman, "Recognition of Foreign Adjudication: A Survey and Suggested Approach," 81 *Harvard Law Review,* 1601 (1968).

(2) No State can require the recognition of its laws beyond its bounds.[266]

This Cyclopean [267] model provides merely a hypothetical starting-point. Just as Polyphemus needed his brethren after Ulysses put out his eye, so no state can operate effectively in "sovereign disregard of all its peers." On the other hand, nations' sovereign independence does provide the basis for selective refusals of recognition—for strictly local reasons and in vindication of what may well be no better than strictly autochthonous values. For human beings, unfortunately, and even states, can exhibit a propensity to mumpsimus just as they can act in the light of enlightened self-interest. In addition, it is possible for states to see their self-interest as calling for the nonrecognition of foreign laws, judgments, and instruments—since recognition in certain circumstances could well be viewed as supporting an unwanted and burdensome *status quo*. Thus, in the absence of an equivalent to a full-faith and credit clause, foreign titles and other characterizations remain possibly contingent upon the hospitality of the receiving state.[268]

There are a number of advantages, from the point of view of the proposed regime as a whole, in imposing strong full-faith and credit obligations. First, it assures the general security and predictability of transactions. Second, it protects the regime from being undermined by activities outside it and under general international law. Because there may well be pickings for states which remain outside a registration regime, it is almost inevitable that not all states would quickly choose to ratify the treaty establishing it.[269] Again some states, while becoming parties to the establishing convention, might leave the initiative of invoking the regime's protection, in any given situation, to their ocean-exploring or exploiting enterprises (*i.e.*, they might operate under the aegis of nonparties). In either case, individuals, enterprises, and even states would still be capable of engaging in submarine activities outside the regime and under the general customary international-law privilege of taking the oceans' resources on an open-access

---

[266] Friedrich C. Von Savigny, *Private International Law*, trans. Guthrie (Edinburgh 1869), 26.

[267] Plato, in his *Laws*, described the Cyclops as follows:

> Mootless were they, and lawless;
> On Mountains high they dwelt in hollow caves,
> Where each his own law dealt to wife and child
> In sovereign disregard of all his peers.

[268] An illustration of this point may be found in Durfee v. Duke, 375 U.S. 106 (1963). One may imagine an opposite outcome, had there been no Full Faith and Credit Clause in the United States Constitution.

[269] This point was made by Goldie, "Davy Jones's Locker" (fn. 73), 53. See also 53–54 for the analogous position regarding defense installations, which, however, is not germane to the present discussion.

basis.[270] For it should be recognized that, on a short-term footing at least, this could provide some activities with greater advantages than would the regime. Furthermore, the regime, while promoting the general advantage of its signatories as a group, might work to an enterprise's or a state's disadvantage in certain circumstances. Since the majority of states cannot impose the regime on all states, the inclusion of a mutual full-faith and credit obligation effective among the participating states could tend to reduce the advantages of staying out of the regime, provided the leading commercial nations of the world were parties to it. If a dispute should arise between an enterprise operating under the regime, and one operating under the general privilege that customary law allows, then, in the event of its coming before the courts of a third state, a party to the regime, the full-faith and credit clause would bind that state's courts and assure that the claim based on the treaty regime would prevail. Hence states participating in the regime would enjoy, among themselves, an unambiguous advantage whenever transactions call for transnationally-merchantable titles. These advantages, possibly, would not accrue in the courts of third states which remain outside the regime. But this merely emphasizes a point already made, namely that the regime should be framed to attract, and include, as many as possible of the states through whose economies the products of the seabed are most likely to flow.

Similar advantages could accrue before international tribunals when rights protected by the clause compete with claims arising under general international law. A state party to the treaty would be internationally bound by the full-faith and credit clause as a treaty obligation and, therefore, be constrained to recognize a title deriving from the regime. This may be illustrated by the following example. A dispute arises between States A and B over title to a product from a zone of special jurisdiction, validly allocated to State C and worked by an enterprise operating under its laws. State B asserts that the product is, under its laws, the property of another enterprise, one whose claim it is now espousing, and since that product has subsequently come into State A in the ordinary course of commerce, State A is under a duty to recognize the title derived from State B's laws. If States A and C are both parties to the treaty regime, but State B is not, then the full-faith and credit clause would call upon the tribunal to uphold A's recognition of the title created under the laws of State C and not the title derived from those of State B. That the treaty may thus effect the claims of State B, a non-party, is not so surprising when one recalls the specific nature of mutual obligation between States A and C

[270] This argument is accepting customary international law as still current and does not attempt to evaluate the General Assembly's so-called Moratorium Resolution, *i.e.*, General Assembly Resolution 2574 D (XXIV).

in this case, for they are obligations which can only be limited by preexisting rules of validity. This advantage is limited to the case where the duty to recognize the priority of the treaty obligation exists. Where it does not, the opposite decision might well be of equal validity, depending on the tribunal's view of the nonrecognizing state's international obligations apart from the treaty. Here again, the advantage of the full-faith and credit clause would be enhanced if the major mercantile states of the world were parties to the regime.

By placing a priority on rights derived from the regime, the full-faith and credit clause is thus able to create inducements for states and enterprises to see that working within the regime, rather than outside it, would most closely accord with their enlightened self-interest.

The International Panel did indicate a sensitivity to the need for some form of international recognition of titles to transnationally moving products of the seabed. It recommended that:

> (f) Registration of a claim to exploit particular mineral resources in a particular area of the deep seas shall confer upon the State Registrant (i) . . . (ii) internationally-recognized title, or the right to confer such title, to the extracted mineral resources. States which are parties to the agreements embodying the new framework shall undertake to enact implementing national legislation protecting such titles.[271]

It has been pointed out elsewhere,[272] however, that this formulation does not really indicate an effective choice on the International Panel's part, and a more viable selection will be outlined below.[273]

### 2. "DAVY JONES'S LOCKER" [274]

The proposals for a treaty regime in the pages which follow are intended to indicate in general terms procedures for allocating among states needed controls over the exploration and exploitation of mineral resources of the seabed and subsoil of the deep oceans, beyond the continental shelves already subject to the sovereign rights of coastal states. Second, these proposals take up a more detailed discussion of an international regime capable of providing for the recognition and reception of transnationally valid and marketable titles to those resources.[275] Third, proposals for a registration regime will be intro-

---

[271] III *Panel Reports* (fn. 5), VIII-37.

[272] See Goldie, "Neglected Problems" (fn. 263).

[273] See §IV 2 (c) below.

[274] This title indicates that the proposals which follow outline those already put forward by this writer in "Davy Jones's Locker" (fn. 73), 38–54.

[275] This treaty regime could equally well be established by adding new articles to the Geneva Convention on the High Seas, or, alternatively, by means of a fifth

duced.[276] Fourth, the outlines will be delineated of an international (or, even better, transnational) regime of recognition—of "Full Faith and Credit"—whereby the authorities of all states who are parties to the regime will recognize the validity, in their own jurisdictions, of titles granted by each state and pertaining to resources won from the bed and subsoil of the deep oceans. To be more explicit: the intention here is to propose the principles of a regime governing the assurances of titles created under the municipal law of each state, by the recognition of these titles in the courts of all the others through an international agreement, and by means of establishing, under public international treaty law, conflict of laws standards and obligations of recognition.

(a) *Procedures for Allocation.* In contrast with *Our Nation and the Sea,* the proposals which follow eschew the Stratton Commission's Cherokee Strip values in whatever guise of "first-come, first-registered" it may appear. Again, any analogies which one may be tempted to draw between the original titles recognized by virtue of the Convention (or Draft Articles) proposed in "Davy Jones's Locker" and those traditionally derivable from the doctrine of *occupatio terrae nullius* and the Law of Capture [277] are illusory—as would be any seeming like-

---

Convention on the Law of the Sea, possibly to be named the "Convention on the Resources of the Seabed and Subsoil of the High Seas." On the other hand, to add these proposed articles to the Continental Shelf Convention could be very misleading. Despite the fact that they also offer procedures for exercising sovereign rights in submarine areas, and create thereby means of securing titles to resources won from the seabed and subsoil of the oceans, the recognition of claims, the allocation of authority, the blueprint proposed in the paper is planned to operate on the basis of quite a different set of principles from those set forth in the Geneva Convention on the Continental Shelf. To place these two sets of operating principles in the same Convention could, therefore, create confusion—especially in matters of interpretation.

[276] See §VI B 2 (b) below.

[277] The classic definition of *occupatio terrae nullius* is to be found in art. 35 of the Berlin General Act, Feb. 26, 1885, x, *Martens Nouveau Recueil,* 2d 384, 396–97. The leading international law cases are: Legal Status of Eastern Greenland Case, [1933] P.C.I.J. ser. A/B No. 53; Clipperton Island Case, 26 *American Journal of International Law,* 390 (1932); Island of Palmas Case (United States v. the Netherlands), Hague Court Reports (2d Ser.) (Scott), 83, 2 U.N.R I.A.A., 829 (Perm. Ct. Arb., 1928). See also Jacobsen v. Norwegian Government (the Jan Mayen Island Case), 1933–1934, Ann. Dig., 109 (No. 43) (Supreme Court, Norway, 1933).
On the occupation of sedentary fisheries see the works cited in fn. 107. See also Vattel (fn. 138), bk. 1, §287. For the right of capture (i.e., the taking of possession of, or occupation of unowned property, e.g., fish, animals and minerals lying *in situ*) in international law, see Grotius, *Mare Liberum,* 25–30, Carnegie Endowment for International Peace edn. (New York 1916); Oppenheim (fn. 54), I, 556, 630; Samuel v. Pufendorf, *De Jure Naturae et Gentium Libri Octo,* bk. 4, ch. 6 (1688); Vatell (fn. 138), §§204–10, at 234, 279–81.
For a minimal number of divergent but landmark examples (over a span of some 1700 years) of the adoption of the "natural" doctrine of occupation in private law see, e.g., (for origins in Roman and civil law) Gaius, *Institutes* 2, at 66–69; Justinian,

ness between the treaty regime proposed by this writer and those traditional principles of international law which justify the reduction of things, including territory, to the mastery of the first taker. The suggestion here is that the policy goals of secure titles, limited access to resources to ensure the prevention of overcrowding and overcapitalization (with consequent increases in costs and prices), and the avoidance of "first-come first-served" tactics (with ensuing conflicts), may best be gained by drawing upon the relevant provisions of the International Telecommunications Convention [278] for analogies for necessary allocation procedures.

Clearly distinctions are also relevant, if only in terms of differences in subject matter. In the present context one purpose of the regime would be to establish effective conference machinery for the allocation of jurisdictional areas—to be designated "Zones of Special Jurisdiction"—in which states may exercise exclusive authority over exploration for and exploitation of the specific mineral resources for which the authority was sought in the first place. Second, the appropriate conference machinery should be able to provide effective demarcations between different uses. In this way some areas, whose resources might otherwise subject them to conflicting multiple uses, or to overuse, would be preserved from becoming arenas of intractable disputes. The premise here is that, since new rights are to be created and have their

---

*Institutes* 2.1, at 12–19. See, further, e.g., (for origins in Anglo-American law) Keeble v. Hickeringill, 103 Eng. Rep. 1127 (K.B. 1809); Pierson v. Post, 3 Gai. R. 175 (Sup. Ct., N.Y., 1805); Eads v. Brazelton, 22 Ark. 499, 79 Am. Dec. 88 (1861); Ghen v. Rich, 8 F. 159 (D. Mass. 1881); State *ex rel.* Scott v. Buzard, 235 Mo. App. 636, 144 S.W. 2d 847 (1940); City of London Corp. v. Appleyard, [1963] 1 W.L.R. 982 (Q.B.); Blackstone *Commentaries*, II, *1–4. For a history of the doctrine see, e.g., Sir Henry Maine, *Ancient Law*, Sir Frederick Pollock, ed. (London 1906), 258–70, 311–15. For the leading cases on the application of the Law of Capture to oil and gas resources in oil pools under lands owned by surface proprietors, see Walls v. Midland Carbon Co., 254 U.S. 300 (1920); Westmoreland Nat. Gas Co. v. De Witt, 130 Pa. 235, 18 A. 724 (1889). For a classic statement of the Rule of Capture as applied in oil and gas cases, see Barnard v. Monongahela Nat. Gas Co., 216 Pa. 362, 65 A. 801 (1907).

[278] *Done*, Nov. 12, 1965, T.I.A.S. No. 6267. A general indication of the analogies which may be profitably drawn from the International Telecommunications Convention is in "Davy Jones's Locker" (fn. 73), 40–43. A detailed study of these analogies in order to fashion procedure for the allocation of authority to regulate submarine industrial activity is to be the subject of a collateral study by this writer. In the second article there will be a more detailed discussion of, and proposals for, the creation and vesting, as distinct from the recording and evidencing, of states' rights over exploration and exploitation activities in submarine areas beyond the continental shelf.

For a study of the radio spectrum as a common property natural resource and proposals for its rational management (at the domestic level only, however) by means of controlled access—the problem now to be faced by the world community in the context of the resources of the ocean floor—see H. J. Levin, "New Technology and the Old Regulation in Radio Spectrum Management," *American Economic Review*, LVI (May, 1966), 339.

boundaries set, rather than existing ones interpreted, questions of allocation and of demarcation call for the "legislative" creativity of a conference rather than the "administrative" activity of a recording agency (which also has its appropriate function in the scheme proposed). This chapter's advocacy of calling Plenipotentiary Conferences to allocate, in general terms, states' zones of jurisdiction and control over the exploration for and exploitation of submarine resources stems, not from an unquestioning support of eighteenth century political theories, but from an evaluation of twentieth century political realities. To confer the tasks of assigning and demarcating the rights proposed in this chapter upon a relatively unrepresentative body (i.e., unrepresentative of the interests of, possibly, a considerable number of states) would be to burden it dangerously with inappropriate tasks—given the present international political climate.[279] Whereas a century of development and practice has evolved to stabilize the procedures of the International Telecommunications Union, many issues which now may be settled at an International Telecommunications Union Administrative Conference would, in the context of more novel kinds of claims, call for deliberation at a Plenipotentiary Conference.

While the recordation of rights already established could be effectively and satisfactorily conducted by an administrative agency, the allocation of new rights, inevitably involving problems of competing for the opportunities of new wealth those rights would represent as well as those of overcrowding, international rivalries, and economic waste, should be left to an equivalent of a Plenipotentiary Conference of the International Telecommunications Union. This international agency, unlike that in Professor Scelle's blueprint, for example, would not have supranational authority with respect to allocations and assignments. It would provide the arena, or forum and market place, for the chaffering and trade-offs of participating states. In such a context, furthermore, Zones of Special Jurisdiction would be allocated among the participating states, while the assignments, within those Zones, of specific privileges to individuals and enterprises would be in terms of

---

[279] The wisdom of advocating that an international judicial tribunal, for example the International Court of Justice, should be invested with a power of granting zones to be recorded under the proposed convention is also doubted. On the other hand, to create the possibility of investing the International Court of Justice with a compulsory jurisdiction over disputes concerning the interpretation of application of the proposed Convention or Articles, bringing them into line with the rest of the Conventions agreed on at Geneva in 1958, and extending to them the terms of the Optional Protocol of Signature Concerning the Compulsory Settlement of Disputes done April 29, 1958, 450 U.N.T.S. 170, is unequivocally advocated. But since no additional articles are suggested for the Optional Protocol, it is not necessary to discuss it at length in the text. It is sufficient to assert that its scope should be extended to cover the additional Convention, or Articles, proposed in "Davy Jones's Locker" (fn. 73), 38–48.

the machinery for the registration of states' Zones of Special Jurisdiction and ensure international protection for them. Third, it should impose upon each of the participating states the obligation of according full faith and credit to the private titles and rights which derive from the laws of all other participating states. Finally, the regime should provide for the countervailing claims of scientific research.

(b) *The Recording Requirements.*[280] This is the second limb of the regime. Recording calls for the public evidences of titles, which enable the carrying out of large-scale exploration and exploitation activities on the seabed and in the subsoil of the deep oceans with the assurance of security, by means of setting up an international recording administration. The proposal is that regional agencies with, necessarily, a central index in the United Nations Secretariat, should be established to carry out *evidentiary* and *recording* functions. (They should have no authority to *grant* exclusive authority over Zones of Special Jurisdiction).[281] The primary function of such institutions would be to ensure that the whole world has effective notice of the existence of recorded rights. Clearly problems could arise as to whether specific Zones of Special Jurisdiction fell within a general allocation by the Plenipotentiary Conference or not. Such problems of interpretation and application, and of the exercise of incidental discretions, should not fall to the recording agency, but to the Plenipotentiary Conference.

At least one United Nations agency, namely the International Frequency Registration Board of the International Telecommunications Union,[282] provides a useful analogy in its sphere of communication activities to the procedures proposed here for evidencing rights on the seabed. It records and assures title to those increasingly valuable property interests, radio frequencies—increasingly valuable because they are increasingly scarce.

[280] See, for an indication of the major rules which the system of registration envisaged herein should include, "Davy Jones's Locker" (fn. 73), 43–48.

[281] This would remain the special function of the Plenipotentiary Conferences.

[282] Art. 21.1.a, of the International Telecommunications Convention (Geneva Revision, 1959), [1961] 2 U.S.T. 1761, 1784, T.I.A.S. No. 4892 at 24, sets out the activity in question, as being one of the "essential duties" of the International Frequency Regulation Board, as follows:

> to effect an orderly recording of frequency assignments made by the different countries so as to establish, in accordance with the procedure provided for in the Radio Regulations, and in accordance with any decisions, which may be taken by competent Conference of the Union, the date, purpose and technical characteristics of each of these assignments, with a view to ensuring formal international recognition thereof.

For an important discussion of the International Telecommunications Union in general, and the International Frequency Regulations Board in particular, see Glazer, "The Law-Making Treaties of the International Telecommunications Unions through Time and in Space," 60 *Michigan Law Review* 269 (1962).

(c) *Full Faith and Credit.* So far the discussion has been concerned with one type of recognition of transnationally moving titles, namely full faith and credit. This requires the receiving state to recognize the original title which the state wherein it first arose conferred on the owner. There is, however, another type. It is to be found in multilateral conventions protecting special kinds of property, for example the Universal Copyright Convention,[283] and the International Convention for the Protection of Industrial Property.[284] These treaties call for the "national treatment" of rights originating in a foreign country, rather than the reception of those rights as originally defined. The Stratton Commission's International Panel did not specify which of these two types of recognition of foreign-based titles it favored. Clarity would have been served if the International Panel, or, better still, the Commission, had stated its choice—or even, perhaps, had formulated a third position tailored to the needs of the international legal-political framework it was envisaging.

Be that as it may, perhaps the most apt model, despite the fact that it merely operates within a federation, may be found in the recognition of perfected security interests in Section 9-103 of the Uniform Commercial Code.[285] While this example is generally relevant, it need not be followed in every detail. Countervailing claims (*i.e.,* claims protected by parochial policies) to those protected by the full-faith and credit requirements adumbrated here should be limited to the extent that the draftsman's skill can make this possible. This result should not be pursued, however, to the extent of doing violence to either significant transnational policies, or national policies upon which acceptance of the regime could depend.

## VII: POLLUTION, INJURY, AND LIABILITY

All of the new and emerging uses of the sea which have already been indicated offer new benefits to mankind. Many of them, however, carry the threat of pollution and harm while others might well be particularly exposed to them. The sources of their pollution are manifold, and some of them are not traceable to individual conduct or responsibility. Other activities result in such nonactionable, continuing deteriorations as the accelerated eutrophication of lakes and estuaries. They can all be tamed, however, by regulation and by making their operators chargeable for the harms they may wreak. The discussion

---

[283] *Done,* Sept. 6, 1952, [1955] 3 U.S.T. 2731, T.I.A.S. No. 3324, 216 U.N.T.S. 132. Entered into force Sept. 16, 1955.

[284] *Done,* Oct. 31, 1958, [1962] 1 U.S.T. 1, T.I.A.S. No. 4931. Entered into force Jan. 4, 1962.

[285] *1962 Official Text (including the 1966 Official Recommendations for Amendment)* 266-68 (1968).

will take up the harmful aspects of three potentially injurious uses of the ocean. A, transportation and pollution; B, blowout oil wells in the deep-ocean; and C, industrial effluent from processing minerals on the high seas. Then the problems which the vulnerabilities of other uses will be canvassed, closing with a proposal of different levels of severity of liability for different uses.

## A. Transportation and Pollution

Some of the impending technological developments in ocean transport have been outlined in an earlier section of this chapter.[286] This mainly pointed out the economies and advantages of the growth of giant bulk-cargo ships, including tankers, and the development of submarine trains and ocean bed pipelines. These all illustrate a foreseeable future trend. The economies of scale which giant tankers, ships carrying bulk cargo, submarine trains, and under-ocean pipelines offer their operators also increases the hazards of pollution they create for the livelihoods of coastal and insular populations and for the environment. The increases in hazard will be, moreover, commensurate with the tankers' increase in size and the pipelines' increase in diameter and distance.

Many large-scale enterprises operating on the frontiers of science and technology, be they involved in the production of nuclear power or outer space activities, in the operation of sub-ocean trains and pipelines or giant tankers, or in the drilling for oil under the seabed, operate at a high degree of cost and risk. These factors, cost and risk, may, furthermore, be seen as reciprocal. The more an enterprise is called upon to shield third parties and the environment from the risks of disasters which may result from its operations, the higher its operating costs tend to become. Conversely, the more such an enterprise is permitted to expose third parties to harm, or the environment to devastation, the more it will be in a position to reduce its operating costs. The costs of protection, however, still remain. They are merely transferred from the enterprise to society. They become "social costs."[287] They should be transferred back to the shoulders of those who create them and have the most to gain from them—the operators of the ships, the submarine trains, and the pipelines—by means of imposing absolute [288]

---

286 See §II G above.

287 For a discussion of this issue, and the thesis that throwing the costs of extra-hazardous activities onto the shoulders of those who are exposed to the risk of harm, see Goldie, "Liability for Damage" (fn. 58), passim and esp. 1212–13. See also Goldie, "Responsibility for Damage Caused by Objects Launched into Outer Space," British Institute of International and Comparative Law, *Current Problems In Space Law* (1966), 49, 54, 56–57 [hereinafter cited as Goldie, "Responsibility for Damage"].

288 For an indication of the meaning of absolute liability in this context see Goldie, "Liability for Damage" (fn. 58), 1216–17. See also Goldie, "Responsibility for Damage" (fn. 287), 55–56.

liability on those operators for the harms their activities bring about. This was recognized at the Inter-Governmental Maritime Consultative Organization's Conference on Marine Pollution Damage held November 10–29, 1969, at Brussels. Article 3 of its (at present unratified) International Convention on Civil Liability for Oil Pollution Damage imposes a more than ordinarily strict liability on owners. This is more than ordinarily strict since its exculpatory provisions are as restricted, *mutatis mutandis,* as the conventions on liability for nuclear harms.[289]

## B. Blow-Out Oil Wells in the Deep-Ocean

A reading of the reports in the *New York Times* between January 31 and April 3, 1969, carrying the history of the oil-drilling catastrophe in the Santa Barbara Channel should indicate to thoughtful people the pressing need, now, to take measures for the protection of our environment against the time when powerful enterprises engage in widespread deep-ocean submarine oil-drilling exploitations. For, as exploration and exploitation activities extend further into the deep oceans, so must the risk of blow-outs increase—and the difficulty of getting them under control if rigorous conditions and regulations are not imposed. Thus it is suggested preliminarily, that no exploration or exploitation activities will be espoused or licensed by states, or by any international organizations, at depths greater than the feasibility of closing blow-outs. Nor should pipelines be permitted below such depths.

In addition, the requirement of absolute liability has a necessary place here, just as it has with regard to the obligations of the operators of giant tankers and sub-ocean trains and pipelines. For those risk-creating enterprises, as with the possibility of blow-out wells in the deep oceans and damaged or deteriorated pipelines discharging their polluting contents into the ocean environment, there should be an absolute liability for harms imposed. For these enterprises also point to the risk of great harms to the environment, and to those who look to the sea for their survival, livelihood, health, therapy, and recreation.

## C. Industrial Effluent from High Seas Mineral Processing

In addition to risks of ocean pollution from the winning of oil and gas from the subsoil of the deep oceans, there is a further risk from the mining of hard minerals by ships—for example, the mining of manganese nodules. The Commission on Marine Sciences, Engineering, and Resources tells us that:

[289] See fn. 67.

Mining operations conducted completely independent of land (as in the deep sea or remote shallow banks) will result in entirely different processing and transportation problems. Ore will be loaded directly in barges, tankers, or ore transports. Immediate initial beneficiation or processing may be necessary at sea to reduce weight or bulk although this may require large processing equipment on the dredging ship. If all operations are conducted from a single vessel, this will further reduce the amount of ore collected on each trip. If multiple vessel operations are anticipated, one collecting and processing vessel could operate continuously while transport vessels shuttle to port.[290]

What this does not tell us is that the waste products, including acids and other processing chemicals, will be dumped into the sea by the mobile processing ship.[291] A number of such ships could turn sea areas (of no great extent initially, perhaps) into maritime equivalents of slag heaps, causing very considerable ecological change and deleteriously affecting the food web. In addition submarine strip mining, e.g., for calcium carbonate, could cause considerable ecological damage over a wide area.[292]

## D. Proposed Perspectives for Liability Doctrines

The inclusive but vulnerable uses of the sea, for example, undersea hospitals, laboratories, recreation centers, and research bases have also been indicated.[293] The doctrine of liability applicable when these are the instrumentality, rather than the victim, of harm should be quite different from that to be called into play when harm is caused by the uses which derive benefit from exposing others to risk. Even though this writer welcomes the appearance of strict and absolute liability in international law, he does not support the elimination of the less stringent doctrines therefrom. They, too, have appropriate areas of application. A relative approach should be adopted, so that the strictness of the liability to be imposed should depend on the activity causing the harm, the type of activity harmed, and the juxtaposition of

[290] II, *Panel Reports* (fn. 5), VI-186; V-184–85; and *Our Nation and the Sea* (fn. 5), 134–35.

[291] But see II, *Panel Reports* (fn. 5), VI-188, where the following recommendation was made: "Research on the problem of waste disposal. . . . [U]nwise dumping of the tailings, if not carefully planned, could quickly foul a mining operation. Furthermore, the compatibility of a marine mining operation with exploitation of the other resources of the sea, particularly the food resources, will depend principally on the effectiveness of the tailings-disposal system."

[292] For a discussion of this method of mining and of the consequent pollution dangers see Bird, "Undersea Bahamas Mine Stirs Conservation Fears," *New York Times*, April 6, 1970, p. 41, cols. 1–4; April 21, 1970, p. 42, editorial cols. 1–2.

[293] See, for example, §II D, II E, and II F above.

the operator and the injured.[294] Five different regimes [295] of liability for harms caused by maritime activities may now be proposed. These have not, it should be emphasized, been developed in order to render the question of liability dependent on the location of the accident (i.e., in an exclusive zone of coastal state jurisdiction or on the high seas). They are dependent on the activities giving rise to, or exposed to, the ensuing injury—on the social relations created by the incident, namely:

(i) When harm to a coastal population or its livelihood is occasioned by a use of the sea which gains economies from exposing others to increased risks, then absolute liability, channeling accountability back to the operator, possibly subject to a maximum limitation of liability sum, should be imposed on the risk-creating operator causing the harm;

(ii) When fish-farming, including intensive or "battery" fish-farming activities, health (including submarine therapy), submarine recreation, and scientific research activities are harmed by the types of activities indicated in (i) above, absolute liability, subject possibly to a maximum limitation of liability figure, should be imposed;

(iii) When harms caused by activities in (i) above are suffered by other activities in the same category, then the injury calls for no higher level of compensability than that given by fault liability;

(iv) When traditional maritime activities, for example fishing with trawls, lines, and nets (including purse-seine nets) cause injury to such activities in (i) above as, for example, submarine pipelines or mining activities, then the liability applicable should be in terms of fault; but negligence should be presumed and the immediate actor, for example, the fisherman, should be permitted to exculpate himself on such grounds as want of notice and knowledge on his part, due care, inevitability and, when the harm occurs in traditional fishing grounds, or under other circumstances where the operator of the tanker, submarine, or other risk-creating activity knowingly increases the risk to others, the assumption of risk by that operator. Indeed, the application of channeling proposed in (i) above may well leave the operator of the risk-creating enterprise as the liable party;

(v) When traditional maritime activities such as indicated in (iv) above are the agents of harms to vulnerable types of emerging ac-

[294] This concept of the relativity of liability in international law to risk creation, exposure, and social desirability was first outlined by this writer in Goldie, "Liability for Damage" (fn. 58), 1220–24, 1254–58.

[295] The concept of "regimes" used here and elsewhere in this chapter is taken from Goldie, "Special Regimes and Pre-emptive Activities in International Law," 11 *International and Comparative Law Quarterly,* 670 (1962) [hereinafter cited as Goldie, "Regimes"]. See also M. McDougal, "The Prospect for a Regime in Outer Space," *Law and Politics in Space,* Maxwell Cohen, ed. (Montreal 1964), 105, 106–09.

tivities, for example those in (ii) above, then liability should be strict, in the traditional sense; but not absolute.

Each of the five sets of social relations inherent in these different classifications of liability varies from the others in terms of the balance of risk and power to do injury while remaining free from the physical harm or financial loss, and with the degree of effective expropriation which the creation of risk in each relationship entails. Thus, the regime appropriate to each set of social relations, by adopting the correct concept of liability, should be viewed as restoring the balance of risk and power so that one group of interests is not permitted to take risks, or carry on its operations, at the expense of the others. On the other hand, those "others," while entitled to protection, should not be protected against the consequences of risks for which, as a result of their own prior conduct, they might well be viewed as responsible. Furthermore, their own protection should be in terms of the risks to which they expose their own operatives, their social desirability, their relative immunity from harm, and the risks they create for other activities. Each set of social relations is seen as providing its own specific means of establishing the concept of liability appropriate to it, thereby adjusting the balance of risk and advantage to the special social situation brought within its terms.[296]

## VIII: CONCLUSION

Because this chapter has concentrated on the theme that impending technological developments will increasingly call for new basic concepts of maritime law to supplement the dichotomy between seas subject to states' exclusive rights and those designated as "free" in an almost entirely negative sense, its writer has observed an ordinance of self-denial. This has led to the elimination of a review of the seabed deliberations in a number of committees, departments, and commission of the United Nations, which, so far, have been indeterminate—although illustrative.[297]

To argue that the new uses of the sea which may significantly increase the risk of injury through pollution can be fitted into tradi-

296 For a fuller discussion of the views outlined in this section see Goldie, "International Principles of Responsibility for Pollution," a paper given March 12, 1970, at the Conference on International and Interstate Regulation of Water Pollution, Columbia University School of Law, *see also* "International Principles of Responsibility for Pollution," 9 *Columbia Journal of Transnational Law* 283 (1971).

297 Similarly, a contrast between the politico-legal problems raised by the recently reported major oil find in the East China Sea (see *New York Times*, Aug. 28, 1969, p. 1, col. 7 and p. 4, cols. 3–5; Sept. 1, 1969, p. 2, cols. 7–8) with those which have already been the subject of judicial settlement in the North Sea, see [1969] I.C.J. 4, has been eschewed since it would not assist in developing this chapter's central theme.

tional legal rules with increasing distortions and difficulties does not mean that those rules will therefore disappear. They could remain virtually unreformulated and unreformed. The consequence of this failure of the law to adapt to social and technological change could be stultifying to many beneficial uses of the sea, and beneficial to a few— or, possibly, even none. One means of change could be through resort to legal fictions. But these carry an inherent danger of deforming growth by imposing fake or distorting classifications or conditions, and add unproductive costs. In the case of the law of the sea, the distorting fictions might either arise from the proliferation of coastal states' exclusive claims to enclose ever-increasing areas of the sea, or alternatively, from claims by a large number of states invoking the freedom of the sea to stultify regional and other specially-oriented or based supranational developments. These claimant states might well call for trade-offs or other advantages, or for the right of direct participation in those regimes' benefits. Such developments would greatly reduce, if not eliminate, incentive to establish equitable special regimes [298] which, in benefiting a region or other special group of states directly, could have long-term salutary effects on world welfare.

The Convention on Fisheries offers some protection to regional fisheries regimes. But none is offered to equivalent regimes aimed at regulating seabed mining, the processing of minerals suspended in seawater, aquaculture in the open sea, recreational and therapeutic installations, and high seas pollution, among many possibilities. Yet, in the long run, these uses, and others like them, may come to need the protection of regional regimes, or of special regimes based on other criteria of selection than regional ones,[299] at least as urgently as fisheries. Thus the conclusion is that while the international law of the sea clearly requires a change from its traditional dichotomy, present-day socio-economic and technological trends cannot, merely by virtue of coming into existence, bring that change about. The possibilities of frustration and distortion as alternatives to legal innovation are very real threats to the optimum uses of the sea.

On the other hand, a preliminary step away from frustration and distortion, and toward a legal environment better facilitating the emerging uses of the sea, may well be taken by providing procedures to enable the creation of exclusive regional and other special regimes. Such regimes should, clearly, be subject to the United Nations Charter, and their conduct should not be immune from the world body's scrutiny. But their independence should be respected sufficiently to ensure a sturdy autonomous growth.

[298] For the concept of special regimes other than treaty or regional regimes see Goldie, "Regimes" (fn. 295), 670.
[299] See fn. 298.

# CHAPTER 6

# Livelihood and Welfare

## LEON GORDENKER

THE IDEA OF international cooperation and law-making to improve
and regulate human living and working conditions has an honorable,
if rather recent history. In a formal sense it is widely accepted by governments and some important associated groups such as trade unions,
and in a practical way it has led to innovations and useful activities
at the international level.[1]

The desire and willingness to deal with living and working conditions as problems appropriate for action at the international level has
given rise to and supports the existence of a bulky handful of active,
special-purpose, universal-membership organizations, the oldest and
perhaps best-known of which is the International Labor Organization
(ILO), the recent recipient of a Nobel Peace Prize. ILO and other international institutions have led in the development of several hundred
international conventions which impose obligatory practices and standards on the governments which adhere to them. Beyond these binding
legal instruments, international organizations have pressed countless
recommendations on their member governments. In some instances,
these governments have a legal obligation to report back their responses to the recommendations, while in others, reports as to governmental action are requested. In either case, the policy-making process
of the international organization is designed so as to encourage member governments to act in accordance with international recommendations and perhaps to create related legislation or regulations.

Yet the development of international law affecting welfare and livelihood and the underlying situations which imply its desirability have
attracted much less interest among governments and scholars than comparable rule-making efforts directed towards the maintenance of peace
and security, even though it may be easier to create law regarding
welfare than regarding international security.[2] The state of normative

---

[1] There are, however, few comprehensive studies. An old but still useful one is
Philip C. Jessup, Adolf Lande, Oliver J. Lissitzyn, and Joseph P. Chamberlin, *International Organization* (New York, Carnegie Endowment for International Peace,
1955). C. W. Jenks, *The Common Law of Mankind* (London 1958) is a more ambitious study that emphasizes the subject. Wolfgang Friedmann, *The Changing
Structure of International Law* (London 1964) contains important comments and
arguments.

[2] For example, G. W. Schwarzenberger, *A Manual of International Law*, 5th edn.
(London 1967), 113–14, treats international social law as part of a discussion of
limitations of state jurisdiction by means of treaties. Ian Brownlie, *Basic Documents*

rules applying at the international level to matters of livelihood and welfare can therefore fairly be judged as underdeveloped and as lagging behind fundamental change in the social environment. This lag has frequently been noted in discussions in international organizations touching on the social implications of programs of economic development, the more concrete features of which tend to attract intense attention and perhaps understanding.[3] Furthermore, some of the regulation that has been undertaken through the mechanisms of international law may appear redundant in national settings: it is relatively painless for a government to accept, say, an international convention regulating employment of children when its own preexisting laws set a higher standard.

The thesis of this essay is, however, that the need for dealing with some problems of livelihood and welfare will assume such proportions that the long-term development of new rules and regulations at the international level probably will, and certainly should, be encouraged. The subject matter of the essay includes those problems which are connected with work and employment, social modernization and change, social well-being and health, and the provision of welfare services for the unfortunate. It will suggest why such problems will demand increasing international attention during the next three decades and how they relate to the development of broader international law.

## I

During the next three decades, growing numbers of the people of the world are likely to feel the effects of two strong tendencies of the immediate past that inevitably introduce changes in their social and working environments. The first of these tendencies comprises rapid

in *International Law* (Oxford 1967) includes no example of the kind of treaty referred to by Schwarzenberger. Louis Henkin, *How Nations Behave: Law and Foreign Policy* (London 1968) deals with law outside the security field only *en passant*. William Coplin, *The Functions of International Law: an Introduction to the Role of International Law in the Contemporary World* (Chicago 1966) indeed does include a chapter on the development of international social and economic welfare legislation, but it is largely a description of the structures of international institutions. D. W. Bowett, *The Law of International Institutions* (New York 1965) also uses a structural organization that hardly permits dealing with law in the general welfare field. A notable and challenging exception is Friedmann (fn. 1).

[3] "While only a handful of developing countries had development plans during the late 1950s, the majority of those countries had plans by 1965. More often than not, however, the foundation of these plans left much to be desired. Objectives and targets were often formulated solely or principally in economic terms neglecting social and institutional bottle-necks to economic growth and ignoring the undesirable social consequences which may accompany such growth." United Nations, Department of Economic and Social Affairs, *1967 Report on the World Social Situation*, E/CN. 5/417/Rev. 1 (New York 1969), VIII.

and largely unplanned, so far as social ramifications are concerned, technological innovation. This has been characteristic of the last fifty years and shows no signs of slackening, either in intensity or in its ability to spread throughout the world, almost unimpeded by national boundaries, differing governmental policies, and varied cultures.[4] The second tendency, already operating to an almost universal extent and strongly supported by the programs of international organizations, is represented by the deliberate attempt to plan and increase the pace of economic development and social change.[5] Although this tendency affects the affluent, developed countries, where production and living conditions have already reached high levels, it is even more striking in the less-developed countries, where many governments strive to transform their societies deliberately with the aid of rationally-directed economic development programs which almost always entail important changes in social practices.

The usual site for the appearance of technological innovations affecting livelihood and welfare has been the highly-developed countries, especially those of North America and Western Europe. These innovations during the last century manifested themselves in such phenomena as the use of the motor car as the basis of local transportation, the replacement of fuels that can be had for the gathering with processed fossil and sophisticated nuclear materials, and the employment of mass communications to reach vast numbers of people. Such technologically-based features and countless others have become essential elements of modern economic production and therefore potent agents of social change. Their use is spreading rapidly to the less-developed lands, partly spontaneously and partly as the result of explicit governmental development programs. Increasingly, the less-developed countries have sought to promote technological innovation, in terms of their present

---

[4] "The world is poised, at the present time, on the threshold of a scientific and technical revolution the dimensions and future course of which cannot be foreseen." International Labour Organisation, Second European Regional Conference, Report of the Director-General, *Technological Change and Social Problems: Some Problems and Perspectives* (Geneva, International Labour Office, 1968), 14.

[5] ". . . the desire to 'develop' has induced one country after another to set up a plan framework within which the compatability of objectives and the consistency of policy measures can be tested. In some cases, especially in countries with a more sophisticated private sector, this has involved chiefly a set of projections to provide guidelines to private decision-making. In others, it has been a more comprehensive and detailed exercise with specific sector and industry targets. In others again, it has focused principally on the acquisition and disposition of government resources. In all cases, it has involved a more systematic approach to the development process and a continuing attempt to use the instruments of economic policy in a consistent fashion." United Nations, Department of Economic and Social Affairs, *The Problem and Policies of Economic Development: An Appraisal of Recent Experience, World Economic Survey 1967*, Part One, U.N. Doc. E/4488/Rev. 1 (New York, United Nations, 1968), 97.

practices, in order to raise productivity and diversify output. The planning for and meeting of the United Nations Conference on the Application of Science and Technology in the Less Developed Countries, and the creation of a permanent committee of eminent scientists to carry on the work, furnishes some evidence of the seriousness and wide acceptability of efforts to foster the use of advanced technology for development.[6] Somewhat less striking but possibly of even greater effect is the employment of technical assistance programs, intended to fit into explicit development plans, in every corner of the less-developed countries.[7] Such assistance frequently promotes the introduction of specific modern techniques, such as the use of insecticides to control malaria and other diseases, over a period of several years. Often the newly-introduced technique becomes a permanent feature of the lives of the people involved.

Even if the less-developed countries do not succeed in reaching their lofty—or in some case, impossible—goals, their efforts to increase and diversify production and to establish appropriate organizational forms for development must necessarily result in the introduction of new working patterns for wide segments of populations in many places. Not every worker in the developing country may expect such a dramatic shift as that from the hoe to the spectroscope, but many will have to make adjustments of similar magnitudes in their skills. Wherever industry appears—which becomes increasingly likely—highly advanced and productive agricultural methods, new standards of time precision, for example, must be imposed on less-structured work regimes. To serve high productivity occupations, dependable and comprehensive communication networks must be created. Such communications facilities in themselves compel a qualitative change in aspects of society.

On a broader scale, enough communications networks now exist so that communication of general ideas and symbols is only slightly inhibited. Electronic communication via artificial earth satellites provides instantaneous contact for television viewers around the world, so that when the Pope visits Uganda or the first man walks on the moon millions of human eyes observe closely. At a less exalted level, rock and roll music sounds in the Siberian forest and West African high-life

[6] For a summary of its recent work, including a World Plan of Action, approved by the U.N. Economic and Social Council, see United Nations, Official Records, General Assembly: 23rd Session, Supplement No. 1, *Annual Report of the Secretary-General on the Work of the Organization* (1967–68), 121–23; and same: 24th Session, *Annual Report . . .* (1968–69), 112–14. See also Sherman E. Katz, "The Application of Science and Technology to Development," *International Organization*, XXII, 1 (Winter 1968), 392–410.

[7] The U.N. System in 1967–68 supported 2814 technical assistance projects, including experts, fellowships, and equipment and supplies, in 134 countries and territories. Same, 165. Additional and, in the aggregate, larger programs are sponsored by individual governments.

dances can be heard in North American night clubs. The Mercedes Benz automobile is known as a symbol of prestige in every hamlet of the less-developed world. Like the network of communication that must grow up around modern means of production, the wider high-speed, partly electronic network can only grow in comprehensiveness and efficiency during the next three decades. With it, both popular and elite symbols will trickle and then flood into still isolated social corners.

Similarly, the long-distance transportation of humans, already unbelievably easy and cheap as compared with a half-century ago, can be expected to become yet more efficient and inclusive with the further application of even existing technology. Travelers will continue to spread ideas and techniques, as they always have. But the ease of traveling may produce migrations of novel character as new groups achieve physical mobility.

In the less-developed countries an almost endless chain of alterations in aspects of the social matrix has begun to emerge from efforts to achieve economic change by deliberate plans. Urbanization is encompassing unexpectedly large segments of the populations. Family structures shift in content and direction and sometimes weaken. Children increasingly seek formal education outside of the family and the values of the clan either tend to give way or are readapted to the new world. With better communications and forced change affecting their ways of life, individuals widen their perspectives. They make strong, novel demands on their societies, seeking such services as advanced medical care, unemployment insurance, compensation for injuries, safety protection, and old age security. Some individuals, perhaps a larger number, react to changes in the form of physical and mental trauma.

Local and national social variations remain despite the recent onslaught of deliberate change, growth of communication, and other unplanned technological innovation. Adaptations appear and old cultural practices can be maintained next to modern techniques; and in some cases new techniques are employed to strengthen the value structure of old societies. But it seems likely that the perception that certain social problems anywhere have a strong kinship with social problems elsewhere has become fairly widespread. Issues involving livelihood and welfare have increasingly been perceived as geographically universal, broad and not parochial in scope, and having a general identity.

Even now, specific transnational programs, most of them operated by international organizations with either regional or universal membership, aid the less-developed country in meeting the problems of livelihood and welfare that grow out of efforts to foster economic development. Although social effects have sometimes been regarded by government as an ugly sister of economic development and unworthy of close attention, a growing awareness of such problems is detectable. The demand for aid to help deal with them is strong, unrelenting, and growing.[8] The response, as usual, falls far short of the perceived needs. Nevertheless, it has grown beyond negligible quantities, as the programs of the United Nations Children's Fund (UNICEF), ILO and the World Health Organization (WHO), indicate.

The attention given the social implications of economic development and the resultant aid programs has been accompanied in international organizations, at least, with the elaboration of doctrines that treat problems of livelihood and welfare as omnipresent and largely identical, whatever the national setting.[9] In this sense, livelihood and welfare is already a matter of international concern and treatment.

Furthermore, the highly-developed countries of Western Europe and North America have essayed numerous cooperative ventures which affect livelihood and welfare. To improve mass communications, that powerful agent of social change, in coverage and efficiency, governments have established programs employing long-lived communications satellites, which make possible routine exchanges of radio and television material for broadcast on national networks. The crossing of national boundaries by travelers has become ever more simple, encouraging the spread of ideas. The affluence which allows long-distance vacation travel for ever-increasing numbers of people also tends to spread ideas.

The governments have identified and dealt with some problems of migration and social welfare for migrants. They have laid down transnational regulations providing for the uniform treatment of old-age pensioners, attempted to rationalize educational standards and much more. Indeed, these efforts, precise and in legal form, suggest that the very achievement of a high level of development itself tends to internationalize some problems of livelihood and welfare.[10]

## II

Within the broad streams of change generated by rapid technological innovation and deliberate stimulation, a number of substantive

[8] For an example of the changing attitude toward social questions in deliberate development programs, see United Nations, Department of Economic and Social Affairs, *Report on the World Social Situation with Special Reference to the Problem of Balanced Social and Economic Development,* U.N. Doc. E/CN.5/346/Rev. 1 (New York, United Nations, 1961), esp. Chap. II and conclusions. See also *Annual Report of the Secretary-General* . . . (1968–1969), 172, for some specific examples of international cooperation on social problems connected with developments.

[9] *Report on the World Social Situation* (fn. 8), Chap. v.

[10] For additional discussion, see Friedmann (fn. 1), Chap. 9. For a summary of some transnational regulations in force in Europe and comments on transnational movements of people, see *1967 Report on the World Social Situation* (fn. 3), 196–99.

problems can be identified as likely to have transnational effects in the future. Some of these will appear as novel at the international level, as compared with the agenda of the past. Others represent a continuation of work in progress or perceptions familiar in the past which have not been followed by much effort to provide regulation. Some problems of the future will stem from the intensification of difficulties already subject to treatment through cooperative action by several governments. With dramatically increasing interdependence among states, old problems of livelihood and welfare can only deepen and broaden.

In many instances, problems of livelihood and welfare appear to fall comfortably within the jurisdictions of existing international institutions which are eager to deal with them. In other examples, attention from international organizations has resulted in early identification of forthcoming difficulties and issues in the realm of livelihood and welfare. The organizations have tried consistently to alert governments and the relevant publics to new and intensifying problems.[11] Yet the establishment of a reasonable and uniform standard of measures to deal with such problems may be impeded by a structure of international relations that preserves wide differences in levels of affluence. Some agreed standards of distributive justice could be essential in providing for satisfactory international handling of problems of livelihood and welfare.

Among the problems long understood as having international implications, and which will certainly figure in the future, are the control of diseases and the promotion of health. Organized interstate efforts to control epidemics and communicable diseases from spreading unchecked around the world began before the turn of this century. More recently, quarantine and other sanitary regulations in seaports and airports have been applied according to international standards. Epidemiological information flashes around the world through an internationally operated radio service. Similarly, international programs have developed to seek control of such disease vectors as the yellow fever mosquito, the tsetse fly, the bilharzia-bearing snail, and certain animal ticks. Information networks trace their progress in an effort to predict and head off epidemics, and receive international support.[12]

Indeed such measures, designed at the international level within a formal organization framework such as that offered by the WHO, are

[11] The rapidity with which international organizations have engaged themselves on issues growing out of technological innovation is striking. These issues include the peaceful use of nuclear energy, the exploration of Antarctica, the exploration of outer space, the uses of the seabed, and the destruction of the natural environment. Not all the attention of the international organizations is specifically directed toward the creation of rules of law, but some of it has been.

[12] *The First Ten Years of the World Health Organization* (Geneva, World Health Organization, 1958), 211–20, 242–48, 259–79.

now commonplace. In many instances, regulations that are binding on the governments of member states can be adopted within the organizational framework. In others, governments adopt parallel regulations according to a pattern agreed on by international organizations. Further efforts are likely to emerge, as the improvement of communications and transport and a rising level of international commerce tend to create preconditions of or actual pandemic situations. It seems likely that governments, perceiving the need for controlling pandemic diseases, will seek further regulation. Yet it is conceivable that some governments at least, perhaps those best equipped to deal with health problems, may opt for isolation rather than expensive cooperation with less well-equipped governments, especially if the pace of regulation lags far behind needs.

Efforts to clamp effective controls on the traffic in narcotic drugs have achieved a useful level, at least with regard to identification of the sources of illicit drugs, and the supervision of permissible commerce in narcotics and other dangerous products for medical purposes. From hesitant beginnings just before the First World War, control measures, supported and strengthened by the League of Nations and the U.N., have grown into a large body of treaty law to which additions are made from time to time. The international accounting procedures are particularly well developed with regard to narcotics produced from plants, including opium and cocaine. National reporting on work by governments to control the traffic comes under the close scrutiny of expert international civil servants and the officials of other governments.[13] The illicit trade in and production of narcotics has certainly not disappeared and at the moment probably is growing, but, to the degree that police control serves to deal with this evil, the international response has been generally helpful.

Furthermore, the U.N. and WHO have substantially expanded the scope of international control of traffic in drugs. To begin with, a long list of synthetic narcotic drugs, which replace or supplement natural products and are susceptible of abuse, have been brought under international supervision.[14] The abusive use of other manufactured drugs has been getting increasing attention. International recommendations have warned of the dangers of trade in and misuse of synthetic drugs, including depressants and stimulants, which contribute to the contemporary "drug culture." The widening use of *cannabis* (marijuana,

[13] Leland M. Goodrich, "New Trends in Narcotic Control," *International Conciliation*, No. 530 (Nov. 1960).

[14] For a vivid view of the number of drugs under international supervision and the complexity of their identification, see United Nations, *Multilingual List of Narcotic Drugs Under International Control*, U.N. Doc. E/CN.7/513 (New York, United Nations, 1969).

etc.) has been the subject of a number of international discussions and recommendations; a recent proposal seeks to control all international trade in hallucinogens.[15] These international activities were undertaken far enough back in time so that they can be judged as having constituted a practical early warning of future difficulties. Current activities perform a similar future-oriented function; they at least point out the opportunities for international regulation.

Controlling international traffic in drugs subject to abusive illegal use does not, of course, deal with the underlying social and psychological causes of the "drug culture" or with its frequently tragic outcome. It cannot, for example, check the flow of colorful information about the way that some of the heroes of popular culture devote their leisure to drug-sampling. With modern mass communication, such information spreads everywhere and stimulates eager and ignorant hero-worshippers to their own trials of drugs, some of which end in injury, addiction, or arrest. Furthermore, the effect of purely police controls on the narcotic trade is controversial. It is even arguable that the control of drug traffic by treaties, which provide one of the bases for local police activity, simply defines the field for illegal operators who can easily elude an official surveillance that varies so greatly in quality and intensity from country to country.

Nevertheless, the long history of international cooperation in the effort to control the drug traffic, its success in accounting and in setting standards for the production of natural products, and its wide acceptability in governmental circles suggests that it will still furnish an approach to the drug problem in the future. Furthermore, recent experience with a lengthening list of synthetic drugs may constitute only the beginning of a program to deal with whole new classes of products that are emerging from pharmaceutical research in many countries. Current attempts to control some of the new synthetic products may at least provide national governments with a kind of early warning of developing problems. It seems likely that additional regulation, perhaps employing new methods of detection of illicit traffic, and perhaps extending deeper within municipal jurisdictions than has been attempted before, may evolve, or at least be sought, during the next three decades. In addition, because present international regulation is based on perceptions of social evils, it seems probable that future regulatory developments will refer to the social effects of new products.

Synthetic pharmaceuticals constitute only one class of modern industrial output which may require controls to prevent the creation of widespread, internationally-ramified, health hazards. It is probable that

15 *Annual Report of the Secretary-General* . . . 1967–68 (fn. 6), 135–36; U.N. General Assembly Resolution 2433(XXIII); and *Annual Report of the Secretary-General.* . . . 1968–1969 (fn. 8), 130.

the dimensions of these dangers remain clouded by ignorance and in-adequate forethought. But it is clear that just as making the phos-phorus match imperiled the health of workers in its day, and as lead-based paints still poison children, so new chemicals and products will affect individuals and groups. An example of such products is the insecticide which, dumped into the Rhine River in Germany, made the water-supply of much of the Netherlands unfit to drink. Other insecticides deposit residues in the bodies of animals and humans who consume sprayed foods and contaminated water. Over a long period these deposits may contribute to the early decline of the affected organ-isms. Some detergents and enzymes used in household cleaning and industrial washing find their way into drinking-water supplies—rivers and lakes—and stay there for indefinite periods. Food additives, em-ployed increasingly for preservation and for improving taste and ap-pearance, may have still unknown but dangerous effects on unwitting consumers. A list of these chemicals with unknown long-term effects could be almost as long as the catalog of factories where consumer products are treated. Furthermore, air and marine pollution accom-panying industrial processes may have cumulative and international effects. Relatively little attention at the international level has been given to such hazards,[16] but the pace of industrial development and innovation, especially in the highly-developed countries, suggests strongly that it will be needed in the future.

Advanced industrial processes and the requirements of ever greater quantities of energy for consumer use, especially in the highly-devel-oped countries, have expanded the use of radioactive materials. In themselves, these materials constitute a health hazard, to which is added the problem of safe disposal of wastes and secondary radio-activity of irradiated materials. Some experience with radioactive fuels and materials has already been strongly reflected at the international level. The increasingly wider distribution of nuclear fuels, radio iso-topes, and irradiation has inspired the drafting of a model interna-tional code of regulations for the safe handling of such substances. Disposal of nuclear wastes has received mounting attention at the international level.[17] Nevertheless, the scope of the problem has prob-ably not yet been defined—even approximately—and the probable fu-ture expansion of the use of such materials will constitute a serious

[16] The U.N. has begun, however, to give specific attention to marine pollution. U.N. General Assembly Resolution 2566(xxiv). The U.N. Conference on the Human Environment in 1972 will take up this and other similar problems on a broad basis. See U.N. General Assembly Resolution 2398(xxiii).

[17] For a recent example, see United Nations General Assembly Resolution 2647 (xxiii), parts A and B on the uses of the seabed in the interests of mankind. See also, Jenks (fn. 1), Chap. 7.

problem that can only be dealt with satisfactorily through international regulation.

The very introduction of sophisticated industrial processes of the sort, for example, that use radio isotopes, and their wider application, demands ever greater numbers of highly-trained workers and professionals. These demands arise both in the highly-developed countries and the less-developed ones. Efforts to meet the demands for such personnel, which will certainly mount in the future, have led to several kinds of international concern. One relates to the training of expert personnel who can make a contribution in the less-developed countries. The response comprises governmental and intergovernmental programs of technical assistance, fellowships, training institutes, and various industrial training exchanges.[18] Direct assistance from outside nongovernmental sources to national educational systems has also evolved to help meet demand for personnel. This kind of operational activity may certainly be expected to continue in the future. The needs for programming such work and the transnational discussion and problem-solving it entails tends to develop working norms which are applied by officials in both national and international structures. It is possible that rather firm norms that can be generally applied will emerge.

The creation and expansion of educational systems, especially in the less-developed countries, and the training offered through fellowships and scholarships abroad have already created some difficulties. National administrations and educational systems frequently find it puzzling to interpret unfamiliar degrees and diplomas and to assign their holders to appropriate work. The subject of equivalence of degrees and uniform standards of education has often been discussed in the past at the international level.[19] But the problem has been intensified by the emergence of new national educational systems in the new states and by the offer of training opportunities from new sources. It seems likely that the problem of educational equivalence, which seriously affects the efficient use of manpower, will intensify and become more complex in the future.

Concern with education (and recently with control of dangerous drugs) relates to more general problems with youth that reach broad proportions and unquestionably transcend national boundaries. One aspect of the problem derives from efforts to widen and deepen education and training in the less-developed countries. Their schools all too

18 The establishment and long-term support and supervision of such training enterprise by the U.N. Development Program probably tends to promote an international standard for such aid. For an indication of how far short of the needs such efforts fall and consequently how remote is a firm standard, see Lester B. Pearson, *Partners in Development* (New York 1969), 202–03.

19 United Nations Educational, Scientific, and Cultural Organization, *World Survey of Education*, 4 vols. (Paris, UNESCO, 1966), esp. vol. IV.

frequently turn out pupils who have some basic skills of literacy but no specialized or vocational training and little prospect of getting it. But such individuals often leave their cultural and social bases to seek employment in a restricted modern economic sector that may actually be developing less rapidly than is the increase in population, especially in the youthful age groups. The result is large numbers of unemployed young men and women who cluster around new urban agglomerations and contribute little to any society.

Such youth represent a sheer waste of valuable life and energy and a potential which the governments of the less-developed countries recognize should be linked to the development process.[20] In addition, these wasted young people contribute to a political and social unrest that has international repercussions. Already fragile governments become more unstable in response to upheavals and pressures among the wasted young. Months and years of national and international development efforts can quickly be lost. Instability of this sort only adds complexity and uncertainty to international aid for development. At the same time, the wasteful handling of the energies of the young stores up social problems for the future and increases the magnitude of developmental issues.

Meanwhile, in some of the highly-developed countries, an extremely visible group of young people, some of them university students, has drifted (or in some instances plunged headlong) into protesting and anomic behavior, also causing social waste. In a sense, this behavior mirrors the obverse of the faulty educational process in the less-developed countries. Instead of too short a period of school to achieve a useful level of specific work skills, the youth of the highly-developed countries finds itself compelled to submit to seemingly endless educational programs before reaching the competence deemed necessary by their elders for responsible work. Young men and women in their mid-twenties find themselves still ranked among the apprentices in specialized training programs although they are at the creative height of their physical and intellectual powers. They show sharp awareness of the intellectual and social challenges implicit in their studies and therefore suffer from intensified frustration at not having responsible roles. Some of them have protested by "dropping out" of society. Sometimes this protest is dramatized by the use of drugs and eccentric behavior designed to shock other groups of the society.

These young, intellectually-inclined protesters, together with various

20 The U.N. General Assembly by acclamation adopted a lengthy resolution in 1969, linking problems of youth, human rights, and participation in natural development. Among other things, it appealed to youth "to affirm solemnly its faith in international law" and the principles of the U.N. Charter. U.N. General Assembly Resolution 2497(XXIV).

leaders of taste in the popular culture, sweep other young people of less sophisticated cultural talents and attainments along with them. Protest of this sort has spread in epidemic waves during the last decade. Because it affects almost every part of the world in some way, it has increasingly been a subject of discussion in international forums.[21] It suggests that governments in the future may have to face widespread problems of mental health which respect no borders, and which spread with the printed word and the electronic message.

Although the "drop-out" protest suggests a new order of transnational concern, dealing with problems of youth, children and their mothers hardly could be termed a novel category for international activity. Conventions regulating international traffic in women and children, working conditions for women, and child labor date back to the 1920's and even earlier. The ILO and the League of Nations devoted much effort to such problems and met them not only with conventions but also with a series of recommendations to governments.

The members of UNICEF turned it into a permanent organization, when it proved its usefulness as a relief agency after the demise of the United Nations Relief and Rehabilitation Agency; it has since broadened its activity to include a wide range of services to aid governmental programs for the benefit of children and mothers. The United Nations Educational, Scientific and Cultural Organization (UNESCO) and the Food and Agriculture Organization (FAO) have also tried to deal with aspects of the welfare of mothers, children, and youth. The United Nations has sponsored consideration of an international covenant on the rights of the child and has also devoted much discussion and research to the rights and welfare of women,[22] a subject that creates real controversy in some parts of the world. Such protective work, as much of it can be characterized, can be expected to continue and perhaps to move at a faster pace in the future, when novel problems connected with development and perhaps with new industrial techniques could conceivably create a new interest in international rule-making.

Problems of health and cross-cutting concerns with youth, children, and mothers connect with a set of equally-widespread problems of food and nutrition, urbanization and migration, and social welfare and defense. All these subjects have had some international treatment and all seem likely to form foci of future activity.[23]

International cooperation to increase and improve food production and distribution, another hardly novel endeavor, has taken on a more urgent character with the perception of how rapidly the population

[21] Pearson (fn. 18), 55–63ff.
[22] See Pearson (fn. 18), 73–77, and U.N. General Assembly Resolution 2263(XXII).
[23] Pearson (fn. 18), 55–63ff.

of the world is growing and with mounting knowledge of the extent of unsatisfactory nutritional standards, especially in the less-developed countries. Accordingly, nutrition has become a subject for international action and aid, especially in connection with economic development and with relief of disaster areas and war zones. Much progress has been made in evolving new plant varieties to increase productivity of the land, and international programs help to spread their use. But in this work little emphasis has been given to international regulation as opposed to operations.[24] With new seeds and new processes for production and preservation of food, however, international standards could conceivably be applied. They could be made to cover the standardization of seeds, limitations on the residual quantities of chemical insecticides in foodstuffs in international trade, and the use of possibly pathogenic preservatives and irradiation.

The fact that much of the less-developed world produces foodstuffs as main sources of foreign exchange, essential for their economic development programs, has inspired numerous attempts to shape trade and commerce so as to ensure stable markets and shelter producers from transitory fluctuations in income. The creation of the United Nations Conference on Trade and Development (UNCTAD), which is intended to have at least some standard-setting capacity, represents an expansion of the commodity board approach: it includes rearrangement of trade conditions so as to benefit the development programs of the emergent countries. Its work, therefore, will indirectly touch on problems of nutrition and agricultural output and it seems likely that its activity, slow and straining though it may be, will be permanent.

Another kind of regulative activity could conceivably appear at the international level when population increases outrun the current improvement in agricultural productivity that is growing out of new plant strains. Numerous suggestions have been made for "banking" surpluses to even out variations in production and thus to prevent starvation. Other programs to study new food sources, such as greater yields from the sea, have been launched by international bodies. But it seems probable that some attention will eventually have to be given to the regulation of trade, in the interest of the fair sharing of scarce supplies should long-enduring food shortages occur. Governments and nations can behave brutally toward others, but it is almost inconceivable that a part of the world's people would by default and indifference be allowed to starve while other groups contentedly enjoyed relative plenty.

Migration, especially that forced by political upheavals and natural disasters, has long been affected by the operation of at least some inter-

24 1967 *Report on the World Social Situation* (fn. 3), 42–45.

national norms. Intense efforts to care for refugees, left by the two world wars and by lesser conflicts such as those in Palestine, Korea and the Congo, have resulted in important international agreements and in the operation of long-continued relief programs that can serve as a minimum standard for the maintenance of forced migrants. In the case of natural disasters, such as earthquakes, established and *ad hoc* international organizations have rushed to provide relief. Provision of travel documents for refugees who lack the protection of their own governments has become standard practice. International conventions guarantee refugees at least some protection, miserable though it may be, and they benefit from the continuing work of the United Nations High Commissioner for Refugees.[25] Unless political and natural disasters disappear from the human environment, refugee problems will not vanish in the future and are likely to call forth continuing, if not augmented, international cooperation along now familiar lines.

Much less attention and effort at the international level has been given to voluntary migration. Those programs that have appeared have been mounted by pairs of governments. In at least one instance, international attention has been directed to slowing the voluntary migration which arises from the demand for highly-skilled professional personnel. The most-developed countries tend to attract much-needed administrators, scientists, and scholars from those lands that offer less scope and fewer rewards for work. This "brain-drain" has even shifted manpower with scarce skills from the less-developed countries to international organization staffs. The "brain-drain" has become the subject of international study and will probably remain under scrutiny for a long period.[26] It is conceivable, if not very likely, that it will be brought under some internationally-sanctioned regulation.

Rapid urbanization, so striking in the less-developed countries and scarcely less so elsewhere, has been both a cause and a product of voluntary migration. Some migrants have caused international repercussions because of crossing national borders to nearby cities. Some of this has been planned, as in the temporary migration of labor to European industrial centers. This kind of work-associated migration seems likely to reach an ever-greater volume during the near future, assuming a differential in the rate of economic development in different areas. It conceivably could require wide international regulation, similar to that used on a smaller scale in the European Economic Community, to provide for the orderly flow of people at a rate that can be

[25] Convention Relating to the Status of Refugees (1951), U.N. *Treaty Series,* 189 (1954), No. 2545. See also U.N. General Assembly Resolution 2594(XXIV) for recent instructions to the High Commissioner for Refugees.

[26] United Nations, Official Records, General Assembly: 23rd Session, Supplement No. 3, *Report of the Economic and Social Council* (1967–68), 59–61.

assimilated in urban communities and in industrial occupations. It might be extended to the protection of the rights and welfare of temporary migrants, and to their return to their original homes when they desire it. Furthermore, assistance given by international organizations to various countries for urban planning could result in the setting of standards for housing and other facilities for migrants.

The social change implicit in growing urbanization, in the shifting of occupations as the result of formal education and deliberate economic development and in more efficient and pervasive communication, takes its human toll in the form of psychic breakdowns, criminality, maladjustment and destitution. Almost inevitably some plans, at least, for social protection and welfare go along with modernizing social change. New concepts of the treatment of social offenders begin to be applied as societies take on the complexities of a money economy or of industrialized, urban centers. And the older, well-developed countries also find themselves faced by social welfare demands of unprecedented magnitude, such as the provision of facilities for the aged and the rehabilitation of youth suffering from psychiatric disorders. These problems have frequently been the subject of international inquiry and of recommendations to national governments. Technical assistance had also been furnished.[27] It seems possible that as the pervasiveness of these and similar problems is increasingly understood, efforts at international regulation may become necessary to provide at least uniform standards of social welfare in similar settings.

## III

The growth of international regulation of livelihood and welfare thus far indicates that law has emerged in four main fields, which may be identified as health law, labor law, social security law and welfare law. Indirectly associated and at an earlier stage is the field of trade and development law. The need for further elaboration of all these kinds of law in the next three decades will probably be strong, and will be directly stimulated by technological innovation, deliberate development, and social change. Yet the existence of a need for international regulation does not compel the emergence of law.

In considerable part, existing law affecting livelihood and welfare derives from social conditions associated with the process of industrialization in the highly-developed countries. Such conventions as those covering working conditions for women and children in industry or for seafarers aboard ships emerged from the work of the ILO and some of them are decades old. Their application, as the result of ratification

27 A brief summary of U.N. activities in these areas can be found in *Annual Report of the Secretary-General . . . 1968–1969* (fn. 8), 116–18. The U.N. General Assembly also has begun to face the problems of the aged.

by national governments, remains spotty and far short of comprehensive in terms of the contemporary states covered.

Regulation approached by the process of drafting international conventions will pose a number of specific difficulties that are already visible. First, the drafting and application of international conventions is a slow process and, if past experience foreshadows the future, lags considerably behind the emergence of social problems. With technological innovation proceeding so rapidly, the lag is likely to become wider than ever. Moreover, with the emergence of new states during the last two decades, the drafting and application of conventions has become more difficult because of the diversity of character, aims, and level of development among states.

Second, the widespread suspicion on the part of the less-developed countries of the usual content and process of creating international law inhibits the use of conventions.[28] A common view identifies international law with the old colonial regimes and with what is called "neo-colonialism." The force of this suspicion is in no way reduced by the fact that most governments accept the international obligations of the colonial period as binding on them as successors, nor by the fact that some governments have never completely surveyed the treaties and conventions which apply to them. Since the term neo-colonialism more often than not simply equates with strong foreign influence in the modern sector, where the less-developed countries often strive hardest to gain local control, it is difficult to see how regulation by convention can be expanded rapidly.

Third, international regulation by convention usually implies that within the municipal realm a sophisticated administration is available to carry out the treaty provisions and apply them by means of bureaucratic processes. In many countries, especially the newest group, the local ability to administer complicated regulations to cope with social problems remains low. Trained manpower is not yet available, and much that is available prefers employment in the more dramatic work of stimulating and activating tangible increases in economic output, rather than in projects of social repair or protection.

Fourth, depending on the views and reactions of individual governments, international regulation of livelihood and welfare generally, and proposed conventions in particular, may be taken as an excessive incursion into the domestic jurisdiction. The widespread suspicion of "neo-colonial" adventures among the less-developed countries applies here. So does the sometimes jealous guardianship of sovereignty, that ties in so well with sectoral and private interests, in the highly-developed

---

[28] B. V. A. Röling, *International Law in an Expanded World* (Amsterdam 1960), Chap. 2.

countries. In addition, many member governments have recently been moving toward a stronger emphasis on nationalistic aims and a lesser interest in international cooperation.[29] Although it is true that no government need accept a treaty, the manner in which such conventions affecting livelihood and welfare develop, especially within international organizations, creates some pressures on the national regimes to conform. Furthermore, governments that do conform may well urge other governments to join them as a means of reducing the competition from lower-cost producers. Such a desire to avoid competition could conceivably lead in the future as it has in the past to quota restrictions, tariff and trade discrimination, and punitive conditions for trading and migration. Or else it could lead to highly nationalistic reactions which inevitably inhibit the creation of norms.

Yet among the highly-developed countries, especially those linked in regional associations such as the European Economic Community or the Nordic Council, the possibility of developing conventions to regulate livelihood and welfare remains relatively favorable. The EEC in particular has proved itself able to sponsor and apply such regulation. It seems likely that as close economic relationships continue and probably expand in the future, additional conventions will appear. The less-developed countries, too, may find certain advantages in attempting regional regulation of problems of livelihood and welfare, but so far their regional organizations have given strong preeminence to increased material production.

If the highly-developed countries, acting in regional organizations, do in fact expand the legal regulation of this area, another set of new problems is likely to appear. It will become necessary to match the increasingly comprehensive and sophisticated regulations of the developed countries with lower standards elsewhere in the world. This asymmetry of standards could well lead to frictions with the less-developed countries and reinforcement of the view that legal methods of social regulation benefit only the wealthy.

A more promising approach to general regulation, at least for the next decade, appears to rely on consultation and recommendation, especially through international organizations. The functional problems of governments can find tentative expression and definition, without major commitment, in international organs. The common interests can be elucidated in a systematic manner without giving rise immediately to permanent or long-term obligations.[30] The performance of the

[29] See Gordenker, "The New Nationalism and International Organization," *International Studies Quarterly*, XIII, 1 (March 1969), 31–45.

[30] The United Nations General Assembly, for example, adopted in 1969 by 119 votes in favor, none against, and two abstentions, a lengthy "Declaration on Social Progress and Development." Although the document covers an excessive amount of

United Nations system of agencies in identifying growing problems resulting from technological innovation in such fields as outer space, nuclear energy, and the use of the sea can be judged generally as good. More development seems possible here.

Furthermore, the views of the less-developed countries can be represented as fully in these international forums as their governments wish or are capable of doing. The record of such contributions so far gives little cause for jubilation, but the permanent attention of international secretariats helps build up a foundation of expertise which can aid the less-developed countries in defining and designing programs to meet emerging needs in the area of livelihood and welfare. Thus, some of the menace their governments may perceive in international instruments that reflect mainly the reactions of the highly-developed countries can be obviated.

International recommendations can be supplemented and supported with technical advice, planning, and training from international sources. Although advisers furnished by international organizations hardly apply a common doctrine and proceed in the same manner on the basis of the same set of international discussions, it is conceivable that changes proposed for the United Nations Development Program may promote greater uniformity of practice.[31] The experience of a large number of countries with aid from international sources, based on defined doctrine and similar procedures, could encourage the adoption of similar standards of livelihood and welfare.

In addition, this experience could lead to an emphasis on positive approaches to problems of livelihood and welfare. Rather than seeking merely to eradicate or to cope with social evils that have international scope, however defined, recommendations could be harnessed to development programs. Eliminating the effects of such diseases as malaria or sleeping sickness may, for example, be the first step towards opening up a new source of food. The identification of such a disease as a limiting factor in development, and planning for its elimination within the framework of a set of international recommendations could represent a decisive forward step for the government mainly involved.

If the international organizations can create a set of standards of general application, it may help greatly in the creation of explicit international law, either through treaties or through the quasi-legislative approaches of the organizations. Moreover, expansion of the

---

ground, it nevertheless offers some sort of standard, however vague, to governments. It can thus be used to measure progress and to spur international cooperation. U.N. General Assembly Resolution 2542(XXIV).

[31] See United Nations, *A Study of the Capacity of the United Nations Development System* (Report by Sir Robert Jackson), 2 vols. (Geneva 1969), esp. Vol. 1, Chap. v.

scope in which international organizations are permitted to produce binding regulations would become easier.

As Wolfgang Friedmann writes: "In the field of international welfare . . . the extent of effective organisation remains far behind the needs and threats created by the population explosion and the threat to the resources of the Earth, by internationally uncontrolled exploitation. But the vast number of international welfare organisations of varying scope and effectiveness that have been created especially since the last World War are beginning to cope with the manifold tasks of human welfare. This 'functional,' as distinct from the 'constitutional,' approach to international organisation is inevitable in the present state of international society." [32]

Beginnings, it may be added, do not necessarily produce desirable conclusions. Much in the welfare field will depend on what happens to the ambitious economic plans of the less-developed countries. At the present stage, it probably is more important to establish the preconditions of the emergence of firmer law regarding livelihood and welfare than to specify the content of that law.

[32] Friedmann (fn. 1), 378–79.

# CHAPTER 7

# The International Legal Order
# on Human Rights

## JOHN CAREY

### I. TODAY'S INTERNATIONAL LEGAL ORDER ON HUMAN RIGHTS

#### (1) *Pre-United Nations Charter*

In order to understand today's international legal order on human rights, it is necessary to retrace developments since World War I. Before that War the plight of individuals at the hands of their own governments was seldom considered the proper concern of other governments or peoples. The only exceptions were the rare instances when forcible "humanitarian intervention" was employed by some governments to rescue oppressed minorities.[1] The notion that the state's relations with its own citizens concerned no one else was part of the concept of sovereignty; the state's powers in its own territory were held to be absolute except where limited by treaty. It was by treaty that the first exceptions to totally domestic control of human rights were made.

At the close of World War I the rights of citizens in relation to their own domestic governments for the first time became the subject of treaties. These were known as Minorities Treaties, and generally sought to protect ethnic groups whose governments had lost the war. One of the costs of defeat was foreign supervision of domestic human rights—an attribute of full state sovereignty was taken away. The experiment was discredited when Hitler, in the name of minorities protection, sought to intervene on behalf of ethnic Germans in Czechoslovakia.

A parallel development following World War I was the mandates system. This involved international regulation of treatment of persons not by their own domestic governments but by foreign governments with temporary hegemony. A number of mandates were awarded, the best known being perhaps those of the United Kingdom over Palestine and South Africa over South West Africa. The Mandatory's obligations toward its charges escaped adjudication in the International Court of Justice in its 1966 decision. More than two decades earlier, however, the mandate system had already, together with the minorities treaties and the work of the International Labor

---

[1] See R. B. Lillich, "Forcible Self-Help by States to Protect Human Rights," 53 *Iowa Law Review*, 325 (1967).

Organization (ILO), established precedents for international concern with human rights which could be relied on by the framers of the United Nations Charter.

The ILO was chartered by the Versailles Treaty and thus has worked for fifty years. It set about establishing international standards for the working man, embodied in either Conventions or Recommendations. These are known collectively as the International Labor Code and number well over one hundred. The relevance of these measures to matters more generally within the "human rights" area is being increasingly recognized.[2]

## (2) *What the Charter Wrought*

The first multilateral treaty containing a generalized commitment by governments as to the treatment of their own citizens—a matter theretofore considered of purely domestic concern—was the United Nations Charter. The horrors of the Nazi period had shown that systematic oppression of citizens can have an external impact. The Charter provisions fell short of the bill of rights some had hoped for, but they still constituted what U Thant has called "perhaps the boldest innovation of the Charter—the unconditional and universal obligation in regard to human rights and fundamental freedoms." [3]

Human rights are mentioned a number of times in the Charter; the provisions to which the Secretary-General doubtless referred were those in Article 56, under which "all Members pledge themselves to take joint and separate action in cooperation with the Organization for the achievement of the purposes set forth in Article 55." This in turn provides that "the United Nations shall promote: . . . . c. universal respect for, and observance of, human rights and fundamental freedoms for all without distinction as to race, sex, language, or religion."

During the three years following adoption of the Charter, the United Nations enumerated the rights therein mentioned, in a Universal Declaration of Human Rights. Some authorities believe that the Declaration has come to enjoy a status akin to that of law.[4] The President of the U.N. General Assembly's 25th session, Edvard Hambro of Norway, submits "that a rule of customary international law has been created forbidding violations of fundamental human rights." [5] The twentieth anniversary of the Declaration's adoption in

[2] See resolution concerning Trade Union Rights and Their Relation to Civil Liberties adopted by the International Labor Conference in June 1970, 53 ILO Official Bulletin, No. 3, 287 (1970).

[3] U.N. Press Release SG/SM/971, ECOSOC/2474 (July 8, 1968).

[4] See E. Schwelb, *Human Rights and the International Community* (Chicago 1964); Louis Sohn, "The Universal Declaration of Rights," 8 *Journal of International Commission of Jurists*, 17, 26 (1967).

[5] E. Hambro, "Human Rights and States' Rights," 56 *American Bar Association Journal*, 360, 361 (1970).

1948 was marked as International Year for Human Rights 1968, proclaimed both by the U.N. and by the President of the United States. The final stage in enumerating an international bill of rights was reached in 1966, when work was completed on treaties putting in legally binding form most of the rights set forth in the Universal Declaration.

## (3) *The International Definition of Human Rights*

Besides the 1966 U.N. treaties, known as the International Covenant on Civil and Political Rights and the International Covenant on Economic, Social and Cultural Rights, a number of other mulilateral instruments have been written since 1945 defining the individual's relations with his own government. Some have been written at the United Nations or its specialized agencies, while others were prepared at the regional level. Only a few can be mentioned here.

The 1966 Covenants were preceded at the United Nations by the 1965 Convention on the Elimination of All Forms of Racial Discrimination, and by the 1948 Genocide Convention. Both of these came promptly into force. Both were signed, but neither has been ratified, by the United States, although Senate approval of the Genocide pact was requested by two Presidents, Truman and Nixon. Each includes compulsory adjudication by the International Court of Justice, carefully reserved against by communist country adherents. The Race Convention set up an international supervisory organ, for the first time at the world level except for UNESCO's treaty on discrimination in education. The Race Convention preceded any other such instrument in providing for receipt of individuals' complaints by this organ, though at the option of the government against which the complaint was lodged.

The most widely adopted human rights treaties are the four Geneva Conventions of 1949 on the treatment of war victims, which apply to internal as well as to international conflict.[6] The approximately 125 parties include such entities as North and South Vietnam. The two Conventions on prisoners of war and civilians raise questions in the context of Vietnam, the Israeli occupied Arab territories, and other areas of conflict such as southern Africa.

Two regional human rights conventions have been written, one in the Council of Europe and the other in the Organization of American States. The European Convention has established a viable system for international supervision of relations between individuals and their governments. The system is activated by complaints coming either from States Parties or, if the respondent government has consented,

[6] The texts are in Vol. 75 of the U.N. Treaty Series.

from aggrieved individuals. A Commission examines the situation and attempts to adjust it. Failing this, final decision is reached by the European Court of Human Rights, if the respondent government has accepted its jurisdiction and if it or the Commission takes the case there, or else, as has happened in thirty cases, by the Committee of Ministers. Nine cases have been adjudicated, the most controversial being the group known as the *Belgian Linguistic Cases.* It was the Committee of Ministers which in April 1970 passed on the *Greek Case,* brought to the Commission by Denmark, Norway, Sweden and the Netherlands. The Committee affirmed the Commission's findings of Convention violations by the regime of the Colonels, and decided to publish the Commission's report. A new complaint by Denmark, Norway and Sweden was found admissible in May despite Greece's denunciation of the Convention, effective in June.

Besides writing a treaty to protect civil and political rights, the Council of Europe has also produced a European Social Charter. This embodies many of the principles covered in the International Covenant on Economic, Social and Cultural Rights, such as the "right to work." Since this is an objective to be sought rather than an absolute right, such a matter is implemented by a different order of procedure, based on periodic reporting by governments of their efforts to achieve the stated goals.

In November 1969 the American Convention on Human Rights was signed at San Jose, Costa Rica, culminating ten years of preparation. Signatures were affixed on behalf of Chile, Colombia, Costa Rica, Ecuador, El Salvador, Guatemala, Honduras, Nicaragua, Panama, Paraguay and Venezuela. Ratification by two-thirds of these countries will bring into force this second regional human rights pact. The American pact is farther advanced in certain ways than the European Convention.

The Pact of San Jose de Costa Rica, as the American Convention alternatively denominates itself, protects eight rights not included in the European Convention or its Protocols: the rights to recognition as a person before the law, to compensation for miscarriage of justice, to a name, to a nationality, to equality before the law, the rights of asylum and correction, and the rights of the child. Only the right to education is covered by the European system but not by the American one. The twenty-six rights found in both include that of property, which was included in the United Nations' 1948 Universal Declaration of Human Rights but not in its 1968 Covenant on Civil and Political Rights.

The American Convention's Means of Protection outstrip the European machinery in an important respect. Governments have no choice about the power of the Commission to consider petitions. The

Commission had already existed for several years and had enjoyed this power since 1965. In contrast each member of the European system can elect whether to allow that Commission to receive individuals' complaints against it. On the other hand, susceptibility to inter-State complaints is optional in the American Convention but mandatory in the European. The jurisdiction of the Court of Human Rights is optional under both systems.

Time will tell whether recent discussions in the Organization of African Unity and League of Arab States lead to definition and protection of human rights on any scale comparable to those of the European and Inter-American regional organizations.

## (4) *International Protection Methods Developed to Date* [7]

The European and the Inter-American protection of human rights through investigation by commissions and adjudication by courts have been mentioned. The ILO has developed comparable procedures, particularly for freedom of association cases, but the United Nations itself has only recently and with halting steps moved in this direction.

Despite the Charter power of both the U.N.'s Economic and Social Council and its Human Rights Commission to promote human rights (Articles 62, 68), it seemed for two decades to be established that U.N. activity would with rare exceptions be confined to making general studies and drafting treaties or declarations. As the U.N.'s second decade neared its end, however, practices grew up, applicable only to colonies and to the Republic of South Africa, which took account of individuals' complaints and gave them wide notice. So extensive a set of practices was bound in the end to lap over into the broader area of human rights complaints generally.

In the first half of the 1960's the Committee on Colonialism of the U.N. General Assembly, followed shortly thereafter by the Committee on South African Apartheid, began holding hearings for complainants and publishing their written complaints. While some felt that this process produced very little, the mere publication of individuals' complaints, either oral or written, was a new field of activity for the United Nations. As a result of some of the complaints which were brought to the surface by this process in the Colonialism Committee, the General Assembly, in its landmark resolution in October of 1966, 1244, invited the Economic and Social Council and the Commission on Human Rights to give urgent consideration to ways and means of improving the capacity of the U.N. to put a stop to violations of human rights wherever they might occur.

---

[7] The methods are more fully described in J. Carey, *U.N. Protection of Civil and Political Rights* (Syracuse 1970).

The U.N. Human Rights Commission in early 1967, shortly after Assembly resolution 1244 was adopted, resolved to ask the Sub-Commission on Prevention of Discrimination and Protection of Minorities to bring to the Commission's attention any situation which the Sub-Commission had reasonable cause to believe revealed a consistent pattern of violations of human rights and fundamental freedoms in any country, including policies of racial discrimination, segregation, and apartheid, with particular reference to colonial and dependent territories. In addition, the Human Rights Commission asked the Sub-Commission to prepare a report containing information on violations of human rights and fundamental freedoms from all available sources.

A little later, in June 1967, ECOSOC in resolution 1235 approved these arrangements, and in addition took a step of great significance: it authorized both the Commission and the Sub-Commission to inspect all of the many thousands of written human rights complaints which flow year by year to the U.N. This authority was granted for the explicit purpose of complying with the duties assigned to the Commission and Sub-Commission with respect to their annual consideration of the question of violations of fundamental rights throughout the world.

Prior to June, 1967, the thousands of written complaints coming to the U.N. each year were handled in accordance with a highly restrictive arrangement contained in ECOSOC resolution 728F under which complaints relating to any parts of the world other than colonies or South Africa were simply filed at U.N. Headquarters, and a form letter sent to the complainant advising him that substantially nothing could be done. A copy was sent without the name of the author to the state complained against, for any comments which it might care to make.

The new procedure under ECOSOC resolution 1235 allowed the Commission and Sub-Commission to look at these complaints in their original form, instead of in the form of mere summaries prepared by the Secretariat. The new procedure was first put into effect at the meeting of the Sub-Commission in Geneva in October 1967. The outcome was a resolution, adopted without contrary vote, recommending to the Human Rights Commission further investigation concerning not only those parts of southern Africa which had become traditional targets of U.N. investigation, but also two other countries, Greece and Haiti. When the Sub-Commission's resolution came before the Human Rights Commission in February, 1968, representatives of Greece and Haiti spoke at length in defense of their policies, a novel situation in U.N. experience. The further investigation of those countries recommended by the Sub-Commission was not approved, but neither was the precedent thus set rejected, despite sharp attacks on that body.

The Sub-Commission in October 1968 discreetly said no more on Greece and Haiti, but merely drew the attention of the Commission to the further discussions it had just conducted, touching not only Greece and Haiti, but also Czechoslovakia, the Middle East, and southern Africa. The Sub-Commission did, however, adopt—by a vote of nine in favor and five abstentions, with only the Soviet and Polish members dissenting—a remarkable resolution proposing detailed procedures for handling complaints regardless of source. The carefully devised provisions, sponsored by Afro-Asians as well as Westerners, adopted a tactic long employed in ILO freedom of association usage, of requiring government consent for full investigation, but providing for extensive preliminary scrutiny in the Sub-Commission and Commission regardless of consent. This ingenious compromise between the U.N.'s human rights authority and the claims of national sovereignty recognized in Charter Article 2(7) received the full support of the U.S. Government in the next higher U.N. body, the Human Rights Commission, where it was approved in a slightly modified version.

ECOSOC, after a year's delay for governments to give their views, followed by reiteration of the Commission's approval, adopted in May 1970, by a 14 to 7 vote with 6 abstentions, a further modified version in its resolution 1503 (XLVIII). The Sub-Commission was thereby authorized to appoint a working group to meet before its annual sessions to consider all complaints received by the United Nations and bring to the Sub-Commission's attention those appearing to reveal a consistent pattern of gross and reliably attested violations. ECOSOC also decided in resolution 1503 that the Sub-Commission should at its August 1970 session, devise appropriate procedures for dealing with the question of admissibility of complaints.

In fact the Sub-Commission took neither action at its 1970 session.[8] Extensive filibustering by the Soviet member prevented a vote from being taken on a three-member proposal to appoint the working group and adopt rules on admissibility. The matter is to be taken up again in 1971 on a priority basis. The Soviet member did in the end introduce his own admissibility rules, as did the Pakistani member. The three sets [9] provide a notable contrast in approaches to the treatment of complaints. The existence of at least minimum common ground provides hope for some U.N. handling of compliants other than those touching South Africa or colonial lands in the near future.

8 U.N. Doc. E/CN.4/1040, E/CN.4/Sub.2/316 at 75 (1970).
9 Same, 75–76, 82–84.

These developments have evolved without a treaty basis other than the general language in the U.N. Charter.

The efficacy of treaties as a means of human rights protection is diminished by ratification problems, as is illustrated in U.S. experience. The submission to the Senate by President Truman of the 1948 Genocide Convention was followed by the Bricker Amendment struggle, the aftermath of which included a State Department stand of declining any substantial role in U.N. human rights treaty-making. No human rights treaty was sent to the Senate until President Kennedy, shortly before his death, asked for advice and consent on the Women's Rights, Forced Labor, and Slavery treaties. Only the last was approved, and ratification followed late in 1967. Meantime President Johnson had submitted the ILO's Employment Policy Convention, which the United Nations classifies as a human rights pact. Late in 1968 the Senate complied with his request to approve a Protocol to the Refugee Convention, another instrument concerned with human rights. The Senate has not to date complied with President Nixon's 1970 request for approval of the Genocide Convention. The U.S. record of human rights treaty ratification ranks near the bottom in the list of U.N. members.

The use of treaties for international legislation is, even by itself, one of the available tools for human rights enhancement and protection, since sometimes merely setting standards promotes their fulfillment. Voluntary compliance is also encouraged by the educational process which the U.N. carries on through seminars and fellowships. Where enforcement is needed, however, various international legal tools have been employed, ranging in coerciveness from force of arms to simple exposure to public view. Where nothing else succeeds, aiding the victims of oppression is the international community's last resort in fighting violations.

Coercion short of force, depriving the offending government of some benefit, is a legal tool now in use against Rhodesia under binding Security Council directions. Another tool is adjudication, employed by the International Court of Justice and the European Court of Human Rights, and used at Nuremberg in criminal proceedings of a type now urged by some to combat South African Apartheid. Nonjudicial investigations by international bodies can be effective, and offer a variety of techniques for information gathering and evaluation. Quiet negotiation to persuade officials is a tool the effect of which is enhanced by the threat of exposure to world opinion through the separate weapon of publicity. Such are the human rights tools developed to date under international law; of them all, investigation has shown the most rapid growth in recent United Nations use.

For several decades the ILO has demonstrated how "supervision," its process of reviewing government reports, can produce results in human rights affairs.[10] The United Nations, too, inquires of governments on many matters, human rights included. But governments alone are often thought insufficient as sources of information on cases to which they are parties, so private groups and individuals are therefore consulted for their versions of the facts.

Private groups may acquire standing under the U.N. Charter, at least for general consultations. Some of them which have played an active role in particular human rights cases have borne the brunt of governmental wrath.[11] Individuals have gained stature in U.N. proceedings, by being permitted to bring their complaints to the attention of a U.N. body, as described above, a possibility previously open to certain Europeans[12] and Americans having access to regional commissions but limited at the U.N. to inhabitants of colonies or South Africa. Individuals will in some cases also have standing to complain to international bodies under the 1965 Convention on Elimination of All Forms of Racial Discrimination and, when it becomes effective, under the Optional Protocol to the 1966 Covenant on Civil and Political Rights.

Investigation has been seized on by the U.N. Human Rights Commission and ECOSOC since 1967. An *Ad Hoc* Group of Experts was first assigned the task of looking into the treatment of prisoners and detainees in South Africa. Later the Group's mandate was expanded geographically to cover other parts of southern Africa, and substantively to include alleged violations of trade union rights. The members of the Group were asked at the Commission's 1969 session to investigate charges that the 1949 Geneva Convention on the treatment of civilians was being violated in Israeli-held Arab lands. Although denied access to those lands and therefore "not in a position to verify juridically the allegations which were received," the Group was "of the opinion that there are violations of the Fourth Geneva Convention."[13] The Human Rights Commission at its 1970 session condemned "Israel's refusal to apply" the Convention and extended the Group's mandate.[14]

The *ad hoc* investigations have suffered from a lack of procedural

10 See E. Landy, *The Effectiveness of International Supervision: Thirty Years of ILO Experience* (London and Dobbs Ferry 1966).

11 The Consultative Board of Jewish Organizations was granted Category II consultative status by ECOSOC in 1970, subject to termination "if at any time the Council is convinced that the organization is engaged in any of the activities alleged." U.N. Press Release ECOSOC/2903 (May 29, 1970).

12 By the end of 1969 the European Commission had received 4300 petitions. U.N. Doc. E/CN.4/L.1117/Add.1 at 3 (1970).

13 U.N. Doc. E/CN.4/1016/Add.2 at 2 (1970).

14 U.N. Doc. E/4816-E/CN.4/1039 at 79-82 (1970).

rules to guide them. Model rules were prepared in 1970 for consideration by the Human Rights Commission session, but the Commission had no time to deal with them.[15] Similarly hampered has been the General Assembly's Special Committee to Investigate Israeli Practices in the occupied territories, which heard witnesses in the spring of 1970.

The dependence of international investigation on the good faith of the respondent government may be seen by contrasting the ILO's Spanish labor inquiry with the European Human Rights Commission's Greek torture probe. The Spanish Government's cooperation is amply shown in the ILO's detailed report.[16] The European Commission, at first allowed to enter Greece, was later rebuffed. Shortly before denouncing the Convention and Council of Europe Statute, Greece rejected the Commission's report.[17]

It thus appears that the international legal order on human rights is in a rudimentary stage. Not only are the procedures so far devised at the global level mostly insufficient and crude where they do exist, but also deficiencies in substantive rules are glaringly apparent. Tomorrow's international legal order has much work to be done on both procedural and substantive aspects.

## II. TOMORROW'S INTERNATIONAL LEGAL ORDER ON HUMAN RIGHTS

### (1) *The Need for Further Procedural Development*

The United Nations' investigative techniques, aside from treaties, must continue to evolve. Only in Europe and the Americas is there regional relief for the oppressed, and even there a final appeal at the global level should exist. When the two Covenants come into effect, there will be many areas where governments will not ratify, or will ratify without the Optional Protocol allowing individuals' complaints.

The preliminary screening of complaints authorized by ECOSOC resolution 1503 in May 1970 must be put to work. This will require concerted effort by the liberal members of the Sub-Commission on Prevention of Discrimination and Protection of Minorities to overcome conservative resistence led by the Soviet member. The Sub-Commission has been charged by ECOSOC with responsibility for writing rules on admissibility of complaints and choosing up to five of its members to make the initial screening. Delaying tactics by the con-

---

[15] Same, 45.

[16] *Report of the Study Group to Examine the Labour and Trade Union Situation in Spain*, ILO Official Bulletin, Second Special Supplement, LII, No. 4 (1969).

[17] Greece asserted that the Commission and Sub-Commission had infringed Convention provisions, international law, and their own rules of procedure. Council of Europe, *Stock-Taking on the European Convention on Human Rights*, DH (70) 1, at 5 (1970).

278 · ON HUMAN RIGHTS

servatives must not be allowed to prevent the Sub-Commission from doing its duty.

After initial screening comes the stage of full investigation. This requires the respondent government's consent under ECOSOC's new rules. ILO's experience with a similar requirement shows that the great bulk of cases will be disposed of at the screening stage. Where cases do go to investigation (an ILO example being the recent Spanish freedom of association case),[18] far tighter procedures will be needed than those employed by the U.N. Human Rights Commission's *Ad Hoc* Group of Experts, which has ranged over southern Africa since 1967 and the Middle East more recently. With scarcely any rules this group of six has heard scores of witnesses, made findings, and issued voluminous reports. The small notice taken by the press may show how little confidence is felt in the impartiality of an investigation without even a rule requiring unbiased investigators. The Commission should set this right for the future by promptly adopting rules based on the models prepared in 1970 by the Secretariat.

Another desirable procedural development would be to endow a high U.N. official with significant executive functions in human rights matters. This could be done either by creating a post of High Commissioner for Human Rights, as now proposed, or by adding to the powers of the existing High Commissioner for Refugees. The latter course is surely the more likely to succeed, since the Refugee Commissioner is a familiar institution and the incumbent is both popular and discreet. His present concern with persons who have fled their countries could, with a few words added to his statute, be broadened to include those who would like to flee but cannot. His present intercession with governments to which refugees plan to return could be slightly extended to guarantee their safety after returning, and to protect those who have not left.

All of these future procedural developments are bound to encounter storms of conservative opposition led by the Soviet Union. Soviet doctrine assigns the protection of the individual to his own government and forbids outside concern.[19] If the government is the oppressor, the individual has no recourse. The Soviets are not alone in their conservative stance. They gain certain allies like Greece from among governments whose oppressions do not bear scrutiny. They gain others for quite different reasons: for example, some Arab representatives join in blocking progress in U.N. human rights investigation even when their own interests are served by inquiries into Israeli

18 See fn. 15.
19 See J. Carey, "Implementing Human Rights Conventions—the Soviet View," 53 *Kentucky Law Journal*, 115 (1964).

acts in the occupied territories. Other governments turn timid when general U.N. jurisdiction is proposed, fearful that the light will shine on skeletons in their closets.[20] For a variety of reasons, delegates speaking for established national authority tend to resist progress toward international protection for the individual.

Given this tendency of governments, the impetus for progress must come from the true parties in interest. These are not only the persons now oppressed but others who join their cause, whether for reasons of principle or for fear that they might become tomorrow's victims. Feelings of affinity among individals the world over, bypassing government authority where necessary, must be galvanized from a state of passive sympathy into one of active solidarity. Only in this way can the massive wall of sovereignty be breached sufficiently to protect the individual against his own government.

## (2) Solidarity versus Sovereignty

"The solidarity of all mankind and the mutual interdependence of all states are overriding considerations of immeasurably greater importance for the future than independence and sovereignty." [21] So said Edvard Hambro, President of the U.N. General Assembly's 25th session, in April 1970. The same month a chilling description of the icy grip of sovereignty on international human rights protection was given by U.S. and Jamaican representatives at the Annual Meeting of the American Society of International Law. Ambassador Rita E. Hauser, United States Representative in the U.N. Human Rights Commission, perhaps reflecting disappointment at the narrow defeat of a move in the American Bar Association to approve U.S. ratification of the Genocide Convention on which President Nixon had shortly before asked for the Senate's advice and consent, urged that U.S. diplomatic rhetoric cease outstripping U.S. human rights action. "We have reached the point in the United Nations that for many our credibility is questioned." [22] She argued that State Department agents should not be asked to join in drafting treaties which the Senate would not support. Some in her audience were reminded of similar expressions from Secretary of State Dulles in the face of the Bricker Amendment threat. Mrs. Hauser criticized governments in general as too politically inclined to be objective in matters of human rights. "It is a simple task to predict

[20] It has been perceptively observed that in view of such skeletons, "a state's willingness to submit certain of its activities to scrutiny by an appropriately constituted international authority is a sign of strength, not weakness." R. St. J. MacDonald, "Petitioning an International Authority" (1970), 140, in Allan Gotlieb, ed., *Human Rights, Federalism and Minorities* (Toronto 1970), 121–44.

[21] Hambro (fn. 5), 363.

[22] See 64 *American Journal of International Law*, 114, 118 (1970).

positions that will be taken by delegates, irrespective of rationales or facts presented. Politics predominate." [23]

Discouragement with governmental unreliability was even more vividly put by Jamaican Ambassador Egerton Richardson. To fill the need for champions of human rights he urged a "fifth column" in each country, in the form of voluntary citizens' groups, able to speak directly for the oppressed in United Nations halls.[24] He contrasted the equal representation of workers' groups, government, and management in the ILO's tripartite scheme with that in the U.N., where governments have no peers. He suggested analogous peoples' representation in U.N. human rights bodies.

Machinery for directly championing the oppressed was already a part of the U.N. table of organization, though little used for this purpose: it was possible for the nongovernmental organizations (NGO's) in consultative status with the Economic and Social Council to play the role of champion. Acting both as sponsors of individuals' complaints and as authors of periodic reports on human rights, NGO's were able in theory to fill the need for objective representation of the oppressed, undistorted by national politics. Many NGO's felt subdued by the close scrutiny of their affairs exercised in 1969 by ECOSOC.[25] Those with substantial concern for human rights banded together in an *Ad Hoc* Committee for mutual support and to exchange ideas on buttressing their role. But it remained for NGO's acting individually to espouse complaints and provide direct representation of individuals at the United Nations.

A plea from American law students bore this out. When President Nixon dispatched U.S. troops to Cambodia, protest took many forms, among them a petition by American law students, framed to allege violation by the Administration of certain of the petitioners' rights under the Universal Declaration. The students put their case before a group of NGO representatives, emphasizing their love of country but their desire to bypass what they deemed a frustratingly unresponsive government. One NGO representative, Professor Gidon Gottlieb, speaking for Amnesty International and having advised the students on procedure, agreed to forward the written petition and supporting legal argument in the name of his organization.

The students' plea, entirely apart from its substance, seemed like a procedural idea the time for which had come, with or without NGO sponsorship. Though fully aware of the limitations of U.N. petition procedure, very shortly to be rectified by ECOSOC, the students ex-

23 Same, 115.
24 The published proceedings merely report that Ambassador Richardson "gave his enthusiastic encouragement to all forms of citizens' human rights organizations."
25 See fn. 10.

pressed a keen desire to be heard at the world level. They saw the international forum as a means of embarrassing their own government and thus employed a method of focusing public opinion different from that of a domestic petition, however widely the latter might be noticed in the foreign press.

The American students' plea resembled that of fifty Soviet citizens who the year before had said: "we address ourselves to the United Nations because our protests and complaints addressed in the course of several years to the highest governmental and judicial authorities of the Soviet Union have remained unanswered." [26] The confidence of both the Russians and the Americans was well-founded, since people-to-people feeling had been growing and a response could be expected.

Affinity of peoples had been nurtured for widely diverse purposes under the rubric of "solidarity." Pope Paul VI in 1965 described as "what is most beautiful in the United Nations" the fact that "you are organizing brotherly cooperation among the peoples. Here a system of solidarity is being set up. . . ." [27] Also in 1965 the First Solidarity Conference of the Peoples of Africa, Asia, and Latin America took place in Cuba. Resolutions proclaimed "that the economic relationships between revolutionary states and movements which lead liberated zones must be based on active solidarity, fraternal aid and common interest of the peoples of the three continents," [28] and referred to "the necessary solidarity, in order to put an end to colonialism and neo-colonialism and to assert the right to self-determination of the peoples." [29]

No mention was made at Havana of securing other rights such as freedom of speech by means of solidarity, or of reciprocal solidarity, but the possibility was born. The cry that "we express our firm solidarity with the right of the people of Cyprus . . . to determine their own future" [30] is not qualitatively different from a cry from abroad of solidarity with American students, or a cry from American students of solidarity with the rights of their East European counterparts to determine their future. Just as a Polish Committee for Solidarity with the Peoples of Asia and Africa could report to the U.N. "mass meetings for solidarity with Guinea Bissau" held "at the factories and youth camps all over the country," [31] a group of Americans of various faiths advertised their "Declaration of Solidarity With Soviet Jews," [32] and the Islamic Conference of Foreign Ministers "designate[d] the 21st of August of every year (the day of the arson of Masjid Al-Aqsa) a Day

26 *Christian Science Monitor*, June 26, 1969, p. 6, col. 3.
27 U.N. Yearbook (1965), 240.
28 U.N. Doc. A/A6611Add. 1 at 2 (1966).
29 Same, 13.
30 Same, 18.
31 U.N. Doc. A/AC.109/PET.1124.
32 *New York Times*, May 29, 1970, p. 5, cols. 1–8.

of Solidarity with the struggle of the people of Palestine." [33] Similarly an American Students' Committee for Solidarity with the Peoples of Eastern Europe, if one existed, might petition the United Nations for freedom of dissent for their Polish counterparts. Certainly U.S. student activists *should* take to the U.N. on behalf of their counterparts in South Africa who protest at greater peril than their own.[34]

The notion of solidarity has been invoked in economics as well as politics. U Thant in 1970 employed the theme that "under-development offers the rich countries the opportunity to demonstrate their concern for the people in the less fortunate areas of the world. The solidarity shown today will lay the foundation for the solidarity needed tomorrow when most nations will be developed and less unequal." [35]

"Solidarity" as a concept may be likened to the "new patriotism" noted by James Reston, "not of the nation alone, but of the human family." [36] He considers that loyalty, which expanded from the family to the tribe and nation, "is going on now, for good or bad, to the even wider circle beyond nations to the world." In the process we are having, he said, "a tremendous battle . . . between loyalty to the nation and loyalty to mankind." And he added that because of widespread questioning of authority all the "establishment characters are in trouble."

United Nations leaders have no taste for sharing the plight of "establishment characters." Just before Reston wrote, U Thant had told the ILO's 50th Anniversary gathering that "our international institutions must never be considered, in the jargon of today, part of the 'establishment.' The active participation of youth, moreover, should ensure that our international institutions, built on the firm foundations of experience, constantly adapt themselves to changing needs." [37] The calling of a World Youth Assembly in 1970 invited youth's attention to the U.N. Seven hundred supposedly uninstructed "representatives of the young people of their lands," [38] were invited. It seemed likely that after twenty-five years the voices of "we the peoples of the United Nations," the purported authors of its charter (as contrasted with "the High Contracting Parties" in the League of Nations Covenant), would again have the chance to express their determination "to reaffirm faith in fundamental human rights."

As the hour approached for the Youth Assembly, U Thant increas-

[33] U.N. Doc. S/9808 at 4 (1970).

[34] A former South African student told the U.N.'s Apartheid Committee in 1969 that "the National Union of South African Students had been the first such organization to draw attention to the problem of students in South Africa through the International Student Conference." U.N. Doc. A/AC.115/SR.114 at 10 (1969).

[35] U.N. Press Release SG/SM/1236 at 7 (1970).

[36] *New York Times,* July 4, 1969, p. 20, col. 5.

[37] U.N. Press Release SG/SM/1118, ILO/1618 at 3 (1969).

[38] U.N. Press Release NV/175 (1970).

ingly sounded the "solidarity" theme. He hailed African Liberation Day, May 25, 1970, as "a day that symbolizes the solidarity of the Member Governments of the Organization of African Unity in their determination . . . to accelerate the unconditional attainment of national independence by all African Territories still under foreign domination." [39] The next day he called for "a second allegiance—that is, allegiance to the international community represented by the United Nations." [40]

While considered a disorderly fiasco by many old U.N. hands, the World Youth Assembly did demonstrate how people-to-people concern can overcome governmental conservatism. Besides excoriating the United States on a number of grounds, the Assembly actually criticized Soviet occupation of Czechoslovakia.[41]

Allegiance to the international community and solidarity of peoples are bound to facilitate protection of human rights at the international level. If private citizens feel intensely about the plight of their opposite numbers in other countries, and if nongovernmental organizations busy themselves with presenting such plights under the new ECOSOC complaint procedures, the political motivations of governments for or against U.N. concern with particular human rights problems will have far less effect in distorting the U.N.'s protection function.

The required concept of solidarity could not be better put than it was by the Secretary-General in June 1970: "We must recognize, in deed as well as in word, that we are all deeply responsible for the well-being not merely of our own relatives and friends, not merely of other members of our community or other citizens of the nation to which we happen to belong, but of every human being anywhere in the world." [42]

### (3) Areas for Future Substantive Law-Making

Several substantive human rights problems are on the U.N.'s agenda or just over its horizon. Two items that have been before the world body for several years are the drafting of declarations or conventions in the areas of religious intolerance [43] and freedom of information.[44] Neither subject is palatable to communist and some other countries, so that progress is slow.

A newer subject of study at the United Nations is the effect of scientific and technological developments on human rights. This involves

[39] U.N. Press Release SG/SM/1263 (1970).
[40] U.N. Press Release SG/SM/1265, PI/89 (1970).
[41] U.N. Doc. 56/WYA/P/10 at 5–6 (1970); U.N. Monthly Chronicle, VIII, No. 8 (Aug.–Sept. 1970), 110.
[42] U.N. Press Release SG/SM/1271 at 2 (June 8, 1970).
[43] See U.N. Doc. A/7930 (1970).
[44] See U.N. Doc. A/8036 (1970).

such matters as respect for privacy, physical and intellectual integrity, and controlling the use of electronic data processing. A Secretariat study [45] was presented at the 1970 Human Rights Commission session, but several years will probably be required before the subject is exhausted. Whether or not a convention or declaration embodying principles results, the process of discussion in United Nations bodies should promote legal development.

The United Nations is moving to cope with other threats to the quality of life. Preparations for a 1972 Conference on the Human Environment include plans for recommendations, agreements, and conventions, as well as a draft universal Declaration on the Human Environment. These proceedings will inevitably deal with the rights of the individual. It is he who suffers from breathing polluted air. His well-being would be better protected if discussions centered on his right to breathe clean air more than on any polluter's alleged right to foul our limited atmosphere. In this area U.N. treatment should clearly lead to new international law as well as to a sharing of ideas on the development of national law. The world has but one atmosphere, and it knows no boundaries. Its preservation, like that of the sea, must be regulated internationally as well as nationally.

The greatest nonmilitary threat to the quality of life is surely the population explosion. A world with 7 billion people, twice the present population, has been forecast in the next thirty-six years by U.N. experts.[46] This unhappy problem is caused not just by increase in the birth-rate but by the happy decrease in the rate of death through control of disease. One solution may come through drastically curtailing births. This will require government suasion, beginning with urging and moving in the direction of requiring. The needs of society will sometimes conflict with the desires of parents. In all this the U.N. can help, both scientifically and legally.

### (4) International Law on Limiting Births

The United Nations and related organizations are increasingly active in promoting birth control.[47] After what U Thant called an "historic" General Assembly resolution in 1966 endorsing an expanded U.N. program of population activities,[48] the 1968 Teheran International Conference on Human Rights stressed, in terms of human dignity, the need for family planning.[49] During 1969 the World Health Organiza-

---

[45] E/CN.4/1028 and Add.1–4 and Add.3/Corr.1 (1970). See also A/7055 (1970).
[46] *New York Times*, Oct. 25, 1970, p. 57, col. 1, citing newly published U.N. Demographic Yearbook.
[47] See summary in E/AC.52/L.72 at 20–22, 106–15 (1969).
[48] U.N. Press Release SG/SM/1132, ECOSOC/2712 at 7 (1969).
[49] *Final Act of the International Conference on Human Rights*, A/CONF.32/41 at 14–15 (1970), Sales No.: E.68.XIV.2.

tion (WHO) provided assistance in the development of family planning services in thirty countries, in all six regions of the world. In 1970 the U.N. Children's Fund Executive Board agreed that UNICEF could provide contraceptives, when specifically requested by a government and with technical approval from WHO.

The U.N. Economic Commission for Asia and the Far East (ECAFE) called on member countries, "in accordance with their national policies and special needs, to adopt practical and effective family planning measures on a voluntary basis," while another regional U.N. affiliate, the Latin American Demographic Center, has been active regarding population questions in its region.[50] The U.N. economic commissions for Africa (ECA) and Europe (ECE) are also concerned with population problems. The Secretary-General established in 1967 a U.N. Fund for Population Activities to provide assistance for member countries wishing to create and evaluate population policies, to which the United States pledged half of the $15 million goal for 1970.[51] The year 1974 has been designated by the Economic and Social Council as World Population Year, during which a World Population Conference is planned.

A serious human rights problem inevitably arising from such governmental promotion of birth control is what governments do about pregnancies which conflict with their policies. The drive to free parents from taboos against birth control has been sold on the theory of parental choice,[52] a notion equally at odds with taboos against procreation. In the long run, some societies may wish they had substituted one taboo for another, instead of declaring parental freedom and later trying to discourage its exercise. A member of the U.N. Joint Inspection Unit recognized the problem late in 1969. Hailing "the acceptance of the principle of family limitation in Singapore," he asserted that, "as so many have stressed, family limitation cannot and must not be imposed from above." [53]

Some thinkers had gone beyond this understandable official response to the problem. Richard Falk perceived several years ago that, "given the ideal of four-five children per family that prevails in the Afro-Asian and Latin American countries, it seems absolutely essential to reconsider this right of parents to have as many children as they want." [54] James Reston pointed out early in 1970 that in U.S. political

[50] See U.N. Secretariat, *Population Newsletter*, No. 8 (March 1970), 14–21.

[51] See U.N. Press Release SOC/3735 (1970) indicating that UNESCO, FAO, and IBRD had also been active. WHO held a symposium which discussed birth control methods and called for rapid development of family planning. U.N. Press Release H/2144 (1970).

[52] See for example A/RES/2211 (XXI) (1960).

[53] E/4766 at 6 (1969).

[54] "World Population and International Law," 63 *American Journal of International Law*, 514, 519 (1969).

usage "family planning" was being replaced by "control of the growth of population." [55] Some persons, he said, are "questioning people's right to have as many children as they can afford." A Colorado legislator believes that: "Society at large may have to discourage the raising of children. At this point, all the case law so useful in giving couples the right to control their child raising turns around and protects them against government action that would directly restrict childbearing. . . . The development of law, strong enough to be effective, wise enough to be acceptable, will be the challenge of the new generation of lawyers and lawmakers." [56]

The lawyers and lawmakers who answer the challenge would do well to employ United Nations' facilities. Expertise now available on physical birth control techniques will doubtless be supplemented by expertise on legal and human rights techniques. In the words of U Thant, "the world should be aware that now the United Nations system stands ready and able to help countries to ascertain the nature of their population problems and to cope with these problems." [57] The United Nations should help governments not only in promoting birth control but in the far more delicate matter of legally discouraging births. Since the problem is global in extent, the solution must be worked out through the international community, particularly in order to avoid any politically motivated resistance to birth control. Inaction by any state in failing to take reasonable steps to combat overpopulation, may come to be regarded as the breach of an international duty.

Conceivably a relation might develop between the duty of states to limit births and their right to receive aid in their economic development. Suggestions have been made that such a right exists,[58] but its acceptance might come sooner if there were a reciprocal duty to prevent the benefits of aid from being eaten up by a galloping population rise. While such a *quid pro quo* basis for population control might be distasteful if offered directly to developing countries by the developed ones, administration by a U.N. agency could furnish useful insulation. Countries could join the agency and secure aid, including that derived from the wealth of the seabed, upon their promise to control their birth rates. The agency could furnish the scientific and legal technol-

[55] *New York Times*, Jan. 21, 1970, p. 46, col. 5. Senator Robert Packwood of Oregon has proposed tax incentives to discourage large families. *The Commentator* (New York University Law School student newspaper), v, No. 1, Sept. 15, 1970, p. 1, col. 1.

[56] Richard D. Lamm, "The Reproductive Revolution," 56 *American Bar Association Journal*, 41, 44 (1970).

[57] U.N. Press Release SG/SM/1264, SOC/3734 (1970).

[58] According to U Thant, "the concept that rich nations have an obligation to assist the poor ones is now widely accepted as a new moral precept in the international community." U.N. Press Release SG/SM/1323 at 4 (1970).

ogy needed for compliance without excessive intrusion on the right of parents to determine the size of their families.

## (5) *Brutality of Men in Uniform*

United Nations studies have begun on "human rights in armed conflict." One may hope that in several years there will result (a) new treaty law controlling the use of modern weapons, (b) new procedures for securing compliance with the rules against brutality by soldiers against civilians and war prisoners, and (c) an extension of the study into the area of police brutality.

The United Nations' active consideration of human rights in armed conflicts started at the 1968 Teheran International Conference on Human Rights, where questions were raised about the adequacy of existing humanitarian law and the implementation of existing law such as the 1949 Geneva Conventions.[59] These had updated earlier conventions, adding protection for civilians to earlier provisions on war prisoners and the sick and wounded. The 1949 Conventions had also added significant rules applying to undeclared international wars and even to civil wars. A parallel branch of law had been developed governing methods of waging war. Regulations concluded at The Hague in 1899 and 1907 were supplemented by the 1925 Geneva Gas Protocol dealing with chemical and biological warfare. The United States has not ratified the Protocol, which the U.N. General Assembly has declared to prohibit tear gas and defoliants.

After Teheran the General Assembly took up the subject. Late in 1968 it adopted three principles urged by the International Committee of the Red Cross (ICRC): (1) that the right of parties to a conflict to adopt means of injuring the enemy is not unlimited, (2) that attacks against civilians as such are prohibited, and (3) that distinction must be made at all times between persons taking part in hostilities and noncombatants.[60] The Assembly also requested a Secretariat study. This was published in preliminary form in time for the 1969 Assembly session,[61] and was supplemented in 1970.[62] The Economic and Social Council at a mid-1970 meeting asked the Secretariat to give particular attention to the question of protection of women and children in emergencies and in wartime.

The internal conflict between contending armies which the international legal order has sought to regulate since the 1949 Geneva Conventions, is logically not far removed from internal conflict between police and organized violent civilians. Stages of escalation can be dis-

[59] Fn. 44, 18.
[60] U.N. Doc. A/RES/2444 (XXIII) (1968).
[61] U.N. Doc. A/7720 (1969); E/CN.4/1033 (1970).
[62] U.N. Doc. A/8052 (1970).

cerned, starting with occasional violence among peaceful demonstrators, progressing to largely violent crowds, then to systematic terror
and sabotage, then to hostilities between quasi-military insurgents and
government forces. The latter may be police, militia, or regular army
units. Whatever the stage and the government unit involved, the rebel
enjoys certain rights along with his obligations and penalties. In the
early stages, he is subject to his country's ordinary criminal procedures.
At a much later stage, he becomes entitled to prisoner of war treatment if captured. This treatment has been urged for "freedom fighters"
in southern Africa,[63] but a ready means for determining entitlement
is lacking.

Because violent protest occurs in many countries, efforts to draft
and apply rules governing the rights of protesters and their police or
military antagonists should proceed in an international forum. Expansion of the U.N.'s consideration of human rights in armed conflict
backward through the stages of civil strife would be a natural development. The process could go as far as the stage of occasional violence
among peaceful demonstrators. The proper limits on the use of force,
both by protesters and police, should be identified by a comparative
U.N. study. Further attempts by single nations to cope with such a
widespread set of problems without regard to other nations' experience
would be a foolish waste of the knowledge and facilities available from
an organized international community.

Rules should be written into international law on the right of mass
demonstration, the degree to which the presence of demonstrators may
interfere with the normal activities of others, and the extent to which
government forces, be they police, militia, or army, may use force to
control or disperse protesting crowds. A code of conduct for all parties
to a peaceable assembly would thus appear. Its implementation would,
like other human rights, be the primary function of domestic government, only thereafter subject to review by regional or worldwide organs of the international legal order.

Besides soldiers and policemen, there is another category of men in
uniform whose brutality causes a widespread human rights problem.
They are those prison guards who victimize civilian prisoners the world
over. The better-known cases of Con Son Island, tortures in Brazil and
Portuguese Territories, and solitary confinement in South Africa are
doubtless only hints of what exists elsewhere. There are standards, but
their application is the problem. The Standard Minimum Rules for

[63] A majority of the General Assembly decided that "all freedom fighters under
detention shall be treated in accordance with the relevant provisions of the Geneva
Convention relative to the Treatment of Prisoners of War of 12 August 1949." U.N.
Doc. A/L.600 at 4 (1970).

the Treatment of Prisoners,[64] written in the U.N., provide a worldwide yardstick. But the prisoner can take no solace from the existence of rules with little or no implementation machinery.

Often closely related to the problem of illegal methods of warfare is that of aircraft seizure. Frequent hijackings in the United States have merely provided transport to Cuba, but those that aroused the international community were a feature of armed conflict in the Middle East, and the object was to obtain hostages. U Thant's reaction was a proposal which should be high on the agenda for development of international legal order, both substantive and procedural. In September 1970 he proposed an advanced type of international criminal jurisdiction. Describing hijacking as "a crime against an international service affecting a diversity of nations, men, women and interests," he declared that "this crime must be brought before an international tribunal defending the interests of all peoples and nations and not of any particular people or nation." [65] He urged extradition to bring hijackers before "an agreed international tribunal," where they "should be prosecuted in the name of the peoples of the world, for the benefit of all travelers and all pilots, irrespective of their nationality, and of all nations, irrespective of their political system."

The Secretary-General's plan transcends previous progress in international criminal law. The 1948 Genocide Convention refers to the possibility of trial in an international court, but none exists. Even piracy, long recognized as a universal crime punishable even by land-locked states, has no such supranational jurisdiction. Nor is it provided for in the latest legislation broadening multinational substantive criminal law, the Convention on Non-Applicability of Statutory Limitations to War Crimes and Crimes Against Humanity. Effective in 1970, this pact, adhered to first by communist countries, defines "crimes against humanity" to include "eviction by armed attack or occupation and inhuman acts resulting from the policy of apartheid." [66] These acts would thus be punishable by any state party, but no common court is established such as U Thant proposed for hijackers.

## CONCLUSION

The evolution of procedures for the protection of individuals against their own governments has moved in recent years along two routes. Not only have treaties been drafted with novel implementation provisions but also enforcement measures have been created apart from treaty. Further progress is needed in both directions.

[64] See U.N. Doc. A/CONF.43/3 (1970); note 2 *New York University Journal of International Law and Politics*, 314 (1969).

[65] U.N. Press Release SG/SM/1333, ANV/87 (1970).

[66] U.N. Doc. A/RES/2391 (XXIII) (1968).

The human rights treaties that have been drafted require wide ratification, a process fraught with difficulties. The wide-ranging U.N. Covenants on Civil and Political Rights and on Economic, Social, and Cultural rights will be especially difficult to put into effect, as will the American Convention on Human Rights. The nontreaty U.N. procedures are at a point where they can be stalled or can break through to higher ground, depending largely on the determination with which their proponents espouse them. Support must come from both governments and nongovernmental organizations. Solidarity of peoples concerned about each others' plight must breach the traditional wall of sovereignty.

The international legal order requires substantive development for its future responsiveness to worldwide human rights problems. The individual must be protected against oppressive features of scientific and technological developments. Efforts to preserve the environment would have a sharper focus if cast in terms of the rights of the individual respecting his surroundings. A right to inhabit an uncrowded planet must be nurtured and reconciled with the emerging right to decide for oneself whether to procreate.

A universal solution to the problem of controlling brutality by men in uniform must be sought. The U.N. program on human rights in armed conflict should encompass conflict in street demonstration and mistreatment of prisoners. Pursuit by single nations of solutions to problems of this order, when U.N. facilities are at hand for comparative study and universal standard-setting, would be as foolish as to seek the cure of disease on a single-nation basis.

# CHAPTER 8

# Individual Responsibility

## HANS W. BAADE

### INTRODUCTION

IT IS USUALLY said that only sovereign states and, lately, international and supranational organizations are the "subjects" of international law —the former being the natural and the latter the artificial subjects of the international legal order. "Subject" is one of those curious terms that have directly contrary connotations depending on the context in which they are used. Etymologically and in classical legal parlance, the reference is to subordination, i.e., to a legal command (*subiectus*— thrown under). In grammar and in philosophy, on the other hand, the subject is not the subordinate but the dominant element.[1]

Classical international law managed to operate with this inherently contradictory term because it was descriptive of the basic structure of the international legal order in both of its connotations. The rules of international law were addressed only to sovereign states (and international and supranational organizations); and only these were *subjected* to its commands. But international law itself was the product of agreements between, and the practice of, these sovereign states themselves. Consequently, they were the law-givers, the dominant elements of the legal order.

These basic structural rules are not founded in unalterable logic. They merely reflect two historical facts: (1) the sovereign states which had the power to make new rules of international law chose to address these rules only, or at least primarily, to sovereign states and international legal entities; and (2) the sovereign states did not choose to exercise their exclusive law-making capacity so as to alter the basic rule that only sovereign states in concert can make international law.

The factual premises of the classical international legal order are presently in the process of erosion. Norms of international law are increasingly addressed directly to individuals, thus subjecting them to international law. These norms can confer both benefits (human rights) or duties (international criminal law). Furthermore, the sovereign states have, through the exercise of their originally exclusive law-making capacity, enlarged the class of international legal persons by

---

[1] See F. A. von der Heydte, "Rechtssubjekt und Rechtsperson im Völkerrecht," *Grundprobleme des Internationalen Rechts, Festschrift für Jean Spiropoulos* (Bonn 1957), 237.

conferring that capacity (albeit with restrictions) upon international and supranational organizations.[2]

This latter process, which is inherently capable of making a profound change in the ground rules of international law, is perhaps not as yet irreversible. Having created Uruguay by treaty, Argentina and Brazil cannot by subsequent treaty abolish this "natural" subject of international law. On the other hand, a single unanimous resolution of the League Assembly (and a patently unconstitutional one) terminated the legal existence of the League of Nations.[3] The constituent instrument of the European Coal and Steel Community (the only "supranational" organization to date) was amended by the contracting parties through a procedure that was directly and intentionally at variance with its amendment provisions.[4] And there seems little doubt that the member states could, if they so chose, abolish the European Economic Community or, for that matter, the United Nations—at least by unanimous decision.

While it is also at least theoretically conceivable that the norms of international law created in the future will no longer (or only to a significantly lesser extent) address themselves to individuals, this seems even more unlikely than a mass slaughter of international organizations. Even if we discount (although, perhaps, we should not disparage) over-enthusiastic assertions in this regard, we can, I believe, safely assume that individuals will continue to be directly subjected to the rules of international law, probably to an increasing extent. This view is based on developments within the last two decades, to be discussed in the central section of this chapter (II). Before proceeding to the "living law" of individual responsibility, however, I propose to deal with the "classical" law as it stood before the Nürnberg principles came to be generally accepted (I). In conclusion, and in keeping with the editors' mandate, I will address myself to policy questions, including a seemingly paradoxical problem, yet one of seemingly telling heuristic value: the international human rights of (suspected) war criminals.

## I. "CLASSICAL" INTERNATIONAL LAW

### A. The Point of Departure

The term in quotation marks here refers to a somewhat mythical period, starting with the extension of international law to non-Chris-

---

[2] D. W. Bowett, *International Organisations*, 2d edn. (London 1970); Hermann Mosler, "Die Erweiterung des Kreises der Völkerrechtssubjekte," *Zeitschrift für ausländisches öffentliches Recht und Völkerrecht*, XXII (1962), 1.

[3] Denys P. Myers, "Liquidation of League of Nations Functions," 42 *American Journal of International Law*, 320, 330–32 (1948); and the relevant documents in Hans Aufricht, *Guide to League of Nations Publications* (New York 1951), 597–649.

[4] Heinz Wagner, *Grundbegriffe des Beschlussrechts der Europäischen Gemeinschaften* (Cologne, Berlin, Bonn, Munich 1965), 114ff., esp. 119.

tian sovereign states and probably terminating with the establishment of the League of Nations. A curious mixture of paleoliberal pipe dreams and imperialist ideology, it rests on the sovereign equality of states, the free *ius ad bellum,* and the voluntary autolimitation theory. This construct is theoretically defective and historically inaccurate. Nevertheless, it has supplied some of the ground rules which have managed to survive to this day.

Our point of departure is a famous passage of the opinion of the Permanent Court of International Justice in the equally famous *Lotus* case: [5] "International law governs relations between independent States. The rules of law binding upon States therefore emanate from their own free will as expressed in conventions or by usages generally accepted as expressing principles of law and established in order to regulate the relations between those co-existing independent communities or with a view to the achievement of common aims. Restrictions upon the independence of States cannot therefore be presumed." Such an approach to international law has recently been termed "anarchy" by a highly learned and respected commentator.[6] Even if I shared his views (which I do not),[7] this would now seem somewhat futile, for the International Court of Justice seems to have accepted the central thesis of *Lotus* in its recent *North Sea Continental Shelf* decision.[8] I shall therefore proceed from the premise that, in the absence of restraints imposed by conventional or customary international law, sovereign states are entitled to act as they wish, and that the presumption is in favor of the absence of such restraints: *in dubio pro libertate.* Such an approach seems all the more justified here because *Lotus* is, of course, the leading authority on criminal jurisdiction in international law.

The premise here adopted leads to two conclusions: (1) States can exercise penal jurisdiction, and apply substantive norms of criminal law of their own choosing, unless *restrained* from doing so by international law. (2) States *do not have* to exercise penal jurisdiction unless *directed* to do so by international law.

It would seem that individual responsibility *under* international law can arise only where the requirements of the second conclusion are met. To illustrate: Turkey did not *have to* prosecute M. Demons, but *could* do so without thereby engaging its international responsibility toward France, the national and flag state of the accused navigation officer. *Lotus* is now overruled as between States who are parties to the

[5] Case of the S.S. "Lotus" (France v. Turkey), P.C.I.J., Ser. A, No. 10, p. 8 (1927).
[6] C. W. Jenks, *The Prospects of International Adjudication* (London and Dobbs Ferry 1964).
[7] H. W. Baade, "Review" (of Jenks), 13 *Kansas Law Review*, 451, 453f. (1965).
[8] Federal Republic of Germany v. Denmark & The Netherlands, 1969 I.C.J. Reports 3, especially at 44.

High Seas Convention; and the flag state has exclusive jurisdiction over incidents of navigation on the high seas.[9] But again, there is merely a right, and not an explicit obligation, to impose penal sanctions.

Nevertheless, it seems reasonable to assume that a deliberate refusal to prosecute a culpable multi-flag collision on the high seas would entail international responsibility. Where the person injured is an alien and the act inflicting the injury is generally regarded as a serious crime, failure to prosecute diligently is said to constitute a denial of justice.[10] This might even be seen as a case of genuine individual responsibility, for in the absence of official involvement in the act, the offending state is, obviously, not responsible for the crime itself. States are not internationally liable for the murder of aliens by private individuals. Still, it would appear somewhat fanciful to contend that the murderer of an alien is internationally responsible for his acts. The penal sanctions applied will be those of national, not international, law; so will the procedure and the rules of evidence. In the final analysis, this kind of individual liability derives from national law, although it is reinforced by an international minimum standard of protective penal law.

It thus follows that rules restricting criminal jurisdiction and the sphere of applicability of substantive criminal law are not directly relevant for present purposes—although their interplay with rules of international law directing the imposition of penal sanctions might be of substantial significance. Even the latter type of rules appears to be in need of closer analysis in order to determine whether the rules are addressed primarily to states or to individuals. To take another example: the Vienna Convention, which to this extent is surely declaratory of classical international law, imposes a "special duty" upon the host state to protect the premises of diplomatic missions, and a similar duty with regard to the personal security and integrity of diplomatic agents.[11] In the absence of specific provisions in the Convention regarding penal sanctions, each member State is free to select its own devices for fulfilling its obligations thereunder, so long as these are not prohibited by international law. The diligent prosecution of an ambassador's murderer is one such way—although, of course, not a very satisfactory one. Still, neither the crime nor its punishment is directly defined by international law.

To sum up: generally prevalent penal norms designed to protect certain basically accepted values like life and personal security are to some extent reinforced by rules of international law, such as those re-

---

[9] Geneva Convention on the High Seas, of April 29, 1958, article 11 (1).

[10] See generally D. P. O'Connell, *International Law* (2nd edn., London and Dobbs Ferry 1971), II, 949f.

[11] Vienna Convention on Diplomatic Relations, of April 16, 1961, articles 22 (2) and 29.

lating to denial of justice and the special protection of diplomatic missions, which are addressed to states rather than to individuals. Nevertheless, the penal norms thus brought to bear on individuals derive from national rather than international law; and the nationality or status of the victim is hardly more than an additional incentive for the diligent prosecution of acts already proscribed internally. This surely is not individual responsibility by virtue of international law.

## B. Criminal Sanctions Imposed by International Law

1. *Peace.* We may well doubt whether classical customary international law directly imposed any sanctions on individuals in peacetime. *Pirata hostis* [12] *humani generis;* and all maritime states have assumed jurisdiction, and indeed perhaps a moral duty, to try and punish pirates who fell into their hands. Nevertheless, in the absence of treaty,[13] there was probably no legal obligation to do so, and the crime as well as the sanction is usually defined by the law of the captor state. When it comes to the private-law consequences of the crime, it seems rather courageous indeed to elevate *pirata non mutat dominium* to the level of a rule of international law.[14]

Treaty law relating to criminal conduct not connected with war is another matter. It ranges from extremely serious subjects such as illicit traffic in narcotic drugs [15] to what Holmes would have undoubtedly regarded as an "uncommonly silly law": the Council of Europe Convention against "pirate" (i.e., unsubsidized) broadcasting.[16] Without an exhaustive survey of relevant provisions, generalization about treaties calling for the imposition of penal sanctions for acts not connected with war seems somewhat risky. Nevertheless, I hazard the guess that the standard pattern has three basic elements: (1) a disapproved conduct that is facilitated or even made possible by modern transnational communication (e.g., white slave or drug trade; sale of obscene publications); (2) an obligation of the member States to proscribe this con-

12 Etymologically, *hostis* would appear to stand for "foe" rather than "enemy" (= *inimicus*). See George Schwab, "Enemy or Foe," *Epirrhosis, Festgabe für Carl Schmitt* (Berlin 1968), 665.

13 Article 14 of the Geneva Convention on the High Seas, of April 29, 1958, provides expressly: "All States shall cooperate to the fullest possible extent in the repression of piracy on the high seas or in any other place outside the jurisdiction of any State."

14 Cf. B. A. Wortley, "Pirata non mutat dominium," 24 *British Year Book of International Law*, 258 (1947).

15 Single Convention on Narcotic Drugs, of March 30, 1961, esp. article 36. For historical antecedents, see Arnold H. Taylor, *American Diplomacy and the Narcotics Traffic, 1900–1939. A Study in International Humanitarian Reform* (Durham 1969).

16 European Agreement for the Prevention of Broadcasts Transmitted from Stations Outside National Territories, European Treaty Series No. 53, 1965; see, e.g., H. F. van Panhuys and M. J. van Emde Boas, "Legal Aspects of Pirate Broadcasting, A Dutch Approach," 60 *American Journal of International Law*, 303 (1966).

duct in their territory and, perhaps, also by their nationals wherever engaged in it; and (3) wide discretion in the shaping, and especially in the enforcement, of the penal sanctions to be used. The latter point might be illustrated by reference to a "post-classical" treaty, the U.N. Single Convention on Narcotic Drugs. Article 36 of the latter, which lists penal provisions in some detail, concludes with the following saving clause: "Nothing contained in this article shall affect the principle that the offenses to which it refers shall be defined, prosecuted and punished in conformity with the domestic law of a Party."

If this clause is indicative of the general pattern, as I believe it to be, it would seem that even penal provisions contained in treaties of the type here referred to do not, strictly speaking, impose liability directly upon individuals. These are still subject to the relevant national penal law, although the contents of the latter have been modified or, as the case may be, "frozen," by treaty obligation. Where a state has failed to enact the necessary penal sanctions it will be violating its treaty obligations, but an individual taking advantage of this convenient gap can hardly be considered a criminal under international law.

2. *War.* It seems to have been quite firmly established before the outbreak of World War I that belligerents were bound to conduct hostilities in accordance with a reasonably discrete body of laws of war, restated in convenient form primarily in the Hague Rules of Land Warfare.[17] These rules were binding upon belligerent states, which in turn were bound to enforce them against armed forces subject to their command. Since the various offenses were defined by international law with a great deal of specificity, and since the relevant rules were intended to be applied directly to individuals, it seems common ground that the laws of war entailed direct individual liability by virtue of international law.

There was, however, some question as to jurisdiction to enforce compliance with these rules. As already mentioned, each belligerent was *required* to enforce them against its own armed forces. Furthermore, each belligerent was *entitled* to enforce penal sanctions, including the laws of war, in occupied territory, and to administer military justice in prisoner-of-war camps with respect to incidents therein. Some of these sanctions did not derive from international law, as witness the case of the spy behind the lines. His activity was not prohibited by international law or even regarded as reprehensible; Major André is

[17] Regulations Respecting the Laws and Customs of War on Land, annexed to Hague Convention IV, concerning the Laws and Customs of War on Land. For comprehensive discussion, see Morris Greenspan, *The Modern Law of Land Warfare* (Berkeley and Los Angeles 1959).

buried in Westminster Abbey.[18] However, the spy was, if caught before rejoining his armed forces, unprotected by that rule of land warfare which gives members of the opposing armed forces immunity from liability for hostile acts. He was, in other words, engaged in unprivileged conduct, and could be punished. That punishment, however, was neither laid down nor required by international law.

The big question, unresolved until the end of World War I or possibly even later, was whether a belligerent was entitled to try members of the opponent's armed forces for war crimes committed antecedent to capture or surrender. Precedents are somewhat sparse or, as in the case of Henry Wirz, the commandant of the Andersonville prison, not entirely convincing. Suffice it to say that the Allied and Associated Powers, including the United States, supported the proposition that "every belligerent has, according to international law, the power and authority to try the individuals alleged to be guilty of crimes" constituting violations of the laws and customs of war, "if such persons have been taken prisoners or have otherwise fallen into its power."[19] Germany challenged this assertion indirectly by flatly refusing to extradite persons accused of war crimes, as required by Article 228 of the Versailles Treaty. In the end, the Allied and Associated Powers accepted a German counterproposal to conduct war crimes trials against German nationals before the German Supreme Court. The results of these trials were widely regarded as unsatisfactory, but there the matter rested.[20]

## Summary

Up to the end of the First World War, peacetime customary international law affected individuals only indirectly by imposing obligations upon sovereign states to punish, or to prosecute diligently, conduct falling short of minimum standards of civilized behavior or directly offending against relations between sovereigns. The catalogue of offenses thus indirectly sanctioned was somewhat enlarged by treaties, without, however, affecting the basic premise of state instead of individual responsibility.

In wartime, belligerents were obliged to enforce compliance with the laws and customs of war by armed forces subject to their command. It was generally accepted that persons offending against these rules and customs had to be punished; and to that extent, individuals

18 Personal observation; for legal aspects, see Hans Heuer, "Adré-Fall," *Wörterbuch des Völkerrechts* (Berlin 1960), I, 46.

19 Commission on the Responsibility of the Authors of the War and on Enforcement of Penalties, Report Presented to the Preliminary Peace Conference, March 29, 1919, 14 *American Journal of International Law*, 121 (1920).

20 *Papers Relating to the Foreign Relations of the United States, The Paris Peace Conference 1919* (Washington 1947), VIII, 377-79.

can be said to have been directly subject to international law. However, there was controversy as to the scope of jurisdiction to punish war crimes. The Allied and Associated Powers asserted such jurisdiction with respect to enemy personnel for acts committed prior to capture or surrender, but this position cannot safely be said to be the one prevailing in 1919.

Let us assume the Allied position to have been the correct one. Even so, it is not so easy to speak of individual liability *under* international law pure and simple. While there was some doubt as to concurrent jurisdiction in coalition wars, it seems to have been quite firmly established that the only opposing belligerent conceivably entitled to assert jurisdiction over enemy personnel for violations of the laws and customs of war was the one whose rights had been infringed by such violations. As stated by the representatives of the United States on the Commission on the Responsibility of the Authors of the War and on Enforcement of Penalties:[21]

> It seemed elementary to the American representatives that a country could not take part in the trial and punishment of a violation of the laws and customs of war committed by Germany and her Allies before the particular country in question had become a party to the war against Germany and her Allies; that consequently the United States could not institute a military tribunal within its own jurisdiction to pass upon violations of the laws and customs of war, unless such violations were committed upon American persons or American property, and that the United States could not properly take part in the trial and punishment of persons accused of violations of the laws and customs of war committed by the military or civil authorities of Bulgaria or Turkey.

Thus, the opposing belligerent's jurisdiction (if, indeed, it existed) might be regarded as something akin to a *lex talionis* or, if one prefers, a "stripping doctrine" that obviated the governmental immunity of those violating international law. Interestingly enough, the American delegation specifically rejected this latter construction so far as the Kaiser was concerned.[22]

## II. Nürnberg and Beyond

### A. The Nürnberg Breakthrough

Let us look once more at the Versailles Treaty. Its provisions here relevant read as follows:

[21] Memorandum on Reservations, dated April 4, 1919, to the Report referred to in fn. 19; 147.

[22] Same, 135f; 147–49.

## PART VII. PENALTIES

### Article 227

The Allied and Associated Powers publicly arraign William II of Hohenzollern, formerly German Emperor, for a supreme offense against international morality and the sanctity of treaties.

A special tribunal will be constituted to try the accused, thereby assuring him the guarantees essential to the right of defense. It will be composed of five judges, one appointed by each of the following Powers: namely, the United States of America, Great Britain, France, Italy and Japan.

In its decision the tribunal will be guided by the highest motives of international policy, with a view to vindicating the solemn obligations of international undertakings and the validity of international morality. It will be its duty to fix the punishment which it considers should be imposed.

The Allied and Associated Powers will address a request to the Government of the Netherlands for the surrender to them of the ex-Emperor in order that he may be put on trial.

### Article 228

The German Government recognizes the right of the Allied and Associated Powers to bring before military tribunals persons accused of having committed acts in violation of the laws and customs of war. Such persons shall, if found guilty, be sentenced to punishments laid down by law. This provision will apply notwithstanding any proceedings or prosecution before a tribunal in Germany or in the territory of her allies.

The German Government shall hand over to the Allied and Associated Powers, or to such one of them as shall so request, all persons accused of having committed an act in violation of the laws and customs of war, who are specified either by name or by the rank, office, or employment which they held under the German authorities.

As already mentioned, the United States (which, in the event, did not ratify the Treaty [23]) did not regard itself competent to patricipate in the adjudication of war crimes not committed against the United States, and also regarded the Kaiser's acts as shielded by sovereign immunity. Furthermore, the United States delegates on the Commission on Responsibility took a dim view of the attempt to arraign Wilhelm II "for a supreme offense against international morality and the sanctity of treaties," as stated in Article 227, §1: [24] "They were averse to the creation of a new tribunal, of a new law, of a new penalty,

---

[23] George A. Finch, "The Treaty of Peace with Germany in the United States Senate," 14 *American Journal of International Law*, 155 (1920).

[24] Memorandum on Reservations (fns. 21 and 19), 147.

which would be *ex post facto* in nature, and thus contrary to an express clause in the Constitution of the United States and in conflict with the law and practice of civilized communities."

. . . *et nos mutamur cum illis.* Less than three decades later, Dr. Stahmer was to advance substantially the same argument, quite unsuccessfully, on behalf of all the defendants at Nürnberg.[25] I can hardly deny that when I first looked at the Nürnberg complex as a law student at Kiel some five years after the event, I was much taken by the fundamental stance taken by the old gentleman—a staunch anti-Nazi, incidentally—who was then our next-door neighbor and family lawyer. Still another two decades later, Lady Lauterpacht graciously showed me through 6 Cranmer Road, and it was with some awe and a good bit of reverence that I contemplated the room overlooking the Cambridge Rugby field, where Professor Lauterpacht (as he then was) and Mr. Justice Jackson had laid the groundwork for the Nürnberg trials. Almost exactly between these two events, I had occasion to write a little piece on the *Eichmann* case.[26] This was, to my knowledge, the first article on the subject by a German law teacher; and response from colleagues in Germany was entirely favorable.

Needless to say, both my conversion and that of my German colleagues came somewhat later than the more or less general acceptance of the Nürnberg Principles in other parts of the world, but this seems of secondary significance. The important thing is that German lawyers, too, have come to accept the new international criminal law, so that today relevant discussion, at least in academic circles, is about the details rather than fundamentals.

What, then, is this new international criminal law? Its contours will emerge rather clearly against the background of Versailles. The Kaiser was to be tried "for a supreme offense against international morality and the sanctity of treaties." This novel and, hence, *ex post facto* charge outraged not only Germany, which had overthrown him, but also the United States, which had contributed most effectively to his defeat. The Netherlands quite expectedly refused extradition, stating that "it cannot recognize an international duty of associating itself with the act of high international policy of the powers," and referring to a national tradition of "refuge for the vanquished in international conflicts."[27] If The Netherlands had done otherwise, we

---

[25] Motion adopted by all defense counsel, November 19, 1945, *Trial of Major War Criminals Before the International Military Tribunal* (Nuremberg 1947), I, 168–70. This motion was rejected, so far as it went to the jurisdiction of the Tribunal, by ruling of November 21, 1945; same, II, 95.

[26] H. W. Baade, "The Eichmann Trial: Some Legal Aspects," *Duke Law Journal*, 400 (1961).

[27] Netherlands note to the President of the Peace Conference, January 23, 1920; excerpts quoted in *The Paris Peace Conference*, VIII, 375.

may well doubt whether it would have escaped lasting opprobrium. We can be quite sure, however, that the whole world would have been stunned if The Netherlands had asserted its own jurisdiction to try the Kaiser. To sum up: the crime against peace, as it was to be called subsequently, was not recognized in 1919 (or, perhaps more accurately, in August, 1914); and the idea that an outsider to the conflict could assert its own international penal jurisdiction even over a belligerent who was in clear violation of preexisting rules would have appeared as futuristic if not absurd. Perhaps not quite the latter, for, while refusing to extradite the Kaiser, The Netherlands had stated: [28] "If, in the future there was instituted by the League of Nations an international jurisdiction competent to judge, in case of a war, acts that are qualified as crimes and submitted to sanction by a prior statute, the Netherlands would properly associate itself with this new regime." Despite persistent efforts in that direction, no International Criminal Court has as yet been created. Nevertheless, there has been remarkable progress in two other areas: the expansion and definition of substantive international criminal law, and the universalization of jurisdiction to enforce it.

Trying the Kaiser for plotting aggressive war seemed a rather odd step in a world where the *ius ad bellum* was unrestricted. Yet the Versailles Treaty incorporated, and indeed started with, the Covenant of the League of Nations. The latter, as eloquently evidenced by its Preamble, was intended primarily "to promote international cooperation and to achieve international peace and security by the acceptance of obligations not to resort to war." These obligations were intended to be enforced by a system of collective security that was not without loopholes. Subsequent developments, however, notably the outlawry of war as an instrument of national policy by the Kellogg-Briand Pact of 1928, completed the process. In 1939, if not in 1914, the category of crimes against peace was a logical concomitant of a new international system dedicated to peace. Furthermore, in view of the obvious threat of every act of aggression to the entire system of international security erected since 1919, an offense against peace against one country could, with some justification, be regarded as an offense against the entire international system. Leaving aside, for a moment, the somewhat over-rated problem of retroactivity, the punishment at Nürnberg of those guilty of crimes against peace was quite consistent with the post-1919 international system, and so was the participation of the non-victim countries in this aspect of the trials.

War crimes and crimes against humanity (especially if limited, as at Nürnberg, to offenses against enemy populations connected with the

[28] Same.

conduct of hostilities) are much more easily fitted into the traditional framework than is the crime against peace. The acts comprised thereunder are clearly prohibited by international law, and are also punishable offenses. Nürnberg essentially brought two essential innovations with respect to these offenses. First, it reaffirmed (or, perhaps, established) a belligerent's right to punish violations of the laws of war and of humanity committed by the members of the opponent's armed forces prior to capture or surrender. Second, and much more important, it took a major step toward the complete universalization of jurisdiction to punish violators of the laws of war and humanity.

At Versailles, it had "seemed elementary to the American representatives that a country could not take part in the trial and punishment of a violation of the laws and customs of war . . . before the particular country in question had become a party to the war." No such scruples existed at Nürnberg with respect to Soviet and United States participation in the adjudication of offenses committed before June and December, 1941, respectively. In 1919, the United States had also completely negated jurisdiction to try offenses not committed against Americans or American property.[29] Again, no such limitations were observed at Nürnberg, both in the Major War Criminals case and, more particularly, in the subsequent cases conducted exclusively under American auspices and styled, *United States v . . . .*[30] Finally, the agreement embodying the statute that established the Nürnberg tribunal was expressly accepted by a large number of countries, some of which either could not reasonably be said to have been Nazi victims at all (e.g., Paraguay), and one of which had not even been in existence as an independent country in World War II (India).

This support of the Nürnberg Charter by countries other than the four Occupying Powers directly responsible for the trial was apparently taken by the Tribunal as an act of recognition of its legitimacy by the civilized world. The Tribunal regarded the law of the Charter not as a one-sided act of political justice by the victors, but as a "contribution to international law" which was at the same time "the expression of international law existing at the time of its creation."[31] It thus conceived its function to be the enforcement of respect for basic rules of international law. Individual responsibility was re-

---

[29] See text at fn. 21.

[30] These twelve cases are conveniently summarized and discussed by John Alan Appleman, *International Crimes and Military Tribunals* (Indianapolis 1954), 137–233.

[31] Judgment of the International Military Tribunal at Nürnberg, of September 30–October 1, 1946, *Trials of the Major War Criminals* (1947), I, 461. In French, this passage reads: "Le Statut . . . exprime le Droit international en vigueur au moment de sa création; il contribua, par cela même, au developpement de ce droit." *Procès des grands criminels de guerre devant le Tribunal Militaire International* (Nuremberg 1947), I, 230.

garded as central in this connection: [32] "Crimes against international law are committed by men, not abstract entities, and only by punishing individuals who commit such crimes can the provisions of international law be enforced. . . . [T]he very essence of the Charter is that individuals have international duties which transcend the national obligations of obedience imposed by the individual state."

Paradoxical as it may seem, this basic position of the Nürnberg Tribunal appears to be based on yet another one of the great ideas or ideals of the post-Versailles era that was to come to fruition in the wake of World War II: the international protection of human rights. The partial universalization of jurisdiction to punish crimes against peace is a logical concomitant of collective security; the warmonger upsets the entire system and thus can be called to account by all its members. War crimes and crimes against humanity stand on a different footing. They can be, and usually are (albeit to varying degrees), committed by both sides. Their punishment has no inescapable connection with collective security; and it is a basic rule of international law that only the state or states adversely affected can, at their own discretions, demand or, in exceptional but here pertinent cases, effectuate reparation or retribution. If states not directly affected participate in the prosecution of war crimes and of crimes against humanity, it stands to reason that they seek to enforce respect for rules that serve the general interests of mankind. This connection between individual responsibility for conduct proscribed by international law and the international recognition and protection of human rights is not spelled out clearly in the judgment of the Nürnberg Tribunal. However, it is basic for further developments in this area.

## B. *The New International Criminal Law*

Article 6 of the Nürnberg Charter had defined the relevant offenses as follows:

(a) Crimes against Peace: namely, planning, preparation, initiation or waging of a war of aggression, or a war in violation of international treaties, agreements, or assurances, or participation in a common plan or conspiracy for the accomplishment of any of the foregoing.

(b) War Crimes: namely, violations of the laws or customs of war. Such violations shall include, but not be limited to, murder, ill-treatment, or deportation to slave labor or for any other purpose of civilian population of or in occupied territory, murder or ill-treatment of prisoners of war or persons on the seas, killing of hostages,

[32] *Trials of the Major War Criminals* (fn. 31), I, 466.

plunder of public or private property, wanton destruction of cities, towns, or villages, or devastation not justified by military necessity.

(c) Crimes against Humanity: namely, murder, extermination, enslavement, deportation, and other inhumane acts committed against any civilian population, before or during the war, or persecutions on political, racial or religious grounds in execution of or in connection with any crime within the jurisdiction of the Tribunal, whether or not in violation of the domestic law of the country where perpetrated.

Leaders, organizers, instigators, and accomplices participating in the formulation or execution of a common plan or conspiracy to commit any of the foregoing crimes are responsible for all acts performed by any persons in execution of such plan.

By Resolution 95(I) of December 11, 1946, the U.N. General Assembly "affirm[ed] the principles of international law recognized by the Charter of the Nuremberg Tribunal and the judgment of the Tribunal." This resolution has been cited as authority in subsequent resolutions,[33] and it seems now quite generally agreed that the Nürnberg Principles are part of present-day customary international law.[34]

The Principles cover crimes against peace, war crimes, and crimes against humanity. They suffer, to varying extents, from lack of precise definition, and there is some doubt as to basic jurisdictional issues. Furthermore, what emerged as the most gruesome of all crimes in World War II, the systematic extermination of whole populations, was covered only partially by Article 6(c) of the Charter as restrictively interpreted by the Tribunal. Developments since 1946 have mainly concentrated on remedying these three deficiencies.

First, as regards definitional problems, progress has been slow. Pursuant to General Assembly mandate, the International Law Commission of the United Nations formulated in its 1950 Report what it

---

[33] E.g., U.N. Commission on Human Rights Res. 3 (XXI), of April 9, 1965; and 3 (XXII), of April 6, 1966, reprinted in Marjorie M. Whiteman, *Digest of International Law*, XI (Washington 1968), 1021, 1023; GA Resolution 2391 (XXIII), of November 26, 1968, below, at fn. 47. On the significance of Resolution 95 (I), see Obed Y. Assamoah, *The Legal Significance of Declarations of the General Assembly of the United Nations* (The Hague 1966), 121–25; and on the re-citation of General Assembly resolutions generally, S. A. Bleicher, "The Legal Significance of the Re-Citation of General Assembly Resolutions," 69 *American Journal of International Law*, 444 (1969).

[34] E.g., Assamoah (fn. 33), 125; and all participants in a recent panel discussion on "The Nuremberg Trials and Objection to Military Service in Viet-Nam," *Proceedings of the American Society of International Law* (1969), 140ff. In the case Concerning the Barcelona Traction, Light and Power Company, Ltd. (New Application: 1962) (Belgium v. Spain), 1970 I.C.J. Reports 3, 32, the International Court of Justice stated the outlawing of acts of aggression and of genocide to be rules of contemporary customary international law.

conceived to be the Nürnberg Principles, but failed to supply a definition of aggression. This issue has vexed the United Nations since that time; and, despite some at least superficially promising recent developments, it seems likely that it will continue to do so in the future.[35]

Second, with respect to jurisdiction, and to some extent also in the area of definitions (if on a more modest scale), a major breakthrough was achieved with the four Geneva Conventions of August 12, 1949, for the protection of war victims. Each of these four Conventions specifically defines "grave breaches" of its provisions. Each Member State undertakes "to enact any legislation necessary to provide effective penal sanctions for persons committing, or ordering to be committed," any of the grave breaches "as defined in the relevant Convention," and to "search for persons alleged to have committed, or to have ordered to be committed, such grave breaches, and [to] bring such persons, *regardless of their nationality,* before its own courts." [36] The language here italicized serves to underline the universal character of these offenses. Within the ambit of the four Geneva Conventions, there is thus not only a right but also an obligation of member states to prosecute violations, irrespective of the *locus* of the offense and of the "national character" of the interest adversely affected.[37]

The four 1949 Geneva Conventions brought substantial advances toward the more precise definition of war crimes, and are landmarks on the road to the establishment of the universality principle in its most extensive form: the positive obligation to prosecute violators wherever they may be found. It is almost needless to add that they also settled (if, indeed, the matter needed settling) the opposing belligerent's right to punish enemy personnel for violations of the laws of war commited antecedent to capture.[38]

Finally, as regards ethnic mass murder (genocide), world reaction has been swift and firm. By Resolution 96(I) of December 11, 1946, the U.N. General Assembly formally *"affirm[ed]* that genocide is a crime

[35] The United States still remains "extremely skeptical" as to the value of even an acceptable definition of aggression, but has recently given its support to a specific draft definition. See 63 *American Journal of International Law,* 565–69 (1969).

[36] Conventions for the Amelioration of the Condition of the Wounded and Sick in Armed Forces in the Field and of Armed Forces at Sea, articles 49 and 50, respectively; Conventions Relative to the Treatment of Prisoners of War and to the Protection of Civilian Populations in Time of War, articles 129 and 146, respectively.

[37] A. R. Carnegie, "Jurisdiction Over Violations of the Laws and Customs of War," 39 *British Year Book of International Law,* 402, 406–08 (1963); G. A. I. D. Draper, "The Geneva Conventions of 1949," 114 *Académie de Droit International, Recueil des Cours,* 63, 153–60 (1965-1).

[38] Article 85 of the Prisoner of War Convention of 1949 provides: "Prisoners of war prosecuted under the laws of the Detaining Power for acts committed prior to capture shall retain, even if convicted, the benefits of the present Convention."

under international law which the civilized world condemns," and requested the preparation of a draft convention on the subject. The Genocide Convention prepared pursuant to this request was approved by the General Assembly on December 9, 1948, and has since that time received almost universal acceptance. The only major Power currently not adhering to this Convention is the United States. This seems all the more regrettable in view of the fact that United Nations action in this area was largely prompted by the very country that remains, more than two decades later, the last major holdout against universal ratification. Several Presidents have sought to rectify this situation; but even if attempts to secure the consent of the Senate should continue to be unsuccessful, it is abundantly clear that the Convention embodies customary international law binding upon all countries, including the United States.[39]

The Genocide Convention is an advance over the Nürnberg Principles because it extends to acts committed in time of peace, contains more exact definitions of the various offenses, and clearly spells out the *obligation* of the states to provide for, and diligently pursue, the punishment of offenders. Its "special characteristics" have been described by the International Court of Justice in the following manner: [40]

> The origins and character of that Convention, the objects pursued by the General Assembly and the contracting parties, the relations which exist between the provisions of the Convention, *inter se*, and between those provisions and these objects, furnish elements of interpretation of the will of the General Assembly and the parties. The origins of the Convention show that it was the intention of the United Nations to condemn and punish genocide as "a crime under international law" involving a denial of the right of existence of entire human groups, a denial which shocks the conscience of mankind and results in great losses to humanity, and which is contrary to moral law and to the spirit and aims of the United Nations (Resolution 96[I] of the General Assembly, Decem-

[39] See, e.g., the Barcelona Traction case, fn. 34 above; Whiteman, 848–74. On December 13, 1967, the U. S. Representative to the Third Committee of the U.N. General Assembly stated that "international law already recognized that, in certain circumstances, genocide, murder, extermination, enslavement and deportation constituted crimes against humanity, regardless of the nature of the political régime under which these acts were committed." U.N. Document A/C.3/SR. 1549, p. 484. For a recent attempt to secure Senate approval of the Genocide Convention, see President Nixon's message of February 19, 1970, *International Legal Materials*, IX (1970), 431.

[40] Reservations to the Convention on Genocide, Advisory Opinion of May 28, 1951, 1951 I.C.J. Reports 15, 23; cited with approval in the Barcelona Traction case, above, fn. 34.

ber 11th, 1946). The first consequence arising from this conception is that the principles underlying the Convention are principles which are recognized by civilized nations as binding on States, even without any conventional obligation. A second consequence is the universal character both of the condemnation of genocide and of the co-operation required "in order to liberate mankind from such an odious scourge" (Preamble to the Convention). The Genocide Convention was therefore intended by the General Assembly and by the contracting parties to be definitely universal in scope. It was in fact approved on December 9th, 1948, by a resolution which was unanimously adopted by fifty-six States.

The objects of such a convention must also be considered. The Convention was manifestly adopted for a purely humanitarian and civilizing purpose. It is indeed difficult to imagine a convention that might have this dual character to a greater degree, since its object on the one hand is to safeguard the very existence of certain human groups and on the other to confirm and endorse the most elementary principles of morality. In such a convention the contracting States do not have any interests of their own; they merely have, one and all, a common interest, namely, the accomplishment of those high purposes which are the *raison d'être* of the convention. Consequently, in a convention of this type one cannot speak of individual advantages or disadvantages to States or of the maintenance of a perfect contractual balance between rights and duties. The high ideals which inspired the Convention provide, by virtue of the common will of the parties, the foundation and measure of all its provisions.

## C. The Retroactivity Issue

"Retroactivity" or, for those who prefer to affect visceral reactions in strange tongues, *ex post facto* or *nulla poena sine lege*, are by now Pavlovian reactions to the mere mention of Nürnberg. Those of us who have shared this reaction at some time or other might be tempted to speculate upon the functions of ideology, "false conciousness," or sublimation—the latter especially if we happened to be the products of a pre- or, rather, anti-Freudian culture where psychoanalysis is still considered godless, dirty, or both. But international lawyers need not be "emancipated personalities" in order to deal with the retroactivity syndrome.

The terms just mentioned refer, in one way or another, to the punishment of offenses that were not punishable at the time they were committed. This immediately excludes the entire category of war crimes (Article 6[b] of the Nürnberg Charter), which manifestly *were* punishable between 1939 and 1945. It also excludes those crimes against humanity (Article 6[c]), which were, at the time of commission, violations of a then-existing system of penal laws applicable thereto by its own terms and consistent with the *Lotus* rules.[41] Despite apparent initial apprehension to the contrary, this seems to have been quite generally the case. Thus, the retroactivity issue does not arise at all in connection with war crimes and crimes against humanity.

Crimes against peace are another matter. Again, there is no doubt that aggression was prohibited by general international law in 1939; that aggression was, in fact, committed; and that the defendants were, in fact, responsible. The only question is whether violations of the prohibition of aggression entailed individual criminal responsibility under international law as it stood in 1939.

The Tribunal appears to have answered this question in the affirmative, but its position in this regard has failed to command universal respect, and perhaps quite rightly so. (Calling the Charter "the expression of international law existing at the time of its creation; and to that extent . . . itself a contribution to international law" [42] seems absurd, Byzantine, or perhaps a bit of both.) A more appropriate justification was offered by the prosecution. *Nulla poena sine lege* and the prohibition against *ex post facto* laws, so the argument runs, apply to statutory rather than customary law offenses; customary criminal law is necessarily "retroactive" as to the first offenders against a newly crystallized rule, be they the warmongering Mr. Goering or the smut-peddling Mr. Shaw.[43] Since the rules of international law relied on at Nürnberg were customary in nature, the only conceivable restraint on this form of retroactivity would be unfair surprise—an element that was singularly lacking.

This line of thinking is irrelevant so far as the status of the Nürnberg Principles and of genocide in contemporary international law is concerned. Whatever the case might have been in 1939 or 1945, these rules now *are* part of general customary international law, and have had that quality since 1948 at the latest. Consequently, the entire issue of retroactivity at Nürnberg is what I call a "mule problem": it is inherently incapable of propagation, and thus of ephemeral existence.

However, while mules are destined to die without issue, the species will not expire if appropriate matings are permitted to continue. Retroactivity is, at least at present, clearly not an argument that can be employed to impugn the *current* validity of the Nürnberg Princi-

[41] See above, text after fn. 8.

[42] See above, fn. 31 and text thereat.

[43] See Mr. Justice Jackson's opening statement of November 21, 1945, *Trials of Major War Criminals* (fn. 31), II, 147; cf. Shaw v. Director of Public Prosecutions, [1962] A.C. 223 (H.L. 1961), the "Ladies' Directory" case, and for criticism, H. L. A. Hart, *Law, Liberty and Morality* (Stanford 1963), Chap. 1.

ples. But the question remains whether international law should continue to be regarded as capable of creating *new* offenses through the future expansion of customary criminal law.

On this issue, there would appear to be a division of opinion. The Universal Declaration of Human Rights provides, in its article 11(2), that "No one shall be held guilty of any penal offense on account of any act or omission which did not constitute a penal offense, under national or international law, at the time when it was committed." The same rule is contained in the 1949 Geneva Conventions on prisoners of war and civilians in occupied territory.[44] Since these conventions have received almost universal adherence and are generally treated as applicable, at least in principle, in conflicts with or between nonmembers (e.g., Korea, Vietnam), it would seem that enemy personnel, at any rate, can no longer be subjected to retroactive customary international criminal law.

On the other hand, the Draft International Convenant on Civil and Political Rights and the European Convention on Human Rights and Fundamental Freedoms, while incorporating the above-quoted language of the Universal Declaration, expressly provide that the nonretroactivity rule "shall not prejudice the trial and punishment of any person for any act or omisison which, at the time when it was committed, was criminal according to general principles of law" recognized by "the community of nations" and/or "civilized nations," respectively.[45] This would seem to indicate that there is still a good deal of sympathy for what might be called the Jackson-Devlin position: the power of constituted authority to punish acts that were manifestly immoral and disapproved by the legal order, but not as yet expressly subjected to penal sanction, at the time of their commission. For instance, during the recent discussions in the Third Committee of the U.N. General Assembly leading up to the drafting of the Convention on the Non-Applicability of Statutory Limitations to War Crimes and Crimes Against Humanity, the United States delegate declared that, as regards crimes against humanity, "it was important not to congeal the convention by incorporating an enumeration which did not allow for the progressive development of international law." [46]

Perhaps the answer to the question here posed is simply that while enemy personnel are now entitled to treatment in accordance with the maxim *nulla poena sine lege*, there is as yet no *general* international human right (even against the offender's own country) that prohibits action in accordance with the conflicting maxim, *nullum crimen sine*

[44] Articles 99 (1) and 65 and 67, respectively.
[45] Articles 15 (2) and 7 (2), respectively. See below, fn. 50, for the West German reservation to this provision.
[46] Cited above, fn. 39.

*poena*, at least where the "crime" is one that is generally regarded as reprehensible by civilized persons everywhere.

## D. *The Prescriptability Issue*

On November 26, 1968, the U.N. General Assembly adopted, and opened for signature, a draft Convention on the Non-Applicability of Statutory Limitations to War Crimes and Crimes Against Humanity. The substantive portions of this Convention deserve setting forth in full. They read as follows: [47]

### Article I

No statutory limitation shall apply to the following crimes, irrespective of the date of their commission:

(a) War crimes as they are defined in the Charter of the International Military Tribunal, Nürnberg, of 8 August 1945 and confirmed by resolutions 3(I) of 13 February 1946 and 95(I) of 11 December 1946 of the General Assembly of the United Nations, particularly the "grave breaches" enumerated in the Geneva Conventions of 12 August 1949 for the protection of war victims;

(b) Crimes against humanity whether committed in time of war or in time of peace as they are defined in the Charter of the International Military Tribunal, Nürnberg, of 8 August 1945 and confirmed by resolutions 3(I) of 13 February 1946 and 95(I) of 11 December 1946 of the General Assembly of the United Nations, eviction by armed attack or occupation and inhuman acts resulting from the policy of *apartheid,* and the crime of genocide as defined in the 1948 Convention on the Prevention and Punishment of the Crime of Genocide, even if such acts do not constitute a violation of the domestic law of the country in which they were committed.

### Article II

If any of the crimes mentioned in article I is committed, the provisions of this Convention shall apply to representatives of the State authority and private individuals who, as principals or accomplices, participate in or who directly incite others to the commission of any of those crimes, or who conspire to commit them, irrespective of the degree of completion, and to representatives of the State authority who tolerate their commission.

### Article III

The States Parties to the present Convention undertake to adopt all necessary domestic measures, legislature or otherwise, with a view to making possible the extradition in accordance with international law, of the persons referred to in article II of this Convention.

[47] A/RES/2391 (XXIII), reprinted in *International Legal Materials* (1969), VIII, 68.

## Article IV

The States Parties to the present Convention undertake to adopt, in accordance with their respective constitutional processes, any legislative or other measures necessary to ensure that statutory or other limitations shall not apply to the prosecution and punishment of the crimes referred to in articles I and II of this Convention and that, where they exist, such limitations shall be abolished.

Why had the United Nations taken the trouble of preparing a convention on this subject more than two decades after the completion of the major war crimes trials? The answer to this question is to be found in the peculiarities of German criminal law.

1. *West Germany.* Pursuant to §66 of the German Penal Code of 1871, the lapse of the statutory period of limitation excludes the prosecution of the offense. This provision has been held to require dismissal of criminal charges *ex officio*, even in the absence of an appropriate motion by the defense.[48] The periods of limitation are laid down by §67. As in force in West Germany after an amendment dated August 4, 1953, these periods are twenty years for felonies punishable by life imprisonment; fifteen years for felonies punishable by imprisonment for more than 10 years; and ten years for all other felonies. Pursuant to §68, any judicial action affecting the offender in connection with the offense tolls the running of the statute, which commences running *de novo* after each such tolling. Finally, §69 provides that the statute is automatically tolled whenever a legal norm prevents the initiation or continuation of prosecution. This latter provision has been held to work an automatic tolling of periods of limitation for the prosecution of Nazi crimes until at least May 8, 1945.[49]

Article 103, sec. 2, of the West German Constitution, or Basic Law provides that "an act can only be punished if a penal sanction had been fixed by statute before the commission of the act." West Germany has consistently taken the position that, consequently, West German courts can exercise only statutory penal jurisdiction based on enactments already in force at the time of the offense. For this reason, West Germany has ratified the European Convention on Human Rights and Fundamental Freedoms subject to a reservation;[50] and §220a of the Penal Code, which provides for the punishment of genocide as required by the Genocide Convention to which West Germany is a

---

[48] Adolf Schönke, *Strafgesetzbuch*, 9th edn., Horst Schröder, ed. (Munich and Berlin 1959), 383.

[49] Same, 392.

[50] This reservation, made on November 13, 1952, is to the effect that the Federal Republic of Germany will apply article 7 (2) of the Convention (above, fn. 45), only within the limits of article 103 (2) of the West German Basic Law, quoted above, after fn. 49.

party, has been held to be operative only as of its effective date under internal West German law, or February 22, 1955.[51]

The result is that under West German law, as it stood in late 1964, Nazi war crimes and crimes against humanity could be punished only by virtue of subtantive German penal law already in effect before May 8, 1945; and that all prosecutions were subject to being tolled by the appropriate statute of limitation. Where prosecutions had not already been initiated, and where no appropriate judicial action had been taken, murder alone remained punishable, as only it carried a life sentence; and even here, the statutory period was bound to expire on May 8, 1965.

In what now appears to have been a total misconception of the temper of the times, the West German cabinet decided, on November 7, 1964, not to introduce legislation on this matter. A few weeks later, it appealed to the world at large for information that could be used in order to initiate prosecution, or at least judicial steps, against as yet undetected criminals, so as to toll the statute before May 8, 1965. This, however, was not enough. Parliament required the Government to submit a report on the prosecution of Nazi crimes by March 1, 1965; and upon receipt of that report, it decided to extend the period of limitation.[52] This extension was effected by an Act of April 13, 1965 which provides that as regards crimes punishable by life imprisonment and not as yet proscribed, statutes of limitation had been suspended from May 8, 1945, to December 31, 1949. This extended the statute of limitations for such crimes to December 31, 1969.

By choosing this expedient, the authors of the 1965 Act sought to evade the issue of the constitutionality of "retroactive" extensions of statutes of limitation in criminal cases. Their apprehensions on this score now appear to be unfounded, for by a decision dated February 26, 1969, the Federal Constitutional Court has upheld the constitutionality of this statute while expressly rejecting the legislative fiction of an automatic tolling between 1945 and 1950. The Court regarded the constitutional prohibition of retroactive penal legislation as inapplicable to legislation extending or suspending statutes of limitation, as such legislation does not alter the punishment prescribed at the time of the act. While nevertheless holding legislative discretion in this area to be subject to the Rule of Law principle embodied in the Basic Law, the Court rejected the contention that this principle had been violated by the 1965 Act. So long as any appropriate judicial action could, pursuant to §68, toll the operation of the statutory

---

[51] Decision of the Federal (Supreme) Court of May 20, 1969, [1969] *Juristenzeitung* 434, 435.

[52] *Verhandlungen des Deutschen Bundestages,* LVI (Bonn 1964), 7457–62; LVII (1965), 7823–25 and esp. 8517–71 (debate of March 10, 1965); LVIII (1965), 8759–90.

limitation at any time, there could be no justifiable reliance on the part of offenders that, after the expiration of a time certain, they would go free. Furthermore, such an expectation would be all the more unjustifiable, in the opinion of the Court, where the maximum possible punishment was imprisonment for life, i.e., quite possibly in excess of the period of limitation.[53]

It would be comforting—if not altogether pleasant—to conclude a discussion of West Germany on that note. Unfortunately, this is not possible. The reprieve obtained by the 1965 Act has proved inadequate; and recently Parliament had to take the somewhat more drastic step of extending the statute of limitations for murder to thirty years.[54] Prescription has been eliminated altogether so far as genocide is concerned,[55] but, for the reason indicated above, this latter change will be of no consequence for present purposes. Only time will tell whether the new extension of the period of limitation will be adequate to deal with murderers—as presently defined by West German law.

On this last issue, West German law has lately taken a remarkable and alarming turn. A recent amendment of §52 of the Penal Code provides that participants in criminal acts, who lack "personal characteristics, situations, or circumstances" of the offender-in-chief which establish the latter's penal liability, are to receive more lenient punishment. This automatically activates, where applicable, the limitation period of fifteen years for participants in murder whose motives fall short of those required for first-degree murder, pursuant to §211 of the West German Penal Code. This amendment of the law, being the more lenient for the accused, is applicable retroactively in favor of the accused by virtue of §2.

In a decision dated May 20, 1969, the West German Federal (Supreme) Court has used this new legal situation to justify the acquittal, because of the running of the statute of limitations, of a police official who had, while a member of the "Jews Desk" of the Nazi police force in occupied Cracow, participated in measures leading to the extermination of—to quote the Court—"a large number of Jews." But Mr. Heinrich had acted not out of *personal* motives; he merely obeyed orders (although, as found by the jury, he knew these to be criminal, and solely motivated by race hatred). Consequently, he was subject to more lenient punishment, with the concomitant limitation of fifteen years. Since no judicial action had been taken

---

[53] 25 Entscheidungen des Bundesverfassungsgerichts 269, 291 (1969).

[54] Penal Law Amendment Act of August 4, 1969, articles 1 and 2; [1969] 1 *Bundesgesetzblatt* 1065.

[55] Penal Law Amendment Act of July 4, 1969, sec. 78 (2), [1969] 1 *Bundesgesetzblatt* 717; Penal Law Amendment Act of August 4, 1969, article 1.

against him with respect to his offense or offenses (seemingly some 2800 in number) by May 7, 1960, the Court directed his acquittal.[56]

Perhaps not unexpectedly, this decision has aroused a good deal of reaction, although it seems rather unlikely that there will be an attempt at legislative rectification.[57] This would raise constitutional problems of some magnitude; and even the new ten-year extension of the statute of limitations for first-degree murder was difficult enough to achieve. Still, developments such as these serve to convey some ideas as to the motives of the authors of the U.N. Convention.

2. *East Germany.* Article 91 of the 1968 Constitution of East Germany provides expressly: "The generally recognized rules of international law on the punishment of crimes against peace and against humanity, and of war crimes, are directly applicable (internal) law. Crimes of this kind are not subject to prescription."

While the drafting of this article was manifestly influenced by the statute-of-limitations controversy in the last five years, its substantive content is hardly more than a restatement of East German law. Pursuant to article 5 of the 1949 Constitution, the generally recognized principles of international law were "binding upon government and all citizens." Since article 135 of the same Constitution expressly permitted actions and rules adopted "for the overcoming of Naziism, Fascism, and militarism, or which are necessary for the prosecution of crimes against humanity" in derogation of the rule requiring all criminal prosecutions to be based on nonretroactive *statutory* norms, East German courts have uniformly regarded the Nürnberg Principles as directly applicable in East German internal law.[58] In a decision dated July 23, 1963, the East German Supreme Court has made the following observations on article 6 of the Charter of the Nürnberg Tribunal: [59] "The significance of this norm in relation to the internal criminal laws of states, which also uniformly make punishable murder, battery, maltreatment, robbery, and the like, lies in the right and the duty of states to designate and to punish such officially organized mass crimes aimed at the murder of whole peoples, their extermination, spoliation, and enslavement, as crimes under international law: as attacks on the peace and the security of peoples, as war crimes, and as crimes against humanity."

As early as 1960, the same Court has held that these crimes are not

---

[56] [1969] *Juristenzeitung* 434.

[57] See, e.g., the comments of Gehrling and Schröder, same, 416, 418.

[58] See the decisions of the Supreme Court of the German Democratic Republic in DDR v. Oberländer (in absentia), April 29, 1960, [1961] *Neue Justiz*, Supplement to no. 10; DDR v. Schäfer, May 20, 1961, same, 440, 446–47; DDR v. Richter, June 21, 1963, [1963] *Neue Justiz* 385, 386; DDR v. Globke (in absentia), July 23, 1963, same, 449, 507; District Court of Schwerin, DDR v. Breyer, April 14, 1961, [1961] *Neue Justiz* 394, 400.

[59] DDR v. Globke (in absentia), [1963] Neue Justiz 449, 507.

subject to prescription.[60] Consequently, there was no need, so far as East Germany was concerned, to take legislative steps on this issue. Nevertheless, by Act of September 1, 1964, the German Democratic Republic enacted a Law on the Non-Prescription of Nazi and War Crimes, which, "in confirmation of the existing legal situation," provides that crimes against peace and humanity and war crimes committed between January 30, 1933, and May 8, 1945, are not subject to prescription.[61]

The legal situation described above has now been codified by the new East German Penal Code, which became effective on July 1, 1968. Section 84 excludes the applicability of statutes of limitations to crimes against peace, humanity, and human rights, and war crimes are not subject to prescription. The punishment of these crimes is provided for in §§85–86, 91, and 93, and, so far as members of the armed forces are concerned, in §§277–282 of the Penal Code of 1968.

There are, thus, some rather remarkable differences in the attitudes of East and West Germany to the new international penal law. Perhaps it was no more than an historical accident that the decision of the Supreme Court of the German Republic spelling out the inapplicability of statutes of limitations to crimes under the Nürnberg Charter was *in absentia* proceeding against Oberlaender, a former West German minister who was forced by the revelation of his past to resign from the federal cabinet, but who nevertheless remained in Parliament to cast his vote with the minority against the 1965 Act extending the statute of limitations for murder. Still, West Germany has yet to acknowledge expressly what all other countries have accepted: the validity of the Nürnberg Principles, the duty under customary international law to enforce these principles, and the nonapplicability of domestic statutes of limitations to violators thereof. Almost perversely, there is still enough international support for West Germany's nonrecognition policy toward East Germany to block the accession to the U.N. Convention on the Non-Applicability of Statutory Limitations to War Crimes and Crimes Against Humanity of the one German state willing to do so.[62]

[60] DDR v. Oberländer (in absentia), [1961] *Neue Justiz* Supplement to no. 10, at p. 19.

[61] [1964] 1 *Gesetzblatt der Deutschen Demokratischen Republik* 127. See the pertinent statement of the Minister of Justice in Parliament, [1964] *Neue Justiz* 545.

[62] Article 5 of the Convention, incorporating the so-called Vienna Formula, reads as follows: "This Convention shall, until 31 December 1969, be open for signature by any State Member of the United Nations or member of any of its specialized agencies or of the International Atomic Energy Agency, by any State Party to the Statute of the International Court of Justice, and by any other State which has been invited by the General Assembly of the United Nations to become a Party to this Convention." Despite encouraging changes in West German policy since October 1969, I reluctantly let the above statement stand, for as of December 1971, it is still correct.

3. *The Convention and Customary International Law.* By its terms, the 1968 Convention is declaratory of international law. This appears quite clearly from the Preamble, which describes the Contracting Parties as

> *Noting* that none of the solemn declarations, instruments or conventions relating to the prosecution and punishment of war crimes and crimes against humanity made provision for a period of limitation,
>
> *Considering* that war crimes and crimes against humanity are among the gravest crimes in international law,
>
> *Convinced* that the effective punishment of war crimes and crimes against humanity is an important element in the prevention of such crimes, the protection of human rights and fundamental freedoms, the encouragement of confidence, the furtherance of cooperation among peoples and the promotion of international peace and security
>
> *Noting* that the application to war crimes and crimes against humanity of the rules of municipal law relating to the period of limitation for ordinary crimes is a matter of serious concern to world public opinion, since it prevents the prosecution and punishment of persons responsible for those crimes,

and as

> *Recognizing* that it is necessary and timely to affirm in international law, through this Convention, the principle that there is no period of limitation for war crimes and crimes against humanity, and to secure its universal application.

However, only 58 states voted in favor of the adoption of this Convention. Seven states, including the United States, the United Kingdom, and Australia, voted against it; and no less than 36 other states abstained. It therefore appears necessary to examine the legislative history of the Convention with a view to determining whether this voting record impairs the authority of the draft Convention as evidence of customary international law. Since there were extensive explanations of the views of the various states before and after the voting, there is no need to go into the entire legislative history at this point.[63]

[63] See, in this connection, Bernhard Graefrath, "Schultz der Menschenrechte—Bestrafung der Kriegsverbrecher," [1967] *Neue Justiz* 393 and 458; Gunter Görner and Günter Schumann, "War Crimes and Crimes Against Humanity," [1969] *German Foreign Policy* 177; Natan Lerner, "The Convention on the Non-Applicability of Statutory Limitations to War Crimes," 4 *Israel Law Review*, 512 (1969); Robert H. Miller, "The Convention on the Non-Applicability of Statutory Limitations to War Crimes and Crimes Against Humanity," 65 *American Journal of International Law*, 476 (1971).

The strongest challenge to the future authority of the Convention came from the United States, whose delegate declared:[64] "My Government must make it emphatically clear that it does not regard this convention, most particularly the language of articles I and II, as embodying generally agreed statements of international law and that it does not believe the provisions of this convention should be considered as evidence of international law as generally accepted or practised by nations." However, even the United States—the most articulate opponent of the Convention as it finally emerged—did not quarrel with what it termed the "original purpose" of the Convention: "to make it clear that under international law there are no periods of limitations applicable to war crimes and crimes against humanity."[65] There were four major objections by the United States to the final text. Since this is the most extensive critique of that text, it may serve as an exhaustive catalogue for present purposes.

First, it was objected that the Convention should not serve the purpose of redefining crimes against humanity, and that *apartheid,* in particular, had no place in this definition. The position of the United States in this respect was expressly shared by the United Kingdom. Second, the United States thought the scope of war crimes under article I(a) too broad; this was an elliptical way of saying that the Convention should not be applicable to "minor offenses committed in time of war." This position, as well, was supported by the United Kingdom. Third, article II, which deals with participation and the like, was deemed to be poorly drafted. The fourth objection is the main one: it is directed at what is termed the "retroactive effect" of the Convention "in reactivating penal liability already extinguished by operation of law." This latter objection was expressly shared by a large number of states.[66]

It would seem that the first and the third objections are only directed at the attempt of the majority to expand the substantive contents of international penal law, especially through the addition of *apartheid.* The practice of the latter had, indeed, been termed a "crime against humanity" by prior General Assembly resolutions, but it was contended, and perhaps rightly so, that these resolutions were not intended to be read in a technical legal sense.[67] It thus seems that

[64] U.N. Document A/PV. 1727, p. 48.
[65] Same, 46.
[66] Same, 46–48 (U.S.); 6 (Belgium); 21–26 (U.K); 26 (El Salvador); 35–36 (Norway); 56 (Sweden); 56–57 (Italy); 61 (Chile); 62 (Japan); 63 (Denmark); 63–65 (Portugal); and 66 (Australia).
[67] In its comments on the draft convention, dated August 21, 1968, the United States had observed, with respect to G.A. Resolutions 2184 (XXI) and 2202 (XXI) which had condemned *apartheid* as a crime against humanity: "These resolutions were not intended to deal with the question of crimes in a legal sense, nor to formulate legal definitions." U.N. Document A/7174, p. 46.

these two objections do not affect the main purpose of the Convention, which is to establish, in an authoritative manner, that statutes of limitations do not apply to war crimes and to crimes against humanity.

The second and the fourth objections are more troublesome. Taken by itself, the fourth is either an error in logic or a rejection of the basic premise of the Convention. As the Polish delegate explained, the principle *lex retro non agit* is plainly inapplicable if customary international criminal law already prohibits statutes of limitation for war crimes and crimes against humanity; and it seems reasonable to assume that to be the case in view of the gravity of these crimes and the "qualified silence" of the various pertinent sources.[68] This position was shared, among others, by the Secretary-General.[69] Was it rejected by the United States and by the other states objecting to the retroactive operation of the Convention with respect to statutes of limitation that have already expired? If so, the Convention cannot be unequivocal authority for the proposition that under present-day customary international law the prosecution of war crimes and crimes against humanity may not be barred by statutes of limitation.

The legislative history of the Convention does not appear to supply a definitive answer to this question. However, the more reasonable interpretation would appear to be that the fourth objection of the United States has to be read in conjunction with the second one, and that the retroactivity objection is limited to lesser offenses. As to these, there is as yet no prohibition of prescription under customary international law. Consequently, states could apply their statutes of limitation to the prosecution of such offenses, so long as they did not thereby circumvent their obligation to prosecute, spelled out, e.g., in the Geneva Conventions of 1949. On the other hand, as to major offenses under customary international law, e.g., those prosecuted at Nürnberg, prescription is already outlawed by customary international law. This position seems to have been adopted, at least indirectly, even in West Germany, as witness the recent elimination of prescription for the crime of genocide.

*Summary*

Present-day customary international criminal law is a universal system which all members of the international community are bound not only to obey, but also to enforce universally. Its substantive contents have been shaped by four major factors: the transition from the *ius ad bellum* to collective security; the international human rights movement; reaction to unprecedented atrocities toward whole populations

---

68 U.N. Document A/PV. 1727, p. 11.

69 U.N. Document E/CN.4/906, pp. 111–12. See Lerner (fn. 63), 520–22.

in the last war; and refinements of the laws of warfare based on past experience. The major sources of the new international criminal law are the Charter of the Nürnberg Tribunal, the 1949 Geneva Conventions, and the Genocide Convention.

So far as this body of law is concerned, retroactivity is not presently an issue. However, there is still some doubt as to whether new norms of international criminal law can be created in the future with retroactive effect. As regards prescription, it seems clear that the prescription of major international crimes, i.e., at least those committed by the Nürnberg defendants and the crime of genocide, may not be limited by internal statutes of limitations, and that states may likewise not evade their duties of enforcement of sanctions against lesser crimes by the prescription device. However, it seems likely that countries failing to ratify the 1968 Convention will still be free, under customary international law, to observe reasonable periods of prescription with respect to minor war crimes.

### III. Policy Questions: Deterrence and Human Rights

*A. Deterrence, Safety, and Security*

All punishment has one of three basic functions, or a combination of them. These are justice through retribution for wrongdoing, short-range safety of society by the removal of the offender, and long-range security by the deterrent effect on future would-be offenders. To what extent does present-day international criminal law serve these functions, and what values are pursued thereby? It seems appropriate to commence our discussion with the latter, as these seem reasonably clear.

1. *Crimes Against Peace.* First, there is world peace. Nürnberg stands for the proposition that aggressive war is an international crime, and that those instigating it bear criminal liability despite their official positions. Punishment of major offenders under this heading has surely served the ends of justice and, perhaps, short-range safety. There is a real question, however, as to deterrent effects. The world has not known peace since 1945. Charges of aggression in more or less localized conflicts abound, and some of them, one suspects, are justified. Perhaps the clearest case, though by no means the only possible one, was the Suez venture of Great Britain and France in 1956.

The mere fact that there have been acts of aggression after Nürnberg is no conclusive indication of the absence of deterrent effects; after all, criminal law needs its "clients." Admittedly, we are dealing with somewhat elusive phenomena, as there have been no prosecutions for crimes against peace committed after the second World War. Nevertheless, at least two indirect effects of Nürnberg are clearly noticeable. First, no state is indifferent to the charge of aggression.

Second, and closely linked therewith, world public opinion condemns the exercise of military power for ethnocentric purposes. As the example of Suez in 1956 shows, this is a factor to be reckoned with even within the state that is thought to be the transgressor.

Whether statesmen are deterred only by the propaganda implications of acts of aggression, or whether there is a real apprehension of criminal liability, cannot be answered with confidence. I incline to answer this question in the negative. There is as yet no clear and generally accepted definition of aggression, and the material facts are almost certain to be in dispute. This militates against the exercise of jurisdiction by outsiders. As between the parties, the *status quo* cemented by the nuclear balance of terror makes conflicts terminating in the capture or surrender of enemy statesmen quite unlikely.

Fortunately, this is not quite the end of the matter. Military actions create legal problems of some uncertainty; and this itself is a deterrent—if only a rather weak one. Without in any way appearing to endorse the legal arguments employed, we might draw some comfort from Theodore Sorensen's argument that to the factors imposing the "limits of permissibility" of Presidential action [70] "must be added international law, which cannot be dismissed as quickly as some claim.

"For example: had the Organization of American States failed in October, 1962, to provide the necessary two-thirds vote authorizing a Cuban quarantine, the Soviets and possibly others might have been emboldened to challenge the legality of our action, creating confusion and irresolution in the Western camp and giving rise to all kinds of cargo insurance and admiralty questions that this nation would not enjoy untangling."

How about the deterrent effect of Nürnberg on military personnel participating in aggressive war? Count 2 of the indictment at Nürnberg charged all defendants with participating "in the planning, preparation, initiation, and waging of wars of aggression." One defendant, Admiral Doenitz, was convicted under this count although he was acquitted under Count 1, which, as limited by the Tribunal, charged participation "in the formulation or execution of a common plan or conspiracy to commit, or which involved the commission of, Crimes against Peace." The Tribunal expressly found that [71] "the evidence does not show that [Doenitz] was privy to the conspiracy to wage aggressive wars or that he prepared and initiated such wars. He was a line officer performing strictly tactical duties."

The Tribunal apparently regarded the "waging of wars of aggression" therein charged as separable, and concluded that Doenitz

[70] Theodore C. Sorensen, *Decision Making in the White House. The Olive Branch or the Arrows* (New York and London 1963), pp. 24f.
[71] *Trial of the Major War Criminals* (fn. 31), I, 310.

"was active in waging aggressive war." This conclusion is based, in essence, on the following finding: [72] "He was not a mere army or division commander. The U-boat arm was the principal part of the German fleet and Doenitz was its leader." It thus seems that military leaders can be guilty of crimes against peace even if they are line officers and have no part in the political decision-making process. Still, they have to be in more exalted positions than "mere" army or division commanders, at least where several of these are simultaneously in command positions. Even if we should fail to be persuaded by recent criticism of this aspect of the *Doenitz* case,[73] it would still seem that very few "unpolitical" career officers, indeed, have grounds to fear personal criminal liability for crimes against peace.

2. *War Crimes, Crimes Against Humanity, and Genocide.* Here, the basic policy goal is "clean fighting" between combatants and the protection of noncombatants. Liability is personal throughout the civilian and military hierarchies, and there is some likelihood of the capture of the offender. Even trial by his own side is a possibility; and we are reliably informed that there have been more than a dozen such trials in Vietnam, with a high percentage of convictions.[74]

Nevertheless, we may well doubt whether penal norms designed to enforce the laws of war are sufficiently effective. It seems likely that unavoidable publicity and the pressure of world public opinion will prevent systematic genocide and large-scale crimes against humanity in the future. However, when it comes to the laws of war, things are different. The substantive law tends to be unsettled in direct proportion to the novelty (and hence, usually the destructiveness) of the means employed. Trial of enemy personnel arouses strong reactions, and might lead to reprisals.[75] Finally, a belligerent is likely to be less than enthusiastic in the prosecution of its own personnel accused of war crimes. Such acts might be attributed to excessive zeal in a just cause; and especially if committed pursuant to superior orders, their prosecution is likely to be regarded as harmful to military discipline and morale. Not unreasonably, a large number of trials, with inescapable publicity, will be considered as a liability in the propaganda war.

These very days (1969), we are witnessing the whole range of this type of reaction. The secret killing of a suspected enemy spy without ante-

---

[72] Same, 310–11.

[73] See, e.g., the comments of Telford Taylor, *Proceedings of the American Society of International Law* (1969), 166, 177.

[74] See the remarks of Benjamin Forman, same, 181. This paper was written before the Calley case which, in any event, would appear to be primarily a laboratory case of mass psychology. That case will not be discussed here.

[75] See Thomas H. Sponsler, "The Universality Principle of Jurisdiction and the Threatened Trials of American Airmen," 15 *Loyola Law Review*, 43, esp. 63–65 (1969).

cedent trial is called the "plain duty" of the perpetrators by a widely read commentator; the mere fact of a criminal investigation is termed a "foul-up" and harmful to morale; and one of the accused sees himself treated in a way reminiscent of Nürnberg. Somewhat to the surprise of at least some of those not engaged in what the Nürnberg Tribunal called "the honorable profession of arms," [76] he manifestly considers such treatment unjust.

To summarize: the direct impact of Nürnberg is not sufficient to assure the attainment of the policy objectives of the new international penal law. Nevertheless, the mere existence of some generally recognized substantive standards, coupled with the impact of charges of violation on world and even home public opinion, is of substantial significance.

Since both crimes against peace and war crimes are likely to continue to pose threats to values generally recognized by the world community, we might speculate on ways to improve the system of penal sanctions for their suppression. One possibility would be the creation of an International Criminal Court—a project that has been discussed, in one form or another, for several decades. This will probably fail, as did the International Prize Court, so long as there is no agreement on the substantive law to be applied. Disagreement is likely to focus on the definition of aggression and the legality of the use of thermonuclear weapons.[77] There might even be unbridgeable conflicts on the legality of chemical warfare [78] and of some smaller-scale devices, such as napalm.

Another approach might be the expansion of substantive international penal law without the creation of an International Criminal Court. Such a step might give rise to serious human rights problems, which will be discussed in the next section. Of at least equal importance, however, is the question of "counterproductive" effects. The most obvious next step would be the punishment of mere participa-

[76] *Trial of the Major War Criminals* (fn. 31), I, 278. See the report by Frank Frosch, "Beret's Aim: To Be Free," *Atlanta Constitution*, August 28, 1969, p. 9A, on Capt. Budge E. Williams, one of the eight "Green Berets" accused of the clandestine murder of a Vietnamese suspected of being a double agent. The eight accused have been released in the meantime. Cf. the decision of the West German Federal (Supreme) Court of August 15, 1969, [1969] *Juristenzeitung* 706, upholding the conviction of the chief of the Gestapo in occupied Norway for causing the "silent killing" of four Norwegian civilians suspected of being members of the Resistance.

[77] As to the latter, see, e.g., Declaration on the Prohibition of the Use of Nuclear and Thermo-Nuclear Weapons, U.N. General Assembly Resolution 1653 (XVI) of November 24, 1961, discussed in Assamoah (fn. 33), 101ff.

[78] See the Declaration on the Question of Chemical and Bacteriological Warfare (Chemical Weapons), U.N. General Assembly Resolution 1603 (XXIV), and the position of the United States in regard thereto, as reported in *Department of State Bulletin*, LXII (1970), 95.

tion in aggressive war. Probably nothing could be better calculated to increase the ferocity of the conduct of hostilities.

Finally, we may speculate upon the utility of the "right to resistance" against participating in violations of international penal law. This subject is of considerable current importance in the United States.[79] It seems clear that a state which punishes noncompliance with orders that are criminal under international law will thereby violate international law. For this reason, states currently permit (or, perhaps, claim to permit) the defense of illegality under international law in prosecutions for refusal to obey superior orders.[80] However, in the field, such refusals are likely to be quite rare. Should members of the Armed Forces, or possibly even prospective conscripts, be given the right to refuse all military service because they would be participating in an illegal war (which is no offense as to them), or because they might receive orders to violate international law (which they would be entitled to disobey)?

Traditional notions of law call for a negative answer.[81] However, it may well be that a movement towards the recognition of an international human right to refuse participating in illegal wars (and possibly also in lawful hostilities characterized by a substantial amount of illegal acts) could be a powerful and beneficial factor in international relations. The basic obstacle to be overcome will be the fear of the asymmetrical operation of such a rule to the detriment of states with open societies.

## B. Suspected War Criminals and Human Rights

The new international criminal law, we have seen, is to a considerable extent the product of the human rights movement. This connection is most obvious in the case of the Genocide Convention. More generally, it was recently underlined by the fact that the 1968 U.N. Convention on statutory limitations had its orgins in the Commission on Human Rights and received its final shape in the Third Committee. The preamble of this convention expresses the conviction of its authors that "the effective punishment of war crimes and crimes against humanity is an important element . . . in the protection of human rights and fundamental freedoms.

But just as basic human rights need to be protected by penal sanctions, so do accused war criminals need the protection of human

---

[79] See generally Louis Loeb, "The Courts and Vietnam," 18 *American University Law Review*, 376 (1969); and the panel on "The Nuremberg Trials and Objection to Military Service in Viet-Nam," *Proceedings* (fn. 73), 140ff.

[80] See Benjamin Forman, "The Nuremberg Trials and Conscientious Objection to War: Justiciability Under United States Municipal Law," *Proceedings* (fn. 73), 157, 164.

[81] The traditional position is well stated by Mr. Forman, same, 163–64.

rights. For reasons that will soon become apparent, this aspect of international criminal law has received scant attention up to date. Still, we are perhaps justified in discerning an increasing general awareness of the problem in the following remark of the United States representative during the course of debates on the 1968 Convention in the Third Committee: [82] "The question of retroactivity should also be seen within the general context of the guarantees of the right to a fair trial enjoyed by any accused person and spelled out, *inter alia,* in articles 9, 10, 14 and 15 of the International Convention on Civil and Political Rights. The preliminary draft convention did not recognize that aspect of the problem." Let us now look at some characteristics of war crimes trials that appear to make international human rights safeguards particularly appropriate.

1. *Uncertainty and Bias of Substantive Law.* Customary law is likely to be uncertain, and those who are the first defendants convicted under an expanding rule of customary criminal law are subjected to a form of retroactive punishment. In internal law, this process might be tolerable because it will be based on a preexisting consensus on what constitutes reprehensible conduct. Even so, the movement toward a purely statutory system of criminal law, and hence toward an exact catalogue of punishable conduct, seems to be a hallmark of advanced civilization.

It may be that international law, being as yet a primitive legal order, should not as yet be saddled with the requirement that all offenses be previously defined by "written" law, i.e., by treaty. However, in that case, utmost care will have to be exercised to assure that the process of norm creation is not biased to the detriment of the current adversaries of those conducting the trials. Unfortunately, no such safeguards exist as yet.

Legal literature has made a major contribution to the development of customary international criminal law, and probably will continue to do so. There is no assurance, however, that the writings of authors on the subject will be free from personal bias, or even that they will live up to generally accepted standards of legal literature. For one thing, until relatively recently at least, a number of those who contribute to the body of literature on international criminal law have not been professional lawyers. Even where authors had this essential qualification, criminal law was usually not their main field of interest. It seems a relatively safe assumption, at least for the United States, the United Kingdom, and—to a lesser extent—West Germany, that the literature on customary international criminal law has been produced, in the main, by strangers to the field of academic criminal law.

[82] U.N. Document A/C.3/SR. 1517, pp. 6–7 (November 16, 1967).

This personal component of the process of law creation poses several dangers, which might perhaps be illustrated by the seemingly far-fetched example of an authoritative medical journal that freely accepts and publishes amateur contributions. The publishers of medical journals are fully aware that published reports of inaccurate or biased medical research can kill patients. I am yet to be convinced that there is a similar awareness among international legal authors that their writings can hang defendants. I might even add, with considerable reluctance, that where such awareness exists, it might not necessarily serve as a brake.

2. *Trial by Publicity.* This brings us to what seems to be the main deficiency of war crimes trials: advance adjudication in public. It takes a good bit of propaganda buildup to hold such trials at all; and in the course of this shaping of public opinion, it is not unlikely that there will be an almost irreversible prejudging not only of as yet unsettled legal questions, but also of some of the more important operative facts. Chief Justice Stone's acid characterization of the Nürnberg trials as Mr. Justice Jackson's "high-grade lynching party" [83] is rather plainly a reaction to this type of pressure. In retrospect, I continue to be appalled to see how few of us even bothered to state, in early discussions of the *Eichmann* case, that our opinions rested on the premise, yet to be established, that the prosecution would be able to prove its case.[84]

An especially reprehensible form of public pressure and prejudging is intimidation of the defense. At Nürnberg, the President of the Tribunal found it necessary to issue a sharp rebuke to a newspaper for an intemperate attack on one of the counsels for the defense, and to assure the person involved of the confidence of the Tribunal.[85] This laudable action does not appear to have had the impact to be desired; and even in legal literature, there has been *ad hominem* criticism of defense counsel.[86]

3. *Judicial Independence.* Nürnberg has been attacked because the Tribunal was staffed by jurists from the victor nations. Criticism on this score is not justified *per se,* for it does not automatically follow that the Bench was unfair or biased. Nevertheless, it seems that the process of selection of judges *ad hoc* by the powers in charge of the

[83] Letter to Sterling Carr, December 4, 1945, quoted in Alpheus T. Mason, *Harlan Fiske Stone: Pillar of the Law* (New York 1956), 716.

[84] Baade, "The Eichmann Trial," 400–401; 405.

[85] *Trial of the Major War Criminals* (fn. 31), VIII, 532–33. Francis Biddle, *In Brief Authority* (Garden City 1962), 369ff., records an astonishing degree of intimacy between the Bench and the prosecution at Nürnberg.

[86] See Sheldon Glueck, *The Nuremberg Trial and Aggressive War* (New York 1946), 71–74; and especially Joseph Berry Keenan & Brendan Francis Brown, *Crimes Against International Law* (Washington 1950), passim and 155–56.

prosecution from among their own ranks is inherently subject to objection. To be sure, a number of the most advanced judicial systems presently have considerable flexibility in the assignment of judges. Nevertheless, the designation of the judge or panel is invariably either a judicial function or a routinized procedure not subject to manipulation by one of the parties. I take this to be a necessary corollary of judicial independence.

It seems unavoidable that a number of persons accused of war crimes will be tried by military tribunals resembling courts-martial. The United States Supreme Court has recently characterized the entire system of military justice as a lesser order of jurisprudence—one that does not live up to normal requirements of due process.[87] In the interest of discipline in activities deemed necessary for national survival, such lesser standards might be deemed to be tolerable. However, there is a real question whether *enemy* personnel should be subjected to a judicial system that administers less than full justice for patriotic reasons.

4. *Illegal Procedures.* Unfortunately, there is some reason for apprehension that in war crimes trials the prosecution might resort to illegal procedures—to procedures that would not only vitiate convictions in civilian courts but would also call for the swift and massive judicial discipline of those who thus sully their robes. This latter sanction is likely to be almost entirely lacking because of the ephemeral composition of the court, and possibly also due to "patriotic" loyalties. The most common example would be the coerced confession. There is no escaping the mention of the Landsberg trials of those accused in the Malmedy massacres[88] in this connection. With some reluctance, I quote the following letter of a United States military guard at Landsberg prison in late 1945 or early 1946:[89] "I have nice padded cells here where I can personally work over my victims! What could give more pleasure? heh! heh! hey! How I love to torture! I have the most ingenious inventions for extracting the most excruciating pains and screams from my murderer victims! They too think it is pleasure so long as it is applied to another prisoner and not to them! We are all mad killers here! heh! heh! heh! If I could only get you in my clutches I could torture you too! That would be

[87] O'Callahan v. Parker, 395 U.S. 258, 265–66 with note 7 threeat (1969). For criticism, see Robinson O. Everett, "O'Callahan v. Parker—Milestone or Millstone in Military Justice?" *Duke Law Journal* (1969), 853.

[88] U.S. Congress, Committee on Armed Services, *Malmedy Massacre Investigations* (2 parts, Washington 1949). Some of the relevant materials are quoted by Charles Fairman, "Some New Problems of the Constitution Following the Flag," 1 *Stanford Law Review*, 587, 597–600 (1949).

[89] Chamberlain v. Chamberlain, 230 S.W. 2d 185, 187 (St. Louis Court of Appeals, 1950).

fun! Yes wouldn't it! heh! heh! heh!" This letter was considered by a Missouri court as pertinent to the successful charge of cruelty in a divorce action.

### CONCLUSION

The new international criminal law, consisting mainly of the Charter of the Nürnberg Tribunal, the Genocide Convention, and the Geneva Conventions of 1949, is directly applicable to individuals, and binding upon all states in the sense that prosecution of violators, irrespective of nationality, is not only a right but also a duty. The main purposes of this new system of criminal law are to safeguard world peace and to protect human rights.

Neither of these two aims has been fully realized to date, and under-performance falls short of the selective enforcement that generally characterizes internal criminal law. Nevertheless, a radical expansion of substantive international criminal law does not seem desirable without the establishment of an International Criminal Court, which, in turn, is not feasible at the present. The best hope would seem to be a sustained effort for the recognition of a new international human right to refuse participation not only in acts incriminating the objecting individual, but in internationally illegal conduct generally.

Whatever the approach chosen, more attention will have to be paid to the protection of the human rights of those accused of war crimes. In keeping with my own injunction against amateur meddling, I have limited myself to mentioning some of the more typical obstacles to the even-handed administration of international criminal justice. Perhaps we should be content only when the professionals, i.e., those who are primarily concerned with *internal* criminal law, have claimed our subject as their own.

# Part  II

## Structures

## CHAPTER 9

# The Nature of International Law: Toward a Second Concept of Law

## GIDON GOTTLIEB*

### I

LAW IN international relations is unlike law in our domestic system. This has led to doubts about the "legal" quality of international law. These emanate, it will be argued, not from the nature of international law but rather from analyses in terms of only one concept of law. Far from being a "problem" area it will be shown that international law is a paradigm for legal ordering in a decentralized power system.

Consideration of the nature of international law imports assumptions about the concept of law.[1] These assumptions currently rest on a number of dominant legal theories. The problem with theories about the concept of law and about the nature of legal systems is their foundation in the political context of nation states. They all refer primarily to *legal* systems operating in the *political* systems of such

---

[1] These are considered in a significant body of recent literature—Richard A. Falk, "New Approaches to the Study of International Law," in Morton Kaplan, ed., *New Approaches to International Relations* (New York 1968); Richard A. Falk, "The Adequacy of Contemporary Theories of International Law—Gaps in Legal Thinking," 50 *Virginia Law Review*, 231 (March 1964); Myres McDougal, Harold Lasswell, William Reisman, "Theories About International Law: Prologue to a Configurative Jurisprudence," 8 *Virginia Journal of International Law*, 188 (April 1968); Wolfgang Friedmann, *The Changing Structure of International Law* (New York 1964); Gregory Tunkin, *Droit International Publique, Problèmes Theoriques* (Paris 1965); Charles de Visscher, *Theory and Reality in Public International Law* (rev. ed., Princeton 1968); Karl W. Deutsch and Stanley Hoffmann, *The Relevance of International Law* (Cambridge, Mass. 1968); Cornelius F. Murphy Jr., "Some Reflections Upon Theories of International Law," 70 *Columbia Law Review*, 447 (March 1970); Hans Kelsen, *Principles of International Law*, R. Tucker, ed. (New York 1966); Gregory Tunkin, "International Organizations and Law," *Soviet Law and Government* IV No. 4 (1966), 3; Oscar Schachter, "Towards a Theory of International Obligation," 8 *Virginia Journal of International Law*, 300 (April 1968); Oscar Schachter, "Law and the Process of Decision in The Political Organs of the United Nations," 109 (1963) 2 *Recueil Des Cours*, 171; Michael Barkun, *Law Without Sanctions* (New Haven 1968); Morton Kaplan and Nicholas de B. Katzenbach, *The Political Foundations of International Law* (New York 1961); H. L. A. Hart, *The Concept of Law* (Oxford 1961), Chap. x; Stanley Hoffmann, "International Systems and International Law," in Klaus Knorr and Sidney Verba, eds., *The International System* (Princeton, N.J. 1960).

* The author is indebted to Oscar Schachter, Executive Director of UNITAR, and to Abraham Edel, Professor of Philosophy, City University of New York, for their stimulating and perceptive comments.

states.[2] That is, to the legal order of societies in which the means of coercion are supposedly monopolized by the state. These are systems in which, to borrow Professor Falk's phrase, there is a vertical or hierarchical relationship between unequal centers of power. This is in contrast to systems in which there is a horizontal or nonhierarchical order between equal centers of power: [3] power, that is, in the sense of a capacity to gain one's ends *over the opposition* of others rather than a generalized capacity to attain goals.[4] Vertical and horizontal relationships are a function of actual power relationships—not of formal social arrangements.

Dominant legal theories all relate to the legal order of vertical systems. None investigates the legal order that is characteristic of horizontal systems. Statements about the nature of law and about the existence of legal systems in the writings of Austin, Kelsen, and Hart implicitly accept the pyramidal model of state power.[5] It is by no means evident that they can be successfully transplanted to the alien grounds of international relations.

A productive analysis of the nature of international law requires an overhaul of the conceptual framework in terms of which it is conducted. The first task is to investigate the features of the concept of law that are peculiar to horizontal political orders. Second, to determine whether it is possible to have more than one concept of law in the same way that we have more than one system of geometry. It may thus be possible to develop an alternative to the state-system analogy—or, to mix an old metaphor, something like a non-Euclidian concept of law. Third, to find out whether it is possible to demarcate meaningful boundaries between a concept of law peculiar to horizontal systems and the neighbor concept of politics.

The need to outline an additional concept of law rests on the necessary connection between the structure of a legal order and underlying

[2] Austin, Kelsen and Hart devote considerable attention to international law. See John Austin, *The Province of Jurisprudence Determined*, Hart ed. (New York 1954); Kelsen (fn. 1) and also Hans Kelsen, *General Theory of Law and State* (Cambridge, Mass. 1949); Hart (fn. 1).

[3] See Richard A. Falk, "International Jurisdiction: Horizontal and Vertical Conceptions of Legal Order," 32 *Temple Law Quarterly*, 295 (Spring 1959). See also Inis L. Claude, *Power and International Relations* (New York 1962), Chaps. VII and VIII.

[4] The concept of power is usefully analyzed in Talcott Parsons, *Structure and Process in Modern Societies* (Glencoe, Ill. 1960), 182; Harold Lasswell and Abraham Kaplan, *Power and Society* (New Haven 1950). See also Talcott Parsons, "On the Concept of Political Power," *Proceedings of the American Philosophical Society* CIII, No. 3 (June 1963). See also B. de Jouvenel, *On Power* (New York 1949); Guglielmo Ferreró, *The Principles of Power* (New York 1942); Adolf A. Berle, *Power* (New York 1969).

[5] In Kelsen's opinion a coercive legal order is an essential feature of law. See Kelsen (fn. 1), 3–177. See also Hart (fn. 1), Chap. X; John Austin, *Lectures on Jurisprudence*, R. Campbell, ed. (New York 1875).

patterns of power relationships. The distortions caused by reliance on the pyramidal model of state power in the analysis of "primitive" legal systems at one extreme and on international law at the other, rest upon the unproven proposition that there is only one ideal model for legal systems.[6] The risks of using conceptual instruments out of context are particularly acute when analysis proceeds in terms of one standard model only. This is precisely what occurs in international law theory: ". . . the more familiar vertical structure of the domestic legal order is taken as the model for the optimum international order. Mere *characteristics* of the domestic model are transformed into *prerequisites* for international order. The acceptance of either vertical model as a decisive test of the existence of legal order generates irrelevant cynicism as to the stabilizing claims of international law."[7]

The mutual interaction of model systems of legal ordering and of the concepts which are their component parts is an unavoidable problem. In physics, for example, it was discovered that it is not possible to describe the atomic system in abstraction from the apparatus used for the investigation. This is a characteristic difficulty of all modes of analysis. The properties of the instruments used in an investigation necessarily determine the scope and the character of that investigation. The problems posed in analysis by inadequate standard models are also familiar to philosophers. In logical theory, for example, attempts to justify induction by analytic standards of certainty were prompted by the expectation of philosophers such as Hume that induction should be shown to be only a variant species of deduction.[8] The "failure" of induction when judged in terms of the analytic model is reminiscent of the "failure" of international law when judged in terms of domestic law models. Conceptual assumptions about the nature of law operate as a perception set determining the scope and the subject of investigation.

This investigation involves reliance upon separate levels of discourse—statements about different models of international systems, statements about different models of legal ordering, and statements about appropriate concepts of law. It involves emancipation from the hold of inapplicable conceptual tools of analysis.

*Conceptual Distortions Caused by Vertical Concepts of Law*

Under the impact of hierarchical concepts of law it is conventional academic wisdom to accept a number of propositions:

[6] See Barkun's well-argued thesis, Barkun (fn. 1); see also Fried, "How Efficient is International Law?" in Deutsch and Hoffman (fn. 1).

[7] Falk (fn. 3), 297.

[8] This is a central theme in Stephen Toulmin, *The Uses of Argument* (Cambridge 1958).

–international law is not as fully law as the law of the domestic legal order;

–what gives all law a peculiar legal quality is the establishment of coercive acts as sanctions;

–international law is only at the beginning of a development which national law has already completed. It is a primitive legal order;

–the prophecies of what courts will do are what is meant by the law;

–the structure which has resulted from the combination of primary rules of obligation with the secondary rules of recognition, change, and adjudication is the heart of a legal system;

–when law is violated, it is necessary either to vindicate rights or to punish offenders to preserve the legal system;

–in the absence of applicable norms, decision makers enjoy full discretion;

–fidelity to law requires deference to constituted authority;

–there is a clear line dividing the law that is from the law that ought to be;

–the existence of law is not a matter of degree;

–the power of a sovereign is incapable of legal limitation;

–there is a clear line between the study of law and the study of behavior and other social phenomena;

–a fully developed legal system relies on separate agencies for changing and making laws, for determining infractions of the law, for enforcing the law, and for settling disputes.

Every one of these statements requires qualification when we speak about law in a horizontal power system. Every one of them is predicated upon a hierarchical power structure alien to the international environment. We shall have occasion to consider them again.

The strategy of this argument involves in the first place the discovery of "limit situations" for international legal arrangements. That is, situations which cannot be changed merely by agreement but which do require appropriate systemic and social changes. Three kinds of limit situations will be discussed, those imposed by the international system, those imposed by survival challenges and those imposed by our conceptual apparatus, attitudes, expectations, and ideologies. Relying on macrosystem structure analysis, characteristic features of legal ordering in horizontal systems will be considered. It will be argued that existing concepts of law all relate to vertical state systems and that they are inapplicable in horizontal systems. Further it will be demonstrated that *it is possible to develop a concept of law characteristic of horizontal system structures, that is, a second concept of law new to legal theory.* After outlining the main ingredients of such a concept of law it will be demonstrated that problems of demarcation between this new concept of law and the neighbor concept of politics are not insurmountable and that meaningful criteria of demarcation can be used to differentiate between legal and political systems in horizontal power relationships. Finally, the implications of the three types of limit situations for the future of the international legal order will be considered.

## The Systems Approach and Horizontal Models

In referring to the systems approach it is necessary to bear in mind the rich and complex flowering of studies based upon general systems theory and its application to international relations. This is a matter that has led to sharp but fruitful divisions of opinion between the so-called traditional approach and the scientific approach to the study of international relations.[9] Advocates of the systems approach, however, do not by any means agree even on matters of method. While the impact of the systems theory on particular substantive norms of international law has not been convincingly demonstrated, fruitful use of systems theory has already been made to study model forms of legal ordering. Such use has involved the relatively permanent elements of structure rather than the substance of specific rules and doctrine. Focusing on permanent factors of structure, systems theory has been helpful in conceptualizing the context in which legal systems operate. Reliance on macrosystems study for this purpose should prove useful in extracting implicit assumptions about system context and in furnishing a less impressionistic foundation for the analysis of vertical and horizontal systems.[10]

In classical studies of factors underlying the nature of international law, emphasis was placed on the civilization of European powers and on their religious and cultural ties. Systems theory on the other hand stresses relationship patterns between states that need not belong to homogeneous cultural or political traditions. Its advantages in an expanding world society composed of culturally heterogeneous units and

[9] On systems theory and international relations see Oran R. Young, *Systems of Political Science* (Englewood Cliffs, N.J. 1968); Kaplan and Katzenbach (fn. 1); Morton A. Kaplan, *System and Process in International Politics* (New York 1957); Kaplan (fn. 1); Richard A. Falk, "The Interplay of Westphalia and Charter Conceptions of International Legal Order," in Richard A. Falk and Cyril Black, eds., *The Future of the International Legal Order* (Princeton 1969), I, 32. See the comments of Rosalyn Higgins, "Policy and Impartiality: The Uneasy Relationship in International Law," *International Organization* xxIII (Fall 1969); Klaus Knorr and James N. Rosenau, eds., *Contending Approaches to International Politics* (Princeton 1969); John W. Burton, *Systems, States, Diplomacy and Rules* (London 1968); Hoffmann (fn. 1); Knorr and Verba (fn. 1); Barkun (fn. 1); M. Banks, "Two Meanings of Theory in the Study of International Relations," *Yearbook of World Affairs* xx (1966), 220.

[10] Emphasis on macrostructure considerations is characteristic of M. Kaplan's work. See Kaplan in Knorr and Rosenau, *Contending Approaches* (fn. 9); see also Kaplan (fn. 1), and Kaplan and Katzenbach (fn. 1).

hostile political systems are evident. Reliance on systems theory for the purpose of establishing macrostructural features does not mean, however, that reliance upon it for predictive purposes is equally fruitful. The explanatory power of systems theory models may indeed be far greater than their predictive capabilities.

Investigations of the concept of law should reflect variations in permanent features of power structures. Differences between such power systems are clearly reflected in normative systems.

Despite the manifestly horizontal character of the decentralized power structure of international society, a number of vertical relationships do coexist and alternate with horizontal ones. Decentralized relationships of a horizontal character may become vertical in time of armed conflict, only to reacquire their previous horizontality immediately thereafter. They display, in other words, a considerable degree of elasticity. The phenomena of the refusal of the defeated Arab states to recognize the Jewish State of Israel and to negotiate direct peace arrangements with it, or, indeed, the refusal of North Vietnam to negotiate with the United States during the bombing of the North suggest that the connection between vertical and horizontal relationships is both troublesome and elusive. Except during combat, the limited effectiveness of armed coercion in international and in domestic conflicts is well established. During combat, military victories can be defined in objective "kill ratio" or destruction terms, and coercion then prevails. At other times however, the will to resist superior power is productive of horizontal relationships which do not reflect coercive capabilities. Horizontal and vertical relationships may thus alternate between the same system units on a time continuum reflecting the alternance of armed conflicts and other forms of coercion. Such modifications may depend also on the character of the issues involved. Resistance to occupation may lead to horizontal relationships in one sphere that are not duplicated in another sphere. The acceptance of the financial and fiscal policies of an occupying power and the rejection of its production goals are not necessarily incompatible phenomena. The events in Czechoslovakia after the Warsaw Pact intervention are rich in nuances and preclude a neat analysis of the links between power, coercion, and submission.

The will and the ability to resist superior coercive power, displayed in Czechoslovakia and in Vietnam, are accompanied in the domestic sphere by similar phenomena.[11] The spontaneous growth of mass

[11] See Arthur Schlesinger, Jr., "Vietnam and the End of the Age of Superpowers," *Harper's Magazine* (March 1969), 41. On violence and resistance see Hannah Arendt, *On Violence* (New York 1969); Wilson C. McWilliams, "On Violence and Legitimacy," 79 *Yale Law Journal*, 623 (March 1970) and literature on violence cited therein.

movements facilitated by television and other mass media, the increasing vulnerability of delicate technological structures to violence, the increasing resistance in labor and youth movements to coercive practices, the hardening of racial hostilities, and the extravagant political and social costs of law enforcement against small dissident groups are likely to have lasting consequences for domestic legal ordering. The proliferation of units with a capability to disrupt and to threaten existing social and political structures is a phenomenon characteristic not only of the international legal order but also of the domestic order of advanced nontotalitarian states. It persists significantly even at a time when military capabilities are of unprecedented magnitude. Modern state systems are endowed with the means to destroy and to subdue but find it difficult to secure obedience, except, that is, by the exercise of quasi-totalitarian powers.

The relevance of a second concept of law for horizontal systems should not be limited to international law. It is likely to have a bearing on areas of domestic constitutional law, civil rights, and labor law as well—on all legal fields dealing with power groups and political organizations rather than with individuals' rights and interests. With the spread of horizontal power relationships in characteristically vertical systems, realistic strategies taking this phenomenon into account must be designed for securing compliance with the law. Student disruptions on campuses have thus led some university administrations to adopt a delicate balance between policies of conciliation and enforcement. Changes in attitude to legal ordering domestically may also find expression in expectations about international law. International phenomena may be more understandable in the light of domestic developments pointing to difficulties with law enforcement against determined power groups.

*Limit Situations.* Limit situations express the nature of the international system. These cannot be drafted away, negotiated into nonexistence or modified unless accompanied by actual changes in social, conceptual, and material circumstances. They represent the point at which the pliability of human arrangements breaks down—at which "realities" exercise a veto over normative conventions.[12] They can perhaps best be conceived of as situations in which choices and decisions are ineffective or weighted down by necessity. The barriers limiting effective decision-making are of distinct kinds. These are the three barriers of natural necessity, of the limitations of power, and more fundamentally, of perception and judgment in terms of which all options are conceived.

12 See Lon L. Fuller, "American Legal Philosophy at Mid-Century," 6 *Journal of Legal Education,* 457 (1954).

Limit situations do not arise only because of the structural characteristics of the effective power system. The two other sets of limit situations mold and determine the operation of the international legal process no less than the system context.

Of these two, the "perception and judgment" set arises out of the "internal" character of social relations first outlined by Vico:

> . . . in the night of thick darkness enveloping the earliest antiquity, so remote from ourselves, there shines the eternal and never failing light of a truth beyond all questions: that the world of civil society has certainly been made by men and that its principles are therefore to be found within the modifications of our own human mind. Whoever reflects on this cannot but marvel that the philosophers should have bent all their energies to the study of the world of nature, which, since God made it, He alone knows; and that they should have neglected the study of the world of nations, or civil world, which, since men made it, man could come to know.[13]

Limit situations do arise out of the concepts we use, our expectations and attitudes. Voluntary behavior in international relations as elsewhere is behavior as to which there is an alternative.[14] This introduces systematic indeterminacy into the system: "One will still not be able to predict any determinate outcome to a historical trend because the continuation or breaking off of that trend involves human decisions which cannot be *definitely* predicted: if they could be, we should not call them decisions."[15] All forms of voluntary behavior carry with them unintended consequences that are not related to the voluntary decisions taken within our conceptual universe. The crucial limit situations arising out of the internal view of the international system have nevertheless been almost totally overlooked in discussions about the future of the international legal order, although it dominates prospects for future normative arrangements.

The second set of limit situations, the "natural necessity" set, arises from challenges that must be met to permit the continuation or organized social life on this planet. These are the twin challenges of armed conflicts with modern weapons technology and of planetary ecological collapse. The imperative of deflecting existing ecological trends away from looming catastrophe, forecast by a nearly unanimous scientific

13 G. B. Vico, *New Science*, ¶331 cited in D. R. Bell, "The Idea of a Social Science," *Proceedings of the Aristotelian Society*, Supp. vol. XLI (London 1967), 115, 120.

14 For a consideration of these matters see Peter Winch, *The Idea of a Social Science and Its Relation to Philosophy* (London and New York 1958), 15. For interesting comments on Winch's work see the papers by Alastair MacIntyre and D. R. Bell in *Proceedings of the Aristotelian Society*, Supp. vol. XLI (London 1967), 95, 115.

15 Winch (fn. 14), 92–93.

community, must therefore be accepted as establishing a limit situation of a new kind. Between the dictates of the international system and the imperatives for survival requiring international action, the range of meaningful options is gradually narrowing.[16]

The three species of limit situations—systems considerations, internal conceptual consideration and challenge considerations—provide the setting for an analysis of the nature of the international legal order. Some contemporary approaches to international law reveal a lack of balance between these three dimensions and consider them to be in conflict rather than complementary. "Future studies" in particular, have not been fully informed by the philosophical and methodological dimensions of the internal conceptual approach to social science. Studies of the future of the international legal order require careful investigation of all three types of limit situations. Methodological sophistication grounded in modern philosophical analysis could do much to strengthen the conceptual grid for mapping future worlds. Disregard of pertinent methodological considerations cannot but weaken the gossamer thread of investigations about the future.

## II

*The Uses of Law in Horizontal Systems*

At the present time the rare international disputes that reach settlement are not generally resolved by judicial organs. In the settlement of disputes the International Court of Justice now performs distinctly secondary functions. This is not due to faulty draftsmanship of Chapter VI of the Charter, or of the Statute of the Court, or to a failure on the part of the Framers at San Francisco. Rather, this fact reflects the true position of courts in horizontal system disputes in times of stress.[17] Under United States constitutional law, for example, judicial restraint in the decision of "political questions" or of issues that would present compliance problems is a familiar phenomenon.[18] The political question doctrine has enabled the Supreme Court to avoid deciding

[16] This is one of the themes of Richard Falk, *This Endangered Planet* (New York 1971).

[17] See Lon L. Fuller, "Adjudication and the Rule of Law," 54 *Proceedings of the American Society of International Law*, 1 (1960), and see also his "Collective Bargaining and the Arbitrator," *Wisconsin Law Review* (January 1963), 3. See also Milton Katz, *The Relevance of International Adjudication* (Cambridge, Mass. 1968).

[18] On the "political question" doctrine in U.S. Constitutional Law see Alexander Bickel, *The Least Dangerous Branch* (Indianapolis and New York 1962); Herbert Wechsler, *Principles, Politics and Fundamental Law* (Cambridge, Mass. 1961); Fritz W. Scharpf, "Judicial Review and the Political Question—A Functional Analysis," 75 *Yale Law Journal*, 517 (March 1966). This doctrine should not be confused with the concept of political disputes under international law. On this second subject, see Rosalyn Higgins, "Policy Considerations and the International Judicial Process," 17 *International and Comparative Law Quarterly*, 58 (Jan. 1968).

cases that would involve serious conflicts with other branches of the government or interfere in the conduct of foreign relations. Disputes between powerful units, between branches of the government, those involving sensitive Federal-State relationships, civil rights issues, and strong labor, racial, or other groups are characteristic of horizontal system disputes. Like international disputes they stand in contrast to vertical system conflicts in which law enforcement presents few problems.

In horizontal disputes, accommodation rather than adjudication is the object generally sought. The goal is conflict settlement, not the vindication of rights. In the *Corfu Channel* case the International Court of Justice's judgment remained unenforceable when Albania was not prepared to accept the Court's jurisdiction or to abide by its judgment.[19] The use of the "power of the sword and of the purse" against state units can be costly indeed, and enforcement can be more damaging to the enforcer than to the victim. Agreed settlements, on the other hand, are by definition effective. This lesson was learned by the Mayor of New York City in a number of bitter disputes with municipal employees' unions, in which judicial decisions enjoining strikes and condemning defiant labor leaders merely aggravated conflict. The illegal Teachers' Union strike and the Sanitationmen's strike highlighted the ineffectiveness of New York State's Taylor Law prohibiting them and of judicial decisions under it. Talk of calling out the National Guard to collect the refuse merely led to talk of a general strike in the City. Domestic statutes and constitutional provisions are liable to become scraps of paper no less easily than treaties.

Legal arrangements disregarding power relationships and underlying systemic factors may in time be doomed to ineffectiveness. Or, to put the matter differently, it is not enough for negotiators and legislators to agree on the terms of an instrument and to rely on good faith for implementation. There is a limit to the pliability of social arrangements. Thus in horizontal system disputes, in which power is not centralized, courts must steer a careful course between the Scylla of ineffective judicial activism and the open defiance of judgments and the Charybdis of exaggerated judicial restraint allowing the erosion of constitutionally binding instruments. But even in matters that do not lend themselves to adjudication, those pertaining to horizontal and to permanent relationships, law may still be invoked and has an important role to play. This has some far-reaching consequences.

[19] On the problem of enforcing the decisions of the International Court of Justice, see Leo Gross, "The International Court of Justice and the United Nations," 121 (1967), *Recueil Des Cours*, II, 319, and also Leo Gross, "Problems of International Adjudication and Compliance with International Law: Some Simple Solutions," 59 *American Journal of International Law*, 48 (Jan. 1965); Corfu Channel (Merits) [1949] ICJ Reports 1. See also Katz (fn. 17).

States invoke legal norms in nonjudicial contexts when making claims and concessions, in negotiations, in the justification of political moves, in arbitration and mediation, and in other attempts to settle disputes peaceably outside courts of law.[20] Legal norms are also invoked in international organizations, in debates and caucuses, in drafting and legitimizing resolutions, in rallying support for them and getting them adopted. Indeed, law is much used in diplomacy, in drawing attention to particular features of conflicts, in defining issues, in characterizing situations, in building up authoritative practices, in conferring and withdrawing legitimacy, and ultimately in shaping policy options.[21] Such nonjudicial uses of law are equally prominent in domestic legal systems, even though they are largely neglected in academic writings and legal education which focus primarily on judicial decisions and on rule formulations.

When dealing with bodies of law that do not lend themselves readily to adjudication—that is, with non-judicial uses of law—clear identification of rules and principles as "legal" is not always appropriate. In the process of making claims and counterclaims, of advancing demands and allowing concessions, much can sometimes be gained by allowing ambiguity about the legal quality of the rules and principles invoked. For it is generally harder to retreat from asserted legal rights than from hoped-for political advantages.

Only courts of law and other rule-applying organs need therefore know *with precision* what the law of the court is or what the law of

[20] For interesting comments on the uses of international law outside law courts see Dean Rusk, "Parliamentary Diplomacy—Debate v. Negotiation," *World Affairs Interpreter*, XXVI (Summer 1955); Philip Jessup, "Parliamentary Diplomacy: An Examination of the Legal Quality of the Rules of Procedure of Organs of the United Nations," 89 (1956) *Recueil Des Cours*, I, 185; Hardy Dillard, "Some Aspects of Law and Diplomacy," 91 (1957) *Recueil Des Cours*, I, 449; Percy E. Corbett, *Law In Diplomacy* (Princeton 1959); Louis Henkin, *How Nations Behave* (New York 1968); Arthur Lall, *Modern International Negotiations* (New York 1966), Chap. 26.

[21] On the uses of international law by organs other than judicial organs see the works cited in fn. 20, and see also Rosalyn Higgins, *The Development of International Law Through the Political Organs of the United Nations* (Oxford 1963); Richard A. Falk, *The Status of Law in International Society* (Princeton 1969); Roger Fisher, "Bringing Law to Bear on Governments," 74 *Harvard Law Review*, 1130 (April 1961); Rosalyn Higgins, "The Place of International Law in the Settlement of Disputes by the Security Council," 64 *American Journal of International Law*, 1 (Jan. 1970); Myres McDougal, "International Law, Power and Policy," 82 (1953) *Recueil Des Cours*, II, 137; Schachter (fn. 1); Oscar Schachter, "Dag Hammarskjold and the Relationship of Law to Politics," 56 *American Journal of International Law*, 1 (Jan. 1962), and "The Development of International Law Through the Legal Opinions of the United Nations," 25 *British Yearbook of International Law*, 91 (1948); A. J. P. Tammes, "Decisions of International Organs as a Source of International Law," 94 (1958) *Recueil Des Cours* II, 264; Leo Gross, "States as Organs of International Law and the Problem of Auto-Interpretation," in George A. Lipsky, ed., *Law and Politics in World Community* (Berkeley 1953).

the organ is. But states are often content to claim as "legal" rules and principles that law courts would in all probability disregard. *Rules of recognition, which identify rules that are "legal," can remain fairly indeterminate in legal systems in which judicial organs perform secondary functions only.* Thus the combination of primary rules of obligation with secondary rules of recognition, change, and adjudication, which Hart claims is the heart of all legal systems, is significant only in systems in which law courts play a major role. In simple forms of social structure rules are said to function without secondary rules of recognition. Hart claims the resulting phenomenon is not a legal system but a "set" of pre-legal rules accepted as binding: Secondary rules of recognition, he says, mark the emergence from the pre-legal to the legal world.[22] But Hart fails to recognize that this combination of primary and secondary rules is of little significance in horizontal systems of legal ordering. It cannot be said to constitute a characteristic feature of such systems.

To characterize international law as a "legal system" rather than a "legal set" does rest on the propriety of conceiving of legal systems in terms of more than one model. It raises the question whether a system of ordering in which accommodation rather than adjudication is the object, should be characterized as a legal system at all. It raises by implication questions about the "best" characterization—assuming that such a judgment can be made. It raises questions about the "politics" of categories and about the covert value preferences underpinning the use of particular models. The characterization of the international order as a legal system requires an investigation of what would be lost or misperceived by a failure to consider as legal also those systems in which adjudication and enforcement are secondary and in which accommodation is the principal object.

## The Creation and Alteration of International Obligations

Authoritative guidance such as "community policies" and "general principles" would not always be characterized as "law" under operative rules of recognition. Yet in the *South-West Africa* case Judge Jessup maintained that accumulations of expressions of condemnation of Apartheid were of decisive practical and juridical value in determining the meaning that was to be given to the mandate provisions dealing with the well-being of the inhabitants of the Territory of South-West Africa. Judges Fitzmaurice and Spender, on the other hand, said "[This] is a court of law and can take account of moral principles only insofar as these are given a sufficient expression in legal form. Law exists, it is said, to serve a social need; but precisely for that reason it

22 Hart (fn. 1) 91.

can do so only through and within the limits of its own discipline. Otherwise it is not a legal service that will be rendered." [23]

This division of approaches fairly demonstrates how preconceptions about what are the proper limits of the legal discipline can color the outcome of a judicial decision. Judges with an ideological commitment to a Hartian concept of law, characterized by a combination of primary rules of obligation with secondary rules of recognition, are more likely to take a restrictive view of what counts as law than judges with no such conceptual parti-pris.

This issue takes on a different complexion where nonjudicial uses of law are involved. While Judge Fitzmaurice would only apply the law of the Court as determined in the rules of recognition in Article 38 of the Statute, the political organs of the United Nations are prepared to claim a much broader and indeterminate set of principles and instruments as being authoritative and "legally" compelling. Secretary General Hammarskjold, for example, considered that not only the rules concerning the various organs of the United Nations were binding but the statement of objectives in the Charter were equally obligatory.[24] This is true also of States engaged in the process of developing international law. In the absence of formal legislative procedures, a wide range of unstructured practices are used to accomplish quasilegislative ends. No secondary rule of recognition can be used to identify the variety of laws and the proliferation of law-making techniques. These techniques share some common features:

–they are based on consensus rather than on consent;

–they erode the status of formal sources of law such as treaties and enhance the importance of informal sources like declarations;

–they favor informal and rapid normative change;

–they involve fairly general principles and standards rather than precise contractual obligations, and therefore leave states with considerable discretion in the interpretation of obligations;

Most of the informal or indeterminate sources of international obligations have their origin in the conference diplomacy of the political organs of the United Nations. Conference diplomacy can be singularly productive of obligations which are not necessarily formulated in legally binding forms. The General Assembly has thus developed over the last twenty-five years a variety of techniques for laying down binding obligations. These include:

–resolutions "declaring" or "affirming" legal principles, i.e. the Resolution Affirming the Principles of International Law Recognized in the Charter and Judgment of the Nüremberg Tribunal; 95(I);

[23] *South-West Africa Cases* [1966] *ICJ Reports* 34. See the discussion of these approaches by Higgins (fn. 18), 6off.

[24] See Schachter's excellent short piece, "Dag Hammarskjold and the Relationship of Law to Politics" (fn. 21) 2.

–resolutions reciting such principles, i.e. in the Resolution on Permanent Sovereignty over Natural Resources; 1803 (xvii);

–resolutions "interpreting" Charter obligations, i.e. in the Declaration on the Granting of Independence to Colonial Countries and Peoples; 1514 (xv);

–resolutions formulating agreed interpretations of Charter provisions, i.e. the Declaration on the Inadmissibility of Intervention in the Domestic Affairs of States; 2131 (xx).

These are examples of processes whereby authoritative principles and rules are formulated otherwise than through the traditionally accepted forms of sources of "law." The demands of advocacy, of multilateral diplomacy, of legal change, and of conflict settlement have all contributed to this development. In the political organs of the United Nations it matters little whether *every* state expressly accepts principles and standards that are claimed to have a legal quality. Legal principles are "declared" by Assembly majorities and Charter provisions are "interpreted" often over the objections of a small number of dissenting states. Thus while in 1965 the United Nations Conference on International Organizations expressly rejected proposals to give the General Assembly legislative authority, this has not prevented Assembly majorities from resorting to such quasi-legislative techniques.[25]

---

[25] See materials cited in fns. 20 and 21 above. On the legal effects of United Nations resolutions see: Gabriella R. Lande, "The Changing Effectiveness of General Assembly Resolutions," *Proceedings of the American Society of International Law* (1964), 162; Krzysztof Skubiszewski, "The General Assembly of the United Nations and Its Power to Influence National Action," *Proceedings of the American Society of International Law* (1964), 153; Rosalyn Higgins, "The U.N. and Lawmaking," *Proceedings of the American Society of International Law,* 64 *American Journal of International Law,* 37 (1970); D. H. N. Johnson, "The Effect of Resolutions of the General Assembly of the United Nations," 32 *British Yearbook of International Law,* 197 (1957); Francis A. Vallat, "The Competence of the United Nations General Assembly," 97 (1959), *Receuil Des Cours,* II, 207; F. Blaine Sloan, "The Binding Force of A 'Recommendation' of The General Assembly of The United Nations," 25 *British Yearbook of International Law,* 1 (1948); 'Pollux,' "The Interpretation of the Charter of the United Nations," 23 *British Yearbook of International Law,* 54 (1946); Richard A. Falk, "On the Quasi-Legislative Competence of The General Assembly," 60 *American Journal of International Law,* 782 (Oct. 1966). Jorge Castañeda, *Legal Effects of United Nations Resolutions* (New York 1969); Oscar Schachter, "The Quasi-Judicial Rôle of the Security Council and the General Assembly," 58 *American Journal of International Law,* 460 (Oct. 1964); Obed Y. Asamoah, *The Legal Significance of the Declarations of the General Assembly of the United Nations* (The Hague 1966); Samuel A. Bleicher, "The Legal Significance of Recitation of General Assembly Resolutions," 63 *American Journal of International Law,* 444 (July 1969). See further Clive Parry, *The Sources and Evidences of International Law* (New York 1965); Leo Gross, "The United Nations and the Role of Law," *International Organization,* XIX (Summer 1965), 537; R. Y. Jennings, "Recent Developments in the International Law Commission: Its Relation to the Sources of International Law," 13 *International and Comparative Law Quarterly,* 385 (April 1964).

Reliance on legal rules and principles in diplomatic practice is not in general designed with litigation in mind. It therefore matters relatively little whether a particular state accepts or rejects principles invoked against it when these have been recognized as authoritative by the vast majority of states. In such a climate, the shift from consent to consensus is an easy one. It is further accentuated by growing international cooperative activities in which exclusion from participation is an effective sanction.[26]

A good illustration of the working of consensus procedures can be found in the action taken at the Twentieth Session of the General Assembly in connection with the Declaration on the Inadmissibility of Intervention in the Domestic Affairs of States. Most of the Eastern European and Latin American States asserted that this Declaration was declaratory of international law. The United States and other Western States asserted that it expressed not a legal doctrine but the political consensus of the General Assembly. The United States thus found it possible to vote for the Declaration. Evidently, the distinction between a legal and nonlegal text is in this context somewhat intriguing, for it appears to have little practical significance.[27] A violation of the Declaration by a Member State is likely to be followed by the same consequences whether it be considered a legal or a political instrument. No enforcement machinery was set up to secure its application, and the General Assembly itself—as a political organ—is not likely, on the basis of its past record, to draw a distinction between legal and political doctrines in considering a resolution against a state violating the Declaration. The point of the distinction, however, may be manifest in a different context. The states which recognize the Declaration as a legal instrument do presumably indicate their commitment to abide by its provisions. In the absence of enforcement machinery they are in practice free to disregard such commitments with impunity, and this is what some of them have already done. The states which are unwilling to assign legal significance to the Declaration do presumably put the other states on notice that they are not committed to give it effect, for the political will of states can be altered at their discretion. In current international practice the two attitudes to the Declaration lead to very similar consequences, for, where one state will violate international law and its treaty obligations with cynical impunity, another state will seek to abide by the expression

[26] See Falk (fn. 25); see also Judge Tanaka's dissent in the *South West Africa Cases* [1966] *ICJ Reports* 248, 292–94. See further Falk (fn. 9), 55, (fn. 21), Chap. 5; on the sanction of non-participation see Friedmann (fn. 1), 88ff.

[27] On demarcating between law and other normative phenomena, see Gidon Gottlieb, *The Logic of Choice* (New York 1968), Chap. IX.

of the mere political will of the community of nations. An opportunity arose for arguments about the alleged status of the Declaration in connection with attempts to develop the principle of Article 2.7 of the Charter in the Special Committee on Friendly Relations.[28] The question was whether the Declaration was or was not expressive of principles of international law.

The weight of interpretive consensus in diplomacy can be easily overlooked. Attempts by the Big Four to reach an agreed interpretation of the November 1967 Security Council Resolution on the Middle East, itself incorporating agreed principles of international law, demonstrate the use of such principles in settling the parameters within which settlement terms must be found. The delicate influence of an agreed interpretation on exchanges through Dr. Jarring suggests that the weight of Big Power consensus could be felt even when no imposed settlement is contemplated. For example, it would be difficult for Israel legally to justify claims for a land corridor to Sharm-el-Sheikh in Sinai if the Big Powers were to agree that the Resolution precludes substantial border changes. This was made plain by the Israeli Embassy in Washington in a response to the United States plan submitted to the Four Power Talks. The Embassy of Israeli said in a policy paper that:

> U.S. policy as unfolding now comes close to the advocacy and development of an imposed settlement. While this may not be deliberate, the mechanics and dynamics are moving in that direction. . . . By addressing themselves in detail to matters of substance, the U.S. proposals do more than to undermine the principle of negotiations; they preempt its very prospect. For there can be little meaningful left for the parties to negotiate once outside powers virtually decide on each and every item for solution. Certainly, the Arabs are not going to give an inch on anything that has already been decided upon in their favor by the powers.[29]

Big Power consensus could then very well lead to a deterioration of Israel's diplomatic hand even when no "imposition" is contemplated. It could also lead to an Israeli refusal to continue exchanges under the terms of the November resolution. The trend from consent to consensus is not likely, however, to hasten the settlement of conflicts in which diplomatically isolated states are determined to hold on to their vital interests in the face of adverse world opinion. On the contrary, it is possible that such consensus might well harden the positions of

[28] A/AC.125/L.38/add.3 page 11 (1966).
[29] Embassy of Israel, Washington, D.C., December 24 (1969), *Policy Background: An Analysis of the U.S. Mid East Peace Plan.*

all and delay the elaboration of acceptable common grounds for settlement. A similar situation seems to have developed in the wake of General Assembly Resolution 2145 (xx) terminating South Africa's mandate in South-West Africa and establishing, in Resolution 2248 (S-V), the Council for Namibia (South-West Africa) to take over the administration of the Territory. These decisions, as well as subsequent Security Council resolutions, have made diplomatic accommodation less likely than ever. The prospects for accommodation have not been enhanced by the 1971 Advisory Opinion of the International Court of Justice on the question of Namibia.

The impact of consensus declarations of a legal character on the settlement of disputes remains to be assessed. Judging from the experience of recent years, consensus declarations and resolutions of a legal character can easily be adopted in situations involving a pariah state such as South Africa and its policy of Apartheid. Almost any law-making resolution designed further to isolate South Africa is likely to secure majority support. But it is also destined to be ignored by that country.

Julius Stone has observed that in a world in which militarily strong states remain the supreme depositories of coercive power, and in which international organs wield only feeble power, military victory by a state is a limit situation for international law, as it is for the vanquished state. But, he writes,

> The choice before international law is in one way more difficult than the choice before the vanquished. For vanquished innocence it may be counted as noble (and for vanquished aggressors at least courageous) if they reject all terms, and choose the path of self-immolation. The interests they thus sacrifice are their own. For international law, however, there is really no alternative to accommodation with the victor as to his terms for the vanquished. Since the victor can have whatever his power (tempered by his conscience) gives him, the effect of international law's refusing limited accommodation will be but to destroy in whole or in part the international legal order generally. And in the case of a war in which the greatest military states are involved, this would only make it easier for the victor to impose on the world a whole new legal order tailor-made to suit his own interest. Insofar as the international legal order exists to mitigate as far as possible the rigors of life among states, and not for its own sake, there can be neither virtue, wisdom, or nobility, much less any duty, to destroy itself in a polite and futile protest against those rigors which it cannot mitigate. The interests which it will thus immolate are not its own. It has neither the right nor the

duty to commit suicide when suicide can only increase the rigors of states and peoples whose interests it exists to protect.[30]

The trend from consent to consensus, however, would seem to point in another direction. United Nations actions in connection with the situation in Southern Rhodesia, in South-West Africa and in the Middle East, i.e. the 1967 General Assembly Resolution on the status of Jerusalem, do not indicate that Assembly consensus must lead to accommodation. These extra-judical uses of international law are not designed to promote accommodation or conflict settlement, but rather to affirm political positions and principles accepted by a majority of states and thus to erode the benefits of military superiority. The dilemma confronting the community of states is on the one hand whether to resist accommodation on the basis of de facto power, thus heightening tensions, and on the other whether to promote accommodation at the cost of disregarding shared principles and policies. The Security Council has shown a disposition to do both. In connection with the Indian invasion of Goa, Soviet intervention in Czechoslovakia, and American operations in the Dominican Republic, the Organization has shown a remarkable ability to shy away from an affirmation of its principles. In the case of Rhodesia, South-West Africa, and the Portuguese territories, however, the Organization has chosen the path of principle over that of accommodation.

Though the shift from consent to consensus is a significant feature of contemporary international law its significance can be easily over-estimated. Its benefits are clear in matters such as self-determination, human rights, and colonialism. In strategies promoting the growth of legal ordering in world affairs, consensus practices have indeed had a catalytic import. But this shift may be an expression of conference diplomacy rather than of a major system change. The trend towards consensus permeated even League practices, despite formal requirements about unanimity voting.[31] The shift may also be characteristic of nonjudicial uses of law in which formal requirements of validity often give way to community expectations. The problems faced by consensus strategies—un-evenhanded applications and limited effectiveness—are likely to be highlighted as African countries soften demands for armed confrontation with South Africa. The impotence of military power in securing political settlements in Vietnam and in domestic situations in the United States is equalled only by the impotence of consensus not backed by force in the face of determined resistance by

[30] Julius Stone, "De Victoribus Victis: The International Law Commission and Imposed Treaties of Peace," 8 *Virginia Journal of International Law,* 356, 359 (April 1968).

[31] Julius Stone, *Legal Controls of International Conflict* (New York 1954), Chap. VI, §II.

minority groups and isolated states. The limitations of coercive power in the vertical model and of consensus in the horizontal model both reflect the essential role played by attitudes and ideologies about resistance to coercion. The impermeability of some societies to outside pressure, whether physical or normative, has been ignored while undue trust has been placed in the effectiveness of coercion and in the authority of consensus. Systemic limitations on the effectiveness of both power and consensus may focus attention on the dependence of power on legitimacy bases and on the dependence of consensus on power bases. Stalemates in East-West conflicts, in regional conflicts like Kashmir, in the struggle against Apartheid and the racist regimes of South Africa, in the Arab-Israeli war, and in Vietnam are all bound to raise questions about forms of legal ordering and procedures for conflict settlement no less acute than those raised by the substantive challenges of economic, social, and technological change to life on this planet.

## Effectiveness of Obligations

Political uses of international law by nonjudicial organs such as the General Assembly and the Security Council of the United Nations exhibit common characteristics. Such uses of law are often designed to justify partisan policy considerations promoting the parochial interests of national governments or groups of states, and they are therefore frequently applied in a manner that is neither principled nor evenhanded. Moreover, the competing and complementary nature of the rules, principles and policies of international law generally permit the justification of a wide range of national policies. The development of vague and general principles of law leaves considerable leeway in their application. Frequent difficulties in law enforcement and in securing compliance with authoritative norms and decisions are complicated by the absence of international legislative organs and the growth of a variety of informal techniques for the development of international obligations.

Political uses of international law also involve the use of authoritative texts and instruments to justify national policies after the event, rather than to guide decision-making in accordance with community expectations and norms.

These characteristic features of the political uses of international law raise questions about the basis of international obligations. Oscar Schachter reviewed more than a dozen "candidate" theories to account for the basis of obligation in international law. The theories which have been put forward can be divided very roughly between theories looking to the enforcement of obligations, theories looking to their acceptance, theories underlining reciprocal and common interests, theories underlining their foundation in natural reason and necessity, and theories looking to the formal validity and recognition of obligations as authoritative. In his analysis, Schachter suggested that there are five processes required for the establishment of an "obligatory" norm:

(i) the formulation and designation of a requirement as to behavior in contingent circumstances;

(ii) an indication that that designation has been made by persons recognized as having the competence (authority or legitimate role) to perform that function and in accordance with procedures accepted as proper for that purpose;

(iii) an indication of the capacity and willingness of those concerned to make the designated requirement effective in fact;

(iv) the transmittal of the requirement to those to whom it is addressed (the target audience);

(v) the creation in the target audience of responses—both psychological and operational—which indicate that the designated requirement is regarded as authoritative (in the sense specified in (iii) above) and as likely to be complied with in the future in some substantial degree.[32]

These features are all designed to enable us to discover underlying factual assumptions that have not otherwise been noticed, and to look beyond words to the realities of obligational phenomena. The five processes outlined by Schachter account for the obligatory force of norms in general. But the problem of discriminating between policy norms and legal norms remains—although we have not seen as yet what the function of this distinction is when adjudication is not involved.

Factors making for the effectiveness of legal norms in international relations are not easily identifiable. Foreign policy pronouncements have a distinctive binding force that tends to tie the hands of even the greatest powers. This is true of proclamations, declarations, statements, joint resolutions, treaties, agreements, and other instruments used in foreign relations. But the use of documents, policy statements, treaties, and other international instruments has certain side-effects unrelated to the purposes they are designed to serve. There are consequences inherent in the very use of texts and other policy pronouncements that bear no relation to their contents and functions. These are side-effects analogous to the unchartered repercussions of the use of certain medical drugs. The effectiveness of these pronouncements does *not* depend upon whether they are in-

[32] Schachter, "Toward a Theory of International Obligation" (fn. 1), 308.

tended to be legally binding. Nor does it seem that effectiveness depends on theories of obligation corresponding to the distinction drawn by Hart in *The Concept of Law* between "being obliged" and "having an obligation." This is the distinction he drew between the "gunman situation" when someone hands over his money at pistol point, and situations in which there is a serious social pressure behind the rules. This distinction corresponds to that between the theory of law as a coercive order relying on the use of sanctions to secure compliance and theories of another kind which point to social pressures and to other subjective factors enhancing compliance.[33] It has, however, been wrongly assumed that these two kinds of theories are mutually exhaustive. The fact that texts, declarations, and other policy pronouncements have a coercive, obligatory force generated independently of their legal quality, enforceability, or acceptance has been largely ignored. Their peculiar force does not rest in either states "being obliged" or "having an obligation." This can be most clearly seen in an analysis of the termination, dissolution, or change of international obligations and policies. Let us take an example. The United States is committed to defend the islands of Quemoy and Matsu under certain contingencies. This commitment is contained in a statement on Formosa and the offshore islands made by President Kennedy in a press conference on June 27, 1962: "The position of the Administration has been that we would defend Quemoy, Amoy and Matsu if there were an attack which was part of an attack on Formosa and the Pescadores."

This commitment has been listed by the Department of State in a communication to the Committee on Foreign Relations of the United States Senate detailing the foreign undertakings of the United States.[34] Let us assume that the Administration would like to terminate this commitment, to get "unstuck." It would then face a number of difficulties:

—termination of the commitment or its erosion may cause bigger dramatic changes on Taiwan;

—it may lead other allies to seek a reaffirmation of our commitments to them:

—it would open up a heated domestic debate as to the wisdom of a change or a shift of policy, and about the continuation of other policies or commitments.

The Administration would probably postpone a decision until a crisis situation, a shift in big power relations, a war, or an emergency

---

[33] Hart (fn. 1), 8off.

[34] United States Senate, 90th Congress First Session, Hearings before the Committee on Foreign Relations, Senate Resolution 151, United States Commitments to Foreign Powers (1967), 70. This chapter was written in 1969 before the onset of changes in U.S.-China relations.

arose which would make it imperative to reassess its position. The hold of the policy outlined by President Kennedy, it will be noticed, lies not in public or social pressure to honor obligations, nor in any other feelings of obligation haunting the President and his advisers. It is rather as if the policy statement binding us to the defense of these islands had acquired a coercive force of its own, as if some genie escaped from the bottle could no longer be governed by its master. This example illustrates the peculiar gravitational pull of authoritative policy pronouncements, authoritative texts, speeches, agreements, and the like. Deviation from them is difficult and states are frequently trapped in webs of past commitments. This gravitational pull, this entrapment is generated by a variety of factors closely related to the nature of the international system and to the very functions of policy guidance:

*Stability.* States and bureaucracies generally face demands for consistent and stable policies both domestically and from allies. Verbal formulations serve as signposts and standards for such policies. Even unilateral declarations and unilateral formulations of a nonlegal character, i.e. the guarantee of the freedom of Berlin, acquire an inertial weight of their own. Attempts to abandon or to erode these commitments may lead to strong political reactions from those with a vested interest in the status quo, and stimulate other demands for more far-reaching policy changes.

*Legitimacy.* Administrations require authority for the conduct of their policies. Such authority is generally derived from authoritative texts, precedents, and past practices. Deviations from past practices and past statements frequently raise questions about the authority or legality of such departures. Reasons must then be given to account for changes. Deference to guidelines, to rules, to institutionally defined goals, and to standard practices are features of all organizations particularly at the bureaucratic level.[35] Changes require leadership, persuasion, authority, and determination. Inertia is not mere laziness, it is the natural temperament of organizations.

*Propaganda.* Some policies and statements evoke emotional responses both at home and abroad. "Contain Communism," or "Punish the Aggressor" are not mere guidelines for treaty making. They are powerful propaganda symbols. They crystallize and fossilize attitudes and expectations. The staying force of such symbols is independent of the will of their creators. Policy symbols rapidly develop an immunity to change and destruction. They easily become live fossils, so to speak. They are not easily forgotten or destroyed—but generate the emotion and support required to assure their survival.

[35] Fisher (fn. 21).

*Deterrence.* Much foreign policy is designed to set the boundaries of permissible actions for other powers. Containment, deterrence, collective security, and collective self-defense are all policies which require putting adversaries on notice of actions we would take to meet hostile moves. A key goal of such instruments is to prevent miscalculations by adversaries about our intentions. The sanctity of commitments, on the altar of which Secretary Rusk has performed public rites, is assured by the jealous God of miscalculation.

These four factors are not exhaustive, common ends, reciprocity, retaliation, the pressure of allies—all these are other factors accounting for difficulties in abruptly terminating obligations, abandoning commitments, changing policies, and suspending agreements, which even the most powerful states must consider. These factors would suggest that some policies are more "sticking" than others, harder to abandon. This again does not depend on their "legal" quality or status. For example, the so-called rules of the game governing spheres of influence between the United States and the Soviet Union, which are based on tacit understandings, on unilateral actions and acquiescence, are among the most effectively enforced rules of any system. While containment is an almost irreversible policy, nonintervention on the other hand, i.e. as set out in Article 15 of the OAS Charter, is more easily abandoned: witness United States actions in Guatemala, the Dominican Republic, and Cuba.

It is now argued that American foreign policy urgently requires an overhauling—to permit the nation to accommodate to the new power alignment and revolutionary pressures in developing countries. In this endeavor a hard second look at policies of containment in Asia is necessary. This is where the problem of reducing commitments arises in its most acute form. Other powers like Great Britain also face the problems confornting the United States, but in less acute form. Great Britain is reducing its former world role and modifying its presence "East of Suez." It is able to do so because such moves will not lead to changes in the planetary balance of power. Other states, like France, find themselves able to pursue very flexible foreign policies and if need be to reverse alliances. France thus moved from an alliance with Israel to a pro-Arab policy in a matter of months, and withdrew her troops from NATO while continuing to rely on U.S. containment of Soviet ambitions in Europe.

Unfortunately, short of war or the threat of war between China and the Soviet Union for example the United States has not yet designed efficient modes for the redirection of foreign policy and the termination of commitments. In this regard, the United Nations and regional organizations may serve useful purposes. They may provide the instrument for transferring responsibilities and retreating from exposed positions through new policies on the seating of China for instance.

Another characteristic of international law doctrines and of foreign policy instruments is their myth-making capability. This arises from treaties, declarations, joint resolutions, and the like. For example, American intervention in Vietnam was justified by the Administration as a response to an armed attack from the North threatening the political independence and territorial integrity of the free Territory in the South under the jurisdiction of the State of Vietnam. Action was taken pursuant to the South-East Asia Treaty and under Article 51 of the Charter. Responding to aggression with armed force is a principle enshrined in Chapter VII of the U.N. Charter (where it is to be done under the Security Council). Punishing aggressor states is a shared expectation of elites committed to the view that law is a coercive order. The rule of law is then equated with the sanctioning of violations. The "cops and robbers" model of the law has a strong hold on the allegiances of elites.

Criticism of U.S. involvement led the Administration to emphasize the claim that we are in Vietnam to assist a friendly sovereign state under external attack. The Administration took great pains to incarnate through elections the myth of a friendly sovereign government in Saigon, insisting that the United States would do nothing to jeopardize its sovereignty or to intervene in its domestic affairs. It thus doomed to failure economic and social projects which alone could have established the Saigon regime on a solid popular base. It is not clear how significant a devotion to governing law—text and treaties—was, in characterizing the Vietnam conflict as an international war rather than as a civil war, though it appears that the Charter and the South-East Asia Treaty influenced the formal justifications advanced by the United States for its intervention. This justification in turn fed theories that the war in the South was essentially foreign-directed, and that the Saigon regime would have no problem in controlling the insurgency but for such outside intervention. This myth in turn strengthened the diplomatic position of the Saigon regime and narrowed the prospects for a negotiated settlement at the Paris peace talks. The pitfalls of justificatory rhetoric are clear: they can lead to confusion, myths, and credibility gaps.

A further characteristic of the use of international law doctrines and foreign policy instruments is their impact on debate and dissent. The use of texts referring to guiding authority and precedents, to legitimacy, to morality, to national goals and interests can have unforeseen consequences. When the government's policies are well within the perimeter of its guidelines and authority, when its policies are clearly designed to meet stated goals, and when its actions do not offend the moral sense of its backers, few problems arise. It is the nature of policy statements, however, to open up issues for debate, for the simple reason that they import standards for criticism in their very formulation.

Grave problems arise when a government's actions skirt the outer edges of the rationales provided for them. When the government's actions are of doubtful legality and of questionable morality, when they do not manifestly appear designed to meet stated aims, and when they are not likely to advance proclaimed goals and interests, then dissent, disobedience, and even resistance can be expected in free societies. Or to put the matter in another way: it is the duty of the government to stay well within the limits of its legal authority, and to stay clearly faithful to its own proclaimed policies and stated goals, if it is not by its own pronouncements and actions to erode its legitimacy and credibility.[36]

Public laws and declared policies put constraints on a government's actions which it can ignore only at the peril of respect for law and authority—the spread of dissent and resistance is part of the cost of the state's disregard of its own authoritative pronouncements and laws. In this regard, criticism of President Pompidou's government sale of Mirage jets to Libya is a good example. Lack of candor about the number of airplanes involved, distinctions between countries in the battle zone and other countries, distinctions that remained utterly unconvincing in terms of the stated intent not to arm the enemies of Israel—all these contributed at the time to an erosion of the government's domestic and foreign credibility.

There are thus inherent features involved in the very use of guidelines in foreign relations. They cannot be willed away and disregarded. Some of these rest on systemic considerations. All guidance devices play roles that we would not expect of a system that is backed neither by the "power of the sword" nor by that of "the purse." These factors account, however, for the weight of all "commitments" rather than for those of a specifically "legal" character. They point to yet a further link between the political and the legal orders of the international system, confirming difficulties about a meaningful demarcation between the two.[37]

*Community Review*

In the case of allied nations acting within the framework of common interests, deference to "community review" by the United Nations or regional organizations may act as a brake on unprincipled

[36] See Gidon Gottlieb, "Vietnam and Civil Disobedience," in Richard Falk, ed., *The Vietnam War and International Law* (Princeton 1969), 597, 599.
[37] See United States Senate (fn. 34).

uses of force. But the legal and moral quality of such review is debatable. The political uses of law in organs for community review suggest that often little more is involved than subjection to political majorities in conference diplomacy dominated by developing, Asian, African, and Socialist states. In conflict situations, conference diplomacy can encourage the accommodation of competing claims, horse-trading, and a moderation of extreme positions. But these benefits dissipate where states in minority positions or with weak political support, like Portugal and South Africa, perceive the futility of their efforts to obtain reasonable compromises in the face of hostile political majorities. Likewise, community review of Big Power decisions involving the use of force may be most effective in homogeneous regional organizations like the OAS, NATO, and the Warsaw Pact, rather than in the Security Council of the United Nations. The trouble with such "review" however is that it often involves review by satellite states of actions by their dominant power. It can also conceivably lead smaller states with extremist policies to encourage drastic actions, as the German Democratic Republic reportedly did in connection with the Warsaw Pact intervention in Czechoslovakia.

In horizontal systems, it is thus still not apparent, despite Professor Falk's insistence that "the essence of a law-oriented approach to the use of force is to submit claims to the *best available* procedure for community review" (my italics). Here it seems he failed to pursue the logic of his investigation of the impact of systemic considerations by insisting at all costs on community review, which is an essentially verticalist concept. Even allowing for a moment that the intervention of law in human affairs necessarily involves a central role for the third party decision-maker who is entrusted with the task of sorting out adversary contentions, not *any* third party procedure will do for this purpose.[38] This requires some elaboration.

The essence of third party adjudication lies in a requirement that the decision reached be informed and impartial, and that it assure to an affected party an opportunity to present proofs and arguments for a decision in his favor. Such a procedure requires deference to law, agreements, principles and community expectations—it certainly precludes decision-making designed primarily to promote the third party's own political claims and interests. Third party involvement can also be directed to an optimum settlement, a settlement in which each protagonist gives up what he values less, in return for what he values more. Mediation therefore requires procedures eliciting the needs, perceptions, and expectations of the parties through private

[38] See Richard A. Falk, *Legal Order in a Violent World* (Princeton 1968), 32; and see the comments by Higgins (fn. 9). See also Thomas M. Franck, *The Structure of Impartiality* (New York 1969), 46.

consultations that would be wholly improper in adjudication. It also precludes the selfish pursuit by a mediator of his own political ends. Authoritative third party decision-making, to be authoritative, always requires that priority be given to community expectations and interests and to those of the parties affected.[39] But third party decision-making of the kind available in international political organs is devoid of such authoritative quality. Not all political uses of law have an authoritative or legal quality about them—as Professor Falk himself recognizes. He condemns, for example, uses of international law to bludgeon or bolster partisan foreign policies as unfortunate, for such uses create the impression that international law serves to inflame debate rather than to guide or shape public policy. Such uses are nevertheless characteristic of State behavior in the Security Council and in the General Assembly. The connection between third party decision-making in the United Nations and authoritative community review is tenuous at best. Myths about the legal quality of review by community processes serving naked political designs that are neither principled nor consistent is a dangerous foundation for legal order of any kind. It may sometimes be good politics, it may sometimes work, but it lacks the essential ingredients of authority.

In the present system of world order, the "best available" third party community-review procedures are therefore not good enough. They may even not be as good as the judgment of independent scholars and experts, and the opinions of legal advisers committed to principled applications of the doctrines of international law.

The failure of community review evidently tends to leave a damaging vacuum in the fabric of the international legal order on the theory that third party adjudication is indeed an essential ingredient of all legal ordering. But, as we have pointed out, in horizontal systems adjudication is quite naturally relegated to a secondary role. The insistence on third party community review is a vestigial remnant of verticalism in essentially horizontal power systems. But the absence of third party review does not deal a death blow to the *legal quality* of international legal ordering at all. It is merely a desirable feature of such ordering, not a prerequisite for its existence.

The writings and opinions of independent scholars and publicists do play a significant role, not so much in replacing unavailable adjudication procedures by *ex parte* pronouncements, but by articulating and identifying principles and rules accepted as binding. The role of scholars and publicists as catalysts of agreements and as molders of consensus is pronounced in systems of horizontal ordering. In such systems, processes for altering and creating obligations are generally

[39] Fuller, "Collective Bargaining and the Arbitrator" (fn. 17).

dependent on consensus rather than on formal legislative procedures. The publicist's role as a crystallizer of consensus should not be confused with his role as *ex parte* adjudicator. The crystallization of consensus is an appropriate scholarly role in horizontal systems in which indeterminacy of obligation is a common phenomenon.

### The Problem of Demarcation between International Law and Politics

This bleak account of political uses of international law could at first sight appear to reinforce arguments for discounting their significance. For if the uses of international law in the political organs of the U.N. are as partisan and unprincipled as is sometimes maintained, what is then the difference between law and politics—or, in other words, what is the point of talking about international law at all when referring to such highly politicized behavior? Is international law then not precisely that positive morality which Austin argued is not law properly so called?

The purists would restrict our concept of law to adjudication contexts, although these are of secondary significance only in the existing horizontal system. To do this, however, would be to exclude from our concept of international law much that states and international organizations do regard as international law. The alternative is to use the concept of law to include also to political uses of international law. We are then led, however, to consider as legal some practices that are not easily distinguishable from political maneuvers.[40]

The demarcation between international law and politics can best be understood in terms of the functions of the demarcation itself. In a well-known essay Brierly wrote that the best evidence for the existence of international law is that every state recognizes that it does exist and is under an obligation to serve it. Significantly, when states violate international law—and this is not an infrequent occurrence—they do not deny its binding force. They characteristically attempt to excuse and explain away their conduct without challenging the validity or the existence of the international legal order.[41] This professed acceptance of law by the community of states cannot be dismissed by rule-skeptics or "realists" focusing on actual state behavior—for, in the very process of disregarding international law, such skeptics would lose sight of the ways in which states act upon policy options

[40] See Stanley Hoffmann, *The State of War* (New York 1965), 130ff.; de Visscher (fn. 1), 106ff.; Higgins, *The Development of International Law Through the Political Organs of the United Nations* (fn. 21), 1–10; Falk, in Deutsch and Hoffmann (fn. 1), 144ff.; J. Fried, in Deutsch and Hoffmann (fn. 1), 116ff.; Gerald G. Fitzmaurice, "Judicial Innovation," in *Cambridge Essays in International Law in Honour of Lord McNair* (London and New York 1965).

[41] J. L. Brierly, *The Basis of Obligation in International Law* (Oxford 1958), Chap. I.

open to them and take into account considerations of a legal nature.[42]

Demarcation problems arise in a number of contexts. First, in accepting rules and principles of international law, states must necessarily demarcate between instruments they accept as "legal" and others they do not. Thus when the General Assembly adopted resolution 2603 (XXIV) on the Question of Chemical and Bacteriological (Biological) Weapons by a vote of 80 in favor, three against and 36 abstentions, declaring that the use of all chemical agents of warfare is contrary to the generally recognized rules of international law, it became incumbent on member states to take a stand on the status of this resolution. This was necessary if only for the purpose of stating the correct rule of international law in their military manuals. This is particularly significant in countries like the United States in which international law is part of the law of the land. In such states the development of the law of nations in the political organs of the United Nations may ultimately have an impact on domestic law.

Questions of demarcation also come up in controversies as to whether a rule of law has been terminated—for example the rule permitting belligerents the right of visit, search, and seizure of ships. This problem arose in the Middle East conflict. The Security Council had adopted a resolution on September 1, 1951, on the passage of Israeli ships through the Suez Canal in which it determined that neither party to the conflict could any longer assert belligerent rights or the right of visit, search, and seizure for any legitimate purpose of self-defense.[43] Needless to say, this was not the Egyptian thesis.

It may also be necessary to determine whether a particular event constitutes a violation of law or a precedent. Leonard Meeker, the former Legal Adviser to the Department of State, thus asserted on one occasion that far from being a violation of international law United States actions in Vietnam were indeed a precedent for future legitimate operations.[44] Questions of demarcation also arise when there are doubts whether a practice under a treaty establishes legal rights. Thus in the case of *Passage over Indian Territory* between Portugal and India, the International Court of Justice had to determine the legal status of the practice under British colonial rule of permitting Portuguese military personnel to cross from Goa to Damão.[45]

[42] See Fisher (fn. 21); Henkin (fn. 20); see also the work of the Panel of the American Society of International Law on Decision-Making in War-Peace Crises.

[43] Security Council Resolution 95 (1951); see also Elihu Lauterpacht, "The Legal Irrelevance of the 'State of War,'" 62 *Proceedings of the American Society of International Law*, 58 (1968); R. R. Baxter, "The Legal Consequences of the Unlawful Use of Force Under the Charter," same, 68.

[44] Leonard Meeker, "Vietnam and International Law of Self-Defense," *Department of State Bulletin*, LVI, No. 1437 (Jan. 9, 1967), 54.

[45] [1960] *ICJ Reports* 6.

Further practical demarcation questions arise in prima facie determinations about alleged violations of international law for the purpose of deciding on appropriate responses. For example, Israel had to reach a preliminary conclusion that Bulgaria had violated international law when it shot down an El-Al plane that had strayed over Bulgarian air space before it decided to bring the case to the International Court.[46] In another illustration, in 1965, the United States determined that South Vietnam was the target of an armed attack from the North constituted by the infiltration of armed personnel. Other practical demarcation problems arise when one country tries to determine whether a commitment is of a legal or a political character. In the *Legal Status of Eastern Greenland* case, the Permanent Court of International Justice had to consider what legal effect should be given to an oral statement made by the Norwegian Minister for Foreign Affairs to the Danish Minister accredited to the Kingdom of Norway.[47]

More complex questions arise about the "legitimacy" of resistance to particular governments or regimes under international law and the right to assist movements engaged in armed struggle for independence. In 1969, for example, Portugal protested to Sweden about financial assistance extended to insurgents in Portugal's African provinces and Sweden responded that it was acting under the authority of a General Assembly Resolution.[48] Similar problems arise in connection with the "authority" of various organs established by a General Assembly resolution. The United States was thus invited to indicate whether it would recognize travel documents for Namibians issued by the Council for Namibia and indicated that it accepted the competence of the Council for this purpose.[49]

The range of problems suggested in these examples illustrates the *practical* need for demarcation between legal and nonlegal instruments and practices. The argument that there is no meaningful use for international law except in the context of adjudication simply fails to meet the practical needs of states in the conduct of their foreign relations. It also fails to reflect the practice of legal officers in foreign ministries and in international organizations in their day-to-day activities.

Adjudication cannot in any meaningful sense be the touchstone of the international legal system so long as its horizontal authority structure subsists. Some other criterion is required to sort the legal from the political. But all available models have failed—neither

---

[46] *Aerial Incident of 27 July 1955 Case,* [1959] *ICJ Reports* 141.
[47] *Legal Status of Eastern Greenland* PCIJ., Ser. A/B, No. 53 (1933).
[48] *New York Times,* October 15, 1969, p. 3, col. 6.
[49] See the response of the United States in A/AC. 131/10 (1969).

Hart's emphasis on primary and secondary rules, nor the Austin-Kelsen concern with sanctions can account for international law. We are thus left with two questions that must be kept separate for they invite different kinds of response:

How can one demarcate between legal and other obligations in the international system?

What does it mean to say that an international legal system exists? [50]

The first question about demarcation invites the articulation of criteria for dealing with the practical problems of sorting obligations. The second question about the existence of an international legal system does not involve the application of criteria of demarcation. It is a meta-system question; a question *about* the international legal system, not about problems arising in its operation.

The relationship between these two questions is a matter of some delicacy. The problem of demarcation between juridical and other obligations points to the *need* for rules of recognition such as those set out in Article 38 of the Statute of the International Court of Justice. State practice discloses no other widely accepted principle of recognition. Strict adherence to Article 38 [51] would, however, rule out the legal status of much that states accept as legally obligatory—the alternative is to accept the indeterminacy of obligations.

This indeterminacy of obligations raises difficulties about the existence of the international legal system as such. For, if rules of recognition are indeterminate and uncertain, we can either conclude with Hart that we are confronted with something other than a fully realized legal system, or we must argue that Hart's thesis about the combination of primary and secondary rules does not apply to legal

[50] There is a vast literature on this subject. See, in particular, Hart (fn. 1), Chap. x; Glanville Williams, "International Law and the Controversy Concerning the Word 'Law,'" 22 *British Yearbook of International Law*, 146 (1945); Herbert Morris, "Verbal Disputes and the Legal Philosophy of John Austin," 7 *U.C.L.A. Law Review*, 27 (Jan. 1960). The first question is generally treated under the heading of "sources" of international law, see Parry (fn. 25), and see also fns. 20, 21, and 25; the second question is one about "legal systems"; in addition to the works cited in fns. 1 and 2 above, see also Hermann Kantorowicz, *The Definition of Law*, A. H. Campbell, ed. (Cambridge 1958); Julius Stone, *Legal System and Lawyers' Reasonings* (Stanford 1964).

[51] "The Court, whose function is to decide in accordance with international law such disputes as are submitted to it, shall apply:

(a) international conventions, whether general or particular, establishing rules expressly recognized by the contesting states;

(b) international custom, as evidence of a general practice accepted as law;

(c) the general principles of law recognized by civilized nations;

(d) subject to the provisions of Article 59, judicial decision and the teachings of the most highly qualified publicists of the various nations, as subsidiary means for the determination of rules of law.

2. This provision shall not prejudice the power of the Court to decide a case ex aeque et bono, if the parties agree thereto."

ordering in horizontal systems however "advanced" they may be.[52] The rejection of Hart's thesis, so far as world order is concerned, would be more persuasive if it were possible to outline a competing idea of legal system. Such an idea would not then be based on a combination between primary rules of obligation and secondary rules of recognition. It should account at least for legal ordering in the international system.

### Two Concepts of Law. The Authority Model and the Acceptance Model

We have rejected characterizations of the international legal system in terms of judicial agencies, judicial pronouncements, enforcement models, or rules of recognition. An attempt has recently been made to ascribe a definite meaning to the statement "a legal system exists." It has been made by Martin Golding, a professional philosopher with a sophisticated mastery of the tools of conceptual analysis, who seeks criteria for establishing the plausibility of his formulation of the issues inherent in the problem of the nature of law.[53] Golding's model is worth analyzing in some detail for the transparency of its widely-held premises. Golding's principal criterion is the "clear case" of the legal system of our community. Taking our vertical system as a model, or taking perhaps somewhat more inchoate notions of the existence of a legal system as a starting point, he comes up with the statement that initially, at any rate,

> An assertion of the form
> a legal system exists in $S$ is true, if, and only if,
> 1. there are laws in $S$ and
> 2. there exists in $S$ an agency for changing and making laws, and
> 3. there exists in $S$ an agency for determining infractions of the laws, and
> 4. there exists in $S$ an agency for enforcing the laws, and
> 5. there exists in $S$ an agency for settling disputes between individuals.
>
> Each of the statements 1–5 is a necessary condition for the truth of the original assertion, and jointly they are sufficient for its truth.[54]

This he asserts is a "clear case" of the existence of a legal system— but even a system lacking one of the features of clear cases would still remain a legal system. That is because "clear cases" are not paradigmatic and that not *every* case falling under the concept need

---

[52] See Hart (fn. 1), 91ff. and Chap. x.

[53] See the forthcoming work by M. P. Golding, *Philosophy of Law* (Englewood Cliffs, N.J. 1971).

[54] Same.

have all of the features—or even all of the central features—of the clear cases of the existence of a legal system in a society. While the existence of a legal system is not a definite and isolable type of phenomenon, Golding asserts that all systems share in certain general features, namely laws and jural complexity.

There is, in his view, a sufficient degree of "jural complexity" in a system in which there are agencies for changing and making the laws, for determining infractions, and for settling disputes between individuals, even though such a system has no agency for enforcing the laws. Yet the absence of an agency for enforcement would in his view seem to rob the laws of their jural character, reducing them to the status of other social norms in the society. He is therefore only reluctantly prepared to recognize the existence of systems that have no agencies for enforcing the law as "legal."

The "clear case" model for the existence of a legal system is rife with questionable premises. It assumes that there is only one model proposal for asserting the truth of the statement that a legal system exists, and that it is not possible to make a totally *different* proposal that in another appropriate systemic context would be equally legitimate. It assumes further that the practice of establishing the plausibility of such a proposal by the clear case of the legal system of *our* own community is legitimate—and that it is not possible to establish the plausibility of a competing proposal by the "clear case" of another kind of community, the community of nations for example. It would also appear to assume that one can say that a legal system does not yet exist or exists only partially in a given community without at the same time inviting inferences with regard to a range of other related matters such as:

—the duty to obey its laws,
—the legitimacy of resistance to its constituted authorities,
—the requisite conditions for the creation or the development of a pre-legal system,
—assertions with respect to the nature of a fully developed (as opposed to rudimentary) legal system,
—assertions with respect to the breakdown or erosion (pathology) of a legal system,
—assertions with regard to responses to violations and the maintenance of the integrity of the system.

The "clear case" model would also suggest that no reference to the functions and ends of the norms of the system is required, and furthermore that the ends of norms, ethical or otherwise, the policy goals of legal norms, are not part of a "legal system."

To take the legal order of *our* community as the clearest case of the existence of a legal order is methodologically unjustifiable. For it presupposes that which must be examined, positing that which is most familiar as the fullest blossoming which "developing" legal systems must strive toward. This error parallels the fallacy of using conceptual sets, imposed on alien forms of social ordering by anthropologists "naturally" formulating subjects for inquiry and hypotheses for verification, that do not reflect the relationships that have acquired significance in the society under study but are those of the anthropologists' own culture.[55] Common methodological errors can be traced in different fields. We have already referred to the Vico-Wittgenstein-Winch tradition and to the Durkheimian scientific method. Both methods can be relied upon to focus attention on related features of all social systems: on the internality of social relations, the role of conventions and the perceptions of actors on the one hand and on observed external regularities that are not dependent upon agreed conventions on the other.

These internal and external relationships are not mutually exclusive. While there is much argument about where one should draw the line between intended meaningful behavior and systemic unavoidable relationships, it is important not to exclude either of these two methods within their somewhat imprecise limits. If investigation of the nature of international law is to move forward, it requires insights garnered from separate fields, from philosophical analysis, from systems theory, and from the unified theory of international relations. It requires, we repeat, consideration of both the "internal" and the "external" views of the legal order. This bears repetition. The internal view rests on the notion that: "If social relations between men exist only in and through their ideas, then, since the relations between ideas are internal relations, social relations must be a species of internal relations too."[56]

The external view, on the other hand, does not stress the notions of those who participate in the social order, but looks for "more profound causes unperceived by consciousness."[57] That is the thesis of Durkheim, and of most social scientists after him who are concerned with observable patterns of behavior, attitudes, opinions, and probabilities from an observer's "external" perspective.

The difficulties encountered in international law theories have arisen in no small measure from an imbalance between these approaches. Systems theory, which could be characterized as an "external" approach method, offers a very incomplete account of the context of the international legal order. The internal approach, on the other hand, fails to account for deviations from normatively prescribed be-

[55] Bell (fn. 13).
[56] Winch (fn. 14).
[57] Emile Durkheim, cited in Winch (fn. 14), 23.

havior, for recurring unavoidable relationships, and for underlying power structures impervious to normative change. An equilibrium between both approaches should forestall the "anthropological fallacy" of attributing to other forms of social ordering a trend towards features characteristic of the investigator's own system.

In line with these considerations I should like to advance the following proposal to account for the existence of a legal system in horizontal power relationships. This is a proposal for an "acceptance model" contrasting with the dominant "hierarchical-enforcement" model. It builds upon systemic distinctions expressed in different types of power relationships. It takes as a point of departure the peculiar features of institutional arrangements in the international society in which power is widely diffused. In such a horizontal system, it is correct to assert that a legal order exists when:

1. international actors (for example, states) accept sets of fairly specific rules, principles, and policies as binding—in the sense that they recognize they are not at liberty to disregard them—and as proper standards for assessing the legality of their own actions;

2. international actors make demands, claims, complaints, and proposals to each other on the basis of such binding rules, principles, and policies and seek to settle their differences by reference to them;

3. international actors attempt to secure compliance with such rules, principles, and policies and there is a measure of congruence between state action and accepted law;

4. there are organizations established under such rules, principles, and policies and acting pursuant to them;

5. there is a measure of consensus between international actors about the content of the rules, principles, and policies accepted as binding, and about criteria for identifying them;

6. these rules, principles, and policies regulate significant aspects of the relationships between international actors and are designed to limit their unfettered discretion in decision-making;

7. international actors are committed to accept the guidance of these binding rules, principles, and policies in good faith and to apply them evenhandedly in all situations.[58]

[58] The reference to "international actors" is not merely a reference to States. It is a reference to all groups and entities with the *capability* to affect international relations. It is a de facto sociological concept—not a juridical construct. The state system happens at this time in history to be the most effective power system in international relations.

There is nothing in this model of law to preclude either reciprocal or common interest arrangements. Horizontal systemic relationships are not confined to barter-like reciprocal associations. Indeed, common enterprises feature prominently in them. Horizontality refers to the distribution of power—power in the sense of a capability to gain one's ends over the opposition of other centers of power. A horizontal distribution of power does not then preclude the agreed subordination of

Such a legal order involves then a *process of authoritative decision-making* leading to unavoidable principled choices between competing goals and policies.[59] It requires a measure of congruence between state action and accepted law. This congruence is a central feature of *the existence of any legal system.*[60] Accordingly, the earnestness with which major powers act upon international law considerations in good faith, and the intensity of their commitment to its principles and objectives, are good measures of the existence of such a system. Deviant practices, invoking one set of standards for oneself and another for adversaries, stretching concepts to legitimize national policies of questionable legality, all these tend to undermine the existence of the international legal order. The health of a legal system is thus subject to fluctuations, declining at times of crisis and tension when legal scruples may be ignored to accommodate pressing political interests.

These seven ingredients can be used as a model concept of law in all horizontal systems. Every one of these ingredients is a goal or target for the fullest realization of the legal nature of the system. At the end of the spectrum farthest from law lie the politics of coercion, in which the strongest but not necessarily the most authoritative influences govern. This formulation evidently contemplates a continuum between law, power, and politics separated by a threshold of considerable indeterminacy. This formulation, as can be noticed, makes no reference to the ingredients featured in Golding's proposal—agencies for changing the laws, for determining infractions, for enforcing the laws, and for settling disputes. Nor does it set much store by the rules of recognition and other criteria for the identification of obligations. For in a decentralized power system indices for the identification of rules, principles, and policies as binding are evolved and applied in a decentralized manner. States and organs of international organizations make their own determinations about the legal status of instruments and doctrines. Such a system can retain its unity only so long as some measure of consensus is achieved. Horizontality, it must be noticed, is not a feature of the concept of law but of systems in which

narrow vested interests to a higher vision of the common good. Nor does it rule out the possibility that another authority or power structure might be established for conflict control or for other objectives.

A nonauthoritarian model of law for horizontal systems does not require the attribution of any special status to sovereignty or nonintervention principles. These principles are merely reflections of the interests and claims of states as the most powerful international actors. These principles do not *logically* form a component of our model.

[59] For a fuller discussion, see Gottlieb (fn. 27), Chaps. VIII, X and XI; see also Rosalyn Higgins, *Conflict of Interests; International Law in a Divided World* (Chester Springs, Pa. 1965).

[60] Lon L. Fuller, *The Morality of Law,* rev. ed. (New Haven 1969), 39ff., 81ff.

it operates. The legal model for horizontal systems merely *reflects* systemic requirements. Actual power relationships are generally situated somewhere on the continuum between vertical and horizontal extremes.

Evidently the unity and coherence of such a system is open to erosion as consensus breaks down not only about the content and application of primary rules of obligation but also about secondary rules of recognition. The unity and universality of the international legal order remains vulnerable and the line between law and non-law undemarcated. This is in contrast to positivist concepts which provide for clear demarcation resting on accepted rules of recognition.

The erosion of such a system can also occur through a failure of congruence between state action and accepted law. States do not admit to flagrant violations of international law. They invoke a variety of diplomatic explanations, rhetorical justifications, and doctrinal innovations in support of their actions. For example, the Brezhnev Doctrine designed by the Soviet Union to legitimize the Warsaw Pact intervention in Czechoslovakia, was shortly afterward reflected in the revised Soviet draft definition of aggression submitted to the Special Committee on the Question of Defining Aggression. The Soviet Union proposed that the use of force by a state to encroach upon the social and political achievements of the peoples of other states is incompatible with the principle of the peaceful coexistence of states with different social systems.[61] Soviet rhetoric to justify the invasion of Czechoslovakia, once it became clear that there had been no invitation from the Czech government for Soviet forces to intervene, demonstrates an extreme reluctance to admit to a violation of accepted norms about nonintervention. In the debate in which he vetoed a draft resolution condemning the armed intervention of the U.S.S.R. and other members of the Warsaw Pact in the internal affairs of Czechoslovakia, the Soviet Representative stressed the special significance of the Warsaw Treaty in protecting the achievements of socialism and the sovereignty of fraternal states.[62] In the international order, cosmetic interpretations of legal obligations are designed to cover up flagrant departures from accepted principles and policies.

But law itself presupposes a commitment by governing authorities to abide by their own rules. Lon Fuller writes that "Fidelity to the Rule of Law demands not only that a government abide by its verbalized and publicized rules, but also that it respect the justified expectations created by its treatment of situations not controlled by explicitly announced rules. Even more plainly it requires that govern-

---

[61] A/AC.134/L.12.
[62] General Assembly Official Records, 24th Session, Supp. no. 2, A/7602 p. 69 and draft resolution S/8761.

ment apply written rules in accordance with any generally accepted gloss written into those rules in the course of their administration." [63] Self-serving political uses of law by states can only erode the legal quality of their own practices. The maintenance of an international legal order cannot long succeed in the face of unprincipled state practices.

The question remains—why do we insist on referring to the system of international rules, principles, and policies as a legal order when political uses and abuses of law are so common, when its "internal morality" is so constantly imperiled? [64] This is a recurring question of considerable importance.

The erosion of the line between legal and political practices has been a contributing factor in the loss of interest in international law among social scientists. Stanley Hoffmann wrote "The tendency of some international lawyers [is] to agree with earlier criticisms so much that they throw out the legal baby with the stale bath. They analyze law in policy terms that miss the distinctiveness of law as a method of social control and that iron out the normative essence of law under the pretext of straightening out the discipline." He added,

> It is essential, however, to understand that law in the hands of statesmen is not merely a policy among others, but that it has very special characteristics and roles: the social scientist who forgets this and advises the Prince accordingly will debase the instrument and mislead the Prince.
>
> Law is distinguished from other political instruments by certain formal features: there is a certain solemnity to its establishment; it has to be elaborated in a certain way. More significantly, the legal order, even in international affairs, has a life and logic of its own: there are courts and legal experts who apply standards of interpretation that are often divorced from underlying political and social factors. . . . Law may be an instrument of policy, but it is one that has an "artificial reason." Not every legal norm can be traced back to political or social realities: this fact should, in turn, give to political sociologists of law a sense of perspective and modesty. [65]

The solemnity of effects, the fact that international law enshrines, elevates, and consecrates the interests it embodies could tend at times to intensify political contests. Law makes it much more difficult to alter or to disregard policies consecrated in legal form. This is missed by those who would identify international law with politics.

But the reasons for insisting on a demarcation between interna-

[63] Fuller (fn. 60), 234.
[64] See Fuller's (fn. 60) discussion of the concept of the "internal morality of law."
[65] Hoffmann (fn. 40), 124, 131.

tional law and politics are perhaps plainest if we were to assert that no international legal system now exists. Such a proposition would clarify what is at stake and would entail a number of conclusions of palpable falsity:

–that every state is at liberty to disregard rules and policies as its interests may dictate and that there is no duty to abide by them or to obey them;

–that there are no legal grounds for impeaching the legitimacy of constituted authorities and the legitimacy of their policies;

–that since there is no international legal system there is no occasion to respond to violations of the law, to affirm standards, and to maintain claims. In the absence of law all a State can do is to use its power to uphold its interests;

–that in the absence of obligations, and of rules and policies of a binding and constraining character, it is useless to negotiate agreements and to draft international instruments;

–that the establishment of an international legal order would require legal arrangements radically different from those currently in effect.

These considerations do not as yet account for all the qualitative differences between political and legal guidance systems. One crucial aspect of these differences lies in the extent to which decision makers are limited in their discretion. Let me elaborate. The hierarchical, vertical model of the legal order has been shown to inhibit consideration of purposes and policies in the application of law. The Austinian command model of law has tended to blur the difference between the separate techniques involved in obeying orders and in complying with rules. The hierarchical, vertical model of law has also distorted the distinctions between relying on rules and on policies for guidance. Policies are one of a set of guidance devices for decision makers.[66] All such devices—whether we have in mind orders, standards, principles, precepts, rules, standing procedures, goals, and the like—are designed to be acted upon by those to whom they are addressed. Acceptance of guidance involves, however, the willingness to limit one's discretion, one's freedom of action. Guidance may be illusory when for every order there is a counter-order, for every rule a competing rule and for every policy a rival policy, and when choices between them are unprincipled.[67] Guidance is also illusory when vagueness and generality are raised to such heights as to provide no direction at all. Though all this is true, the fact remains that some orders, some rules,

[66] Gottlieb (fn. 27), Chap. VIII.
[67] Same. See also Falk, "The Adequacy of Contemporary Theories . . ." (fn. 1), and Stanley V. Anderson, "A Critique of Professor Myres McDougal's 'Doctrine of Interpretation by Major Purposes,'" 78 *American Journal of International Law* 378 (April 1963).

and some policies do involve a measure of guidance, some limitation of discretion. This is a necessary effect of all authoritative efforts to guide, control, and direct. Free decisions, by way of contrast, involve a choice unbounded by external or public considerations. In this sense both rule and policy do not merely guide, but also limit discretion and tend to exclude naked demands as a proper ground for choice and judgment.[68] It is immaterial what the sources of policies happen to be, whether they are found in specific rules or stated in general instruments. Policies are designed to guide inferences towards fixed results or, to use Dewey's term, towards ends-in-view. Rules contemplate specific contexts or settings of application, and fixed decisions designed to promote specific objects. They provide relatively firm guidance not only with respect to ends but *also* as to the means to be adopted; they elaborate what has to be done, when and to what end. The reasoning appropriate to decisions in terms of policies differs from reasoning required by rules. When policies only are available to direct decisions, their executants are free to determine when and what to do provided their decisions lead to the required goal. Policies contemplate the delegation of a considerable degree of authority to their executants and presuppose a correspondingly significant area of indeterminacy in measures to be adopted. For example, the principle contained in Article 2 paragraph 4 of the Charter—that all Members shall refrain in their international relations from the threat or use of force against the territorial integrity or political independence of any state, or in any other manner inconsistent with the Purposes of the United Nations—functions as a policy directive. It is of such generality that it cannot meaningfully guide the decisions of States. In attempting to develop these principles, the Special Committee on Principles of International Law Concerning Friendly Relations and Cooperation Among States considered proposals that would narrow the ambit of legitimate discretion of states with regard to uses of force under this Article. The United Kingdom, for example, proposed that this principle be taken to mean, among other things, that "Every State has the duty to refrain from instigating, assisting or organizing civil strife or committing terrorist acts in another State or across international lines of demarcation, or from conniving at or acquiescing in organized activities directed toward such ends, when such acts involve the threat or use of force." [69] This attempt to reduce a general principle to harder levels of concreteness would involve a reduction in a state's legal liberty to act as it pleases with regard to terrorist acts. It is easy,

[68] Gottlieb (fn. 27), Chap. VIII; see also Ronald Dworkin, "Judicial Discretion," *Journal of Philosophy* LX (1963), 624; see also Fuller (fn. 60) on managerial discretion, 207ff., 212ff.

[69] General Assembly Official Records, 23rd Session, A/7326 p. 12.

however, to exaggerate the contrast between rule and discretion. Ronald Dworkin has ably challenged the widespread assumption that these are mutually exclusive.[70] Indeed, it can be shown that commands, rules, and policies each preclude complete discretion, in the sense that they all set a limit to authorized or required behavior. It can however also be shown that none of these can entirely exclude discretion, although the discretion of the recipient of a command is clearly narrower than that of an addressee of a rule or of the executant of a policy. But policies are not the only authoritative mode for guiding decisions. Specific rules and provisions limit a state's discretion more sharply than broad policy goals.

Legal as distinct from political guidance requires that there be a "marked degree" of firmness of guidance, limiting discretion not only with respect to the goals to be achieved but also as to the means to be adopted. Under policy guidance the pursuit of posited ends may take a variety of forms and the means are left to the discretion of executants. Rule guidance, on the other hand, typically requires the performance of specific acts in predetermined circumstances for stated ends. Rules guidance looks not only to the acceptance and pursuit of policy goals, but also to compliance with certain procedures and requirements in promoting them. Arguments that rules are always competing pairs of opposites can be overdone. Similar arguments can be made that policy goals are so vague as to amount to functioning legal fictions. The fact remains that rules no less than policies can be designed to guide, to limit discretion, and to circumscribe unfettered authority. Only in this fashion can we account for the hard bargaining and time-consuming drafting involved in the production of international instruments. Rules and policies operate through the instrumentality of language and of text. Initially at least, they call for deference to verbal guidance rather than to the expectations of their authors.[71] A legal system as distinct from a political system relies on specificity in language about what is required, when, and to what end. This is by way of contrast to systems in which one would only postulate abstract goals, in which general principles, broad standards, and loose precepts permit decision-makers to do pretty much as they please. In such systems, general and frequently conflicting aims provide the only signposts to permitted or required behavior. Here again there looms a vast undemarcated terrain between the legal and the political—but

70 Dworkin (fn. 68).

71 See Gidon Gottlieb, "The Conceptual World of the Yale School of International Law," *World Politics* xxi (October 1968), 108–32, and David Weisstub, "Conceptual Foundations of the Interpretation of Agreements," *World Politics* xxii (January 1970), 225–69; see further Gidon Gottlieb, "The Interpretation of Treaties by Tribunals," and Myres McDougal, "Comments," in *Proceedings of the American Society of International Law* (1969), 122–34.

the more specific the guidance in a system becomes, the more specific the norms, the policy goals and their application, the more "legal" this system becomes. On the other hand, a system which requires merely obedience to very specific orders, directives, and commands without regard to policy considerations would not necessarily present a true picture even of a vertical legal system. It should be more accurately characterized as a bureaucratic structure resembling the military, severing consideration of policies from the application of rules and standing orders.

Inevitably, the accretion of strata of authoritative precedents in the practice of political organs, international and domestic, fosters tendencies to legal modes and procedures of argument.

This leads to yet another point about the distinction between law and policy. Malinowsky's concern with deviant conduct in anthropology is matched by current concern about deviant conduct of states under international law. Discrepancies between proclaimed norms and actual conduct is a characteristic of many legal systems indeed. It suffices to compare the Periodic Reports on political and civil rights submitted to the UN Commission on Human Rights with the situation known to prevail in countries filing the Reports. State violations of human rights generally involve violations of their own domestic laws. This as an aspect of legal theory fittingly characterized as the "pathology of law." But while states may violate laws and not live up to their requirements, states do not "violate" political goals. They may alter them, abandon them, or qualify them—they are not obligated to steer a steady course in political matters, although, as we have already observed, it is often awkward in the existing international system for a big power to alter the course of its policies. Evidently, the reductionist urge to assimilate international law with international politics born from impatience with fine distinctions can only, as Hoffmann suggested, mislead the Prince. It threatens, moreover, to cast a long shadow on the prospects for the survival of international order itself. The adoption of a model concept of law for horizontal systems makes the distinction between international law and politics plain for all to see. It is a distinction that must be maintained if force alone is not to be allowed to govern international relations.

Preoccupation with the foundations of decision-making in the international legal process leads us to another central feature of legal systems, which sets them well apart from political processes. It involves the neutrality and the principled quality of choices between rival rules and competing goals. Clearly, political decisions do not labor under a requirement of consistency nor need they be characterized by deference to the authoritative policy choices of others, by disinterested choosing or again by choices made on some principled grounds. Deference to third party decision-making, to community processes, is one obvious method for avoiding partisan choices of one's own, but it presupposes that these community processes are themselves principled. The search for a system that would provide government officials with a scientific alternative to human judgment, which is somewhat unfairly attributed to Richard Falk, is a search for the impossible.

With the recognition of the fact that rules and principles of all sorts promote policies and goals, the unavoidable nature of choices between them becomes manifest. What is less manifest is that the range of alternative methods for making these choices is strictly circumscribed:

> The resolve to make principled and consistent choices whenever possible leads to a limited number of alternatives:
> 1. to follow one's own commitment to prefer a specific recurring interest in its recurring clashes with other interests;
> 2. to defer to the commitments of others in such circumstances whenever they can be said to exist, whether they be the commitments of exemplars, judges, drafters of legislation or commitments which can be derived from . . . kindred texts such as the U.N. Charter.[72]

The problems raised in the international legal process about such choices are hard to resolve. The most articulate alternatives to date are those advocated by McDougal and by Falk. McDougal would have a public official apply the law only when it promotes the policies of the moral community that he serves.[73] Falk would have officials defer to the best available centralized community processes even if they are as unprincipled and as partial as U.N. organs. The substitution of law for force involves, he argues, gradual replacement of the ideology of self-help by that of third party judgment. We have already considered this argument, but we have not yet seen how any *principled* decision can be reached internationally through community review. Deference to shared world-policy goals, rather than to national or ideological policy imperatives, is called for by the very concept of a world legal order.[74] But only independent scholars, impartial judges, and some international civil servants can at this time be expected to strive for principled decisions grounded in *international* public policy. On them devolves the responsibility which in vertical systems falls on the judiciary. Placing trust in the Security Council for collective security is one thing, relying on it for authoritative "community review" is an-

[72] Gottlieb (fn. 27), 164.
[73] For a discussion of these differences see Higgins (fn. 9).
[74] See n. 38 above on community review.

other. There is no escaping the fact that principled community review is now beyond reach. Political organs serve the political objectives of their participants. This, after all, is not so far removed from the realities of the domestic legal order.

## Characteristics of Legal Systems—a Recapitulation

Common elements in the two model legal systems suggest that there are some essential qualities for legal ordering that are not shared by other forms of ordering. They possess salient features of their own.

Perhaps the first and most prominent element is the acceptance of guidance. Legal decisions involve primarily guided reasoning—reasoning that relies whenever possible on the authoritative guidance of texts and of enunciated policies formulated in binding fashion. Such reasoning requires *deference* to the preferences of authoritative decision-makers rather than reliance on one's own preferences. In clear contrast, political reasoning looks to no authority to defer to but is designed to promote the claims, needs, and expectations of relevant constituencies. Guided legal reasoning, guided decision-making, accordingly requires "good reasons" for departing from established practices.

A second and closely related feature of legal ordering is the commitment to abide by governing rules and principles and authoritatively enunciated policies. That commitment and the resulting congruence between decision-making at all levels and declared law express the guided nature of legal reasoning. To accept legal guidance in good faith necessarily involves congruence between official action and accepted law. Good faith compliance and deference to rules, principles, and their objectives are essential ingredients in legal ordering. In these circumstances unauthorized modifications and departures from practice are impermissible. The acceptance of legal guidance signifies the acceptance of rules and binding policies that one cannot unilaterally alter at will. In political systems, by way of contrast, policies and objectives can be modified and abandoned without impropriety.

Third, good faith deference to authoritative texts and policies calls for their evenhanded and consistent application. Evenhandedness and consistency in application are no mere moral virtues. They express the essence of legality. Unequal applications of the law or inconsistent decisions that are not based upon "good reasons" are essentially arbitrary. But nonlegal decisions, political decisions for example, those that are concerned neither with justice nor with principle but primarily with the attainment of posited ends, these need be neither evenhanded nor consistent.

A fourth requirement of legal ordering can be discerned in procedures for choosing between competing rules, principles, and binding policies. Legal choices for which no authoritative guidance is available must be made on a principled basis transcending the requirements of each case. In such choices consistency, evenhandedness, and principle express the essentially legal character of the choices involved. Choices expressing merely the preferences of the decision-maker are devoid of this feature. They are political.

A fifth characteristic of legal ordering lies in yet another aspect of authoritative guidance—in a limitation of discretion. The crucial point is the fairly simple one that all acceptance of guidance involves a limitation of discretion. Free decision, as we have observed, involves a choice unbounded by any prior authority. The continuum from discretion to authority spans the full breadth of the division between legal and political reasoning.

A sixth characteristic of legal ordering can be found in the procedures adopted in adjudication. Impartial and informed decisions can be made only when affected parties have an opportunity to present proofs and arguments for a decision in their favor. Procedure is here inseparably related to the very concept of legal ordering.

Then, in addition, reference should be made to the seven ingredients of the acceptance model outlined above. They are, however, peculiar to legal systems operating in societies in which power is widely diffused. But the emphasis on the authoritative quality of the guidance is fundamental. The seven ingredients are a shorthand statement of the specifically juridical character of decision-making in horizontal systems.

In the repeated references placed in this essay upon the distinction between the legal and political systems, no concept of political system was either proposed or attempted. Instead, the strategy of the argument has been to outline what is involved in the existence of a legal system and to proceed by exclusion. The emphasis was placed on models of legal ordering and to contrast the different modes involved in juridical and "other" forms of ordering. *The emphasis in this contrast lies not in institutions but on modes of decision-making and on procedures of reasoning.* The contrast between juridical and political processes does not depend upon the existence of particular institutional settings. Both horizontal and vertical institutional structures and political arrangements can accommodate juridical processes. The combination of vertical institutional structures, characteristic of the state, and of juridical modes and procedures of decision constitute the principal elements of what is commonly known as a "legal system." The essence of my argument is that a combination of horizontal institutional arrangements and of juridical modes and procedures of decision are no less capable of producing a "legal system," albeit a different one, not based upon enforcement but on acceptance. Patterns of power relations, patterns of authority structures and of institutional arrangements provide the fluid context in which juridical modes and procedures of decision function. They account for the varieties of legal systems. Common juridical modes and procedures can therefore be traced to both models of legal ordering. The distinct features of those two models turns on their institutional and societal context, on the power relationships prevailing in that society. The consistent qualities of legalness are system-free, relating instead to modes and procedures of decision-making. The requirements of legalness in patterns of power relationships remain constant. We thus face three separate sets of statements regarding

–different model legal systems which are

–appropriate for different systemic power structures but which

–express the underlying requirements and procedures of juridical decision-making.

Insistence on erecting the legal system of the nation state, that is of a particular system of power relationships, as the only acceptable form of *legal* ordering (as distinct from extra-legal) reveals an implicit value bias, a bias for hierarchical power and authority relationships in political arrangements.

Much of our argument is therefore reduced to a matter of definitional policy—the adoption of one unitary "hard" concept of law grounded in hierarchical, pyramidal state structures, characterizing all nonconforming phenomena as nonlegal, or the acceptance of a second, complementary concept of law appropriate for pluralistic relationships between diffuse power centers. The two-model approach is reluctant to exclude law-affected phenomena as nonlegal. It also remains neutral as between the two forms of social ordering. Since the essential qualities of legal ordering are system-free, insistence on a particular power system context for the concept of law cannot be justified except in political terms. It amounts to a covert preference for a particular form of authoritarian order. That it is possible to formulate two concepts of law, and that it is not necessary to use only a single hard unitary one, exposes the value bias of the unitary concept advocates.

The use of two flexible and complementary sets of concepts of law has policy implications of its own. Severing the characteristics of legal ordering from its systemic context should weaken legal objections both to systemic changes and to a shift from enforcement models to acceptance models. Such shifts, under the two models theory, do not entail an abandonment of legal methods but rather an adjustment to new societal relationships. On the other hand, a unitary state-oriented concept of law resists such characterization as a move from law to politics. There is nothing in the concept of law to wed it so irremediably to the concept of state and to permit the dismissal of other binding normative arrangements as "political." On the contrary, it is this very dismissal which is "political" in a true sense, that is, neither called for by analytical considerations nor justifiable by reference to neutral criteria.

The "two concepts of law" theory permits also a more faithful account of the manner in which authoritative rules, principles, and policies are invoked by states and by other international actors. While this of itself is not conclusive it draws attention to the greater explanatory power of *two* model concepts. The problem of choosing between conceptual models is not unique. It is a recurring feature of scientific theory. But all unverifiable, uncontestable theories about the concept of law must be assessed with reference to criteria such as

–their explanatory powers,

–their impartiality between different forms of societal arrangements and competing political systems,

–their internal consistency,

–their capability to resolve conceptual problems.

While these matters of theoretical policy are best left to professional philosophers, I should nevertheless like to conclude with a reference to Sir Karl Popper's discussion of conjectures. He wrote that he much prefers an attempt to solve an interesting problem by a bold conjecture, even if it soon turns out to be false, to any recital of a sequence of two—but irrelevant—assertions. New scientific theories proceed from some simple, new, and powerful unifying idea about some connections or relation between hitherto unconnected phenomena. Much the same can be said of conceptual analysis in legal theory.

## The Future of the International Legal Order

The development of the international legal order, we have observed, must of necessity take place in the context of three sets of "boundary situations," situations that cannot be avoided come what may. These situations, as we have suggested, arise from:

–the limitations imposed by the international political system—"systemic considerations" arising from patterns of power relationships between states and other international actors;

–the limitations arising from the internality of social relations at all levels—the "internal considerations" connected with the expectations, perceptions, and attitudes of states and other international actors;

–the limitations imposed by challenges that must be met if organized social life is to continue on this planet—the "challenge considerations" connected with the control of international conflicts, population growth, and environmental issues.

These constraints have serious implications for studies of the future of the international legal order. Legal structures do not only reflect a faithful image of the international system but in some measure help mold and direct the development of the system itself.[75] In other words, internal considerations can within limits modify systemic relationships. We have seen that the impact of ideology, of the capability and will to resist coercive power, is in no small measure the outcome of ideology and policy objectives. Since predictions about perceptions, ideological attitudes, and values rest in large measure on intuitive foundations, a major element of indeterminacy necessarily enters into all predictions about the international system and its legal order. But predictions and projections about future developments can themselves have an impact on the history of the future, inasmuch as they may form an integral part of "internal" considerations of years to come.[76]

Second, internal considerations are likely to be deeply influenced by perceptions of emerging perils, by concerns with new technologies of warfare, with environmental catastrophes and with analyses of the economic, racial, and social causes of conflict. The development of credible alternative policy options and of models for guided change, designed either to promote systemic modification or to meet emerging challenges, may assist in the drawing of meaningful maps for possible preferred futures.

Third, challenge considerations pertaining to perceived threats require a realistic strategy, realistic, that is, within the twin context of systemic and internal considerations. The interdependence of these sets of variables suggests that the limitations within which the international legal order must operate are by no means inflexible. From this perspective, some cautious comments about the future of the international legal order may be ventured.

a. The further growth of major industrial and military powers in Europe and Asia will mark a return to 19th-century style balance of power diplomacy modified by the dictates of nuclear deterrence of socialist ideologies and modernization problems. New power alignments are to be expected. The development of communications and media technologies and the accelerated growth of weapons technologies is likely to affirm horizontal system trends, internationally and domestically, which are characterized by an increased will and capability among international actors to resist coercion.

b. Firm forecasts of population growth, the growing gap between rich and poor nations, and concomitant racial, economic, and social tensions will provide a favorable terrain for the proliferation of international conflict situations and internal disturbances offering numer-

[75] Hoffmann, "International Systems and International Law" (fn. 1).

[76] On prediction in social studies see Quentin Gibson, *The Logic of Social Enquiry* (New York 1960); Winch (fn. 14), 91ff.; see generally Robert K. Merton, *Social Theory and Social Structure*, rev. edn. (Glencoe, Ill. 1957); see further Walter G. Runciman, *Social Science and Political Theory*, 2nd edn. (London 1969).

ous opportunities for Big Power involvement, often by balance-of-power diplomacy. Increasingly, civil strife and instability in very advanced societies and in the Third World will cast a long shadow over international peace and security.

c. These developments are not likely to favor the development of international judicial or third party organs for the settlement of disputes. Nor is it likely to brighten the prospects for peace enforcement and collective security. Accommodation modes may acquire increasing significance as enforcement models fail to achieve hoped-for results. But the limited effectiveness of consensus law is already becoming apparent in the situation in Southern Africa. Disillusionment both with the effectiveness of limited coercion and with the effectiveness of authoritative consensus may encourage the freezing and hardening of local conflicts and renewed attention to negotiated settlements and diplomacy.

d. Nor are these developments likely to enhance the authority—as distinct from the coercive power—of national state governments. Both domestic order and international order are facing challenges arising from new perceptions about the limitations of power and the limitations of authority. The erosion of domestic authority structures is expressed in their failure to command either the loyalty or commitment of the intelligentsia and the younger generation.

e. States may be tempted to respond to common challenges by resort to regional organizations sharing common ends, ideologies, and interests rather than to the more universal United Nations. Tendencies favoring regional organizations and groupings could therefore gain momentum. Arms control issues and regional settlements may nevertheless continue to be handled in Big Power conferences with limited outside participation. Environmental problems, technological questions, ocean resources, satellite transmissions, and other specialized matters in which common interests outweigh political rivalries, these may all continue to be dealt with under United Nations auspices. But voting majorities may yet render the Organization too uncomfortable for the big powers even on issues of this character. Conference diplomacy under United Nations auspices provides convenient machinery for international consultations that states are not likely to forego. But it is also unlikely that modernizing societies, bent on preserving the benefits of hard-gained independence, will accept the development of international institutions encroaching upon their sovereignty. Small states grouping together may increasingly attempt to counterbalance the weight and influence of the Superpowers in the political organs of the United Nations.

These factors are not encouraging, as we have seen in the even-handed application of the norms of international law. The crises of modernization sweeping developing societies are bringing to the fore military and technological elites primarily concerned with maintaining their shaky control, and with the attainment of economic goals rather than with human rights, democratic principles, and considerations of legality. States are not likely to be more preoccupied with the rule of law internationally than they are domestically. But counter-elites may continue to exert a strong influence in technologically advanced societies which rely on the services of scientific personnel and intellectual classes. The influence of these elites may be felt most clearly in the Superpowers. There too, however, extremist provocations of state authority may lead to a heightening of repressive policies and the stifling of dissent. Casual terrorism, massive insecurity, and government repression in these states could have unsettling consequences for the international order.

f. Short of cataclysmic conflict and short of ecological collapse no major changes are likely to transform the international system itself. The fragility of planetary survival is becoming more apparent day by day—and so is the capability of small states and dissatisfied groups to inflict unacceptable damage. Preoccupation with conflict control and environmental control may increasingly conflict with claims for economic development, social and human rights. Wise adjustments between these rival sets of claims may well hold the key to our planetary future. In technologically advanced societies loss of faith in the concepts of economic growth and progress may trigger off a variety of nonmaterialistic movements and ideologies with unchartable consequences for their destinies. Postmaterialistic ideologies, practices, and fads may have an unsettling domestic effect in the United States and in Western Europe in particular.

This brief inventory of factors points to the central role of internal considerations in the future of the international legal order in which systemic and technological considerations will continue to impose their side effects. Since ideological and normative transformations are relatively undetermined, model building and the design of credible future worlds may well exert some influence of its own over state policies.

Institution design for horizontal systems requires a realistic appraisal of the capabilities of adjudication and law enforcement agencies. Greater attention might be paid to collective bargaining techniques, to the refinement of negotiation practices and accommodation procedures guaranteeing the functioning of essential relationships. The range of international actors participating in settlement procedures might be widened to include significant nongovernmental forces. Arrangements could be designed for leaving primary responsibility for modernization in the hands of the societies concerned, while providing for international sources of capital from international public utilities and financial institutions. This would lessen the political dependence of modernizing societies upon the Big Powers and reduce the risks of involving them in Third World civil strife. Such trends could conceivably be pushed to extremes. Advanced societies would thus increasingly seek to insulate themselves from the teeming and desperate struggle of the populations in Third World ghettos, paving the way for the growth of parallel communities of nations divided in the same manner in which slum areas are separated from wealthy neighborhoods in modern cities.

The successful operation of an ever-increasing number of international functional agencies, planetary telecommunication systems, and increased international travel may help catalyze rapid changes in the expectations and values of political elites. Visual media replacing written communications will put new stress on practices and conditions deriving their authority from custom, law, and government. Visual communications may lead to yet further emphasis on sensibilities, style, and manners to the detriment of principle and written law.[77]

Finally, reference should be made to the future power structure of the international system. Credible future world order models should not be exclusively based upon vertical system concepts—an attempt should be made to design such models on horizontal lines cutting across state structures. There should be an attempt to design "liberated" utopias, liberated, that is, from the overbearing shadow of more effective and more centralized authority establishments. The difficulty with a proliferation of decentralized authority structures rests in the magnitude of emerging challenges which appear to call for more effective controls. It is by no means clear, however, that vertical authority structure limited to functional tasks, designed to meet the demands of population growth and of environmental protection that are necessary to sustain life on earth, should be broadened to include other political concerns. International public utilities, multinational corporations and specialized agencies may well be structured on a vertical basis to perform essential functions and tasks. On the other hand, centralized vertical world power models of a political character could easily degenerate into Orwellian dystopias. More power to technologically omnipotent elites and bureaucracies, with demonstrated indifference to genocide and human suffering, is not a convincing panacea for widespread disasters. One may reasonably dread the onset of vertical

[77] Marshall McLuhan, *Understanding Media: The Extension of Man* (New York 1965), 81; see also an imaginative work on modern sensibility by Theodore Roszak, *The Making of a Counter-Culture* (New York 1969), John Kenneth Galbraith, *The New Industrial State* (New York 1967), and Herbert Marcuse, *One-Dimensional Man* (New York 1964) which furnish insights into the requirements and operations of authority structures in advanced societies.

authority—of centralized world government or a Big Power condominium—even at a time when it is said that such authority alone can
manage planetary security, ecological and ecosocial concerns. But such
distrust of a centralized world authority does not preclude the design
of automated, computerized, vertical bureaucratic structures for international functional agencies performing economic and technological
tasks. Indeed, in considering future power structures, the connection
between political agencies primarily affecting human relationships and
eco-technological agencies controlling things and their environment
must be reexamined. Automation and computerization may increasingly dissolve the link between these two types of agencies. The establishment and operation of eco-technological agencies may be regulated
independently of the regulation of political and social behavior. Political control of economic behavior, of labor, and of consumption may
well become less compelling as automation and computerization progress. Control and planning in political and in social relationships
may no longer be feasible in advanced societies without resort to the
kind of techniques outlined in Orwell's *1984*. Relevant horizontal
utopias do not therefore necessarily conflict with vertical functional
structures undertaking essential but narrow tasks. Control over vertical
eco-technical structures may be maintained in horizontal political systems asserting a wide range of demands and expectations. The establishment of planetary functional agencies and of planetary corporations such as Comsat may continue to occur simultaneously with the
weakening of existing authority structures at the national level—these
two trends are not contradictory. The policies of such functional
agencies, however, have to be increasingly responsive to claims for
social justice, economic progress, and environmental integrity. In horizontal power relationships, consensus rather than enforcement serves
as the basis for legal ordering, but consensus is seriously vulnerable
to deeply felt grievances.

Vertical agencies concerned with effectiveness may increasingly depend on automation and computer technology to reduce labor problems and other disruptive factors. They may also rely on transnational
solutions to functional problems—transcending in the process purely
national considerations. St. Simon's well-known prophecy may then
come true that "the government of man will be replaced by the
administration of things."

Far from tending to greater homogeneity, popular loyalties may increasingly be commanded by groups that also disregard state boundary
lines and by small tribe-like national units putting big state structures
under yet additional stress. The impact of television and other communications media may have already reversed the process of assimilation of racial, social, and cultural groups, enhancing instead claims

for autonomy, distinct life styles, and separate identity. The spreading fragmented mosaic of relatively small states and of racial and affinity groups should have consequences favorable to the spread of liberty, if by liberty we refer to the diversity of open roads one can take, to the possibility of mobility from group to group.

The variety and availability of meaningful options and life-styles promoting different kinds of individual self-realization should be placed high on the list of specifications for a preferred future. The "capacitation" of people for the full enjoyment of their liberties and the realization of their options, for the development of "conditions of liberty," should be key ingredients in relevant utopias. "Giving full freedom to human nature to expand itself in innumerable conflicting directions" is what is at stake here.[78] No serious argument about preferred futures will be able to dodge consideration of social ends and the ends of life. Centralizing authority, "turning a people into a flock of timid and industrious animals of whom the government is a shepherd," or allowing the dissolution of the social texture and the growth of anarchy—these are ancient alternatives indeed.[79] Nothing in the discussion of desirable utopias permits us to shirk these choices and to disregard arguments debated from Plato's time, by Burke, by Hegel, by Mill, and by Isaiah Berlin in our day. The advocacy of a centralized world authority to meet survival necessities must be tempered by an awareness of the formidable technology of surveillance and repression already in existence. The clear and present dangers of nuclear conflict, of civil disorders, of environmental catastrophe, and of population growth do not render authoritarian centralized governments more attractive—be they national, transnational or indeed global.

There is a need to reassess world government and Big Power condominium models inspired by the vertical structure of nation states, ideas of collective security, and peace enforcement concepts. There is room for the design of more acceptable constructs, based upon the recognition of the systemic realities of horizontal relationships and the changing character of power relations inside states. This is the reality of an international system in which the strong have the power to destroy everything but little authority to govern, in which the weak have the capability to terrorize and disrupt, and in which all tremble at the fragility and precariousness of life on this planet.

[78] Isaiah Berlin, *Four Essays on Liberty* (Oxford 1969), especially the fourth essay on John Stuart Mill.
[79] Same.

# CHAPTER 10

# Domestic Institutions *

## RICHARD B. LILLICH

THAT THE role of domestic institutions in the prescription and application of international law has been an important one goes without saying. From the substantive standpoint, state practice, usually divined from foreign office documents conveniently if belatedly reprinted in various national digests, undoubtedly has been the major source of customary international law.[1] Judicial decisions of national courts, whether viewed as additional evidence of the practice of states or as an independent source of international law, also have had a significant effect upon its development.[2] From the procedural perspective, moreover, the foreign offices and national courts of the various states have been the principal means, the use of force aside, for enforcing legal rights against other states.[3]

The traditional approach outlined in the preceding paragraph, which limited the consideration of domestic institutions to certain government officials in the executive and judicial branches, has been supplemented in recent years by a more sophisticated, policy-oriented analysis of the social and power processes within states. At the highest level of abstraction, this new approach defines the term institution "to refer to the pattern of practices by which values are shaped and shared. Such patterns include . . . both myth and technique, or both rules and operations." [4] Shaping and sharing these values are the participants in the national social and power processes, namely, government officials, political parties, pressure groups, and private associa-

---

[1] Clive Parry, *The Sources and Evidences of International Law* (Manchester 1965), 61–82.

[2] Same, 94–108.

[3] For a description of how a foreign office operates to enforce international rights, see Gordon A. Christenson, "International Claims Procedure Before the Department of State," 13 *Syracuse Law Review*, 527–43 (1962). National courts, of course, adjudicate numerous cases involving foreign states. See, e.g., Frank G. Dawson, "International Law, 1968 Survey of New York Law," 20 *Syracuse Law Review*, 237–57 (1969), discussing international law cases arising in the State of New York during a single year.

[4] Myres S. McDougal, "International Law, Power and Policy: A Contemporary Conception," Hague Academy of International Law, 82 *Recueil des Cours*, 168 (1953).

* This chapter, in slightly revised form, was published previously as "The Proper Role of Domestic Courts in the International Legal Order," 11 *Virginia Journal of International Law*, 9–50 (1970).

tions.[5] Individuals, both by themselves and as members of the above organizations, also participate in these processes.[6]

A comprehensive study of the way in which the power processes of the various states operate within the context of the world power process still awaits writing. Any such study, in the words of McDougal, first must identify participants and then "describe arenas of interaction and influence, methods of access or admission to such arenas, bases of power, practices, and effects."[7] This essay, of course, does not purport to be such a study. Indeed, to invoke an oft-quoted phrase, it is not even "a framework for future inquiry." Rather, taking the participants falling within the broad category of United States government officials,[8] it puts aside such tempting topics as the Office of the Legal Adviser,[9] the numerous other departments and agencies involved in international matters,[10] and such quasi-judicial bodies as the Foreign

[5] Myres S. McDougal, "The Impact of International Law Upon National Law: A Policy-Oriented Perspective," 4 *South Dakota Law Review*, 36–39 (1959), reprinted in Myres S. McDougal and associates, *Studies in World Public Order* (New Haven 1960), 170–173. For a recent restatement of this approach, see Myres S. McDougal, Harold D. Lasswell, and W. Michael Reisman, "The World Constitutive Process of Authoritative Decision," in Richard A. Falk and Cyril E. Black, eds., *The Future of the International Legal Order* (Princeton 1969), I, 81–94.

[6] Individuals often underestimate the contribution that can be made to the international legal order through participation in such organizations. "A large proportion of the people of the world are connected with one or more of these organizations, for they include in their membership nearly all the large churches, trade unions, businessmen's associations, co-operative societies, farmers' groups, and women's organizations, as well as numerous professional, scientific, humanitarian, and social reform organizations. They deal with almost every possible subject from theology to the Olympic Games, from child welfare to astronomy, from cancer to the problems of labor, from aviation to women's rights." Lyman White, "Peace by Pieces—The Role of Nongovernmental Organizations," *The Annals of the American Academy of Political and Social Science*, No. 264 (July 1949), 88.

[7] Myres S. McDougal, "The Comparative Study of Law for Policy Purposes: Value Clarification as an Instrument of Democratic World Order," 1 *American Journal of Comparative Law*, 42 (1952), reprinted in Myres S. McDougal and associates, *Studies in World Public Order*, 969.

[8] That is, "officials established by formal authority . . . who are expected to make the important decisions sustained by community coercion. . . ." Same.

[9] For the authoritative, albeit admittedly uncritical, article on the Office of the Legal Adviser, see Richard B. Bilder, "The Office of the Legal Adviser: The State Department Lawyer and Foreign Affairs," 56 *American Journal of International Law*, 633–84 (1962). A thorough study of the purpose, structure, and recent conduct of this Office is badly needed. Cf. Wolfgang Friedmann, "United States Policy and the Crisis of International Law," 59 *American Journal of International Law*, 857–71 (1965). See generally H. C. L. Merillatt, ed., *Legal Advisers and Foreign Affairs* (Dobbs Ferry 1964).

[10] No adequate survey, much less thorough study, exists of the role of international law in the operations of the United States Government. A questionnaire circulated by the Association of American Law Schools in 1954, which received 59 replies from 24 separate departments and agencies and their subdivisions, revealed that legal questions involving international matters arose frequently. The writer is indebted to Richard W. Edwards, Jr., sometime Assistant Director, American Society of International Law, for a copy of the Association's report, a summary of

Claims Settlement Commission,[11] to examine, it is hoped from a fresh perspective, that old and honorable domestic institution—the domestic court.[12]

There are several reasons for restricting the scope of the present essay to this particular domestic institution. In the first place, given the basic horizontalism of the international community, surprisingly little thoughtful work has actually appeared on the role of domestic courts in the international legal order.[13] Moreover, far too few commentators, much less judges, correctly perceive the domestic court as "an agent of an emerging international system of order, an agent that accords precedence to the norms of international law when these norms come into conflict with the dictates of national policy." [14] Finally, whether domestic courts in the United States, after a long period of "judicial abdication" to the executive branch in cases involving international law issues, can redeem their abandoned prerogatives, while simultaneously accommodating themselves to new limits and standards being prescribed by an increasingly assertive legislative branch, is a question the answer to which may affect the international weight to be accorded future decisions of domestic courts in general.[15]

After setting forth briefly the historical background, this essay will examine the decisions of courts in the United States on three topical international law questions: the immunity of foreign states, the act of state doctrine, and the Vietnam War. From this survey will be drawn some general conclusions about the proper role of domestic courts in the international legal order.

---

which appears in Association of American Law Schools, "Report of the Committee on International Law," *Proceedings* (1955), 199–201.

[11] See, e g., Richard B. Lillich, *International Claims: Their Adjudication by National Commissions* (Syracuse 1962). For a policy-oriented study of French national claims commissions, see Burns H. Weston, *International Claims: Postwar French Practice* (Syracuse 1970).

[12] In keeping with this perspective, no attempt will be made to provide definitive answers to such long-standing doctrinal questions as why "[i]nternational law is part of our law. . . ." The Paquete Habana, 175 U.S. 677, 700 (1900). See fn. 21 below. For an excellent analysis and critique of five suggested answers to this question, see Harold L. Sprout, "Theories as to the Applicability of International Law in the Federal Courts of the United States," 26 *American Journal of International Law,* 280–95 (1932). See also fn. 37.

[13] The singular exception is Richard A. Falk, *The Role of Domestic Courts in the International Legal Order* (Syracuse 1964).

[14] Richard A. Falk, "The Interplay of Westphalia and Charter Conceptions of International Legal Order," in Falk and Black, eds. (fn. 5), I, 69.

[15] "With numerous new states now contributing, however modestly in quantity, to the accumulation of authoritative expression of rules of international law, national courts are one medium by which the values of societies once submerged under European domination can have their influence, good or bad as it may prove, upon the future development of the rules of international law." Lambertus Erades and Wesley L. Gould, *The Relation Between International Law and Municipal Law in The Netherlands and in the United States* (New York 1961), 224. See also Richard A. Falk, *The Status of Law in International Society* (Princeton 1970), 525–26.

## I. The Historical Background

Domestic courts are a place where the claims of the international and national legal orders frequently converge. Given the relatively primitive character of international society, they often "must be relied upon to perform the international function of upholding rights and duties grounded in international law."[16] When they act in this capacity, as unofficial agents of the international legal order, they do so subject to the claims of the particular national legal order that gave them their jurisdictional competence and of which they remain a part.[17] This built-in tension has produced an abundance of doctrinal debate on the relationship between international law and municipal law.[18] The monists, on the one hand, contend that international law should have primacy over municipal law in domestic courts,[19] while the dualists, on the other hand, maintain that municipal law prevails.[20]

Without entering this long-standing debate,[21] it nevertheless is important to an understanding of domestic courts to appreciate the practical impact these theoretical arguments have had on them.[22] This impact can best be seen by tracing the effect of changing concepts upon the doctrine of incorporation in Anglo-American law.[23] This

[16] Erades and Gould (fn. 15), 223.

[17] "Domestic courts are generally understood to be national institutions even when called upon to apply law emanating from extranational sources in private and public international law cases. It is also understood, but not often articulated, that domestic courts function as part of the international legal system: in applying and developing its norms and in giving them effectiveness, publicity, and prestige." Falk (fn. 13), 4 fn. 5.

[18] The literature, all somewhat dated, is collected in Daniel P. O'Connell, *International Law* (London 1965), I, 37 fn. 1. See also Marjorie M. Whiteman, *Digest of International Law* (Washington 1963), I, 103–16.

[19] See generally Hans Kelsen, *Principles of International Law* (rev. edn., New York 1966), Part v.

[20] See, e.g., Lassa F. L. Oppenheim, Introduction to Cyril M Picciotto, *The Relation of International Law to the Law of England and of the United States of America* (New York 1915), 9–12.

[21] See fn. 12. Here the writer fully accepts Falk's approach. "The relationship between national and international authority remains at the core of my inquiry into the proper functioning of domestic courts. However, the relationship is not conceived of as a problem calling for doctrinal reconciliation. It is instead approached as a matter of social and political dynamics—as a search for a conception of domestic judicial function that is broad enough both to acknowledge the national setting and to explain the duty of upholding international law." Falk (fn. 13), 170.

[22] See Edwin D. Dickinson, "Changing Concepts and the Doctrine of Incorporation," 26 *American Journal of International Law*, 239–60 (1932).

[23] "It is an ancient doctrine of the Anglo-American common law that the law of nations is incorporated in and in some sense forms part of the national law. This doctrine had its origin in the acceptance of certain fundamental concepts with respect to the law of nations. As fundamental ideas have changed, there has been a transformation of the doctrine affecting both its theoretical significance and the processes of its practical application. It is impossible to understand either the doctrine or its application without reference to fundamental ideas." Same, 239. For a

doctrine, which holds that the norms of international law are part of the common law, first was articulated by Lord Chancellor Talbot in *Barbuit's Case*, a 1735 decision wherein he reportedly held that "the law of nations (which in its fullest extent was and formed part of the law of *England*) was the rule of decision. . . ." [24] As for the doctrine's origin, Brierly reminds us "of the original conception of international law as simply the law of nature applied to the relations between sovereign princes, and of the fact that the Common Law too professed to be an embodiment of reason. It was natural therefore that judges should think of the two kinds of law not as two unrelated systems, but as the application to different subject-matters of different parts of one great system of law." [25]

Gradually, however, this eighteenth and early nineteenth century natural-law approach to the law of nations gave way before the writings of the positivists, who "conceived of the law of nations as preëminently a law of human institution derived from custom, treaties, and the common understanding of states. . . ." [26] While the English courts retained the rhetoric of incorporation, the substance of the doctrine underwent significant modifications.[27] In contrast with earlier decisions, which made no mention of the requirement of "assent," [28] by the turn of this century English courts were holding that only "that to which we have assented along with other nations in general may properly be called international law. . . ." [29] Thus international law "became a source, rather than an integral part, of the national system." [30] As a mere source, it has validity in domestic courts today only insofar as its principles are adopted by such courts.[31]

---

study of the enforcement of international law through the courts of Germany, Switzerland, France, and Belgium, see Ruth D. Masters, *International Law in National Courts* (New York 1932).

[24] 25 Eng. Rep. 777, 778 (Ch. 1735). Lord Mansfield later ruled in several cases that the law of nations was in full force in England, and that the statute of 7 Anne, c. 12, §3 (1708) granting immunity to foreign diplomats was merely declaratory of the common law. Dickinson (fn. 22), 254–55. Blackstone took the same view in his Commentaries. 4 Blackstone, *Commentaries** 67.

[25] James L. Brierly, *The Law of Nations*, 6th edn. (Oxford 1963), 87.

[26] Dickinson (fn. 22), 250.

[27] Same, 255–59.

[28] "For the judges of those days International Law could rest entirely on an *a priori* basis, or on an *a priori* basis fortified by a modicum of practice. It would seem that they did not require a uniformity of practice even among a substantial majority of States, still less did they require the assent of the State of whose law the international rule under discussion was said to form part." Picciotto (fn. 20), 83.

[29] West Rand Central Gold Mining Co. v. The King, [1905] 2 K.B. 391, 406–07. See Picciotto (fn. 20), 95–103.

[30] Dickinson (fn. 22), 260, citing Picciotto (fn. 20), 105–06: "The true view would seem to be that so far from International Law being in any sense whatever a part of the Common Law of England it is merely a source of law, and that this fundamental confusion between cause and effect has vitiated the whole controversy."

[31] See O'Connell (fn. 18), 50–51.

From the viewpoint of one concerned with the development of general international law norms of universal applicability, this outcome has two major drawbacks. First, by treating international law as just another source of common law, it subjects it to the fatal syllogism that "under the British Constitution an Act of Parliament is paramount; international law is part of the common law, and in a British court any rule of the common law must yield before an Act of Parliament." [32] Second, decisions by English courts on international law questions are subject to the rule of *stare decisis*.[33] "The courts are limited in their power to neglect precedent and apply new or modified international law. Hence, it is possible for English law and international law to take divergent paths." [34] When the possibility of executive intervention in the process of judicial decision is added to these drawbacks,[35] it can be seen that in England the doctrine of incorporation no longer has the significant meaning it once possessed.[36]

In the United States, the doctrine of incorporation followed roughly the same evolutionary path.[37] Unlike England, of course, domestic court decisions had to take into account the relevant provisions of a written Constitution. The key provisions are found in Article I, Section 8, which gives Congress the power "to define and punish piracies and felonies committed on the high seas, and offenses against the law of nations," and "to declare war, grant letters of marque and reprisal, and make rules concerning captures on land and water," and Article

[32] Brierly (fn. 25), 88, citing Mortensen v. Peters [1939] A.C. 160. See Felice Morgenstern, "Judicial Practice and the Supremacy of International Law," 27 *British Yearbook of International Law*, 68–73 (1950).

[33] "[E]nglish courts hold themselves bound to apply English rules about the force of precedents to questions of international law in exactly the same way as they apply them to questions of domestic law, and if there is an English precedent available, no amount of foreign authority will displace it. English courts sometimes seem to the lawyers of other countries to be applying purely English law when they themselves profess to be applying international law." Brierly (fn. 25), 92. See Morgenstern (fn. 32), 80–82.

[34] O'Connell (fn. 18), 59. "This is particularly the case in the law of sovereign immunity, where earlier decisions, allegedly based on international law but which are now seen to have taken a false, or at least outmoded view of it, continue to bind." Same. See the next section of this essay for a discussion of the divergency problem in the sovereign immunity context.

[35] Cf. A. B. Lyons, "The Foreign Office Certificate: Some Recent Tendencies," 33 *British Yearbook of International Law*, 302–10 (1957).

[36] "Indeed, in its modern version, the doctrine . . . means simply that the national law governing matters of international concern is to be derived, in the absence of a controlling statute, executive decision, or judicial precedent, from such relevant principles of the law of nations as can be shown to have received the nation's implied or express assent." Dickinson (fn. 22), 260.

[37] See fn. 12. See generally Picciotto (fn. 20), 109–26. For an excellent two-part treatment of the subject, see Edwin D. Dickinson, "The Law of Nations as Part of the National Law of the United States," 101 *University of Pennsylvania Law Review*, 26–56, 792–833 (1952–53).

II, Section 2, which gives the President the power, with the advice and consent of the Senate, to make treaties. Moreover, Article VI provides that "all treaties made, or which shall be made, under the authority of the United States, shall be the supreme law of the land. . . ." Aside from this last provision, the relation of international law to municipal law is left undetermined.[38]

The first cases decided under the Constitution which raised the question involved federal criminal prosecutions for breaches of President Washington's neutrality proclamations during the early 1790's.[39] As Wright has pointed out, "[t]he contents of these proclamations indicate the belief that breaches of neutrality by individuals could be punished without specific statute, and this view was upheld by the court in the case of Gideon Henfield." [40] However, at Henfield's trial for illegally serving on a French privateer, the jury, despite a charge by the court that breaches of neutrality constituted violations of the law of nations which was part of the common law, "refused to find Henfield guilty largely on account of the popular republican sympathy for revolutionary France." [41] The upshot of this and similar acquittals was the Neutrality Act of 1794,[42] which made such offenses punishable by statute.[43]

Although indictments similar to Henfield's were returned from time

[38] Since it is not essential to the main thrust of the above commentary, the many ramifications of this last provision will not be considered at length. Suffice to say that while a self-executing treaty supersedes inconsistent provisions of an earlier statute, Cook v. United States, 288 U.S. 102 (1933), a subsequent federal statute also will override inconsistent treaty provisions. Reid v. Covert, 354 U.S. 1 (1957). In other words, as between a treaty and a federal statute the last in time prevails. Whitney v. Robertson, 124 U.S. 190 (1888).

[39] Proclamation of April 22, 1793, 11 Stat. 753.

[40] Quincy Wright, *The Enforcement of International Law Through Municipal Law in the United States* (Urbana 1916), 115. "That the first Judiciary Act was intended to give the district and circuit courts of the United States a jurisdiction of crimes at common law and under the Law of Nations as part of the common law is supported in the strongest terms by what we know now of the Act's legislative history. Had the jurisdiction been exercised initially in cases of piracy or ambassadorial privilege, it may be confidently surmised that there would have been no significant opposition on the part of either law or professional critics. As history would have it, however, the initial exercise fell in the more debatable and the much more explosive area of offences against neutrality. In consequence the basic questions of constitutional power and statutory purpose were soon lost to view in the gathering clouds of political controversy." Dickinson (fn. 37), 793.

[41] Wright (fn. 40), 116. See fn. 40. The records of this fascinating case are found in Francis Wharton, *State Trials of the United States* (Philadelphia 1849), 49–89.

[42] Act of June 5, 1794, ch. 50, §1, 1 Stat. 381.

[43] "And though the law of nations had been declared by Chief Justice Jay . . . to be capable of being enforced in the courts of the United States criminally, as well as civilly, without further legislation, yet it was deemed advisable to pass the act in view of controversy over that position. . . ." The Three Friends, 166 U.S. 1, 53 (1897).

to time in the years immediately following the statute's enactment,[44] within two decades the Supreme Court decided, almost by default, that federal courts had no common law jurisdiction in criminal cases.[45] "Thus the premise that individuals might offend against the Law of Nations and become punishable in the federal courts in the administration of a federal common law of crimes, so recently affirmed by framers of the Constitution and implemented by the draftsmen of the first Judiciary Act, came to be somewhat unceremoniously abandoned."[46] Henceforth, to make individuals subject to international law in the criminal context, the courts required a specific statute incorporating the international offense into national law.[47]

On the civil side, at an early date, the courts in the United States invoked international law under the theory that it was part of the country's municipal law.[48] As in England, however, a federal statute was deemed to override inconsistent norms of customary international law.[49] The bluntest restatement of the relation of international and national law undoubtedly is found in *The Over the Top:* "International practice is law only in so far as we adopt it, and like all common or statute law it bends to the will of Congress. . . . There is one ground only upon which a federal court may refuse to enforce an act of Congress and that is when the act is held to be unconstitutional. The act may contravene recognized principles of international comity, but that affords no more basis for judicial disregard of it than it does for executive disregard of it."[50] Furthermore, once again as in England, the doctrine of *stare decisis* provides for the possibility of additional "built-in" provincialism.[51]

The incorporation doctrine, of course, occasionally is supplemented in the United States by legislative provisions requiring domestic courts to apply international law to a case or group of cases. As Jessup observes generally, "[n]o one doubts that the appropriate authorities of

[44] "For some time after the passage of this act there was doubt whether such offenses were not indictable at common law, in the federal courts, in the absence of a specific act. It was only gradually that the doctrine that federal courts enjoy no common law jurisdiction, developed." Wright (fn. 40), 116. Cf. Talbot v. Jansen, 3 U.S. (3 Dall.) 133, 161 (1795).

[45] United States v. Hudson and Goodwin, 11 U.S. (7 Cranch) 32 (1812); United States v. Coolidge, 14 U.S. (1 Wheat.) 415 (1816).

[46] Dickinson (fn. 37), 795.

[47] The statute making piracy a federal crime is a good example. 18 U.S.C. §1651 (1970) (corresponds to Act of March 3, 1819, ch. 77, §5, 3 Stat. 510, 513). See Edwin D. Dickinson, "Is the Crime of Piracy Obsolete?" 38 *Harvard Law Review,* 342–50 (1925).

[48] See, e.g., The Schooner Exchange, 11 U.S. (7 Cranch) 116 (1812). See fn. 12 above.

[49] See, e.g., The Nereide, 13 U.S. (9 Cranch) 388 (1815). See fn. 32 above.

[50] 5 F.2d 838, 842 (D. Conn. 1925). But see fn. 55 below.

[51] Sovereign immunity cases, discussed in the next section, are a good example. See fns. 33 and 34.

a state may by constitutional or legislative enactment direct that this shall be done. Witness the wholesale incorporation of international law by the constitutions of the German Federal Republic, Austria, and other states, and the common statutory enactments of the rules providing for diplomatic immunities." [52] In the United States, Congress during this century has authorized the Court of Claims to decide a case according to international law principles,[53] while its 1885 statute authorizing the same court to adjudicate the many French spoliation claims stated that international law was to be the basis for decision.[54] Cases decided under this act are especially interesting, since they frequently find the court holding that international law prevails over inconsistent federal statutes.[55]

The above cursory examination of the historical relation between international and national law in the domestic courts of England and the United States lends credence to Falk's assertion that "even in advanced countries with long-cherished traditions of judicial independence, it is unclear whether a domestic court is generally free to apply international law in an impartial fashion." [56] The situation is even less clear in many recently independent states.[57] Pending a general survey of judicial practice, this essay seeks both to call the international community's attention to several areas where courts in the United States have muddled international law matters, and to construct from the

[52] Philip C. Jessup, *Transnational Law* (New Haven 1956), 36–37.

[53] Act of March 3, 1927, ch. 463, 44 Stat. 1838. See Royal Holland Lloyd v. United States, 73 Ct. Cl. 722 (1932).

[54] Act of Jan. 20, 1885, ch. 25, §3, 23 Stat. 283. See generally J. H. Toelle, "The Court of Claims: Its Jurisdiction and Principal Decisions Bearing on International Law," 24 *Michigan Law Review*, 686–97 (1926).

[55] In the Schooner Nancy, 27 Ct. Cl. 99, 109 (1892), for instance, the court noted that "[i]t has been urged that a statute of the United States authorized resistance by our merchantmen to French visitation and search, to which there is the simple answer that no single State can change the law of nations by its municipal regulations." See also The Ship Rose, 36 Ct. Cl. 290, 301 (1901), where the court stated that in case of "any conflict between the municipal law of the United States, as exemplified in the statute, and the well-recognized principles of international law, the latter must prevail in the determination of the rights of the parties." "Accord, The Schooner Jane," 37 Ct. Cl. 24, 29 (1901). But see text at fn. 50 above.

[56] Falk (fn. 15), 526. He adds: "Foreign policy and ideological considerations often dominate the domestic legal scene." Same. On this score see the next two sections of this essay.

[57] Falk suggests that "it would be useful to discover whether by constitutional provision or by statute international law is the supreme law of the land and to find out under what circumstances a specific rule of international law must be received by an act of the national legislature as a precondition of its internal validity." Same. The Procedural Aspects of International Law Institute, of which the present writer is Director, has on its agenda a series of books entitled *International Law in National Courts*, which will contain individual essays on the application of international law by the domestic courts of states in Africa, Asia, Europe, and North and South America.

mistakes of these tribunals a workable theory about the proper role of domestic courts in the international legal order.

## II. The Immunity of Foreign States [58]

The international law doctrine of sovereign immunity is generally traced back to Chief Justice Marshall's historic opinion in *The Schooner Exchange*,[59] the landmark case granting immunity to a warship of a friendly foreign power. While this decision is often regarded as simply declarative of "one of the oldest-established principles of international law," [60] actually Marshall broke new ground when, in the absence of any constitutional or statutory provision,[61] he upheld the immunity of a French vessel.[62] His opinion, reflecting common sense reasoning rather than abstract conceptualism, rests upon the belief that "the immunity of a foreign sovereign flows from considerations of comity and practical expediency in friendly international intercourse." [63]

*The Schooner Exchange,* of course, was decided in an era when the "sovereign" activities of a state encompassed far less than they do

[58] The first part of this section is based upon Chapter 1 of *The Protection of Foreign Investment: Six Procedural Studies* (Syracuse 1965), 3–44, in which the present writer's views on sovereign immunity are developed at length and all the recent legal literature on the question is gathered. In addition to articles cited throughout the section, for the best recent literature see Lawrence A. Collins, "The Effectiveness of the Restrictive Theory of Sovereign Immunity," 4 *Columbia Journal of Transnational Law,* 119–50 (1965); Richard C. Pugh and Joseph McLaughlin, "Jurisdictional Immunities of Foreign States," 41 *New York University Law Review,* 25–66 (1966); and K. R. Simmonds, "The Limits of Sovereign Jurisdictional Immunity: The Petrol Shipping Corporation and Victory Transport Cases," 11 *McGill Law Journal,* 291–309 (1965). See also Comment, "Restrictive Sovereign Immunity, the State Department, and the Courts," 62 *Northwestern University Law Review,* 397–427 (1967); and Comment, "Sovereign Immunity of States Engaged in Commercial Activities," 65 *Columbia Law Review,* 1086–1100 (1965).

[59] See fn. 48.

[60] U.N. Conference on the Law of the Sea, Off. Rec., Second Committee, Doc. No. A/Conf. 13/40, at 69 (1958) (U.S.S.R.).

[61] "The immunity of a foreign state is judge-made law. It does not rest on the Constitution or any federal statute." Wacker v. Bisson, 348 F.2d 602, 609 (5th Cir. 1965). In its last sovereign immunity decision, the Supreme Court noted that the doctrine has "become part of the fabric of our law . . . solely through adjudications of this Court." National City Bank v. Republic of China, 348 U.S. 356, 358–59 (1955). See text at fns. 104–121 below for discussion of a proposed statute governing sovereign immunity.

[62] He prefaced his opinion with the following statement: "In exploring an unbeaten path, with few, if any, aids from precedents or written law, the court has found it necessary to rely much on general principles, and on a train of reasoning, founded on cases in some degree analogous to this." 11 U.S. (7 Cranch) at 136. After reviewing the reasons for granting immunity to foreign sovereigns, their diplomats and their armies in transit, he used these old precedents to justify placing the judicial imprimatur upon a new class of immunity case. Same, 145–46.

[63] John G. Hervey, "The Immunity of Foreign States When Engaged in Commercial Enterprises: A Proposed Solution," 27 *Michigan Law Review,* 761 (1929).

today, and when the idea that a sovereign state might engage in ordinary commerce was obviously alien to the international community.[64] Unfortunately, subsequent English decisions extended the rule of the case to situations where the practical considerations which Marshall deemed controlling were not present, or if present existed to a lesser degree.[65] Finally, in *Berizzi Bros. Co. v. S.S. Pesaro*,[66] a 1926 case correctly called "one of the most unfortunate decisions ever made by the Supreme Court," [67] the highest court in the United States, ignoring the Department of State's contention that foreign state-owned vessels engaged in commercial pursuits should be treated like privately owned ships,[68] granted immunity to an Italian government-owned merchant-man.[69] For the past forty-five years, this "absolute" immunity concept has held sway in Anglo-American, if not customary international, law.[70]

A dozen years after sovereign immunity reached its high-water mark in the United States, an undertow commenced. In *Compania Espanola v. Navemar*,[71] the first of a trio of immunity cases to be decided by

[64] Bernard Fensterwald, Jr., "Sovereign Immunity and Soviet State Trading," 63 *Harvard Law Review*, 614 (1950).

[65] In The Parlement Belge, 5 P.D. 197 (1878), a Belgian mail packet, secondarily engaged in transporting merchandise and passengers, was held to have immunity. While the decision represented an extension of The Schooner Exchange, the rationale of the latter did give it some support, since a public function of a foreign sovereign was involved. However, in The Porto Alexandre, [1920] P. 30, the court granted immunity to a Portuguese government-owned merchantman, stating that "[i]t has been held . . . in *The Parlement Belge* that trading on the part of a sovereign does not subject him to any liability to the jurisdiction." Same, 36–37. The effect of this decision was to bestow immunity upon all government ships without regard to whether "comity and practical expediency" necessitated it.

[66] 271 U.S. 562 (1926).

[67] Frederic R. Sanborn, "The Immunity of Government-Owned Merchant Vessels," 39 *American Journal of International Law*, 794 (1945).

[68] Green H. Hackworth, *Digest of International Law* (Washington 1941), II, 437. In light of subsequent developments, it should be noted that the Department of State then took the position that "the questions involved are particularly suitable for determination by Courts, rather than by political departments of the Government." Same, 429.

[69] 271 U.S. at 574. The court, reasoning syllogistically that "public ships" were entitled to immunity, that government-owned merchant vessels were public ships, and that hence such merchant ships might claim immunity, failed to give sufficient consideration to the fact that the doctrine of sovereign immunity "grew up in an age when the operation of merchant vessels by the state was unknown, and when all state-owned or operated ships were in a real sense public vessels, and when there was some excuse for the immunities which were accorded them." J. W. Garner, "Legal Status of Government Ships Employed in Commerce," 20 *American Journal of International Law*, 766–67 (1926).

[70] The latest edition of Oppenheim states that "there are now only a few States which adhere without qualification to the practice of conceding jurisdictional immunities to State-owned ships engaged in commerce." Lassa F. L. Oppenheim, *International Law* (8th edn., London 1955), I, 857. See also Joseph M. Sweeney, *The International Law of Sovereign Immunity* (Washington 1963), 20–23.

[71] 303 U.S. 68 (1938).

the Supreme Court, Chief Justice Stone, after restating the *Pesaro* rule, indicated in dictum a willingness to bestow immunity in all cases where the claim was "recognized and allowed" by the Department of State.[72] Since the Department had not forwarded such a suggestion, however, Stone did not consider the court bound to accept Spain's claim of immunity as conclusive. There being no evidence that the ship actually was in the possession of a foreign state, a prerequisite to immunity according to the *Pesaro,* the court denied it. While paying lip service to precedent, the decision clearly evidences an intention to construe the *Pesaro* holding as strictly as possible.

*Ex parte Peru,*[73] a libel against a Peruvian steamship, afforded the court an excellent opportunity to reconsider the *Pesaro.* Instead, Stone converted his *Navemar* dictum into holding by stating that the Department of State's suggestion of immunity, apparently made in an attempt to follow the decision in *Pesaro,*[74] "must be accepted by the courts as a conclusive determination by the political arm of the Government that the continued retention of the vessel interferes with the proper conduct of our foreign relations."[75] The rationale behind this relinquishment of jurisdiction was the desire not "to embarrass the executive arm of the Government in conducting foreign relations."[76] Presumably this embarrassment would have occurred had the court denied immunity, and had Peru then claimed that such denial violated its rights under international law.[77] Although international law no longer requires immunity in such a case,[78] thus eliminating this possible source of embarrassment, the argument is still used by advocates of executive supremacy in sovereign immunity matters.[79]

The last of the immunity cases decided by the court since *Pesaro,* the case of *Mexico* v. *Hoffman,*[80] also involved a libel in rem, this time against a ship owned by the Mexican government on lease to a private corporation. The Department of State, exercising "courteous neutrality,"[81] submitted a note accepting as true the Mexican claim

---

[72] Same, 74. In the *Pesaro,* it will be recalled, the court had not believed itself bound by a suggestion to deny immunity. See text at fn. 68 above.

[73] 318 U.S. 578 (1943).

[74] American Law Institute, *Restatement (Second) of the Foreign Relations Law of the United States* §69, Reporters' Note 1 at 212–13 (1965). See also §72, Reporters' Note at 226–27 (1965).

[75] 318 U.S. at 589.

[76] Same, 588.

[77] American Law Institute, *Restatement (Second) of the Foreign Relations Law of the United States* §69, Reporters' Note 1 at 215 (1965).

[78] Same. See also text at fn. 70 above.

[79] See, e.g., Michael H. Cardozo, "Comments," 63 *American Society of International Law Proceedings,* 193–94 (1969) [hereinafter cited as *Proceedings*].

[80] 324 U.S. 30 (1945).

[81] Ulen & Co. v. Bank Gospodarstwa Krajowego, 261 App. Div. 1, 4, 24 N.Y.S. 2d 201, 204 (2d Dep't 1940).

of ownership but expressing no opinion about the asserted immunity. Stone, once again writing for the court, declined to grant immunity since such action had not been requested by the Department of State and since the vessel was not in Mexico's possession. Thus the holding reaffirms the *Navemar's* strict interpretation of *Pesaro*.[82] The case is far more important, however, especially for the purposes of this essay, as an illustration of the role now played by the Department of State in the determination of sovereign immunity cases.

In the two prior decisions, Stone had indicated a willingness to be bound by the Department's affirmative suggestion of immunity, believing the question to be an appropriate subject for judicial inquiry only in the absence of such a suggestion. While in *Mexico* v. *Hoffman* he reiterated this view,[83] he unhappily clouded the issue by adding that "it is therefore not for the courts to deny an immunity which our government has seen fit to allow, or to allow an immunity on new grounds which the government has not seen fit to recognize." [84] This further injection of the Department of State into the process of determining and applying the international law rule of sovereign immunity constitutes a complete "judicial abdication" by the court.[85] In the view of most commentators [86] and almost all courts,[87] the refusal by the Department of State to suggest immunity is now considered the equivalent of a binding determination of no immunity.[88] "One can summarize the situation of immunity claims in United States courts," concludes Falk, "by observing that the subject is governed by executive action." [89]

The above exposition is of practical interest only to international lawyers in the United States, but it has a much wider relevance in that

[82] See text following fn. 72.

[83] The opinion states that, "in the absence of recognition of the claimed immunity by the political branch of the government, the courts may decide for themselves whether all the requisites of immunity exist." 324 U.S. at 34–35.

[84] Same, 35.

[85] Philip C. Jessup, "Has the Supreme Court Abdicated One of Its Functions?" 40 *American Journal of International Law*, 168–72 (1945).

[86] See, e.g., Philip C. Jessup, *The Use of International Law* (Ann Arbor 1959), 83.

[87] See, e.g., Amkor Corp. v. Bank of Korea, 298 F.Supp. 143, 144 (S.D.N.Y. 1969).

[88] The Supreme Court, although it has declined to clarify the question, remarked in a 1955 dictum that the Department's "failure or refusal to suggest such immunity has been accorded significant weight by this Court." National City Bank v. Republic of China, 348 U.S. 356, 360 (1955). Lower courts, taking heed, uniformly hold that the Department's view is "conclusive" upon them. Et Ve Balik Kurumu v. B.N.S. Corp., 25 Misc. 2d 299, 301, 204 N.Y.S. 2d 971, 974 (Sup. Ct., N.Y. Co. 1960), 12 *Syracuse Law Review*, 270 *(1960)*. A detailed consideration of the basis and weight of Department of State suggestions of immunity may be found in Lillich (fn. 58), 20–32.

[89] Falk (fn. 13), 164. Or, in blunter words, "with respect to immunities the court agrees to play dead whenever the executive chooses to act." Same, 160.

it also highlights precisely how domestic courts should *not* act when confronted with difficult international law issues. Initially, the Supreme Court in the *Pesaro,* by a mix of Austinian conceptualism and misread national precedent, ignored what even in the 1920's was probably the emerging customary international law norm of restrictive sovereign immunity, opting instead for the doctrine of absolute immunity that had few supporters then and even fewer now.[90] Subsequently, rather than admit its error and get back on the proper jurisprudential course, it attempted to distinguish rather than overrule *Pesaro,* but effectively ended up delegating its functions in sovereign immunity cases to the Department of State. This delegation, apparently unknown elsewhere,[91] has created a host of due process problems nationally.[92] More importantly, however, it has lessened the stature of United States domestic courts in the international community by requiring them to act in sovereign immunity cases as virtual arms of the executive branch of government.

Ironically, the supremacy of the executive in immunity cases became a major problem only in 1952, when the Department of State issued the "Tate Letter" indicating its willingness "to follow the restrictive theory of sovereign immunity in the consideration of requests of foreign governments for a grant of sovereign immunity." [93] "The practical effect of the Tate letter," a leading practitioner has noted, "has been to make the *Pesaro* decision a dead letter," [94] a fact which the Restate-

[90] See fn. 70. Note especially that with respect to ships the Geneva Convention on the Territorial Sea and the Contiguous Zone adopts the restrictive rule. U.N. Doc. No. A/Conf. 13/L.52 (1958), reprinted in 52 *American Journal of International Law,* 834 (1960). See Lillich, "The Geneva Conference on the Law of the Sea and the Immunity of Foreign State-Owned Commercial Vessels," 28 *George Washington Law Review,* 408-20 (1960). The United States ratified this convention, which now has come into force.

[91] An attorney in the Civil Division of the Department of Justice has stated that "[i]t was the Department's experience that the American suggestion practice was unique and [he] knew of no other country, anywhere in the world, where the Executive 'suggests immunity' to the courts and it is considered binding." Bruno A. Ristau, "Remarks," *Proceedings* (fn. 79), 202. The closest practice is in England, where Foreign Office certificates are limited "to questions of fact as distinct from questions of law. It is not for the certificate to say whether the person concerned is entitled to any privilege or immunity, but only to state the relevant facts." Francis Vallat, *International Law and the Practitioner* (Manchester 1966), 59.

[92] A detailed consideration of the due process problems raised by Department of State suggestions of immunity may be found in Lillich (fn. 58), 32-40.

[93] 26 *Department of State Bulletin,* 985 (1952). While the Department "realized that a shift in policy by the executive cannot control the courts," in a fine display of understatement it also perceived "indications that at least some justices of the Supreme Court feel that in this matter courts should follow the branch of the Government charged with responsibility for the conduct of foreign relations." Same. See William W. Bishop, Jr., "New United States Policy Limiting Sovereign Immunity," 47 *American Journal of International Law,* 93-106 (1952).

[94] Sigmund Timberg, "Expropriation Measures and State Trading," 55 *American Society of International Law Proceedings,* 114 (1961).

398 · DOMESTIC INSTITUTIONS

ment recognized when it adopted a rule denying immunity to the commercial activities of foreign states.[95] Numerous lower court cases citing the Tate Letter also attest to the rejection of the absolute sovereign immunity theory by the United States.[96] Yet this very shift in executive policy, designed to free the courts to adjudicate claims against foreign sovereigns in accordance with customary international law, has had the effect of making them even more dependent upon suggestions by the Department of State.

The reason for this development is the fact that the courts, with no backlog of national precedents to guide their decisions under the new restrictive immunity test, have followed the Supreme Court's lead and treated the Department's pronouncements as determinative, despite Jessup's observation that "an abundant jurisprudence in many countries as well as the position of the Department of State itself, attests the validity of the conclusion that the granting or withholding of immunity is a legal question." [97] While the Department's suggestions generally are compatible with customary international law, thus making the courts' reliance upon executive guidance immaterial to the outcome of most cases, the possibility always exists that the Department, for some supposedly overriding reasons of policy, will recommend immunity in a case where none is warranted. This possibility was illustrated most graphically in *Rich* v. *Naviera Vacuba, S.A.*,[98] where the courts considered themselves bound by precedent to follow, without question, an executive suggestion clearly contrary both to international law and to the principles enunciated in the Tate Letter.[99]

[95] American Law Institute, *Restatement (Second) of the Foreign Relations Law of the United States* §69 (1965).

[96] The most important of these cases are Victory Transport Inc. v. Comisaria General de Abastecimientos y Transportes, 336 F.2d 354 (2d Cir. 1964), cert. denied, 381 U.S. 934 (1965), and Petrol Shipping Corp. v. Kingdom of Greece, 360 F.2d 103 (2d Cir.), cert. denied, 385 U.S. 931 (1966), discussed in K. R. Simmonds (fn. 58), 291–309. See Note, "The American Law of Sovereign Immunity Since the Tate Letter," 4 *Virginia Journal of International Law*, 75–97 (1964). Additional cases may be found in the articles on "International Law" which have appeared since 1965 in the annual *Survey of New York Law* published by the Syracuse Law Review.

[97] Jessup (fn. 86), 83.

[98] 295 F.2d 24 (4th Cir. 1961), affirming 197 F.Supp. 710 (E.D. Va. 1961). The Supreme Court denied applications for a stay on September 11, 12, and 14, 1961. "The Chief Justice, in denying the applications for a stay . . . , relied on the classic sovereign immunity decisions of this Court, endorsing on the papers 'Application for stay denied. See *Ex Parte Peru*, 318 U.S. 578, and *Republic of Mexico* v. *Hoffman*, 324 U.S. 30.' " Petition for Writ of Certiorari, p. 19, Banco Nacional de Cuba v. Sabbatino, 376 U.S. 398 (1964).

[99] For a critique of this international legal monstrosity, see Lillich (fn. 58), 17–20. Cardozo, whose article contains the best arguments advanced to date for giving the executive "almost absolute control" over sovereign immunity cases, justifies the decision as a proper application of "the rule of law that provides for sovereign immunity when required in the interest of comity and denies the immunity when it would not serve that interest." Michael H. Cardozo, "Judicial Deference to State

The concept of judicial deference, as exemplified by the decision in *Rich,* reminds Falk of "a notion developed by men who are skeptical about the role of law as a regulator of international matters, for what could be more embarrassing to the development of the habits of law than a bland endorsement of an inconsistent pattern of disposition?" [100] Judicial self-reliance, on the other hand, reaffirms the commitment by the United States to settle disputes, at least in the domestic court context, according to international law norms. While the present writer's observation that the courts "are not anxious to rethink their views on the subject" still holds true,[101] remedial action by Congress no longer appears as remote as it did a half-dozen years ago.[102] Indeed, a proposed statute now being considered within the executive branch would wipe away the cobwebs of judicial deference that have gathered during the past quarter-century and, with appropriate revisions to be suggested below, would restore to the courts of the United States their abdicated role as expositors of the international law of sovereign immunity.[103]

The draft statute, which generated a lively debate at the 1969 Annual Meeting of the American Society of International Law,[104] "would make foreign states answerable in the courts of the United States for activities carried on in the United States or having a direct effect in this country in the same manner that private persons or firms are

---

Department Suggestions: Recognition of Prerogative or Abdication to Usurper?" 48 *Cornell Law Quarterly,* 471 (1963). See also fn. 79 above.

[100] Falk (fn. 13), 161.

[101] Lillich (fn. 58), 41. "If and when the State Department concludes that a foreign Nation is entitled to Sovereign Immunity that determination, we repeat, is conclusive no matter how unwise or, in a particular case how unfair or unjust the Department's determination appears to be (a) to injured American citizens and (b) to vast numbers of the American people and (c) to our Courts. . . ." Chemical Natural Resources, Inc. v. Republic of Venezuela, 420 Pa. 134, 147, 215 A. 2d 864, 869–70, cert. denied, 385 U.S. 822 (1966). For an excellent comment upon this case, see Note, 51 *Cornell Law Quarterly,* 845–53 (1966).

[102] For a discussion supporting in principle remedial legislation like S. 1894, 89th Cong., 1st Sess. (1965), first introduced by Senator Ervin in 1962, see Lillich (fn. 58), 40–44. Of course, pleas to Congress for the enactment of a statute abolishing or limiting the immunity of foreign sovereigns are not new. See, e.g., Sanborn (fn. 67), 28; Hervey (fn. 63), 774–75; Note, "Sovereign Immunity for Commercial Instrumentalities of Foreign Governments," 58 *Yale Law Journal,* 182 (1948). See also Comment, "The American Doctrine of Sovereign Immunity: An Historical Analysis," 13 *Villanova Law Review,* 603 (1968).

[103] The statute, appended to a perceptive article by its drafter, may be found in Andreas F. Lowenfeld, "Claims Against Foreign States—A Proposal for Reform of United States Law," 44 *New York University Law Review,* 936–38 (1969). It differs only slightly from an earlier draft made available to the present writer on a confidential basis. Letter from Murray J. Belman, Deputy Legal Adviser, Department of State, to Richard B. Lillich, Aug. 8, 1968.

[104] Panel, "New Departures in the Law of Sovereign Immunity," *Proceedings* (fn. 79), 182–203.

answerable for such activities." [105] Specifically, it would permit actions against a foreign state, or an agency or instrumentality of a foreign state, upon:

> (1) an express or implied contract entered into, to be performed, or arising out of transactions in the United States; or
>
> (2) a claim for personal injury or death or damage to property caused by an act or omission of any officer, agent, or employee of such foreign state while acting within the scope of his office, agency, or employment within the United States, its territories or possessions,
>
> under circumstances where the foreign state, agency, or instrumentality, if a private person, would be subject to suit in accordance with the law of the place where the action is brought. [106]

All other actions, "and in particular those relating to political acts of foreign states or to activities occurring outside the jurisdiction of the United States, would be barred." [107]

Of key importance is the draft statute's authorization of service of process by mail. [108] "Commencement of actions against foreign states," according to its drafter, "would be by the simple means of the clerk of court serving a summons and complaint by registered mail upon the foreign state's embassy or other representation in the United States." [109] As a partial *quid pro quo* for this liberalization, the statute eliminates the right to attach the property of foreign states in order to obtain jurisdiction, [110] and codifies the present practice of prohibiting the attachment of such property for purposes of execution of final judgments. [111] These procedural innovations combine to permit the most startling and welcome development of all, namely, the removal of "the State Department from a decision-making rôle in sovereign immunity cases." [112] Needless to say, this long-overdue attempt to reorder "the

---

[105] Lowenfeld (fn. 103), 902–03.

[106] Same, 937.

[107] Same, 903. See fn. 117 below.

[108] Same, 937.

[109] Same, 903. "Under the new procedure service on the foreign government would serve a notice function only. Therefore, service could be sent to foreign Ambassadors in Washington or to the foreign capital itself." Murray J. Belman, "New Departures in the Law of Sovereign Immunity," *Proceedings* (fn. 79), 186.

[110] Lowenfeld (fn. 103), 937. This innovation has been the subject of criticism. See Monroe Leigh, "New Departures in the Law of Sovereign Immunity," *Proceedings* (fn. 79), 188.

[111] Lowenfeld (fn. 103), 937. This codification also has been the subject of criticism. See Leigh, *Proceedings* (fn. 79), 192–93. Cf. Lowenfeld (fn. 103), 926–29.

[112] Belman, *Proceedings* (fn. 79), 186. "[I]f attachment and execution are no longer permitted, there would seem to be no need for the Executive Branch to intervene in the judicial process." Lowenfeld (fn. 103), 930.

law of sovereign immunity on more rational and less feudalistic lines"[113] has met in principle with almost unanimous approval.[114]

While this effort at reform warrants strong support, it nevertheless must be noted that in rectifying one problem the draft statute creates another. It immunizes domestic courts from executive intervention, true, but it also supplants customary international law with a unilateral legislative standard to be applied in actions against foreign states.[115] In so doing the statute seriously misperceives what the role of domestic courts should be. Legislative intervention through the prescription of so-called international law norms, rightly criticized in the case of the Sabbatino Amendment, is no less undesirable than executive intervention through the "suggestion" technique.[116] Under the statute as presently worded, the defense of sovereign immunity might be available in some instances where it is not now,[117] and certainly would be denied foreign states in other situations where it is now allowed.[118] Consequently, as a practical matter both plaintiffs and foreign states might have occasion to protest the statute's departure from international law norms.

Granted the difficulties in applying the restrictive theory of sovereign immunity in practice,[119] it remains the customary international law norm, and its replacement by a statutory standard, no matter how enlightened, would be an unfortunate and retrogressive development.[120] "Why," asks Sweeney about the draft statute, "is the Legal

[113] Leigh, *Proceedings* (fn. 79), 187.

[114] See fn. 104. But see Cardozo, *Proceedings* (fn. 79), 193–94.

[115] See text at fn. 106 above. "The proposal would modify the standards now applied in sovereign immunity cases. . . ." Belman, *Proceedings* (fn. 79), 185.

[116] See the discussion in the next section at fns. 180–184. "In effect, the proposal would scrap customary international law to the extent such law is not consonant with the statute's standard. If we are going to object in the case of the Hickenlooper [Sabbatino] Amendment to a unilateral pronouncement on matters of international law, instructing our courts to apply a certain rule, then consideration should be given to the same problem here. Mr. Belman cites customary international law to support the statute's granting immunity from execution. Perhaps, then, it would be wise to use customary international law to determine immunity from suit as well." Richard B. Lillich, "Comments," *Proceedings* (fn. 79), 195.

[117] E.g., in the case of an intentional as opposed to a negligent tort. Same, 195. See Samuel A. Bleicher, "Remarks," same, 196–97. See also Lowenfeld (fn. 103), 916.

[118] "We do not believe that the new standards would not [sic] require foreign governments to defend themselves in a substantial number of new cases. Most contract cases now fall within the commercial side of the Tate letter dichotomy, and tort claims against foreign governments are infrequent. Foreign governments may even appreciate the rationality that the new standards would bring." Belman, *Proceedings* (fn. 79), 185.

[119] See Lowenfeld (fn. 103), 906–07, 914–15. Compare Leigh, *Proceedings* (fn. 79), 187.

[120] In addition to the basic objection raised at fn. 116 above, a statutory standard of necessity would "freeze" the ability of domestic courts to reflect changes in international practice. See Remarks from the Floor, *Proceedings* (fn. 79), 201.

Adviser's Office so afraid of international law?"[121] There has been no convincing explanation to date, just as there has been no persuasive argument advanced in favor of the statutory standard.[122] Hence, one must hope that before Congress acts the draft statute will be revised to make customary international law the basis for decision.[123] This step will guarantee United States courts complete autonomy in the sovereign immunity decision-making process for the first time in many years, thereby restoring them to their rightful role in the creation and application of international law in this area.

## III. THE ACT OF STATE DOCTRINE [124]

Under the "act of state doctrine," courts in the United States have refused to inquire into the validity of certain acts of foreign states, whether alleged to violate the municipal law of the foreign state or the public policy of the United States,[125] on the ground that by applying the foreign state's law as "a rule for their decision" [126] they prevent disturbance of the peace of nations.[127] The Supreme Court acknowledged the doctrine in a sovereign immunity case, *Underhill* v. *Hernan-*

[121] Joseph M. Sweeney, "Remarks," *Proceedings* (fn. 79), 198. "He submitted that there is sufficient guidance offered by the international law cases on this point, and a viable rule of law may be culled from these cases." Same. See fn. 70 above.

[122] See Lowenfeld (fn. 103), 914–21.

[123] Lillich, *Proceedings* (fn. 79), 200–01. "Mr. John Wolff observed that the question of sovereign immunity is deemed to be one of customary international law in Europe, not a question of policy, and to be answered by the courts. Thus, the proposal is only partially consonant with this practice, since, although it delegates to the courts the power to render decisions they should have been making all along, it dictates the standards to be applied. Query: Why not delegate the power without strings?" *Proceedings* (fn. 79), 199.

[124] The first part of this section is based upon Chapter 11 of Lillich (fn. 58), 45–113, in which the present writer's views on the act of state doctrine are developed at length and all the relevant legal literature on the question is gathered. The literature since 1965, to quote Dickinson in another context, "includes some things provocative, more that is merely informative and much that is likely to impress a practitioner as having become incautiously confused." Edwin D. Dickinson, "The Law of Nations as National Law: 'Political Questions,'" 104 *University of Pennsylvania Law Review*, 452 (1956). In addition to a monograph by Eugene F. Mooney, *Foreign Seizures: Sabbatino and the Act of State Doctrine* (Kentucky 1967), 62 *American Journal of International Law*, 800–01 (1968), and articles cited throughout the section, for the best recent literature compare Myres S. McDougal, "Act of State in Policy Perspective: The International Law of an International Economy," in Southwestern Legal Foundation, ed., *Private Investors Abroad—Structures and Safeguards* (New York 1966), 327–59, with Louis Henkin, "Act of State Today: Recollections in Tranquility," 6 *Columbia Journal of Transnational Law*, 175–89 (1967). See also Stanley G. Mazaroff, "An Evaluation of the Sabbatino Amendment as a Legislative Guardian of American Private Investment Abroad," 37 *George Washington Law Review*, 788–815 (1969).

[125] See American Law Institute, *Restatement (Second) of the Foreign Relations Law of the United States* §41, comments f and g at 129–30 (1965).

[126] Ricaud v. American Metal Co., 246 U.S. 304, 309 (1918).

[127] Oetjen v. Central Leather Co., 246 U.S. 297, 304 (1918).

*dez,*[128] where Chief Justice Fuller prefaced his opinion with the following dictum: "Every sovereign State is bound to respect the independence of every other sovereign State, and the courts of one country will not sit in judgment on the acts of the government of another done within its own territory."[129] While variations of the doctrine have been applied by the courts of a few other countries,[130] it is not a rule of public international law,[131] but "a principle of judicial self-restraint and deference to the rôle of the executive or political branch of government in the field of foreign affairs."[132]

Recently, foreign nationalizations have given rise to many act of state cases. In the typical case, a foreign state takes the property of a United States national located within its territory and transfers it to a third party, who subsequently brings the property into the United States. If courts in the United States applied the act of state doctrine, an action by the former owner against the third party to recover the property would be dismissed without consideration of the international validity of the property seizure. Some courts[133] and most commentators,[134] however, have taken the position that the doctrine does not preclude a domestic court from examining the validity of foreign nationalization laws and decrees under international law. This view, which received substantial support in 1959 from a well-known report by the Committee on International Law of the Association of the Bar of the City of New York,[135] was acknowledged in 1962 by the proposed draft of the American Law Institute's Restatement of the Foreign Relations Law of the United States.[136] By this time, of course, *Banco Nacional de Cuba* v. *Sabbatino,* undoubtedly one of the most impor-

---

[128] 168 U.S. 250 (1897).

[129] Same, 252.

[130] See American Law Institute, *Restatement (Second) of the Foreign Relations Law of the United States* §41, Reporters' Note No. 1 at 134–35 (1965).

[131] Same, §41, Reporters' Note No. 4 at 135–37 (1965). "No international tribunal has ever held a refusal to apply the 'act of state' doctrine to be a violation of international law, and there has been no diplomatic protest against a judicial decision which has failed to apply it." J. Anthony Kline, "An Examination of the Competence of National Courts to Prescribe and Apply International Law: *The Sabbatino Case Revisited,*" 1 *University of San Francisco Law Review,* 128 (1966).

[132] International Law Association, *Report of the Fiftieth Conference* (Brussels 1962), 155.

[133] A collection of cases may be found in the opinion of the Court of Appeals in Banco Nacional de Cuba v. Sabbatino, 307 F.2d 845, 855 n. 6 (2d Cir. 1962).

[134] A list of authorities may be found in the opinion of the District Court in Banco Nacional de Cuba v. Sabbatino, 193 F.Supp. 375, 380 n. 7 (S.D. N.Y. 1961).

[135] Association of the Bar of the City of New York, Committee on International Law, *A Reconsideration of the Act of State Doctrine in United States Courts* (New York 1959), 11.

[136] American Law Institute, *Restatement (Second) of the Foreign Relations Law of the United States,* Explanatory Notes §44, comment b at 145 (Proposed Official Draft 1962).

tant international law cases to be decided by a domestic court in this century, was already working its way up through the Federal courts.

In the District Court for the Southern District of New York, Judge Dimock, after balancing the reasons for refusing to examine the validity under international law of a Cuban nationalization decree against the reasons supporting such examination, reached the "inescapable" conclusion that "the decree . . . is subject to examination in the light of principles of international law." [137] Although his opinion did not expressly adopt the Restatement's tentative position, the latter's rationale is apparent in it.[138] Moreover, the opinion, refusing to follow the "green light" theory of the *Bernstein* cases,[139] where the Court of Appeals for the Second Circuit held that it would not invoke the act of state doctrine when the Department of State had shown a "positive intent" to relax its application, expressly avoided making domestic courts mere "conduits for the fulfillment of executive policy." [140] At the same time the decision raised hopes "that individuals injured by foreign acts of state in violation of international law might more often obtain a day in court," [141] thereby contributing to the clarification of international law on such questions as nationalization.

Upon appeal to the Court of Appeals for the Second Circuit, the decision of the District Court was affirmed.[142] The affirmance, however, turned out to be a pyrrhic victory,[143] since Judge Waterman's opinion exchanged the international law for the *Bernstein* exception as the basis for permitting the consideration of the case on its merits.[144] Effectively, then, the District Court's broad exception to the act of state doctrine, based upon an alleged violation of international law, was replaced by a much narrower exception conditioned upon the permission of the Department of State. This shift was rationalized on the ground that the wholesale examination of foreign acts of state might occasionally embarrass the executive in its conduct of foreign affairs.[145] The argument, one of the most overrated in the annals of American legal history, is no more appealing in the context of the act of state

[137] 193 F.Supp. at 382.

[138] See Lillich (fn. 58), 51–54.

[139] Bernstein v. Van Heyghen Freres S.A., 163 F.2d 246 (2d Cir.), cert. denied, 332 U.S. 772 (1947); Bernstein v. Nederlandsche-Amerikaansche Stoomvaart-Maatschappij, 210 F.2d 375 (2d Cir. 1954).

[140] Falk (fn. 13), 95 fn. 95.

[141] Association of the Bar of the City of New York (fn. 135), 15.

[142] 307 F.2d 845 (2d Cir. 1962).

[143] See Richard B. Lillich, "A Pyrrhic Victory at Foley Square: The Second Circuit and *Sabbatino*," 8 *Villanova Law Review*, 155–76 (1963).

[144] 307 F.2d at 857–58. For a critique of Judge Waterman's use of *Bernstein*, see Lillich (fn. 58), 61–67.

[145] For a well-presented yet unpersuasive argument to this effect, see Stanley D. Metzger, *International Law, Trade and Finance* (Dobbs Ferry 1962), 66–77.

doctrine than it is when the question of sovereign immunity is involved.[146] Toleration of executive intervention, as Falk warns, "is itself a deprecation of the commitment to international law. The prestige of international law in domestic courts is undermined if its application depends upon a prior political authorizaton." [147]

When the case reached the Supreme Court, Mr. Justice Harlan, writing for a majority of eight, quoted "the classic American statement of the act of state doctrine" [148] from *Underhill v. Hernandez*,[149] surveyed later decisions including *Oetjen* and *Ricaud*,[150] and concluded that "none of this Court's subsequent cases in which the act of state doctrine was directly or peripherally involved manifest any retreat from *Underhill*." [151] Noting that the decision by the Court of Appeals relied upon the *Bernstein* exception, the Supreme Court expressly stated that if any such exception existed it did not apply to the facts of *Sabbatino*.[152] The case turned, therefore, upon whether the Court accepted either of the other two contentions advanced against the doctrine's application: (1) that it did not apply to acts of state which violated international law; or (2) that it was inapplicable unless the executive branch specifically interposed it in a particular case.

Commendably, Mr. Justice Harlan's decision, although noting that "the plain implication of all these opinions . . . is that the act of state doctrine is applicable even if international law has been violated," did not apply "the wisdom of the precedents" mechanically. Indeed, it acknowledged that the doctrine's continuing validity depended upon its capacity to meet present needs. Balancing the "relevant considerations," the Court rejected claims of an absolute act of

146 For a discussion of this argument in the sovereign immunity context, see the previous section. Domke has cautioned that in this area too "the courts should not abdicate their function to determine the private rights of American citizens, irrespective of the attitude the government has to take, the latter being guided by expediency which may be justified under existing political circumstances." Martin Domke, "The Present American Attitude Towards Nationalization of Foreign-Owned Property," 1963 *Duke Law Journal*, 289–90.

147 Falk (fn. 13), 93. Despite the fact that he found the Second Circuit's opinion to be "a distinct improvement over Judge Dimock's opinion with regard to the external or foreign relations aspects of the case," Falk nevertheless agreed that "in the matter of the proper character of executive-judicial relations in an international law case—the internal aspects— . . . [t]he ideal of judicial independence is shamelessly sacrificed without any development of defensive or limiting principles." Same, 116, 116–17.

148 376 U.S. 398, 416 (1964).

149 See text at fns. 128–129.

150 See fns. 126–127.

151 376 U.S. at 416.

152 "This Court has never had occasion to pass upon the so-called *Bernstein* exception, nor need it do so now. For whatever ambiguity may be thought to exist in the two letters from State Department officials on which the Court of Appeals relied . . . is now removed by the position which the Executive has taken in this Court on the act of state claim. . . ." Same, 420; see also 436.

state doctrine and reached a narrower holding, a holding covering only those acts which involve the taking of property.[153]

> Therefore, rather than laying down or reaffirming an inflexible and all-encompassing rule in this case, we decide only that the Judicial Branch will not examine the validity of a taking of property within its own territory by a foreign sovereign government, extant and recognized by this country at the time of suit, in the absence of a treaty or other unambiguous agreement regarding controlling legal principles, even if the complaint alleges that the taking violates customary international law.[154]

Finding a lack of consensus on the controlling legal principles involved in *Sabbatino,* the Court applied the act of state doctrine and reversed the decision of the Court of Appeals.[155]

What the Court did, then, was to adopt Falk's consensus argument, which mandates the application of the doctrine unless "the subject matter of dispute is governed by substantive norms of international law that are adhered to by an overwhelming majority of international actors." [156] Although the Court's approach to ascertaining the presence or lack of consensus may be faulted on various grounds,[157] the real defect in its opinion, noted by Mr. Justice White in his able dissent, is the fact that it completely "ignores the historic role which this Court and other American courts have played in applying and main-

[153] Writers with such opposite viewpoints as John R. Stevenson, "The State Department and Sabbatino—'Ev'n Victors Are by Victories Undone,'" 58 *American Journal of International Law,* 707 (1964), and Richard A. Falk, "The Complexity of Sabbatino," 58 *American Journal of International Law,* 935 (1964), agree on this point. But see Interamerican Refining Corp. v. Texaco Maracaibo, Inc., 307 F. Supp. 1291, 1299 (D. Dela. 1970).

[154] 376 U.S. at 428.

[155] "It should be apparent that the greater the degree of codification or consensus concerning a particular area of international law, the more appropriate it is for the judiciary to render decisions regarding it, since the courts can then focus on the application of an agreed principle to circumstances of fact rather than on the sensitive task of establishing a principle not inconsistent with the national interest or with international justice." Same.

[156] Falk (fn. 13), 9. Falk argues that "rules of deference applied by domestic courts advance the development of international law faster than does an indiscriminate insistence upon applying challenged substantive norms in order to determine the validity of the official acts of foreign states." Same, 6–7. "Rather than risk the bias of decentralized review," he contends, "it is preferable to insist upon deference, relying upon diplomatic pressure and supranational review for the application of substantive standards of international law." Same, 106. Compare Kline (fn. 131), 89: "Why this should be so is left unexplained. One would think that the insulation of the judiciary from the political demands of special interests, and the judicial experience in clarifying long-range interests would make the courts the most dispassionate of all possible decision-makers. 'Institutionalized bias,' if and when it exists at all, is far more likely to be found in political than in judicial decision-making."

[157] See Lillich (fn. 58), 81–85.

taining principles of international law." [158] Of course, as the Court points out, domestic court decisions are a patchwork process and often conflict with each other, but from such stuff is customary international law made and modified.[159] Indeed, by refusing to clarify and apply the relevant international law standards, the Court actually perpetuates the supposed lack of consensus so damaging to customary international law.[160] Its decision creates expectations throughout the world, expectations which unfortunately will work in many areas to undercut the international standard in this area.[161] "The impact of the decision and reasoning, at a time when we have only the rudiments of an international judiciary," concludes McDougal, "can only be to embarrass and minimize the indispensable role of national courts in the making and application of international law." [162]

Having disposed, to its own satisfaction, of the international law exception to the act of state doctrine, the Court turned next to the second contention, namely, that the doctrine should be applied only "when the Executive Branch expressly stipulates that it does not wish the courts to pass on the question of validity." [163] This "reverse-twist *Bernstein* exception," [164] first recommended as the Court notes by the

[158] 376 U.S. at 458. In McDougal's more sprightly phraseology, "it forsook the historic, creative role of the Supreme Court for the expression of timid and suicidal conceptions." Myres S. McDougal, "Comments," 58 *American Society of International Law Proceedings*, 49 (1964).

[159] "Although foreign courts, in passing on expropriation decrees, have not yet arrived at a demonstrable consensus, the majority's argument overlooks the fact that the only likely alternative is a collection of still more divergent and conflicting statements by various foreign offices. Indeed, it seems likely that the availability of opinions from municipal courts would aid the International Court of Justice if it were ever called upon to review an expropriation case." Note, "The Supreme Court 1963 Term," 78 *Harvard Law Review*, 303–04 (1964). See Robert Y. Jennings, "Comments," in Lyman M. Tondel, Jr., ed., *The Aftermath of Sabbatino* (Dobbs Ferry 1965), 88–89. For "numerous other circumstances [where] our courts have applied rules of international law, many of which were far from certain or universally accepted at the time," see Carlyle E. Maw, "Application of International Law in United States Courts—Immunity of States and the Act of State Doctrine," in Southwestern Legal Foundation, ed., *Rights and Duties of Private Investors Abroad* (New York 1965), 393–94.

[160] See F. A. Mann, "The Legal Consequences of *Sabbatino*," 51 *Virginia Law Review*, 625 (1965). According to Jennings (fn. 159), 94, "the emphasis that the Supreme Court put upon consensus seems to me to be altogether too positivist a notion of international law—one that stems indeed from the nineteenth century rather than the twentieth."

[161] "If the courts of the leading power of the free world support by their silence or by their jurisprudential verbiage the notion that there is no international law, they certainly lend no support to the Department of State when it seeks to protect American interests abroad." Jessup (fn. 86), 85.

[162] McDougal (fn. 124), 341–42.

[163] 376 U.S. at 436.

[164] Stanley D. Metzger, "Act-of-State Doctrine Refined: The Sabbatino Case," [1964] *Supreme Court Review*, 241. For discussion of the *Bernstein* exception, which the Court found inapplicable, see fns. 139–140 and 152 above.

Association of the Bar of the City of New York,[165] was also rejected by Mr. Justice Harlan, citing "representations of the Government that such a reversal of the Bernstein principle would work serious inroads on the maximum effectiveness of United States diplomacy." [166] Although this argument, for changing the *Bernstein* presumption of non-review in the absence of an executive "green light" to a presumption of review unless a "red light" was signaled subsequently, would be deemed persuasive by Congress, it found no favor with the Court. "We do not now pass on the Bernstein exception," wrote Mr. Justice Harlan, "but even if it were deemed valid, its suggested extension is unwarranted." [167]

The reaction to the Supreme Court's decision in *Sabbatino* was swift. Although some commentators supported the Court's reformulation of the act of state doctrine, most observers agreed with McDougal that "[t]he doctrine of automatic, blanket abstention announced by the Court is clearly a new, and bizarre, creation." [168] Since even supporters of the decision recognized "the authority of Congress to deal with Act of State under its foreign affairs power," [169] numerous international lawyers urged the enactment of a statute embodying an international law exception to the doctrine.[170] Perhaps because the specter of Cuba lurked in the background, Congressional support proved easier to mobilize than when sovereign immunity reform was at issue. In any event, within eight months after the Supreme Court had spoken a statute was pushed through Congress adopting, in substance, the international law exception approach originally advocated by the Association of the Bar of the City of New York.[171] The wheel had come full circle.

The vehicle used to accomplish this speedy reversal of *Sabbatino* was the Foreign Assistance Act of 1964. To this act Senator Hickenlooper proposed a new amendment providing that no court in the United States should decline, on the ground of the federal act of state doctrine, to determine on its merits any case in which an act of a

---

[165] See fn. 135.

[166] 376 U.S. at 436.

[167] Same. See fn. 172 below.

[168] McDougal (fn. 124), 341. "Professor Falk's conclusion amounts to a repudiation of the historic role of domestic courts as clarifiers and promoters of the long-range common interest of all peoples, and a repudiation as well of the process of customary prescription of law." Kline (fn. 131), 85.

[169] Louis Henkin, "The Foreign Affairs Power of the Federal Courts: *Sabbatino*," 64 *Columbia Law Review*, 821 (1964).

[170] See, e.g., John G. Laylin, "Holding Invalid Acts Contrary to International Law—A Force Toward Compliance," 58 *American Society of International Law Proceedings*, 36–39 (1964).

[171] 78 Stat. 1013 (1964), 22 U.S.C. §2370(e)(2) (1970).

foreign state was alleged to be in violation of international law, subject only to "the reverse-twist *Bernstein* exception that was specifically rejected by the Court." [172] "The effect of the amendment," according to the Senate Foreign Relations Committee, was merely "to achieve a reversal of presumptions." [173] To the person whose property has been taken this reversal makes all the difference in the world. Instead of having to wait in vain for an executive "green light," he is assured his day in court unless the executive, for overriding reasons of national policy, flashes a "red light" in his particular case.[174]

While the Sabbatino Amendment is a vast improvement over the Supreme Court's decision, it must be reiterated that it only modifies the decision in the matter of presumptions, with the courts now being able to consider the international validity of foreign acts of state in the absence of an executive veto.[175] Thus the amendment, unlike Judge Dimock's opinion, does not read out the possibility of executive intervention.[176] On the other hand, the amendment is much preferable on this score to the decision of the Second Circuit, under which executive approval rather than an alleged violation of international law became the key to judicial freedom of inquiry.[177] Nevertheless, as the present writer urged immediately after the amendment's enactment, the provision allowing executive intervention should be excised,[178] since in Falk's words it "tends to politicize the courts and to reinforce their image as nationalized decision-making tribunals." [179]

[172] Metzger (fn. 164), 242.

[173] S. Rep. No. 1188, 80th Cong., 2d Sess. 24 (1964).

[174] "We are perfectly prepared to leave to the discretion of the President the decision as to whether the foreign policy interests of the United States require that a private litigant be denied his day in court and that the court be denied the ability to apply principles of international law in such a case. What we are not willing to do is to leave it as an inflexible presumption that the courts are absolutely precluded from making an inquiry into the validity of an uncompensated foreign taking when no one in the Government has even taken the trouble to determine whether the litigation would impinge upon the foreign policy interests of the Government." 110 *Congressional Record*, 19548 (daily edn., Aug. 14, 1964) (Senator Hickenlooper).

[175] Same, 19547. To the extent that the Sabbatino decision eliminated the possibility of an executive veto when a consensus existed, the amendment modifies the decision on this score too.

[176] See text at fns. 139–140.

[177] See text at fns. 143–147.

[178] Lillich (fn. 58), 112–13.

[179] Richard A. Falk, "The Sabbatino Controversy," in Lyman M. Tondel, Jr., ed., *The Aftermath of Sabbatino* (Dobbs Ferry 1965), 51. Falk realistically recommends that the executive branch be required "to formulate in advance some principles to govern the use of the power to intervene. The court will then, at least, be in a position to review adherence by the Executive to these principles. The use of such a set of principles will also give the entire process of Executive intervention less of an *ad hoc* appearance." Same. His preference, however, is "to go further and leave the option of Executive intervention completely out of the statute." Same.

The Sabbatino Amendment also contains another major flaw, a flaw similar to one found in the draft statute governing sovereign immunity.[180] The amendment defines "the principles of international law" that the courts are to apply to include "the principles of compensation and other standards set out in this subsection," thereby incorporating the standards which the 1962 Hickenlooper Amendment enjoins the President to follow when determining whether to suspend foreign aid to a country which has taken United States property.[181] These standards, especially insofar as they require the payment of full compensation in convertible foreign exchange, clearly exceed the requirements of customary international law.[182] Undoubtedly this provision, which instructs courts in the United States to follow Congress's parochial view of customary international law when invoking what purports to be an international law exception, is the weakest and least desirable one in the Sabbatino Amendment. It deprives the courts of their right to apply and develop international law, as they have been able to do occasionally in sovereign immunity cases, and it mocks the efforts of persons "who supported the Amendment in the hope that it marked a step toward, not away from, the rule of international law in American courts and the world community."[183] The provision should be eliminated at the earliest possible opportunity if the opinions of courts in the United States on the validity of foreign acts of state are to carry any international weight.[184]

The Sabbatino Amendment has withstood attack on various constitutional grounds,[185] and has been applied and interpreted in a number of cases to date.[186] Enough has been said in this section to indicate the

---

180 See text at fns. 115–123.

181 "These principles as applied by our courts are to include the requirement for prompt, adequate, and effective compensation in cases of expropriation spelled out in the first part of section 620(e)." 110 *Congressional Record*, 22849 (daily edn., Oct. 2, 1964) (Mr. Adair). For an analysis of the Hickenlooper Amendment, see Lillich (fn. 58), 117–46.

182 Same, 130–33. "These standards seem, if anything, to be in excess of the traditional rules of customary international law." Falk (fn. 179), 37.

183 Samuel A. Bleicher, "The Sabbatino Amendment in Court: Bitter Fruit," 20 *Stanford Law Review*, 869 (1968).

184 Writing shortly after the amendment's enactment, Metzger commented that if it were applied "we would be witnessing the spectacle of American courts deciding cases upon the basis of 'international law' principles known not to be accepted as such by the international community. This would indeed be a curious way of showing that the rule of law as practiced in the United States deserves respect." Metzger (fn. 164), 246.

185 Banco Nacional de Cuba v. Farr, 243 F. Supp. 957 (S.D. N.Y. 1965), aff'd, 383 F.2d 166 (2d Cir. 1967), cert. denied, 390 U.S. 956 (1968).

186 The most significant being French v. Banco Nacional de Cuba, 23 N.Y. 2d 46, 242 N.E. 2d 704, 295 N.Y.S. 2d 433 (1968), discussed in Richard B. Lillich, "Interna-

present writer's disenchantment with an act of state doctrine that precluded the application of international law to the conduct of foreign states. The Sabbatino Amendment, to the extent that it removes the bar of a near-absolute act of state doctrine and permits the examination of the validity of foreign acts relating to the taking of property, is a desirable piece of legislation that warrants retention by Congress. As Falk reminds us, "an increase in the use of domestic courts to settle the controversies that arise in international life is, other considerations aside, a vital and progressive step toward an orderly and just world." [187] Yet, consistent with the proper role of domestic courts in the international community outlined above, the provisions in the amendment permitting executive intervention and prescribing so-called international law norms have no place in the act. Their deletion would allow courts in the United States, for the first time since *Bernstein,* to contribute impartially to the maintenance and development of international law in this important area.

## IV. THE VIETNAM WAR

The cases discussed in the previous two sections involve the invocation of international law in domestic courts to challenge the validity of acts of foreign states. Such cases historically have been the basis for scholarly analysis of the role of domestic courts in the international legal order. Recently, however, a number of cases involving the Vietnam War have arisen in United States courts where, almost for the first time, nationals of a state have attempted to invoke international law to challenge the acts of their own government. In this category of cases, "the main issues concern the availability to individual litigants of judicial remedies in situations in which executive action is alleged to transgress limits on governmental action set by rules of international law." [188] While each attempt to bring international law to bear upon the litigant's own government has met with failure, these cases presage

---

tional Law, 1969 Survey of New York Law," 21 *Syracuse Law Review,* 470–74 (1970). See Comment, "Sabbatino Property: A French Twist," 58 *Georgetown Law Journal,* 1298–1312 (1969).

An equally if not more important case, in that it gives the Supreme Court an excellent opportunity to pass upon the *Bernstein* exception, is Banco Nacional de Cuba v. First National City Bank, 270 F. Supp. 1004 (S.D.N.Y. 1967), rev'd, 431 F. 2nd 394 (2nd Cir. 1970), cert. granted, judg. vacated and case remanded, 400 U.S. 1019 (1971), prior decision followed, 442 F. 2nd 530 (2nd Cir. 1971), cert. granted, 40 U.S.L.W. 3141 (Oct. 12, 1971). See Richard B. Lillich, "International Law, 1971 Survey of New York Law," 23 *Syracuse Law Review* (1972).

[187] Falk (fn. 179), 63.

[188] Falk (fn. 15), 426. He notes that "[t]here is an unfulfilled need for comparable scholarly attention being devoted to category 2 problems." Same, fn. 2.

important developments with respect to the role domestic courts may play in the not too distant future.[189]

If domestic courts in the United States are to reach the substantive international law issues raised by the Vietnam War cases, however, they first must learn to surmount what Mr. Justice Stewart has called "serious preliminary issues of justiciability."[190] These procedural issues, whether couched in terms of "standing" or the "political question" doctrine, so far have been deemed to preclude judicial activism in the war-peace area of international law. The initial standing case, *United States v. Mitchell*,[191] involved a prosecution for failure to report for induction in violation of the Universal Military Training and Service Act. The defendant, *inter alia*, claimed that the intervention of the United States in Vietnam was unconstitutional and contravened various treaties and international conventions to which the United States was a party. The District Court, in an opinion revealing more bias than learning,[192] held that "defendant lacks standing to claim that the Act is being unconstitutionally applied in drafting him to go to Viet Nam to fight an 'undeclared war.' He stands guilty of the felony of refusing to report for induction. Had he been inducted, he might never have been sent abroad, much less to Viet Nam. Until inducted and ordered to Viet Nam, his claim of unconstitutional application of the Act is premature."[193] The court also applied the same reasoning to defendant's international law arguments, finding them "utterly irrelevant as a defense to the charge of willful refusal to report for induction in the armed forces of the United States. . . ."[194]

Upon appeal to the Court of Appeals for the Second Circuit, defendant's constitutional arguments were deemed "not to be premature,"[195] but nevertheless "not a defense to a prosecution for failure to report for induction. . . ."[196] Thus the court concluded that it

[189] Cf. Falk (fn. 14), 64: "Individuals are increasingly appealing above the heads of their elected national officials to global norms and procedures. These patterns of protest and appeal are currently at a rudimentary stage of assertion, but they represent important indications about what is going to happen in international society in the near future in the event that further cosmopolitan support develops."

[190] Mora v. McNamara, 389 U.S. 934, 935 (1967) (dissenting).

[191] 246 F. Supp. 874 (D. Conn. 1965).

[192] The court, after referring to the "sickening spectacle" of a United States citizen asserting that his government had violated international law, characterized the proffered argument as "tommyrot. . . ." Same, 899.

[193] Same, 898.

[194] Same, 899.

[195] 369 F. 2d 323, 324 (2d Cir. 1966). "The court of appeals in the *Mitchell* case, while disagreeing with the district court that raising the issue of the war was premature, nonetheless went on to hold that any proof Mitchell might present on the question would go to the issue of the President's use of the armies raised by Congress, not to the power of Congress to raise those forces." Louis Loeb, "The Courts and Vietnam," 18 *American University Law Review*, 385 (1969).

[196] 369 F.2d at 324. See text accompanying fn. 195 above.

"need not consider whether the substantive issues raised by appellant can ever be appropriate for judicial determination." [197] With respect to the international law arguments, however, the court apparently adopted *sub silentio* the District Court's determination that, given the posture of the case, defendant would always lack standing to raise such issues.[198] The Supreme Court subsequently denied certiorari in *Mitchell*,[199] although Mr. Justice Douglas dissented on the grounds that serious international law issues concerning the Vietnam War were involved and that "extremely sensitive and delicate questions," including whether the defendant had standing, were present.[200]

Lower court decisions in subsequent induction cases uniformly have denied defendants standing to raise international law issues. Typical is *United States* v. *Valentine*,[201] where the District Court noted that "the authority of the government to impose the duty of military service upon its citizens does not depend upon a judicial determination that American activities in Vietnam accord with international law and treaty obligations." [202] The court, in language similar to that used in *Mitchell*, reasoned that the "defendants have no standing to raise the issue, since they are charged only with refusing induction, not with refusing to obey an order assigning them to Vietnam, and it is entirely a matter of conjecture whether their induction ever would have led to their receiving such an order." [203] For purposes of the standing question, then, induction into the armed forces and participation in the Vietnam War are not deemed synonymous.[204] Thus it is settled beyond doubt, at least for the present, that a citizen of the United States cannot raise the question of the international validity of his government's use of force abroad "by refusing to obey induction orders

[197] 369 F.2d at 324.

[198] "[A]s appellant asserts that the Selective Service, *and not merely the conduct of the war in Vietnam*, is illegal, his defenses would seem not to be premature." Same (emphasis added). The implication of this sentence appears to be that the international law issue alone would not satisfy the standing requirement. Compare text at and accompanying fn. 195.

[199] 386 U.S. 972 (1967).

[200] "This case presents the questions:
  (1) whether the Treaty of London is a treaty within the meaning of Art. VI, cl. 2;
  (2) whether the question as to the waging of an aggressive 'war' is in the context of this criminal prosecution a justiciable question;
  (3) whether the Vietnam episode is a 'war' in the sense of the Treaty;
  (4) whether petitioner has standing to raise the question;
  (5) whether, if he has, the Treaty may be tendered as a defense in this criminal case or in amelioration of the punishment." 386 U.S. at 973.

[201] 288 F. Supp. 957 (D.P.R. 1968).

[202] Same, 984.

[203] Same.

[204] See Simmons v. United States, 406 F.2d 456, 460 (5th Cir.), cert. denied, 395 U.S. 982 (1969).

and by interposing international treaty obligations as a defense in a criminal prosecution for refusal to be inducted." [205]

If a potential draftee has no standing, what about a soldier in the typical "Vietnam case" who seeks an injunction against his being sent to participate in what he believes to be an illegal war? [206] Such a case was *Luftig* v. *McNamara*,[207] where an Army private sought a declaratory judgment and injunctive relief to prohibit the Secretary of Defense from sending him to Vietnam. The District Court, *sua sponte*, dismissed the complaint on the ground that the plaintiff had raised "obviously a political question that is outside of the judicial function." [208] Noteworthy, however, is the fact that the District Court's opinion nowhere questions plaintiff's standing. In its *per curiam* opinion affirming the decision of the District Court, the Court of Appeals for the District of Columbia also implicitly sustained his standing.[209]

The Supreme Court's subsequent denial of certiorari, of course, sheds no additional light on the matter, but the two dissenting opinions appended to its refusal to grant certiorari in *Mora* v. *McNamara* [210] provide some evidence that the political question doctrine and not the issue of standing would be a litigant's chief obstacle should the Court ever accept a Vietnam case.[211] The Court of Appeals for the

[205] United States v. Owens, 415 F.2d 1308, 1316 (6th Cir. 1969), cert. denied, 397 U.S. 997 (1970). If a potential draftee lacks standing to raise such issues, it goes without saying that other persons, such as mutilators of Selective Service records, also lack standing. "It is not clear what standing these defendants have to raise the legality of this country's involvement in Vietnam when they have not been called to serve in the armed forces, are not directly affected by our government's actions in that country, and are not even directly affected by the Selective Service apparatus." United States v. Berrigan, 283 F. Supp. 336, 341 (D.Md. 1968), aff'd, 417 F.2d 1009 (4th Cir. 1969), cert. denied, 397 U.S. 909 (1970).

[206] For an analysis of "the Vietnam case," see Warren F. Schwartz and Wayne McCormack, "The Justiciability of Legal Objections to the American Military Effort in Vietnam," 46 *Texas Law Review*, 1033 (1968), who argue persuasively that "soldiers seeking to avoid participation in the Vietnam war do satisfy the criteria functionally required to have standing. They surely meet the threshold requirement of a substantial enough interest to assure a serious presentation of the issues. . . . Moreover, there can be no more appropriate plaintiff to challenge the war, since— discounting the possibility of suit by a Vietnamese—the most direct objects of the challenged activity cannot be before the Court." Same, 1039.

[207] 252 F. Supp. 819 (D.D.C. 1966), aff'd, 373 F.2d 664 (D.C. Cir.), cert. denied, 387 U.S. 945 (1967).

[208] 252 F. Supp. at 819.

[209] 373 F.2d at 665–66. See Schwartz and McCormack (fn. 206), 1037 fn. 18. See text accompanying fn. 206 above.

[210] 387 F.2d 862 (D.C. Cir.), cert. denied, 389 U.S. 934 (1967). The Court of Appeals held *Mora* in abeyance pending the Supreme Court's determination of *Luftig*. They were two separate cases, though, a fact frequently overlooked by commentators. See, e.g., Loeb (fn. 195), 387 fn. 64.

[211] Admittedly these dissenting opinions by Mr. Justice Douglas and Stewart refer to possible problems of justiciability, but they seem to assume that the three Army

Sixth Circuit so interpreted the emanations from *Mora* when it later observed that "[t]here is respected authority for the proposition that at some point a member of the Armed Services who is assigned to combat duty in Vietnam should have the right to have the issues raised . . . as to international treaty obligations determined by a constitutional court." [212] The "unsettled question," added the court, "is at what point can these issues be raised." [213]

Assuming, *arguendo,* that a particular litigant can satisfy the standing requirement, what hope does he have of surmounting the "political question" doctrine? The answer at present is nil. The leading case again is *Luftig* v. *McNamara,* where the District Court invoked the doctrine to dismiss a complaint based upon the alleged illegality of the war.[214] The Court of Appeals, in a *per curiam* opinion which reads more like a government brief than a reasoned decision, held that this proposition was

> so clear that no discussion or citation of authority is needed. The only purpose to be accomplished by saying this much on the subject is to make it clear to others comparably situated and similarly inclined that resort to the courts is futile, in addition to being wasteful of judicial time, for which there are urgent legitimate needs.
>
> It is difficult to think of an area less suited for judicial action than that into which Appellant would have us intrude. The fundamental division of authority and power established by the Constitution precludes judges from overseeing the conduct of foreign policy or the use and disposition of military power; these matters are plainly the exclusive province of Congress and the Executive.[215]

---

privates at least had standing. 389 U.S. at 934–39. Compare Mr. Justice Douglas's dissenting opinion in *Mitchell,* fn. 200 above, where "whether petitioner has standing" was stated to be one of the major issues in that induction case.

[212] United States v. Owens, 415 F.2d 1308, 1316 (6th Cir. 1969), cert. denied, 397 U.S. 997 (1970).

[213] Same. Or, in Taylor's more detailed question, "[w]hen does the individual have standing to raise these objections, either by refusing induction, by refusing to train, or by refusing to get on the plane for Viet-Nam?" Telford Taylor, "Comments," *Proceedings* (fn. 79), 166. For the contention that the only individual who has standing is the serviceman "who refuses to obey a specific combat order or to carry out a specific combat mission on the ground that the action ordered is contrary to the laws and customs of war," see Benjamin Forman, "The Nuremberg Trials and Conscientious Objection to War: Justiciability Under United States Law," same, 164.

[214] See fn. 208 above.

[215] 373 F.2d at 665–66. "Random leafing through the pages of any volume of the Federal Reporter might leave one quite perplexed at what are, and what are not, legitimate demands made on courts to settle controversies." Loeb (fn. 195), 387 fn. 63.

Subsequent Vietnam cases citing *Luftig,* including *Cooper,*[216] *Simmons,*[217] and *Valentine,*[218] all reaffirm how "futile" it is to resort to domestic courts.

Despite some sharply-worded academic criticism,[219] the courts have maintained the view that their invocation of the political question doctrine "is not an abdication of responsibility by the judiciary. Rather, it is a recognition that the responsibility is assumed by that level of government which under the Constitution and international law is authorized to commit the nation." [220] Just why the courts should defer so readily to the claims of exclusive executive responsibility in the war-peace area has never been articulated satisfactorily, however, at least to persons who believe it necessary "to reappraise the political-question doctrine that has so far insulated from judicial appraisal most executive action in the area of foreign policy." [221] A perusal of lower court opinions in the Vietnam cases reveals that these courts obviously have failed to carry out the "discriminating analysis" which the Supreme Court in *Baker* v. *Carr* [222] stated was the hallmark of its own political question decisions.

[216] "Little need be said on this point because it is so patently without merit. It is not the function of the judicial branch of the Government to entertain litigation challenging the legality or wisdom of the executive branch in sending troops abroad or to any particular region. The point seeks judicial review of political questions not within the jurisdiction of the courts and is clearly not a defense to the charge [draft card mutilation] in this case." Cooper v. United States, 403 F.2d 71, 74 (10th Cir. 1968).

[217] "The appellant urges that the United States' participation in the war in Vietnam is in violation of various treaties, Articles 2(4) and 33(1) of the United Nations Charter, and the norms of international behavior, and that hence his induction would force him to become a party to war 'crimes.' . . . We are unable to find any constitutional authority for such interference by the judiciary in matters charged exclusively to the Congress and the Executive." 406 F.2d at 460.

[218] "More importantly, a judicial inquiry into the conduct of foreign policy or the use and disposition of military forces by the executive branch would violate the doctrine of separation of powers which is at the heart of our constitutional system of government." 288 F. Supp. at 984.

[219] E.g., "It would seem that the federal judiciary will have to confront the issues raised by . . . Nuremberg and international law, or else add another chapter to the record of judicial retreat before the determined advances of the Executive in pursuit of its broad powers to conduct foreign relations and national security affairs. If this is to be the case, perhaps a somewhat more charitable view might be taken with respect to those defeated enemies of World War II who were also often caught up in the domestic laws, practices, and personal dilemmas of wartime and were treated as war criminals." William V. O'Brien, "Selective Conscientious Objection and International Law," 56 *Georgetown Law Journal,* 1130–31 (1968).

[220] 283 F. Supp. at 342. For additional cases regarding relief, see Richard B. Lillich, "International Law, 1970 Survey of New York Law," 22 *Syracuse Law Review,* 289–90 (1971). See also United States v. Garrity, 433 F. 2nd 649 (8th Cir. 1970).

[221] Richard A. Falk, "Six Legal Dimensions of the United States Involvement in the Vietnam War," in Richard A. Falk, ed., *The Vietnam War and International Law* (Princeton 1969), II, at 244.

[222] 369 U.S. 186, 211 (1962).

This failure, which was capped by the Supreme Court's unfortunate denial of certiorari in *Mora*,[223] is all the more regrettable when one recalls, somewhat ironically, the Court's own admonition in *Baker* v. *Carr* that "it is error to suppose that every case or controversy which touches foreign relations lies beyond judicial cognizance."[224] Indeed, the Court in that case laid down six specific criteria for determining the applicability of the political question doctrine,[225] noting that "[u]nless one of these formulations is inextricable from the case at bar, there should be no dismissal for nonjusticiability on the ground of a political question's presence."[226] These criteria should have been given "discriminating analysis" in the context of a Vietnam War case long before now.[227] As Mr. Justice Stewart trenchantly observed in his dissenting opinion in *Mora*, "[w]e cannot make these problems go away simply by refusing to hear the case of three obscure Army privates."[228]

Although the weight of professional opinion in the United States still may favor the invocation of the political question doctrine in Vietnam War cases,[229] a growing number of international lawyers agree with Falk that the doctrine should be repudiated, or at least revised, "to allow questions of executive policy to come before the courts as part of a wider effort to bring law effectively to bear on a government's action with regard to war-peace issues."[230] Only if domestic courts reassert themselves and "assume an active role in the process of confining the scope of governmental action to those limits that are internationally permissible," continues Falk, can they serve as a check to questionable international behavior by the executive.[231] "The only convincing reason to refuse adjudication of such substan-

---

[223] See fn. 210 above.

[224] 369 U.S. at 211.

[225] "Prominent on the surface of any case held to involve a political question is found a textually demonstrable constitutional commitment of the issue to a coordinate political department; or a lack of judicially discoverable and manageable standards for resolving it; or the impossibility of deciding without an initial policy determination of a kind clearly for nonjudicial discretion; or the impossibility of a court's undertaking independent resolution without expressing lack of the respect due coordinate branches of government; or an unusual need for unquestioning adherence to a political decision already made; or the potentiality of embarrassment from multifarious pronouncements by various departments on one question." Same, 217.

[226] Same.

[227] Cf. United States v. Valentine, 288 F. Supp. 957, 986 (D.P.R. 1968).

[228] 389 U.S. at 935. See also the dissenting opinion of Mr. Justice Douglas, who contended that "[t]hese petitioners should be told whether their case is beyond judicial cognizance. If it is not, we should then reach the merits of their claims, on which I intimate no views whatsoever." Same, 939.

[229] See, e.g., Forman, *Proceedings* (fn. 79), 162.

[230] Falk (fn. 221), 250.

[231] Same, 254.

tive issues," he concludes, "is in order to insulate the exercise of power, however arbitrary, from serious legal challenge."[232] This eloquent plea for judicial activism has been complemented by a number of careful studies suggesting that the courts are under no constitutional compunction to invoke the doctrine in the typical Vietnam case.[233]

A final and generally overlooked hurdle facing the Vietnam litigant, either related to or part of the political question doctrine, is the possibility that for certain practical reasons a court might exercise its judicial discretion and abstain from deciding the case. Although there are a number of "practical political considerations" favoring such a decision, given the high stakes involved in the Vietnam cases judicial abstention would not seem justified.[234] This conclusion especially applies to the most commonly mentioned ground for possible abstention—lack of readily ascertainable international legal standards.[235] While a serious problem admittedly exists which cannot be overcome merely by general references to "Charter norms" or "the precedents of war crime trials,"[236] the past fifty years have seen the gradual development of legal standards by which a State's use of force in the international arena can be appraised.[237] These standards obviously still need substantial clarification, but surely here, as in the act of state area, the courts should not defer to the executive merely because an "overwhelming" consensus on substantive standards is lacking.[238] Rather, as Falk rightly stresses, they should assume an activist role and seek to clarify and apply the evolving international law norms governing war-peace issues.[239]

[232] Same.

[233] See, e.g., Schwartz and McCormack (fn. 206), 1041–45.

[234] For a comprehensive discussion of this point, see same, 1045–52.

[235] "Assuming that the question of aggressive war is not a political question, the facts that (i) no definition of aggression has been agreed to by the United Nations, (ii) different standards for defining aggression have been proposed by nations with divergent interests and social ideologies, and that (iii) the political effect of a municipal adjudication of the issue would have sensitive implications for our relations with third countries, strongly argue for judicial abstention. Those of you who are familiar with the *Sabbatino* opinion will realize that I am paraphrasing the court there." Forman, *Proceedings* (fn. 79), 162. See text accompanying fn. 239 below.

[236] See, e.g., Falk (fn. 14), 63. But see Falk (fn. 15), 599 fn. 12.

[237] E.g., the Kellogg-Briand Pact, the United Nations Charter, the Nuremberg Principles and the Geneva Conventions of 1949.

[238] See text at and accompanying fns. 156–158.

[239] Falk (fn. 221), 256. In a footnote he comments that "[s]uch a view is endorsed by the most conservative elements of the legal community when the question in controversy is whether the foreign expropriation of alien property conforms with international law. See any of the extensive literature associated with the Sabbatino controversy." Same, n. 54. Some irony surrounds this comment. Unfortunately, Falk's own views on judicial self-restraint, adopted by the Supreme Court in *Sabbatino*, now cut against his arguments in the Vietnam context. See text accompanying fn. 235 above. Cf. O'Brien (fn. 219), 1092 n. 37. Well taught by the Supreme Court, lower courts have failed to grasp why they should intervene in Vietnam but not

Two other possible grounds for judicial abstention, both mentioned by Chief Judge Wyzanski in *United States* v. *Sisson*,[240] also have not received the attention they warrant. First, assuming a domestic court was to consider a Vietnam case, serious evidentiary problems would arise in determining whether United States action comported with international law. To quote from *Sisson*, "the facts would surely be difficult to ascertain so long as the conflict continues, so long as the United States government has reasons not to disclose all its military operations, and so long as a court was primarily dependent upon compliance by American military and civilian officials with its judicial orders." [241] Second, the difficulty of rendering a "wholly disinterested judgment" led the court in *Sisson* "to conclude that a domestic tribunal is entirely unfit to adjudicate the question whether there has been a violation of international law during a war by the very nation which created, manned, and compensated the tribunal seized of the case." [242] In view of the attitude already manifested by some courts in the Vietnam cases,[243] the likelihood of "a provincial interpretation of the norms of international law" [244] cannot be discounted.[245] Neither of these problems, however, is necessarily insurmountable, and both are outbalanced by the desirability of encouraging domestic courts to invoke international law in this new and different context.

One concluding caveat must be entered to the above discussion. Even were a domestic court in the United States to reach the substantive merits of a Vietnam case, there is no assurance that it would be able to utilize international legal standards to determine it. The first section of this essay, it is hoped, adequately demonstrated the fallacy of merely assuming "that they have been assimilated into our domestic legal system." [246] However disagreeable the fact may be,[247] "[a]mple

---

in expropriation cases. See, e.g., Simmons v. United States, 406 F.2d 456, 460 (5th Cir. 1969). Falk has yet to reconcile his conflicting positions in these two areas. The thesis of this essay, of course, is that domestic courts should adopt the same activist approach regardless of the subject matter of the dispute or the character of the State involved.

[240] 294 F. Supp. 515 (D. Mass. 1968). For subsequent developments in this case, see 297 F. Supp. 902 (D. Mass. 1969), appeal dismissed, 399 U.S. 267 (1970).

[241] 294 F. Supp. 517.

[242] Same.

[243] See fn. 192.

[244] Falk (fn. 13), 127.

[245] "With effort, self-discipline, and judicial training, men may transcend their personal bias, but few there are who in international disputes of magnitude are capable of entirely disregarding their political allegiance and acting solely with respect to legal considerations and ethical imperatives. If during hostilities a trustworthy, credible international judgment is to be rendered with respect to alleged national misconduct in war, representatives of the supposed offender must not sit in judgment upon the nation." 294 F. Supp. at 517.

[246] Schwartz and McCormack (fn. 206), 1040.

[247] "In today's debate, arguments have been propounded which a great and proud

precedent has been established for the proposition that the domestic validity of a Presidential or Congressional action is not affected by the fact that such action is violative of international law." [248] Unless it can be demonstrated to the court's satisfaction that a specific provision of some treaty or other international agreement applies to the particular case,[249] or that some federal statute incorporates by reference similar international obligations into domestic law, a court in the United States is highly unlikely in the near future to hold that the government's use of force abroad is invalid.

This state of affairs, seemingly necessitated by the dualist precedents set forth in the first section of this essay, calls for an urgent reassessment of the status of international law in United States courts.[250] Sohn, for instance, contending that "[t]he obsolete doctrine that international law is not controlling in United States courts when confronted with a later statute is a product of the jurisprudence of a period when international law was quite different from what it is today," has recommended that the Supreme Court announce "that the rules derived from the Charter prevail not only over earlier law but also over later statutes." [251] Other observers have suggested the possibility of a constitutional amendment.[252] While the likelihood of either event occurring may seem remote, the general dissatisfaction with the lack of actual, as opposed to doctrinal, commitment to international law on the part of the United States, revealed by the Vietnam cases, guaran-

---

nation should hardly insist upon: for example, that 'our courts are bound to follow [any] statute regardless of its compatibility with international law'; and that 'if the United States is engaging in conduct contrary to international law,' the United States has nevertheless not lost the 'right to enforce any duty upon its citizens . . . and to engage in such conduct.' These are the types of arguments we heard at Nuremberg by the defense. Such contentions run counter to the letter and spirit of the Nuremberg law and Judgments." John H. E. Fried, "Comments," *Proceedings* (fn. 79), 172. The commentator was attacking the assessment of current United States law presented by Forman, same, 162, 163.

[248] William N. Lobel, "The Legality of the United States' Involvement in Vietnam—A Pragmatic Approach," 23 *University of Miami Law Review*, 793 (1969). "Whether the actions by the executive and the legislative branches in utilizing our armed forces are in accord with international law is a question which necessarily must be left to the elected representatives of the people and not to the judiciary. This is so even if the government's actions are contrary to valid treaties to which the government is a signatory. And the Supreme Court has held that Congress may constitutionally override treaties by later enactment of an inconsistent statute, even though the subsequent statute is in violation of international law." United States v. Berrigan, 283 F. Supp. 336, 342 (D.Md. 1968), aff'd, 417 F. 2d 1009 (4th Cir. 1969), cert. denied, 397 U.S. 909 (1970).

[249] See fn. 237. Even in this situation lower courts have warned that "[n]o treaty can authorize the judiciary to undertake an inquiry forbidden to it by the Constitution." United States v. Valentine, 288 F. Supp. 957, 986 (D.P.R. 1968).

[250] See O'Brien (fn. 219), 1130.

[251] Louis B. Sohn, "Remarks," *Proceedings* (fn. 79), 180.

[252] See e.g., Beverly Woodward, "Remarks," same, 180.

tees an exhaustive inquiry in coming years into the role of domestic courts in applying international legal standards to the government's conduct in the war-peace area.

## V. Conclusion

Starting with the assumption that domestic courts are unofficial agents of the international legal order as well as national institutions of the particular State which created them, this essay has examined the decisions of United States courts in three important and topical areas. Eventually, of course, it will be "essential to disentangle what is American from what is universal about the role of domestic courts in the international legal system." [253] Nevertheless, without being provincial in the matter, it seems possible to develop a general thesis favoring judicial activism from United States practice.[254] If only because judges in the United States are relatively independent compared to their brethren in many other States,[255] the recent decisions concerning sovereign immunity, act of state and the Vietnam War "are important indicators of the extent to which domestic courts will be permitted to examine the validity of governmental action—foreign as well as domestic—in response to a legal complaint by an individual." [256]

In any evaluation of domestic courts in general, it would be wise to remember Friedmann's warning that historically their role has been "severely limited and distorted by the predominance of national prejudice, in matters where the interests of nationals have to be adjudicated in an international context. Few national courts have been able to resist the temptation of modifying doctrine when national passions are aroused." [257] Moreover, as the last section has shown, domestic

[253] Falk (fn. 15), 427. "Such disentanglement must await, however, detailed comparative studies of constitutional tradition, political reality, and public expectation in the major domestic societies of the world. In the interim an assessment of the role of domestic courts within the international legal order will have to remain incomplete and tentative." Same, 427–28. See text accompanying fn. 57 above.

[254] "This line of argument is not intended as an endorsement of a provincial outlook. On the contrary, domestic courts should be encouraged by international lawyers to construe the character of international law from as nonnational a perspective as possible." Same, 428.

[255] Falk observes that in recently independent States "solidarity at a national level produces political interpretations of international law," and that "there is no judicial independence in antidemocratic societies. . . ." He notes that these factors put "a significant limit upon the role that domestic courts can be expected to play in the international legal system." Falk (fn. 13), 19, 20. See generally Frank G. Dawson and Ivan L. Head, *International Law, National Tribunals and the Rights of Aliens* (Syracuse 1971).

[256] Falk (fn. 15), 526. The present writer would substitute "may" for "will" in the above quotation.

[257] Wolfgang Friedmann, *The Changing Structure of International Law* (New York 1964), 147. He recognizes that "their contribution will become much more valuable if and when they are able to be truly agents of international law rather

courts have revealed substantial ingenuity in avoiding the necessity of deciding international law cases where the local sovereign's conduct has been called into question.[258] Yet the ideal of impartial national tribunals dispensing justice in international matters has been acknowledged for several centuries. Blackstone recognized the desirability of applying international law domestically,[259] Lord Stowell analogized British prize courts to international tribunals,[260] and in the United States Mr. Justice Story somewhat enthusiastically declared that "[t]he Court of prize is emphatically a Court of the law of nations; and it takes neither its character nor its rules from the mere municipal regulations of any country."[261] How the ideal, or at least an improvement on the present situation, can be attained is what deserves attention now.

Without restating all the specific recommendations, express or implied, contained in earlier sections of this essay, it might be useful to

---

than spokesmen of national interests in questions of international legal importance." Same, 148. See also Wolfgang Friedmann, "National Courts and the International Legal Order: Projections on the Implications of the Sabbatino Case," 34 *George Washington Law Review*, 443–55 (1966). Compare text accompanying fn. 260 below.

[258] McDougal, who acknowledges the "hard reality" that at the present time "inclusive prescription by internal application is not achieved and is probably not achievable," specifies as one limiting factor judges who "seek to escape responsibility for the internal application of inclusive policies by passing the issue of international commitment to the executive under the doctrine of political questions. . . ." McDougal (fn. 5), 206, 225.

[259] In words relevant to the recent prosecutions of American servicemen for alleged massacres in Vietnam, he observed that while offenses against international law were "principally incident to whole states or nations . . . where the individuals of any state violate this general law, it is then the interest as well as duty of the government under which they live to animadvert upon them with a becoming severity, that the peace of the world may be maintained." 4 Blackstone, *Commentaries*\* 68. See fn. 24 above.

[260] "[T]his is a Court of the Law of Nations, though sitting here under the authority of the King of Great Britain. It belongs to other nations as well as to our own; and what foreigners have a right to demand from it, is the administration of *the law of nations*, simply, and exclusively of the introduction of principles borrowed from our own municipal jurisprudence, to which, it is well known, they have at all times expressed no inconsiderable repugnance." The "Recovery," 165 Eng. Rep. 955, 958 (Adm. 1807). It is interesting to note that contemporaneous commentators from other States greeted Lord Stowell's dictum with a certain degree of skepticism. "How far the practice of recent times, or of any times, has corresponded with this theory, will always be a matter of doubt with those whose rights and interests are affected by the adjudications of these *ex parte* tribunals. This will be more especially the case with respect to a great maritime country, like Great Britain, depending on the encouragement of its navy for its glory and safety, where the national bias is so strong in favour of the captor, that the judge must, unconsciously, feel its influence." Henry Wheaton, *Elements of International Law* (3rd edn., Philadelphia 1846), 48.

[261] The Schooner Adeline, 13 U.S. (9 Cranch) 244, 284 (1815).

summarize its major conclusions. They may be classified conveniently, if not wholly accurately, under two general headings: judicial administration recommendations, that is, steps which the courts themselves, alone or in conjunction with the executive and legislative branches, should take to improve their capability to decide international law cases; and institutional (or constitutional) recommendations that would require either a significant change in judicial precedents or perhaps even a constitutional amendment.

Under the heading of judicial administration, the courts first should reclaim the role in sovereign immunity cases which they abdicated several decades ago. Pursuant to the statute discussed in the second section if it is enacted, or by repudiating the rationale that led to the *Rich* case if it is not, they should free themselves from the binding effect of Department of State suggestions. Secondly, in the act of state cases the courts, consistent with the policy suggested for the sovereign immunity area, should eschew the extreme deference exhibited by the Supreme Court in *Sabbatino*. While the "reverse-twist" *Bernstein* exception and the purported codification of international law contained in the Sabbatino Amendment constitute continued executive and legislative infringements upon the role of the judiciary that should be eliminated as soon as possible, until the amendment is revised the courts can lessen its negative impact by an ameliorative construction of its terms. Finally, in all international law cases, but especially in cases touching sensitive national nerves as the Vietnam cases have done, the courts should avoid the parochial bias which, in its extreme, saw one district judge characterize an appeal to international law as "tommyrot." [262] Such flagrant displays of prejudice toward international law can only undercut its viability in both the United States and the international community.[263]

Under the heading of institutional (or constitutional) recommendations, the courts ultimately must reassess the precedents by which international law, although doctrinally incorporated into the law of the United States, actually is accorded second-class status. The implications of a constitutional system which can recognize the domestic legitimacy of a course of action while acknowledging its international invalidity also must be faced. As Falk has warned, "[t]here is no way to compromise or otherwise avoid the thorny issue of paramountcy." [264] If the Supreme Court is unwilling or unable even to approach this

[262] See text accompanying fn. 192.

[263] As Falk has stated, "[d]omestic courts provide an excellent arena within which to exhibit either a scornful or a constructive attitude toward the relevance of international law to international behavior." Falk (fn. 13), 12.

[264] Falk (fn. 15), 433.

issue, then surely the possibility of an amendment to the Constitution requires consideration. While either step would constitute "a revolutionary breakthrough in the relations between the individual and the sovereign state," [265] one or the other will have to be taken some day. Nothing would be a better herald of the recommitment of the United States to the principle of the rule of law than speeding that day's arrival.

[265] Same, 599.

# CHAPTER 11

# Regional Institutions

## JOSEPH S. NYE

THE NUMBER and proportion of international regional institutions has been increasing, as shown in Table 1, but it is not clear what conclusions we should draw from this fact. In the opinion of Jean Rey, "the political life of the world is becoming less at the level of national states and more at the level of continents." [1] Even Charles deGaulle has said that, "it is in keeping with the conditions of our times to create entities more vast than each of the European states." [2] We shall argue, however, that there is not a clear trend toward regionalization of world politics in the sense that the most important sets of interdependence are based on geographical contiguity. At best the evidence

### TABLE 1

NEW REGIONAL AND QUASI-REGIONAL INTERGOVERNMENTAL ORGANIZATIONS FOUNDED, 1815–1965

|  | Intergovernmental Organizations Newly Founded | | |
|---|---|---|---|
|  | Total | Regional | Regional as Percent of Total |
| 1815–1914 | 49 | 14 | 28% |
| 1915–1944 | 73 | 27 | 37% |
| 1945–1955 | 76 | 45 | 60% |
| 1956–1965 | 56 | 41 | 73% |
| Founded | 254 | 127 | 50% |
| Terminated | (65) | (27) |  |
| Total | 189 | 100 | 53% |

SOURCE: J. David Singer and Michael Wallace, "Intergovernmental Organization in the Global System, 1815–1964," *International Organization*, 24 (Spring 1970). This table was constructed by the author and David Handley (scoring regional and quasi-regional on the basis of geographical restriction in an organization's name or practice) from an early version of the list kindly made available by J. David Singer. The trends are corroborated by Kjell Skjelsbaek, "Development of the Systems of International Organizations," International Peace Research Association Paper, September 1969.

[1] Quoted in *European Community*, No. 103 (June 1967), 8.
[2] Press Conference, September 9, 1965.

is ambiguous, and there are alternative hypotheses for explaining the meaning of the growth of the number of regional institutions.

## I. REGIONAL TRENDS

Has world politics become increasingly "regionalized"? The evidence is varied, and different types of behavior point in different directions. On the one hand, those who see a trend toward regionalism cite the fact that non-regional organizations like the Commonwealth, which once represented the paragon of effective international organization, has undergone a decline,[3] and Britain has sought to limit its military obligations "East of Suez" and prove its Europeanness.

Intra-Commonwealth trade in 1967 was roughly a quarter of the total trade of member countries, but the figure has declined steadily and even the report of the Commonwealth Secretariat refers to "the drive towards regional economic emphasis" among its members.[4] At the same time, the countries of the European Community more than tripled their intraregional trade in the first decade. This striking success caused other countries to try to imitate it. Further evidence frequently cited is the fact that regional voting blocs have come to characterize the politics of the United Nations and the principle of regional representation within the U.N. is firmly established. Finally, not only has the number and proportion of new intergovernmental organizations increased but, what is probably a more accurate indicator of transactions, the same has been true for nongovernmental organizations. From 1957 to 1963 international nongovernmental organizations of the regional type increased some five times as rapidly as other nongovernmental organizations.[5]

This evidence, however, is far from conclusive. In some cases, for example the broadening of the "Atlantic" OECD to include Japan in 1964, or the establishment of the nonregional Group of Ten in the politically important international monetary system, the important trend does not seem to be regional. As for behavior in the U.N., many of the caucuses are "regional" only in a loose sense of the word,[6] and

---

[3] "The Commonwealth stands today as a foremost example of international cooperation." Daniel S. Cheever and H. Field Haviland, *Organizing for Peace* (Boston 1954). In addition, other nonregional selective efforts such as Francophone or Afro-Asian organizations have not prospered.

[4] Commonwealth Secretariat, Second Report of the *Commonwealth Secretary-General* (London 1968), 3.

[5] Robert Angell, "The Growth of Transnational Participation," *The Journal of Social Issues*, XXIII (Jan. 1967), 125. See also *Peace on the March* (New York 1969), Chap. 9.

[6] For instance, UNCTAD groups are partly by region and partly by level of development. See J. S. Nye, "UNCTAD," in Robert Cox and Harold Jacobson, New Haven, 1972. In the words of Robert Keohane, "the most striking feature of the

TABLE 2

TRADE GROWTH

|  | 1958 $billion | 1967 $billion | 1958 = 100 |
|---|---|---|---|
| US/Canada | 3.3 | 13.9 | 420 |
| US/Japan | 1.7 | 5.7 | 340 |
| Intra EEC | 7.5 | 24.5 | 326 |
| Intra EFTA | 2.8 | 7.0 | 249 |
| World Trade | 108.0 | 214.1 | 194 |

SOURCES: United Nations, *Yearbook of International Trade Statistics* OECD, *Overall Trade by Countries.*

"regional" caucusing behavior in the U.N. arena is not a reliable indicator of political behavior outside the U.N. Turning to international trade, it is true that geography remains an important determinant [7] and there have been dramatic increases in trade among members of regional organizations, but there have also been dramatic increases between distance partners such as the United States and Japan [8] (see Table 2).

Steven Brams and Bruce Russett have made systematic efforts to map the pattern of transactions in the international system. Looking at exchange of diplomatic personnel, trade, and shared membership in intergovernmental organizations in the early 1960's, Brams found that "geographical proximity seemed to be the dominant influence in the structuring of most of the sub-groups." However, bearing out our suspicions, he also found that neither diplomatic exchanges nor trade showed as clear a regional principle as was apparent in memberships in international organizations. [9]

Russett factor analyzed socioeconomic homogeneity, U.N. voting patterns; trade; shared memberships, and geographical proximity among states in the 1950's and 1960's. He notes that for the indicators

Regional Groups is their weakness," "Political Influence in the General Assembly," *International Conciliation*, No. 557 (March 1966).

[7] See Hans Linnemann, *An Econometric Study of International Trade Flows* (Amsterdam 1966).

[8] Indices of relative acceptance which correct for the effects of the size of trading partners show a more marked rise from 1954 and 1964 in trade from Japan to the U.S. than vice versa. On the other hand, there is a slight decline in the indices of relative acceptance between the U.S. and Canada. I am endebted to Karl Deutsch, Richard Chadwick, I. Richard Savage, and Dieter Senghaas for this data from their forthcoming *Regionalism, Trade and Political Community*.

[9] Steven Brams, "Transactions Flows in the International System," *American Political Science Review*, LX (Dec. 1966), 889.

## TABLE 3

### "REGIONAL GROUP" FACTORS AS A FRACTION
### OF TOTAL NUMBER OF FACTORS

|  |  | *Early 1950's* | *Early 1960's* | *Change* |
|---|---|---|---|---|
| ¾ of states in the factor are "re-gional" | U.N. Voting | ¾ | ⅟₇ | decline |
|  | Trade | ⅛ | 2/9 | small rise |
|  | I.O. Membership | 2/7 | 9/7 | large rise |
| ⅔ of states in the factor are "re-gional" | U.N. Voting | ¾ | 4/7 | decline |
|  | Trade | ⅜ | 2/9 | slight decline |
|  | I.O. Membership | 4/7 | 9/7 | slight rise |

he chose, "the lowest correlation for a given analysis is almost always between it and the pattern of geographical proximity," and that the average correlation among his factor analyses for the 1960's is slightly lower than for the 1950's.[10]

One of the problems of interpreting Russett's results is that his factor analysis is designed to find the fewest and thus often the largest) clusters of states to account for the variance in the data.[11] The resulting factors are then given "regional" labels though in some cases the fit between the general meaning of the labels and the factors is very imperfect. However, if we take the three factors for which Russett has data over time and rather arbitrarily give regional labels only to those factors of which three-quarters (or alternatively two-thirds) of the states listed fall in an intuitively recognizable contiguous region, we find that Russett's data, like Bram's, seems to substantiate our suspicion that there may have been more regionalization in international organization than in other international behavior (see Table 3).

In a more recent factor analysis of Bram's data on the exchange of diplomatic personnel in the early 1960's, Russett and Lamb found that most groupings were regionally based, but three of their nine factors were nonregionally labeled "Large powers; China and friends; Commonwealth and Outer Seven." Moreover, several of their "regional" factors included distant nonregional large powers.[12]

## II. THE NATURE AND USES OF REGIONAL INSTITUTIONS

If there does not seem to be a strong trend toward or away from regional systems as the dominant sets of interdependence, how then

[10] Bruce Russett, *International Regions and the International System* (Chicago 1968), 213.

[11] This tendency to find quasi- and macroregional clusters also means that a number of Russett's generalizations about regions are not relevant (and sometimes misleading) when applied to microregions.

[12] See also Bruce Russett and W. Curtis Lamb, "Global Patterns of Diplomatic Interchange," *Journal of Peace Research*, No. 1 (1969), 42.

do we explain the increase in the number and proportion of regional institutions? To answer the question, we must look more carefully at the nature and functions of regional organizations.

First, regions are relative. There are no absolute naturally-determined regions. Relevant geographical boundaries vary with different purposes, and these purposes differ from country to country and change over time.[13] Regional core areas can be determined and various boundaries delineated by analysis of mutual transactions and other interdependences, but which of a large number of potential regions become relevant for organization depends on political decision. Physical contiguity can be misleading, not only because technology, history, and culture can make "effective distance" differ from linear distance,[14] but also because images of what constitutes a region is affected by different political interests.

A political region "needs essentially a strong belief. Regionalism has some iconography as its foundation."[15] But even these beliefs or icons change, or are differently applied. For example, do "oceans divide men" or do "oceans unite men"? For Western Europeans at the time of NATO's foundation, the Atlantic Ocean was the historic highway of Atlantic culture. Less is heard of this in recent years. In the eyes of African anticolonialists, however, salt water was a clear dividing line. "France belongs to the continent of Europe; Algeria belongs to the continent of Africa"—though Algeria and France are both Mediterranean and close, while Algeria and Ghana (fellow members of the OAU) share neither of these characteristics. In short, geographical milieu may be interpreted in very different ways by decision-makers.[16]

Added to the confusion stemming from the relativity of regional images has been the value-laden character of the regional organization label. Diplomatic efforts to define regional arrangements or agencies under both the League and the United Nations were not successful because they were essentially political struggles over legitimacy. For example, at the San Francisco Conference on International Organization in 1945, Egyptian diplomats pressed for a definition of a regional organization that closely resembled the recently founded Arab League, while American delegates pressed for language on regional organiza-

13 In Russett's words, "there is *no* region or aggregate of national units that can in the very strict sense of boundary congruence be identified as a subsystem of the international system" (fn. 10), 69.

14 Karl Deutsch and Walter Isard, "A Note on a Generalized Concept of Effective Distance," *Behavioral Science* (January 1961), 308–10.

15 Jean Gottmann, "Geography and International Relations," in W. A. Douglas Jackson, ed., *Politics and Geographic Relationships* (New York 1964), 28.

16 E. N. van Kleffens, "Regionalism and Political Pacts," 43 *American Journal of International Law*, 668 (1949). Kwame Nkrumah's views quoted in Ali Mazrui, *Towards a Pax Africana* (Chicago 1967), 43; Harold and Margaret Sprout, *The Ecological Perspective* (Princeton 1965).

tion that would clearly benefit the Inter-American system without giving too much leeway to organizations like the Arab League. Similarly, the Soviet Union has consistently denied that NATO was a legitimate regional organization.[17]

Academic authors have also used the term "regional organization" in a variety of ways. Some use the term "regional" for all organizations which are not globally inclusive in their membership (including, for instance, the Commonwealth), no matter how geographically dispersed the members are. Others use the term to refer to geographically contiguous states, but differ on the degree of contiguity necessary. Still others apply "regional" to selective membership organizations which restrict membership on the basis of a geographical principle regardless of geographical contiguity.

Definitions are not right or wrong, but more and less useful. As Oran Young has argued, a conception of region that abandons geographical contiguity as a necessary condition means that "the term 'region' is apt to become so inclusive that it is useless." [18] Since we wish to distinguish the effects of geographical contiguity from selective membership, we will define a regional organization as one in which (1) membership is restricted in principle and in practice on a basis of geographical contiguity (i.e., there are no nonregional members); and (2) this contiguity involves a proximity and compactness.[19]

We will define as "quasi-regional" an organization (1) whose membership is restricted in part on the basis of geographical contiguity or a geographical area of concern; but (2) which in practice includes nonregional members. We will treat all other restrictive membership organizations (as well as universal ones) as nonregional.

Where one draws the line between regional or quasi-regional organizations is, of course, an arbitrary decision. So also are the lines we use to distinguish different types of regional and quasi-regional organizations by their degree of contiguity. We shall call "macroregional" those organizations that encompass vast "regions"—where the maximum distance between members' capitals is one-fourth to one-half that of the "global" United Nations (i.e., 3100 to 6200 miles). We shall use the term "microregional" for those organizations where the

[17] Ruth B. Russell, *A History of the United Nations Charter* (Washington 1958), Chap. 27; and Arthur H. Vandenburg, Jr., *The Private Papers of Senator Vandenburg* (Boston 1952), 190; G. I. Morozov, "Notion et Classification des Organisations Internationales," *Associations Internationales*, No. 6 (1967), 412.

[18] Oran Young, "Professor Russett: Industrious Tailor to a Naked Emperor," *World Politics*, XXI (April 1969), 488.

[19] The precise degree of contiguity one demands is a matter of choice. For example, 6000 miles between the most distant capitals (half the maximum distance between capitals of U.N. members) and no country more than 1500 miles from the others makes NATO "quasi-regional." To make NATO "regional" would require a threshold of 3000 miles.

maximum distance between members' capitals is less than one-eighth that of the United Nations (i.e., less than 1500 miles). Of course, one can object that these distances are arbitrary. But some such arbitrary decision is essential in constructing typologies, and this one leads to interesting patterns as we shall see in Table 4. Also one might object that "effective distance" measured in communications cost is more important than linear distance. Such an objection misses the point, however, since we are interested in analyzing the (perhaps mistaken) regionalist belief in a relationship between linear distance and effective international organization.

Finally, in constructing a typology we also categorize regional organizations by whether their primary declared or manifest function is military security (defense against an external military threat), primarily political (including diplomatic and cultural activities affecting a group's security, rank, or identity); or primarily economic (concerned with the creation, acquisition, or allocation of resources). Table 4 takes a table of "principal regional organizations in 1966" from a recent text and reconstructs it according to the geographical criteria that we have elaborated above.[20]

Table 4 provides evidence for our earlier statement that the role of contiguity in what is conceived of as a region for organizational purposes varies with the type of function involved. One of the things apparent from the table is that military security organizations tend to be of the low contiguity macroregional type and quasi-regional membership. Political organizations tend to be divided between macro- and microregions, but tend to be regional rather than quasi-regional— perhaps because of the important role of identity. Economic organizations involved in promoting high levels of trade integration or common services among their members tend to be microregional, with high geographical contiguity and identity seemingly playing an important role. This pattern would not hold, however, if regional and quasi-regional economic organizations involved in providing aid and finance (e.g. U.N. Regional Commissions and Regional Development Banks) were added to this table. Like military organizations, the relevant power for their functions seems frequently to be beyond the microregional scale.

20 Jack C. Plano and Robert Riggs, *Forging World Order* (New York 1967), Table 4-1. The "principal" organizations selected by Plano and Riggs correspond with eighteen of the twenty-five regional organizations given by Donald Blaisdell, *International Organization* (1966); eighteen of twenty-five in Ruth Lawson, *International Regional Organizations* (New York 1962); eighteen of twenty-one nonmilitary regional organizations in J. S. Nye, *International Regionalism* (Boston 1968); and ten of ten military organizations in Philip Jacob and Alexine Atherton, *The Dynamics of International Organization* (Homewood, Ill. 1965). ANZUS, OECD and the Commonwealth are nonregional and not included in our table.

TABLE 4

### Types of Regional Organization

| | Principal Declared Function | | | | | |
| --- | --- | --- | --- | --- | --- | --- |
| | I. *Military Security* | | II. *Political* | | III. *Economic* | |
| (Mileage between most distant capitals) | Regional | Quasi-Regional | Regional | Quasi-Regional | Regional | Quasi-Regional |
| 6,000 (and over) | | SEATO 11,500<br>NATO 5,500 | ASPAC 6,000<br>OAU 5,800<br>OAS 5,300 | | | COLOMBO PLAN |
| 5,000 | | | | OCAM 4,900 | LAFTA 4,700 | |
| 4,000 | WTO 3,900 | CENTO 3,700 | Arab League 3,100<br>Council of Europe 3,100 | | CMEA 3,900 | |
| 3,000 | | | | | | |
| 2,000 | | | Nordic Council 1,500 | | EFTA 1,900<br>UDEAC 1,100 | |
| 1,000 | WEU 900 | | Entente 700<br>ODECA 500 | | Eur. Com. 800<br>E. Af. Com. 700<br>CACM 500<br>Benelux 200 | |

MILEAGE BETWEEN MOST DISTANT CAPITALS — Macro-Region / Micro-Region

To return to our question of why the number and proportion of regional organizations have increased though the evidence of increased importance of regional systems is ambiguous, perhaps the most useful perspective is to ask what incentives there are for elites and statesmen to use them. From this perspective, it would be a mistake to see the politics of regional organizations as purely the politics of cooperation. Regional organizations, like all international organizations, have derivative uses as well as declared ones. They may serve a number of diplomatic purposes, whether as a means of holding conferences without quibbling over schedules, gathering information, or exerting pressure on other states. In a world in which communications make other societies "penetrable," an aspect of power is the ability to communicate over the heads of governments (*i.e.*, not by diplomacy alone) to create sympathy and a basis for legitimizing one's policies. The conference or parliamentary diplomacy aspects and sometimes the administrative actions of regional organizations are among the many means available for communicating to foreign populations. In some cases, regional secretariats act as pressure groups in domestic political processes. These derivative uses may also include a symbolic role, for example, something comparable to statements of good will, nonaggression treaties, or an indication of a weak alignment. A seemingly useless organization today may provide a useful diplomatic instrument in the future.[21]

These derivative uses often seem more important than the declared functions for the political regional organizations, particularly the macroregional political ones such as the Arab League, OAU, OAS and Council of Europe. But military and economic regional organizations can also be put to the same diplomatic use. Control of Germany was a major derivative function of the ECSC. More recently De Gaulle tried to use the EEC as a means to press his economic partners toward a French conception of a European foreign policy. A 1969 struggle over the right of the WEU to discuss the Middle East was in reality a pretext for some of the EEC states to associate with Britain.

One can speculate that these derivative uses have made regional organizations particularly attractive to the statesmen because of the nature of power in the current international system. As Stanley Hoffmann has described the current system, the combination of the self-defeating costliness of nuclear weapons; the sanctification of the legitimacy of the nation-state (enshrined in the United Nations), and the costliness of ruling socially mobilized (rather than colonially inert) alien populations have reduced the role of force and enhanced the

[21] There are also "private-regarding" derivative uses. International organizations may become cozy little clubs staffed by routineers; or be promoted by diplomats who see them as an opportunity for such personal goals as prestige, exile, or corruption.

psychological components of power in world politics today. For the large powers, milieu goals (concern with the general environment of the international system) have become more important than possession goals (direct territorial, economic, or other concrete interests). Prestige and capacity to communicate effectively have taken on special importance. Loose arrangements among small weak states are no longer useless.[22]

The following examples show the way in which these characteristics of the current international system has enhanced the attractiveness of regional organization as a diplomatic tool. 1. As the less tangible psychological components of power have increased in importance, statesmen have sought the prestige of regional leadership as a symbol of power—witness the foreign policies of France, Ethiopia, and Egypt in the EEC, OAU, and Arab League respectively. 2. Given the increased importance of domestic populations in world politics, coupled with the legitimacy of national sovereignty, regional organizations provide an opportunity to appeal over the heads of governments to groups in other states (despite the sovereignty clauses often written into the charters), as the successful and unsuccessful efforts of the Ivory Coast and Ghana to influence their neighbors through the Conseil de l'Entente and the OAU, respectively, demonstrate.[23] 3. With the diminished utility of military force, in many settings traditional military alliances have lost some of their attractiveness. Nonetheless, statesmen still feel the need to draw lines and introduce even a faint element of predictability into their search for security by creating political alliances under the guise of regional organization—witness ASPAC, RCD, and the Association of Southeast Asian Nations.[24] 4. With the predominance of milieu goals over possession goals, regional organizations can serve as useful tools for shaping conditions beyond one's national boundaries, whether it be creating more favorable conditions for aid for economic development (e.g. the regional development banks); or creating regional balances of power (a major motive for ASPAC). 5. Finally, with the increased importance of communications and signals, regional organizations have been useful as "no trespassing" signs, either between the Superpowers (the OAS or the Warsaw Pact) or from the weak to the Superpowers (OAU).

[22] For these arguments see Stanley Hoffmann, *Gulliver's Troubles* (New York 1968), Part I; also Karl Deutsch, "The Future of World Politics," *Political Quarterly* (Jan. 1966); Robert Rothstein, *Alliances and Small Powers* (New York 1968).

[23] I. William Zartman, *International Relations in the New Africa* (Englewood Cliffs, N.J. 1966); also Claude Welch, *Dream of Unity* (Ithaca 1966); and Scott Thompson, *Ghana's Foreign Policy, 1957–1966* (Princeton 1969).

[24] "They may properly be seen as publicizing cherished ideas, as providing a forum, or rather forums, and as a means of launching pilot schemes which might possibly lead to future political unification . . . ," Peter Lyon, *War and Peace in Southeast Asia* (New York 1969), 156.

In addition to the incentives provided by the derivative diplomatic uses, political leaders may create and use regional organizations in response to personal or elite desires to express a collective identity in world politics. Particularly in less-developed areas where foreign policy is less bureaucratized, a leader may succumb to the heady wine of "instant brotherhood" sometimes felt at summit conferences, or he may shrewdly calculate that he must make a token concession to regional identity to satisfy domestic elites who wish to assert their status or defend their culture in the world arena.

The results are sometimes paradoxical. For example, East African leaders met under U.N. ECA auspices in Lusaka in 1965 and agreed to the formation of an Eastern African Common Market at the same time that they were unable to work out the more immediate problems plaguing their existing common market. Central Americans have a long history of agreeing to protocols at regional meetings and then failing to ratify them after the leaders have returned home.[25] Similarly, a Latin American president could have chosen either to break the spell of brotherhood at the 1967 Summit Conference or agree to the formation of a Common Market by 1985—when he would almost certainly be out of power. At approximately the same time, the member states of LAFTA were unable to agree on the more modest (but immediate) goal of a contractually overdue second list of goods to be freely traded.

This is not to suggest that the fault lies solely with the leaders. The demands for a sense of identity and status as a larger group in world affairs may be sufficiently widespread among politically relevant groups to make the creation of regional organizations "good politics" from a leader's point of view. But public opinion is not monolithic. Nor as the literature on opinion polls has shown, is it always consistent, even in the same person. Most people have multiple loyalties and senses of identity, and they can switch from one to another according to the situation and their perception of the personal cost involved. For example, Ugandan trade unionists called for a Pan-African foreign policy at the same time that they demanded the exclusion of Kenyan workers.[26] A leader may feel impelled by domestic political needs to agree to the foundation of a regional organization, and later severely limit his commitment to it in response to foot-dragging by civil servants, representatives of low-income areas, or threatened industries (not to mention the possibility of a threat to his personal position).

[25] A crucial protocol on standardization of industrial incentives was delayed for seven years. In early 1968, one-third of the protocols signed during the life of the CACM have not been ratified. See *Latin America* (April 11, 1969), 114.

[26] J. S. Nye, *Pan-Africanism and East African Integration* (Cambridge, Mass. 1965), 199.

In other words, we have suggested two alternative hypotheses (derivative diplomatic uses, ambivalent political identities) as possible ways to account for the increase in the number and proportion of regional institutions. If they are valid, the equilibrium condition for most regional organizations may be a minimal existence that fills the identitive or diplomatic needs without incurring any additional costs. This appears to be particularly true of such manifest "political" organizations as ODECA or the Arab League, but it is probably also true of a number of manifest "economic" organizations such as the Association of Southeast Asian Nations, the Maghreb Council, RCD, or the proposed West African Customs Union. The type of organization which is based on these derivative or identitive functions alone could be said to represent "token integration" at the international level. The increase in the numbers of such regional institutions would not mean an increase in the effectiveness of regional institutions in the future international legal order.

### III. THE FUTURE OF REGIONAL INSTITUTIONS

If the existing evidence about the importance of regional institutions is rather mixed, what can we say about future trends? Will the future remain as ambiguous as the present or will there be clear trends toward or away from a greater importance for regional institutions? Obviously we can merely speculate about the future of these institutions, and the longer the time we assume, the less likely to remain the same are the other things we hold constant.

Nonetheless we can inform our speculations by making explicit our projections of four important determinants: (1) the policies of the Superpowers; (2) technological changes that may affect economic and political decisions; (3) the systems transformation effects of existing regional organizations; and (4) large-scale changes in public opinion resulting from particular events, new issues, or generational change.

Predicting the policies of the U.S. and the U.S.S.R. is beyond the scope of this enterprise. If we project current policies, we find that the United States has been a major promoter of regional organizations in the past quarter decade. United States attitudes toward regional organizations stemmed from a series of *ad hoc* responses: in the Western Hemisphere, from a long historical tradition; in Europe, from a desire to reconstruct a continent left fragmented by war and threatened by cold war; in Africa, representing a response both to economic logic and isolationist impulses; in Asia, relating to American efforts to create a non-Chinese pole of power. A policy toward regional organization *per se* has been raised as an issue in foreign policy debate only twice: once, in the period of planning for a new world organization during the latter part of World War II, and again in the late 1960's, as part of the Vietnam imbroglio.

For the Johnson administration, regionalism offered a means of promising that the costs incurred in Vietnam would not be repeated endlessly by a United States acting as a global policeman. In President Johnson's words, "Our purpose in promoting a world of regional partnerships is not without self interest. For as they grow in strength inside a strong United Nations, we can look forward to a decline in the burden that America has had to bear in this generation." [27] As the London *Economist* noted in 1968, the word regionalism "pops up regularly and has established itself in the Administration's vocabulary to connote a vague kind of principle by which distant continents may get themselves into better order." [28] Not only in declaratory policy, but in practice as well, the rising costs of Vietnam created constraints which increased the emphasis on regionalism in U.S. policy. One of the strands underlying the incorporation of regional criteria in U.S. aid programs for Africa was a Congressional "neo-isolationism" which was heightened by the Vietnam situation and came to be expressed in Congressional resolutions limiting the number of countries to which aid could be given. Similarly, the need to offer something dramatic yet with minimal budgetary implications, at the meeting of Western Hemisphere presidents in 1967, was an important reason for upgrading U.S. support for Latin American regional organization.[29] And in Asia the connection was even more clear. As one administration spokesman told Congress in 1967, "a better Southeast Asia . . . less likely to produce a series of Vietnams can be furthered by regional integration. . . ." [30]

Critics point out that efforts to create regional balances of power—from which the United States as the stronger superpower could stand back and intervene only occasionally to right the scales, in an analogy to Britain's nineteenth century European policy—were at odds with the ideological doctrine of containing Communism sometimes expressed as a goal. So long as ideological containment had priority, the United States could only intervene on one side of the scales. In any case, after the 1968 election and change of administration, there was a marked decrease in the rhetoric of regionalism in U.S. foreign policy,

[27] Lyndon Johnson, *Department of State Bulletin* (September 26, 1966), 453.

[28] *The Economist* (January 27, 1968), 31.

[29] See Robert Denham, "The Role of the U.S. as an External Actor in the Integration of Latin America," *Journal of Common Market Studies*, VII, 3 (March 1969). Also confirmed in interviews by this author.

[30] Rutherford Poats before the House Appropriations Committee, *Foreign Assistance and Related Agencies Appropriations for 1968* (April 26, 1967), 837. I am indebted to Robert Denham for the research that uncovered this and several other references in this chapter.

and, more important, a diminished emphasis on support of regional organization in specific areas such as Europe and Africa.

At the same time that U.S. support for regional organizations was becoming less intense, the interest of the U.S.S.R. in regional organization began to increase. While the U.S.S.R. had consistently followed a policy of a *de facto* regional sphere of influence in Eastern Europe in the postwar period, it had shown far less interest in supporting, and in some cases even a hostility toward, regional organizations in other parts of the world.[31] At the end of the 1960's, however, the U.S.S.R. promoted the idea of an Asian regional collective security idea to include India, Pakistan, Afghanistan, Burma, Cambodia and Singapore as well as a regional trade plan that might also include Turkey and Iran.[32] Initial Soviet efforts were met with coolness, and there is reason to believe that the U.S.S.R. would meet the same limitations in the promotion of regional organizations that confronted the U.S.[33] External actors are only one of a number of factors that support the growth of effective institutions. A rapid growth in the power of China, however, and a concerted Chinese foreign policy effort to create its own regional sphere and organizations might change the situation. Indeed, the unintended effects of superpower policies could have a more important impact on the growth of regional institutions than will their policies of deliberate promotion of such institutions. For example, policies that are perceived in Europe or Asia as a rapid expansion of Soviet power or a rapid withdrawal of American power might seriously alter public attitudes toward transferring power from existing states to regional institutions. We will return to this question below.

A second factor, technological changes that affect political and economic decisions, is likely to have indeterminate effects. On the one hand, skeptics about the future of regional organizations tend to base their argument on the probable direction of technological change. They argue that the revolution in transport, communications, and defense technology is rapidly foreshortening effective distances and calling into question the basis for regionalist schemes.[34] For example,

[31] Klaus Tornudd, *Soviet Attitudes Towards Non-Military Regional Cooperation* (Helsinki 1963).

[32] *New York Times*, September 20, 1969. The ironies were not missed by the Chinese who accused the Russians of having "picked from the garbage-heap of the notorious warmonger John Foster Dulles." *The Economist* (July 5, 1969), 26.

[33] J. S. Nye, "United States Policy Toward Regional Organization," *International Organization*, XXIII (Summer 1969), 724–25.

[34] Albert Wohlstetter, "Illusions of Distance," *Foreign Affairs* (Jan. 1968), 250. Also Institute for Strategic Studies, *The Implications of Military Technology in the 1970s* (London, Adelphia Paper 46, 1968).

the creation of jumbo air-freighters, giant supertankers, and large-scale data-processing that facilitates capital movements and central control in multinational corporations, will make reduction of trade barriers and achievement of economies of scale less dependent on geographical contiguity. Paul Streeten argues that "modern economic facts make for inter-continental groupings because sea freights have fallen compared with land transport costs." [35] According to Samuel Lawrence, "From a transport viewpoint, it is now essentially immaterial whether the manganese brought to the United States originates in Africa or Brazil or whether the iron ores discharged in Rotterdam are brought from one of those regions or Australia." [36]

The growth of global corporations may be a more significant trend in international organization than the growth of regional organizations. In 1965, the 87 largest corporations (of which 60 were domiciled in the United States) had sales greater than the gross national product of the 57 smallest sovereign states. Increasingly such corporations are developing global strategies and absorbing the business done abroad into the mainstream of corporate strategy.[37] In the eyes of some, they are seen as private global decision systems, staffed by Saint-Simonian technocrats responding to criteria of economic rationality rather than regional or national identity in their choices as to the location of industry, employment, or earnings.[38]

In the defense field, nuclear and missile technology has already reduced the role of geographical distance in military security, and further changes of a similar type can be expected from satellite technology, and possibly also from developments in chemical and biological warfare. From a satellite in a synchronous orbit 22,300 miles above the earth, distances beneath are immaterial. It costs no more to send a signal between Alaska and Madagascar than between next door neighbors.[39] In the view of Thomas Schelling, a new type of global geography may be taking over, in which earth spin and cloud cover may become as important in the world of satellites as Suez and Gibraltar were for seapower. In Albert Wohlstetter's words, "the upshot of these

[35] Paul Streeten, "A New Commonwealth," *New Society*, 353 (July 3, 1969).

[36] Samuel A. Lawrence, "Ocean Shipping in the World Economy," *World Affairs*, CXXXII (Sept. 1969), 123.

[37] George Modelski, "The Corporation in World Society," *Yearbook of World Affairs* (1968), 68; Raymond Vernon, "Economic Sovereignty at Bay," *Foreign Affairs*, XLVII (Oct. 1968), 115.

[38] See Sidney Rolfe, *The International Corporation* (Paris 1969); Howard Perlmutter, "Multi-national Corporations," *Columbia Journal of World Business* (Jan.–Feb. 1969); and Charles Kindleberger, *American Business Abroad* (New Haven 1969). For a skeptical view, see "Notes on the Multinational Corporation," *Monthly Review* (Oct.–Nov. 1969).

[39] *The Economist* (Feb. 22, 1969), 58.

considerations of technology in the 1970's, is that basic interests in safety will extend further out than they ever have before." [40]

It would be mistaken, however, to conclude from the projection of technological trends that there will not also be important regional systems—whether economic or military. For one thing, such a conclusion would be somewhat premature, at least for the early 1970's. Despite falling transport costs, geography will still have an impact on price. Despite missile and satellite technology, local and conventional defense techniques will remain relevant, particularly for less-developed countries. Moreover, some technological changes may have a positive effect on regional organization. Technological changes may reduce the autonomy of the nation-state, but if for historical or psychological reasons this leads to the redistribution of only *part* of these national powers at the regional level, the result would be a strengthening of regional organization. For example communications technology may make possible direct and inexpensive regional communications in areas like Latin America or Africa, where intraregional communications now often have to go through New York, London, or Paris. Large international corporations, to take another example, may prove to be important catalysts by regarding groups of countries as regions and acting accordingly.[41]

Technology and systems of transactions are not the only determinants of international politics. As Pierre Hassner points out, "political geography is made of history, anthropology, and psychology, as much as of physical geography." Oceans, skin, color, and other crude images of regions constitute points of salience "which emerge out of history and leave their mark on psychology." Unlike the United States, China need not establish the credibility of her long-term presence in Asia.[42] Nor is it technology that made three Arab states contribute two-thirds of Jordan's budget after the June war of 1967.[43] Moreover, popular images tend to lag considerably behind technology changes—witness the relative indifference in American public attitudes toward Japan, or the limitation of public commitment to geographically proximate areas.[44] As long ago as 1943 some commentators were predicting that

[40] Speech to Foreign Policy Association, New York (May 1968); Wohlstetter (fn. 34), 252.

[41] For evidence of this type of effect, see Raymond Vernon, "Multinational Enterprise and National Sovereignty," *Harvard Business Review*, XLV (March–April 1967), 156ff.

[42] Pierre Hassner, "The Nation-State in the Nuclear Age," *Survey* (April 1968), 12, 13.

[43] *International Herald Tribune*, February 19, 1969. By the end of 1969 Kuwait, Saudi Arabia, and Libya had contributed $321 million to Egypt and Jordan. *New York Times*, December 24, 1969.

[44] See *The Economist* (November 15, 1969), 44; Louis Harris poll in *Time* (May 2, 1969).

the development of modern transport and communications would probably "destroy both the objective and subjective grounds for regionalism." [45]

If there were a one to one relationship between systems of interdependence, as measured by transactions or technological links and states' willingness to consent to international organization, we might have more confidence in projections about regional organization that are based solely on technology or transactions. In fact, the relationship is made more complex by the fact that elite perceptions of different types of interdependence is an essential link in the causal chain. For example, when there are various types of interdependence, why do states choose to form organizations on the basis of some rather than others?

If we think of "states" in terms of elites or groups of competing bureaucracies instead of as single rational units, we can see that different types of interdependence will affect the interests of (and be recognized by) different groups in different ways. An insecure political elite may be more concerned with interdependence in public opinion (and might create an organization in response to such opinion), while a technocratic elite might pay more attention to trade interdependence. For example, in Central America in 1951, the traditional political elite founded an organization reflecting diplomatic and domestic political interdependence, while a new generation of technocrats was allowed by default to found another (and ultimately more successful) organization—not on the basis of actual trade transactions (which were extremely low) but on the basis of *anticipated* transactions.

A third factor that might determine the future is the effect of existing regional organizations on their related state systems. Given the impact of its demonstration effect on the rest of the world, this is particularly interesting in the case of Europe. In Haas' words, one model of international system transformation "credits the international organization with the capacity to produce feedbacks that result in changed perspectives on the part of national actors." The other model "puts the emphasis on autonomous changes within nations. Developments in the various domestic social, economic and political sectors are conceived as proceeding more rapidly and decisively than the learning of lessons fed back from the international system." [46] According to the regionalist doctrine, microregional economic organizations serve as particularly effective generators of the forces that can lead to the overcoming of national sovereignty and the transformation of the international system.

45 Pittmann B. Potter, "Universalism Versus Regionalism in International Organization," *American Political Science Review*, XXXVIII (1943), 852.
46 Ernst Haas, *Tangle of Hopes* (Englewood Cliffs, N.J. 1968), 29.

We would argue, however, on the basis of a model elaborated else-where, that integration processes slow down rather than accelerate over time, particularly in less-developed areas.[47] First, in most settings the process of politicization means that low-cost integration and tech-nocratic style decision-making procedures are unlikely to last very long; certainly not until widespread popular support or a powerful coalition of intensely concerned interests have developed to the point where they determine the decisions of political leaders.

Second, the ability to reach difficult political agreement on "positive integration" measures to cope with the problems created by redistri-bution is likely to lag behind the forces created by more easily agreed-upon liberalization measures. Alternatively, in settings where market forces are weak and liberalization cannot be agreed upon, it seems likely that process forces will also be weak.

Third, the sense of reduced alternatives and the precipitation of larger crises will probably fail to have an integrative effect the closer the issues come to the security and identitive areas that are of greatest concern to popular political leaders. These are also the areas in which they are least likely to have the clear overriding common interests that make crises productive rather than destructive. Finally, the pres-sures both inside and outside the region for a common external policy are likely to develop more rapidly than popular or group support for a high degree of integration in these generally more controversial fields.

In brief, unless the structure of incentives offered by the interna-tional system is seriously altered, the prospects for microregional eco-nomic organizations leading in the short run of decades to federation, or to some sort of political union capable of an independent defense and foreign policy, do not seem very high. This does not mean, of course, that coordination of economic policies cannot help provide a basis for more coordination of foreign and defense policies so long as that is desired by the relevant political leaders. But this is a far cry from political union and a single external policy.

If common markets do not lead to federation, does this mean that they must slip back or fall apart? Is there no point of equilibrium in between? The belief that common markets must go forward or fall back is widely accepted. It has even been accepted by such skeptics as Stanley Hoffmann, who argues that "half-way attempts like supra-national functionalism must either snowball of roll back." [48]

Our basic hypothesis is that most political decision-makers will opt for the *status quo* at any level so long as the process forces or popular

[47] J. S. Nye, *Peace in Parts: Integration and Conflict in Regional Organization* (Boston 1971), Chap. 3.

[48] "Obstinate or Obsolete? The Fate of the Nation State and the Case of Western Europe," in J. S. Nye, ed., *International Regionalism* (Boston 1968), 229.

pressures are not so strong as to make this choice unbearable for them. If the process forces are too strong, political decision-makers may downgrade commitments to a point where they are tolerable, as happened in East Africa. But though equilibrium may not be tolerable at a given level, it does not follow that the only equilibrium point is in the cellar of disintegration. On the contrary, a certain amount of economic integration, particularly if it can be handled by the "hidden hand" of market forces and thus not involve costly political decisions, may go part way to meet the concerns of those who argue that existing states are too small to provide adequate welfare. Half-measures may take the edge off the urgency of the situation, reduce the force of the demands of the "new feudalists" who wish to reduce the role of the sovereign states, and strengthen regional institutions at the subnational and supranational levels.

Moreover, as Krause and Lindberg have pointed out and the case of EFTA shows, this type of market integration need not greatly strengthen the regional institutions.[49] In short, it seems most likely that under the current structure of international incentives, most political decision-makers will find some point of equilibrium at which they would rather tolerate the inconvenience of the existing level of process forces than incur the greater political costs of full integration or disintegration.

Barring dramatic events or pressures from the international environment and barring forces released by generational change, a rapid transformation as the result of existing integration processes is unlikely. System transformation will occur, indeed has occurred, in the sense of altering the locus of decision-making between states and region in a number of issue areas. But the result is what we might call a functional-region, rather than a highly unified region.[50] Even under relatively favorable conditions, such as in Europe, it seems doubtful that the integration process forces will be strong enough to bring about major shifts in the locus of decision-making for most spheres of activity between member states and regional organizations in the next decade or so.

This leads us to the fourth factor we will consider—large-scale changes in public opinion resulting from factors exogenous to our model. Public-opinion studies show that mass opinion determines elite behavior only when it is strong and intense. Despite popular expres-

[49] Leon Lindberg, "Integration as a Source of Stress on the European Community System," in Nye (fn. 48). Lawrence Krause, *European Economic Integration and the United States* (Washington 1968), 24.

[50] This term implies that some functions, e.g. nuclear defense, may be handled in large part outside the region. See Alastair Buchan, *Europe's Future, Europe's Choices* (London 1969).

sions favorable to regional organization, opinion in Europe and elsewhere has tended to provide only a permissive consensus rather than a clear direction.[51] When probed for intensity, public opinion tends to become rather ambiguous. While 60 percent to 80 percent of Europeans favored a united Europe, only half that number favored a federation.[52] A majority of Frenchmen voted Gaullist and supported the political unification of Europe at the same time.[53] Nor was elite opinion consistently intense. For instance, a majority of French and German elites favored limited sovereignty in principle, but preferred to rely on national defense measures in practice.[54]

One potential source of a more intense public opinion is generational change. There is evidence to show that younger groups in regions like Europe are more favorable to unity than their elders.[55] In addition many activist youth groups respond to a technologically transmitted transnational culture that deliberately downplays national identity.[56] But their attitude that "Europe exists," without paying attention to institutional ways to replace existing national organizations, probably means that they will either be socialized by the existing pattern of interests and institutions that respond to the needs of the more national majority or will be relegated to ineffectiveness.

Another possible source of intensification of opinion could be the impact of particular cataclysmic events in one of the Superpowers, between the Superpowers, or in their policies toward given areas. The rise of a dictatorial regime, inadvertent wars, a renewed military threat, or sudden withdrawal of support might have such an effect.[57]

A less dramatic source of change in public opinion might come from the gradual politicization of the environmental pollution problem. Pollution is not merely a regional problem; nor is it a problem that attracts the attention of elites in all regions. Nonetheless, there are signs of a growing awareness of the regional aspects of pollution in Europe. Pollution of the Rhine and North Sea has become some-

[51] See Leon Lindberg and Stuart Scheingold, *Europe's Would Be Polity* (Englewood Cliffs, N.J. 1970); also William E. Fisher, "An Analysis of the Deutsch Sociocausal Paradigm of Political Integration," *International Organization* (Autumn 1969), 289.

[52] Jacques René Rabier, *L'Opinion Publique et L'Europe* (Brussels 1966), 23.

[53] See Alain Lancelot and Pierre Weill, "Les Français et l'Unification Politique de l'Europe, d'Après un Sondage de la SOFRES," *Revue Française de Science Politique*, XIX (February 1969), 166, 147.

[54] See Robert Weissberg, "Nationalism, Integration and French and German Elites," *International Organization* (Autumn 1969), 341.

[55] See Ronald Inglehart, "An End to European Integration?" *American Political Science Review* 67 (March 1967); also Anitra Karsten, *Comment les Jeunes Allemands Voient Les Autres Peuples* (Brussels 1969).

[56] See the description in Anthony Sampson, *The New Europeans* (London 1968), Chap. 21.

[57] See the argument on withdrawal of American troops in Buchan (fn. 50).

thing of an issue between the Netherlands and Germany. Newspapers have carried accounts of "black snow" falling in Norway as the result of pollutants dispersed into the air in the Ruhr.[58] The UN Economic Commission for Europe has begun to look at pollution in both Eastern and Western Europe. As yet, however, environmental pollution tends to be treated as a problem requiring technical cooperation rather than as a problem calling for a major regional political solution.

Barring such changes, the growing obsolescence of the nation-state is unlikely to induce a dramatic shift in public opinion. As Herz describes it, the rise of the nation-state followed the invention of gunpowder and the development of professional infantry, which destroyed the impenetrability of the medieval castle. Now with air warfare, nuclear weapons, economic blockades, and ideological warfare, the hard protective shell of the state has become "permeable." Or in Boulding's terms, there are no longer any snugly protected centers of national power, and all states are only "conditionally viable." [59] But this is already accepted in a verbal way by many European elites.[60]

The argument that the state is obsolete, in terms of welfare functions, emphasizes the enormous costs of research and development in such technologically modern industries as electronics, aircraft, space satellites, and nuclear energy, and cites the fact that the United States spends more on research and development in three weeks than Germany or France spends in a year.[61] For many developing countries, the argument is that their internal markets are too small to achieve economies of scale in any but a small range of industries.

But the obsolescence of the nation-state is nowhere near as complete as it is sometimes claimed to be. Take the failure to provide security. Nuclear deterrence has made viability conditional, but not as a fact of daily life in such a way as to weaken national loyalties. In terms of welfare, the argument is mainly against the *size* of some states, and tends to neglect the question of distribution. After all, one role of the state has been to preserve inequality of welfare vis-à-vis outsiders, and this it has done and will continue to do all too well— witness the response of the wealthy states to poverty in the Third World.

One thing that many nation-states no longer successfully provide,

[58] *New York Times,* January 11, 1970. See also "Europe Unfit to Live In," *Agenor,* No. 14 (Dec. 1969), 27–43.

[59] John Herz, "The Rise and Demise of the Territorial State," *World Politics,* IX (July 1957), 473–93. Kenneth Boulding, *Conflict and Defense* (New York 1962).

[60] See Morton Gorden and Daniel Lerner, "The Setting for European Arms Control: Political and Strategic Choices of European Elites," *Journal of Conflict Resolution,* IX (December 1965), 428.

[61] See Robert Gilpin, *France in the Age of the Scientific State* (Princeton 1968), Chap. 2.

however, is a sense of identity, of pride, of "counting for something in the world" for some of their elite groups. As we argued earlier, in Africa, Latin America, and Europe, the desire by some elites to achieve equality of status and to project an image of power in world affairs is an important motive for the creation of regional organizations. But we also argued that the strength of the organizations that can be built on this sense of regional identity has not so far been such as to challenge the nation-states.

Welfare and security often prove to be stronger incentives than the sense of identity that is expressed at the regional level.[62] Take, for example, European responses to the "challenge" of direct investment by large American corporations. Some Europeans urge a nonregional response of accepting close economic linkages with the North American (and to a lesser extent Japanese) economy, carving out areas of comparative advantage through specialization as the Swiss and Swedes have done. Others like J. J. Servan Schreiber argue that maximizing welfare is not enough, and that European identity and power are also important. Too close linkages with the global or Atlantic economy could hinder these objectives by making Europe overly dependent on imports of technological innovations. It is not enough for Europeans to live like Swiss or Swedes.[63] Rather they must build a strong regional unit capable of being an independent power in world politics. An individual European manufacturer, however, much as he might agree with Servan Schreiber in principle, would probably put welfare first if faced with the choice of merging with another weak European firm to counter the threat of an American intruder, or merging with the American firm to reap the profits of the imported technology and skills.[64]

The net effect of these four factors is, unhappily, indeterminate. Technology is shrinking the importance of distance. Other factors, however, work to enhance the importance of the iconographic aspects of geographical images.[65] Most believers in regionalism do not see "regions" as a technocratic planner might—as a set of variable and overlapping or, in some cases, concentric geographical units. On the contrary, regionalists see regions as groups of states with a similar con-

[62] In 1969, among British reluctant to join the Common Market, a possible rise in cost of living outweighed all other fears by ten to one. *The Economist* (September 27, 1969), 1.

[63] J. J. Servan Schreiber, *The American Challenge*, trans. R. Steel (New York 1968), 111.

[64] See Raymond Aron, quoted in Gilpin (fn. 61), 425.

[65] The novelty of elites' concern for world status should not be overestimated. *The Economist* (October 15, 1864) noted "the desire now manifesting itself in so many quarters of the world for aggregation, the wish to belong to a great and powerful community able to defend itself, and able also to exert a powerful influence on the progress of the world."

cern about loss of status or defense against outside forces, who have chosen a geographical symbol around which to aggregate their power, at either high or low levels of integration.[66]

Given the growing imbalance among nations in the world, the disproportionate size of the United States and its capacity to penetrate other societies, the increasing role of multinational corporations, and the perceived threat to indigenous cultures from mass communications, there will continue to be strong incentives for elites to create and use regional organizations.

If the demand for identity should lead to widespread dissatisfaction with existing nation-states and the development of strong regional attitudes, the technological changes that are reducing—but not eliminating—the importance of proximity could lead statesmen to support more *effective* regional institutions. If identitive demands are not intense at the regional level, it seems more likely that technological changes will lead in the direction of functional type organizations. Such organizations might have a regional core such as the OECD or the Group of Ten have, but the common denominator would be less a geographic proximity or imagery than a mutual high level of development.[67] Such institutions at different levels may fulfill various needs —if not perfectly, at least sufficiently to reduce pressing problems to second-order ones of inefficiency. We reach these conclusions, however, with awareness that the unknowns are generally the most important terms in equations about the future.

[66] See Gustavo Lagos, "The Political Role of Regional Economic Organizations in Latin America," *Journal of Common Market Studies*, VI (June 1968).

[67] See Edward L. Morse, "The Politics of Interdependence," *International Organization* (Autumn 1969).

# CHAPTER 12

# The Future Role of International
# Institutions

## DONALD W. McNEMAR

INTERNATIONAL institutions have become an accepted phenomenon in the contemporary international system. Although such intergovernmental organizations developed only after the Congress of Vienna, it is impossible to imagine the operation of international politics today without such structures. While states remain the primary actors in the contemporary world, international institutions provide an important arena for interaction and introduce a new set of participants into international politics. These institutions represent an important variable in the international system, and therefore, raise the significant question of what will be their function and impact in the future.

One indication of the increasing relevance of international institutions to world politics is the rapid growth in the number of such organizations. Wallace and Singer found that the number of intergovernmental organizations had risen from 1 in 1815 to 192 in 1960.[1] The authors report that the total growth rate for such organizations is exponential; and even controlling for the expanding number of nations within the system, a linear relationship remains between the number of international organizations and the passage of time. This rapid growth in the number of institutions produced a 64.0 percent increase between 1956 and 1963, and the most noticeable gains were in regional organizations. The number of worldwide institutions grew by 33.5 percent and particularistic organizations by 28 percent, while regional institutions increased 167.2 percent.[2] The formation of the Common Market during this period inflated the number of regional groups, but even if these particular organizations are excluded, the remaining number of regional organizations increased by 76.5 percent. Not only has the number of institutions grown, but the number of nation memberships in globally oriented organizations has multiplied as well with a 7 percent annual increase in the 1956–1963 period.[3]

[1] Michael Wallace and J. David Singer, "Intergovernmental Organization in the Global System, 1815–1964: A Quantitative Description," *International Organization*, XXIV (Spring 1970), 272.

[2] Robert C. Angell, "An Analysis of Trends in International Organizations," *Peace Research Society (International) Papers*, III (1965), 186.

[3] Same, 193.

Although the Wallace and Singer article (fn. 1), represents the most extensive analysis of international organizations and the trends relating to their development,

This expansion in the number of organizations and the participation by states indicates the importance of international institutions. The rate of increase in numbers of institutions may lessen in the future, since the expansion of the system via new states is ceasing and nongovernmental organizations are assuming more functions.[4] However, these trends away from the formation of new organizations must be balanced against the increase in technological functions and the continued need for cooperation within an organizational setting. The rate of formation of new organizations cannot be accurately predicted, yet there are no trends suggesting a dissolution of such organizations. The number of international institutions has risen rapidly over the last 150 years, and there is every indication that they will remain important actors in the future international system.

In assessing the impact of these structures on the international system, the relationship between such organizations as the United Nations and the system must be viewed as a two-way relationship with influence flowing in both directions.[5] In the past much emphasis has been placed on the nature of the international system as a determinant of United Nations behavior.[6] Such analysis often describes the UN as the dependent variable, and the international system as the independent variable. This approach can be used to explain the inability of the UN to insure peace and social change, but such an emphasis obscures the impact which international institutions may have on the international system.

An alternative conception of this relationship is one in which the international system determines constraints on the organizations, and

---

other studies of this nature include Bruce M. Russett, *International Regions and the International System* (Chicago 1967), 94–121 and Paul Smoker, "Nation State Escalation and International Integration," *Journal of Peace Research*, No. 1 (1967), 61–73.

[4] Wallace and Singer predict "a decreasing rate of growth into the 1980's and a nearly total cessation of growth by the early 21st century." Their forecast is based on the lack of new states that will arise in the future, a reevaluation of the cost-to-effectiveness ratio of these organizations, and a rise in nongovernmental activity. Wallace and Singer (fn. 1), 284.

[5] The impact of organizations such as the United Nations has always been difficult to judge. For two interesting attempts to evolve strategies for evaluating this influence see Gabriella Rosner Lande, "An Inquiry into the Successes and Failures of the United Nations General Assembly," in Leon Gordenker, ed., *The United Nations in International Politics* (Princeton 1971), 106–29 and Ernst B. Haas, "Collective Security and the Future of the International System," in Richard A. Falk and Cyril E. Black, eds., *The Future of the International Legal Order*, Vol. 1, *Trends and Patterns* (Princeton 1969), 226–316.

[6] For analysis of the impact of the structure of the international system on the operation of the United Nations see Wolfram F. Hanrieder, "International Organizations and International Systems," *Journal of Conflict Resolution*, x (September 1966), 297–313 and Stanley Hoffmann, "International Organization and the International System," *International Organization*, xxiv (Summer 1970), 389–413.

the institutions, in turn, affect the operation of international politics.[7] Such characteristics of the international system as the type of units, the power relationships, and the goals of actors all serve to define the limits placed on the capabilities and functions of the international institutions. However, the organizations, once established have an impact on world politics by forcing states to examine their goals and conduct in light of the procedures and purposes of the existing institutions.[8] In examining the future of international institutions one must start with the characteristics of the international system as determinants of the nature of the institutions, and then also examine the impact of the organizations on that system.

In emphasizing this two-way flow of influence, it is necessary to conceive of international institutions as both instruments of states *and* as actors in the international system.[9] These organizations are often analyzed from the instrumental perspective which views them as an additional channel states can use in pursuing their national interests. Certainly to the policy-maker within a state faced with solving a problem, regional or international organizations represent one of many alternatives. States may or may not choose to use these instruments. In a situation such as Vietnam, where states chose not to use this particular structure, the capabilities of the institutions evaporate and the role they can play is restricted. Because the international organizations are instruments of states, it is always necessary to consider the political support among members in any given situation. The primary factor determining the effectiveness of an organization in this decentralized international system is the attitude of member states. Therefore, international organizations must be viewed as instruments of states.

However, to think of international institutions like the UN as only tools with no capacity to act is to misunderstand the organizations. International institutions possess certain characteristics which do enable them to contribute independently to the process of international politics. The organizations provide a multilateral forum for debate and action which enjoys legitimacy and popular support. The secretariats for these organizations can take initiatives for action and serve as world spokesmen. Institutions can also grant or withhold approval

[7] Young emphasizes "the proposition that the United Nations is an actor in world politics." Oran R. Young, "The United Nations and the International System," in Gordenker, ed., *The United Nations in International Politics* (fn. 5), 10–14.

[8] This phenomenon is pointed out by Falk when he notes that "there is a refraction effect discernible, such that the United Nations setting may be said to influence the ways in which conflicts are conducted and justified." Richard A. Falk, "The United Nations: Various Systems of Operation," in Gordenker, ed., *The United Nations in International Politics* (fn. 5), 191.

[9] For emphasis on this dual conception see Linda B. Miller, "International Organization and Internal Conflicts: Some Emerging Patterns of Response," in Gordenker, ed., *The United Nations in International Politics* (fn. 5), 131.

for unilateral state policies. Once an action is undertaken by an international organization it can influence the policies of individual states, thus making the institution an actor in international politics.

Effective analysis of international institutions must combine these two views of such organizations since neither is satisfactory by itself.[10] International institutions do represent instruments which states use in their relations, but at the same time the organizations act within the system affecting state policies.

## TYPES OF INTERNATIONAL INSTITUTIONS

The term international institution is used to refer to intergovernmental organizations possessing formal, ongoing structures, such as charters, regular meetings, or secretariat staff.[11] These organizations draw together a number of states for regularized interaction. The types of international organizations are indeed varied, and can be divided on the basis of the extent of membership or the nature of their purpose.

The two primary categories concerned with the size of membership are regional and global institutions. Regional bodies are made up of states from a particular area and the membership is limited to a specific continent or region of the world, for example the Organization of African Unity, the European Economic Community, and the Organization of American States.[12] The rapid development of numerous regional organizations has been an important addition to the types of institutions operating in the international system. During the period from 1949 to 1967 global intergovernmental organizations increased from 33 to 88, but the number of regional organizations increased from 5 to 111.[13] Nye reports that regional organizations represent 53

[10] In discussing the conceptualization of the United Nations Hanrieder suggests that: "In performing its designated functions, which presumably affect the conditions of the system by solving tasks, the organization may also be viewed as an *actor* of the international system. Depending on the analytical purpose and vantage point, an international organization may therefore be viewed either as an *actor*, along with other actors in the system including the members of the organization, or as one of many possible *structures* through which the members of the system address themselves to tasks and projects which arise from the ends-means relationhips of the system." Hanrieder (fn. 6), 297.

[11] Hanrieder has defined international organization as "an institutionalized arrangement among members of the international system to solve tasks which have evolved from systemic conditions." Same, 297.

[12] For further discussion of the concept of regionalism see Joseph S. Nye, ed., *International Regionalism* (Boston 1968) and Joseph S. Nye, *Peace in Parts: Integration and Conflict in Regional Organization* (Boston 1971), and Ellen Frey-Wouters, "The Prospects for Regionalism in World Affairs," in Falk and Black, eds., *The Future of the International Legal Order*, Vol. 1, *Trends and Patterns* (fn. 5), 463–555.

[13] William D. Coplin, *Introduction to International Politics* (Chicago 1971), 164.

percent of the new organizations founded between 1815 and 1965.[14]
These regional organizations draw together contiguous states which
tend to be homogeneous and share similar problems. To date such
organizations have suffered either from a lack of resources for effective
action as in the case of the OAU or they have fallen under the hegemony of a superpower such as the case of the OAS.[15] While the role of
regional organizations has been limited in the past, the desire of states
to handle problems on a local rather than a global plane could lead
to a significant increase in the role played by regional organizations.[16]

In contrast to the regional structures are the global institutions
which include nations from throughout the world. The United Nations
is the best example of such an institution which has members from
all regions of the world and is concerned with a variety of purposes.
Although universality of membership has not been achieved, the variety of cross pressures and splits between the East and West and North
and South are all represented in the UN. This diversity makes global
institutions, such as the International Labour Organization, the International Atomic Energy Agency, and the International Monetary Fund,
forums for resolution of a variety of world problems.

International institutions may also be categorized on the basis of
the functions performed. Certain organizations have generalized tasks,
while others specialize. The UN, OAU, and OAS are good examples
of general organizations since they have responsibilities in such widespread areas as security, human rights, development, and arms control.
In effect there are many issues which can be brought before these
organizations. On the other hand, such institutions as the International
Bank for Reconstruction and Development, NATO, the Warsaw Pact,
and the Food and Agriculture Organization are all organizations with
specific functions. Such functional organizations are not void of politics, but because they handle fairly technical issues, they may exhibit
a greater willingness to disengage these functions from other issues and
cooperate on a particular service which needs to be accomplished and
can only be achieved through interstate cooperation.[17] The theory of
some functionalists that success in technical fields will lead directly
to political integration cannot be assumed.[18] These specialized insti-

[14] Nye, *Peace in Parts* (fn. 12), 4.

[15] For discussion of the hegemonic nature of US participation in this regional
organization see Minerva M. Etzioni, *The Majority of One: Towards a Theory of
Regional Compatibility* (Beverly Hills 1970).

[16] Oran R. Young, "Political Discontinuities in the International System," *World
Politics*, xx (April 1968), 369–92.

[17] The impact of politics on development programs is analyzed in Leon Gordenker, "The United Nations and Economic and Social Change," in Gordenker, ed.,
*The United Nations in International Politics* (fn. 5), 151–83.

[18] The traditional functionalist approach positing spillover from nonpolitical to
political issues is developed in David Mitrany, *A Working Peace System* (London

tutions may produce significant cooperation based simply on the common interest of states in achieving a specialized function.

In this discussion of the nature of the future of international institutions, particular emphasis is placed on the United Nations as a global, general institution with high visibility and moderate successes. The UN was chosen since it seems to include the characteristics of many other institutions, yet not bias the analysis in a favorable direction. It reflects every cleavage and disruption within the system. The UN is given minimal amounts of resources and support and at the same time called upon to produce the most phenomenal results. Furthermore, the UN most broadly reflects the general international system. For these reasons the illustrations and analyses in this chapter are based on this organization, although much of what is suggested is equally applicable to other regional or specialized institutions as well. If the UN is capable of a particular impact or function, then those organizations with fewer members and more technical roles may also be capable of certain influences on the international system.

## Predicting the Future

In examining the future of international relations various strategies may be undertaken in an attempt to understand future events and thereby to influence them in a desired direction.[19] One approach is an examination of alternative models.[20] By explicating the possible future developments an increased understanding about their operation can be gained and evaluations made about their desirability.[21] An additional means of examining the future is through extension of current trends.[22] Such a practice makes one quickly aware of the implications of present practices by extending them into the future and suggesting what is likely to occur if these trends and rates of change are continued. Finally, one may undertake to present causal statements about the future developments. This practice isolates factors

---

1946), and an evaluation of this approach is found in James Patrick Sewell, *Functionalism and World Politics* (Princeton 1966).

[19] Haas suggests three approaches to studying the future: 1) construction of utopias, 2) various types of projections, and 3) use of selective developmental models which he describes as "contingent forecasting based on articulate assumptions, established trends, and probable logical connections between these." Haas (fn. 5), 228.

[20] One imaginative attempt to formulate alternative futures is the World Order Models Project of the World Law Fund.

[21] The Clark-Sohn model has been used as an explicit diagram of one future alternative. Grenville Clark and Louis B. Sohn, *World Peace through World Law* (Cambridge 1966). For a set of readings directed toward evaluation of this model and strategies of transition toward that end see Richard A. Falk and Saul H. Mendlovitz, eds., *The Strategy of World Order* (New York 1966).

[22] Bruce M. Russett, *Trends in World Politics* (New York 1965).

responsible for actions and predicts that certain circumstances will result in particular events.[23]

The rapid rate of change in the international system and its extensive impact on all individuals has made efforts to understand the future essential.[24] In order to plan rational policy today, statesmen must be in a position to make intelligent judgments about the implications of their actions for the future. By making judgments about desirable alternative futures, by examining the positions toward which the present trends are leading, and by making clear the causal links, the future may be incorporated into policy-making so that a transition may be attempted from the current situation to a more desirable world order.

To appreciate the nature of the future environment within which states will interact, it is necessary to examine the role of international institutions. Given the expanding number of international institutions and their continuation as actors and instruments of the international scene, the role they will play and the impact they will have on the actions of nations in the future should be judged. The tasks undertaken here are an explication of assumptions about the future international system which will determine the course of international institutions, an examination of the capabilities possessed by these institutions, and an assessment concerning functions such institutions will fulfill in the future international system. On the basis of this analysis it is possible to suggest the contributions of international institutions to the international legal order in the coming decades.

## Assumptions about the International System

A series of assumptions about the nature of the international system in the near future can be made based on current trends. The characteristics of this system constrain the nature and functions of institutions within world politics. Therefore, expectations about the future international system form the basis for judging the role of international institutions as a factor in the international environment.

The first assumption made is that the nation-state will remain the primary actor within the international system. Although there are increases in transnational politics and a shift in certain functions from the states to other actors, the ultimate resort to force rests with the individual state. Although there may be powerful arguments for a

---

[23] Claude describes this process of prediction about the future, but warns about the unknowable factors in the UN's future. Inis L. Claude, Jr., "Implications and Questions for the Future," *International Organization*, XIX (Summer 1965), 835–37.
[24] The importance of examining the future is persuasively argued in Alvin Toffler, *Future Shock* (New York 1970), 446–87.

new form of organization to meet world order problems,[25] there seem to be no forces at work at the moment which would produce a shift away from organization as nation-states by the turn of the century. Therefore it is safe to predict that the international system will remain a decentralized one in which the primary actors are sovereign states.

Concomitant with this survival of sovereign states will be a continued reliance on deterrence as a means of maintaining peace within the system. As long as the decision to fight resides within the nation-states the primary mechanism for limiting the use of the prerogative is the balance of force.[26] Nuclear deterrence will continue to be the primary restraint on the major powers which prevents escalation of conflicts into open war. While efforts at disarmament and peaceful change may supplement and contain this process, the ultimate means of maintaining peace will continue to be a balancing of military power.

Shifts in the distribution of power within the international system may well occur. The trend toward multipolarity can be expected to continue and the assumption of major roles by countries such as China will definitely contribute to the obscuring of the bipolar complex. The increase in power and influence of the new great powers such as Germany and Japan insures that the multipolar structure is enhanced. Furthermore, the disassociation of various spheres such as economics and security produces a much more diversified multipolar framework in which countries align differently on various issues.[27] Although states will remain as the primary actors, the power relationships may shift significantly, demonstrating increased flexibility in the pattern of alliances.

A second major assumption about the future international system is a change in emphasis from foreign to domestic concerns. Two developments have helped to insure that states will place greater importance on domestic policy rather than on international policy in the future. One development is the increased salience of internal issues in both developing and developed countries. The need for modernization

[25] For an analysis of the severity of problems relating to the war system, overpopulation, depletion of resources, and the environment, and a discussion of the necessity for new forms of government to deal with these problems see Richard A. Falk, *This Endangered Planet* (New York 1971).

For a discussion of trends and forces which might lead to a world altered along transnational lines consult Robert O. Keohane and Joseph S. Nye, eds., "Transnational Relations and World Politics," *International Organization*, xxv (Summer 1971).

[26] Emphasis on the continued importance of the balance of power in controlling military force is found in Alastair Buchan, *War in Modern Society* (New York 1966), 142–98 and Raymond Aron, *Peace and War* (New York 1968), 665–702.

[27] Haas places strong emphasis on the fact that tasks of international organizations are becoming "self-encapsulating and self-sufficient" rather than being closely intertwined. Ernst B. Haas, *The Web of Interdependence: The United States and International Organizations* (Englewood Cliffs, N.J. 1970), 113.

and rapid advances in the standard of living forces the new states into an emphasis on nationalism and progress on the domestic scene. At the same time older states are also becoming increasingly aware that problems with poverty in the midst of affluence, discrimination against minorities, and dissatisfaction with traditional methods are apt to occur in old as well as in new states.[28] Another development is the perception of an increased impact of international issues on national politics.[29] No longer is foreign policy an entirely separate preserve in which heads of state can operate autonomously. Rather foreign interventions and involvements are perceived as directly detracting from the resources available for the solution of domestic issues. The domestic scene is sensitive to international ventures such as the war in Vietnam or distribution of foreign aid. Given this increasing awareness of domestic problems and of the influence of international operations on these concerns, states are devoting more attention to internal rather than external issues.[30] This emphasis on avoiding foreign involvement in order to concentrate on domestic issues may result in a transfer of certain tasks to international institutions.

While states may shift their concerns to domestic issues, the third major trend assures that they will not withdraw altogether from world politics. Interdependence is also a predominant trend in the future.[31] States are being drawn into greater and greater reliance on each other for achievement of their goals. The increased capability for communication provides the opportunity for interaction. The expansion of the number of tasks which need interstate cooperation to solve them, such as environmental problems, are drawing states together. The necessity of cooperation in the economic sphere and the irreverence displayed by corporations for national entities also demonstrate this developing interdependence. Such interconnections between states will continue to develop and will be an important factor in the future international system. This phenomenon may have both positive and negative effects

[28] This emphasis on domestic priorities is noted in Miller (fn. 9), 135.

[29] Hoffmann describes this as the "increasing interpenetration between domestic politics and international politics." Hoffmann (fn. 6), 400.

[30] In recommending policy for the United States toward international organizations, Haas points out that "the first duty of American politics is to work toward the perfection of American society itself," and recommends a policy of "prudential withdrawal and selective recommitment" toward the tasks of international organizations. Ernst B. Haas, *Tangle of Hopes: American Commitments and World Order* (Englewood Cliffs, N.J. 1969), 236.

[31] Edward L. Morse, "The Politics of Interdependence," *International Organization*, XXIII (Spring 1969), 311–26 and Oran R. Young, "Interdependencies in World Politics," *International Journal*, XXIV (Autumn 1969), 726–50. For an argument against the interdependence thesis see Kenneth N. Waltz, "The Myth of National Interdependence," in Charles P. Kindleberger, ed., *The International Corporation* (Cambridge 1970), 205–23.

on the development of the international community,[32] but the mounting interdependence will have an impact on the functions of international institutions.

A fourth characteristic of the future international system will be the continuing demand for change. There will be no significant slackening in the pleas for changes of all sorts, from colonized to decolonized, from developing to developed, from capitalist to socialist. In short the system will continue to have revolutionary tendencies.[33] While certain conflicts such as the East-West struggle may become more muted than at the height of the cold war, there is no real indication that a status quo orientation will prevail. Rather a variety of tensions will continue to exist, with insistent demands by the parties to these disparities that they be remedied. While a certain amount of moderateness may be applied, the international system will remain one in which the need for mechanisms for peaceful change will be important.

Given the expectation that at the turn of the century the international system will be composed of states which place emphasis on domestic issues and which are increasingly interdependent but still produce demands for significant changes, what role will international institutions play in this particular system? Three alternative roles can be hypothesized and examined in light of how they would operate in such a system. One alternative would be the development of a world government. Despite the needs for such a structure to insure international peace, it seems unlikely that transition to such an organization will be accomplished in the twentieth century. Although solution to such problems as nuclear war, the environment, and population may require greater centralization of authority,[34] the continued primacy of states precludes the development of world government.

A second alternative might be the dissolution of international institutions, with increasing emphasis on the autonomous role of states. This alternative also appears unlikely. Aside from the bureaucratic fact that few organizations wither away once they are established, there seem to be no real indicators that international institutions will diminish in importance in the international system. On the other hand, the increasing interdependence of states seems to suggest that international institutions may still serve a useful function and would be expected to continue in the future international system.

[32] Young notes the "new interdependencies may produce either positive or negative results from the perspective of international community." Young (fn. 7), 56.

[33] For discussion of the revolutionary aspects of the contemporary international system see Stanley Hoffmann, *Gulliver's Troubles, or the Setting of American Foreign Policy* (New York 1968), 17–51 and Richard A. Falk, *The Status of Law in International Society* (Princeton 1970), 60–83.

[34] For a discussion of the centralization needed to insure future world order see Falk (fn. 25), 285–352.

The alternative future which seems most likely would be a continuation of international organizations in the system with variations occurring in the functions they fulfill. Some traditional tasks will diminish in importance, while others may become more significant.[35] The continuation of states along with increasing interdependence suggests that international institutions may be a significant means of encouraging cooperation. Likewise, the ongoing need for a balancing of force in an era when the failure of the balance portends nuclear holocaust and the continuing demands for change which may produce violence and escalation, suggest that international institutions may have important functions as moderating mechanisms in the future international system.

## CAPABILITIES OF INTERNATIONAL INSTITUTIONS

International institutions lack many of the capabilities that traditionally enable organizations to take effective action. These organizations are frequently in financial difficulties as illustrated by the UN's problems with financing peacekeeping and the Article 19 dispute. Since they rely on the contributions of member states, they are at the mercy of their constituents and when a major contributor such as the United States chooses to withhold its contribution (as in the case of the International Labour Organization), the existence of the international institution is threatened. Proposals have been put forward to provide independent sources of income for organizations, such as international control of the seabed, with the UN receiving the fees for leasing. To date, however, no independent sources of financial support exist for international institutions.

Another traditional basis for influence has been the possession of instruments of force such as police, armies, or nuclear weapons. Although an international force was envisioned in Chapter VII of the UN Charter, the cold war prevented the development of a unified UN military force. Peacekeeping efforts are circumscribed since their action is limited by host consent and the use of force only in self-defense. There have not yet been enforcement actions in which the UN used force against a state. Although African states have requested this type of action on the part of both the UN and the OAU regarding the colonial questions in southern Africa, the international and regional organizations do not have the capabilities to undertake any type of military action.

The capacity to take authoritative decisions binding on other political bodies has also been crucial to governments and organizations.

---

[35] Haas points out that in the future multibloc asymmetric system he envisions, tasks of the United Nations will become increasingly autonomous and each will be legitimate only in its own right. Haas (fn. 30), 230.

Although certain decisions taken by such groups as those connected with the European Economic Community are binding on states, most resolutions and requests of international institutions remain contingent upon the compliance of the members. Little has really been given up in terms of binding decisions, and the real locus of authoritative decision-making remains within the state.

The fact that these usual capabilities for influencing the behavior of actors are denied to international institutions suggests that their impact may be limited. The members of the organizations do in fact deny the organizations these capabilities to insure that the organizations will not assume dominance over them, but in so doing, states also guarantee that the international institutions can not accomplish many of the needed world order tasks, such as prevention of nuclear war.[36] Although traditional capabilities of resources, force, and binding authority are not readily available to international institutions, these organizations do possess other capabilities which enable them to act.

International institutions represent a focus of communication and a mechanism for decision-making. In the deliberative bodies of international institutions states are constantly in contact dealing with a variety of specialized and general world issues. The parliamentary format allows for communication about formal agenda items. All nations are involved in the deliberation of these issues and forced to take stands on the questions under consideration. Aside from the formal communication procedures, an informal network of dialogue exists among the delegates to these international institutions.[37] This informal means of exchange allows bargaining and negotiating on agenda items to be carried out backstage as well as in the glare of publicity. Furthermore, this network provides easy access to the representatives of all nations for communication on all issues. The mere fact that representatives of over 130 states are located in New York or Geneva represents a significant change in the nature of diplomacy. Contact on an informal basis has been greatly enhanced through the variety of international institutions. For small or new states the opportunity to be in contact with all other states through a single diplomatic mission may be particularly important. This potential for extensive communications on both a formal and informal basis is a significant development in the history of diplomacy.

International institutions also possess regularized channels for reach-

[36] Falk notes that "the lack of autonomous United Nations capabilities is itself a way of maintaining the preeminence of principal sovereign states and of sustaining traditional modes of diplomatic interaction." Falk (fn. 8), 201.

[37] Chadwick F. Alger, "Personal Contact in Intergovernmental Organizations," in Herbert C. Kelman, ed., *International Behavior* (New York 1965), 523-47.

ing decisions. Through the established rules for deliberation and passage of resolutions, in the variety of organizations from the General Assembly and Security Council to the Council of Ministers of the EEC or the OAU, the process for reaching conclusions has been agreed upon whether it is unanimous consent, majority vote, or vote with certain states holding a veto. To be sure these resolutions may vary from laws to simple statements of preference in different circumstances. The actual impact of the resolution may depend on factors such as the size of the vote, the nature of the issues, and the parties involved.[38] In spite of differences about the legal nature of resolutions, the fact remains that international institutions offer an established formula for reaching collective decisions. Because of the opportunity for communication and the existence of mechanisms for collective action, the international institutions provide the basis for greater centralization of decision-making within the international system. As the need for cooperative and collective action increases, the availability of these means of communication and decision-making become important capabilities of the organizations.

A second capability that international institutions possess is the multilateral machinery for action in a variety of fields. These organizations possess multilateral structures, which are already set up and able to administer and implement the joint efforts of states. International institutions currently have established a variety of ongoing programs which have the necessary personnel to run them and the combined experience to enable them to carry out their tasks. Some of these are specialized programs with a particular function, such as the FAO, the ILO, and UNICEF, while others are general institutions which have spawned a variety of programs within their framework. The types of existing machinery that could be used in the future include the International Court of Justice, the United Nations Development Programme, UN peacekeeping forces, and economic common markets. These programs could be rapidly expanded if member states chose to invest increased resources in them. As the desirability of multilateral rather than bilateral programs increases in the eyes of states, the existing multilateral machinery of international institutions represents an important capability.

A third asset of international institutions is their emphasis on the systemic perspective in dealing with international problems. Given the

---

[38] For discussion of the impact of UN Resolutions see Obed Y. Asamoah, *The Legal Significance of the Declarations of the General Assembly of the United Nations* (Hague 1966), Rosalyn Higgins, *The Development of International Law through the Political Organs of the United Nations* (London 1963), Jorge Castaneda, *Legal Effects of United Nations Resolutions* (New York 1969), and Richard A. Falk, "On the Quasi-Legislative Competence of the General Assembly," *American Journal of International Law*, LX (October 1966), 782–91.

traditional focus on national interest, it is indeed important that some attention be given to the overall effects of each unit pursuing its particular interest. There is no guarantee that in following individual interests, states will inevitably insure the general good of all states. In fact in many instances quite the contrary may be true, each state maximizing its own interest may produce disaster for the whole world. Therefore, it is essential that some attention be given to the implications of actions for the entire system over the long run. As the potential for disaster increases, the importance of focusing concern on the effects of actions on the world order likewise increases.[39]

The secretariats of the international organizations offer a leadership potential for examining proposals and the actions of nation-states from an international perspective. As the concept of the secretariat has evolved from that of a mere administrative setup doing the bidding of states under the League of Nations to that of world spokesman in the UN setting, the office of Secretary-General of the United Nations has become a source of initiative in raising issues and implementing programs. Naturally the extent to which international leadership is available depends on the individual occupying the office, but most international institutions today have a secretariat that not only does the bidding of members but also takes the initiative in proposing programs, furthering the goals of the institutions, and encouraging cooperation among states. Such international administrators approach issues from a different perspective than those of states, since their focus is international rather than national.[40] As international politics becomes more interdependent, it is crucial that the systemic view be injected into issues, and international institutions possess a rather unique ability to perform this function.

The power to grant legitimacy is the fourth capability that international institutions possess. Actions with collective support are considered more legitimate than those undertaken unilaterally. In an international system with individual states making divergent justifications for their actions, collective approval has become a means of moderating and adjusting unilateral efforts. This desire for collective approval makes the capacity to grant legitimacy an important one for international institutions.[41] All states desire approval for their actions, and the current arena in which this can be secured is in the existing international institutions. Presumably there is a hierarchy for approval:

[39] For recommendations concerning world order needs see Falk (fn. 25), 215–84.

[40] Hammarskjold describes his concept of the independent international civil servant and the problems regarding neutrality in Dag Hammarskjold, "The International Civil Servant in Law and in Fact," in Robert W. Gregg and Michael Barkun, eds., *The United Nations System and Its Functions* (Princeton 1968), 215–28.

[41] Inis L. Claude, Jr., "Collective Legitimization as a Political Function of the United Nations," *International Organization*, xx (Summer 1966), 367–79.

endorsement by the United Nations is most significant, with sanctions from a regional organization following, and unilateral action being least legitimate.[42] Examples of states seeking this type of multilateral approval may be cited, such as the efforts of the United States to secure support of the OAS in the cases of Cuba and the Dominican Republic or the insistence that the invasion of Czechoslovakia was an act carried out under the Warsaw Pact or that Vietnam was a SEATO action. Likewise, the debates within the UN justifying and denouncing such moves all illustrate attempts to secure the approval of multilateral bodies. Because such an endorsement of policies is perceived as desirable, states may in fact alter or moderate their policies in order to secure this consent of international institutions.[43] The ability to grant or withhold legitimacy for the actions of a state represents an important capability that international institutions will possess in future international relations.

Although the international institutions may be lacking in traditional sources of influence such as money, force, and binding legal authority, they do possess a series of capabilities as a center for communication and decision-making, a provider of multilateral machinery, a protector of the international interest, and a dispenser of legitimacy. All of these capacities represent important assets in a future international system which is expected to continue its reliance on independent states while the units become increasingly interdependent. As states are faced with the necessity for cooperative actions in spite of their sovereign independence, these capabilities of international institutions may assume more saliency, and permit the institutions to fulfill a variety of significant functions in the international environment of the future.

## FUNCTIONS OF INTERNATIONAL INSTITUTIONS

A wide range of functions—from erasing illiteracy to preserving world peace—have been posited as purposes for various international institutions. To be sure the limited capabilities with which such organizations are endowed have not permitted them to achieve fully the variety of goals set forth.[44] However, international institutions will

[42] The value of this hierarchical form of legitimacy is questioned in Linda B. Miller, *World Order and Local Disorder* (Princeton 1967), 211–14.

[43] In a case such as the Cuban Missile Crisis the desire of the United States to secure collective support of the OAS may have contributed to the selection of the quarantine as one of the more moderate strategies available. Because the approval of multilateral bodies is desired by states, they may tailor their unilateral actions toward securing this legitimacy.

[44] Young makes a useful distinction between the mythology surrounding the Charter and the realities of the operation of the UN in the international system. Young (fn. 7), 11.

continue to carry out a wide range of functions, and the nature of the future international system will thrust some functions of organizations into prominent roles, while precluding fulfillment of other tasks.[45] In turn, the various functions which the organizations are able to fulfill form an important part of the context in which states interact and make foreign policies.

*Security Guarantees*

The assurance of security has been an important purpose of international institutions. With the establishment of the United Nations an attempt was made to shift the method of providing this security from a balance of power to a collective security system.[46] Claude has described the ideal form of this system as calling for "an international organization with authority to determine when a resort to force is illegitimate and to require states to collaborate under its direction in suppressing such use of force."[47] Under the UN system for security a presumption is made that the threat or use of force is not allowed and that those violating this norm will be met by the combined force of all other parties. Such a system requires sufficient centralization to determine the aggressor and direct the response. In terms of centralization the collective security system lies between the balance of power system and the establishment of world government.

The United Nations Charter delineates the nature of the collective security system in Chapters VI and VII: states are called upon to refrain from the use of force, to report all actions regarding force to the Security Council for decision, and to supply military troops to the Council in case of aggression. The UN proposed to handle the prob-

[45] The types of functions attributed to the United Nations by other authors have varied. Young suggests the UN can act as: regulator, effector of great power agreements, a partisan political instrument, a force for political change, a creator of long-term viability, and a norm creator. Young (fn. 7), 25–35. Haas divides the tasks of the UN into the fields of world peace and disarmament, trade and finance, economic and social development, colonialism and human rights, and science, technology, and planning. Haas (fn. 30), 65–223. Gregg and Barkun use a systems approach suggesting that the functions of the UN should be considered under the divisions of articulation and aggregation of interests, communication, socialization and recruitment, conflict management, redistribution, and integration. Robert W. Gregg and Michael Barkun (fn. 40), 3–9. Falk analyzes the functions as promotion of social change, aggregation of claims by new states, facilitation of technical forms of cooperation, publication and censure of human rights violations, and formulation of a world public interest. Falk (fn. 8), 197.

[46] The operation of the UN as a collective security system is considered in Inis L. Claude, Jr., "The United Nations and the Use of Force," *International Conciliation*, No. 532 (1961) and Ernst B. Haas, "Collective Security and the Future International System," *Monograph Series in World Affairs*, Vol. 5, No. 1 (University of Denver 1967–1968).

[47] Inis L. Claude, Jr., "The Management of Power in the Changing United Nations," *International Organization*, xv (Spring 1961), 221.

lem of peace not through establishment of a superior force, but rather through a mechanism for the collaboration of individual states in opposing aggression. The viability of this mechanism was immediately threatened with the rise of the cold war as a barrier to joint action among the powerful states.

The Korean War represents an insistence on the part of the U.S. that the collective security concept be applied, and illustrates the failure of the system when nations are incapable of working together because of ideological differences.[48] The Security Council authorized a response in the absence of the Soviet Union which was boycotting the Security Council meetings, and the United States took up the role of opposing aggression on the part of the UN. However, because the Chinese and Soviet supported the North Koreans against the United States the collective security system was doomed. The ideological division ruined the collective aspects of the security system by producing wars with a potential for escalation rather than presenting aggressors with a united front of all nations.

The outcome of the cold war on the United Nations in this area of security was twofold. The first result was the development of international institutions within each bloc based on the idea of collective security.[49] The functions of NATO and the Warsaw Pact were to insure that the group of nations would respond jointly to an attack against any single nation in the group. These regional or bloc security organizations guarantee collective effort for members, but because there are two such blocs world peace is not necessarily insured by these groups. The second development was an attempt to disassociate conflicts outside the spheres of influence of the two superpowers from the cold war. The UN assumed the role of attempting to control conflicts in the third world as a means of avoiding confrontations between the great powers. Thus the idea of collective security came to be applied within the regional institutions of the superpowers, with the UN trying to insulate conflicts outside the spheres of influence of the superpowers.

Although there has been a decline in the unity of the regional security institutions such as NATO and the Warsaw Pact and there have been specific instances of superpower cooperation such as the Suez crisis in 1956, one must conclude that the outlook for collective security through the United Nations as a means of insuring world peace

[48] On the specific question of collective security in Korea see Arnold Wolfers, "Collective Security and the War in Korea," in Richard A. Falk and Wolfram F. Hanrieder, eds., *International Law and Organization* (Philadelphia 1968), 202–14. For information on the factors affecting the US decision-making regarding Korea see Glenn D. Paige, *The Korean Decision* (New York 1968).

[49] The role of security pacts as regional groups is considered in Lynn Miller, "The Prospects for Order through Regional Security," in Falk and Black, eds., *The Future of the International Legal Order*, Vol. I, *Trends and Patterns* (fn. 5), 556–94.

among the great powers does not seem promising in the next decades.[50]
As long as states remain sovereign and retain their right to resort to
nuclear weapons, the UN lacks the necessary degree of centralization
to define aggressors and coordinate responses that would permit a
successful collective security system to function. Therefore, the relations among the great powers will continue to be dependent on a
balancing act based on their military abilities. International institutions may provide a set of norms and procedures which help to constrain this balancing through efforts toward disarmament, expectations
about the threat and use of force, and requests for moderation in the
use of force.

*Conflict Control*

Concomitant with guaranteeing security is the field of conflict control.
Conflict control is defined as those actions and strategies which separate local struggles from the rest of the international system in order
to prevent escalation into international war. Under the doctrine of
peacekeeping, conflict control has become an important UN task.[51]
While its abilities in the area of collective security are limited, the UN
has assumed a major role in preventing the escalation of wars through
great power involvement. In an era when many countries are undergoing internal disruptions and the superpowers are attempting to extend ideological influence through indirect involvement in these struggles, the function of conflict control is significant.[52] Hammarskjold
realized the need for such actions in developing his strategy of preventive diplomacy.[53] He developed the international peacekeeping
forces of the United Nations as a means of limiting the outside involvement of the great powers in struggles beyond their spheres of
influence.

The primary components of the UN effort to control such conflicts
are field operations deployed to patrol the struggle, mediation efforts

[50] Haas includes both peacekeeping and security for the great powers under his
concept of collective security. Haas studied 108 disputes which threatened the peace
in the 1945–1965 period, and found that 75 percent of these were referred to international or regional organizations. Of the 55 disputes referred to the United Nations
18 were settled wholly or in part on the basis of UN resolutions, giving the UN a
"success score" of 33 percent. Haas (fn. 5), 260, 268.

[51] Arthur M. Cox, *Prospects for Peacekeeping* (Washington, D.C. 1967) and Oran
R. Young, "Trends in International Peacekeeping," *Research Monograph*, No. 22
(Princeton Center of International Studies 1966).

[52] Huntington points out the altered nature of violence and the new emphasis
on internal struggles. Samuel P. Huntington, "Patterns of Violence in World Politics," in Samuel P. Huntington, ed., *Changing Patterns of Military Politics* (New
York 1962), 18.

[53] Introduction to the Annual Report of the Secretary-General on the Work of
the Organization, 16 June 1959–15 June 1960, *General Assembly Official Records*,
15th Session, Supplement No. 1A (A/4390/Add. 1).

to resolve the issues involved, and norms regarding the participation of outside states in the fighting. The best examples of UN efforts are the Middle East, Congo, and Cyprus cases.[54] In each of these examples the United Nations sent a UN force composed of national contingents supplied for use by the organization and under international command. These troops went into the conflict with the consent of the host country and were limited to use of force in self-defense. They assumed mandates ranging from the patrol of borders to prevention of civil war. The impact of the presence of such international forces has been to dampen the fighting under way and to separate hostile factions by interposing international troops between them.

The mediation efforts have not been attempts to impose solutions on the conflicts, since the United Nations is incapable of dictating resolutions to conflicts. Rather international institutions have offered good offices, encouragement, recommendations, and procedures to the parties involved in the hope that they would reach a solution. While the impact of a UN peacekeeping force may be to freeze a situation rather than producing resolution of the underlying issues, the coupling of a peacekeeping force to minimize the fighting and a mediator to bring the parties together can contribute to settlement. It is essential for conflict control that the peaceful resolution of conflicts be encouraged as well.

A primary concern of these efforts is avoidance of escalation into international wars through the intervention of outside states. One means of accomplishing control has been the development of the norm that once the United Nations has become involved in a struggle unilateral intervention is no longer permissible. Actions and expectations in the Congo and Cyprus cases suggest that while the UN is operating in a conflict, unilateral military assistance is impermissible.[55] Because such unilateral involvement is the basis for escalation, the multilateral presence is designed to preempt the role of intervenor and thereby control the conflict and avoid a potential superpower confrontation within the context of local wars.

In order to evaluate the degree to which conflict control will be a vital function in the future, it is necessary to understand the attitudes

[54] The Congo case is analyzed in Ernest W. Lefever, *Uncertain Mandate: Politics of the U.N. Congo Operation* (Baltimore 1967) and the UN effort in Cyprus is discussed in James A. Stegenga, *The United Nations Force in Cyprus* (Columbus 1968).

[55] Donald W. McNemar, "The Postindependence War in the Congo," in Richard A. Falk, ed., *The International Law of Civil War* (Baltimore 1971), 271–82. For a general discussion of international law and internal war see Rosalyn Higgins, "Internal War and International Law," in Cyril E. Black and Richard A. Falk, eds., *The Future of the International Legal Order*, Vol. III, *Conflict Management* (Princeton 1971), 81–121.

of potential intervenors in these conflicts. Much of the drive for such indirect involvement in wars of liberation and struggles against Communism has been generated by the ideological competition and the accompanying efforts to make advances at the expense of the other side. A primary objective has been to prevent any step which might be claimed as a victory by the other side. If each side could be assured that there would be no gain for the opposing cold-war camp in any particular conflict, its own incentive to intervene would be lessened.[56] The injection of an international peacekeeping force into these situations may function to reassure each side that no gains are to be made in the struggle by their opponent. Acting as a neutral referee in such fighting, the international peacekeeping body may be able to reassure the superpowers that their participation is not necessary. The presence of observers from international institutions can encourage definition of the conflict in local and nationalistic rather than ideological terms, and can discourage indirect involvements which might escalate into great power confrontations.

Given the recent unhappy experiences with unilateral interventions in such places as the Dominican Republic, Czechoslovakia, and Vietnam and the increasing emphasis on domestic issues, states may become more reliant on multilateral efforts at conflict control in an attempt to avoid unilateral involvements while maintaining some assurance that other states are not making gains at their expense in the struggle. Such multilateral efforts may take a variety of forms.[57] In the Nigerian civil war the OAU demanded that the UN and outside states not become involved, and this produced a relatively noninterventionist policy on the part of foreign states, although some arms were supplied. In the Soccer War between Honduras and El Salvador, the OAS served an important role in facilitating mediation, while the US refrained from dominant involvement. Already there have been proposals for an international team as a potential means of facilitating US withdrawal from Vietnam.[58] The UN peacekeeping force continues its

[56] Miller suggests that "if the leaders of governments that are potential 'intervenors' come to regard the outcomes of future internal conflicts as less vital to security requirements or to ideological struggles, 'benign' forms of competition, based on tacit agreements, could prevail." Miller emphasizes perception and self-restraint of third parties as the primary factors determining control of internal wars. Miller (fn. 9), 136.

[57] For evaluation of regional efforts in this area see Linda B. Miller, "Regional Organization and the Regulation of Internal Conflict," *World Politics*, xix (July 1967), 582–600. For recommendations about future UN peacekeeping see United Nations Association of the USA, *Controlling Conflicts in the 1970's* (New York 1969). Discussion of various strategies for keeping conflicts localized is found in Lincoln P. Bloomfield and Amelia C. Leiss, *Controlling Small Wars* (New York 1969).

[58] Lincoln P. Bloomfield, *The U.N. and Vietnam* (New York 1968), 19–37.

role at present in Cyprus,[59] proposals have been made that a joint peacekeeping force of US and Soviet soldiers might be a part of a Middle East solution,[60] and UN relief workers have been stationed throughout East Pakistan.[61] All of these examples seem to suggest that as states pursue their domestic interests and learn from past mistakes regarding unilateral interventions, the function of conflict control may become increasingly important in the future of international institutions.

*Peaceful Change*

International institutions seek to accommodate change by peaceful means. Given the tremendous pressures for alterations in the status quo resulting from the rapid pace of technology and the emergence of a variety of new states, the facilitation of peaceful methods of change is tremendously important. For many of the new members of international institutions and for many socialist states, the traditional organizations have been too European-centered. Therefore they are insisting on a variety of changes in the laws and institutions.[62] Perhaps three of the most important demands that have been voiced to date have been for the end of colonialism, increased modernization, and redistribution of wealth.

In the area of decolonialization the United Nations has facilitated the birth of nations. The UN provided acceptance of and support for the right of self-determination. Once nations gained their independence, UN membership was an important recognition of their new status. Furthermore, the General Assembly represented an arena in which the new nations could voice their demands on an equal basis with older members and could express their concerns about colonialism and development. The United Nations continues to pursue this tradition of decolonialization with denunciations of the remaining colonies in areas such as southern Africa.

In the realm of development and redistribution of wealth the United Nations has played a vital role in establishing multilateral

[59] James A. Stegenga, "UN Peace-Keeping: The Cyprus Venture," *Journal of Peace Research*, No. I (1970), 1–16.

[60] Robert B. Semple, "U.S. Says It Favors Joining Russians to Police Mideast," *New York Times*, August 27, 1970, p. 1.

[61] Benjamin Welles, "U.N. to Send Team to East Pakistan," *New York Times*, August 1, 1971, p. 1.

[62] The tension between the attitudes of old and new states is discussed in A. A. Fatouros, "The Participation of 'New' States in the International Legal Order," in Falk and Black, eds., *The Future of the International Legal Order*, Vol. I, *Trends and Patterns* (fn. 5), 317–71 and Richard A. Falk, "The New States and International Legal Order," *Recueil des Cours* (Hague 1966), Vol. II.

channels for the provision of aid and technical assistance.[63] Through the variety of programs within the UN Development Programme and the Specialized Agencies, assistance has been available to new nations in meeting technical problems and undertaking modernization. Obviously the flow of aid from the rich to the poor nations has not been terribly significant. The results of the first Development Decade were disappointing and the hope remains that more progress can be achieved in the second Development Decade.

While these efforts represent attempts to alter the status quo through the peaceful channels of international institutions, the success of such programs remains in question. Great strides forward have not been made, yet these institutions are a means of accomplishing the needed changes through peaceful rather than violent means. Whether those nations which are benefiting from the current status will realize that it is in their interest to undertake peaceful change is doubtful. The attempts to end the last vestiges of colonialism have already moved toward violent means, and the longer these colonies continue the greater the likelihood that fighting will be involved in the attainment of their eventual independence. Similarly, the rich continue to enjoy their privileged position with only minimal assistance to the poor. The limited response and the great disparities are producing increased pressures toward violent action.

International institutions can provide channels for peaceful change, but there is no real evidence that greater advantage will be taken of these organizations in the future. On the colonial question more consensus may develop on enforcement measures aimed at those countries in which a white minority rules a black majority. If a regional or international organization undertakes to use force to accomplish this change, the predominance of collective force may be able to subdue the opponent with minimal violence. In the realm of foreign assistance there may be increases in funds through multilateral channels. Aid by international institutions tends to be more acceptable to recipients and will relieve the donors of the necessity of deciding which countries will receive assistance. Such shifts may increase the aid given through international institutions, but there are no indications that countries might begin granting assistance on a scale large enough to alter significantly the gross disparity; on the contrary, the emphasis on domestic issues suggests a decrease in such aid. The capacity for peaceful change through decolonialization and development will remain with

[63] Past performance and future needs in the area of development is analyzed in Report of the Commission on International Development, *Partners in Development* (New York 1969) and R. G. A. Jackson, *A Study of the Capacity of the United Nations Development System* (Geneva 1969).

international institutions in the future, but there is no evidence at this time that states will increase their support for such activities to such a level that meaningful change will be achieved.

*Protection of Human Rights*

Respect for human rights has been an important purpose of the United Nations and of regional organizations such as the Council of Europe. The Universal Declaration of Human Rights established standards for the treatment of all individuals. However, the implementation of such standards by international institutions has not been an effective function of these organizations in the past.[64] Whenever suggestions are made that the United Nations should investigate alleged violations of civil rights in such places as Haiti and Greece, similar accusations are immediately made against a variety of other states, and the UN shrinks away from any efforts to enforce the guidelines. Some regional bodies have gone even further than the UN in this area; the Council of Europe established a Court of Human Rights with binding jurisdiction permitting it to adjudicate allegations of violations. The willingness of the European community to take protection of human rights seriously is illustrated by the withdrawal of Greece from membership in the Council of Europe when threatened with sanctions after the European Commission on Human Rights released a report about violations of human rights in Greece.[65]

Human rights issues are ignored on the basis of strong respect for state sovereignty and the concept of domestic jurisdiction. International institutions are often unable to become involved in adjudication regarding human rights simply because states insist on total control of their own nationals. States are reluctant to support investigations of and sanctions against other states regarding treatment of their own citizens. Each time a country like the United States or the Soviet Union takes an initiative in this area, they are met with accusations about their own treatment of Negroes or Jews. States, therefore, tend to avoid any explicit investigation of human rights complaints through international institutions.

It does not seem that the future international system will be any more conducive to rigorous enforcement of these standards than in the

64 For elaboration on the role of international institutions in protecting human rights see William Korey, "The Key to Human Rights—Implementation," *International Conciliation*, No. 570 (1968), Vernon Van Dyke, *Human Rights, the United States, and World Community* (London 1970), and John Carey, *UN Protection of Civil and Political Rights* (Syracuse 1970).

65 Alvin Shuster, "Inquiry on Greece Reports Tortures," *New York Times*, November 29, 1969, p. 1, and Henry Giniger, "Greece, Facing Expulsion, Quits Council of Europe," *New York Times*, December 13, 1969, p. 1.

past. Since the sovereign state may show an even greater interest in its domestic scene than in the past, there seems to be little room for international policing of the treatment of nationals. Therefore, the primary role of international institutions seems to be limited to assertion of the principle that individuals are entitled to protection against certain actions by states—a rather revolutionary doctrine in terms of international law. However, the enforcement of the application of these rights is restricted to publicizing the violations and censuring those states that are guilty of abuses. In the case of apartheid which is perhaps the most blatant violation today, the efforts of African states before the International Court of Justice saw this international body refuse to decide the case on a technicality in order to avoid a decision which might have called for some action to eliminate apartheid.[66] The African states have succeeded in drawing world attention to the situation in the societies practicing apartheid and have passed motions of censure within the United Nations. In the future one can expect international institutions to function as proponents of the rights of individuals, but to limit their protection of human rights to the strategies of publicizing the offenses and censuring the violations. Effective enforcement does not yet seem to be a function of international institutions.

## Creation of Norms

International institutions can function to create norms governing the interaction of states. Through the various mechanisms for treaty preparation and passage of resolutions, these organizations can serve to coalesce consent among states. By asking nations to take positions on these issues, and then recording them in the documents of the institutions, a form of legislative process is undertaken.[67] Although different resolutions may carry different weights, international institutions do represent a potential for performing the legislative function in the creation of new norms.

The view that a majority of nations indicating an intention through international institutions can be a basis for international law has been illustrated by the teleological approach to jurisprudence.[68] Judge Tanaka took this position in the South West Africa case, arguing that general agreement expressed in the United Nations could become the basis for law, even though South Africa insisted that she had not

[66] For further discussion of the issues involved in the South West Africa cases see Falk (fn. 33), 378–402.

[67] Falk considers the legislative possibilities of the United Nations. Falk (fn. 38), 782–91.

[68] Alexander J. Pollock, "The South West Africa Cases and the Jurisprudence of International Law," *International Organization*, XXIII (Autumn 1969), 767–87.

given her consent.[69] Rather than demanding the consent of every state or the evolution of law through decades of practice, international institutions offer a mechanism by which states can make and change the norms governing their interaction.

In the future one might expect the international institutions to continue to play a particularly important role in the area of norm formation.[70] In an era of rapid technological and scientific change it is imperative that the law as a social instrument be capable of alteration to meet new conditions. While custom may have been an adequate means of changing the law in the nineteenth century, the increased pace of change today requires speedier means of altering the law, such as that of relying on international institutions. New states are insisting that the old laws contain a European bias and must be altered in order to meet the needs of an expanded international system including many new nations, emphasizing again the need for a mechanism for changing laws.[71] Furthermore, as new areas of development such as outer space, weapons systems, and the seabed are opened to exploration there is a need for agreement on new norms prior to the beginning of these new ventures, so that once again practice simply cannot be relied upon. All of these characteristics which will be accentuated in the future international system require that new and faster mechanisms for achieving consensus than practice or tradition need to be further developed. Although states may have important reservations and differences which impede norm formation in particular areas, international institutions represent an important mechanism for procuring consent from states and thus centralizing the legislative function in future international systems.

*Preservation of World Interests*

One particular function of international institutions has been the establishment of cooperation to insure protection of world resources and interests beyond the bounds of single states. In such areas as outer space and the seas, international institutions have been used to provide the cooperation which is necessary in order to preserve the interests of all states. Such areas may be viewed in terms of a world interest as opposed to the national interests, and international organizations

[69] Dissenting opinion of Judge Tanaka, South West Africa Cases, Second Phase, Judgment, *I.C.J. Reports* 1966, 287–94.

[70] Young emphasizes the role of international institutions in norm creation. Young (fn. 7), 34.

[71] The interaction of old and new nations over the formation of the law of the sea is described in Robert L. Friedheim, "The 'Satisfied' and 'Dissatisfied' States Negotiate International Law: A Case Study," *World Politics,* xviii (October 1965), 20–41.

function to preserve this interest in the light of competing and conflicting national concerns.

The increasing number of areas of interest which lie beyond a single national jurisdiction and require cooperation among states has given additional importance to this function. Several characteristics of these issues contribute to making international institutions an effective means of action. First, they are frequently related to developments in science and technology. With the rapid discoveries in these fields, new areas are constantly being opened in which no regulations have previously been in force and the need for new rules is quickly realized. Second, many of the issues in this field have not yet been politicized to the extent that every nation considers a vital national interest to be at stake. Nations have various interests in these issues, and they can become politicized quite readily. However, when a new field of discovery is made available through scientific development (such as outer space or a concern about river pollution), the issues have not been involved in long disputes among nations and may be dealt with on an apolitical plane. Third, world interests require cooperation among states in order to achieve any form of solution. Pollution of the seas can never be controlled by a few states. The most stringent controls by one nation can not clean the environment if a neighbor is continuing to pollute. Therefore, the nature of these issues, i.e., those which hold interest for the entire world, necessitate universal cooperation in order to achieve solution of the problems.

International institutions are currently being asked to handle a variety of these world interest issues. Perhaps one of the earliest cases dealt with economic cooperation. With the demands for increased trade and finance across state boundaries, traditional business law and organizations were particularly confining. One development has been the formation of regional common markets in an effort to open up certain areas to free trade, such as the European Economic Community and the Latin American Common Market.[72] These efforts have been designed to expand the area in which trade could take place freely through the establishment of international or supranational institutions to regulate cooperative efforts in an economic field. An additional response to these needs in the economic area has been the rise

[72] For discussion of the developing economic communities see Karl W. Deutsch and others, *Political Community and the North Atlantic Area* (Princeton 1957), Richard N. Cooper, *The Economics of Interdependence: Economic Policy in the Atlantic Community* (New York 1968), J. S. Nye, "Central American Regional Integration," *International Conciliation*, No. 562 (1967), Ernst B. Haas and Philippe C. Schmitter, "The Politics of Economics in Latin American Regionalism," *Monograph Series in World Affairs*, Vol. 3, No. 2 (University of Denver 1965–1966), and Ernst B. Haas, *The Uniting of Europe* (Palo Alto 1958).

of multinational corporations.[73] These institutions have met the problem of doing business in different trade areas by forming new organizations which are incorporated in a variety of states to overcome the problems of a single national jurisdiction.

As nations advanced into outer space, they used international institutions for developing principles to govern the exploration of heavenly bodies and to assist in the regulation of these efforts.[74] Through treaties negotiated within the institutions and the practice of registering vehicles sent into space, international institutions assisted in dealing with problems relating to who owns the moon, who has responsibility for debris in outer space, and procedures for the safe return of astronauts. While further forms of cooperation, possibly even including joint exploration of space may be facilitated through international structures, it is clear that intergovernmental organizations have been contributing to the evolution of norms and machinery for the preservation of joint interests in the newly opened field of outer space.

A similar response is being made to the prospect of scientific discoveries which will allow for the exploitation of the seabed.[75] The Malta Proposal for UN control of the seabed provides for international control over the exploitation of the seabed, as well as for a source of revenue for the United Nations that could be used for development.[76] The United States responded with a working paper suggesting that the general principle of international control of the seabed was acceptable to it.[77] Again on this issue the emphasis is on preparing international machinery which will enhance cooperative control of the seabed and the sharing of these resources, rather than encouraging haphazard and rapid moves by individual sovereign states to secure claims to the ocean.

One of the most recent areas of concern which has led to coopera-

[73] Raymond Vernon, "The Multinational Enterprise: Power versus Sovereignty," *Foreign Affairs*, XLIX (July 1971), 736–51; Kindleberger (fn. 31); Raymond Vernon, *Sovereignty at Bay* (New York 1971).

[74] For discussion of the legal issues raised in regard to outer space see Ivan A. Vlasic, "The Relevance of International Law to Emerging Trends in the Law of Outer Space," in Richard A. Falk and Cyril E. Black, eds., *The Future of the International Legal Order*, Vol. II, *Wealth and Resources* (Princeton 1970), 265–325.

[75] On the issues raised regarding the seabed see Juraj Andrassy, *International Law and the Resources of the Sea* (New York 1970), Wolfgang Friedmann, *The Future of the Oceans* (New York 1971), and William T. Burke, "Ocean Sciences, Technology, and the Future International Law of the Sea," in Falk and Black, eds., *The Future of the International Legal Order*, Vol. II, *Wealth and Resources* (fn. 74), 183–264.

[76] A discussion of the seabed issue by the UN ambassador from Malta who introduced the item into the agenda of the General Assembly in 1967 is found in Arvid Pardo, "Who Will Control the Seabed," *Foreign Affairs*, XLVII (October 1968), 123–37.

[77] Richard D. Lyons, "U.S. Alters Draft on Seabed Riches," *New York Times*, August 2, 1970, p. 27.

tion is the control of the environment.[78] The United Nations Conference on the Human Environment to be held in Sweden in 1972 illustrates the increasing concern that these issues arouse, and the efforts to handle them through existing international machinery such as the United Nations.[79] In order to effectively control environmental problems such as air and water pollution it is essential that states cooperate since no individual state can effectively meet these problems alone. Therefore, international institutions are undertaking the task of educating people to the problems involved, establishing standards for effective control of the environment, and developing worldwide monitoring.

In the field of articulating and protecting common world interests, international institutions can carry out a series of tasks that contribute to the effectiveness of this function. First, the institutions may provide the forum for agreement regarding basic principles to govern the field, such as freedom of exploration in the seas, or the inability of individual states to claim heavenly bodies. Second, the institutions can help establish specific regulations governing these fields. Rules covering the liability for space accidents, the granting of permits for seabed exploitation, or the permissibility of dumping in the oceans can all be agreed upon through international organizations. Third, the machinery for implementing and enforcing such principles and regulations can be incorporated into new or existing international institutions. Registry, monitoring, and inspection systems run by such intergovernmental organizations can contribute to the effectiveness and reliability of these standards. Finally, the institutions can play an important role in educating people and states regarding the relevance of these world issues. Through continual programs to acquaint people with both the necessity for cooperation and the benefits to be gained from collaboration, international institutions can enhance their work in the area of world issues.

The functioning of international institutions to protect world interests can be expected to continue to grow in the future international system. The continual discoveries of science and technology can be viewed as a generator of new areas of concern and exploration. As new areas needing joint solutions arise, the development of cooperation within international institutions may be a means of creating solutions to the issues before they become enmeshed in other political con-

[78] A plea for international machinery to control the environment is found in George F. Kennan, "To Prevent a World Wasteland: A Proposal," *Foreign Affairs*, XLVIII (April 1970), 401–13. Environmental control as a primary function of the UN in the future is suggested in Richard N. Gardner, "Can the United Nations be Revived?" *Foreign Affairs*, XLVIII (July 1970), 669–70.

[79] For discussion of the UN Conference on the Human Environment see Richard N. Gardner, "U.N. as Policeman," *Saturday Review* (August 7, 1971), pp. 47–50.

cerns. As long as they are perceived as technical or economic issues, their solution is easier than when they become embroiled in politics. Because the solving of many of these issues rests on cooperation among states, international institutions present a good forum and mechanism for dealing with them. As organizations become more universal (with the inclusion of states like China and East and West Germany), they will be in an even better position to deal with these concerns. International institutions have been developing an expertise in handling technical and functional problems requiring cooperation, and with the continued development of new problem areas and greater interdependence among nations, international institutions can be expected to play an even greater role in protecting world interests.

## INTERNATIONAL ENVIRONMENT OF THE FUTURE

Having discussed the primary characteristics of the international system and examined the capabilities and functions of international institutions in that system, it is possible to evaluate the contribution of these organizations to the future international environment. The model which seems most useful in examining this relationship is one which conceptualizes international institutions as mechanisms at the interface between the state system and the international legal order. The basis of the future international system is the independent state with control over its internal politics and power over the resort to force. However, overarching these independent actors is a set of norms and structures governing their interaction.[80] International institutions represent an important structure by which the independent states can create, transform, and apply the "rules of the game" governing their interaction. The impact of the international institutions in the future environment can be understood through examination and correlation of the components of this model.

In the state system of the future which has been discussed there exists a tension between the continued reliance on the sovereign state and the increasing interdependence of these actors. Short of a cataclysmic disaster there seems to be no form of transition which would alter the nature of the sovereign units composing the international system by the turn of the century. Despite tendencies toward supranational units, the assumption is that the sovereign state will remain in existence. Yet at the same time the degree of interdependence among these units is increasing and the need for cooperative behavior in

[80] Falk defines the international legal order as "an aggregate conception embodying those structures and processes by which authority is created, applied, and transformed in international society." Richard A. Falk, "The Interplay of Westphalia and Charter Conceptions of International Legal Order," in Falk and Black, eds., *The Future of the International Legal Order*, Vol. I, *Trends and Patterns* (fn. 5), 33.

order to achieve common interests is expanding. In this world of both dependence and independence, states are using international institutions as a means of fostering and regulating cooperative behavior. Thus states view international institutions as a mechanism for producing interdependent actions without demanding that they relinquish their sovereignty to some supranational unit. As the necessity of cooperative strategies increase, the significance of international institutions will likewise increase, so that these organizations can be expected to play an important part in the future international environment.

The primary condition for development of the role of international institutions is the attitudes of member states. Although the organizations have a variety of capabilities of their own, the approval and support of their members remains a primary determinant of their actions. The active support, or at minimum, the acquiescence of the great powers is necessary, the approval of a majority of the organizations' members, and provision of resources in terms of money, equipment, or troops are all essential to the success of operations by these institutions. Such consent may indeed be forthcoming for particular functions of institutions for two primary reasons. First, states may wish to avoid certain roles, and therefore request the United Nations or a regional organization to act in order to avoid a unilateral entanglement or commitment. This position may be the result of increasing domestic involvement or an avoidance of intervention after the Vietnam experience. The second reason for increased consent to multilateral action is the inability to achieve common interests without joint efforts. In these instances, the nations will consent to an international operation in order to achieve their common goal. For these two reasons, the consent of states may be more readily forthcoming for certain actions by international institutions.

Changes in the nature of the international institutions may likewise produce increased capabilities for action. Moves toward universal membership will better equip such organizations to handle a variety of problems. With the inclusion of China in its membership the capacity of the United Nations to deal with such issues as disarmament or problems in Asia is greatly enhanced. Likewise, universality is an important characteristic for an organization dealing with the environment. As institutions like the UN move toward universal membership their usefulness increases. Second, as institutions slip from the hegemonial grasp of a single country or bloc, their relevance is increased. Now that such organizations as the OAS and UN are no longer entirely a policy tool of the United States, they reflect more clearly the divergent power structures on a variety of issues, and thus are more likely to have an effect on the actions of states. Thirdly, these organizations have acquired functional capacities of increasing value. They possess skills which allow them to offer states an important avenue of action. As the institutions develop their universality, more accurately reflect the divisions in the system, and expand their functional skills, their role can be expected to increase.

It is indeed difficult to predict which particular international institutions will be dominant in the future. The expansion of regional institutions has been significant and they may become a powerful layer of subglobal actors interposed between the state and the global body. This approach has the advantage of institutionalizing the discontinuous nature of world politics and possibly compartmentalizing issues to their particular region. Likewise, functional organizations may play an important role in a future dominated by science and technology. At the same time the United Nations has demonstrated adaptive capabilities and a willingness to assume new functions. A variety of international institutions will be available in the future to act as mechanisms for state action.

The functions which international institutions will perform in the future can be divided into stable and expanding functions on the basis of the degree to which they will be important. At present it does not seem likely that any of the functions will disappear as important roles for international institutions. Those tasks which will continue to be performed at roughly the same level are classified as stable, while those areas in which international institutions can be expected to play a greatly increased role are called expanding functions.

Among the stable functions are security guarantees, peaceful change, and protection of human rights. All of these will remain important tasks of international organizations, but in none of them will the institutions take on increased roles. In the field of collective security, institutions may help to stabilize the situation through arms control agreements or pacts for joint defense, but in the last analysis the security of states will continue to rest on their military capabilities. Although the demands for change, particularly in the relations between rich and poor nations may be great, there is no indication that they will be met with any increased grants or support than at present. Multilateral programs of aid will flourish, but the resources placed in these will not be anywhere near the amounts needed for significant redistribution of wealth. The nations with resources and political leverage are patently satisfied with the status quo, so that international institutions will continue to contribute to peaceful change at roughly the same level as in the past. Despite acclamation of standards, the protection of human rights will remain a prerogative of the sovereign state. Publicity and censure may be wielded through the organizations, but effective protection will not be forthcoming.

Those functions that may be expected to expand greatly in the future are control of conflicts, norm creation, and protection of new international interests. Because nations are discovering increased interest in conflict avoidance as a means of limiting unilateral involvements and maintaining the moderateness of the international system, international institutions can be expected to assume an increased role in this area. By permitting states to avoid interventions and possible confrontations through the presence of international observers to verify that the conflict is not producing gains for ideological opponents, international institutions can provide a valuable function. As the need for new norms in a rapidly changing system increases, the political forums of international assemblies and conferences offer an effective means of legislating new norms or altering old ones. Therefore, the formation of consent around new norms and evaluation of the actions of states in light of these norms will expand in the future. Finally, the necessity for cooperation in meeting a variety of worldwide interests coupled with the functional skills of the organizations, suggests that articulation and protection of global interests will become increasingly important as new scientific developments continue throughout the final decades of the twentieth century.

In those fields in which international institutions assume expanded functions, the legal order will take on an increased degree of centralization. As states support the use of these organizations for cooperative efforts, the institutions become the focus for legislating and adjudicating the norms in those areas. States seeking effective cooperation through such organizations must grant them the power to formulate rules and to scrutinize varying claims in order to have an approved set of norms for a working relationship within the international community. In the future international environment, international organizations will serve as important mechanisms by which sovereign states achieve cooperative behavior in an increasingly interdependent world. International institutions will thereby produce increasing centralization of authority and institutionalization of procedures in the future legal order.

# CHAPTER 13

# Functional Agencies

## JAMES PATRICK SEWELL *

SUPPOSE, for the moment, that an historic planetary disjuncture had led to reconsideration of various schemes for structuring an international system as yet unexperienced on earth. What would determine the blueprint actually wrought from these individual proposals? How might the divergence of reality from design best be explained? How could the observer then account for its subsequent evolution? And how could he estimate or even affect the future?

## I. A FRAMEWORK OF EXPECTATIONS

*Value Preferences*

The value preferences of those who advanced their outlines for the new world to follow World War II may be expressed as security, autonomy, well-being, and community. *Security* (order, stability, mutual defense or protection, freedom from fear, or "peace and security" in the United Nations Charter) served of course as the chief justification for a postwar framework of international organization, especially from the viewpoint of spokesmen for United Nations allies engaged in hostilities with Germany, Japan, and Italy. *Autonomy*—the capacity to be oneself and to do one's own thing, a sentiment expressed also as freedom, liberty, absence of exploitation, independence, self-determination, autarchy, privacy, the sovereignty and equality of states or nations—gained utterance by those predisposed to such a value preference either as their way of life or as their aspiration. Gracing Article 55 of the Charter, *well-being* in these pages renders such allusions as welfare, equality (or equity), social justice, prosperity, freedom from want, freedom from hunger, freedom from disease, and freedom from ignorance through enlightenment or the acquisition of skills. Well-being relates most directly to that sector of the international system to be considered below. *Community*, a word here used synonymously with fraternity or brotherhood, received scattered individual championship but only rhetorical governmental articulation and perfunctory Charter embodiment in a preambular resolve "to practice tolerance and live together in peace with one another as good neighbors"—a phrase as redolent of autonomy as of community.

* The author is grateful to the Yale Concilium on International and Area Studies for support, and to Richard Johnson, II, for research assistance and critical stimulation during this project.

Even on an abstract plane, reflection upon these value preferences, aided by the illumination of hindsight, suggests difficulties in aligning values. "Who shall be autonomous?" for instance, frames a level-of-action problem which will continue to exercise those who act in United Nations roles on issues of self-determination and human rights. Equalizing states does not always prove congruent with equalizing social categories or individuals. With security and well-being as with autonomy, furthermore, one man's meat may be, or seem to be, another's poison. *Status quo* and revisionist dispositions cut across value preferences.

Moreover, conflict between differing value preferences appears to be unavoidable. In practice the ubiquitous scramble for security and its artifacts, sanctioned in part by Charter Article 51, has militated against the autonomy of some and against the well-being of others. And autonomy may restrict the development of well-being when the effective right to be left alone in splendid affluence means exemption from social claims.

We should note that those who advanced their proposals for postwar international intercourse also sometimes projected hopes that various values might prove mutually supportive. Thus genuine security was acclaimed as a harbinger of well-being if not indeed of community. True autonomy (within the newly-cast *status quo*) would serve as a major condition of security. And well-being might, as Charter article 55 intimated, contribute to "peaceful and friendly relations among nations. . . ."

Beyond questions of mutual value contradiction or supportiveness loomed a greater and inevitable difficulty: the differing priorities among participants' values. For the allied states of the United Nations, especially those hardest hit by the war, security came first. The United States, which would emerge as the paramount victor, also rated high the value of autonomy—less autonomy in terms of isolation than autonomy as boundless freedom of action in every field of endeavor and perhaps in every quarter. Well-being animated other participants. Ezequiel Padilla of Mexico spoke eloquently for his own government and for many absent from the San Francisco conference: "The Charter is not only an instrument of security against the horrors of war. It is also, for the people who have been fighting to uphold the principles of human dignity, an instrument of well-being and happiness against the horrors of a peace without hope, in which men would be subjected to humiliating privations and injustices. 'Blood, sweat, and tears' comprised the glorious but provisional rule of war. It must not become the rule of peace."[1]

[1] Quoted in Inis L. Claude, Jr., *Swords Into Plowshares* (New York 1964), 61.

## Organizational Conceptions

Picture two images of authority and initiative, one extolling authority united and centralized, the other lauding initiatives functionally separated and spatially dispersed. To look later at actual developments, it will be helpful to envisage these as the extremities on a continuum along which other possibilities also may be drawn. And for our purposes these organizational conceptions should be seen, initially at least, distinct from the substantive value preferences of government participants. Let us then assume, tentatively, wartime planners' agreement on a common postwar destination. Organizational conceptions suggest alternative answers to the question: how to organize to get there from where they stood?

The first conception is well represented by Herman Finer's conclusion about a permanent seat for the international organizations in process of establishment during 1945: "there must be one spot, the center of all . . . collaborating bodies. The buildings and apparatus, archives and libraries serving them all must be centrally and immediately available; and economies are to be obtained thereby. One of the best known and most effective ways of securing co-operation is permanently to lodge the operating, planning and consultative agencies next door to each other, and, if possible, even to house them in the same building." The Preparatory Commission of the United Nations, meeting in London late in 1945, reached a similar though qualified conclusion about site. It also entertained the possibility of a consolidated budget voted by the General Assembly, common fiscal services and personnel arrangements, and other instruments for the control of activities associated with the United Nations.[2]

Short of a central organizational complex, some planners suggested the desirability and means for close coordination of separate endeavors. Coordination aimed at "unified action both in time and space; short-range and long-term thinking, planning, and programming." It assumed that "the human and financial resources available for the conduct of international economic and social programs in a world emerging from the ruin of war are very limited. The primary object of coordination, therefore, is to facilitate maximum utilization of available resources, the avoidance of conflicting or duplicating efforts, and the selection of tasks that are most urgent."[3]

On the other hand, certain commentators, taking as their point of

---

[2] Herman Finer, *The United Nations Economic and Social Council* (Boston 1946), 110; *Report of the Preparatory Commission of the United Nations*, PC/20 of 23 December 1945, 40–48.

[3] Walter R. Sharp, "The Specialized Agencies . . . II," *International Organization*, II (July 1948), 266; Sharp, *Coordination of Economic and Social Activities* (New York 1948), 101.

departure the League of Nations experience with economic and social problems, foresaw great advantages in separate, dispersed organizations only loosely affiliated with principal United Nations organs. Perhaps David Mitrany offered the most extreme version of this argument. "The essential principle," he wrote in 1943, "is that activities would be selected specifically and organized separately—each according to its nature, to the conditions under which it has to operate, and to the needs of the moment. It would allow, therefore, all freedom for practical variation in the organization of the several functions, as well as in the working of a particular function as needs and conditions alter." Mitrany did not exclude coordination, though he certainly did not emphasize it. "As the whole sense of this particular method is to let activities be organized as the need for joint action arises and is accepted, it would be out of place to lay down in advance some formal plan for the co-ordination of various functions. Co-ordination, too, would in that sense have to come about functionally." [4]

## II. FROM EXPECTATIONS TOWARD REALITY

The commonplace that war's conflagration heated those particles from which United Nations' designs for organs and agencies were hammered out, while a helpful generalization, must be viewed in the perspective of time and circumstance as well as alternative values and organizational conceptions. The dislocated world of 1945 is understood only in relation to the shattered Europe of 1919. Organized international efforts following the Second World War can best be seen against a prewar background of global depression and widespread, if incipient, civil conflict. United Nations structures should be viewed, as they were constructed, upon the residuum of interwar years.

### Emergent Structures

More through circumstance than authoritative choice, the United Nations makeup emerged as a complex of scattered, functionally diverse organs and agencies—a "diaspora" of prewar European organization. Several developments help to account for this.

First, the nascent experiment in international organization, though christened anew with hopes for peace and for United States' (and

[4] *A Working Peace System* (Chicago 1966), 70, 73ff. Mitrany elsewhere: "The worst that could be done would be to try to force . . . developments into some general pattern, to give priority to form over performance. . . ." *Public Administration,* XXIII (1945–46), 7; see also fn., 11–12. For other projections of coordination as a piecemeal process progressively blending autonomous units, see Sir Arthur (later Lord) Salter, "From Combined War Agencies to International Administration," *Public Administration Review,* IV (Winter 1944), 1–2, 4–5; Salter (M.P.), *Public Administration,* XXIII (1945–46), 1; Leo Pasvolsky, "Dumbarton Oaks Proposals for Economic and Social Cooperation," *International Conciliation,* No. 409 (March 1945), 206ff.

others') participation, included existent institutions and remnants of the League of Nations. The Universal Postal Union (Berne) and the International Telecommunication Union (Geneva), with roots in the nineteenth century, were after the war "brought into relationship" (Charter Article 57.2) to the United Nations as specialized agencies. The semi-official International Meteorological Organization, born in 1878 and staffed near Utrecht until 1939, when it moved to Lausanne, was conventionally transformed into another specialized agency after the war. The International Labor Organization, located in Geneva until the war, constituted a bastion of agency autonomy long antedating organization of the United Nations.[5] The League itself, though in principle centralized, had over the years been directed to meet definable international problems with organizational responses which would reemerge as specialized agencies concerned with health, education, and culture.

Second, both manifest need and political consideration suggested piecemeal, diffused creation of the successor organizational firmament for international relations. The necessity for massive efforts at relief and rehabilitation was acknowledged early in the war; their possibilities for wartime and peacetime strategic purposes likewise were recognized by Britain and subsequently by the United States. The United Nations Relief and Rehabilitation Administration (UNRRA), a palpable if temporary outcome of these calculations, served as an experiment in organizing the allies and a nominal forerunner for the coming general effort.[6] In Washington, short- and longer-range estimates of food and fiber problems momentarily converged during the war years. The U.S. Department of State, having detected "some public feeling that international discussion of postwar problems was being too long delayed," contemplated food as "a relatively noncontroversial subject on which to proceed for the first full United Nations Conference at this still exploratory stage." President Franklin D. Roosevelt, personally interested in nutrition problems and urged to act on them

[5] According to the former Belgian Prime Minister Paul van Zeeland, previous ILO experience demonstrated "a vitality which has enabled it to pursue its work, to act and to confirm its existence while the League remained in the shadows. This autonomy has proved its worth, and it must at all costs be maintained. There might even be serious arguments for increasing its autonomy [vis-à-vis the new organization]." International Labor Conference, Twenty-Sixth Session, Provisional Record No. 7, 62; quoted by Carter Goodrich, "The International Labor Organization and the United Nations," American Interests in the War and the Peace series, (New York 1944), 19.

[6] Daniel S. Cheever and H. Field Haviland, Jr., *Organizing for Peace* (Cambridge, Mass. 1954), 227–31; U.S. Department of State, *Postwar Foreign Policy Preparation* (Washington 1950), 90–91; Robert H. Johnson, "International Politics and the Structure of International Organization . . . ," *World Politics*, 3 (July 1951), 524ff., 529ff.

by Sir John Boyd Orr of Scotland, F. L. McDougall of Australia, and members of his own administration, "favored at this time the establishment of entirely separate functional agencies in the economic field and chose food and agriculture as the subject offering the best chances for success. . . ." [7] At the 1943 Food and Agriculture Conference at Hot Springs, Virginia, early groundwork was laid for the Food and Agriculture Organization, established in Rome, like its predecessor, the International Institute of Agriculture. Issues of international monetary policy, the financing of reconstruction, postwar air transport, and education and culture were likewise discussed, though hardly settled, well before the San Francisco conference at various sites in the United States and the United Kingdom. These discussions would eventually result in the International Monetary Fund and International Bank for Reconstruction and Development (destined for Washington), the International Civil Aviation Organization (to Montreal), and the United Nations Educational, Scientific, and Cultural Organization (like an antecedent, the *Institut internationale de coopération intellectuelle*, claimed by Paris).

Third, dispositions among government creators of certain agencies contributed mightily in immediate postwar years to further distancing of agencies from close coordination through the United Nations General Assembly and the Economic and Social Council. The Fund and Bank soon superseded ILO as the members of the United Nations family most reluctant to be "brought into relationship." Located in Washington rather than New York in order to insulate them from both the United Nations "political forums" and "economic, financial, or commercial private interests" (as was protested at the time of the formal decision on site), IBRD and IMF insisted upon the sanctity of their staffs, their inner councils, and their financial and administrative planning. To an early charge by a spokesman for the nonparticipating Soviet Union that these institutions were subordinated to United States foreign policy and should hence be tied more closely to EcoSoc, the U.S. representative retorted that the Charter contemplated merely "discretionary" Council control of the specialized agencies.[8] With the Bank and Fund as pacesetters in agency autonomy, it is scarcely surprising that kindred agencies would argue less ambitious briefs for independent action.

The regional commissions introduced yet another "element of complexity in the task of coordinating international economic programs." [9] Economic commissions for Europe (ECE, in Geneva), Asia and the Far

[7] Department of State, *Postwar . . . Preparation* (fn. 6), 143; L. K. Hyde, *The United States and the United Nations* (New York 1960), 31f.

[8] Sharp, "The Specialized Agencies" (fn. 2), 248–49.

[9] Same, 247.

East (ECAFE, in Bangkok), and Latin America (ECLA, in Santiago) would later be joined by the Economic Commission for Africa (ECA, in Addis Ababa). While these provided new liaison points for evolving United Nations activities, including programs fitted to the World Health Organization's regionally decentralized constitution, they also contributed to the overall pattern of decentralization and loose affiliation so rapidly apparent in the structure of the United Nations "family."

Functional agencies, a category which includes United Nations specialized agencies yet need not exclude certain related U.N. activities, by 1948 numbered twelve units established or contemplated: [10]

Universal Postal Union (UPU)
International Telecommunication Union (ITU)
World Meteorological Organization (WMO)
International Labor Organization (ILO, relocated in Geneva)
Food and Agriculture Organization (FAO)
International Monetary Fund (IMF)
International Bank for Reconstruction and Development (IBRD)
International Civil Aviation Organization (ICAO)
United Nations Educational, Scientific and Cultural Organization UNESCO)
World Health Organization (WHO, in Geneva)
Inter-Governmental Maritime Consultative Organization (IMCO, in London, launched in 1957)
International Trade Organization (ITO, remains unrealized; General Agreement on Tariffs and Trade [GATT], unofficially associated with the United Nations, and United Nations Conference [etc.] on Trade and Development [UNCTAD], both in Geneva, operate in this area)

During 1948, reports circulated that "various influential members" of EcoSoc had decided "among themselves to . . . call a halt on any further additions to the specialized agency family." [11]

*Values as Government Preferences*

The preferences or "interests" of a nation-state are defined and redefined by its government—the individuals who act in that state's principal roles. Governments organize or join international institutions because they expect to gain benefits or avoid costs. Both benefits and costs should be seen by the observer in a very broad sense even

[10] At this time the International Refugee Organization also was viewed by some as a specialized agency. Created in 1948, IRO was dismantled in 1951.
[11] Sharp, "The Specialized Agencies" (fn. 2), 251–52.

though they are usually perceived by would-be member governments in a restricted context.

In several respects the Atlantic declaration, negotiated and promulgated by Roosevelt and Winston Churchill in 1941, was the prototype of the new generation of charters negotiated and promulgated for the international organizations which here concern us. All these charters enshrined value preferences in grandiose rhetoric and qualified promises. Yet they all sprang from immediate no less than from remote considerations. "The promises of closer international cooperation were a part—and a most needed part—of the efforts to keep up morale amongst the soldiers and the people back home." They were "also meant to broaden the forces of rebellion in the enemy countries. People had to believe that, once the war had been won, the world would be radically re-made into a happier, more harmonious and stable place, where broadly planned progress and security would result from joint efforts by all peoples in their common interests." [12]

The Atlantic Charter, even more purely than succeeding organization charters, signified the zeal of the American and British Governments in preparing and disseminating their visions of postwar international economic relationships. The Soviet Union initially demonstrated little interest in organizing nonsecurity international matters. France and China, devastated and politically riven by the war, tended to stress immediate needs and specialties (e.g. *coopération intellectuelle* for France, and health for China) when ultimately they joined in these discussions. Others, notably Canada and Australia, figured principally in modifying the proposals already drafted by representatives of the United States and Great Britain.

American and British preferences hardly coincided. Both wanted security; both sought economic recovery and expansion. The Government of the United States, though characteristically plural in enunciating a desirable future, foresaw essentially a world free of political and monetary blockages to commerce and investment in which the U.S.A. might continue its ascendancy. The Churchill Government, on the other hand, though also divided in its counsel, sought to preserve Empire and Imperial preference against all challenges. Yet the warborn charters managed to paper over most disparities in Anglo-American expectations about return to or revision of the *status quo ante bellum*.

The charters fuzzed even sharper differences between other Government participants. Some of the questions unresolved by charter-making would later reappear in different form. How, for instance, reconcile

[12] Gunnar Myrdal, *Beyond the Welfare State* (New Haven 1960), 268.

claims to autonomy by the powerful with claims by the weaker to well-being?

Words in an international organization charter provide a façade of commonality among its member Governments. That façade hides not only differences in governmental objectives, but also more subtle differences in the intensity of various governments' commitments to the same objectives. Membership is only the most apparent threshold betokening a Government's calculation of the costs and benefits of participation or nonparticipation. The United States, the United Kingdom, France, China, and a number of other states became members of most of the newer agencies; at the outset the Soviet Union joined only a few. Most of Asia and Africa remained outside the membership circle.

*Tasks Amplified*

Particular interests posed as universal charter principles. If economic expansion was a major aim of the chief organizing powers, appropriate means toward their versions of economic expansion are scarcely surprising as early tasks assigned to the newer international organizations.

The Government of the United States sought to open new markets and investment opportunities. Among other ramifications, this meant trade and related concessions by the British and French in the Middle East and in other areas of prewar preference or exclusivity, concessions consecrated in phrases such as "equal access to trade and raw materials by all nations," "non-discrimination in international commercial relations," and simply "free trade."

But the United States Government also viewed with grave concern the civil unrest which was threatened by hunger and uprootedness. No American goal exceeded that of avoiding yet another war. Economic and social pacification and an open world on the American model were simply taken as part and parcel of security in this sense.

Beyond such temporary channels as UNRRA and IRO, and the measures, primarily unilateral in character, which superseded them, "international political stability" [13] demanded a more comprehensive and continuing response. Politically-tempered humanitarian considerations along with both the certain present and uncertain future of American agricultural surpluses implied an international instrumentality—FAO—through which information might be obtained to guide production and facilitate the distribution of foodstuffs. Both Americans attuned to banishing famine and raising nutrition standards and those sensitive to fluctuations on world markets could endorse "freedom from want."

[13] *Postwar . . . Preparation* (fn. 6), 26.

Various considerations pointed toward concerted international efforts to avoid a return to competitive economic nationalism. IMF was intended to facilitate trade expansion and to provide alternatives to such restrictive unilateral measures as exchange control manipulation.

IBRD's first tasks, as outlined in 1946 by John W. Snyder, Chairman of the International Bank Board of Governors and subsequently U.S. Secretary of the Treasury, were "assisting in the restoration of war-devastated areas" and "stimulating the flow of international capital. . . ." After the end of hostilities, Assistant Secretary of State Dean Acheson had earlier reminded the Commonwealth Club of California, most nations would face

> a great need for imports; they will have to rebuild their cities, their factories, and their transportation systems. Much that they need will have to come from abroad at the outset, because the very machinery with which they make things will have been destroyed. . . . [They will] wish to borrow money. If they borrow money, they spend the money in places where the goods can be produced. We have the greatest productive plant in the world. While the rest of the world has been undergoing destruction, we have been building up this plant in order to carry the great burden of the war. One of our problems in the future will be to keep that great plant employed and to keep the people employed who are now working in it or who come back from the armed forces.[14]

Trade expansion, given the U.S. Government's objectives, led to a draft code of conduct—with exceptions—intended to guide international commercial behavior (including the treatment to be accorded traders outside preferential areas) and to a proposed bargaining forum in which tariff and other trade barriers might be reduced. The projected International Trade Organization aspired to both tasks. Regulation of "arrangements, public or private, to restrict production and trade in individual commodities" was also contemplated, and several arrangements for individual commodities "in chronic over-supply or subject to extreme variation in prices" were actually organized.[15]

Peacetime air transport, itself a form of commerce, was seen as another potential lever for "open trade and open relations." American access to trade and raw materials in areas previously closed to it would be aided by several of the "five freedoms" urged at the Chicago conference in late 1944 and by Part Four of the ICAO Constitution. The needs of the airlines of other states, similarly enticed by these freedoms, might be filled in large measure by sales of U.S. transport planes.

14 "The Place of Bretton Woods in Economic Collective Security," Department of State Pub. 2306 (Washington 1945), 3, 9.
15 Postwar . . . Preparation (fn. 6), 561.

Freedoms three through five expounded rights to carry traffic from a plane's homeland to another country, to pick up in another country traffic destined for a plane's homeland, and to carry traffic between two or more countries other than a plane's homeland. When read in conjunction with the preamble and Article 44(g) of the Convention on International Civil Aviation, which call respectively for "international air transport services . . . on the basis of equality of opportunity" and avoidance of "discrimination between contracting States," ICAO Constitution articles 81 through 88 imply disclosure of all existing international air transport agreements and the elimination, through ICAO negotiating procedures, of any discriminatory concessions.

A free and open world—that is, a peaceful world—demanded greater objectivity in reporting news, and more reliable access to this news by all peoples. Prejudicial information had in American eyes contributed to the war and to its course. After the U.S. Government sent official representatives to the wartime London talks on a postwar international organization for education, these sentiments were expressed on behalf of mass communications as a UNESCO task and a worldwide United Nations radio network, perhaps under the aegis of UNESCO.

Though perhaps of lesser priority to U.S. official planners, the ILO task revaluation of 1944 in Philadelphia also found some American support. A far-reaching Philadelphia Charter, drafted by International Labor Office (staff) members and unanimously endorsed by participants, urged attainment of conditions under which all men might pursue "their material well-being and their spiritual development in conditions of freedom and dignity, of economic security, and equal opportunity." In Philadelphia at its 26th International Labor Conference, ILO thus seemingly broadened its mandate to include, in the phrase of U.S. delegation chairman and Secretary of Labor Frances Perkins, a "war against poverty." [16]

Some of these aims the British shared. Britain as well as America feared a postwar recession with its chain of international consequences. The Great Depression, it was widely held, had contributed to malignant economic nationalism, to psychic preparation for militarism and totalitarianism, and—because of the failure to alleviate underlying conditions by appropriate action through the League of Nations—to war. Keynesian analysis now pointed toward preventive measures which might be applied through international institutions. At the outset Britain enthusiastically joined the Roosevelt Administration in preparing for "freedom from want," although Lord Keynes (like U.S. Vice President Henry Wallace and others, for slightly differing reasons) also

---

[16] "Twenty-Sixth International Labor Conference . . . ," *U.S. Department of State Bulletin*, XI (10 September 1944), 258–59; Ernst B. Haas, *Beyond the Nation-State* (Stanford 1964), 155ff.

exhorted the deployment of primary commodity buffer-stocks for use as a major global counter-cyclical instrument. Centrally important to British planners was a world monetary institution along the lines of Keynes' Clearing Union proposal. Whereas the American Stabilization Fund plan by Harry Dexter White limited U.S. liability and others' access to internationally acceptable currencies, thereby restricting possible operations by a monetary fund, the Clearing Union plan proposed substantial and automatic drawing rights for all members and authorized the Union in time of dire need to create additional international credit without further subscriptions from members. IMF bore marks of both proposals, but more closely resembled the White project in the limited scope of its assignment and resources. As such, the Fund reassured those Americans who feared an unlimited commitment without reassuring the British who feared an inadequate response.[17]

Following the American lead, British planners applauded the U.S. outline for a banking institution to encourage international loans for reconstruction and development. "This task was of very direct interest to Great Britain. In the first place, she was very conscious both of the lag in development during the war in many of her dependent territories and of the general need to encourage the appreciable and steady flow overseas of American investment upon which the attainment of an expanding and balanced world economy would so greatly depend. In the second place, bearing in mind past difficulties over the 'tied' loans of the United States Export-Import Bank, it was a particular British interest to secure a flow of 'untied' capital, in the hope that borrowers would spend in Britain a proportion of the dollars they received."[18] This time Keynes, mindful of Britain's financial status and immediate prospects, sought and got a more restricted institutional capital base than White had proposed.[19] IBRD's subscription-weighted votes, like IMF's, accorded the highest status to the United States and the second highest to the United Kingdom. Though London wanted the financial institutions, Washington got them.

Commerce was more difficult. Certain segments of the British Government perceived with misgivings that pledges exacted for freer trade, from the Atlantic Charter and Article VII of the Anglo-American Mutual Aid Agreement of 1942[20] through a projected trade convention, were meant, *inter alia*, to whittle down Imperial preference. In other quarters, as U.S. Ambassador John G. Winant discerned in his London soundings, "there is a genuine desire for multilateral trade

---

17 Geoffrey L. Goodwin, *Britain and the United Nations* (New York 1957), 273, 333. On Anglo-American negotiations in finance and trade during this period, see Richard N. Gardner, *Sterling-Dollar Diplomacy* (Oxford 1956), passim.
18 Goodwin (fn. 17), 277.
19 Sewell, *Functionalism and World Politics* (Princeton 1966), 81.
20 See Cheever and Haviland (fn. 6), 188–89, for pertinent excerpts.

and nondiscrimination and a groping for means of reconciling them with a greater degree of forward planning and large scale operations than were practiced in the 19th and early 20th centuries." [21]

In part because Britain would benefit more from multilateral arrangements, in part because America since the birth of its liberalized commercial policy in 1934 had known only bilateral reciprocity, transatlantic conceptions tended to diverge on the character of a bargaining forum. More accurately than American prophets, the British foresaw a postwar recovery hiatus during which a moratorium on applying commercial and monetary codes of conduct would prove a practical necessity. They insisted that balance of payments problems should permit a Government to effect quantitative trade controls without international authorization. Like the Australian and Canadian Governments, who also feared a postwar slump, the British were determined to press full employment policies by every means possible. Cartels, in British somewhat less than American estimation, were demonic devices apt to touch off a new holocaust.[22]

As might be imagined from the rather transparent American aims, the British Government accorded lower priority to negotiations on the postwar status of civil aviation. Virtually all parties to negotiations favored some means for preventing "rate wars" and other forms of "unfair competition." Even the competitive and expansion-minded Americans, whose Chicago delegation included several representatives from major U.S. airlines, "kept the door open for regulatory controls, in view of the strong opposition in certain quarters in the United States to a truly open system." But while most Americans spoke for "freedom of the air" and "non-exclusivity of international operating rights," Churchill and Lord Beaverbrook (then Lord Privy Seal), in particular, wanted understandings reflected in "operational agreements and also spheres of activity" supervised by international authority.[23]

During the International Civil Aviation Conference late in 1944 the Anglo-American rift opened dramatically. With negotiations at an impasse, Roosevelt cabled Churchill his displeasure at the prospect of "a form of strangulation" that might well "place a dead hand on the use of the great air trade routes," and warned the British Prime Minister that "Congress . . . will not be in a generous mood if it and the people feel that the United Kingdom has not agreed to a generally beneficial air agreement. They will wonder about the chances of our two countries, let alone any others, working together to keep the peace if we cannot even get together on an aviation agreement."

[21] *Foreign Relations of the United States . . . 1944*, II (Washington 1967), 13.
[22] Cf. Hyde (fn. 7), 34; Goodwin (fn. 17), 278.
[23] Material on civil aviation negotiations is drawn from *Foreign Relations . . . 1943* (fn. 21), II, 355–613.

Churchill in turn reminded Roosevelt of the prior agreement, so as best to prosecute the war, that the U.S. should concentrate upon transport aircraft and the British upon "fighting types." Thus the United States stood "in an incomparably better position than we are to fill any needs of air transport that may arise after the war is over, and to build up [your] civil aircraft industry." "Let me say also," he added, "that I have never advocated competitive 'bigness' in any sphere between our two countries in their present state of development. You will have the greatest navy in the world. You will have, I hope, the greatest air force. You will have the greatest trade. You have all the gold. But these things do not oppress my mind with fear because I am sure the American people under your re-acclaimed leadership will not give themselves over to vainglorious ambitions, and that justice and fair-play will be the lights that guide them."

In Chicago, the discussion assumed some of the characteristics of multilateral diplomacy in years to come. Lord Swinton, the British representative, argued a questionable brief on behalf of protecting small nations from competition, only to see representatives from most of these states ultimately line up behind the United States. The Americans lofted grand principles. A French representative confided to an American that although he was under instructions to follow the British lead, he was striving to get his orders changed. The Labour Governments of Australia and New Zealand proposed international ownership and operation of air services on certain routes. Canada sought to play the broker's part. And ICAO emerged as the product of an exercise by the most reluctant parties to a series of questions. Technical standards for navigation and air safety encountered minimal opposition. More controversial matters were deferred, or relegated to the unilateral voluntarism of two draft conventions on the "freedoms."

Other agencies precipitated little apparent disagreement on postwar tasks. In 1944, at least, Government, labor, and management ILO conferees endorsed the Office's ambitious bid to scrutinize "all national and international policies and measures, in particular those of an economic and financial character," which bore upon ILO objectives of social justice.[24] UPU, ITU, and WMO were given stronger constitutional foundations during early postwar convocations and authorized to establish interplenary consultative arrangements. At Moscow, in the fall of 1946, governments participated in an international telecommunication conference widely regarded as highly successful.[25] Between visits to the Kremlin, the Moscow Opera, and the countryside, dele-

[24] Haas (fn. 16), 156, 159. Other contemporary metaphors for ILO's assignment were watchdog, overseer, and monitor.
[25] F. C. DeWolf, "Moscow Telecommunications Conference," *Department of State Bulletin,* xv (24 November 1946), 943–46.

gates authorized for ITU a Central Frequency Registration Board of experts to help accommodate increases in ship, air, and other loads. The Frequency Registration Board was asked to review any member's request for frequency allocation; to determine whether its use would interfere with existing communications; then either to register the new frequency, urge the use of another, or, in the event of recalcitrance by the applicant, publish a "Notification" in principle denying ITU protection to the encroaching member. Previously ITU merely published radio information in a list of frequencies. With the transformation from IMO to WMO, the newer agency was instructed to establish a worldwide network of weather-observation stations, facilitate the rapid international exchange of weather information, promote the standardization of meteorological observations, and further the application of meteorology to aviation, shipping, agriculture, and other human activities.[26] And an expansive though nonetheless largely uncontested assignment awaited the World Health Organization, called for by a San Francisco conference resolution co-sponsored by Brazil and China and prepared by an interim commission while awaiting states' ratifications. The preamble to the WHO charter defined health as "a state of complete physical, mental and social well-being" rather than "merely the absence of disease or infirmity." Its enjoyment was held to be a fundamental right of every human being.

## Tasks Constricted

United Nations specialized agencies entered the postwar era under several auspicious signs. Membership, though far from universal, extended well beyond the League of Nations locus. Measured against organized attempts during League days, the endeavors in every field now addressed, including those claimed by ILO, had been strengthened by expanded writs and by organizational modification. Some agencies braced for action on new problems or on older problems previously neglected. FAO, IMF, IBRD, and even ICAO, despite wartime Anglo-American mandates cut to the more reluctant constituent in each case, started with capacious or potentially elastic commissions. Yet performance was not to match promise.

Some of the shortfall is explained merely by deflation of overblown charters after the end of hostilities, some by changing relations among the victorious United Nations allies, particularly between the United States, the United Kingdom, and the Soviet Union. And some can be traced to shifts of governmental (including legislative) figures and postures, especially in the United States. For the specialized agencies owed

[26] John M. Cates, Jr., "Meeting of International Meteorological Organization . . . ," *Department of State Bulletin*, XVIII (11 January 1948), 43–46.

very much to the Roosevelt Administration, and with that Administration's gradual departure came differing perceptions of what was bound in any case to be, and what was additionally made to become, harsh reality.

The choice of alternative instruments for U.S. foreign policy strongly reflected this evolving configuration of international actors with shifting perceptions. Specialized agencies were regarded by Roosevelt, and by Secretary of State Cordell Hull and others, as significant devices to promote American objectives. The British wartime coalition Cabinet likewise saw many of them as useful contrivances. In these priorities both Governments had active segments of their publics behind them, pushing. Given critical and increasingly recognized European recovery demands and the quickening of differences with the Soviet Government, however, the Truman Administration reverted to the American predilection for unilateralism which its predecessor had for a time tactically modified.

Herbert Hoover's advice, drawn from the ex-President's recollection of his own use of anti-Bolshevik food relief in Europe after World War I, strengthened an acknowledged predisposition of Secretary of War Henry L. Stimson and his assistant, John J. McCloy. In mid-1945, Stimson urged Truman to circumscribe multilateral UNRRA aid and to augment resources administered by the military occupation which he oversaw.[27] Individual Congressmen swung behind an allegation that the Soviets were utilizing UNRRA resources, largely American in origin, for their peculiar purposes. A few months before the 1946 elections, Under-Secretary of State William L. Clayton announced that American support for UNRRA would cease. After hard bargaining and not a little bitterness, the faltering British had received an American loan, augmented by Canadian credits, in 1945. France, the Netherlands, Denmark, and Luxembourg received IBRD reconstruction loans totaling about $500 million in 1947 before Bank lending languished; Britain purchased $300 million from IMF with sterling in 1947–48, before a decision was made to husband Fund resources for future use by barring them to European Recovery Program beneficiaries. Marshall Plan aid was then directed to these selected areas. IRO for a time undertook the burden of resettling the homeless, but it was dissolved in 1951 and superseded by a less expensive U.N. High Commissioner for Refugees and by the more tractable United States Escapee Program and the U.S.-sponsored Intergovernmental Committee for European Migration. Although early hopes for a worldwide radio network sanctioned by UNESCO did not materialize, the official Voice of America

27 Gabriel Kolko, *The Politics of War* (New York 1968), 498.

was later joined by the semi-official Radio Free Europe, Radio Liberation, and Radio Free Asia.

The European and North Atlantic collective self-defense arrangements of the late forties and the Asian-focused pacts of the fifties bespoke further reassessment of alternative instruments and a shift from the quasi-universal U.N. to particular arrangements with selected memberships. And more and more, substantive policy, whether unilateral or channeled through "regional" organizations, would emphasize security by military means. A crisis atmosphere—in part composed of very genuine elements—spawned headlines, redirected attention, bled off resources, and built up new vested interests. In the eyes of U.S. policymakers, specialized agencies became "back-burner stuff." [28]

The occasion of the Truman Doctrine provides an illuminating instance of the transition from qualified multilateralism toward other strategies. With UNRRA being liquidated and the Food and Agriculture Organization still inadequately supported by its founders despite FAO's potential for recovery, the overextended British, speaking now through a Labour Government, in 1947 asked the Truman Administration to take up the burden of supporting the Greek regime in its struggle with local guerrilla forces. The British Government also asked that either the United States or IBRD assume the task of aiding Turkey. As an American participant, Joseph M. Jones, was later to interpret these two notes and their ramifications, "Great Britain had within the hour handed the job of world leadership, with all its burdens and all its glory, to the United States." [29]

The form of the future was perhaps less bound to the immediate fact. But one conclusion Americans drew more clearly than before: Britain was no true rival to the postwar United States; she was not even up to the Anglo-American condominium obliquely suggested by Churchill as recently as the spring of 1946 in Fulton, Missouri, before the President of the United States. Henceforth Britain would be regarded as a loyal, if junior, partner. The sole adversary indeed seemed to lie beyond Churchill's iron curtain, an iron curtain that threatened to enclose Greece and Turkey with its next expansion.

Less clear as a necessary consequence of British withdrawal is the U.S. choice to act unilaterally. An FAO mission had recommended economic and humanitarian support to Greece, from U.N. agencies as well as from Britain and the United States. But Jones recorded that, as far as he knew, no suggestion was even offered during formulation of a U.S. direct-aid policy to Greece and Turkey that action might rather be taken through a component of the United Nations. A White

[28] Cf. Harlan Cleveland, *The Obligations of Power* (New York 1966), 35.
[29] Joseph M. Jones, *The Fifteen Weeks* (New York 1955), 7.

House address did incorporate the justification by Dean Rusk, Director of the State Department Office of Special Political Affairs, for bypassing the U.N.: the situation was urgent "and the United Nations and its related organizations are not yet in a position to extend assistance of the kind that is required."

The Rusk draft had also suggested that the United States was "stepping into the breach in order to help maintain conditions in which the United Nations can grow in international confidence and authority. The United States has already taken a lead in the establishment of international agencies designed for the rehabilitation of devastated areas and for long-term economic reconstruction. We will continue to study ways and means through which the United Nations and related international agencies might undertake financial and economic responsibilities in such areas." This portion was not used. Jones speculates that Truman wanted "a simple and unadorned statement of American policy, an incomparable assumption of responsibility, in the United States' own right, of a kind never assumed before, for strengthening free nations and protecting freedom in the world," a message that would "contain no hint of ways of avoiding full and direct responsibility." Truman's aim was "a fearless confrontation of the American people with the responsibilities involved in the use of the tremendous and unique power of the United States to promote peace and well-being and preserve freedom. . . ." [30]

Arthur Vandenberg, Chairman of the Senate Foreign Relations Committee in the new Republican Congress, had told Truman that the only way he could get Congressional approval was to "scare hell out of the country." Truman's proposal succeeded with Congress. But Vandenberg later wrote that the White House "made a colossal blunder in ignoring the U.N." [31] The Truman Doctrine led the way to future U.S. military and economic support for beleaguered, often unpopular, governments elsewhere. It also signaled a further decline of the U.N. specialized agency profile in the perception of U.S. officials and the American people.

Even when not pressed by cold-war calculations, the principal Government participants in the United Nations complex during the early postwar period sometimes acted in ways which deprived agencies of responsibilities initially mooted for them. When the separate ICAO international agreements for Two Freedoms and Five Freedoms of the air failed to gain many signatories, U.S. negotiators set out to get bilateral agreements with desired partners. The outstanding Anglo-American disputes over civil aviation were largely settled "out of court"

[30] Same, 161.
[31] Eric F. Goldman, *The Crucial Decade* . . . (New York 1960), 59; Jones (fn. 29), 180.

and at the expense of a stronger ICAO. To be sure, the foundation of these developments had been laid earlier. In April 1944, several months before the Chicago conference, British negotiators had proposed an "International Air Transport Authority" to allocate civil aviation opportunities, and the chairman of the U.S. delegation in Chicago, Adolph A. Berle, Jr., recognized the possibility of an extra-ICAO arrangement to avoid "rate wars and other violences of competition" by means of "conferences of air operators analogous to ship operators' conferences." This procedure, Berle had been assured by the U.S. Attorney General, was legal—provided the federal Civil Aeronautics Board (as it was then called) approved. Implementing agreements, Berle concluded, presented no real problems. "While the Civil Aeronautics Board does not have general power of enforcement, it could make it plain to any United States operator who violated an agreement that he would thereby forfeit diplomatic protection for his landing and transit rights abroad. It was the opinion of our operating advisers that no airline would violate an agreement thus made."

But to avoid "a new version of a cartel organization," the Chicago understanding contemplated that operators' conference decisions "must come up for scrutiny before the international organization where any complaint of injustice or hardship could be heard"—a principle reminiscent of hopes (likewise unfulfilled) for international commodity arrangements representing the interests of consumers no less than those of producers. The airlines' IATA (International Air Transport Association) has proved at least equal to the operators' expected part; ICAO, where IATA is domiciled, has fallen far short in representing consumers' interests.

Non-cases among functional agencies further illustrate the deemphasis of U.N.-affiliated possibilities. An International Office of Business Practices was proposed by the U.S. Special Committee on Private Monopolies and Cartels but never seriously negotiated. International modes for assuring full employment, pressed by the Australian Government and others, never achieved more than the reserved pledges of Governments to act separately in doing what they could. Some embryonic elements of both cartel and full-employment international policy went down with the ITO charter, finally abandoned in 1950 to a "second-class funeral," as an Italian periodical called it, by the Truman Administration. For some American interests the proposal went too far; by others it was held not to go far enough. The Executive Committee of the United States Council of the International Chamber of Commerce, taking essentially the latter tack in its *Statement of Position* on ITO, also revealed the political temper of the day: "It is a dangerous document. . . . It places the United States in a permanent minority position owing to its one-vote-one-country voting procedure. Because of that, membership in the ITO based on this Charter would make it impossible for the United States to engage in an independent course of policy in favor of multilateral trade." [32] And if the sponsoring United States was not going to ratify ITO's Havana Charter, other Governments were certainly not interested in doing so.

Some agencies simply never received the support necessary to fulfill earlier promises. "No steps had been taken to expand the general scope and functions of the ILO" at the 26th Labor Conference, an official U.S. account soberly reported five years later.[33] ILO's Philadelphia Charter and Conference resolutions had been endorsed without cost; its follow-up conventions and recommendations might be ignored with impunity. Nor would dynamic construction of ILO's authority to apply international standards be countenanced in the manner hinted at in 1944. Secretary of State James Byrnes' instructions the following year to U.S. delegates attending another ILO meeting were: "The United States Government does not want international pressures encouraged or supported which look to extending the legal sanction of collective agreements beyond the groups represented by the parties to the agreement." [34] Soon thereafter, an American employer delegate to ILO thought talk of the Philadelphia declaration referred to a statement adopted on the Fourth of July, 1776.

Newer agencies were meeting much the same fate. FAO was beseeched by its first Director General, Sir John Boyd Orr, to lead the coming race between world population and food supplies. Boyd Orr wanted a powerful World Food Board with adequate financial resources to direct this long-term effort, but his proposal was turned down. FAO budgets were either trimmed to fit "the present difficult financial world situation," as an FAO finance subcommittee justified one cut in June 1947, or restricted at the outset by the U.S. ceiling of 25 percent imposed upon its subscription to this agency—despite larger U.S. proportions authorized for certain other parts of the United Nations complex. Told by U.S. Department of Agriculture delegate Leslie Wheeler that Congress had established this absolute limit by law, a United Kingdom delegate once asked, without gaining real satisfaction, why then Congress could not *change* the limit by law. Under such circumstances, Boyd Orr soon resigned.[35]

[32] Quoted in William Diebold, Jr., "The End of the I.T.O." (Princeton 1952), 20, 21.

[33] *Postwar . . . Preparation* (fn. 6), 240.

[34] *Foreign Relations . . . 1945* (fn. 21), I, 1551.

[35] FAO member Governments did approve a weaker version of Boyd Orr's Board which they named the World Food Council. Its terms of reference replaced such words as "decide," "direct," and "enforce" with "review," "examine," and "advise." In an interview with the *Daily Mail* shortly before his resignation, Boyd Orr said: "America talks about Russian misuse of the veto but the United States itself has

From the outset it was clear that budgetary resources would likewise be a crucial factor in effecting the ambitious aims outlined by the UNESCO and WHO constitutions. UNESCO for a time enjoyed a U.S. budgetary percentage substantially higher than FAO's, but both absolute totals remained negligible. Jaime Torres Bodet, who followed Julian Huxley as UNESCO Director General, resigned in 1950 on a budget issue, resumed his position at the plea of General Conference delegates, again resigned over another budget crisis two years later and did not return. WHO, finally under way in 1948, found its efforts constrained by the ceiling of $1.92 million set upon United States participation. Dr. Brock Chisholm, first WHO Director General, later helped to negotiate a compromise whereby "operational" and "administrative" budgets would be separated so as to accommodate American reservations [36] without totally shackling WHO efforts. Nonetheless, these efforts were sharply delimited.

*Regular Budgets per annum*

|      | FAO | UNESCO | WHO |
|------|-----|--------|-----|
| 1947 | $6,782,000 | $6,000,000 | |
| 1948 | $5,000,000 | $7,682,637 | |
| 1949 | $5,000,000 | $7,780,000 | $5,000,000 |
| 1950 | $5,000,000 | $8,000,000 | $7,501,500 |
| 1951 | $5,025,000 | $8,300,000 | $7,300,000 |
| 1952 | $5,250,000 | $8,718,000 | $9,077,782 |
| 1953 | $5,250,000 | $9,017,849 | $9,832,754 |

After early hopes, the dominant British public feeling toward the U.N. specialized agencies turned to disappointment. Some Americans feared them. Chosen instruments for the Roosevelt Administration's free-enterprise open-world policy, they now were viewed by a few critics, including the National Economic Council, as the bestial artifice of statism and collectivism. "The method of putting this deception over on the American people is simple. While we are lulled into imagining that the UN is all mouth, a harmless debating society, the Planners are busy attaching tentacles to its body—tentacles specially designed to grip hard just where they are intended to grip. These tentacles are 'agencies' of the UN. We are counted upon to assume

---

vetoed and therefore destroyed a world plan to feed the world. We had a blueprint and we [were] ready to go ahead. Then America said 'No.'" Sir John (as he then was) later extended his criticism to the Soviet Union for its unwillingness to participate, an unwillingness which, he held, foredoomed any major grain stabilization scheme. In later years Lord Orr did not spare the British Government for its own sins of omission and commission.

[36] Another reservation attached to U.S. participation was freedom from any domestic American obligation to enact programs referred to in the WHO Constitution.

naively that the agencies of a harmless body must be harmless too." [37] But by most Americans they were not so much rejected as quietly forgotten.

## III. NEW PARTICIPANTS, NEW MISSIONS

Thus far our account has followed the American and British viewpoints on the United Nations specialized agencies. These governments fundamentally shaped the newer agencies and the revaluation of those which existed already. Their preeminence in structuring the organizational setting owed something to farsightedness and to a will to form, or reform, the postwar world; it owed much, as already suggested, to the unequal impact of war, and because of this, to their available resources for various actions. Given the timing of the Anglo-American bid to reach tentative decisions during the course of the war, it was inevitable that negotiations would occur among governments and governments-in-exile on unoccupied territory. Who would participate, when they would participate, where they would participate, and what the participants would formulate, questions of considerable interest to many states, proved to be choices exercised largely by host governments in Washington and London.

Anglo-American aims and resulting agencies and tasks during the immediate postwar period were discussed in the previous section. A brief consideration of how other participants came to fit into the functional agencies sheds additional light on their establishment, partial dystrophy, and further evolution.

### From Particularity Toward Universality

A measure of the effectiveness of American and British initiatives is provided by Anglo-American skirmishes for pride of place, and their consequences for participation by others with some claim to charter status in United Nations organizations. Thus, the Soviet Government refused to participate in the Inter-Allied Committee on Post-War Requirements, UNRRA's precursor created in September 1941, on grounds that its constitution by Governments-in-exile domiciled in London and its British chairman and secretariat "placed it under British domination." The Soviet observer to the London Conference of Allied Ministers of Education confided much the same to his American counterpart before dropping out of talks leading to UNESCO. Keynes' original Clearing Union draft proposed an institution "designed and initiated by the United States and the United Kingdom," with the Soviet Union "and perhaps one or more other members of the United Nations . . .

[37] Quoted in Gabriel A. Almond, *The American People and Foreign Policy* (New York 1960), 204.

invited to join them as founder States. Other members would then be brought in. . . ." Regarding the Food Conference and beyond, the British Embassy in Washington suggested in 1943: "His Majesty's Government have always believed that the most satisfactory way of making progress would be by reaching preliminary agreement between the United States and the United Kingdom. The two governments would then consult the Soviet and Chinese Governments and subsequently approach the other members of the United Nations." When prior consultation with the White Commonwealth furthered British aims, however, this was done. In response to a Soviet request for information on the forthcoming Chicago conference on civil aviation, Lord Beaverbrook offered to inform the Russians that they would be brought into talks only after the British and Americans had concluded their preliminary discussions.[38]

Once they entered the field of agency-making, the Americans demonstrated their own tactical skill and, in addition, the advantages of preponderant resources. A donor-oriented UNRRA with a strong staff headed by an American would best fit official U.S. purposes, and there was ample benefactor leverage to achieve it despite British efforts to secure decentralized multipower consultative arrangements. When it called a constitutional meeting on American soil, the U.S. Government was capable of organizing it in much the same manner as the British. "Administratively," Hull wrote Roosevelt about Hot Springs preparations, "the Secretariat will be independent of the United States Delegation, although close liaison and cooperation of course will be maintained." Soon thereafter, the governmental choice of a State Department official as executive head of the Food and Agriculture Conference was communicated to those invited.[39]

The Americans, though by no means alone in this, saw advantages in wider, extra-European participation in some negotiations. Canada, Australia, and other Dominions became objects of American courtship, in circumstances which allowed the broader opening of a particular British initiative such as the Conference of Allied Ministers of Education. Ultimately the U.S. would encourage appropriate declarations of belligerency toward the Axis states by Latin Americans, so that they might be invited to the San Francisco conference. In the meantime, the participation of the Soviet Union and the friendly Chinese Government shortly after each American démarche was judged helpful to U.S. objectives. Shortly before Hot Springs, Harry Hopkins recorded the results of a meeting with Roosevelt and Under Secretary of State Sumner Welles:

[38] Johnson (fn. 6), 522; *Foreign Relations . . . 1942* (fn. 21), I, 206; *Foreign Relations . . . 1943*, I, 826.

[39] *Foreign Relations . . . 1943* (fn. 21), I, 828ff.

I raised the question as to whether or not our government was going to agree to the various setups which must be made within the United Nations to discuss various matters and whether or not the main committee should be made up of four members, representing the British Empire, Russia, The United States and China. The British are going to push for committees of 7 or 8, which will include separate membership for Canada and Australia. I said I believe by this technique we would be constantly outvoted and that I thought we should put our foot down in the very beginning in this Food Conference and insist on the main committee of 4 members only and let the British Government decide whether they want their membership to come from England or Canada. Both Welles and the President agreed to this.[40]

The immediate effect of these British and American tactics was to hold the Soviet Union, the Chinese Government of Chiang Kai-shek, the exiled French C.N.F. (which had begun postwar planning for France's return to the eminent place due "sa valeur and son génie," in Charles de Gaulle's words, early in 1942), and others at bay, and to invite their participation when it became tactically expedient. Many words have been offered in explanation of the Soviet refusal to join various United Nations specialized agencies, of General de Gaulle's pique at *les Anglo-Saxons,* of disagreement among the "great powers," the "middle powers," and the "small powers" at San Francisco and elsewhere. Only the Soviet pause at the membership threshold warrants recounting here, for this, most profoundly, affected the specialized agencies during the late forties and early fifties.[41]

The Soviet Union remained a member of UPU; ITU, whose 1946 meeting it hosted; and the reconstituted WMO. It refused a 1944 return to ILO, which it had left shortly after Soviet ejection from the League some five years earlier, although in turning back Roosevelt's plea, Stalin intimated some interest in rejoining if League associations with ILO were dissolved in favor of United Nations links, and if "more

---

[40] Robert E. Sherwood, *Roosevelt and Hopkins* (New York 1950), II, 314. The Soviet Union was not, however, equally welcome to all follow-up negotiations. The Roosevelt Administration felt little inclination to include the U.S.S.R. in 1944 talks on future shipping arrangements. On the other hand, FDR personally sought vigorously, if unsuccessfully, to secure Soviet participation at the ILO's Philadelphia meeting the same year. See *Foreign Relations . . . 1944* (fn. 21), I, 1007ff.; "What Is the ILO?," *Fortune,* XXX (September 1944), 223.

[41] See e.g. Alexander Dallin, *The Soviet Union at the United Nations* (New York 1962), 61–66; Harold Karan Jacobson, *The USSR and the UN's Economic and Social Activities* (Notre Dame, 1963), esp. 265ff.; Alvin Z. Rubinstein, *The Soviets in International Organizations* (Princeton 1964), esp. 102–04; Haas (fn. 16), 228–33; Sewell (fn. 19), 211ff. and sources cited; Wojciech Morawiecki, "Institutional and Political Conditions of Participation of Socialist States in International Organizations: A Polish View," *International Organization,* XXII (Spring 1968).

democratic forms of organization" were effectuated—i.e. more say for Socialist spokesmen. The Soviet Union joined WHO in advance of the United States, but then withdrew after U.S. entry and agency retrenchment because, as Vice Minister of Foreign Affairs Andrei Gromyko later told U.N. Secretary General Trygve Lie, the agency was useless. Soviet refusal at the outset to join UNESCO apparently stemmed not only from what was seen as British control of the Conference of Allied Ministers of Education, but also from fear of the potential domestic impact of an international education organization. Soviet Foreign Minister V. M. Molotov protested Anglo-American exclusivism in the Food and Agriculture Conference arrangements. Although a Soviet delegation participated at Hot Springs, and another journeyed to Quebec in 1945 to witness the charter signing, the Soviet Union did not join FAO. Despite early disquiet over its exclusion from civil aviation preliminaries, the Soviet Government submitted a plan for limited air access to the U.S.S.R. via Soviet aircraft, and sent a delegation as far as Minnesota en route to the Chicago conference before recalling it, ostensibly because certain German satellites had been invited, and governments, such as that of Switzerland, which did not recognize the Soviet Union. A Soviet delegation was dispatched to Bretton Woods, where it received a late cable from Moscow authorizing it to increase the U.S.S.R. subscription to IBRD as well as IMF (and thereby augment the Soviet vote and its status). While Soviet observers came to the spring 1946 meeting of Fund and Bank in Savannah, the Soviet Union did not join these most capitalist of specialized agencies.

Thus after 1949, when it left WHO, the Soviet Union belonged only to UPU, ITU, and WMO. The Socialist Governments of East European states, too, had for the most part dropped out of active participation. Soon thereafter the Soviets began a reassessment of their nonparticipation. During Trygve Lie's Moscow mission in May 1950, about a month before the Korean outbreak, he plied Stalin with reasons why he should "join actively . . . to help support the work of [the specialized agencies] in Asia, Africa, South America, and other underdeveloped parts of the world." Lie continued: "Stalin leaned forward, remark[ed] that he had listened with great interest, and promised that the question I had raised would receive serious thought. However, he could not promise a quick answer: it was a rule in the Soviet Union that they took time for a thorough consideration before making any decision." [42]

The Soviet Union reentered ILO and joined UNESCO in 1954, and at about the same time it assumed a more active part in collateral U.N.

[42] *Foreign Relations . . . 1943* (fn. 21), 1, 823; Trygve Lie, *In the Cause of Peace* (New York 1954), 304.

financing negotiations such as the proposed Special United Nations Fund for Economic Development (SUNFED). Newborn Soviet activism in the economic and social realms of the United Nations complex was soon followed by resurgent, if restrained, interest by the United States and others in some of these same activities.

Meanwhile, non-Communist participation in specialized agencies grew apace. United Nations membership qualified states for entry to its affiliated agencies, and many of the original fifty-one U.N. members immediately joined them. From 1946 through 1950, nine more states became eligible for specialized agency participation in this manner. No states were admitted to the United Nations between 1950 and the "package deal" of 1955, when sixteen European, Asian, and Arab states of varying political predilections entered on the same day. In the early fifties, however, several states were voted into individual specialized agencies, though not without heavy criticism from beyond their membership circles. The German Federal Republic and Japan joined IMF and IBRD in 1953, for instance, and Franco's Spanish Government gained admission to UNESCO in the same year. Six additional states, besides Japan, became U.N. members before 1960. By this time the United Nations comprised 83 members, and several nonmembers, including Switzerland as well as Bonn, participated widely in the specialized agencies.

Aside from the continuing nonrepresentation of the Chinese People's Republic and the Socialist domains of divided Germany, Korea, and Vietnam, in early 1960 the most visible evidence of incomplete universality in the U.N. and the specialized agencies was the absence of most of sub-Saharan Africa. Ethiopia and Liberia had been original U.N. members. Ghana joined in 1957, Guinea the following year. In 1960, sixteen more African states became U.N. members. This surge, followed by yet more waves of new participants in the United Nations complex from Africa and elsewhere, by 1968 raised the total number of members in one or more specialized agencies to 138.

Largely through the efforts of those outside to gain their place in the sun, partly through an inclination by some of those inside to ring in new support for their aims, but more and more under a momentum of its own, universality has been approached within the U.N. specialized agencies. Though hardly displaced, the Anglo-American particularism of early postwar years first broadened to a "Western" cast, then to a more heterogeneous composite in which Asian and African nations and cultures increasingly partook. And whether formally inside or out of the specialized agencies, the Communist states—including the Chinese People's Republic—assumed greater prominence over the years in their affairs and in the concerns of their older members.

For many of the new states and their newer governments, membership in United Nations organs and agencies is before all else "collective legitimization." [43] But changes in membership brought to bear claims quite different from those advanced at the founding ceremonies.

## Development—A Sacred Calling and the Structures of International Action

It would be wrong to regard development as an international task assumed only after the states from Asia and Africa found their places throughout the United Nations system. In 1942, for instance, the U.S. Treasury Department offered its draft proposal for a "Bank for Reconstruction and Development of the United Nations"—the germ of IBRD —and three years later in San Francisco, thanks to a Canadian intervention, U.N. Charter Article 55(a) acknowledged the worthiness of "economic and social progress and development." Other premonitions of development as a serious duty of international institutions abounded along the way toward universal membership. But with accession to participation by governments from low-income states, development— economic development, social development, and other kinds of development—attained the quality of a solemn mission, sanctified in 1961 even by the blessing of the new United States Government.

Some steps merit recalling. Technical assistance, a phrase whose many senses usually emphasize training or the field application of skills or know-how to readily agreed-upon problems without much cost to anyone, had for some time prior to 1945 been directed by U.S. officials to parts of Latin America. After the war, the United Nations, two regional commissions (ECAFE and ECLA), and several specialized agencies, notably ILO, IBRD, FAO, ICAO, UNESCO, and WHO, experimented with small, regular-budget programs of this nature.

In January 1949 technical assistance received a boost. After Truman's unexpected victory, requests for inaugural address themes reached the State Department from the White House. A Department group convened routinely under the Director of the Office of Public Affairs, and it listed three points: a protestation of support for the United Nations, a pledge to persist with ERP, and a statement of intent regarding common defense among North Atlantic states. Upon an invitation for other suggestions, the Deputy Director of American Republic Affairs ventured a fourth point—technical assistance. He and Louis J. Halle of the Department's Policy Planning Staff, who remembered the State Department side of this happening, had one evening talked informally about the possibility of such a program for parts of the world beyond Latin America. Though listed by the compiling group, the fourth point was dropped during the Department's clearance proceedings.

[43] Inis L. Claude, *The Changing United Nations* (New York 1967), Chap. 4.

Halle conjectured on its fate: "Any responsible officer was bound to ask what thought and analysis had entered into the proposal of a program for giving technical assistance to countries all over the world. What countries specifically? What kinds of technical assistance, specifically? On what scale? How much would it cost? Until at least rough answers to these questions were available, until at least the feasibility of such a program had been determined, it would be irresponsible to have the President announce it."

But the White House was unhappy with the "boiler-plate" ("slang," as Halle translates, "for the cant statements that are always thrown into speeches") which remained. From a White House perspective, special counsel Clark Clifford later recounted the quest for "something fresh and provocative that would make people think" in order to spice the "old hat" program already "talked to death in the campaign." Did the State Department not have something original for this triumphant occasion?

The fourth point went back in. Halle calls it "a public-relations gimmick, thrown in by a professional speech-writer to give the speech more life." Front-page treatment greeted the "bold new program" proposed in "Point Four"—some newspapers labeled it a "World Fair Deal" and one reported transatlantic hopes for a TVA on the Jordan River—and astounded White House and State Department alike. Both now began "to look into the possibilities of such a program and make plans." Congress, of course, had still to be approached by the planners. Many months later, the U.S. program, under the Technical Cooperation Administration, actually started. But in the meantime United Nations participants, already engaged in resolving measures to aid economic development, had been stirred by Truman's allusion. The U.S. delegate to EcoSoc, pressed on capital assistance for development by representatives from several Latin American and Asian states, proposed that the Secretary General plan for a program of technical assistance to expand existing activities. His proposal led quietly to *Technical Assistance for Economic Development: Plan for an expanded cooperative programme through the United Nations and the specialized agencies* (U.N. Pub. Sales No. 1949.II.B.1), and to the Expanded Programme of Technical Assistance (EPTA), which in 1950 commenced allocating limited funds, volunteered annually by governments, for augmented services by the United Nations and the specialized agencies.[44]

Traces of most elements present in subsequent development assistance encounters can be found in the origins of EPTA. These encoun-

[44] Louis J. Halle, *The Society of Man* (New York 1965), 21–23; Cabell Phillips, *The Truman Presidency* (New York 1966), 272–74; W. R. Sharp, *International Technical Assistance* (Chicago 1952), 59ff.

ters show growing assertiveness and improving organization among spokesmen for economically underdeveloped states, as they press for greater quantities of appropriate development aid without political, or even "buy-here," ties. They offer increasing evidence of attempts by varying parties to exploit Communist bogeymen. In the West, particularly the United States, brave slogans and programmatic tokens also continue to be locally justified in crude economic terms.[45] The statement triggering vast development hopes by an American, possibly an American in a semi-official capacity, occurs sporadically from 1949 onward.[46] And skirmishes from time to time recur between a U.S. President seeking domestic political exposure, a State Department worrying over its checklist of pre-takeoff safeguards, and a Congress tuning in to many still different frequencies. Burden-sharing among Western allies, it is true, becomes a major theme in development-program negotiations only later with persistent U.S. balance of payments difficulties; by this time Germany, out of the picture in 1949, is economically strong and in most eyes politically reborn; and resurgent though self-restrained Japan will receive increasing pressure to underwrite various programs. Finally, and most pertinent to the current discussion, the part of development-program initiator played by specialized agency protagonists, though little felt in 1949, would become more and more salient through the years. Some of these agencies were caught just as unprepared by EPTA as U.S. officials had been by Point Four. By the sixties, however, development had become a sort of talisman carried by have-not, specialized-agency spokesmen to all interagency conversations which promised an allocation of extrabudgetary funds.

This combination of elements has since produced several functional agency permutations. UNICEF, the United Nations International Children's Emergency Fund, had been established in 1946 as a temporary agent for some of UNRRA's wasting assets. By 1950, with its mandate under review in the U.N. General Assembly, UNICEF had gained so many avid supporters in the United States and elsewhere that it was placed on a trial extension. Three years later it was re-

---

[45] Writes Phillips (272, 274): "[Point Four] was a novel plan to use the leverage of American technical skills and know-how, rather than its dollars, to pry the underdeveloped nations of the world into the twentieth century—and, it was hoped, out of Moscow's reach. . . . There was a twofold motivation behind the plan. The first was humanitarian and political: If the people of Asia and Africa could be helped out of their centuries-old rut of ignorance and poverty, they would become better world citizens and less likely pawns for Communist exploitation. The second was economic: As producers of much of the world's raw materials, the underdeveloped nations had become increasingly important to the reviving economies of the West. Not only was it desirable to protect these sources of supply, but also to offer a potential future market for the West's output."

[46] Cf. Sewell (fn. 19), 290.

named the United Nations Children's Fund (still abbreviated as UNICEF) to connote its permanence yet retain its popular profile. UNICEF owes its creation and its modified status to resolutions of the General Assembly, unlike the specialized agencies, and its financial resources to voluntary donations by governments, nongovernmental organizations, and especially individuals. In recent years UNICEF's activities have brought it into close conjunction with WHO, FAO, and UNESCO. Since the Children's Fund more than pays its own way in any joint endeavor, little or no interagency friction occurs. In 1965 UNICEF won the Nobel Peace Prize. A Sierra Leonean, John Karefa-Smart, has called it the "most widely publicized United Nations body in the field of rendering assistance." [47]

IBRD in 1956 added an affiliate agency, the International Finance Corporation (IFC). IFC ventures debt capital and equity investments in private enterprises. It does not underwrite programs by other specialized agencies, but its assignment and its activities include financial and other relations with regional, sub-regional, and national development corporations and banks.

The mounting diplomatic battle over capital assistance for development, with bids offered in the forties for a United Nations Economic Development Agency by V.K.R.V. Rao of India and in the fifties for SUNFED by others, in 1958 finally produced authorization for a United Nations Special Fund (SF), an abbreviated version of these hopes. From its inception to its "merger" with EPTA as the United Nations Development Programme in 1965 the Special Fund (and afterwards UNDP) was led by Paul Hoffman. Hoffman's "pre-investment" resources come from the same governments who pledge annually to EPTA. The Special Fund's field projects are executed by contracting agent, usually one of the specialized agencies. EPTA resources tempted the specialized agencies to move increasingly into the field; SF, probably more than any factor, has enticed them into development-oriented and development-rationalized work. FAO, UNESCO, and ILO resources especially have been augmented for these multiform programs. Currently, FAO's financial component from UNDP exceeds its regular budget, and UNESCO's resources fall just about equally into these two categories.

SF did not dissipate pressures for a SUNFED. Back in 1953 Stringfellow Barr had called for a U.N.-affiliated International Development Authority able to allocate financial resources for endeavors which were deemed socially desirable rather than strictly bankworthy. All members would contribute financially to Barr's IDA, though addi-

[47] "Africa and the United Nations," *International Organization*, xix (Summer 1965), 768.

tional resources would be garnered through bonds issued to participating individuals and corporations the world over. In 1960 an International Development Association was established, with member Governments initially contributing about $1 billion in public money. IBRD President Eugene Black allowed that IDA, in its latter incarnation, was "really an idea to offset the urge for SUNFED"; U.S. Treasury Secretary Robert Anderson conjured up the specter of SUNFED in negotiating IDA with the Erhard Government and other reluctant North Atlantic partners; and Paul Hoffman, bound to SF, offered U.S. Senators the bluntest testimonial of all: ". . . I don't believe we want to get ourselves in a position of competing with Russia, but Russia has become the principal backer of SUNFED, which is the United Nations Development Fund, about which many questions could be raised." And in a paraphrase of traditional American political wisdom, Hoffman concluded: "we can't fight something with nothing." [48] IDA, actually, a soft-loan window of IBRD rather than a separate agency, extends fifty-year, interest-free credits, generally with ten-year grace periods. Several recent projects involve FAO or UNESCO in joint agency operations.

Besides IDA's beginning and the accession of sixteen African states to United Nations membership, 1960 marked the election of John F. Kennedy to the United States Presidency. During his first year the new President announced America's man-on-the-moon commitment and proposed to the General Assembly that the 1960's be designated the United Nations Decade of Development. "[T]he mysteries of outer space must not divert our eyes or our energies from the harsh realities that face our fellow men," said Kennedy. "Political sovereignty is but a mockery without the means of meeting poverty and illiteracy and disease. Self-determination is but a slogan if the future holds no hope." A United Nations Development Decade, with objectives specified in GNP growth percentages, was soon proclaimed by Assembly resolution. Optimism and scientism again converged in 1963 at the United Nations Conference on Science and Technology, where a new development panacea was celebrated.

IFC and IDA were in large measure strategic innovations, shaped by IBRD backers and added as specialized agencies to what thereafter was touted as the "World Bank Group." SF was a timely tactical concession meant to calm turbulence in the General Assembly, and to its Managing Directorship Hoffman carried both his skills as diplomatic entrepreneur guiding development missionaries and the unarticulated

---

[48] Barr, *Citizens of the World* (Garden City 1952), cited in James H. Weaver, *The International Development Association* (New York 1965), 35–36; Weaver, 28, 46–47, 90. A contemporary saying in some quarters was "A bank a day keeps the Russians away."

questions which had troubled him. By the early sixties, however, the offspring of the constitutive General Assembly bore less outward resemblance to the preferences of United Nations founding fathers or, for that matter, to those of the Soviet and associated governments. The convening of a United Nations Conference on Trade and Development and later the establishing of UNCTAD's permanent complex of arenas for ongoing "conciliation" were resisted bitterly by certain governments, though these initiatives recalled United Nations Development Decade aims. The U.S. chief delegate to UNCTAD I, which met during 1964 in Geneva, voted against a series of "principles" which were overwhelmingly adopted. These and subsequent "decisions," including some approved four years later in New Delhi, remain largely inoperative. In 1965 the United Nations Industrial Development Organization, earlier proposed as a new specialized agency, was authorized by the General Assembly as an agency within the United Nations. UNIDO [49] was to be financed administratively from the regular United Nations budget and, unlike UNCTAD, operationally by voluntary donations from governments—either directly or indirectly through UNDP allocations. An Assembly majority in 1966 voted a United Nations Capital Development Fund. As of June 1969, its assets, voluntarily given, remained at the equivalent of $2.6 million, mostly in nonconvertible currencies. Though the agency rate of Assembly production was setting records, Assembly *productivity* implied a more debatable criterion.[50]

As new participants were precipitating new agencies they were also remodeling older ones. Postwar U.N. organizations invariably included three organs: a plenary (often called the assembly or conference), convoked periodically for delegations from all member states; a smaller executive body (frequently called the council or board), scheduled at shorter intervals for representatives from the principal member states and others chosen during plenary session; and a secretariat (sometimes called the staff or bureau), comprising selected individuals, organized as an international civil service and headed by an elected administrator or executive manager. Each organ showed the impact of the added members.

Plenaries directly reflected the membership surge. Although it is probably true that specialized agency assemblies, much less than the U.N. General Assembly and UNCTAD, have prompted steam-roller

[49] Sometimes pronounced "You-nee-dough."
[50] For more extended analysis of ITU, ILO, UNESCO, WHO, the International Atomic Energy Agency, IMF, GATT, and UNCTAD, see Robert W. Cox and Harold K. Jacobson, eds., *The Anatomy of Influence: Decision-Making in International Organization*, 1972.

majorities without apparent lasting aftereffect, they do occasion spasmodic votes of recorded principle, however symbolic the outcome. Moreover, the influence of new plenary delegations bent on substantive and procedural revision is far more subtle and pervasive than majority voting, of which the specialized agencies as a whole have relatively little. Third World presences and voices in plenary meetings, in the committees and commissions which concurrently assemble, and "behind the screens," affect what is proposed and, insofar as plenaries actually choose, how it is disposed.

The caucus, which arose early as an adjunct in selecting authorized "regional" nominees for plenary election to limited-membership organs such as executive bodies, owes much of its subsequent development to its increasing use on substantive questions, first for action concerted by assembly participants eager to bring change, later for reaction concerted by others who wed themselves to the *status quo.* Bandoeng (1955), Cairo (1962), and Addis Ababa (1963) were notable extra-U.N. caucus landmarks; [51] Geneva (1964), where 77 UNCTAD delegations from all across the earth's southern tier first flaunted their assembled strength, also featured the inauguration of a "Geneva Group" which thereafter convened its delegates from eleven affluent states at the sites of several specialized agencies.

Executive bodies serve to further various Government preferences. Election to them indicates, and in some measure confers, presumptive influence. On an international level they may at the same time offer one means by which the differential intensity of interest among various Governments can be acknowledged and partially provided for, especially to the extent that many different issue areas and executive bodies are viewed and acted upon in the same multigovernment bargaining context. Access to secretariats and their directors is facilitated through executive bodies. Membership on one of them makes it easier for a representative (and sometimes also those whose concerted efforts helped him achieve election) to oversee policy—program, finance, and personnel selection—and even to participate in certain decisions. And executive body seats have been known to provide a refuge or exile for persons out of political favor at home.

As agency tasks outran plenaries' capacities, the executive bodies were looked to more and more; when by governments' agreement the larger meetings were called less often and the smaller conclaves more frequently, assemblies declined further at the expense of the councils. As secretariats grew in stature and in other ways, the executive bodies seemed increasingly important to governments as means of control or animation. For all these reasons, plus a generous measure of concern

---

[51] Cf. Samaan Boutros Farajallah, *Le groupe afro-asiatique dans le cadre des Nations Unies* (Geneva 1963).

for the added legitimacy which executive-body status might bestow upon new states and governments, Third World representatives sought to expand the executive circles. In 1948, according to figures compiled from the *Yearbook of International Organizations,* executive bodies for functional agencies herein addressed averaged 20 seats; in 1958 the figure was 22 seats; by 1968 it had risen to 30. Many of the additional placed were occupied, as they had been conceived, by representatives of the newly admitted states.

Secretariat participation was viewed initially as a matter of right, increasingly as a means to affect policy choices. The belated admission of Third World members meant that secretariat rosters had already largely been filled. Staff candidates from the poorer lands often came with inadequate educational background and administrative training, as officials from Western—sometimes ex-colonial—states found ample occasion to remark. For this and other reasons, including differences in cultural background and administrative style (even among Western founders) magnified in complex bureaucracies, the Asian or African secretariat recruit commonly entered his new milieu as an alien. Since the dearth of well-prepared individuals was felt equally in his own polity, he was apt soon to be called to duty at home. Sometimes his acquisition of skills while an international civil servant operated as a factor in his domestic redeployment. Despite such difficulties, governments of low-income states soon recognized the desirability of strategically-placed secretariat officials, as well as that of representatives on the executive body. Swelling executive bodies grew somewhat less effective in directing secretariats while organization tasks grew more ambitious. Asian and African participants contributed to both tendencies. Through constant pressure for secretariat reapportionment to fit "geographical" criteria—a consideration the application of which Western spokesmen held pernicious to objectives of "efficiency, competence, and integrity" deemed vital by U.N. Charter Article 101—southern-tier nationals gradually entered all levels of the secretariats of functional agencies.

Just as the caucus developed outside the infrequently convoked plenary gathering, the permanent national liaison office (also called permanent mission or permanent delegation) proliferated outside the recurrently convened executive body and the perpetually active secretariat. Because of financial and personnel cost, the governments of poorer states have not established permanent national liaison offices at the headquarters sites of specialized agencies as readily as have the Governments of pillar states. Nonetheless, their growth is striking.[52]

[52] At UNESCO during 1966, for instance, members reported 92 permanent liaison offices, and eight additional states indicated that they maintained liaison officers at their embassies.

UNCTAD I and the continuing activity in its several rings induced a number of governments to establish multiple-agency liaison offices in Geneva. Today various conferences and committees drawing permanent national liaison officers meet between plenaries and executive body sessions. Not surprisingly, the caucus has taken hold just beyond these interim meetings.

Throughout the sixties, the touchstone of functional agency work remained *development*. As the United Nations Development Decade neared its end, consensus continued but results had still hardly materialized; some spoke of a "decade of disappointment." A second period of equal duration was officially proposed and passed along to a new generation of international planners.

## IV. FUTURES CONDITIONAL

The historic cataclysm of 1945, marking the end of World War II and the beginning of new organized experiments in international relations, befell a world partly dazed, partly sleeping. Today, at another juncture in human affairs, the whole world is awake, watching or actively participating upon many global stages. We have entered an era of universal history, yet our planet is sorely troubled by the divergent hopes and fears of its inhabitants.

For some years after the war an ascendant United States, first with the resistance and later the acquiescence of British Governments, dominated those international organizations which its leaders selected as major foreign-policy instrumentalities. Subsequently this preponderance passed to a broader Atlantic-centered and American-led Western alliance; by this time the United Nations organizations had yielded their significance in Western strategies to limited-membership organizations and to relations between the United States and individual alliance partners. Bipolar tendencies characterized the U.N. specialized agencies after the Western retrenchment and the Soviet and East European participation in some of them. Even agencies without Socialist participants were sometimes impelled by bipolarity. Participation by Asian, African, and other relatively nonaligned Governments in various U.N. arenas has modified the play of bipolarity, especially during the past decade. Kwame Nkrumah in 1961 stated majestically that "We have adhered strictly to our policy of positive neutralism and nonalignment and whatever we have done, we have always placed Africa first." ECA, it has been said, stands for "Every cent for Africa," though the two first letters fit ECAFE and ECLA (no less than ECE) equally well.

The international system, conditioned by prevalent conceptions among the international actors which comprise it, in turn conditions these conceptions. To our rhetorical question "How reconcile autonomy with well-being?"—a question which brings together two values written into wartime agreements—the United States first responded with allusions to reconstruction aid and its side effects. Janez Stanovnik benignly recalls this phase: "The concept prevailed during the first postwar period that financial aid to the industrially developed countries would stimulate their economies and that this would indirectly help the developing countries by increasing the demand for raw materials." With the onslaught of the cold war, Western spokesmen began to picture well-being as freedom through the provision or continuation of Western protection from totalitarian aggression for non-Western peoples, so that these peoples, aided by private international investment, might develop economically. In the course of the fifties and beyond, Western trade and aid policies shifted tactically under the continuing pressure of "competitive coexistence." Techniques and justifications were changing, but fundamental conceptions remained stable.

These shifts within one substantive sector of a changing international system, though oversimplified by our depiction, can perhaps aid in exploring some conditions of further evolution by the functional agencies and their activities. Perhaps the key to the next major change in the international system lies with the Chinese People's Republic, although the Chinese stance in turn is deeply affected by domestic conditions and by the state of Sino-Soviet relations. Like Soviet activism vis-à-vis the Third World earlier, the C.P.R. impact does not hinge upon formal membership in U.N. organs and agencies, although membership undoubtedly will amplify the effect. Stanovnik contends persuasively that militant international activism by the Chinese makes a different game in the well-being sector of the international system, which we here analytically strive to isolate.

> [A]id does not guarantee political alliances in the new circumstances. Aid could be conceived as an instrument of policy as long as there were only two main centers of power in the world and as long as both competed for influence over the governments of the developing countries. Now, however, Peking is increasingly asserting itself as an independent protagonist, not so much in the field of economic aid to the governments in those countries as with demagogic slogans addressed to the "revolutionary masses" there. Bilateral aid with political motives and based on political criteria might possibly secure the loyalty of the governmental circles which receive it, but it cannot affect the behavior of the peoples who have had little benefit from it so far, given its failure to promote general economic and social progress. . . . The basic accent no longer is: With which side will the governments of the developing countries become allied?

The question is much more: What will be the real internal economic and social progress in these countries? . . . The developing countries can no longer be an object in world policy; they must become a subject on an equal footing with others.

And, most assuredly, representatives from the emerging nations are asserting themselves as subjects on an equal footing with all others. The behavior of African, Asian, and Latin American delegates in U.N. arenas, with its aggressive insistence upon material results, reflects the peoples' hot breath, which their governments feel now as never before.

As though sharing Stanovnik's diagnosis regarding the inefficacy of aid for alliance-keeping—a diagnosis to which events since lend their credence—some Western governments (including the U.S. Congress) have shown growing reluctance to continue bilateral assistance at previous magnitudes, although they have not seized upon the balance of his prescription. "In these [changing] circumstances," concludes the Yugoslavian Executive Secretary of ECE, "it seems a logical solution to supply aid more through multilateral agencies." [53]

A related factor in pluralizing the well-being segment of the international system deserves consideration now and observation into the future. Dispersed functional agencies have already contributed to the loosening of global bipolarity in this nonsecurity systemic sector. Their functioning promises to contribute further to an international system which is becoming ever more involuted. This happens in at least two ways. First, by inducing the multiplication of tasks and issue areas, these agencies widen the range of questions over which governmental intensities of interest vary, further attenuate the willingness of even the most powerful government to exercise vigorous control over all international policy-making, and thereby encourage additional intergovernmental trade-offs across substantive questions. Second, they offer the Third World alternative platforms for expression,[54] and training centers and staging areas for international political activity on other diplomatic fronts. Plenary, executive body, and secretariat positions all serve. Caucuses socialize newer representatives and, with majority southern-tier "victories," build their confidence. Liaison-office duty imparts other skills. Some Third World diplomatic techniques may indeed lead to future innovation by forcing others to emulate them. Like economies suddenly driven by war's devastation or other shock into modernizing so rapidly that their competitors are outdistanced, the African states, in particular, have adapted to the challenges of on-

[53] "The Changing Political Context," *Foreign Affairs*, XLII (Jan. 1964), 242, 245, 249–50.
[54] Thus, e.g., the Latin Americans have found a respite from U.S. supervision within ECLA and UNESCO. Bryce Wood and Morales M. Minerva, "Latin America and the United Nations," *International Organization*, XIX (Summer 1965), 726.

scene decision-making far better than some "developed" states—whose representatives still labor under precise though often irrelevant instructions written by superiors back in the capital.

A global system diverse in constituent actors and their varied objectives, informed by a large and growing corpus of international questions, and replete with scattered cockpits for actor initiative and avenues for collaborative action, is certain to be a global system indeterminate in many of its outcomes. The coming system, like previous systems, will set limits upon actor autonomy. To some actors these may seem unwanted limits. But more future participants are apt to share in creating world history than has yet been imagined in any scholar's unipolar or bipolar scheme, and prevision of actors' creations, or for that matter their configurations, would necessitate something other than an extrapolation of trends.

Previewing functional agency futures demands more than simply projecting technological change with a normative twist. Technology does not afford a sure enough guide to the future of man, unless we assume the default of further human intervention. Many functional agency tasks are directed toward offsetting or beneficently channeling the social and related transformations which technology brings in its train. But this observation, too, is of minimal benefit in calculating what may lie ahead. Let us briefly examine these perplexities in the light of several fairly familiar "horribles."

We need not linger upon these futures quite plausible to envisage yet terrible to contemplate. The Bomb and its aftermath lie within easy reach of consciousness. Too many mouths and too little food is a nightmare we share increasingly. The apparition of a polluted planet drifting lifeless in space bothers us more and more. These eventualities already engage us—engage us as comfortable and literate individuals concerned about *our* personal futures and the futures of *our* offspring and even perhaps the future of civilization as *we* know it. And if exponentially advancing threats have thus far provoked only tiny increments of response, we are at least awakening to intimations of doom. Our own skins, after all, are at stake. Yet the future remains in doubt.

Just as the Bomb threat has agitated many minds and some scant action through international organizations, the Overpopulation and Famine and Pollution threats undoubtedly will muster us to undertake a certain amount of joint effort in functional agencies and, of course, outside them. Though still rather cautious and limited in their approaches, WHO and IBRD principals are inching toward the hazard of overpopulation; FAO spokesmen have always warned of the peril of famine; UNESCO representatives have recently addressed the menace of pollution and other ecological threats.

Perhaps the universal threat in these onrushing terrors will even bring us more clearly to recognize related present dangers—an impatient, overcrowding urban world mobilized in part by the sensate, and all too often unredeemable, appeals of the city; the injustice and the political risks in a visible reign of hunger alongside food glut; the offensiveness, not to mention absurdity, of public poverty at all levels beneath massively communicated images emitted by a waste-making culture the motto of which, at least in America, might be "no deposit, no return." By such reasoning one might have inferred that the Bomb threat would likewise alert us to the relatively more susceptible problem of controlling international arms sales from industrial states with various political affinities to "developing" countries, or that cold-war tensions would have prepared us to avert further cleavage between the materially-blessed and materially-deprived, northern-dwelling and southern-dwelling, lighter-skinned and darker-skinned peoples of the earth. Does experience make us sanguine?

Surely as social scientists and as lawyers we cannot depend upon manifest universal danger as a predictor of adequate response; nor as beings with a stake in the future should we await imminent danger as a spur to further action. By then it may be too late.

Who will participate in determining this indeterminate future? And what will limit them?

We can begin with a few simple, probably unexceptionable, propositions. Individuals will make the future. They will make it by individual acts and by acts in concert with each other and by acts against other individuals and their groups. To an unknown extent they will limit each others' actions either by the necessities of concerting action or by counter-action. They will make the future by acting upon nature, whether restlessly and with exceedingly limited consciousness of broader and longer social consequences, or otherwise. By such individual acts, insignificant alone but consequential together, they may extend or constrain the range of possible future actions by themselves and their progeny. They will make the future by acting in the disparate roles cast up by the contemporary stage of world history. Their acts will be conditioned—restricted and predisposed—by innate and acquired personality attributes and by the roles and the resources they command. Both personality and role render men's capacities for action unequal. But today's situation draws roles at some levels, with their individual actors, into closer and closer interplay with other roles and individuals: interaction, too, affects actions and may even modify the roles conditioning subsequent action. Interplay, as maintained already with regard to governments, tends to reduce the discrepancies in potential action among interrelated actors.

Let us continue in a more concrete vein. Individuals will determine the future of the functional agencies by acting, preeminently, as intellectuals and as citizen members of an attentive transnational public, as leaders of the mass media, as agency officials, and as governments. Many will act by observing and commenting upon, or choosing not to observe and comment upon, what these agencies are doing—or upon what they should, and conceivably might, be doing. A smaller number will act by transmitting, or choosing not to transmit, the information without which public observation and critical assessment cannot take place. Some will act by moving beyond, or remaining within, the special parochialisms so common in international organizations. An elect few will continue to act by defining and redefining nations' objectives, their respective priorities, and the tactics by which these will be sought, whether in the functional agencies or elsewhere.

The functional agencies remain low on the horizon, at least in the West. They seem distant in space and perhaps remote in time—phenomena of a dim future and sufficient unto that day. By the judges of newsworthiness they are generally deemed unfit or fit only as filler. Media choice-makers sometimes pride themselves as educators of the public, though almost always they stress the limits of that public's education without boggling over any inconsistency.

As a result, many more ideas for invigorating agency activities reside in the public domain, I dare say, than in the public's consciousness. Although IMF's Special Drawing Rights rated prominent coverage, the proposal to allocate a percentage of SDRs to low-income member states, perhaps through IDA, has been exposed to very little public attention.[55] Other proposals to augment Governmental appropriations to IDA, including that of Governor David Horowitz of the Bank of Israel,[56] have likewise received sparse commentary. ICAO has, it appears, fallen miserably short of potential in serving the interests of air passengers;[57] should an internationalized airline be established as a cost and price standard and a source of income for the work of U.N. organizations? Why not create an internationally-owned merchant marine under IMCO or other auspices, with landlocked low-income states as participating shareholders, for the same purposes? Would functional-agency credits to national housing authorities in order to build units in towns and rural areas ease urban overcrowding? Would it draw local hoardings into more socially productive investment as well as helping to shelter the needy? How about IBRD loans to mod-

---

[55] Robert Triffin has suggested several alternative dispositions of Special Drawing Rights. An internationally accessible version of this proposal appears in *Ceres: FAO Review*, III (Jan.–Feb. 1970), 26–28.

[56] See, e.g. his "Soft Loans and Hard Realities," *Columbia Journal of World Business*, I (Summer 1966), 31–35.

[57] Cf. Temple Fielding, *Fielding's Travel Guide to Europe, 1963–64* (New York 1963), 53ff.

ernize antiquated public transportation facilities within and between American cities? Why not institute a United Nations Youth Service Corps for volunteer training and duty, divided between agency or organization headquarters and the field? How about a convention extending advance authorization for UNICEF, FAO-World Food Programme, or WHO to enter famine areas in order to feed victims of starvation in time of war and perhaps in other circumstances? [58]

No doubt many ideas proposed for vitalizing agencies are undesirable, implausible, or both. We need their critical consideration by the media, the universities, and other public forums to weigh them against their alternatives, including the *status quo*.

Interested individuals, whether acting alone, as media taste-makers, or as participants in other private associations (including the nongovernmental organizations associated with functional agencies), are the chief producers and disseminators of ideas for major changes. International officials in the functional agencies are also in a peculiarly excellent position to contribute to healthy innovation by mediating between the preferable and the possible. Sometimes a certain proneness to exaggerate limitations must be overcome. With the continuing support of organizational skills and "memory" at his disposal, a competent and motivated director may, over time, partially reconstruct the expectations and preferences of agency participants along lines of an endeavor he chooses to emphasize.[59] Nevertheless, role attributes among functional agency posts restrict and predispose some managers more than others. The IBRD President (*qua* Bank and IFC head) and the IMF Managing Director, for instance, have long acted with considerable discretion, in part because the Bank Group and Fund, alone among functional agencies, enjoy an income from their operations sufficient to underwrite their own administrative budgets. Moreover, the Bank Group President's pecuniary status provides him with leverage for negotiating with FAO, UNESCO, and possibly with others in the future. While UNESCO's Director General and UNCTAD's Secretary General also are strong leaders, this depends somewhat more upon the strength and knowledge of the persons who occupy (or, in UNCTAD's case, have recently left) these positions. And, notwithstanding strong leadership, UNESCO and UNCTAD may be destined to continue as international gadflies in the fashion of third political parties in American history, promoting ideas but watching others seize upon them—if only in self-defense.

[58] Jean Mayer recently proposed a similar plan as adjunct to a primary convention banning starvation as an instrument both by belligerents who mount a blockade or siege and by those whose civilians are subject to these actions.

[59] On reconstructive leadership, see Charles E. Lindblom, *The Policy-Making Process* (Englewood Cliffs 1968), 105–06.

Governments more than anyone else will determine the future of the functional agencies. As Lester Pearson noted in his 1969 report to IBRD urging greater efforts in financing development, "Governments . . . dispose of what commissions propose."

Southern-tier strategists may yet find effective means of inducing West and East to take these agencies seriously. In my opinion, ritualistic resolution-passing in plenaries today works not for but against this objective, much as in "Uniting for Peace" days its occasional use contributed to perverting the objectives of other U.N. members who then could trigger automatic majorities in the General Assembly. It does not follow that political leverage should be eschewed, only that there are better points and ways to apply it. Timely and concerted governmental participation during the formative and executive phases of agency-program activity demands much greater effort. Standards set previously for future performance need continuing application to specific cases, which only persevering access to executive body and secretariat can provide. Programmatic extension requires cultivation of secretariat members and able, strong-minded officials at home.[60] Above all, the future as Third World spokesmen may shape it depends upon whether they find and utilize means to make the functional agencies more visible and meaningful to peoples and governments in both West and East. Efforts to this end at agency headquarters thus far have failed. Hence it may be found necessary to drive home the message where fundamental decisions are actually reached. Observing how the two rival blocs hold each other in check, Frantz Fanon bids the earth's dispossessed to "take advantage of this paralysis" and to "burst into history, forcing it by our invasion into universality for the first time." What is the international equivalent of a James Foreman in the chancels and naves of sacrosanct Washington and Moscow?

By choices of the governments of high-income industrialized states with "capitalist" and "communist" economies, finally, the future of the functional agencies will be determined. To speak of choosing will to some no doubt seem quaint. Individual seers of Marxist and capitalist persuasions occasionally share a premise that capitalism can never allow the genuine development of underdeveloped areas because a continuation of their underdevelopment is necessary to the capitalist system or, in a variant, is necessary to national capitalist systems at loggerheads with each other. And others contend that Soviet Com-

---

[60] For more on these and other processes and conflicting participant strategies, see the present author's "Policy Processes and International Organization Tasks," in R. W. Cox, ed., *International Organisation* (London 1969) or in *The Politics of International Organizations* (New York 1970).

munism, in seeking world conquest, will in its pursuit never come to utilize U.N. instruments forged by the Free West.

But I believe that the political vortex of functional agency activity has already become too compelling to permit pulling out, however seductive the tactical threat of picking up one's pieces and leaving. To continue implies, at a minimum, to be forced to choose how to survive in this international maelstrom. Contingencies such as greater commitment by others—East or West—would further condition, but hardly eliminate, choosing. Let me offer a flat prediction that if the Soviet Union comes up with positive positions in the specialized agencies to which it belongs, joins FAO (thereby following East European returnees) and ICAO, and proposes that IDA be detached from the Bank Group, reorganized and staffed, and moved to Delhi, Kinshasa, or an internationalized Jerusalem as the sufficient condition of contributing membership by the U.S.S.R., we will see not Western resignation but Western activation. I think a genuine Western commitment would provoke a similar reaction from the Soviets. Let me go farther out on the limb: participation by the Chinese People's Republic will drive both the Soviet Union and the West forward, not out.

At most these political circumstances define the minimal conditions of existence in the future world of the functional agencies. Contingencies aside, the governments of northern-tier states may choose to do other than simply exist.

Without discounting other crucial factors, we can observe that future action by the functional agencies depends heavily upon financial support by the more affluent states of various political inclinations. A 1969 report on operational United Nations programs prepared by Sir Robert Jackson and others foresees expansion of these capabilities, giving special attention to augmented use of UNDP auspices. The Jackson Report is of course merely recommendation, not authorization or appropriation. Assuming for the present that agreement proves possible upon an adapted UNDP financially more capable and universally more acceptable—an assumption which demands critical consideration beyond this essay—the question of implementation remains. No less than a mutual pledge of national honor is required, and it must be a precise commitment, not a hazy one. "Just as the only way out of the almost stagnant poverty of the developing countries is to be found in a visible acceleration of their production," warned Jan Tinbergen of the United Nations Development Planning Committee early in 1970, "the only way out of the antiquated international structure is a shock therapy consisting of the simultaneous acceptance of commitments." If at this juncture we are not yet prepared to finance

UNDP as part of the regular assessed expenses of the United Nations,[61] perhaps at least it is time to base the expanding UNDP operations upon indicative state quotas, or "fair shares," which follow the prevailing assessment percentages assigned members of the U.N. and associated agencies.

This is a time when the peoples of several Western states, notably America, Britain, and France, are groping for a new, post-hegemonial raison d'être. It is a time of crisis but also of opportunity. The United States, like Britain and France earlier,[62] has entered a phase of bitterness toward the United Nations, or at least toward its perceived embodiment in New York. The historic American cycle of manic intervention followed by depressive withdrawal from reality seemingly moves inexorably along its one-track path, at the moment tending toward a negative answer to our single-minded question: to deploy, or not to deploy, force by unilateral edict. This is a propitious moment for our leaders to remind us, and for us to remind them, that there are other dimensions to contemporary international life and alternative approaches to future international living. Aside from working for revolution or waiting for Godot, either of which suggests consequences but dimly foreseen by its protagonists, vitalizing multilateral instrumentalities offers the only known alternative means of grappling with certain imminent international problems. And, unpromising though it now appears, our time may yet cause future historians to remark that this was when human affairs reached a crucial turning-point and ventured onto a new course, through the functional agencies and elsewhere.

[61] Cf. Dudley Seers, "International Aid: The Next Steps," *Journal of Modern African Studies*, II (Dec. 1964), 477ff.; Sewell (fn. 19), 323ff.

[62] See J.-B. Duroselle, "France and the United Nations," *International Organization*, XIX (Summer 1965), 712; Andrew Boyd, *The United Nations* (Baltimore 1964), Chaps. 1 and 2.

# CHAPTER 14

# Transnational Movements and Economic Structures

## GERALD A. SUMIDA

INTERNATIONAL LAW may be regarded essentially as one of the most important means by which participants in the world social process seek to allocate fundamental values in order to attain an optimum maximization of the interests of both the world community and of the various participants.[1] It is now clear that, in addition to states and international organizations, these participants include transnational pressure groups, political parties and private associations—which are often elements in broader transnational movements—and the individual human being. Of the transnational private associations, the multinational business enterprise has only recently been recognized as one of the most important participants in the world social process.

The international legal order,[2] which is the framework within which this authoritative allocation of values is conducted, serves to order and to regulate the relationships and interactions among various participants in the world social process, but at the same time it is itself shaped and influenced by these same interactions and relationships. For this reason, it is necessary to examine both transnational movements and transnational economic relations as part of the structure of the world social process before turning to the interrelations between these and the international legal order.

The transnational movements which will be considered may be divided into five categories: movement-parties, namely, the Socialist, Communist, and Christian Democratic movements; social welfare move-

[1] The concept of "world social process" embraces the total sum of interactions among all participants in the global human community. See Myres S. McDougal, "International Law, Power and Policy: A Contemporary Conception," 82 *Recueil des Cours*, 137–259, esp. 165–79 (1953); McDougal and Harold S. Lasswell, "The Identification and Appraisal of Diverse Systems of Public Order," in McDougal et al., *Studies in World Public Order* (New Haven 1964), 3–41; as well as McDougal, Lasswell and W. M. Reisman, "The World Constitutive Process of Authoritative Decision," in R. A. Falk and C. E. Black, eds., *The Future of the International Legal Order* (Princeton 1969), I, 73–154.

[2] The contemporary international legal order—contrary to the classical definition of international law—does not govern the relations solely of states; rather, the scope of this legal order has been rapidly expanding in response to the requirements, extent, and intensity of activities being undertaken by other participants in the world social process. Ironically, this expansion in the kinds of participants in this world social process has rendered the term "international law" etymologically inaccurate.

ments, specifically the international labor, humanitarian, and antislavery movements; the peace movement; state-creating movements, including the South American, Middle Eastern and African independence movements and Zionism; and religious movements, especially Roman Catholicism and the Christian ecumenical movement. Each of these movements is transnational in nature, although they vary markedly in terms of objectives, kind and degree of institutionalization and size. Each, however, has had, and continues to have, an important impact upon the world social order as well as upon the international legal order. Other illustrations could have been chosen; these, however, are among the more prominent and interesting examples.

Before examining these transnational movements, it might be useful to describe their nature somewhat more precisely. An analysis of their roles in the world social process and their relations to the international legal order can then be undertaken.

### THE NATURE OF TRANSNATIONAL MOVEMENTS

In recent years there has occurred an increasing interest in transnational movements [3] and associations,[4] particularly the transnational business corporation, and several scholars [5] have explicitly noted the effects of these associations upon the international legal order. There also exist numerous excellent studies on various aspects of certain transnational movements, especially those of an ideological nature, although these tend to be generally historical in approach. But one searches the relevant literature in vain for any even limited theoretical studies of transnational movements and phenomena.

While transnational movements *per se* have been ignored by scholars, social movements in general have been the subject of intensive inquiry,

[3] See Wolfgang Friedmann, *An Introduction to World Politics,* 5th edn. (New York 1965), passim.

[4] See Lyman C. White, *International Non-Governmental Organizations: Their Purposes, Methods, and Accomplishments* (New Brunswick 1951); J. J. Lador-Lederer, *International Non-Governmental Organizations and Economic Entities: A Study in Autonomous Organization and Ius Gentium* (Leyden 1963); Arthur Barber, "Emerging New Power: The World Corporation," *War/Peace Report,* VIII (Oct. 1968), 3–7; and George W. Ball, "Making World Corporations Into World Citizens," same, 8–10. The most comprehensive and authoritative compilation of transnational organizations is the *Yearbook of International Organizations* [hereafter cited as *Yearbook*], published annually since 1948 by the Union of International Associations in Brussels. As of 1968, it listed 2188 nongovernmental organizations, excluding transnational business corporations.

[5] McDougal (fn. 1); Wolfgang Friedmann, *The Changing Structure of International Law* (New York 1964); C. Wilfred Jenks, *The Common Law of Mankind* (New York 1958); and Philip Jessup, *Transnational Law* (New Haven 1956). Indeed, Friedmann and Raymond Aron have called attention to the existence of "transnational societies." See Friedmann, 37–39, and Raymond Aron, *Peace and War: A Theory of International Relations* (New York 1966), 104–10.

particularly by sociologists.[6] Their studies and theories are almost entirely limited to movements of a national or subnational scope. Yet in all fundamental respects social movements appear to exhibit identical patterns of origination and evolution, regardless of whether they are subnational, national, or transnational in scope, and consequently it is not entirely accurate to state that there exists no theoretical framework for studying transnational movements. The beginnings of such a theory are found in the extant work on social movements, which must now be extended, with necessary and appropriate modifications, to encompass transnational movements. It remains true, nonetheless, that almost no theoretical work has been done on the impact of such movements upon the international legal order.[7]

For the purposes of this essay, a transnational movement may be described as a large-scale and continuing collective social action which transcends national boundaries and which seeks to affect and shape the world order in some fundamental respect.[8] Before describing the general characteristics of these movements, it might be useful to clarify certain aspects of this definition.

First, transnational movements are phenomena involving collective human action. That is, such movements are not merely aggregates of unorganized individuals and groups; they are social collectivities which possess a certain minimum of organization and direction from the leading individuals or groups. The degree of institutionalization in any movement, however, may vary over time, depending upon a number of factors both internal and external to the movement.

Second, the transnational scope of these movements refers to persons,

[6] Originally included as part of the more general phenomena of collective behavior, social movements emerged as a distinct field of study in the late 1940's. A pioneering study was Rudolf Heberle's *Social Movements: An Introduction to Political Sociology* (New York 1951), which sought to develop a framework for the study of all social movements. Subsequent studies have both expanded and refined Heberle's outline, but none has entirely superseded it. See also R. Heberle, "Social Movements I: Types and Functions of Social Movements," in David L. Sills, ed., *International Encyclopaedia of the Social Sciences* [hereafter cited as *International Encyclopaedia*] (New York 1968), XIV, 438–44; and William B. Cameron, *Modern Social Movements: A Sociological Outline* (New York 1966).

[7] Lador-Lederer (fn. 4), is principally concerned with the international legal personality of transnational organizations and his analysis is thus limited solely to this problem.

A theoretical framework of analysis does exist which could be adopted to study the impact of transnational movements upon the international legal order within a policy-oriented context. This is the scheme devised by McDougal and Lasswell and used by them in their various studies of the international legal order. A study employing this approach would be of great value, but it is beyond the scope of this introductory essay.

[8] This definition is adapted from that of Kurt and Gladys Lang, *Collective Dynamics* (New York 1961), 491. Most definitions of "social movements" are essentially similar. See Heberle, "Social Movements I" (fn. 6).

things, events, and relations flowing across national boundaries, generally, though not necessarily, upon nongovernmental levels.[9] This does not mean, of course, that such movements are never the object of intergovernmental concern and of attempted regulation through diplomatic means. Strictly speaking, a movement can be genuinely transnational and involve only two states, but those considered in this essay encompass a much larger number of countries.

Third, the basic objective of transnational movements is to bring about some kind of fundamental change in a part or in all of the world social order, thereby realizing certain desired values. In some instances their objectives necessarily involve radical alterations in the existing social order: the peace movement essentially seeks a restructuring of this order which would render recourse to war as an instrument of national policy virtually impossible; the international Communist movement, at least at one time, sought the revolutionary transformation of all societies into a particular kind of Communist society. There is, of course, no *a priori* guarantee that the movement will be successful and that the intended change will be effectuated. In fact, it is possible that the changes which do occur are unintended ones and that the original goals remain unfulfilled. Nevertheless, some change almost always results from the endeavors of such movements.

Transnational movements may be described in terms of the following general characteristics: ideology, motivations of members and constituents, social foundations, structure, mode of operation, and functions.

The ideology of a transnational movement, which may be very comprehensive, elaborate and formal or quite general and amorphous, comprises the constitutive ideas of the movement and defines it in terms of its aims.[10] It justifies the existence of the movement, in part by providing a system of beliefs which all members as well as partisans and sympathizers can adopt and which legitimizes their struggles against the values of the existing order.[11]

Individuals may join a movement for a number of reasons—a belief in the truth of its constitutive ideas, the charismatic appeal of the

[9] Special note should be taken of social movements that are national in scope but which have had significant transnational effects. Putting aside for the moment deliberate efforts to export the style and brand of a particular revolution, such movements as the French, Russian, Chinese, Mexican, Algerian, and Cuban revolutions have profoundly influenced the thinking, attitudes, and aspirations of other peoples and governments. In almost all instances, much of the discussion of these great social events centered upon whether they could serve as models for the development of other countries. Nonetheless, these revolutionary movements, with the exception of the Bolshevik revolution, remained basically national, and not transnational, in scope.

[10] Heberle, *Social Movements* (fn. 6), 24. The term "constitutive ideas" is his.

[11] Joseph R. Gusfield, "Social Movements II: The Study of Social Movements," in *International Encyclopaedia* (fn. 6), XIV, 447.

leader, or individual self-interests—and every movement includes individuals who became members because of one or more of these motivations. Nonetheless, what is perhaps most important in binding the members together regardless of their initial motivation is the solidarity, the sense of "we-ness," that membership and participation in the movement engenders. Indeed, the social and psychological rewards that emanate from the mere fact of participation may be motivation enough for many.[12]

Whether, to what extent, and by whom the ideology will be spread depends largely upon the social foundations of the emerging movement; that is, to what groups and/or classes and to what extent among these groups and/or classes the movement appeals. Socialism and Communism, for example, are largely class movements, whereas national independence movements have drawn upon a wider variety of groups and individuals within particular societies. The fact that a movement originated with a particular class- or group-basis does not necessarily mean that its appeal and subsequent membership will be limited to that class or group.

That a transnational movement has a structure does not mean that it is organized in a corporate form. Although social movements do require a minimum of organization through which their spokesmen and representatives can act, they are not corporate entities. Thus the transnational Socialist movement possesses a definite structure consisting of periodic congresses, labor and Socialist parties, trade unions, various international secretariats, affiliated associations and groups, etc. Yet the movement itself has never been formally organized into one all-embracing institution with the usual traits of corporate organization. To a large extent, the structure that the movement assumes is contingent upon its objectives and its strategic and tactical programs. Certain movements may choose to work through the "totalitarian political party," while others may utilize genuine political parties [13] and trade unions. Furthermore, there are also two parts to the structure of most transnational movements. There is the organized portion which embraces constituent groups, leadership structures, formal ideology, and officially identified members. But there is another portion which encompasses those individuals and groups whose perspectives and values are such that they have become the movement's partisans and supporters, and whose assistance is often invaluable to the successful realization of the movement's objectives.

The movement's *modus operandi*—its strategy and tactics—which may be set forth in its ideology, constitutes its program of action for the

[12] This point is made by Lucian W. Pye, *Politics, Personality, and Nation Building: Burma's Search for Identity* (New Haven 1962), 5.
[13] See Heberle, "Social Movements I," (fn. 6), 441.

ultimate achievement of its objectives. What strategy and/or tactics are adopted by a particular movement depend not only upon the goals sought but also upon the environment within which the movement operates and hopes to alter, and upon the general values held by the leaders and members of the movement. The Communist movement by choice and necessity adopted clandestine and conspiratorial tactics. To an extent this was also true of those state-creating movements the activities and very existence of which were proscribed and severely sanctioned by the colonial authorities. In contrast, the Christian Democratic movement conducts its organizing programs in an open manner, seeking to attain political power through parliamentary means and then to realize its objectives through legislation.

The functions performed by transnational movements raise at least two considerations. First, the publicly proclaimed goals of the movement are generally, but not necessarily, the actual goals sought by the leadership elite. Once the movement has attained power, its leadership may then be in a position to pursue objectives other than those which were stated during the ascent to power. Second, the existence of the movement may give rise to a counter-movement which aims to resist the changes being sought in the *status quo*. Yet, even if the movement is only partially successful in accomplishing its objectives, or even if it fails, the very fact of its existence and activities in the long run often causes certain changes in the social order—or it may spur subsequent reform and revolutionary movements. By forcing the established order to confront directly the grievances and demands of a part of the society, and by creating a public opinion on these issues as well as by training political leaders, the movement may succeed in causing many of its objectives and values to be incorporated into the social order. This process of cooptation is often anathema to many more radical movements, but it is one time-tested mechanism of social change. As Heberle remarks, "The great changes in the social order of the world which have occurred during the past two centuries are very largely the direct or indirect result of social movements. For even if a movement did not achieve all its goals, parts of its program were accepted and incorporated into the ever-changing social order. This has been the main, or 'manifest,' function of these movements." [14]

Finally, several observations about the genesis of transnational movements should be mentioned. Social movements may be regarded as "formative processes arising from some unrest, from some threat, deprivation, or aspirations keenly experienced by rather large numbers of individuals." [15] The nature of this generalized social condition which

[14] Same, 273–74.
[15] Muzafer and Carolyn W. Sherif, *An Outline of Social Psychology*, rev. edn. (New York 1956), 722.

creates the popular predisposition toward participation in a movement cannot, of course, be precisely predicted, and the general structure that the movement gradually assumes depends in part upon the particular environment within which it must function. Three factors, nonetheless, appear to be prerequisites for the formation of social movements.[16] First, a relatively large number of individuals within a particular geographical area must consciously recognize their grievances and aspirations and share this recognition among themselves and with others. Second, men must believe in their ability to bring about changes in the existing social order. Third, men must live under conditions which do not preclude effective collective action to bring about even rather fundamental changes in aspects of the social order. Once a movement has been created, and assuming that it is not destroyed by a counter-movement or by the public authorities, it may then disband upon having accomplished its goal, it may itself be transformed into an institution performing a distinct role within the social order that it originally sought to alter, or it may adopt new objectives.

## HISTORICAL AND TRANSNATIONAL MOVEMENTS

A critical distinction must be made in this discussion between transnational movements and sociohistorical phenomena that may be termed "historical movements." Transnational movements, although they may be somewhat loosely organized, are nonetheless essentially social collectivities and act as such. Their members may include individual human beings as well as groups and associations, but all are drawn together by a feeling of solidarity in a common enterprise. "Historical movements," on the other hand, are basically trends which are brought about by the aggregate effects of many unguided and uncoordinated individual efforts.[17] There is no sense of common identity, of belonging to a larger collectivity, or of joint pursuit of articulated goals. This does not mean that historical movements may not generate a vague but pervasive feeling among people that some vast force is somehow affecting the entire social order. Nor does it mean that historical movements may not involve profound attitudinal and institutional changes within the social order. But, while historical movements may give rise to social movements, they are not themselves social movements. Imperialism, especially as it motivated the Western European governments in the nineteenth century, was a historical movement. A feeling of "getting on the bandwagon" and obtaining colonial possessions seemed to pervade the thinking of European ruling elites, regardless of the particular rationalizations that were devised to justify such empire-building. Yet the governmental policies remained separate

16 Cameron (fn. 6), 10.
17 Heberle, *Social Movements* (fn. 6), 8–9.

and uncoordinated, and the several international conferences convened to allocate territories among the various powers were primarily efforts to facilitate and confirm these policies. In contrast, the Socialist movement is a transnational movement which pursues a definite set of stated goals and which unites trade union organizations, political parties, and other groups and associations working to bring about the changes sought by the collective movement.

To avoid any possible confusion, the following prominent historical movements will be mentioned: imperialism, nationalism (which is related to, but not identical with, state-creating movements), colonialism, pan-movements, liberalism, and conservatism. Most of these movements were accompanied by a pervasive sense of "something of great historical significance happening." Others were basically philosophical attitudes or, like Pan-Americanism, official governmental policies. None, however, is described by the definition of transnational movement stated earlier.

## MOVEMENTS AND THE WORLD SOCIAL PROCESS

Transnational movements constitute an important element in the structure of the world social process, and in several instances have brought about significant alterations in the social order itself as well as in the international legal order. What implications these developments portend for the future will be discussed in the later sections of this essay.

### 1. *Movement-Parties*

The highly organized and institutionalized transnational Socialist, Communist, and Christian Democratic movements constitute movement-parties: they are comprised of quite diverse organizations, of which the most important are political parties through which they hope to attain power in countries throughout the world and thereby begin to create distinctive public-order systems. Each aspires to universality, as evinced in its ideology and programs and operations. Each, furthermore, derives its inspiration and direction from an elaborate and definitive ideological foundation which also describes in varying degrees the political and social programs that are to be effectuated. In essence, these may be the rudimentary structures for a world political-party system.

### A. SOCIALISM

Socialism as a transnational movement is presently embodied in a Socialist International, consisting of 52 affiliated parties in 49 countries and representing approximately 17.4 million voters. The central organs of the International comprise a Congress as well as an executive

Council, a Bureau, and a Secretariat. Its auxiliary organizations include regional secretariats and conferences, women's, youth, and professional organizations, and several parliamentary pressure groups.

The "Aims and Tasks of Democratic Socialism," [18] the constitutive document adopted by the First Congress of the International in 1951, defines the movement's objective as the liberation of all peoples from any political and economic order that results in the exploitation of men by other men. It consequently regards economic and political democracy as of equal importance as fundamental goals. Although the movement seeks to create a democratic socialist commonwealth, it also acknowledges that no one socialist model is to be imposed upon every society, and recognizes that each society must resolve for itself the problem of social planning in a manner consistent with its particular conditions.

The movement has passed through several institutional stages [19]— the First International or International Workingmen's Association (1864–76), the Second International (1889–1923), the Labor and Socialist International (1923–40), the Socialist Information Liaison Office– Committee of the International Socialist Conference (1946–51), and the Socialist International (founded in 1951)—but throughout, especially in times of war, it has sought to preserve and expand the transnational bases of the movement, cooperate closely with the non-Communist labor movement, and bring about the adoption through national legislation of extensive social welfare programs. More generally, in one summary, it has "fought dictatorship and the suppression of civil liberties and . . . educated and propagandized for the elimination of poverty and the root causes of economic exploitation, unemployment, colonialism, imperialism, and war. It [has] advocated regional, political, and economic integration; expanded East-West industrial and cultural relations; greater social and economic aid to the developing nations; democratic economic and social planning; and vastly increased health, education, housing, and social security programs in the various countries of the world." [20]

### B. COMMUNISM

The "international Communist movement" is presently more of a battered idea than a vigorous revolutionary movement. Yet, it does em-

[18] Reprinted in Julius Braunthal, ed., *Yearbook of the International Socialist Labour Movement* (London 1956), Vol. I (1956–57).

[19] Comprehensive histories of this movement are G. D. H. Cole, *A History of Socialist Thought*, 5 vols. (London); Harry W. Laidler, *History of Socialism* (New York 1968); Carl Landauer, *European Socialism*, 2 vols. (Berkeley 1959); and Max Beer, *The General History of Socialism and Social Struggles*, 2 vols. (New York 1957).

[20] Laidler (fn. 19), 759–60.

brace 88 Communist parties—including the fourteen ruling parties—with an estimated 45.9 million members, numerous transnational mass organizations, several international organizations, and a regular pattern of interparty and interstate relations. Of the 45.9 million Communists in 1969, approximately 43.3 million or 94.3% were within the fourteen Communist countries.[21] However, many of the nonruling Communist parties, particularly those in the underdeveloped countries, are suffering from legal proscriptions, loose discipline, and competition from indigenous left and radical parties.[22]

The original aim of the movement was the revolutionary transformation of all societies into Communist societies, and this was to be accomplished through the Communist International, or Comintern, which Lenin molded into a highly centralized and disciplined world revolutionary organization modeled upon the Bolshevik party. As a world party the Comintern possessed an elaborate structure: its principal organs were a supposedly annual World Congress, an Executive Committee (ECCI) and a praesidium. The ECCI had a number of important administrative sections that handled agitation and propaganda, international relations among constituent parties and organizations, recruitment and training as well as discipline of cadres, and possibly even military affairs. In addition, transnational mass organizations were created in order to extend Communist influence over many groups, including labor, youth, women, teachers, lawyers, scientists, and journalists.[23] The Comintern under Stalin, however, became merely another instrumentality of Soviet policy, with the consequent identification of the movement's objectives with those of the Soviet Union.[24]

The Comintern structure was dissolved in 1943, but by then its functions had been assumed by the Communist Party of the Soviet Union. The Communist states that emerged in the wake of the Second World War were the result not of an international Communist movement but of the Red Army or of indigenous nationalist-Communist groups. Since the dissolution of the Communist Information Bureau (1947–56), which served mainly as an information exchange center for Communist states and organizations, the Communist leaders have cautiously searched for some appropriate institutional structure for the

[21] United States Department of State, *World Strength of the Communist Party Organizations* (Bureau of Intelligence and Research, 22d Annual Report, 1970), i–ii.

[22] Same; and Edward Taborsky, "The Communist Parties of the 'Third World' in Soviet Strategy," *Orbis*, XI (Spring 1967), 128–48.

[23] See Günther Nollau, *International Communism and World Revolution: History and Methods* (New York 1961), 146–56; Iain Phelps-Fetherston, *Soviet International Front Organizations: A Concise Handbook* (New York 1965); and Robert Orth, *International Communist Front Organizations* (Munich 1963).

[24] This process is described in Nollau (fn. 23), 125–87. See also Milorad M. Drachkovitz and Branko Lazitch, "The Communist International," in M. M. Drachkovitz, ed., *The Revolutionary Internationals, 1864–1943* (Stanford 1966), 159–202.

movement. Since 1956, however, polycentric tensions among Communist states and parties have precluded the reestablishment of any kind of universal Communist organization, and indeed have made very difficult the convening of conferences of all Communist parties. Nonetheless, during this same period distinct patterns of Communist interstate and interparty relations have managed to preserve a façade—albeit a badly mauled one—of a transnational Communist movement, and in the case of several Communist states have given rise to a "socialist commonwealth of nations" with its own international organizations.[25]

The level of institutionalization of the Communist movement remains minimal. The Soviet Union continues to occupy a prominent position in the eyes of most Communist parties, but this has not served to dampen the polycentric tendencies nor to lessen the intensity of the Sino-Soviet conflict. The long-term evolution of the movement is difficult to predict precisely, but it is exceedingly doubtful that the kind of transnational institutionalization that originally characterized the movement will or can be re-created.

While the Communist movement appears to have had no great impact upon the international legal order,[26] and while Communist states explicitly regard international law more as an instrument of policy than as a body of norms of conduct transcending the policy objectives of any one state,[27] it is not entirely accurate to conclude that the movement has contributed little to the contemporary international legal order. The fact that virtually all international commercial and trading activities of Communist states are conducted through public corpora-

[25] See Robert H. McNeal, ed., *International Relations Among Communists* (Englewood Cliffs, N.J. 1967), esp. 1–46, for a detailed discussion of these patterns of Communist interparty and interstate relations. McNeal notes that the closest the Communists have come to a universal organization has been the conference of 81 Communist parties which met in Moscow in 1960. No permanent institutions or procedures of dispute settlement and/or decision-making were created, however. Subsequent efforts to convene similar meetings have not been successful. Same, 15–16. See also George A. Modelski, *The Communist International System* (Princeton: Center of International Studies Research Monograph No. 9, 1961); Kurt L. London, " 'The Socialist Commonwealth of Nations': Pattern for Communist World Organization," *Orbis*, III (1959–60), 424–42; and Kazimierz Grzybowski, *The Socialist Commonwealth of Nations: Organizations and Institutions* (New Haven 1964).

[26] T. A. Taracouzio, "The Effect of Applied Communism in International Law," *Proceedings of the American Society of International Law* [hereafter cited as *Proceedings*] (1934), 105–20. See also Oliver J. Lissitzyn, "International Law in A Divided World," *International Conciliation*, N. 542 (March 1963), esp. 14–36; and "The Impact of Fifty Years of Soviet Theory and Practice on International Law," *Proceedings* (1968), 189–214.

[27] John N. Hazard, "The Soviet Concept of International Law," *Proceedings* (1939) (fn. 26), 34; and James L. Hildebrand, *Soviet International Law: An Exemplar for Optimal Decision Theory Analysis* (Cleveland 1968), esp. 42–45. For a correlation of different emphases in Communist international legal theory with different foreign policy objectives, see Hungdah Chiu, "Communist China's Attitude toward International Law," 60 *American Journal of International Law*, 245–67 (1966).

tions has led to a necessary expansion of international commercial law. Within the Eastern European region the existence of the Council of Mutual Economic Aid, the Warsaw Treaty Organization, and the other more specialized bodies has necessitated the development of various kinds of regional—perhaps "socialist commonwealth"—law, partially analogous to the regional law of the European Economic Community. Finally, the Soviet Union's demand that the existing international legal order be supplanted by one based upon the principles of peaceful coexistence had certain dramatic qualities, but these principles were never clarified and, at least rhetorically, are identical with the fundamental principles of the existing international legal order.[28]

## C. CHRISTIAN DEMOCRACY

The Christian Democratic movement, like the Socialist and Communistic movements, constitutes a world political party with far-reaching strength in Europe and in Latin America and with an impressive transnational structure. At present it embraces organized national political parties and movements of Christian social inspiration, their associated organizations (trade unions, employer and youth groups, etc.), regional organizations of Latin American, European, and exiled Central European parties, and a World Union of Christian Democrats founded in 1961.[29] The movement's traditional strength is in Western Europe, but it has also made great strides in Latin America where it has been regarded as the only real alternative to Communism.[30]

The origins of Christian Democracy are in the Christian—that is, Catholic and Protestant—social movements that began to emerge during the nineteenth century in Europe in response to the more secular, if not outright antireligious, movements of liberalism and Socialism.[31] By 1890 patterns of political Christian Democracy had emerged in Belgium, Holland, Germany, and Switzerland, but the movement as a whole then experienced a tremendous increase in strength as the workers' movement itself gained in organization and numbers. The Papal encyclical *Rerum Novarum* (1891) was a recognition of the rapid and profound social changes occurring in European society, and many of its ideas as well as those of *Quadragesimo Anno, Pacem in Terris,*

[28] See Hildebrand (fn. 27), 46–68; Edward McWhinney, " 'Peaceful Co-Existence' and Soviet-Western International Law," 46 *American Journal of International Law,* 951–70 (1962); and Bernard A. Ramundo, *Peaceful Coexistence: International Law in the Building of Communism* (Baltimore 1967).

[29] Charles R. Dechert, "The Christian Democratic 'International,'" *Orbis,* XI (Spring 1967), 106–27.

[30] For a general discussion, see Edward J. Williams, *Latin American Christian Democratic Parties* (Knoxville 1967).

[31] J. Salwyn Schapiro, *Movements of Social Dissent in Modern Europe* (Princeton 1962), 34–39. A comprehensive history is Michael A. Fogarty, *Christian Democracy in Western Europe, 1820–1953* (Notre Dame 1957).

and *Mater et Magistra* have been incorporated into the developing philosophy of Christian Democracy.

Two basic problems that the movement has had to confront are its relation to the Church and the attainment of internal unity among quite diverse groups in a single movement that lacked even a clear-cut statement of its general philosophy.[32] The first problem was resolved in 1920 when the International Federation of Christian Trade Unions was established, thereby permitting the movement gradually to dissociate itself from any confessional overtones, a process which was completed by the end of World War II.[33] The second problem was also resolved by the end of the First World War, when the three principal tenets of the Christian Democratic philosophy had become generally accepted. These are an acceptance of some degree of public ownership and national planning, but with the twin objectives of achieving a decentralized order based upon industrial self-government, and of according special attention to the basic unit of social and economic life, the family; a substitution of employer-worker collaboration for class warfare and revolution; and a reemphasis, while recognizing the validity of class interests and economic factors, upon the quality of individual personalities as the decisive factor in social life.[34]

The Christian Democratic movement has attempted to fashion an ideology and a political program intended to be of universal application. Whether in fact, however, it can gain a firm foothold in essentially non-Christian societies remains quite speculative.

### 2. Social Welfare Movements

One of the salient characteristics of the contemporary era is a deeply felt and increasingly impatient concern on the part of the world community with the general social welfare of the human race. Not only is there a diverse and expanding group of national and international public and private organizations devoted to bettering the economic, social, and environmental conditions in which men live, but the same aspirations have been solemnly proclaimed as fundamental goals of the international community in such documents as the Universal Declaration of Human Rights and the International Covenant on Economic, Social, and Cultural Rights. There are a number of transnational movements which not only reflect this general concern but also are playing important roles in shaping the social welfare and humani-

---

[32] Margaret Lyon, "Christian Democratic Parties and Politics," *Journal of Contemporary History*, II (1967), 86.

[33] Luigi Sturzo, "The Philosophic Background of Christian Democracy," *Review of Politics*, IX (January 1947), 5; and Rafael Caldera, "Christian Democracy and Social Reality," in John J. Considine (ed.), *Social Revolution in the New Latin America: A Catholic Appraisal* (Notre Dame 1965), 68.

[34] Fogarty (fn. 31), 191.

tarian perspectives of the world community. Three that will be considered here are the transnational labor movement, the humanitarian movement embodied in the International Red Cross, and the antislavery movement.

## A. LABOR MOVEMENT

The transnational labor movement [35] has succeeded in attaining a high degree of institutionalization that currently includes three global internationals—the World Federation of Trade Unions (1945), the International Confederation of Free Trade Unions (1949), and the International Federation of Christian Trade Unions (1920)—and eighteen International Trade Secretariats. The movement, moreover, is aided in its efforts to improve the general social, economic, and political conditions of workingmen by the existence of certain international organizations, most notably the International Labor Organization, which are seeking to achieve the same goals through national and international legislation.

Before the Second World War the labor movement was structured largely within the International Federation of Trade Unions, founded in 1913, and about 27 International Trade Secretariats affiliated with the IFTU. Both worked very closely with the ILO and the movement itself gained in strength, extending with the help of the American Federation of Labor into South America.[36] The IFTU was destroyed by the Second World War, however, and the legacy of the Cold War was a split in the labor movement: the majority of the members of the WFTU, once it became clear that it was Communist-controlled, withdrew to form the ICFTU, which is now the strongest and most influential transnational labor organization.

The several structures that constitute the labor movement may most conveniently be grouped according to their geographical scope and their functional operations.[37] Three main global organizations exist: the ICFTU, with 122 affiliates of 63.4 million members in 94 countries; the WFTU, with a claimed total of 138 million members in its affiliated organizations in 59 countries; and the smaller IFCTU, largely Catholic in membership and orientation, with affiliated organizations in 63 countries.[38] The ICFTU also has regional organizations in Europe (ERO), the Americas (ORIT), Africa (AFRO), and Asia (ARO),

---

[35] A standard history of the transnational labor movement is Lewis L. Lorwin, *The International Labor Movement: History, Policies, Outlook* (New York 1953). See also John Price, *The International Labour Movement* (London 1945).

[36] Sinclair Snow, *The Pan-American Federation of Labor* (Durham 1964).

[37] See John P. Windmuller, "International Trade Union Organizations: Structures, Functions, Limitations," in Solomon Barkin et al., eds., *International Labor* (New York 1967), 81–105.

[38] *Yearbook* (fn. 4), 122–132.

and maintains very close ties with the eighteen International Trade Secretariats. The IFCTU, which has generally supported the policies and programs of the ICFTU, has three regional organizations and eleven Trade Internationals. The WFTU has no dependent organizations but does have eleven Trade Union Internationals of a highly centralized nature. Several independent regional labor organizations also exist in Africa and the Middle East, and specialized transnational organizations are also found clustering around the ILO, EFTA, OECD, OAS, and COMECON.

The movement's high degree of institutionalization has made it possible for the IFTU and subsequently the ICFTU not only effectively to assist national labor groups in obtaining enactment of national legislation guaranteeing certain basic rights of union organization and activities, but also to work within certain international organizations, particularly the ILO, to bring about similar international legislation and to create effective international supervisory and enforcement machinery. The ILO, in fact, was established to devise an international code of labor standards which would offer both minimum protections and legislative guidelines for national legislative efforts.[39] As of 1966 the International Labor Conference of the ILO had produced 126 Conventions, of which 106 were in force, and 127 Recommendations.[40]

## B. HUMANITARIAN (RED CROSS) MOVEMENT

The transnational humanitarian movement, the objectives of which are the care, treatment, and safety of prisoners of war, as well as of the sick and wounded in the armed forces and of the civilian populations in times of armed conflict, was set in motion largely by the indefatigable efforts of Henri Dunant, a Swiss businessman, in the mid-nineteenth century. By 1864 almost every European country possessed a national voluntary committee for relief of the wounded in time of war, and in the same year a diplomatic conference produced the first of several international conventions concerning the welfare of armed forces wounded in war.[41] The efforts of the movement resulted in the requirement—in the rules of war as formulated by the 1899 and 1907

[39] Francis G. Wilson, *Labor in the League System: A Study of the International Labor Organization in Relation to International Administration* (Stanford 1934), 163–64.

[40] International Labour Organization, *Conventions and Recommendations Adopted by the International Labour Conference, 1919–1966* (Geneva 1966).

[41] See James A. Joyce, *Red Cross International and the Strategy of Peace* (New York 1959). A history of war relief in the period before the founding of the Red Cross is presented in Mabel T. Boardman, *Under the Red Cross Flag: At Home and Abroad* (Philadelphia 1915), 17–31; and Giorgio Del Vecchio, "On the History of the Red Cross," *Journal of the History of Ideas*, XXIV (Oct.–Dec. 1963), 577–83.

Hague Conventions—that belligerent powers respect the work of relief societies,[42] in the recognition in Article 25 of the League of Nations Covenant of the work of the Red Cross, and in 1949 in the four Geneva Conventions.[43] These Conventions, which are already recognized to be inadequate in light of modern techniques of warfare, nonetheless for the first time were extended to apply in situations of formally declared war, *de facto* hostilities and internal conflicts.

The humanitarian movement is comprised of the International Red Cross Committee, the League of Red Cross Societies, and the National Red Cross Societies.[44] It is the International Committee, an independent body of twenty-five Swiss citizens, which is authorized to act as a neutral intermediary in time of war and which heads the Central Tracing Agency (before 1960 known as the Central Prisoner of War Agency). The League is a world federation of some 95 National Red Cross, Red Crescent, Red Lion, and Sun Societies with a membership of over 214 million persons in 110 countries. It maintains technical bureaus concerned with planning, training, and executive functions, health and social services, nursing, relief, junior red cross, and public information, and works closely with ECOSOC, FAO, UNESCO, WHO, UNICEF, the United Nations High Commissioner of Refugees, the ILO, and the Council of Europe.

In many respects the humanitarian movement is unique among transnational movements. Not only has it been primarily responsible for the creation of international humanitarian law, but its private International Committee has been accorded by these Conventions an international legal status that permits it to assist in the implementation of the Conventions. Perhaps its concern with vital humanitarian interests and its private, highly expert, and strictly neutral qualities have made the movement's role and activities readily acceptable to governments. But whether it can bring about a more effective international humanitarian law of interstate and internal conflict remains uncertain.[45]

[42] Article 15 in both the 1899 and 1907 Regulations Respecting the Laws and Customs of War on Land, Annexed to the Hague Conventions of 1899(II) and 1907(IV).

[43] International Committee of the Red Cross, *The Geneva Conventions of August 12, 1949* (Geneva 1949). See also G. I. A. D. Draper, "The Geneva Conventions of 1949," 94 *Recueil des Cours*, 63–162 (1965).

[44] A good description is given in Laszlo Ledermann, "The International Organization of the Red Cross and the League of Red Cross Societies," 42 *American Journal of International Law*, 635–44 (1948). See also Joyce (fn. 41), passim.

[45] Josef L. Kunz, "The 1956 Draft Rules of the International Committee of the Red Cross at the New Delhi Conference," 53 *American Journal of International Law*, 132–38 (1959).

## C. ANTISLAVERY MOVEMENT

The antislavery movement, largely under the leadership of the British and Foreign Anti-Slavery Society, founded in 1823 [46] and now the Anti-Slavery Society, succeeded in bringing about a fundamental advance in the international protection of human rights. Of course, the dogged determination of the British Government to abolish both slavery and the slave trade may be cited as a special circumstance of this case. Yet in Britain, as elsewhere, antislavery organizations not only created a favorable public opinion but also were able to act as effective pressure groups, in part because several of their members and sympathizers occupied important governmental positions. This, in essence, is one of the most effective ways in which transnational movements are able to realize their goals.

The antislavery movement, which originated in Britain in the latter part of the seventeenth century, had succeeded by 1811 in obtaining legislation prohibiting the slave trade within Britain and her possessions.[47] By the end of the nineteenth century slavery itself had been abolished in Mexico (1829), the British possessions (1838), the French colonies (1848), the Dutch possessions (1863), the United States (1863), Brazil (1888), and Cuba (after 1898). Most of the South American republics had abolished slavery soon after gaining their independence.

Abolition, however, was by itself an inadequate remedy, for the Portuguese, French, Spanish, and Americans simply took over the now even more lucrative slave trade that flourished between Africa and those countries which had not yet abolished slavery. Until the Second Brussels Conference (1890), previous international efforts to suppress the slave trade—the first Paris Peace Treaty (1814), the Congress of Vienna (1814–1815), the Berlin Conference (1885), and the First Brussels Conference (1889)—had resulted in little more than official declarations of intent, with the result that Britain singlehandedly developed and enforced a conventional network for proscribing the slave trade on the high seas.[48] The General Act of the Second Brussels Conference established international machinery—including the International Mari-

[46] In 1909 this Society was amalgamated with the Aborigines Protection Society, founded in 1837, and henceforth became known as the Anti-Slavery Society. It has 800 subscribing members in 26 countries and has consultative status with the ILO and ECOSOC. It publishes annually the *Anti-Slavery Reporter*. A comprehensive and recent history of the antislavery movement is found in "Slavery," *Encyclopaedia Britannica* (Chicago 1969), xx, 628–44.

[47] See O. A. Sherrard, *Freedom from Fear: The Slave and His Emancipation* (New York 1959).

[48] See H. H. Wilson, "Some Principal Aspects of British Efforts to Crush the African Slave Trade, 1807–1929," 44 *American Journal of International Law*, 505–26 (1950).

time Office at Zanzibar and the International Bureau at Brussels—to enforce the Act's provisions, and for the first time the Anti-Slavery Society, upon whose initiative both Brussels Conferences had been convened, succeeded in bringing into being effective means to prohibit the slave trade.

The subsequent Convention of Saint-Germain-en-Laye (1919) substituted declarations of intent for the international machinery that had functioned so effectively, and the later International Convention on Slavery (1926),[49] which included a definition of slavery, and the Supplementary Convention on the Abolition of Slavery, the Slave Trade, and Institutions and Practices Similar to Slavery (1956) failed to reconstitute any similar enforcement structures. However, the prohibition of the slave trade on the high seas and the right of search that Britain had once exercised are specifically provided for in the Geneva Convention on the High Seas (1958).

Slavery and practices similar to slavery continue to persist;[50] indeed, the Anti-Slavery Society has cited evidence of slavery in various forms in twenty-six countries[51] including Yemen, where an estimated 100,000 slaves are to be found.[52] The United Nations, nevertheless, has at present buried this problem by referring it to a sub-committee, apparently because of resentment on the part of African and Asian countries over public airing of an issue that involves many countries in those regions.[53] In the meantime the Anti-Slavery Society, whose contribution to the present level of international protection and awareness is immeasurable, has continued to pursue its goals, acting as a highly expert advisory body as well as a transnational pressure group primarily within the United Nations and the ILO.[54]

49 It was clear by this time that slavery could appear in a number of guises, such as forced labor. While the International Convention of 1926 did not deal with forced labor, a Convention on Forced Labor was adopted in 1930 by the ILO. See C. Wilfred Jenks, *Human Rights and International Labour Standards* (London 1960), 27.
50 See Mohamed Awad (Special Rapporteur on Slavery), *Report on Slavery* (New York 1966), Doc. E/4168/Rev.1. See also, "British Group Finds Evidence of an Increase in Human Slavery since End of World War II," *New York Times,* April 7, 1967, p. 13, col. 1.
51 "Group Urging U.N. to Halt Slavery," *New York Times,* December 4, 1966, p. 166, col. 3.
52 "Saudi Arabian Slavery Persists Despite Ban by Faisal in 1962," *New York Times,* March 28, 1967, p. 16, col. 3.
53 "U.N. Unit Sends Slavery Issue to Subcommittee," *New York Times,* March 22, 1967, p. 6, col. 4.
54 The International Abolitionist Federation should also be mentioned with the Anti-Slavery Society as a part of more general social welfare movements. Founded originally in 1875 as the British and Continental Federation (the name was changed in 1896), it works primarily to bring about the abolition of prostitution. The Federation currently has national branches and affiliated organizations in 24 countries.

### 3. Peace Movements

The contemporary peace movement dates from the founding of the first peace societies in the United States (1815) and in Britain (1816).[55] At the present time it embraces three general approaches to the problems of war and peace.

The first approach is taken by those individuals and organizations that seek to cope with the problems of international conflict and of modern warfare through reforms, if not radical alterations, in international law and international relations. The activities pursued are very diverse, encompassing the highly publicized Pugwash Conferences;[56] the World Peace Through Law movement of lawyers, jurists, and statesmen; the *Pacem in Terris* Conferences; the codification of international law carried on by various private and public bodies; and efforts of the Churches to determine how religion can make effective contributions to world peace.[57] This approach is the continuation of a tradition begun in the latter third of the nineteenth century by scholars, statesmen, and international lawyers who sought to create a peaceful international order through a systematic improvement in international law, specifically by its codification and by the use of international arbitration.[58] During this period thirteen organizations were founded to promote this work, including the Institut de Droit Internationale (1873), the International Law Association (1873), the Inter-Parliamentary Union (1888), the Pan-American Union (whose first conference was held in 1889), and the International Maritime Committee (1897). In addition, the International Peace Bureau (1892) was established as a secretariat for the Universal Peace Congresses which had been periodically convened since 1843.

[55] Several good histories of the peace movement include A. C. F. Beales, *The History of Peace: A Short Account of the Organised Movement for International Peace* (New York 1931); Norman Angell, "Peace Movements," in Edwin R. A. Seligman and Alvin Johnson, eds., *Encyclopaedia of the Social Sciences* (New York 1934), XII, 41–48; and Francis H Hinsley, *Power and the Pursuit of Peace: Theory and Practice in the History of the Relations between States* (London 1963). See also Jerome Davis, *Contemporary Social Movements* (New York 1930), 749–868.

[56] Joseph Rotblat, *Science and World Affairs: History of the Pugwash Conferences* (London 1962); Betty G. Lall, "Pugwash: Progress and Prospects," *War/Peace Report*, VI (Nov. 1966), 6–7; Marvin Kalkstein, "Pugwash: The Tenth Year," *War/Peace Report*, VII (Nov. 1967), 15–16. The conferences were begun in 1957.

[57] See Carl Soule, "Christian Peace Conference of 1964," *War/Peace Report*, III (Dec. 1963), 14–15; *Peace, The Churches, and The Bomb* (New York 1965); Homer A. Jack, ed., *World Religions and World Peace: The International Inter-Religious Symposium on Peace* (Boston 1968); and Homer A. Jack, "Uppsala: Peace and the Churches," *War/Peace Report*, VIII (Oct. 1968), 18–19. The World Council of Churches has also entered into working relations with the Vatican and the World Buddhist Council on problems of peace and war.

[58] Ernest Nys, "The Codification of International Law," 5 *American Journal of International Law*, 871–900 (1911).

The accomplishments were many. Arbitration was adopted by the Universal Postal Union (1874), and in the decade after the Anglo-French Arbitration Treaty (1903) 162 similar international agreements were concluded, although most reserved questions concerning "vital national interests." The Hague Conferences of 1899 and 1907 both originated under the auspices of the Inter-Parliamentary Union, and the Convention for the Pacific Settlement of International Disputes as well as the Permanent Court of Arbitration were based on reports of the Union.[59] The Women's International League for Peace and Freedom (1915) may have influenced the provisions of Wilson's famous Fourteen Points.[60] The end of the First World War, moreover, brought the establishment of the League of Nations and the Permanent Court of International Justice at The Hague, two innovations in international law and relations that were in no small way the result of the peace movement's efforts.[61] Individuals also contributed to the movement in quite different ways: in 1901 the Nobel Peace Prizes were established, and in 1910 Edwin Ginn founded the World Peace Foundation and Andrew Carnegie the Carnegie Endowment for International Peace. The Kellogg-Briand Pact (1928) was itself originally suggested by an American citizen active in the peace movement.[62] Yet, as the conflicts of the twentieth century have shown, these efforts proved inadequate to prevent war.

The second approach, which has emerged only since the Second World War, is an intensive scientific research effort to uncover the causes and dynamics of both conflict and peace. A growing number of academicians and several research institutes, most notably the International Peace Research Institute (Oslo) and the Institute for Policy Studies (Washington, D.C.), are engaged in the emerging field of peace research.[63] The World Order Models Project of the World Law Fund (New York City) is similarly concerned with possible ways in which a future world order may be structured.

The third approach has been adopted by persons who have broadened the concept of pacifism from one based upon rather narrow religious grounds to one based upon a deep-seated repugnance to war in the modern era.[64] The impetus for this new form came originally

[59] William I. Hull, *The New Peace Movement* (Boston 1912), 165–83.

[60] Beales (fn. 55), 281; and Gertrude Bussey and Margaret Tims, *Women's International League for Peace and Freedom, 1915–1965: A Record of Fifty Years' Work* (London 1965).

[61] For a general discussion, see F. P. Walters, *A History of the League of Nations* (London 1952), I, 4–24.

[62] See Davis (fn. 55), 832–35.

[63] Elise Boulding, "Peace Research Around the World," *War/Peace Report*, v (Jan. 1965), 13–15.

[64] See, for example, Vera Brittain, *The Rebel Passion: A Short History of Some Pioneer Peace-Makers* (London 1964).

from Britain, but it has now shifted to the United States: students and the younger generation particularly, confronted with the Vietnam War, the American military arsenal, and the implications that they draw from great-power foreign-policy commitments, have rejected to varying degrees the use of force in international relations, if not also many of the goals of traditional great-power foreign policy.

A. C. F. Beales' characterization of the peace movement at the end of the nineteenth century as "diverse in origin, ununited in principles, and rudimentary in organization" remains an appropriate description of the movement today.[65] There are roughly over 1700 organizations around the world currently working for peace and disarmament.[66] Several of the older and more prominent organizations include the Women's International League for Peace and Freedom (1915), the War Resisters' International (1921), the International Fellowship of Reconciliation (1919), and the International Peace Bureau (1892, reorganized in 1962). While many of these are transnational in scope, two umbrella-organizations also exist, a reflection of the Cold War: the World Council of Peace, founded in 1950, with individuals and representatives from associations in over 100 countries, and the International Confederation for Disarmament and Peace, an independent organization founded in 1964 by the majority of the groups composing the WPC which objected to its adherence to the Soviet foreign-policy line. The International Confederation has 42 national organizations in fifteen countries, as well as five transnational organizations.

The lack of unity and the inability of component groups to cooperate in an integrated fashion on various projects has always been a defect of the peace movement, but it is more glaring today in the face of modern techniques of warfare and destruction. That it had an important impact upon the international legal order in the past is unquestionable. Today, while perhaps more dramatic but less directly influential upon governments and international organizations, the peace movement nonetheless serves as an "imperfect substitute" for an international foreign-policy assembly.[67] Whether this public-opinion function will in the long run prove sufficient to bring about peace is a highly speculative matter.

4. STATE-CREATING MOVEMENTS

The rise of nationalism, which began in the European colonial empire as early as the eighteenth century, was accompanied by the rise of a number of transnational movements seeking the overthrow of

[65] Beales (fn. 55), 196.

[66] Lloyd Wilkie and L. M. Wilcox, eds., *International Peace/Disarmament Directory*, 3rd edn. (York, Penna. 1963).

[67] Johann Galtung, "Peace," in *International Encyclopaedia* (fn. 6), XI, 495.

colonial rule and the creation of new states out of the often quite heterogeneous imperial domains. Each of these state-creating movements differed quite markedly, and one in particular—the Zionist movement—is unique. It created a *de facto* state by populating a territory with persons previously scattered throughout the world, established an effective parallel governmental structure that rivaled the administrative machinery of the Mandatory Power, and then sought international recognition and support for an independent state. In addition to the Zionist movement, state-creating movements that will be considered are those of South America, the Middle East, and Africa.[68]

The South American independence movement basically consisted of a handful of distinguished army officers, their military forces, and a sympathetic Creole population, and its main task was to defeat Spanish power on the continent permanently, a goal accomplished by the mid-1820s.[69] By the end of 1826 both the United States and Britain had extended formal recognition to the new republics, and the movement itself simply expired. The period of the independence struggle, however, raised anew difficult problems in international law concerning policies of recognition and neutrality that had remained unsettled from the period of the American war of independence.[70]

The Arab nationalist movement first emerged in Beirut in 1875 [71] and grew rapidly, until in 1916 the Arabs, with British encouragement, commenced their revolt against Ottoman rule. Independence was brief, however, for the secret Sykes-Picot Agreement (1916) and more particularly the San Remo Conference formally divided up these territories, with the exception of the Arab Peninsula, between Britain and France. The future disposition of these countries was now very much in the hands of the Mandatory—or in certain cases simply the occupying—Powers, but ultimately Iraq, Syria, and Lebanon were granted their independence. The movement failed to gain a favorable settle-

[68] The nationalist movements in Asia remained generally limited to their own respective countries and established no significant transnational bases of action. Nor did Japan create such a basis when she established her Co-Prosperity Sphere. See Willard H. Elsbree, *Japan's Role in Southeast Asian Nationalist Movements, 1940 to 1945* (Cambridge, Mass. 1953) and Michael Edwardes, *Asia in the European Age, 1948–1955* (London 1961).

[69] The history of this movement is treated in most standard texts on Latin American history. See John F. Bannon and Peter M. Dunne, *Latin America: An Historical Survey* (Milwaukee 1947); and Herman G. James and Percy A. Martin, *The Republics of Latin America: Their History, Governments and Economic Conditions*, rev. edn. (New York 1923).

[70] F. L. Paxson, *The Independence of the South American Republics: A Study in Recognition and Foreign Policy*, 2d edn. (Philadelphia 1916).

[71] This story is masterfully told in George Antonius, *The Arab Awakening: The Story of the Arab Nationalist Movement* (Philadelphia 1939). See also Francesco Gabrieli, *The Arab Revival* (New York 1961).

ment of the Palestine question, however, and to that extent it continues to support the goal of liberating Palestine from Israeli control.

A number of African nationalist movements of transnational scope existed before and during the period of African independence—roughly from 1958 to 1966—but their actual impact is somewhat speculative and moreover depends upon the particular movement under consideration. The Pan-African movement was used from the time of its first congress (1919) by African nationalists to fight against colonial rule. In 1958 the All-African People's Conference was established, which served to bring together nationalist leaders who had won or were still striving for independence and thereby helped to spur demands at the United Nations for decolonization.[72] On the regional level the Rassemblement Democratique Africaine, founded in 1946, encompassed six countries of French West Africa and not only pressed its demands upon the French but also trained party members from the various territories. Yet the unity that initially characterized these movements dissipated in the post-independence period, perhaps not unexpectedly, when it became apparent that the new African leaders had immediately to begin the difficult task of creating "new political and cultural nationalities out of the heterogeneous peoples living within the artificial boundaries imposed by the European master." [73]

The state-creating movement in South America almost completely expired once the republics had gained independence. This was not true of the Arab and African movements, although the fact that these movements do not consider their goals to be fully accomplished is only a partial explanation. The Arab and African movements from their emergence stressed the theme of creating a unity of regional or continental scope.[74] Thus the Arabs founded the Arab League in 1944, and the Africans the Organization of African Unity in 1963. Paradoxically, both organizations are composed of states, though the original aspirations, at least, of both nationalist movements were that such bodies would assist in the dual processes of national integration and regional unification. In fact the Arab League, largely dominated by the United Arab Republic, remains a "confederation of egotists," [75] although it has performed significant functional services.[76] The Or-

[72] Immanuel Wallerstein, *Africa, The Politics of Unity: An Analysis of a Contemporary Social Movement* (New York 1967), 34.

[73] James Coleman, "Nationalism in Tropical Africa," in Peter J. M. McEwan and Robert B. Sutcliffe, eds., *The Study of Africa* (London 1965), 177. This same point is stressed in Robert I. Rotberg, "African Nationalism: Concept or Confusion," *Journal of Modern African Studies*, IV (1966), 33–46.

[74] Immanuel Wallerstein, "Larger Unities: Pan Africanism and Regional Federations," in McEwan and Sutcliffe (fn. 73), 217–28.

[75] Emile Bustani, *March Arabesque* (London 1963), 65.

[76] Robert W. McDonald, *The League of Arab States: A Study in the Dynamics of Regional Organization* (Princeton 1965).

ganization of African Unity has also failed to realize its aspirations of unity, and even its African Liberation Committee has proved a great disappointment to those seeking elimination of the remaining outposts of colonial rule in Africa.[77] Even the RDA was unable to maintain its strength and transnational structure once French West Africa had gained its independence.[78] Nonetheless, and notwithstanding these harsh realities, greater unity—cultural, social and political—remains an important goal of these formerly state-creating movements.

Of the transnational state-creating movements, Zionism is *sui generis,* for its organizational structure, single-minded pursuit of its objectives, and successful accomplishment of a major portion of its goals far surpass the accomplishments of other movements of this class. The Zionist movement—a secular, rather than a religious, movement that sought to resolve the universal problem of anti-Semitism by the creation of a Jewish state with all the attributes of sovereignty [79]—was founded by the first Zionist Congress in 1897 which voted to establish for the Jewish people "a Home in Palestine secured by public law." [80] Efforts by Theodor Herzl, the founder of the movement, to secure an international agreement to resettle Jews in a territorial area proved futile,[81] but intensive Zionist pressure succeeded in eliciting from the British Government the explosive Balfour Declaration in 1917.[82] The Palestine Mandate, moreover, gave the Zionist organization a unique status in international law as the Jewish Agency for Palestine, as well as the

[77] Wallerstein (fn. 72), 174.

[78] Immanuel Wallerstein, "How Seven States Were Born in Former French West Africa," *Africa Report,* VI (March 1961), 3ff. See also, Thomas Hodgkin, *Nationalism in Colonial Africa* (New York 1957), 139–68.

[79] Several good histories of Zionism include Nahum Sokolow, *History of Zionism, 1600–1918,* 2 vols. (London 1919); Leonard Stein, *Zionism* (London 1932); and Israel Cohen, *The Zionist Movement* (New York 1946) and *A Short History of Zionism* (London 1951).

[80] These are the words used in the Basle Program, which was adopted at the Zionist Congress in 1897. The inherent ambiguity of this phrase was subsequently to plague statesmen, but Herzl himself apparently stated: "No need to worry [about the phraseology]. The people will read it as 'Jewish State' anyhow." Quoted in Alan R. Taylor, *Prelude to Israel: An Analysis of Zionist Diplomacy, 1897–1947* (New York 1959), 6.

[81] J. L. Talmon, "Israel Among the Nations: Reflections on Jewish Statehood," *Commentary,* XLV (June 1968), 37.

[82] This complex history is told (from different perspectives) in Antonius (fn. 71); Cohen, *The Zionist Movement* (fn. 79); Taylor (fn. 80); and the ESCO Foundation for Palestine, Inc., *Palestine: A Study of Jewish, Arab, and British Policies,* 2 vols. (New Haven 1947). The Balfour Declaration, in pertinent part, states that "His Majesty's Government view with favour the establishment of a national home for the Jewish people, and will use their best endeavors to facilitate the achievement of this object, it being clearly understood that nothing shall be done which may prejudice the civil and religious rights of existing non-Jewish communities in Palestine, or the rights and political status enjoyed by Jews in any other country."

responsibility to act with the Mandatory Power in all matters concerning the establishment of the Jewish national home in Palestine.[83] When Zionist-British relations deteriorated in the early 1940's, Zionist leaders ceased to cooperate with the British, turning instead to the United States for political and financial support. The Biltmore Program of 1939, which expressly called for the creation of a "Jewish Commonwealth" in Palestine,[84] only confirmed Arab nationalist fears of the movement's intentions. The Zionist organization had in fact succeeded in creating an effective state governmental structure, and in March, 1948, less than six months after the United Nations General Assembly had voted to endorse the partition of Palestine, the State of Israel was proclaimed.

The Zionist movement—now the Jewish Agency for Israel—continues to exist; it now consists of federations in 49 countries. Part of its strength is revealed in the more than $100 million it receives each year from voluntary contributions. In a real sense, its task was not completed with the launching of the state of Israel, for the vast majority of Jews remain in the Diaspora. Though the movement has apparently not attempted to interfere in the governmental policies of Israel, it has expressed concern over the state's seeming lack of interest in Jewry outside Israel from the standpoint of "practical Zionism." [85] Perhaps the fact that Israel is now a state with some rather pressing national and international problems is primarily responsible for the indifference to what the Zionist movement still regards as the essential problem for Jews.

### 5. Religious Movements

Religions, whether considered as organized bodies of doctrines and practice or as definable groups found in society, do constitute social movements, and the more prominent world religions—Christianity, Islam, Hinduism, and Buddhism—are unquestionably of a transnational nature, involving both a system of internal organization and a set of beliefs and loyalties that transcend the more limited political and social boundaries of states and societies. Two particular religious movements, both Christian, will be discussed here: Roman Catholicism, unique among the world's religions for its extensive and highly centralized institutional structure, and the Christian ecumenical movement, involving Protestant, Catholic, and Orthodox Churches.

[83] See text of League of Nations Mandate for Palestine, reproduced in Cohen, *The Zionist Movement* (fn. 79), 349–57.

[84] The story of the creation of a pro-Zionist public opinion in the United States is told in Samuel Halperin, *The Political World of American Zionism* (Detroit 1961).

[85] William R. Polk, David M. Stamler, and Edmund Asfour, *Backdrop to Tragedy: The Struggle for Palestine* (Boston 1957), 213.

## A. ROMAN CATHOLICISM

Roman Catholicism is one of the largest religious movements in the world with over 450 million members and a highly institutionalized structure that includes an ecclesiastical hierarchy of several ranks, numerous religious orders of priests, brothers, and nuns, an ecclesiastical government with eleven Congregations or departments, a temporal sovereign in the Vatican State, and a Papal diplomatic corps. It constitutes, in almost a literal sense, a "perfect society" which coexists with, but also interpenetrates, the other "perfect society," the state.

The Pope, in his person and in his office, has traditionally been the supreme head of the Church, his authority being based upon Christ's prescription: "Thou art Peter, and upon this rock I will build my Church." The creation of the Christian empire in Europe in the Middle Ages found the Church exercising many functions of civil government in addition to fulfilling her religious mission.[86] In the later centuries that witnessed the disintegration of Christendom and the gradual rise of nation-states, the Church herself emerged exercising a sovereignty that was at one and the same time a Papal and a temporal sovereignty, and at least one, if not both, was formally respected by other sovereign states. Whatever basis in international law a particular state might adopt to justify its consideration of the Vatican as a sovereign power, neither Papal sovereignty nor Papal moral authority has been dismissed as nugatory by the international community, not even during the period from 1870 to 1929 when the Pope was generally not regarded as a temporal sovereign.[87]

The overarching concern of the Vatican, and consequently the main task of Papal diplomacy, is to ensure that Catholics in all societies are permitted to practice their religious beliefs and that the Church can carry on her work in freedom.[88] Thus the Church, while it has solemnly condemned Nazism, Fascism, and Communism, does not necessarily demand that a government relinquish its ideologically hostile position if that government is willing to grant the Church certain

[86] See Walter Ullman, *The Growth of Papal Government in the Middle Ages: A Study in the Ideological Relations of Clerical to Lay Power,* 2d. rev. edn. (London 1965). During the fifteenth and sixteenth centuries the Papacy also allocated vast areas of Latin America and Africa among European powers. See Carlos E. Castaneda, "Social Developments and Movements in Latin America," in Joseph E. Moody, ed., *Church and Society: Catholic Social and Political Thought and Movements, 1789–1950* (New York 1953), 733–73, esp. 735–51; and J. Lloyd Mecham, *Church and State in Latin America: A History of Politico-Ecclesiastical Relations,* rev. edn. (Chapel Hill 1966), 3–87.

[87] Robert A. Graham, *Vatican Diplomacy: A Study of Church and State on the International Plane* (Princeton 1959), 30.

[88] Same, 6–7, 383, 392. See also, Edward L. Heston, "Papal Diplomacy: Its Organization and Way of Acting," in Waldemar Gurian and M. A. Fitzsimons, eds., *The Catholic Church in World Affairs* (Notre Dame 1954), 33–42.

freedom of action within its borders. The Church, for example, has been willing to improve its relations with Communist authorities, in the hope of securing certain liberties for Catholics in those societies as well as of entering into closer ties with the Orthodox Church, especially in Russia.[89]

Of course, the Papacy does not restrict itself to protecting only its own interests in any particular country; it also assumes a very deeply felt responsibility and moral authority to offer guidance to the world in times of especial tension and difficulty. In the past the Papacy has acted as an international mediator in disputes between Spain and Germany (1885), Belgium and Portugal (1891), and Brazil, Peru and Bolivia (1905), and has even offered itself as a universal arbiter for international disputes. Moreover, Popes have traditionally made appeals for peace, and in more recent times Pope John XXIII called for the creation of a new international order in his *Pacem in Terris* and Pope Paul VI attempted—albeit unsuccessfully—to bring about an end to the Nigerian civil war.[90]

Roman Catholicism is at present undergoing the long and difficult process of seeking to determine its position and role in the modern world in light of its more timeless mission. Since the Second Vatican Council, which began this *aggiornomento,* the Church has begun to confront squarely, if sometimes haltingly, pressing religious and world problems. What the final outcome will be is difficult even to speculate about at this early date, but it is certain to have important implications far beyond the confines of the Church herself.

### B. CHRISTIAN ECUMENISM

Throughout the history of Christianity the divisions that have rent it have brought forth periodic appeals to restore its original unity, and the history of ecumenical efforts has been traced as far back as 1517.[91] The contemporary transnational movement, however, originated only within the last four decades, and the initiative was taken by the Protestant Churches of Europe and North America at the first World Conference on Faith and Order at Lausanne in 1929. The direct result of this movement was the creation in 1948 of the World Council of Churches—the coming together of three earlier movements: the International Missionary Council (1921), Life and Work (1925) and Faith

---

[89] Peter Nichols, *The Politics of the Vatican* (New York 1968), 202–04.

[90] Various peace efforts of the Popes are recounted in Harry Koenig, "The Popes and Peace in the Twentieth Century," in Gurian and Fitzsimons (fn. 88), 48–68; and E. E. Y. Hales, *The Catholic Church in the Modern World: A Survey from the French Revolution to the Present* (New York 1960), 280.

[91] A comprehensive treatment is Ruth Rouse and Stephen C. Neill, eds., *A History of the Ecumenical Movement, 1517–1948,* 2d edn. (Philadelphia 1967).

and Order (1927). Both Protestant and Orthodox Churches are members of the WCC.[92]

While the Protestants were engaging in conversations among themselves and with the Orthodox Church concerning Christian unity, the Roman Catholic Church officially remained aloof. Nonetheless, Catholics continued to talk informally with the Anglicans during the Malines meetings (1921–26), work with Lutherans from 1920 on in the Una Sancta movement in Germany, and establish various institutes for ecumenical studies, such as those in Holland.[93] In 1949 an instruction of the Holy Office encouraged Catholic awareness of the movement and Catholic observers began to attend meetings of the various departments of the WCC, including the annual meetings of its Central Committee. It was the convening of the Second Vatican Council (1962–65) by Pope John XXIII, however, that totally involved the Church in the ecumenical movement. The Council itself was indicative that the Church was willing to reexamine herself in the light of modern world conditions and to begin the process of adjustment and change where this was deemed necessary. The creation of the Secretariat for Christian Unity—now a permanent part of the Curia—under Cardinal Bea, and the Council's *Decree on Ecumenism* made possible an unprecedented rapprochement between the Vatican and representatives of the major Protestant Churches, the Orthodox Church, and the WCC.[94] In 1965 the WCC and the Vatican Secretariat formed a Joint Working Group of fourteen members to study the possibilities of dialogue and collaboration. One concrete result was the coordination of "Christian aid" for famine relief in India and Africa in 1966.

It has been noted that "the quest of the ecumenical movement necessarily includes a quest for ecumenical institutionalization."[95] In addition to fundamental doctrinal differences, this problem has continued to trouble all members of the movement. Churches embracing Christianity include the Roman Catholics, Orthodox, Anglicans, Protestants, and other "sects." The Anglican Churches, legally and canonically independent, are represented in the Lambeth Conference, a consultative body that meets every ten years. The Protestants are grouped into

[92] A. H. van der Heuvel, "The World Council of Churches," in Leo Alting von Geusau, ed., *Ecumenism and the Roman Catholic Church* (London 1966), 49–58. The WCC publishes *The Ecumenical Review*, devoted to problems and progress of the ecumenical movement and, more recently, to contemporary social, economic, and political problems of the world.

[93] For the history of Catholic approaches to ecumenism see George H. Tavard, *Two Centuries of Ecumenism: The Search for Unity* (New York 1962).

[94] See Bernard Leeming, *The Vatican Council and Christian Unity* (New York 1966).

[95] Nils Ehrenstrom, "The Quest for Ecumenical Institutionalization," in Nils Ehrenstrom and Walter G. Muelder, eds., *Institutionalism and Christian Unity* (New York 1963), 23.

five "families"—Baptists, Congregationalists, Lutherans, Methodists, and "Reformed" or Presbyterians—which, together with the Anglicans, comprise 94–95 percent of all Protestants. Smaller groups include the Disciples of Christ and the Brethren. These main "families" have formed their own transnational organizations and belong to various other religious organizations that cut across denominational lines.[96] Assuming that doctrinal differences are not now—if they will ever be—susceptible to resolution, there remains the problem of the appropriate structural form that the ecumenical movement should take. Dr. Visser 't Hooft of the WCC has argued that the Churches should move toward "a positive pro-existence accepting responsibility for the spiritual influence which we exert upon each other, and cooperating except when deep differences of conviction compel us to act separately." [97] Circumstances in fact necessitate this procedure, which permits cooperation among the various Churches while they continue to seek for ways in which a more complete Christian unity can be created.

### TRANSNATIONAL ECONOMIC STRUCTURES

Transnational structures of the world social process are being created not only by transnational movements but also by the ever-expanding network of economic relations involving essentially private business enterprises and organizations. Transnational business enterprises existed 5000 years ago—for example, the Mesopotamian merchant trading companies engaging in interkingdom, interregional and intertribal trade—but what might be termed emerging "transnational economic structures" are a very recent phenomenon.[98] Such structures include the cartel systems, far less powerful and influential today than they were during the 1920's and 1930's, but even more importantly the patterns of relationships and interactions being developed by multinational business enterprises and such organizations as the International Chamber of Commerce. These latter in particular have recently attracted much interest; they will be discussed in terms of being the principal constitutive elements of transnational economic structures.

[96] Leeming (fn. 94), 34–46.

[97] Quoted in Thomas F. Stransky, "Roman Catholic Membership in the World Council of Churches?" *The Ecumenical Review*, xx (July 1968), 205–06. This article and Lukas Vischer, "The World Council of Churches—Fellowship of All Churches," same, 225–44, are a discussion of the structural problems confronting the WCC and the Roman Catholic Church.

[98] The evolution of multinational business is discussed in Endel J. Kolde, *International Business Enterprise* (Englewood Cliffs, N.J. 1968); and Mira Wilkins, *The Emergence of Multinational Enterprise: American Business Abroad from the Colonial Era to 1914* (Cambridge 1970). Comprehensive studies of this subject include Sidney E. Rolfe, *The International Corporation* (Paris 1969); Charles P. Kindleberger, ed., *The International Corporation* (Cambridge 1970); and Raymond Vernon, *Sovereignty at Bay* (New York 1971).

The multinational business enterprise [99] is a quite recent phenomenon, having become rather widespread and prominent only within the last decade. These enterprises have attracted attention basically because of sheer size and individual and aggregate wealth. For instance, in 1967 the combined worldwide sales of less than 100 such enterprises whose parent companies were based in the United States were greater than the gross national product of any country in the world except the United States and the Soviet Union. It has been estimated that within two decades, more than half of the world's gross national product may be accounted for by less than 300 such enterprises.[100] General Motors, with production facilities in twenty-four countries, in 1967 had a total sales of $20 billion, which is greater than the GNP of all but fourteen of the 124 nations in the United Nations [101] and of all but seventeen nations in the world.[102] Other examples are Standard Oil of New Jersey, with facilities in 45 countries and total sales in 1967 of $13.3 billion, and Corn Products, with facilities in 33 countries and total sales in 1967 of $1.1 billion.[103] Multinational business enterprises are predominantly, though by no means exclusively, an American phenomenon. The OECD estimates current total direct investment by corporations outside their own national base at about $85 billion, with United States corporations accounting for $54 billion and European and Japanese corporations $31 billion. It has been further estimated that this $85 billion contributes to roughly $170 billion of world commerce.[104]

In terms of the number of countries in which multinational business enterprises have subsidiaries and affiliates, a partial list—with the number of countries in parentheses—includes the following: of the American corporations, IBM World Trade Corporation (80), Singer Sewing Machine (62), National Cash Register (56), Pfizer and Co. (46); of the British corporations, British-American Tobacco (54), British Petroleum

[99] These organizations are variously termed "transnational," "international," or "multinational" companies or corporations. In this essay the term "multinational business enterprise" will be used for two basic reasons: first, this term is most frequently used to describe this new corporate phenomenon; second, and more importantly, this term embraces a number of different corporate organizational structures used by corporations engaging in worldwide business operations. These different structures are described in the text. Also, "enterprise" is used instead of "corporation" or "company" because connotatively it includes both the corporate organizational structure and the nature, manner, and scope of business operations, which together comprise part of the emerging transnational economic structures.

[100] Business International Research Report, *The United Nations and the Business World* (New York 1967), 2.

[101] Barber (fn. 4), 3.

[102] "Money Power," *War/Peace Report,* VIII (Oct. 1968), 9.

[103] Sanford Rose, "The Rewarding Strategies of Multinationalism," *Fortune,* LXXVIII (September 15, 1968), 100ff.; table on 105.

[104] Same, 100.

(50), Imperial Chemical Industries (46); and finally the Dutch corporation Royal-Dutch Petroleum (43) and the Danish Det Østasiatiske Kompagni, A/S (42).[105] According to one definitional scheme the United States has about 269 multinational business enterprises, Britain 165, Germany 72, France 48, and Switzerland 27.[106]

The concept of the multinational business enterprise remains undefined, in part a reflection of continuing management efforts to create organizational forms most appropriate for their needs. There is, nevertheless, a consensus that its essential criteria are a manufacturing base or some other form of direct investment in at least one foreign country, and multinational ownership and control combined with a "truly global" perspective. Such a global perspective exists when the management makes fundamental decisions on marketing, production, and research in terms of alternatives that are available to it anywhere in the world.[107]

In operational as well as conceptual terms the multinational business enterprise encompasses at least three different corporate organizational structures: the international headquarters corporation, the world corporation, and the transnational corporation.[108] Traditionally, a company which engaged in foreign commerce had an export department or a foreign operations division simply as one of several departments or divisions in a basically nationally-oriented company. In many instances this department or division has been replaced by a company-controlled organization, operationally and often legally separate—the international headquarters company—which assumes all responsibility for the international aspects and operations of the business. In addition to exporting and importing operations, it also establishes its own facilities abroad for purposes of production, distribution, and service. This is, in essence, an internationally-oriented subsidiary of a nationally-oriented parent. In a world corporation, on the other hand, this dualistic structure is eliminated, and the entire top echelon of the company is reoriented to worldwide business opportunities and re-

[105] *Yearbook* (fn. 4), 1203.

[106] A. J. N. Judge, "Multinational Business Enterprises," in *Yearbook* (fn. 4), 1198. This American predominance was, of course, the main theme of J. J. Servan-Schreiber's best-seller, *The American Challenge* (New York 1968).

[107] Ernest W. Ogram, Jr., *The Emerging Pattern of the Multinational Corporation* (Research Paper No. 31, Bureau of Business and Economic Research, School of Business Administration, Georgia State College 1965), 10; Robert L. Heilbroner, "The Multinational Corporation and the National State," *New York Review of Books* (February 11, 1971), 20–25; and Robert O. Keohane and Joseph S. Nye, eds., "Transnational Relations and World Politics," *International Organization*, xxv (Summer 1971).

[108] These distinctions are set out and analyzed in Endel J. Kolde, "Business Enterprise in A Global Context," in Richard N. Farmer, ed., *International Management* (Belmont, Calif. 1968), 8–32; and Kolde (fn. 98), 245–51.

sponsibilities.[109] A transnational company, finally, differs from the world company in that both ownership and control of the corporate structure are international. There is no parent company and the top management, which is divided among several headquarters in different countries, functions as an international coalition. It is essentially a group of management centers jointly administering a network of operating companies. Unilever and Royal Dutch-Shell are examples of the transnational corporation.

The operations of these multinational business enterprises and their intermeshing economic and commercial relationships are almost entirely governed by the national laws of the countries in which the parent company and its subsidiaries and affiliates are domiciled. There does exist a legal framework within which international trade takes place; it governs sales of goods abroad, legal aspects of international banking, insurance, and carriage of goods by air, sea, and inland transport. But beyond the international conventions on patents, trademarks, and postal rates, there is little applicable international law that even attempts to regulate the multinational business enterprises and their operations.[110] As Henry Fowler put it: "There is no international law applicable to transnational business because there is no supranational authority to issue and enforce it." [111]

The paradox of quite different national—and nationalistic—legal systems attempting to govern the organization, operations, and conduct of business enterprises that are becoming increasingly global in every respect has led to a multitude of inordinately vexatious problems. For every country in which a multinational business enterprise does business, there are different tax systems, accounting systems and procedures, chartering and licensing procedures, and often a host of other special rules and regulations imposed by the host country for any number of reasons, not the least of which may be the government's fear of the economic leverage which the entire enterprise, let alone the national subsidiary, wields.[112] Another problem for both these enterprises, as well as for the host countries, is the extension of United States antitrust laws to the overseas operations of American business, particularly in countries which may look more leniently upon actions

109 See Business International, *Organizing for Worldwide Operations: Structuring and Implementing the Plan* (Research Report 65-2; New York 1965).

110 Howe Martyn, *International Business: Principles and Problems* (New York 1964), 4.

111 Henry H. Fowler, "National Interests and Multinational Business," in George A. Steiner and Warren M. Cannon, eds., *Multinational Corporate Planning* (New York 1969), 129.

112 For a general discussion of these problems, see Donald P. Kirchner, "Now The Transnational Enterprise," *Harvard Business Review*, XLII (March–April 1964), 6ff.; and Raymond Vernon, "Multinational Enterprise and National Sovereignty," same, XLV (March–April 1967), 156ff.

which American antitrust legislation would prohibit.[113] Finally, there is also the perhaps inadvertent use of the multinational business enterprise as an instrument of American national policy. For instance, the United States forbids its nationals, which includes business corporations, from trading in certain goods with certain Communist states. Since this legislation applies to subsidiaries operating in foreign countries, at least part of the foreign economic policy of these countries is willy-nilly determined for them, not to mention the foreign exchange that would be earned from such transactions and which is now denied them.[114]

The absence of a comprehensive body of international law regulating multinational business enterprises does not mean that there is no legal order seeking to control transnational economic associations and relations. Such an order does exist—albeit in quite disorganized and not always consistent form—although its basis is for the most part in the national laws of various countries. Much of the foundation for emerging international business law and many of the uniform international standards in certain areas of worldwide commercial intercourse which have been enacted into national laws have been created primarily by the International Chamber of Commerce, a nongovernmental body which has sought in general, since its founding in 1920, to promote international economic relations and to encourage uniform international commercial legislation.[115] The ICC is a world federation of business organizations and of businessmen; membership is open to any association, not organized for private profit, which legally represents commercial and industrial interests: Chambers of Commerce, Municipal Boards of Trade, voluntary businessmen's associations, federations of corporations, etc. It has national committees in 41 countries, with organizations and associations in 36 more. Its secretariat consists of 45 regional and technical commissions, and the latter are divided into four main groups dealing with economic and financial policy, production-distribution-advertising, transport-communications, and law and commercial practice. The ICC also works closely with the OECD, ECOSOC, and UNESCO as well as with other international organizations concerned with agricultural and food production, air, land and sea transportation, and international trade.

The ICC performs a number of critical functions for its membership

---

[113] "Antitrust Tries Going Multinational, Too," *Business Week*, February 24, 1968, 42; and See Walter Guzzardi, Jr., "Two Recent Antitrust Actions Illustrate the Dangers of Applying U.S. Law to the Overseas Operations of American Business," *Fortune*, LXXVIII (August 1968), 47–48.

[114] Neil W. Chamberlain, *Enterprise and Environment: The Firm in Time and Place* (New York 1968), 198.

[115] Charles H. Alexandrowicz, *International Economic Organizations* (New York 1953), 92.

as well as for the broader world community. It has served to collect and canalize the public opinion of the business community in areas of vital concern to them and to governments. It has initiated numerous studies and made recommendations that have been adopted in many instances by governments and international organizations. In the area of international trade, it brought about the adoption of uniform commercial terms and of regulations dealing with bills of lading and commercial documentary credits; in transportation, it pioneered studies of railway usage in various regions; in communications, it recommended the adoption of certain telegraphic rates; in finance, it made recommendations concerning stabilization of currencies and double taxation.[116] Moreover, it regularly provides experts to serve in different capacities in international conferences and in projects undertaken by international organizations.

The great importance of the ICC in transnational economic relations also stems from its Court of Arbitration and to a lesser extent from its International Council on Advertising Practice, which settles claims of alleged unfair competition in the field of international advertising according to the ICC Code of Advertising Practices. In cases submitted to the Court for arbitration, the ICC Rules of Conciliation and Arbitration prescribe a prior conciliation effort, which resolves most of the disputes. Those remaining are settled by an arbitrator appointed by the Court, rather than by the parties, and there is no appeal from his decision. In virtually all cases, national courts have upheld the arbitrator's award.

The ICC has played such a critical role in fashioning the framework within which transnational economic operations can be facilitated at least partly because, for whatever reasons, no international body has been established to accomplish these tasks. Indeed, in certain respects the ICC has come to play a role functionally somewhat equivalent to that of such an international or supranational body. The transnational economic structures which have already begun to take shape—the multinational business enterprises, their relations among themselves as well as with national governments and international organizations,[117] the regulatory network devised and partly enforced by such organizations as the ICC—will continue to evolve, becoming in all likelihood even more extensive and complex. What the nature of these structures will be, in what ways they can and should be regulated, and how they can contribute to the amelioration of problems common to all mankind are questions that are just now beginning to be asked.

[116] Same, 91–97; Kurt Wilk, "International Organization and the International Chamber of Commerce," *Political Science Quarterly*, LV (June 1940), 231–48; and White (fn. 4), 19–32.
[117] See Business International Research Report (fn. 100).

## IMPLICATIONS FOR THE INTERNATIONAL LEGAL ORDER

The relationship of transnational structures to the international legal order raises a number of questions which can only be discussed here in general terms. Specifically: how have these movements and organizations, and the emerging structures which they have created, shaped the international legal order, and how have they been affected by it? What prognostications might be made regarding the future evolution of transnational structures? Finally, what recommendations might be made to extend the international legal order to encompass these transnational phenomena?

Transnational movements, associations, and structures have shaped the international legal order fundamentally in two ways: directly, by adding to or altering the set of norms regarded as international law by states, international organizations, and transnational associations; and indirectly, by altering the social order of which the legal system is a part and reflects its basic values, and by formulating certain standards of quality and conduct that states and international organizations might formally adopt or approve. It should be recognized, of course, that the category into which a particular movement or association is placed is largely dependent upon the forum or fora of authoritative decision in which it participates.[118] The International Committee of the Red Cross, for example, has ready access to certain international organizations and international conferences where its recommendations may be incorporated into international legislation. This is also true of the labor movement as represented by the ICFTU, a permanent participant in the forum provided by the ILO. Yet the labor movement had to alter fundamental economic relations within a large number of societies, gain substantial political and economic power, and build up a strong transnational movement before it could even hope for an organization such as the ILO and for effective international labor legislation.

Direct access to fora of authoritative decision often enables an organization to participate in an international legislative process. In cases where organizations such as the International Committee of the Red Cross, the ICFTU, or the ICC are involved, they frequently play a major role in preparing initial studies, recommendations, and drafts of proposed conventions. Moreover, they assist in implementing many of these conventions, engaging in a continuous process of recommending a certain action, evaluating its effect, and making subsequent suggestions for improvement and extension.

Where access to fora of authoritative decision is blocked, or where such fora are deemed inappropriate because of the kind of change

---

[118] See McDougal, Lasswell and Reisman (fn. 1).

sought, certain movements have attempted to influence and alter the international legal order in more indirect ways. The *raison d'être* of each movement-party, for instance, is the establishment of a particular system of public order—a system which seeks to create or maintain basic goal values by means of a distinct institutional framework.[119] It is assumed that once a change has been effectuated in the underlying social order, a change will necessarily result in the legal order, be it national or international. Communist theorists originally contended that the transformation of the world social order into a "single world-wide, denationalized, class-less society" would eliminate the need for an international law regulating the relations between independent states.[120] This revolutionary transformation has not occurred, but the Communist countries, while generally conforming to the extant norms of the international legal order, continue to proclaim the existence of a fundamentally different and more advanced Communist legal order.[121]

Another way in which transnational movements may indirectly shape the international legal order is by defining certain standards of quality and of conduct that should guide the actions of states and of international organizations—among themselves as well as with respect to fundamental world problems. Before appropriate international fora of authoritative decision were created, the social welfare and humanitarian movements could only define standards that they felt should apply in a number of situations in the hope that national legislatures would adopt them. From the start the ICC called for the application of relevant standards of quality and conduct in transnational economic relations, in order to facilitate and promote world commerce. Finally, perhaps most notable for their trenchancy but also for their apparent lack of impact upon political leaders are the religious—especially the Papal—pronouncements on world problems. The Papacy has often been considered as the "conscience of the world," and many Popes, regardless of their seeming lack of influence, have continued to expose the moral perspectives of problems in such a way that statesmen cannot remain unaware of their implications.

Transnational movements have influenced the international legal

---

119 This is essentially similar to the definition of McDougal and Lasswell. See McDougal and Lasswell (fn. 1), 15.

120 T. A. Taracouzio, *The Soviet Union and International Law* (New York 1935), 10.

121 See same; and Y. A. Korovin, *International Law: A Textbook for Use in Law Schools* (Moscow n.d.), esp. 7–26; and Bernard A. Ramundo, *The (Soviet) Socialist Theory of International Law* (Washington 1964). Ann Van Wynen Thomas, *Communism Versus International Law: Today's Clash of Ideals* (Dallas 1953), deals more with the clashes between the ideological foundations of the international law derived from Western European civilization and Communism.

order, but they have also been shaped by it—and even more by the international system upon which that order is based. Certain movements have been the object of both international and national proscription, for example, the Communist movement. A number of alliances and mutual security arrangements may be construed as at least in part an attempt to contain the operations of the movement. But the main factor conditioning the nature and effects of transnational movements is the paramountcy of the state and of the international system in the world social order, a reality which the international legal order substantially reflects. Movements must thus work with and through—perhaps against—states to attain their objectives. The rise of international organizations, particularly the specialized, functional organizations, has proved very beneficial for many of these movements, giving them access to fora in which they can influence public opinion, affect state behavior, and perhaps make a contribution to international law. When a movement gains the support of an international organization or organizations, its cause is, of course, immensely enhanced.

In the final analysis, the vast majority of transnational activities and organizations are not subject to international regulation. Even transnational economic phenomena, which constitute one of the most important aspects of world political and economic affairs, are governed only peripherally by national laws and generally by private contractual arrangements, not at all by international law. Whether and to what extent these transnational phenomena should be subject to international regulation, and to what kind of regulation, depends in no small measure upon how these movements and structures will evolve in the coming decades.

To speculate upon the future evolution of transnational structures and to suggest ways in which the international legal order can and should respond to these developments is a difficult and hazardous undertaking. It is, nonetheless, the original task of this essay and can be most conveniently discussed in terms of prospects for a world political-party system, the international protection of human rights, the promotion of world economic welfare, the furtherance of peace, and the outlook for supranational integration.

## 1. World Political-Party System

There now exist at least three transnational political parties—the Communist, Socialist, and Christian Democratic parties—although only the latter two are expressly committed to democratic procedures and to open participation in national parliamentary systems. The adherence of the Communist movement to revolutionary means of seizing political power has led to its legal proscription in most countries, thus drastically curtailing its organizational strength, though not always its popular influence. The existence of these parties, however, does not mean that there is a world political-party system in which they compete regularly for political power in various national parliamentary systems. In fact, the Socialist and Christian Democratic structures share many of the same philosophical and programmatic objectives, and while national Christian Democratic and Socialist parties have competed in elections, this has not been the result of a world political-party strategy but of the political-party configuration in that state.

The strength of a world political party depends partly upon the number of its national affiliates. Whether the existing parties can create bases of power in societies quite different from the Western European society in which these three movements originated is difficult to answer. The Christian Democratic party has developed strong roots in Latin America, whose culture is strongly European, but not elsewhere. The Socialist party has made some inroads in Asia and Africa, but it has had to cope with nationalism as well as with social conditions quite different from those in Europe.[122] In fact, it may be possible that transnational political-party systems will emerge first on a regional, rather than a global, pattern. It should also be noted that the Socialist and Christian Democratic parties currently act as pressure groups in various fora of European parliamentary organizations and of the United Nations. Such parties might, therefore, essentially compete both within national parliamentary systems and within whatever international parliamentary fora may be open to them.

Among the obstacles that a regional or world political-party system would inevitably encounter is the objection by strictly national parties that the participation of a world party in national elections through its national affiliate, or the assistance tendered by the world party to its affiliate, is an interference in the domestic affairs of the state. Such alleged interference might be countered by domestic legislation as well as by an international alliance to restrict the operations of the world party. How the balance should be struck between the influence and power of the world party and the power configurations of the national political party system is impossible to determine in the abstract.

Perhaps the fundamental legal consideration is that such parties are based upon the universally recognized freedom of association, although the exercise of this freedom is often encumbered with various restrictions. Not only the Universal Declaration of Human Rights (Articles 20 and 21), but, more importantly, the legally binding European Convention for the Protection of Human Rights and Fundamental Freedoms (Article 11), and the International Covenant on Civil and Polit-

[122] See, for instance, the essays in William H. Friedland and Carl G. Rosberg, Jr., eds., *African Socialism* (Stanford 1964), 15–127.

ical Rights (Articles 21 and 22) seek to protect this freedom within national contexts. Somewhat effective enforcement machinery is provided for by the European Convention, but these kinds of procedures as well as freedom of association must be extended to the plane of transnational political parties and associations. This, in effect, has already been accomplished for the right of association within both national and transnational trade-union structures.

## 2. Human Rights

In the broadest sense, most of human history has been a struggle by men to achieve a continually expanding body of what are regarded as fundamental human rights for as much of mankind as possible. Transnational movements have contributed significantly to this struggle. Although the antislavery, humanitarian, and labor movements may appear to be seeking only limited sets of freedoms and rights, actually their operations rest upon philosophical bases that are necessarily linked to the entire human rights system. For example, the core of any system of human rights in general is the cluster of rights and freedoms necessary for free trade unionism that international labor legislation seeks to protect, the most fundamental of which is the freedom of association.[123] Consequently, by emphasizing the need for international legislation and protection, both the ILO and the broader transnational labor movement are shaping legal norms that underlie not only trade-union rights and freedoms but also the entire framework for human rights.[124]

Zionism may also be considered as a form of humanitarian intervention. In this case, however, it was accomplished by a transnational Jewish organization on behalf of Jews scattered throughout the world.[125]

Structures for the international protection of human rights are gradually emerging, both on the regional and global levels, but the central problem is effective enforcement machinery. The International Covenant on Civil and Political Rights establishes a Human Rights Committee which, under stated circumstances, may receive complaints about a signatory state's conduct from an individual citizen of that state or from another signatory state. A much more promising development is the machinery established by the European Convention, under which an individual may initiate a complaint against his government which

[123] C. Wilfred Jenks, *The International Protection of Trade Union Freedom* (New York 1957).

[124] See Jenks (fn. 49), and "The International Protection of Trade Union Rights," in Evan Luard, ed., *The International Protection of Human Rights* (New York 1967), 210–47.

[125] For an interesting thesis, see Nathan Feinberg, "The Recognition of the Jewish People in International Law," in N. Feinberg and J. Stoyanovsky, eds., *The Jewish Yearbook of International Law*, 1948 (Jerusalem 1949), 1–26.

is then processed by a special committee and in certain cases by a judicial panel.

It should be noted that the modern concept of human rights includes both rights and freedoms from certain forms of control and power, but also rights and freedoms to participate fully in the political, economic, and social orders. Many of the rights in the International Covenant on Economic, Social, and Cultural Rights fall into this latter category and, since in many instances their realization is contingent upon greater improvements within and modernization of the society, they are more in the nature of standards of achievement than legally enforceable rights.

Until effective regional and international enforcement machinery for the protection of human rights is established, transnational movements can continue to press their advocacy of such a system, mold a favorable public opinion, publicize flagrant human-rights violations, and intervene where possible on behalf of threatened or injured individuals or groups. It is interesting that the Catholic Church long ago created a system for the protection of human rights—primarily though not exclusively for its own members—clustering around the religious liberty of Catholics. This is another form of humanitarian intervention exercised mainly by the Papal diplomatic corps. The Declaration on Religious Freedom [126] of the Second Vatican Council may signal the willingness of the Church to use its interventionary procedures in all cases involving deprivation of religious liberties, and perhaps even to extend this to the broader field of human rights.[127] Once effective international machinery has been created, the role of transnational movements will probably continue as it is now, but complementary to the new structure.

### 3. Economic Welfare

The emergence of transnational economic structures simply reveals the growing economic interdependencies that bind all societies of the world, a trend which is very likely to intensify despite occasional surges of nationalistic protectionism. This fact alone—or even more strikingly when coupled with the problems of great magnitude associated with the need for effective programs of international economic and social development—means that any consideration of the future of transnational economic structures must be undertaken from the perspective of the economic welfare of mankind.

---

[126] Declaration on Religious Freedom: On the Right of the Person and of Communities to Social and Civil Freedom in Matters of Religion (Dignitatus Humanae), promulgated by Paul VI on December 7, 1965. See John C. Murray, ed., *Religious Liberty: An End and A Beginning; The Declaration on Religious Freedom: An Ecumenical Discussion* (New York 1966).

[127] Graham (fn. 87), 393–94.

Part of these emerging economic structures has been created by the interactions and relationships developed by multinational business enterprises. They can already draw upon an international banking system, and may soon bring about the establishment of an international securities market. They exert immense economic power, particularly in their ability to transfer vast amounts of capital, technology, and highly-skilled human beings to any part of the world, and they possess great potential political power over countries large and small. The first capability suggests that such enterprises could play a critical role in international economic development.[128] On the other hand, both characteristics make the smaller and economically less-developed countries extremely apprehensive about the purported desirability of such organizations, especially for purposes of assistance in economic development.[129]

The expansion of multinational corporate structures will undoubtedly raise prospects of transnational unionization and even "corporation-by-corporation" or "industry-by-industry" collective bargaining.[130] National labor federations may find, as many governments have found, that by themselves they are unable to deal adequately with the national subsidiary of a multinational business enterprise, simply because of the economic power wielded by the enterprise—not to mention its credible threat to leave the country, which would perhaps disastrously affect the nation's economy. Whether transnational unions *per se* will be formed of either regional or global scope, or whether certain powerful national labor federations will merely extend their organization remain questions for the future. A transnational labor-management relations structure governed by a supranational labor relations board (perhaps evolving from the ILO) with an international labor-management relations code may seem a somewhat far-fetched projection at this point. A moment's reflection, however, will reveal that the kinds of problems likely to arise in the future may very well require this kind of regulatory machinery.

Virtually all transnational economic relations are governed by contractual agreements entered into by the parties concerned as well as

[128] Chamberlain (fn. 114), 192–99. But see Harry G. Johnson, "The Multinational Corporation as a Development Agent," *Columbia Journal of World Business,* v (May–June 1970), 25–30.

[129] Martyn (fn. 110), 80; and see Arpad von Lazar, "Multi-National Enterprise and Latin American Integration: A Sociopolitical View," *Journal of Inter-American Studies,* XI (Jan. 1969), 111–28. See also "Nationalism Sets Boundaries for Multinational Giants," *Business Week* (June 14, 1969), 94–98, and Edith T. Penrose, *The Large International Firm in Developing Countries: The International Petroleum Industry* (London 1968), esp. 264–73.

[130] For a provocative discussion of the effects of multinationalism on labor, see Elizabeth Jager, "Multinationalism and Labor: For Whose Benefit?" *Columbia Journal of World Business,* v (Jan.–Feb. 1970), 56–64.

by an expanding body of international commercial law.[131] But the problem of the international regulation of transnational economic relations has only recently been faced squarely. Such international regulation would encompass legal codes dealing with business ethics, fair trade practices, product quality standards, patents and trademarks, and antitrust matters. An "international companies law" has been suggested as one means of denationalizing the multinational business enterprise and subjecting it to regulation by a supranational authority.[132] The arbitration system of the ICC might very well be expanded, and might also be placed under the authority of whatever supranational regulatory body is established.[133] Whether the settlement of future transnational industrial and labor-management disputes by arbitration should be compulsory is an immensely problematic issue, but so is the forbidding specter of labor strikes and other disputes on a regional or global scale.

Finally, the problem of international protection of consumer welfare must also be mentioned. Standards of product quality are not always adequate safeguards for consumer well-being. Conceivably, some kind of supranational consumer protection organization may be created—perhaps growing out of organizations like the International Co-Operative Alliance [134]—with procedures permitting individual and collective recourse against the corporations concerned.

The major question underlying this possible future is, of course, how such regulatory structures are to be established. The consent and cooperation of governments, whether directly in a multilateral treaty or indirectly by a delegation of power to some international organization such as the ILO, remain necessary. The answer is unknown at this juncture. Transnational movements and economic organizations, however, can serve to create the enlightened public opinion required before even the initial steps can be taken.

[131] See Clive M. Schmitthoff, "International Business Law: A New Law Merchant," in R. St. J. MacDonald, ed., *Current Law and Social Problems* (Toronto 1961), II, 129-53; and Peter Hay, "The United States and the International Unification of Law: The Tenth Session of the Hague Conferences," in Wayne R. LaFave and Peter Hay, eds., *International Trade, Investment, and Organization* (Urbana 1957), 426-77.

[132] See Ball (fn. 4). See also Raffaello Fornasier, "Toward a European Company," *Columbia Journal of World Business*, IV (Sept.–Oct. 1969), 51-57.

[133] See Louis B. Sohn, "Proposals for the Establishment of A System of International Tribunals," in Martin Domke, ed., *International Trade Arbitration: A Road to World-Wide Cooperation* (New York 1958), 63-76; and Karl-Heinz Böckstiegel, "Arbitration to Disputes between States and Private Enterprises in the International Chamber of Commerce," 59 *American Journal of International Law*, 579-586 (1965).

[134] The International Co-Operative Alliance as founded in 1895 and in general works for consumer protection and welfare through promoting cooperatives. It has 612,282 cooperative societies with 224 million members in 61 countries.

## 4. World Peace

"World peace" is a frustratingly difficult concept to define, but operationally it connotes a world characterized by a mutual tolerance of and peaceful coexistence among different systems of public order, and by a general recourse to pacific means for the settlement of disputes, even fundamental ones. Since the fateful decisions on when to commence war as well as what kind of war to commence remain in the hands of ruling elites of states, the role of transnational movements in seeking world peace is by force of circumstances a peripheral one.

The role of transnational movements has two basic aspects. The first is directly working against a specific application of military force, against war as a means of pursuing national objectives, and against the "military-industrial" complex. The creation of a favorable public opinion and the application of pressure upon the executive establishment and upon parliamentary institutions have been frequently-used tactics. On the other hand, more direct attempts of the Socialist movement to bring a halt to war production failed when national loyalties triumphed over "international proletarianism." Direct attempts to oppose a government's policy also often risk legal proscription.

The second aspect involves creating a global perspective among the world's peoples, a worldwide system of communication and interaction among peoples and a general support for international and transnational structures working to meet the needs of mankind.[135] The effort to extend the control of international law and of international organization over the conduct of ruling elites is a most crucial task, but also an extremely difficult one. The religious movements, especially the Catholic Church, have at times called for the adoption of policies to promote peace, but the ruling elites have usually managed to justify pursuing quite different courses of action. Perhaps the emergence of strong world political parties and even a party system may bring about more effective controls. The peace movement as such, unfortunately, does not have equal access to the ruling elites of the most powerful states. Even if it did, however, its proven inability to persuade certain governmental leaders and other decision-makers of the folly of the national policies being pursued augurs ill for its future effectiveness.

## 5. Supranational Integration

The state-creating movements in Africa and the Middle East, and to a lesser extent in South America, were originally deeply committed to the creation of institutions embodying the profound sense of unity that was felt to imbue the peoples of these regions. This unity, how-

---

[135] See William M. Evan, "Transnational Forums for Peace," in Quincy Wright, ed., *Preventing World War III: Some Proposals* (New York 1962), 393–409.

ever, has tended to survive only in the realms of culture and of political rhetoric. As soon as the states were established, divisive nationalisms arose that have debilitated institutions such as the Arab League and the Organization of African Unity—a turn of events not entirely unexpected, since the tasks of modernization and national integration remain for all these societies.

The state-creating movements and their various transnational associations can nurture perspectives and structures that will constitute the foundations for more extensive future international cooperation.. They may even be able to achieve eventual supranational integration along functional bases. Yet these same movements can also be used for more provincial political ends, and this is a real danger that may finally destroy even the limited effectiveness of such movements.[136]

## CONCLUSIONS

This essay has sought to show how transnational movements and structures have not only shaped the international legal order but also altered the social order underlying the legal order. Two concluding observations arise from this discussion.

To contend that in the present era the state is an anachronistic form of social organization is merely to reiterate the obvious. The existence of varied and flourishing transnational movements and structures itself reveals this. Yet this analysis has also exposed some of the immense complexities, not often considered, with which the future legal order must deal. The necessary international regulation of certain aspects of transnational movements and structures can only be effectively accomplished by some form of adequately empowered supranational authority. The discussion has also adumbrated the kind of international and supranational organizational and legal structure that will be required in the future. Even more problematic is the question of who or what body is to determine what policy goals these structures still to be created will pursue. The traditional diplomatic conference may be able to set up the initial structures. But the need for frequent policy decisions necessitates regulatory structures empowered to make and to implement decisions, similar to the High Authority of the European Coal and Steel Community. This is not to argue that some kind of world government is essential. Conceivably, the United Nations General Assembly may be able to assume some genuine legislative functions within specifically defined areas that would permit it to establish the necessary machinery. Some body, in the final analysis, must assume the basic responsibility.

On a more jurisprudential level, it seems still to be the consensus

136 See Claude Ake, "Pan-Africanism and African Governments," *Review of Politics*, XXVII (Oct. 1965), 532–42.

that individual human beings are not "subjects" of international law; only states and international organizations are. But, in a fundamental sense, international law, like domestic law, is for the welfare of the individual human being. States, after all, are political and legal concepts—albeit very powerful ones—and exist only to the extent that men organize themselves and their interactions in particular patterns, agree in general to this system of order, and enforce a measure of legitimated conformity upon dissident individuals. Transnational movements and structures provide individuals with access to arenas from which they can influence to varying degrees the policies and conduct of states. Until the individual human being becomes a recognized subject of international law, it is almost entirely through transnational structures that he can most effectively avail himself of and participate in the international legal order.

## CHAPTER 15

# The Ecological Viewpoint—and Others

## HAROLD AND MARGARET SPROUT

IN THEIR general introduction in Volume One, the editors stated certain presuppositions that guided their planning of this inquiry on the future of the international legal order. They said, in part:

> A serious concern with the future of the international legal order needs to begin with a clear distinction between what is feasible and what is desirable. It is in the spirit of delimiting the domain of what is feasible that we find that the sovereign state is here to stay for the rest of the century. More specifically, states will retain predominant command over human loyalties and physical resources in the period that we propose to deal with. A world of sovereign states also implies a complex set of relationships involving conflict, competition, and cooperation. The competitive element in international life pervasively threatens to erupt into violence.

The editors also explicitly recognized that "it may well be that no decentralized system of international order, even if reformed in several respects, is capable of meeting the emerging challenges posed by political change, weapons of mass destruction, over-population, pollution, and resource depletion. Nevertheless, we are skeptical about building public and elite attitudes and incentives that would be needed to induce national governments to merge their sovereignty and create a single world state in the near future." [1]

Only time can tell whether this assessment was substantially correct: whether in the final quarter of the twentieth century the sovereign-state system was in fact as durable and resistant to change as it appeared upon the surface to be, or whether the system was gradually and subtly evolving toward something that, in retrospect, would appear to be significantly different in structure and mode of operation. Even if the state system survived the next quarter-century pretty much intact, it was difficult to find firm grounds in the early 1970's for predicting that functional cooperation would, or would not, expand to cope effectively with rising threats to human welfare and even survival. And it was just as speculative whether the epitaph for the twentieth century would be, in the often quoted words of Thomas Hobbes: "no arts; no letters; no society; and which is worst of all, continual

[1] R. A. Falk and C. E. Black, eds., *The Future of the International Legal Order: Trends and Patterns* (Princeton 1969), I, vii–viii.

fear and danger of violent death; and the life of man, solitary, poor, nasty, brutish, and short."[2]

Conjectures regarding the future state of the human condition vary widely these days, as they always must in periods of revolutionary flux and turmoil, transition and transformation. Expectations, in this as in other sectors of human affairs, depend at least in part upon the viewing point and presuppositions of the observer. For example, any image of the future international order, informed by the technocratic perspective, must inevitably differ radically from an image informed by a genuine ecological perspective. It seems to us to be one of the virtues of the latter, the perspective from which we approach the "structure of the international environment," that it directs attention so explicitly to forces and trends working toward a more viable international order as well as to formidable obstacles that must be overcome along the way.

## THE ECOLOGICAL VIEWPOINT AND MODE OF INQUIRY

We are often asked what an ecological approach entails, and how it differs from other viewpoints and approaches. These questions are sometimes accompanied by the suggestion that human ecology is simply a fashionable new label for social science.

Such reactions are perfectly understandable in the light of the current fad for ecological terms and modes of speaking. More often than not, it appears that the adjective "ecological" has simply displaced the older adjective "environmental." Concepts of environment and of environmental relationships are elements of an ecological frame of thinking; but ecology is not synonymous with environmentalism, and includes much besides the idea of environmental relationships.

From earliest recorded history, men have been speculating about the ways in which their lives and fortunes are affected by conditions prevailing upon the earth. Philosophers and historians have attributed the rise and decline of civilizations and empires, and of hegemonies and other regimes of power and influence, to the geographic layout of lands and seas, to variations of climate, to the distribution of fertile land and minerals, to periodic famines and epidemics, to other natural catastrophes, to technological innovations, to forms of political rule, to corruption and mismanagement, and to other environing conditions and events. Indeed, some idea of environment, and some theory of human relations to environment, are implicit, even when not explicit, in every serious discussion of human affairs.

Propositions regarding the quality of life achievable in particular environments, propositions regarding the ways by which individuals

[2] Michael Oakshott, ed., *Leviathan* (Oxford 1946), Pt. 1, Chap. 13, 82.

and communities adapt to environing conditions, or try to modify these, and (in the specific context of international relations) propositions regarding the effects of these interactions on the vitality of political communities and on the distribution of power and influence over the earth, are plainly among the central concerns of an ecological viewpoint and mode of inquiry and analysis.

There is a pervasive tendency, we repeat, to assume that this is all that such an approach entails. But that is a mistake. The ecological perspective embraces something important and distinctive in addition: a distinctive "way of seeing." [3] It is this distinctive way of seeing—and of comprehending—that brings to the study of international order a relevant and fruitful new dimension under conditions prevailing in the final quarter of the twentieth century.

Anticipating ideas to be examined further in a moment, the ecological way of seeing and comprehending envisages, in the context of international relations, a system of relationships among interdependent, earth-related human communities that share with one another an increasingly crowded planet that offers finite and exhaustible quantities of basic essentials of human existence and well-being. Despite an appearance of abundance in a few favored countries, food and other essentials are chronically in short supply in many more countries, and the earth as a whole is being denuded, depleted, and polluted at a rising rate that portends, unless arrested and reversed, a progressively degraded future for most of mankind, if not a terminal catastrophe for all.

Ecologically focused thinking takes off from the following simple proposition: some organism, or population of organisms, is conceived to be surrounded, or encompassed—that is to say, environed—by some set of conditions in ways that are judged to be significant for the present and future of the individual or population in question.

The focus is neither on the behavior and/or state of the individual or population per se; nor on the properties of the environment per se. The focus is on individual or population interacting with the environment in describable patterns called ecological chains.

The most elemental, or basic, of these is the chain-of-life. Plants transform energy received from the sun by the process called photosynthesis: this process releases free oxygen into the atmosphere and into water, converts nonliving matter into chemicals that sustain the plants, and provides food for animals that consume the plants, which in turn provide food for other animals—all of which (plants and animals) eventually die and are decomposed by microorganisms that

[3] The quoted phrase is from Paul Shepard's introductory essay, "Ecology and Man," in the collection of ecological writings, Shepard and Daniel McKinly, eds., *The Subversive Science* (Boston 1969).

transform the dead tissues into nutrient forms that sustain other plants and animals, and thus continue the chain-of-life.[4]

Hypothetically, these processes can continue indefinitely, provided (1) enough but not too much energy continues to be received from the sun, and (2) enough of the nutrient elements derived directly or indirectly from the earth are recycled into forms capable of reuse by plants and animals, including humans.

Failure of either condition could terminate life upon the earth. Such a failure could be sudden and cataclysmic, as might occur if a cosmic catastrophe in the sun should drastically reduce or increase the amount of energy transmitted to the earth. Or failure might be progressive and gradual from various causes. One possibility is that progressive pollution of the oceans (where a large part of photosynthesis occurs) might break the chain-of-life at its source. Another possibility is that progressive destruction of land and water vegetation, increase of population, burning of fossil fuels, and other events might (in the aggregate) so alter the composition of the atmosphere as to reduce critically the quantity of energy received from the sun. Ecologists are identifying many adverse possibilities that are active or latent in our deteriorating environment. Complex interrelated trends, that may portend a state of the earth progressively less congenial for human welfare and even survival, constitute the essence of what ecologists envisage when they assert that we are deep in a spreading and worsening ecological crisis.

A corollary of the chain-of-life is the linkage of all life processes to the physical earth and atmosphere. In the words of biologist René Dubos, "we are bound to the earth's crust, drawing breath from its shallow envelope of air, using and re-using its limited supply of water. . . ." Dubos continues:

> The fact that modern man is now moving into nonterrestrial environments might . . . be interpreted as evidence that he has escaped from the bondage of his evolutionary past, and is becoming independent of his ancient biological attributes. But this is an erroneous interpretation. The human body and brain have not changed significantly during the past 100,000 years and there is no ground for belief that they will change appreciably in the foreseeable future. The biological needs of modern man as well as his biological capabilities and limitations are essentially the same as those of the paleolithic hunter and the neolithic farmer. Civilization provides man with techniques that greatly enlarge the scope of his

---

[4] See, for example, E. J. Kormondy, *Concepts of Ecology* (Englewood Cliffs, N.J. 1969), or E. P. Odum, *Ecology* (New York 1963).

activities, but it does not change his fundamental character. Wherever he goes and whatever he does . . . man must maintain around himself a microenvironment similar to the one under which he evolved. . . .[5]

If there are no credible grounds for expecting that future scientists and engineers can liberate the human species from bondage to the earth for biological life-support, then it must follow, of course, that the fate of our species as well as the quality of human life will continue to depend on conditions prevailing upon our planet.

## MAN AND THE EARTH: SOME ELEMENTAL REALITIES

Salient in the ecological mode of thinking are certain elemental realities of the earth and of human relationships to the earth. One of these, previously noted, is the finite quantity of each and every material essential to human existence—excepting possibly energy received directly from the sun, or derived from the fusion of light atoms. The amounts of these earth materials vary widely. Until recently, some of the basic essentials were assumed to be inexhaustible. But we are learning that this is not so. Even the "free oxygen" in the air we breathe might become insufficient within a few generations at the present rising rate of depletion by fixation into $CO_2$ and other oxides. This is already happening in countless lakes and rivers, where reduction of free oxygen dissolved in water is destroying fish and other marine life.

Another earth reality is the essential global unity of the great natural carriers—atmosphere and seawater. What is discharged into the air over Nevada, or Sinkiang, or Siberia, or anywhere else spreads over larger areas, sometimes over the entire earth. The global circulation of seawater is less rapid, and possibly less globally complete, but materials put into the oceans and connecting seas are likely to show up hundreds or thousands of miles away.

A third earth reality is the uneven distribution of phenomena over the earth surface. For example, arable land, rainfall, fossil fuels, high-yield minerals, and other "natural resources" are (or have been) relatively abundant in some parts of the world, while absent or scarce in others. Uneven distribution also characterizes the knowledge, equipment, and skills that have enabled some societies to prosper and dominate, while others have lagged and languished.

Though regionally uneven, the total volume of knowledge, especially science-based engineering technology, has been, and still is, expanding at a phenomenal rate in the world as a whole. It is estimated that

[5] From a lecture entitled "The Human Landscape," delivered by René Dubos at the Department of State, December 9, 1968.

80–90 percent of all scientists who have ever lived are alive today. Various indicators suggest that scientific knowledge and technological capabilities have been doubling every fifteen years or so since the mid-1600's.[6] Nearly as significant from the standpoint of future international order is the geographical concentration of knowledge and technology, to date predominantly in North America, Europe and the Soviet Union.

This globally immense, but regionally uneven, expansion of scientific knowledge and engineering technology correlates quite closely with the process we now call modernization. A universal element of modernization has been the progressive substitution of inanimate forms of energy for human and animal muscles, and the consequent exponential increase of productivity through multiplication of power-driven machines. This process has raised proportionally the demand for earth materials, thereby accelerating denudation and depletion of our natural endowment.

Another by-product of the expansion of knowledge and the growth of economic productivity has been the concomitant exponential growth of population. More people are living longer, even in those parts of the world least directly affected by the technological revolution. Taking the world as a whole, the number of people is currently doubling every two generations or less. Coupled with the destructive propensities of the human animal, such an increase of population speeds up pollution and denudation, making the earth progressively less healthful and less safe.

For these and other reasons to be considered later, we are deep in a spreading environmental crisis. It is a crisis in the sense that only radical changes in human values, attitudes, economic practices, and styles of living, accompanied by massive changes in the allocation of goods and services, and concerted international as well as national action of a scope and on a scale only dimly imagined as yet, will be required if the earth is to continue to be a congenial habitat for its human population. Thus, to the terminal threat of nuclear war, one must add the comparably somber potentiality of progressive unchecked piecemeal depletion, denudation, and pollution of the human habitat.

## COMMUNITY AND ECOSYSTEM

Central to the ecological mode of seeing and comprehending is the concept of an interrelated whole. This concept is expressed at rising levels of abstraction by such terms as biotic community, web-of-life, ecological complex, and ecosystem. In the idiom of environmental biology (from which these terms come), a population of organisms liv-

[6] D. de S. Price, *Little Science, Big Science* (New York 1963), Chap. 1.

ing within a specified geographic space constitutes a biotic community. The complex of things within that space, living and nonliving, to which that population's subsistence and survival are linked, constitutes its habitat—a near synonym for environment but with stronger territorial connotations. Habitat and population, viewed as an interrelated whole, constitute an ecosystem.[7]

Dubos (previously quoted) applies this integrative concept to human affairs as follows: "The most pressing problems of humanity . . . involve relationships, communications, changes of trends—in other words, situations in which systems must be studied as a whole, in all the complexity of their interactions. This is particularly true of human life. When life is considered only in its specialized functions, the outcome is a world emptied of meaning. To be fully relevant to life, science must deal with the responses of the total organism to the total environment."[8]

Dubos is speaking specifically of individuals. But the same ecological bias against excessive analytic reductionism applies equally to communities of individuals. This point is made explicit by another well-known ecologist, Barry Commoner, who contends that a complex living system cannot be understood "simply by looking at the properties of its isolated parts."[9]

Viewing human complexes as interrelated wholes directs attention to side-effects, by-products, and chains of interactions that flow from particular courses of action. It contrasts strongly with the narrow technocratic, or engineering, perspective that focuses on discrete tasks (for example, building faster automobiles, or more lethal weapons), with insufficient regard to the side-effects that may ramify throughout a political community, larger region, or the world as a whole.

Narrow tunnel-like focus is characteristic of international statecraft, in which parochial conceptions of national interest nearly always take precedence over the welfare or survival of other nations. It is evident, for example, in the current savage struggle to preempt large areas of the international oceans, in ruthless aggressions of the strong against

---

[7] This integrative concept is expressed in various ways. The British ecologist, W. H. Pearsall, says for example: "The environment . . . is not merely the place where the animal lives, but the whole association of factors, inert and living, of which the organism is a part." *Chambers' Encyclopedia* (New York 1967), IV, 758. Marston Bates, American ecologist, puts it as follows: "Environment may be defined as the sum of all factors or conditions acting on an organism or community of organisms. It is thus a very complex concept, and any analysis into single factors or groups of factors is apt to be both difficult and misleading." *Collier's Encyclopedia* (New York 1965), VIII, 516.

[8] René Dubos, *So Human an Animal* (New York 1968), 27.

[9] Barry Commoner, "Development in the Poor Nations: How to Avoid Fouling the Nest," *Science* (March 7, 1969).

the weak, and in other operations conducted with little or no regard for ramifying consequences for the human condition as a whole.

The integrative concept of an ecological complex, or community, or system, is analogous to the gestalt idea of personality, to the geographic concept of region, and to holistic concepts in historiography, anthropology, sociology, and other special fields. All such integrative concepts are susceptible of reification, the attribution of material substance to abstracted patterns. Ecologists, like nearly everyone else, are prone to reify abstractions—and sometimes to clothe them in a mystical overlay in addition. However, if care is taken to avoid these pervasive vices, the concept of ecosystem, adapted from environmental biology, can be fruitfully applied to a great variety of human complexes, including some that are vast in size and rudimentary or amorphous in institutional structure. In this broad sense, one can (and we shall) speak of a world community, and envisage it as an ecosystem.

Social scientists often, perhaps generally, envisage a community as a population living in a specific geographic area, and exhibiting substantial self-awareness of common identity and concerns. In other contexts, however, community may denote simply a population whose members are observed to be interrelated with one another and with their habitat in ways that are judged to be significant to the population's well-being or survival.

In the first instance, psychic self-awareness is the essence of the concept; if absent, no community exists. In the second, such self-awareness is not essential. Significant interrelatedness is the essential condition. This is substantially the sense in which environmental biologists appear to conceive of an ecological community, or ecosystem.

The distinction here is between cognition of interrelatedness and condition of interrelatedness. From the ecological perspective, the latter is always significant; the former may be, but not necessarily. That is to say, if events within Country A affect behavior or the conditions of life in Country B, the two populations are manifestly interrelated, and may (from an ecological viewpoint) constitute a community, or elements of a larger community, irrespective of whether their members recognize this to be so.

Of course a sense of community, or at least self-awareness of interrelatedness and resulting mutual concerns, may be an essential condition of achieving effective action to deal with the consequences of interrelatedness. But, we repeat, it is the condition of interrelatedness that justifies, from the ecological perspective, the judgment that an ecosystem exists, even in the absence of widespread internal recognition thereof.

The secular trend toward ever-expanding mastery over nature has entailed a corresponding growth of interrelatedness. This derives in part from the progressive specialization that inevitably accompanies the development of more efficient machines and processes. It derives also from the greater mobility of people, goods, and ideas. The ancient Chinese and Roman empires could coexist for several centuries with only intermittent and superficial contacts and no significant collisions. Communities in the Americas lived for centuries in even greater isolation. But the explosive expansion of Europeans overseas, from about the middle of the fifteenth century, progressively overcame the previous insulation of empires and regions.

Interrelatedness has become the predominant characteristic of our era. It is especially evident in unanticipated and undesired side-effects of all kinds of undertakings. The makers and users of motor vehicles, for example, do not desire or intend to pollute the atmosphere and produce scarcely tolerable congestion in the cities and along the highways—but these conditions are nonetheless by-products of the mobility that modern Americans and others value so highly.

Moreover, interrelatedness is no respecter of sovereignty and jurisdictional boundaries. American and Russian scientists and engineers who tested the early hydrogen bombs manifestly did not intend to poison the atmosphere of other countries—but that was what occurred in varying degrees throughout the world. Americans clearly have not intended, as a rule, to instigate discontent when they travel over the earth and reside in foreign countries—but the psychological impact of their comparative affluence has not been less disruptive because unintended.

The ecological principle here is as simple as its operation is inexorable  Any substantial change in one sector of an ecosystem is nearly certain to produce significant, often unsettling, sometimes severely disruptive consequences in other sectors. With few exceptions, the secular trend has been for effects to diffuse over larger areas—for effects that would once have remained purely local to become regional or global.

A corollary of this principle is the growing irrelevance, from an ecological standpoint, of the historic separation of domestic and foreign affairs. This separation, sanctified in the venerable legal doctrine of exclusive national jurisdiction over "domestic questions," is further buttressed by the archaic conception of the nation-state as a discrete entity with an existence, set of goals and imperatives, code of behavior, and personality and will, that transcend the human individuals from whom the state organization is derived and for whose welfare it presumably exists.

Numerous epigrams, as well as other evidence, indicate some awareness of transnational interrelatedness and its implications: for example, "the United States cannot long survive as an island of affluence in an ocean of want"; "war anywhere is a threat to peace every-where"; "the ultimate meaning of the nuclear era is one world, or none."

However, viewed in the large, there is very little firm evidence that a sense of community, extending beyond the national polity, is spread-ing. But that does not affect in the slightest the empirical reality of the condition of interrelatedness that characterizes larger regions, and increasingly characterizes the world as a whole. In this sense, we re-peat, the earth and its population are becoming, if indeed they have not already become, a single ecosystem, the component elements of which become more complexly and more tightly interdependent with every passing year.

### ECOLOGICAL RELATIONSHIPS

Elsewhere we have examined in some detail the various ways in which the relational links of a human community, or ecosystem, can be explained and predicted.[10] Here we confine the discussion to cer-tain general aspects of such relationships: in particular, aspects of special relevance to the study of the international order.

Explanations of ecological relationships, and assessments of their significance, are derived from two sets of factors: (1) factors of en-vironment, and (2) attributes of the environed organism or popula-tion, hereafter called entity attributes. More precisely, such explana-tions and assessments are derived from some combination of environ-mental factors and entity attributes.

Suppose, for example, that a farmer plants a lemon orchard in Min-nesota. Winter comes, and the trees die. One observer says that the severe frost (an environmental factor) killed the trees. Another says that the trees died because of their limited tolerance for frost (an entity-attribute). Both explanations are correct, but incomplete. This is so because it is not merely the one or the other but the combination of entity attribute and environing condition that explains the event. This principle applies just as strictly and consistently to human indi-viduals and populations as to lemon trees.

An important corollary is entailed in this proposition: if there is substantial change in either part of the combination—in the attributes of the entity (or entities), or in the environment—a different state of affairs emerges. Changes of either kind are relevant, and may be criti-cally significant for the individual or population concerned, and/or for the future state of the environment.

Put in other words, an ecological approach directs attention ex-plicitly to the implications and consequences of all kinds of changes—

10 See our *Ecological Perspective on Human Affairs* (Princeton 1965); also chapters 2 and 9 of our *Toward a Politics of the Planet Earth* (New York 1971).

innovations, trends, transformations—both changes in the environment (for example, consumption or destruction of natural resources, pollution of air, water, soil and food, increase of noise, deterioration of buildings and public transport, etc.), and changes in the environed population (for example, increase in numbers, changes in health and vitality, in knowledge and skills, political awareness, etc.).

### CONCEPTS OF ENVIRONMENT

The term "environment" carries a standard core of meaning, as previously indicated. However, biologists, psychologists, sociologists, anthropologists, geographers, political scientists, and other specialists have redefined and varied the concept to suit their needs. The result is a semantic chaos beyond anyone's ability to resolve in a manner acceptable to all.[11]

There is a persistent tendency, especially strong in America, to think of environment in purely nonhuman terms that is, the "natural landscape," together with such man-made changes in it as might persist for a time if the human inhabitants were removed. This way of conceiving environment is too restrictive, since a wide variety of social conditions, intangible as well as tangible, affect individuals and populations.

For example, we are members of a university community. The university environment to which our behavior and achievements are relatable includes libraries, laboratories, lecture halls, classrooms, offices, and other nonhuman structures. But this is a small part of our total university environment, which also includes the trustees and officers of administration, faculty colleagues, students, secretaries, librarians, research technicians, patterns of interpersonal relationships, and many other conditions to which our lives are related. Precisely analogous things can be said about any other human ecosystem: family, church, business firm, government, the national community, or the world community as a whole.

Since the ecological perspective encompasses human as well as nonhuman, social as well as nonsocial, environing conditions, we need a

[11] The following specimens illustrate the semantic chaos which has grown up around the concept of environment: natural environment, nonsocial environment, physical environment, nonhuman enviroment, geographic environment, social environment, cultural environment, ecological environment, preperceptual environment, nonpsychological environment, objective environment, subjective environment, behavioral environment, psychological environment, life space, and still other technical terms. In some instances the same term stands for widely different referents in different technical vocabularies, and sometimes even within the same vocabulary. No one has straightened out this semantic jungle satisfactorily. We tried, without much success, in our *Man-Milieu Relationship Hypotheses in the Contest of International Politics* (Princeton Center of International Studies 1956) 11ff. We have come to doubt whether further work along this line is worth anyone's effort.

term that circumvents the restrictive conventional connotations of the word environment. Such a term is the French word milieu, which carries stronger social connotations than the English word environment. As a term of most general reference, milieu includes social as well as nonhuman phenomena to which human behavior and achievements may be related. Such usage frees the word environment for the narrower concept—land, air, water, subhuman organisms, and other nonhuman phenomena—which is in accord with standard American usage.

## ENTITY-ATTRIBUTES

In the study of human populations, genetic characters are usually treated as a set of constant parameters that are rarely even mentioned. This practice may not be justifiable much longer. Release of radioactive and other pollutants into soil, water, and atmosphere opens the possibility of more frequent consequential human mutations. To this possibility one must add biological experiments that envisage deliberate modification of hereditary characters. Such developments would manifestly enlarge one's concern with the genetic dimensions of human ecology.

Even as things now stand, heredity in the human species may be more significant than is generally assumed. For instance, humans everywhere exhibit a common core of biological needs. They require an atmosphere with sufficient free oxygen, and constant access to relatively pure water. They can survive only within a fairly narrow range of thermal variation. They have imperative requirements for certain nutrients, and little or no tolerance for a long list of chemical elements and compounds. Major changes in the environment—for example, progressive depletion of free oxygen in the atmosphere—could render the earth increasingly less congenial to the human species, and might even destroy its habitability altogether.

Relatively less adverse conditions can have severe consequences for individuals, even for entire populations. Take, for example, the significance of malnutrition. It is well confirmed that malnourished infants, especially those deprived of sufficient good-quality protein during the first six months or so after birth, are likely to suffer permanent neural damage, with mental impairment for life. It has been estimated that "as many as two-thirds of the children of most developing countries are now suffering from some degree of malnutrition." [12]

Commenting on the social significance of severe malnutrition, René Dubos says that: "Physical and mental apathy and other manifestations of indolence have long been assumed to have racial or climatic

[12] A. D. Berg, "Malnutrition and National Development," *Foreign Affairs*, XLVI (1967), 126.

origin. But in reality these behavioral traits are often a form of physiological adjustment to malnutrition. . . . Populations deprived during early life commonly exhibit little resistance to stress. They escape disease only as long as little effort is required of them and find it impossible to initiate and prosecute the long-range programs that would improve their economic status. They are prisoners of their nutritional past." [13]

If this assessment is correct, it carries manifest implications for future international relations. What is depicted is a vicious circle of malnutrition contributing to partial disability contributing to mediocre achievement contributing to continued malnutrition. Implicit is the question whether societies so handicapped can ever break out of the cycle without drastic reduction of population growth and infusions of food and capital from abroad.

Other pathological conditions may impose comparable, if not always as permanent ceilings on achievement. Individuals infested with worms or other parasites do not die immediately as a rule. Much the same is true of most victims of tuberculosis and other debilitating diseases. But capacity for achievement may be severely diminished nontheless. When such pathological conditions afflict entire populations, or large segments thereof, especially when the damage is magnified by concomitant malnutrition, the debilitating effect on the whole society may be disastrous.

Capacity for achievement also varies with the kinds and qualities of learned skills available within the society. These are transmitted socially from generation to generation, with each adding its own creative increments to an expanding cultural aggregate. Since human relationships depend heavily upon the relative capabilities of the interacting individuals or populations, the knowledge and skills that contribute to capabilities are manifestly relevant data for the better understanding of human affairs in any context.

The conclusion that emerges at this point is that human attributes as well as environing conditions—more precisely the combination of attributes and environment—have a bearing on patterns of power and influence, on the processes of modernization, on attitudes of the poor and afflicted toward the rich and affluent, and vice versa, and hence on the character of the international order.

## From Adaptation to Manipulation to Crisis

With reference to subhuman species, the general hypothesis of organism-environment relationship is adaptation. Organisms adapt (that is, they conform or accommodate) to environing conditions, or they

13 Dubos (fn. 8), 87.

fail to survive, or at least to flourish. Applied to the human species, this hypothesis itself requires adaptation.

This necessity arises from the far greater ability of even the most primitive humans to modify environing conditions. This human capacity has tended everywhere to enlarge, despite occasional setbacks from natural disasters or other causes. Expressed in general terms, the trend of human history has been from a condition of necessity to conform, in order to survive, toward ever-enlarging capacity to modify and manipulate environing conditions and events.

For tens of thousands of years, progress in this direction was painfully slow and recurrently interrupted. Severely limited power over large sectors of the environment (for example, control of disease) was painfully evident, even in the most technically advanced societies, until well into the twentieth century. But by then a radical transformation was well under way, a transformation that appears in retrospect as a major historical discontinuity.

The transition from necessity to conform to rising ability to modify and control has been, as is well known, largely a function of the advancement of knowledge, especially the developing linkage between theoretical science and engineering technology. Concurrently, human attitudes toward nature became increasingly exploitive, and human activities increasingly destructive of the physical earth and its subhuman inhabitants.

The idea of Nature as a heap of plunder to be possessed and consumed without thought for the future can be traced to numerous sources. Biblical passages and theological doctrines are cited to identify it with the Judeo-Christian ethic—in particular, the injunction to man in the book of Genesis to "subdue" the earth and "have dominion . . . over every living thing" upon it. The historian Lynn White, Jr., concludes that ". . . the present increasing disruption of the global environment . . . cannot be understood historically apart from distinctive attitudes toward nature which are deeply grounded in Christian dogma. The fact that most people do not think of these attitudes as Christian is irrelevant. . . . Both our present science and our present technology are so tinctured with orthodox Christian arrogance toward nature that no solution for our ecologic crisis can be expected from them alone." [14]

Prominent theologians concur. For example, in 1970, a conference of Protestant theological scholars "agreed that the traditional Chris-

[14] Lynn White, Jr., "The Historical Roots of our Ecologic Crisis," *Science* (March 10, 1967), reprinted in Garrett de Bell, ed., *The Environmental Handbook* (New York 1970). See also C. J. Glacken, "Changing Ideas of the Habitable World," in W. L. Thomas, Jr., ed., *Man's Role in Changing the Face of the Earth* (Chicago 1956), 70.

tian attitude toward nature had given sanction to exploitation of the environment by science and technology and thus contributed to air and water pollution, overpopulation and other ecological threats." [15]

The late nineteenth-century philosophy of pragmatism explicitly rationalized the exploitive science-based technology that gave human societies progressively greater mastery over Nature. In contrast to "deterministic philosophy . . . pragmatism looked upon the environment as something that could be manipulated. . . . As [Herbert] Spencer had stood for . . . control of man by the environment, the pragmatists stood for freedom and control of the environment by man." [16] In the caustic epigram of the American geographer Isaiah Bowman, "most men take the view that the world is their oyster. They are out for conquest." [17]

This attitude is as pervasive today as when Bowman composed the epigram in the early 1930's. It is evident in callous destructive attitudes and behavior toward the earth and its subhuman inhabitants, typically most ruthless where the capacity to exploit is greatest. This attitude toward nature inspires the endless stream of fanciful scenarios that predict technological miracles by which future generations will remake the earth to suit their purposes. Implicit in such scenarios is unlimited faith in human ability to go on exploiting the earth, overcoming or circumventing the restraints that shackled previous generations, and ignoring with impunity the progressive denudation of the landscape, destruction of wildlife, depletion of high-yield natural resources, and worsening pollution of air, water, and land.

From the ecological perspective, this image of the future is unrealistic, to say the least. It contrasts in every respect with the view that human populations, including those individuals who innovate, lead, and rule, are all parts of complex living systems, inescapably dependent upon the finite earth for present well-being and future survival.

This way of viewing the human condition need not denigrate in the slightest the achievements of science and technology. Nor does it minimize the consequences of the transforming trends discernible in nearly all sectors of human society. Nor, indeed, need one deplore the prospect of continuing expansion of knowledge and increasingly sophisticated tools and processes. Unless nuclear war or other overwhelming catastrophe abruptly terminates human life altogether, it seems likely that continuing technological innovation will transform the next quar-

15 As reported by E. B. Fiske, *New York Times,* May 1, 1970.

16 Richard Hofstadter, *Social Darwinism in American Thought* (New York 1955), 123–24.

17 Isaiah Bowman, *Geography in Relation to the Social Sciences* (New York 1934), 7.

ter-century at least as much as it has changed the past half-century.

No perspective could alert one more explicitly to the constructive as well as destructive, liberating as well as imprisoning, effects and potentialities of innovative technology. But, as stated at the outset, the ecological perspective finds no credible ground whatever for the arrogant technocratic expectation that science and engineering can enable mankind to escape from the finite and exhaustible essentials of his earthbound existence.

The exponential growth of population, itself a by-product of advancing technology, adds severity and urgency to the spreading and worsening erosion of the human habitat. Not only have more populations acquired more efficient tools wherewith to exploit the earth and its subhuman inhabitants; there are ever more humans to do the exploiting, and in the process to deplete the nonhuman environment, to accumulate rising mountains of debris, to poison soil, water, and air, and otherwise to degrade their habitat.

Stated more generally, the greater the concentration of population, and/or the higher the level of industrial technology available to a population, the more extensive has been the environmental deterioration. The resulting state of affairs in some of the richest societies, above all in the United States, can be characterized as a condition of affluent squalor. It is a condition with many dimensions and ramifications. At the political level, it is a crisis in the sense that it challenges long-standing values and priorities, and will require vast changes in the allocation of resources, to check the drift towards the final phase of the secular trend—from adaptive accommodation to manipulative exploitation to progressive despoliation to eventual catastrophe, a catastrophe, eminent ecologists warn us, that would be worldwide in scope and possibly as terminal in its human impact as a full-blown war fought with thermonuclear weapons.

### ELEMENTS AND ASPECTS OF THE ECOLOGICAL CRISIS

The spreading ecological crisis is a complex phenomenon, exceedingly difficult to comprehend and assess. It is a complicated mixture of conditions and trends, interrelated in ways that are sometimes self-evident but often obscure. It is a compound of subjective impressions and objective realities. Local and/or topical problems are often approached and handled without sufficient regard for their broader context and implications. Any analytic device that helps to identify and delineate problems, and to grasp their elements and dimensions, should be useful at the present stage, which is still more exploratory than operational. Figure A suggests one possibly helpful device for this purpose.

FIG. A

ECOLOGICAL EFFECTS

| | diagnostic aspects | | | | | technical aspects | | political aspects | | | |
|---|---|---|---|---|---|---|---|---|---|---|---|
| types of adverse effects observed or predicted → & implications of preventive or remedial actions ↑ | attributed cause of observed or predicted adverse effect: agent or process | severity of effect observed or predicted | whether & at what point irreversible in present state of knowledge | population (human or other) affected | geographical area involved | technically feasible solutions, if any, in present state of knowledge | relative costs of feasible solutions | political jurisdictions & institutions available | available & feasible modes of operation | allocation of costs: who pays & how much | impact of costs on other values |
| esthetic effects: inconvenience, nuisance, otherwise offensive | | | | | | | | | | | |
| other behavioral effects | | | | | | | | | | | |
| physio-pathological effects | | | | | | | | | | | |
| genetic effects | | | | | | | | | | | |
| ecosystemic effects: life-support, carrying capacity, habitability | | | | | | | | | | | |

The organizing principle, and some of the categories in Fig. A were suggested by Dr. H. H. Landesberg, of Resources for the Future, Inc. (Washington, D.C.).

Figure A is designed to identify certain important aspects of environmental problems that may arise in any context, but considered here with particular reference to the environmental aspects of international order. The vertical axis differentiates five categories of adverse effects that may be attributed to environmental causes. The horizontal axis formulates some of the questions—diagnostic or situational, technical-engineering, and political-administrative—relevant to deciding what if any preventive or remedial actions can, or should, be undertaken.

Esthetic effects, one type of behavioral effects, are defined here as subjective preferential responses to environing conditions. They are identified by such words as inconvenience, nuisance, dislike, etc. Such responses may be individual and eccentric, or they may be widespread and indicative of substantial consensus. In the latter case, they may become political issues of high priority, irrespective of other considerations.

Physio-pathological effects are adverse in the physical functioning of living organisms, with or without significant anatomical changes. These effects can be diagnosed by means other than (or in addition to) the subjective awareness of the individual(s) concerned. Physiopathological effects cluster around the concepts of health and longevity.

Genetic effects would be mutations transmittable by heredity. So far as we are aware, no recent genetic changes have been confirmed as yet. But adverse genetic mutation *is* definitely within the purview of ecological inquiry, in particular with reference to the discharge of radioactive materials into air, water, and soil.

Ecosystemic effects are changes in the capacity of the earth to support organisms and populations of organisms. Until quite recently virtually no attention was given to this elemental reality in the context of human affairs. It was well understood that imbalance between subhuman populations and their environment could be disastrous. But, with very few exceptions, students of human affairs simply took for granted that the "carrying capacity" of the earth was ample to accommodate any foreseeable human population. Warnings that the human species was crowding "the limits of the earth" were received with skepticism and derision, or simply ignored altogether.[18] Such attitudes are still prevalent in all countries. But within the United States and a few other countries, it is beginning to be appreciated that the combination of landscape denudation, natural-resource de-

18 Warnings in the late 1940's that received such treatment included those by Fairfield Osborn and William Vogt. See Osborn's *Our Plundered Planet* (Boston 1948), and *The Limits of the Earth* (Boston 1953). Also Vogt's *Road to Survival* (New York 1948).

pletion, and progressive poisoning of air, water, and land is building up to a world wide ecological crisis that threatens every community in every continent.[19]

With respect to any adverse effects, observed or predicted, there may be agreement, disagreement, or ignorance as to the causative agent or process. However, knowledge is rapidly accumulating with regard to the psychic, physiological, and ecosystemic effects of discharging noxious wastes into waterways, into the atmosphere, and upon the land, effects of pesticides upon humans as well as wildlife, effects of excessive noise and crowding, and other causative agents and processes.

Comparable variation occurs with regard to assessments of the severity of observed effects, and estimates of the severity of future effects. An especially important aspect of severity is presented by such questions as whether the effect is irreversible in the present state of knowledge; and if not yet irreversible, at what point it is likely to become so.

The population (number of organisms, human or other) adversely affected, and the geographical area involved are manifestly relevant to determination of the severity of effects on the ecosystem as a whole, as well as to decisions on whether and how to act on the premises.

All environmental problems, excepting possibly those that have definitely passed the point of reversibility, pose engineering questions. In the present or prospective state of engineering knowledge, there may be no technically feasible solution; or there may be one or more than one. In the latter case, relative costs of alternative solutions (as well as technical feasibility) are relevant data for the policy maker.

The last four "boxes" on the horizontal axis suggest (but by no means exhaust) political questions certain to be posed. What polity (or polities) has (have) jurisdiction to act? What structures of authority are available? What new structures are needed in order to achieve the end in view? What strategies are likely to be acceptable as well as effective? How should the cost be allocated—that is, who is to pay and how much? What will be the impact on other values, especially intangible values such as personal convenience, esthetic preference, individual freedom to choose, and the like?

Figure A, it should be emphasized, is an analytic device for posing questions. It provides no automatic answers. It is designed simply to identify and differentiate the kinds of adverse effects attributed to environmental causes, especially to changing conditions; and also to indicate the kinds of questions likely to be posed by demands for action to remedy or to prevent environmental conditions that are believed to affect human individuals and populations adversely.

[19] See, for example, P. R. and A. H. Ehrlich, *Population, Resources, Environment* (San Francisco 1970).

## Values and Priorities

Ecological values, it must be apparent, have lurked in the wings throughout this discussion. It could scarcely be otherwise. The ecological perspective directs attention explicitly to the effects of advancing technology and other trends on the quality of life sustainable in various kinds of human communities in various settings.

However, it is equally apparent that quality of life, and the related idea, quality of environment, are terms with various meanings. One encounters such expressions as "optimum environment," "maximally desirable environment," "minimally acceptable environment," "environmental deterioration," and the like. None of these terms has been objectively defined; we doubt that it is possible to do so.

Research has identified some of the conditions under which human organisms cannot survive, or at least cannot retain health and vigor. It is also possible to identify at least some of the requisites of a prescribed standard of quality. Whether such a standard is set with reference to subjective preferences, biological health, or to other criteria is often far from clear.

Even greater ambiguity enshrouds the notion of acceptable quality. In some instances, acceptability denotes merely a set of conditions which a population has come to tolerate more or less submissively and mindlessly, irrespective of biological or other systemic effects. In other contexts, acceptable quality denotes the conditions that particular reformers deem to be desirable or imperative, for reasons that may or may not be specified. Sometimes particular esthetic values—for example, getting rid of highway billboards—are linked with health and safety. Just as often, such values are advocated as good per se. More explicit delineation of criteria will plainly be needed if expensive environmental programs are to progress much beyond the stage of exhortation. This seems to us especially so if environmental quality becomes increasingly a subject of international negotiation and action.

The effects attributable to environmental causes (in Fig. A) are relevant only with reference to some set of values to be protected or achieved. This is explicit in the category of esthetic effects, in which subjective preferences are the essence. Underlying values are implicit rather than explicit in the other three categories—physiological, genetic, and ecosystemic effects.

In our view, the most elemental values are associated with health and longevity. In more specifically ecological terms, these values can be summed up as the need to make the earth a reasonably safe and salubrious place to live, not only for a few favored populations but for all mankind through an indefinite future. We do not contend that there is either consensus as to what actions these goals entail, or full agreement among individuals or among different communities as to where these existential values should rank in the ordering of all values. Nor do we minimize the political importance of adverse effects measurable mainly in terms of esthetic or other subjective responses.

We simply assume, on the basis of such evidence as we have seen, that (whatever else may be desired) most people in most countries desire to live long and to be as healthy and fit as possible. To the caveat that these are Western values not fully embraced by non-Western peoples, we would reply that longevity and health are goals nearly everywhere, emergent with the transition from preindustrial to modernized forms of society. We take note of an apparently spreading conviction, at least among life scientists and other informed persons, that existing conditions and trends imperil the attainment of these existential goals even in the most modernized societies, including the United States.

It is true, of course, that only a tiny fraction of the earth's population comes close to attaining the level of health and vigor that has been achieved on the average in the more technologically advanced societies. But the thrust of our argument is that the by-products of advancing technology are already affecting adversely the lives of people, not only where living standards are low to begin with, but even where, as in the United States, material affluence is a loudly-proclaimed achievement.

Much remains to be learned about the ways in which ideas about environmental quality are formed—and re-formed in response to changing conditions. There is plenty of evidence that hundreds of millions of people still tolerate fatalistically a milieu that undermines health and shortens life. There is evidence that even the most "advanced" societies adjust to environmental deterioration; in time most of their members recall only dimly if at all that conditions were ever any better. But even more notable is the massive awakening of ordinary folk, in one society after another, to conditions that are perceived to menace health and to shorten life needlessly.

However defined, ecological values fit into some ordering, or preferential scale, of all values. Ecological values are often subordinated to others: for example, the air traffic industry's subordination of noise abatement and wildlife protection to the need they feel for more capacious and convenient airports; or the high priority that many farmers give to cheap and effective pesticides even at considerable risk to public health; or American public insistence on private motor transport at whatever cost in lethal pollution of the atmosphere.

Prescribed environmental standards tend to reflect complex mixtures of public values. They are public in the sense that their cost is spread more or less widely and their benefits are presumptively available to all or most members of the community. Environmental norms tend also to reflect long-range values, since there is likely to be considerable time-lag before benefits become readily discernible. Moreover, actions to improve environmental quality are apt to curtail both personal freedom and accustomed access to goods and services. Finally, where environments are deeply eroded from long exploitation, abuse, and neglect, as is notoriously the case in many countries, the estimated cost of arrears alone may run to astronomical sums, with the prospect of large continuing outlays for future protection.

For these and other reasons, public authorities in virtually all countries have been chronically tardy in coming to recognize environmental quality as a value of high priority. More often than not, it has required widespread fear of imminent catastrophe, or even experience of catastrophe, to convert exhortation into effective action, with no assurance of adequate follow-through even then. In short, a pervasive feature of the deepening and spreading environmental deterioration is its disruptive impact on long-standing commitments and priorities, and consequently on the allocation of resources within and among sovereign political communities.

## Demands and Resources

Demands for resources to cope with multiple pollutions and destructive exploitations of the earth and of subhuman species coincide with expanding demands from other sectors. These encroach on traditional allocations: in particular on allocations for military defense, military-related commitments, and nonmilitary foreign policies. The dilemma of disposable resources grossly insufficient to meet both standing commitments and new demands and imperatives is becoming a focal issue in numerous countries and is likely to become increasingly so in many others. It should help in coming to an appreciation of the dimensions of this crisis of priorities if one reads the next few pages in the light of the statesmen's dilemma, depicted schematically in Figure B.

This diagram does not present the total allocation picture. It covers only the part that is represented by expenditures of government. For example, in numerous societies including the United States, various social programs are supported in part from public funds (old-age pensions, medical service, subsidized housing, public welfare, and many others), but also in part from private sources. The same is true of education, research, abatement of environmental pollutions, and other objects of public and private expenditure. But it is also true that certain categories are exclusively, or almost exclusively governmental (pay of civil servants and military personnel, provision and maintenance of roads, etc.). The larger the "public sector," the larger is

## FIG. B

### DEMANDS AND RESOURCES—THE STATESMEN'S DILEMMA

social programs (welfare, pensions, poverty, cities, etc.) →←

public authorities at all levels

← military & military-related → commitments & projects

education and research ←→

environmental imperatives (abatement of pollutions, repair of environmental damage, etc.) →←

nonmilitary external commitments & projects (diplomacy, international organizations, grants & loans, etc.) ← →

demands not included in other categories →←

civil government (including law enforcement, tax administration, etc.) ← →

the fraction of the national product that is allocated by governmental action. In any case, the main purpose of this particular diagram is to emphasize the dilemma of allocation directly confronting statesmen.

This dilemma is not new. Public revenues have rarely if ever covered all the purposes envisaged by rulers and their constituents. But in former times the gap between ends and means rarely challenged the allocation of resources to military and other external purposes as sharply as it does today. This is so, in part, because the internal or domestic costs of government were relatively much smaller in traditional societies. The process of modernization, and the social and environmental concomitants of modernization, have run up the internal costs of government and progressively widened the gap between demands and disposable resources. Moreover, in our time, in the case of the United States, the Soviet Union, and a few other states, the costs of military power and of military-related and other external commitments have risen enormously as the sources of perceived threats have multiplied and as military technology has become more and more sophisticated and expensive. Gross insufficiency of disposable resources bedevils the statecraft of all the major powers, and many of the lesser ones too.

The diagram of this dilemma yields no automatic recipe for scholars or statesmen. But it does identify some of the salient elements of an increasingly intractable problem that confronts most governments in one form or another. This intractability derives in part, we repeat, from chronic neglect and abuse of the physical environment. But it derives also from the concurrent politicization of populations and the increasing complexity and vulnerability of modernized societies.

Until quite recent times, most of the population in nearly all countries were undernourished, ill-clothed, poorly housed, illiterate or barely literate, largely immobile and unorganized, ignorant, and politically powerless to improve their miserable condition. It was a condition of virtual servitude, a servitude that prevailed in many countries long after legal slavery was abolished. It was a servitude that more or less rigorously excluded large blocks of the population from effective access to those who ruled in the name of the state of which they were nominally citizens. It was a condition staunchly defended by eminent economists as well as by self-serving entrepreneurs and entrenched aristocrats, defended as an unavoidable if deplorable condition of economic progress.

A different, though no less disabling, servitude was imposed on the non-European subjects of the nineteenth century colonial empires. Colonial servitude expedited the production of foodstuffs and raw materials, and thereby contributed to the rapid industrial development of Europe and societies of European origin in other continents. It helped for a century or more to sustain the colonial empires, and the racist and other myths by which Europeans rationalized and defended their dominion over non-European peoples.

Virtual servitude has long been a notorious concomitant of forced-draft industrialization under Communism; and it is evident in one form or another in many if not most of the modernizing societies today. Even within the richest and most affluent of all societies, the United States, grinding poverty and minimal ability to escape from it are still the lot of millions of nominally free citizens.

However, it is scarcely news any longer that demands for change are pressing hard on rulers nearly everywhere. Common folk, though far from well informed, are becoming increasingly aware of the gap between poor and rich both within their own country and between their own and other countries. Spreading awareness stimulates demands, hesitant at first, then more insistent, and in many instances insatiable and peremptory—and public authorities nearly everywhere are finding it expedient to pay more attention than formerly. In the main, this process has proceeded faster and is more visible in democratic and relatively open societies, but the same forces are at work everywhere and the trend appears to be universal or nearly so.

The rising capacity of ordinary folk, as well as their more affluent fellow-citizens, to make their needs heard and their demands effective, derives in some part from more and better education, from the spread of information by television and other media, and from more effective leadership and organization. But the voices of the lowly gain added strength from quite a different source: the vulnerability of modern urban societies to disaster in case of any prolonged interruption of essential public services.

What this might portend for the future has been fleetingly revealed in London, Paris, New York, and other great cities—by strikes of garbage collectors, postmen, air-controllers, fire-fighters, teachers, and other performers of vital civic services. The possibilities were starkly evident in the chaos produced in a single day by the police strike in Montreal.

Politicians, news media, and affluent citizens generally may protest that strikes in vital services, especially strikes against the government itself, are unpatriotic and intolerable. But these disruptive stoppages keep right on recurring—and there is no indication when they will cease. This is so for the simple and obvious reason that those who perform the services have large backlogs of unsatisfied needs, and in one country after another they are discovering the leverage that they can exert on government and society.

For these and other reasons, we repeat, governments are giving more heed than formerly to the demands of their less-favored constituents. Frequently, from conviction or from expediency, politicians promise more than can be delivered at existing or prospective levels of production and taxation. But, as politicians in a few countries have lately discovered, cutting back social programs, as well as disruption of civic services, can pose threats to the domestic community as grave as those posed by foreign enemies.

To operate and maintain a technologically advanced society requires costly education for adults as well as for children and youth. Greater outlays are also required to protect health, maintain public order, and in general to keep the society viable. Politicians and civil servants in all urbanized modern societies, as well as in many modernizing ones, quail at the staggering price of checking environmental decay, restoring damage, and maintaining a social as well as physical environment in which people can live a civilized existence, or indeed continue to live at all.

Concurrently rising demands and imperatives, coming to peaks simultaneously in many societies today, collide not only with each other but with long-established priorities. In many countries, these press hard on military budgets, and in a few on fantastically expensive sorties into outer space and other projects on the scientific and engineering frontiers.

The resulting dilemma of insufficient disposable resources exhibits many variations and degrees of severity. Among these, three patterns are especially notable:

(1) Cases in which the primary focus of the dilemma is the conflict between massive military and other external commitments on the one hand, and on the other hand domestic demands and imperatives, exemplified most vividly in the United States, but increasingly in the Soviet Union, and to a declining degree in Western Europe;

(2) Cases in which the primary focus is the conflict between public demands for more food and better living generally, and the need to divert goods and services to the tasks of modernization—the conflict between "pie now" and "pie in the sky by and by"—exemplified in most of the countries of Asia, Africa, and Latin America; and

(3) A few cases in which governments are attempting to support heavy military commitments on top of domestic conflicts arising from the drive for modernization, exemplified plainly in the case of China, and to a lesser degree in India, Egypt and other countries that will come to mind.

In our present context, interest focuses both on the impacts of escalating domestic demands on allocations of resources for military and other external purposes, and on the international implications of domestic crises resulting from the dilemma of insufficient resources. In this connection the breakup of colonial empires is instructive. The British Empire and other historic empires were viable so long as lowly folk at home and in the colonies could be kept working at relatively low cost in money and in violence. Empires have become increasingly insupportable as rising demands on the home front and resistance in the colonies coincided with escalating costs across the board. Study of past empires suggests also that previously viable systems tended to become unviable when the imperial rulers' moral claims (superior rule, "civilizing mission," and the like) became unconvincing and implausible, with the result that they had to rely ever more heavily upon the exercise of violence to sustain their imperial rule.[20]

Do these historical cases cast light on the dilemma confronting today's new-style imperialisms, represented chiefly by the United States and the Soviet Union? Are these systems already becoming insupportable both on moral grounds and even more because of concurrent peaking of domestic and external costs? This question suggests others. How many billions of dollars (or rubles) will it take to pay the most pressing arrears of long-continued environmental neglect and abuse? How many additional billions annually to cope with the mountains of wastes that bedevil all modernized societies? How many billions to meet other rising costs that inexorably accompany modernization? How will Soviet and American politicians respond to these imperatives? Will they continue to neglect their deteriorating physical habitat, and strive to repress or divert domestic demands? Will they continue the dangerous and potentially self-destructive course of competitive military escalation? Will they persist in their efforts to achieve global

[20] For an overview of British imperial experience from this perspective, see our "Dilemma of Rising Demands and Insufficient Resources," *World Politics*, xx (1968), 66off.

hegemony? Or will they curtail external commitments and reduce their military budgets the better to sustain the domestic society? Will they continue to spend extravagantly on sorties into outer space? Or will they redirect the fruits of future research more toward alleviating and improving the human condition in their own and in other less-favored societies?

Different perspectives yield different answers to such questions. Many economists envisage endless economic growth, with ever-rising production per capita. Power-oriented politicians and military planners look forward to generations of new weapons and counter-weapons, produced at increasing cost and increasing rates of obsolescence. Space scientists and engineers envision endless vistas of exploration and eventual occupation of the moon and planets. Rarely do they show much concern for the future of the planet Earth, upon which they, like all humans, are ineluctably dependent for the biological requisites of existence. Nor do they often seem even to be aware of the social consequences of their projects. "It may or may not be worth while to support missile research to the hilt," says science-historian Derek Price, "but no man can make such a decision without considering the possibility that this work will ruin the chances of half a dozen other fields for an entire generation" [21]—such fields, for example, as alleviation of hunger, redesign of cities, abatement of noise, restoration of polluted lakes and rivers, and cleaning up the increasingly poisoned air we breathe.

As we have previously emphasized, such narrow, tunnel-like social vision, inherent in much engineering discourse and action, contrasts in toto with the ecological perspective which directs attention explicitly to the inescapable interrelatedness of individuals, groups, and societies, to the side-effects of innovations and the allocation of resources, and to their impacts on the ecosystem as a whole. From the ecological perspective, for reasons already given, it seems unlikely to us that the United States, the Soviet Union, or any other polity can pay the concurrent costs of global political commitments, competitive military expansion, and other fantastically expensive undertakings, without progressively crippling the domestic society upon which all such commitments and projects depend for support. There are signs, gratifying from the ecological viewpoint, that this view is gaining adherents in at least some of the major countries.

One should not concentrate on the Washington and Moscow versions of the dilemma of increasingly insufficient resources to the neglect of the dilemma's constraining effects on other governments, and eventually on all. As previously indicated, the configuration of demands and commitments varies from one society to another. But our thesis is that

21 D. de S. Price, *Science Since Babylon* (New Haven 1961), 123.

the dilemma in one form or another is universal, or potentially so. No polity is likely to be exempt from increasing disparity between rising and proliferating demands and disposable resources to cover them. And all evidence known to us suggests that the severity of the dilemma is likely to vary in proportion to the stage of modernizing economic development attained.

This prospect poses still other questions. How will the dilemma affect flows of capital to the less-modernized societies? How will it affect alliances and coalitions? And the size and composition of military forces at different levels of the international hierarchy of power? How will the dilemma affect the competition for food and raw materials, in particular the terms of permissible access to the international oceans? Will it have minimal or more substantial effects on the development of international institutions? Will it conceivably impel rulers, even those of the most powerful states, into collaborative actions that progressively erode the principle of sovereignty and the time-honored claim to exercise exclusive jurisdiction over so-called domestic questions?

The magnitude and intensity of pressures converging on public authorities vary widely from one polity to another. There is comparable variation in the degree to which authorities are responsive to the needs and demands of the constituents. There is also variation in the degree to which disposable resources can be expanded to cover increasing demands. There is no assurance that statesmen will make prudent, far-sighted decisions; but one thing is certain—they cannot escape the consequences of the decisions they do make. Moreover, established patterns of allocation are everywhere in flux, with even the traditional precedence of military defense being challenged as never before in recent times.

### PATTERNS OF INTERDEPENDENCE

We have emphasized the integrative quality of the ecological mode of thinking. We have shown how this approach directs attention to a wider range of conditions—unintended as well as intended, undesired as well desired—than do approaches more narrowly focused. We have stated as a general hypothesis that change anywhere is likely to ramify beyond the place where the activating event occurs, affecting well-being, subsistence, even survival in remote parts of the ecosystem. This is the principle of interrelatedness, and the interdependencies that interrelatedness entails. Despite indications that a psychic sense of community transcending the national polity is growing very slowly and unevenly if at all, a condition of interdependence increasingly characterizes the affairs of individuals, nations, larger regions, and indeed the world as a whole.

Interdependence poses issues of many kinds, some of which we have previously noted. In the specific context of international order, we would emphasize two types in particular: (1) issues that derive from increasing inability of all governments to prevent disruptive or other adverse or unwanted intrusions into areas of exclusive sovereign jurisdiction as defined by law; and (2) issues that derive from increasing inability of all governments to impose single-handed their demands outside the territorial limits of their jurisdiction.

Both types of issues are relevant not only within the context of national sovereignty and power, but also within the context of the requisites of an enduring international order. Some of the policy problems of both types have been considered in the preceding chapters. Here we shall merely review certain problem areas, in which state sovereignty and parochial nationalism provide increasingly ineffective approaches to the protection of vital interests.

## Loss of Military Viability

Viewed historically, a prime justification of the sovereign territorial state has been its mission to make the national community secure against violent attacks from abroad. By the end of the First World War, there was considerable evidence that advances in military technology had undermined the defensibility of all but two or three states of continental size. In World War II, for the first time in history, cities, transport, and other installations hundreds of miles inside a country's perimeter were attacked and destroyed from the air. The vastly more destructive thermonuclear weapons of the next decade further depreciated the military value of boundaries and space. Development of paramilitary techniques of so-called internal war have still further eroded the territorial façade of defense. The fighting in Algeria, Vietnam, and elsewhere revealed the extreme difficulty, if not utter impossibility, of sealing any territory against violent intruders.

We are not suggesting that the sovereign land-based state is about to wither away through loss of military viability. The thrust of the evidence is simply that the prime goal of security, as traditionally conceived, and still very much alive in the minds of military professionals, diplomats, politicians, and citizens generally, presents problems increasingly resistant to military solutions.[22]

When one turns the military problem around, a comparable attri-

---

[22] The problem is partly technical, but with strong ecological connotations. Some experts cling to the hope that a tactically effective military defense can be achieved through still more sophisticated weapons systems. Others are skeptical of ever achieving any viable military defense against the massive destructive capabilities of contemporary missiles with thermonuclear warheads. And this skepticism extends to the still unsolved problem of defense against biological killers and chemical poisons that might utterly disrupt the ecology of any country.

tion of capability is evident. More destructive weapons and longer-range carriers have not produced corresponding enlargement of useful political influence. Those who command the most lethal weapons can undoubtedly render the earth uninhabitable, but they are notoriously less able than their counterparts a century ago to exert effective influence in distant places.

"At the peak of British power and influence, the decade of the 1860's, total expenditures for military purposes averaged less than £30 millions per year. Adjusting for inflation and changes in the dollar price of sterling, this works out to something in the range of one to two percent of average U.S. military expenditures in the 1950's and early 1960's. In short, mid-nineteenth-century British governments policed a worldwide empire and a global net of seaways and exerted on other nations an influence as great as, if not considerably greater than, the United States can achieve today at a real cost fifty to one hundred times larger." [23]

This comparison emphasizes not only the areal shrinkage of effective military hegemony; it emphasizes even more dramatically the astronomical rise in the cost of attempting to achieve it. Military establishments have become insatiable, ever-increasing consumers of scarce goods and services. For reasons outlined previously, it may be doubted that any polity—not even the United States—can continue much longer to pay the price of competitive military primacy, without progressively eroding and corroding, and eventually destroying the domestic society for the defense of which the armaments are ostensibly provided. This condition has already produced a crisis of priorities in a few countries, above all in the United States. This priorities crisis, we contend, is spreading, is potentially universal, and is likely to become an enduring feature of the international milieu.

To the extent that the dilemma of insufficient resources is appreciated, it narrows the statesmen's probable range of choice. This trend was evident long before the advent of nuclear weapons and ballistic missiles. When British statesmen, between 1900 and 1910, substituted formal or informal military alliances with Japan, France, and the United States, in place of previously greater reliance on their own resources, they were buying—more precisely, trying to buy—greater security for a lower price and at substantial sacrifice of autonomy. Precisely the same is true of post-1945 Russian efforts to build a coalition of Communist polities, and of American counter-efforts to support a worldwide anti-Communist coalition.

Taking a still broader view, one finds further indications of the insupportability of contemporary military policies. In the Soviet Union,

[23] H. and M. Sprout (fn. 20), 667–68.

the military establishment is preempting resources needed to meet targets of economic growth as well as rising consumer demands from the civil society. In the United States, domestic social crisis and environmental imperatives are putting military budgets under heavy and increasing pressure. Domestic pressures have impelled the governments of subordinate allies to curtail their military programs, thereby increasing the burden upon the Superpowers. Continuing rise of military expenditures in the "Third World" jeopardizes developmental programs, and to the extent that military demands receive priority, they will continue to obstruct significant progress toward modernization. At least one of the possibilities implicit in the current spreading crisis of priorities is the emergence, in many countries, during the coming years, of stronger incentives to seek ways of stabilizing military commitments and outlays, with the side-effects of further tightening interdependence and stimulating the search for less costly ways of achieving security.

## Some Implications of Economic Modernization

A parallel growth of interdependence is evident when attention is shifted from the military to the economic condition of sovereign polities. As noted earlier, the process of modernization everywhere includes progressive increase of per capita productivity through substitution of power-driven machines for human and animal muscles. This transition reduces in several ways the autonomy of modernized and modernizing societies, some more than others, but all to an increasing extent. Modernization has stimulated specialization, with consequent expansion of traffic across national frontiers. It has enlarged demands for natural resources, thereby accelerating depletion and denudation of the earth. It has resulted in accumulation of productive and increasingly mobile aggregates of capital. It has brought into existence the complex mechanisms of international finance, especially limitations imposed by the rigors of the balance of payments. And it has opened the way for growth of entrepreneurial structures that penetrate many countries simultaneously, and challenge at numerous points the political sovereignties under which they conduct their operations.

Above all, as previously emphasized, modernization entails progressive politicization of the population, with expansion of their demands on disposable goods and services, and enlargement of their effective leverage on a society increasingly vulnerable internally to disruption. In short, economic modernization puts a government's external commitments and capabilities increasingly at the mercy of domestic politics. Far-reaching international implications derive from the paradox that governments with the largest and most insupportable external commitments are, in the main, those that represent societies further advanced in the process of modernization, and thereby hypothetically more capable of paying the price.

## PSYCHOLOGICAL PENETRATION AND INTERDEPENDENCE

Another dimension of interdependence is the increasing psychological penetrability of political communities. No government is able to isolate its constituency completely. The farther the process of modernization goes, the more psychologically penetrable a society becomes.

This is so for the following reasons, among others: relative widespread functional literacy is a concomitant, probably a requisite, of modernization; increased mobility of people, goods, and ideas also accompanies modernization; greater awareness of the larger world can be, and often is, a prime source of discontent, especially in the less affluent societies.

We have previously noted the generally disruptive impact of American (and to a lesser extent, European) affluence on poverty-ridden societies. It may be difficult for Americans to conceive of their material culture as a force inspiring revolt and even fostering the spread of revolutionary communism. Yet a by-product of the display of American affluence since World War II appears to have been precisely that. American soldiers, civil servants, business men, and tourists have carried the message that ordinary folk can possess and enjoy the material amenities that are restricted in most Asian, African, and Latin American countries to a tiny privileged elite at the top of the social pyramid.

## INSIDIOUS INTRUSIONS

Among the most intractable intruders into the sovereign space of national polities are the environmental pollutants that defy all man-made jurisdictional boundaries. In general, environmental pollution is most severe where productivity is high and the consuming population is large. It becomes a transnational menace when rivers, ocean currents, winds, and other carriers convey pollutants from their source across political boundaries into other jurisdictions.

Long before the advent of nuclear explosives, polluted rivers and lakes were a persistent if relatively minor source of international concern, chiefly in Europe. Airborne pollution was recognized as a major international problem only after the testing of nuclear weapons that followed World War II. In recent years there have been recurrent charges that airborne pollutants, chiefly from industrial areas in Western Europe, are endangering health in neighboring countries, even in areas a thousand miles or more away. Largely because of prevailing winds and geographic location, the massive airborne pollution from the United States, and increasingly from Japan, has not yet become a self-evident source of much international concern.

After nuclear explosions in the air, lethal fallout has invariably been detected at great distances from the site of explosion, and frequently over vast areas, emphasizing the global continuity of the atmosphere and of the oceans and connecting seas. Scientists and engineers engaged in weapons research, as well as those involved in nuclear power development, generally minimize the risk to plants, animals, and humans. But counter-views persist, and are reflected in the recurrent demands for more comprehensive and effective international control of such operations.

A form of insidious intrusion, still very conjectural, is the effect of airborne pollution on climate. The continuing rise of the $CO_2$-content of the atmosphere from automotive exhausts, factory stacks and other sources, has been repeatedly asserted to entail the long-range danger of excessive warming of the atmosphere, with resultant melting of the polar ice and other disastrous ecological consequences. According to a contrary hypothesis, discharge of huge and ever-rising quantities of material into the atmosphere and stratosphere may cause disastrous lowering of surface temperatures by reducing drastically the amount of solar energy reaching the earth.

Numerous scientists and others have ridiculed the possibility of climatic catastrophe resulting from man-made changes in the atmosphere. But G. H. T. Kimble, a leading authority on climate, warns against optimism: "Most of the people who give this answer are not meteorologists, but 'bomb' scientists and technicians. . . . If they were meteorologists, I have a feeling that some of them would be rather more impressed . . . by the delicacy of the atmospheric balance." [24]

From time to time one reads of research toward the objective of macroclimatic control. A few scientists envisage a time when climatic patterns can be modified to serve military-political as well as other purposes. The late John von Neumann viewed such an achievement as a greater threat to the global ecosystem than was the advent of thermonuclear weapons. Climatic control, if achieved, he contended, would be exploited for political purposes unless suitable "new political forms and procedures" were instituted in time to prevent it. [25]

Still another category of insidious intruders into sovereign national space consists of the host of insects and microorganisms that injure or destroy plants, animals, and humans. Such intruders filter through the tightest quarantines. Their potential for damage has risen with the expansion of intercountry and interregional traffic. The influenza pandemic of 1918–19 stands as a stark portent of the deadly potential of these invasive intruders, a potential that might be released either

[24] G. H. T. Kimble, "But Somebody Does Something About It," *New York Times Magazine*, June 8, 1962.
[25] John von Neumann, "Can We Survive Technology?" *Fortune* (June 1955).

spontaneously by natural forces, or deliberately by sinister purveyors of biological warfare.

## THE GLOBAL OCEAN

From a geographic viewpoint, there is only one ocean, a vast expanse of interconnected bodies of water that cover 70 percent of the earth's surface. From a political-ecological standpoint, the global ocean presents a problem just the reverse of the one examined in the preceding sections. That problem was how to exclude unwanted intruders from areas over which particular states have undisputed legal jurisdiction. With respect to the global ocean, the problem confronting every sovereign polity is (1) how to get a fair share of the oceanic resources that are largely outside the legitimate jurisdiction of any state, (2) how to prevent contamination and wanton destruction of those resources which every year become a more important source of life-support upon the earth, and (3) how to curtail upon and beneath the water's surface military or other operations that are inimical to development of a viable international order.

According to traditional international law, the ocean and connecting seas (except for a narrow coastal zone) constituted the "high sea," outside the territorial jurisdiction of any state. The coastal zone of "territorial waters" historically extended about three miles from shore. During the past half-century, various governments have asserted a "right" to exercise jurisdiction for various purposes farther from the shore. In 1958 a major breach in the traditional law was made by a convention that extended the jurisdiction of maritime states over the resources upon and beneath the seabed of the continental shelf to a depth of about 600 feet, or "beyond that limit to where the depth of the superjacent waters admits to the exploration of the natural resources of the said areas."

There are indications that this is only the beginning of another phase of ruthless international competition and conflict. As things stand in the early 1970's, the only effective constraints on exploitation of the sea floor to any depth were those imposed by the transient limitations of a rapidly advancing technology and the availability of huge amounts of capital. Since only a very few political communities commanded both the necessary technology and the capital, the outlook was that those few—U.S.A., U.S.S.R., Japan, and a few others—would progressively preempt development and control of the resources of the more remote ocean depths.

A review of the situation in 1969 concluded that "the great powers will not accept control by an independent body," and that "the great industrial complexes that have been doing preliminary work will not look favorably on the idea of sharing profits" with other nations which lack the maritime frontier and/or the requisite technology and capital to exploit the ocean depths.[26]

In the same year, an authority on submarine technology noted a "worldwide trend by maritime nations to claim more offshore territory," a concomitant trend toward "head-on confrontation between rival claimants," and reluctance of governments and corporations in the forefront of deep sea exploration to accept the principle of internationalization—the principle that the resources upon and beneath the ocean floor are part of the common wealth of the world community as a whole.[27]

While nationalistic giants mobilize to contest control of the resources of the seabed, two sets of forces are eroding the ecology of the ocean as a whole. These are excessive fishing and progressive pollution of the environment in which fish and other marine organisms subsist.

The fact and the potentially disastrous consequences of large-scale industrialization of fishing—especially but not exclusively by Russians and Japanese—have evoked protests of alarm from ecologists in numerous countries. In the measured rhetoric of a recent United Nations report, "destruction or depletion of marine resources has been a continuing process in the absence of effective control and management."[28]

The U.N. report cites specifically the ecological damage caused by oil-spills from tankers and from underwater oil-drilling and pumping rigs. But these are by no means all, or necessarily the most serious, sources of marine pollution. Hundreds of millions of tons of sewage and industrial wastes from scores of countries are being dumped annually into coastal waters, and thence out to sea—with the volume rising year by year. Destruction of spawning sites by these pollutants, by draining tidal marshes, by damming rivers that discharge into the sea, and by other projects and operations go on around the world without regard for their destructive effects on marine ecology.

Recurrent testing of nuclear weapons in the Western Pacific has released incalculable quantities of lethal radioactive debris, carried around the world by the currents of the global ocean. Some radioactive matter as well as a large amount of heat find their way into coastal waters via the spent coolant of atomic power plants, the number of which is steadily increasing. Ecologists view with concern the tendency of radioactivity to accumulate and concentrate in marine organisms through time, to become in the not distant future a menace to human consumers of the products of the sea.

26 *New York Times*, Nov. 24, 1969.

27 Paul Cohen, *The Realm of the Submarine* (New York 1969), 258–59.

28 *Problems of the Human Environment*, par. 48. Report of the Secretary-General, United Nations, May 26, 1969. Economic and Social Council, 47th Session, Agenda item 10.

It is further regarded as virtually certain that, in the absence of adequate and rigorously enforced regulations, the mining of minerals upon and beneath the ocean floor will produce at least as much environmental pollution as comparable operations on land have produced, and are still producing, in scores of countries.

One notes the grim warnings from ecologists that continued drainage of DDT and other long-persistent pesticides into the ocean will sooner or later slow down photosynthesis in marine life, starting chain reactions that would eventually so transform the ecology of the ocean as to endanger all life upon the earth.[29] And finally, as previously noted, there are the conjectures that progressive pollution of the atmosphere might so reduce the energy received from the sun as to produce a disastrous reduction of photosynthesis.

Whether and when marine catastrophe materializes as predicted from these or other causes depends in large degree upon human response, not in one but in many countries. So far these responses are not especially encouraging. But, sooner or later, what happens within and beneath the global ocean seems likely to produce major consequences for the human condition everywhere, even in communities hundreds or thousands of miles from tidewater.

Unregulated nationalistic competition for, and exploitation of, marine life and the minerals upon and beneath the seabed are likely to hasten the worst ecological effects predicted. The ancient British maxim "the sea is one" should be amended "the sea and the land are one," an international reality that picks up new dimensions with every passing year.

## A FINAL QUERY

The thrust of the preceding sections, indeed of this concluding chapter as a whole, poses queries regarding the future of the sovereign state and of our contemporary international order characterized by fragmentation of authority and power, buttressed by narrow tribal nationalism. As previously emphasized, we do not predict that the sovereign state is about to wither away. Social structures usually persist long after they become obsolete—even after they become a menace to the welfare of those who ostensibly derive benefits from their existence. Such may well be the future of the contemporary international order.

On the other hand, historians of the twenty-first century might just possibly conclude that the combination of nuclear explosives, long-range missiles, chemical-biological weapons, unchecked population growth, increasing economic interdependence, psychological penetrability of all polities, vulnerability to insidious invasive intruders, ruth-

---

[29] See, for example, Paul Ehrlich, "Eco-Catastrophe," *Ramparts* (Sept. 1969).

less competition to possess the living and nonliving products of the sea, progressive pollution of the global ocean, and other dimensions of interdependence, had rendered the sovereign territorial state unviable as a unit for providing security and public order and other essential requisites for the survival of the human species, indeed as unviable as the medieval castles and walled towns became after the "gunpowder revolution" of the fifteenth and sixteenth centuries. Is it unreasonable to speculate that future historians may even find grounds for concluding that the final quarter of the twentieth century, like the concluding phase of medieval Europe, was a period of transition in attitudes and institutions, toward a regime better suited to the governance of a world that was no longer many but one? Be that as it may, the conditions and trends sketched in the preceding pages, especially the spreading and tightening interrelatedness that limits the capabilities of even the Superpowers, are ineluctable realities for the architects of a more viable international order.

# Index

BOOKS WRITTEN
UNDER THE AUSPICES OF THE
CENTER OF INTERNATIONAL STUDIES
PRINCETON UNIVERSITY

Gabriel A. Almond, *The Appeals of Communism* (Princeton University Press 1954)

William W. Kaufmann, ed., *Military Policy and National Security* (Princeton University Press 1956)

Klaus Knorr, *The War Potential of Nations* (Princeton University Press 1956)

Lucian W. Pye, *Guerrilla Communism in Malaya* (Princeton University Press 1956)

Charles De Visscher, *Theory and Reality in Public International Law*, trans. by P. E. Corbett (Princeton University Press 1957; rev. ed. 1968)

Bernard C. Cohen, *The Political Process and Foreign Policy: The Making of the Japanese Peace Settlement* (Princeton University Press 1957)

Myron Weiner, *Party Politics in India: The Development of a Multi-Party System* (Princeton University Press 1957)

Percy E. Corbett, *Law in Diplomacy* (Princeton University Press 1959)

Rolf Sannwald and Jacques Stohler, *Economic Integration: Theoretical Assumptions and Consequences of European Unification*, trans. by Herman Karreman (Princeton University Press 1959)

Klaus Knorr, ed., *NATO and American Security* (Princeton University Press 1959)

Gabriel A. Almond and James S. Coleman, eds., *The Politics of the Developing Areas* (Princeton University Press 1960)

Herman Kahn, *On Thermonuclear War* (Princeton University Press 1960)

Sidney Verba, *Small Groups and Political Behavior: A Study of Leadership* (Princeton University Press 1961)

Robert J. C. Butow, *Tojo and the Coming of the War* (Princeton University Press 1961)

Glenn H. Snyder, *Deterrence and Defense: Toward a Theory of National Security* (Princeton University Press 1961)

Klaus Knorr and Sidney Verba, eds., *The International System: Theoretical Essays* (Princeton University Press 1961)

Peter Paret and John W. Shy, *Guerrillas in the 1960's* (Praeger 1962)

George Modelski, *A Theory of Foreign Policy* (Praeger 1962)

Klaus Knorr and Thornton Read, eds., *Limited Strategic War* (Praeger 1963)

Frederick S. Dunn, *Peace-Making and the Settlement with Japan* (Princeton University Press 1963)

Arthur L. Burns and Nina Heathcote, *Peace-Keeping by United Nations Forces* (Praeger 1963)

Richard A. Falk, *Law, Morality, and War in the Contemporary World* (Praeger 1963)

James N. Rosenau, *National Leadership and Foreign Policy: A Case Study in the Mobilization of Public Support* (Princeton University Press 1963)

Gabriel A. Almond and Sidney Verba, *The Civic Culture: Political Attitudes and Democracy in Five Nations* (Princeton University Press 1963)

Bernard C. Cohen, *The Press and Foreign Policy* (Princeton University Press 1963)

Richard L. Sklar, *Nigerian Political Parties: Power in an Emergent African Nation* (Princeton University Press 1963)

Peter Paret, *French Revolutionary Warfare from Indochina to Algeria: The Analysis of a Political and Military Doctrine* (Praeger 1964)

Harry Eckstein, ed., *Internal War: Problems and Approaches* (Free Press 1964)

Cyril E. Black and Thomas P. Thornton, eds., *Communism and Revolution: The Strategic Uses of Political Violence* (Princeton University Press 1964)

Miriam Camps, *Britain and the European Community 1955–1963* (Princeton University Press 1964)

Thomas P. Thornton, ed., *The Third World in Soviet Perspective: Studies by Soviet Writers on the Developing Areas* (Princeton University Press 1964)

James N. Rosenau, ed., *International Aspects of Civil Strife* (Princeton University Press 1964)

Sidney I. Ploss, *Conflict and Decision-Making in Soviet Russia: A Case Study of Agricultural Policy, 1953–1963* (Princeton University Press 1965)

Richard A. Falk and Richard J. Barnet, eds., *Security in Disarmament* (Princeton University Press 1965)

Karl von Vorys, *Political Development in Pakistan* (Princeton University Press 1965)

Harold and Margaret Sprout, *The Ecological Perspective on Human Affairs, With Special Reference to International Politics* (Princeton University Press 1965)

Klaus Knorr, *On the Uses of Military Power in the Nuclear Age* (Princeton University Press 1966)

Harry Eckstein, *Division and Cohesion in Democracy: A Study of Norway* (Princeton University Press 1966)

Cyril E. Black, *The Dynamics of Modernization: A Study in Comparative History* (Harper and Row 1966)

Peter Kunstadter, ed., *Southeast Asian Tribes, Minorities, and Nations* (Princeton University Press 1967)

E. Victor Wolfenstein, *The Revolutionary Personality: Lenin, Trotsky, Gandhi* (Princeton University Press 1967)

Leon Gordenker, *The UN Secretary-General and the Maintenance of Peace* (Columbia University Press 1967)

Oran R. Young, *The Intermediaries: Third Parties in International Crises* (Princeton University Press 1967)

James N. Rosenau, ed., *Domestic Sources of Foreign Policy* (Free Press 1967)

Richard F. Hamilton, *Affluence and the French Worker in the Fourth Republic* (Princeton University Press 1967)

Linda B. Miller, *World Order and Local Disorder: The United Nations and Internal Conflicts* (Princeton University Press 1967)

Wolfram F. Hanrieder, *West German Foreign Policy, 1949–1963: International Pressures and Domestic Response* (Stanford University Press 1967)

Richard H. Ullman, *Britain and the Russian Civil War: November 1918–February 1920* (Princeton University Press 1968)

Robert Gilpin, *France in the Age of the Scientific State* (Princeton University Press 1968)

William B. Bader, *The United States and the Spread of Nuclear Weapons* (Pegasus 1968)

Richard A. Falk, *Legal Order in a Violent World* (Princeton University Press 1968)

Cyril E. Black, Richard A. Falk, Klaus Knorr, and Oran R. Young, *Neutralization and World Politics* (Princeton University Press 1968)

Oran R. Young, *The Politics of Force: Bargaining During International Crises* (Princeton University Press 1969)

Klaus Knorr and James N. Rosenau, eds., *Contending Approaches to International Politics* (Princeton University Press 1969)

James N. Rosenau, ed., *Linkage Politics: Essays on the Convergence of National and International Systems* (Free Press 1969)

John T. McAlister, Jr., *Viet Nam: The Origins of Revolution* (Knopf 1969)

Jean Edward Smith, *Germany Beyond the Wall: People, Politics and Prosperity* (Little, Brown 1969)

James Barros, *Betrayal from Within: Joseph Avenol, Secretary-General of the League of Nations, 1933–1940* (Yale University Press 1969)

Charles Hermann, *Crises in Foreign Policy: A Simulation Analysis* (Bobbs-Merrill 1969)

Robert C. Tucker, *The Marxian Revolutionary Idea: Essays on Marxist Thought and Its Impact on Radical Movements* (W. W. Norton 1969)

Harvey Waterman, *Political Change in Contemporary France: The Politics of an Industrial Democracy* (Charles E. Merrill 1969)

Richard A. Falk and Cyril E. Black, eds., *The Future of the International Legal Order,* Vol. I, *Trends and Patterns* (Princeton University Press 1969)

Ted Robert Gurr, *Why Men Rebel* (Princeton University Press 1970)

C. S. Whitaker, Jr., *The Politics of Tradition: Continuity and Change in Northern Nigeria, 1946–1966* (Princeton University Press 1970)

Richard A. Falk, *The Status of Law in International Society* (Princeton University Press 1970)

Henry Bienen, *Tanzania: Party Transformation and Economic Development* (Princeton University Press 1967, rev. ed. 1970)

Klaus Knorr, *Military Power and Potential* (D. C. Heath 1970)

Richard A. Falk and Cyril E. Black, eds., *The Future of the International Legal Order,* Vol. II, *Wealth and Resources* (Princeton University Press 1970)

Leon Gordenker, ed., *The United Nations in International Politics* (Princeton University Press 1971)

Cyril E. Black and Richard A. Falk, eds., *The Future of the International Legal Order,* Vol. III, *Conflict Management* (Princeton University Press 1971)

Harold and Margaret Sprout, *Toward a Politics of the Planet Earth* (Van Nostrand Reinhold Co. 1971)

Francine R. Frankel, *India's Green Revolution: Economic Gains and Political Costs* (Princeton University Press 1971)